Introduction to Politics of the Developing World

CONTRIBUTORS

Ervand Abrahamian
BARUCH COLLEGE

Amrita Basu
AMHERST COLLEGE

Merilee S. Grindle
HARVARD UNIVERSITY

William A. Joseph
WELLESLEY COLLEGE

Mark Kesselman
COLUMBIA UNIVERSITY

Darren Kew
UNIVERSITY OF MASSACHUSETTS,
BOSTON

Atul Kohli
PRINCETON UNIVERSITY

Joel Krieger
WELLESLEY COLLEGE

Peter Lewis
AMERICAN UNIVERSITY

Alfred P. Montero
CARLETON COLLEGE

Introduction to Politics of the Developing World

THIRD EDITION

GENERAL EDITORS

William A. Joseph
WELLESLEY COLLEGE

Mark Kesselman
COLUMBIA UNIVERSITY

Joel Krieger
WELLESLEY COLLEGE

Houghton Mifflin Company
Boston   New York

To our children, who are growing up in a complex and ever more challenging world:
MK—for Ishan and Javed
JK—for Nathan and Megan
WAJ—for Abigail, Hannah, and Rebecca

Sponsoring Editor: Katherine Meisenheimer
Senior Development Editor: Frances Gay
Senior Project Editor: Ylang Nguyen
Editorial Assistant: Wendy Thayer
Senior Manufacturing Coordinator: Marie Barnes
Production / Design Coordinator: Jennifer Meyer Dare
Marketing Manager: Nicola Poser

Printed in the U.S.A.

Library of Congress Control Number: 2003106257

ISBN: 0-618-21447-X

123456789-MV-07 06 05 04 03

BRIEF CONTENTS

CONTENTS

PREFACE

We began the preface to the second edition of this book: "These are exciting yet daunting times to teach about politics in the Third World. For decades, most of the countries of Africa, Asia, and Latin America seemed trapped in a vicious cycle of dictatorship and underdevelopment. But the recent spread of democracy and the improved economic prospects in many less developed nations have challenged scholars and teachers to think anew about the Third World. . . . *Introduction to Third World Politics* deals with a subject matter whose intellectual, as well as political and economic boundaries are very much in flux."

The first obvious change in this edition is in the title, which is now *Introduction to Politics of the Developing World*. This title reflects better, we think, the increasing diversity and complexity of the more than 150 countries that are usually considered to be economically less-developed—though, as discussed in Chapter 1, we believe that the term "Third World" still retains significant symbolic power in conveying the deep, and in some ways deepening, gap between the richer and the poorer nations.

But at a more profound level this thoroughly revised edition seeks to take into account some of the momentous global trends and unforeseen events that have shaken and shaped our world in recent years. It appears that a reshuffling of the geopolitical order is in progress–the results of which cannot be predicted. We are all struggling to make sense of the awesome challenges of globalization, ethnonationalism, and state-sponsored and non-state-based violence in the brave new world of the twenty-first century. These developments fundamentally affect the internal politics and policies of countries throughout the world in complex and highly variable ways. We hope this book will help students analyze new (and old) political challenges and changing (and persistent) agendas in six important and diverse countries and, though them, gain a better understanding of the particular challenges and special agendas facing the developing world.

Structure of the Book

The core elements of *Introduction to Politics of the Developing World* have not changed. We are pleased that instructors and students have generously praised the analytical framework, lively writing, and high level of scholarship of the previous edition. In this edition, we have retained the basic framework and approach of the second edition. We aim to make the book accessible to students with little or no background in political science. We have used readable, direct prose as free of jargon as possible, and have maximized symmetry among chapters in order to facilitate comparison.

Introduction to Politics of the Developing World emphasizes patterns of state formation, political economy, domestic politics, and the politics of collective identities within the context of globalization. A distinctive feature of the book is the use of four comparative themes to frame the presentation of each country's politics. We explain the themes in Chapter 1 and present an intriguing "puzzle" for each to stimulate student thinking. These themes—treated in each country study—focus attention on the continuities and contrasts among the six countries:

- **The Democratic Idea** explores the challenges posed by citizens' demands for greater control and participation in both democracies and non-democracies.
- **A World of States** highlights the importance of state formation and the interstate system for political development.
- **Governing the Economy** analyzes state strategies for promoting economic development and stresses the effects of economic globalization on domestic politics.
- **The Politics of Collective Identities** considers the political consequences of race, ethnicity, gender, religion, and nationality and their complex interplay with class-based politics.

Through our four themes, the methods of comparative analysis come alive as students examine similarities and differences among countries and within and between political systems. This thematic approach facilitates timely and comprehensive analysis of political challenges and changing agendas within countries.

Introduction to Politics of the Developing World uses a country-by-country approach and strikes a balance between the richness of each country's national political development and more general comparative analysis. Chapter 1 explains the comparative method, analyzes the four key themes of the book, and describes core features of political institutions and processes. Each country chapter that follows consists of five sections. **Section 1** treats the historic formation of the modern state, its geographic setting, and critical junctures in its political development. **Section 2** describes the political economy of past and current national development. **Section 3** outlines the major institutions of governance and policy-making. **Section 4** explains the widely varying processes of representation, participation, and contestation. Finally, **Section 5** reflects on the major issues that confront the country and are likely to shape its future.

Several special features assist in the teaching and learning process.

At the beginning of each chapter, students will find a page of basic demographic, social, economic, and political information to aid in comparing countries. Throughout the chapters a wide array of maps, tables, charts, photographs, and political cartoons enliven the text and present key information in clear and graphic ways. Each country study includes four to six boxes that highlight interesting and provocative aspects of politics—for example, **Leaders,** biographies of important political leaders; **Institutional Intricacies,** important features of a political system that need clarification; **Citizen Action,** unconventional forms of participation; **Global Connection,** examples of connections between domestic and international politics; and **Current Challenges,** issues of today and the future. Key terms are set in boldface when first introduced and are defined in the Glossary at the end of the book. Students will find that the Glossary defines many key concepts that are used broadly in comparative politics.

New to This Edition

We have updated the material on each of the countries to take account of major events and regime changes. We pay particular attention in this edition of *Introduction to Politics of the Developing World* to challenges posed by globalization and issues involving security in a world reshaped by the events of September 11.

The present edition also provides instructors with much greater flexibility and choice regarding the countries that they may include in their course. For those who prefer the convenience of a preselected set of countries, the regular third edition contains the same six countries covered in the second edition. However, instructors who would prefer to cover a different selection of countries can now easily and inexpensively arrange for a **customized edition** of *Introduction to Politics of the Developing World* to be produced for their course. All the chapters of this "Editors' Choice" version of the book are posted in an **online database.** Also in the database of developing countries will be five additional country choices, which will only be available in a customized edition. South Africa is already in the database. In 2004, we will add chapters on the Republic of Korea and Indonesia. In 2005, Cuba and Turkey will be included in the database of countries that instructors can select for their course. To learn more about the database, or to create a custom edition, visit the Houghton Mifflin online catalog at *http://www.college.hmco.com* or contact your Houghton Mifflin representative.

Acknowledgments

We want to thank the following for their assistance in preparing some of the country chapters for this edition: Nagraj Adve (India); Bertha Angulo (Mexico); and Jason Richardson (Brazil). We are also very grateful to those colleagues who have reviewed and critiqued the previous editions of this book:

Michael Bratton, Michigan State University; **William Crowther,** University of North Carolina,

Greensboro; **Louise K. Davidson-Schmich,** University of Miami; **Chris Hamilton,** Washburn University; **Kenji Hayao,** Boston College; **Maria Perez Laubhan,** College of Lake County; **Richard Leich,** Gustavus Adolphus College; **Mahmood Monshipouri,** Quinnipiac University.

Finally, our thanks to the talented and professional staff at Houghton Mifflin, especially Katherine Meisenheimer, sponsoring editor; Fran Gay, senior development editor; Ylang Nguyen, senior project editor; and Nicola Poser, senior marketing manager.

W. A. J.
M. K.
J. K.

Introduction to Politics of the Developing World

CHAPTER 1

Introducing Politics of the Developing World

William A. Joseph,
Mark Kesselman, and Joel Krieger

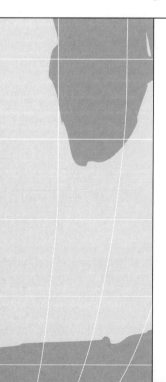

Section ❶ The Global Challenge of Comparative Politics

Politics throughout the world seems more troubled today than even a few years ago, when celebrations around the globe ushered in the new millennium. Of course, no one expected that the start of a new century would spell an end to ethnic cleansing, brushfire wars, horrifying epidemics, famine, currency crises that wiped out years of economic development, and the growing marginalization of whole regions of the globe.

Yet there were positive developments on the horizon. The new century began with vivid accounts of the widening circle of opportunities associated with democratization and economic development. (In the United States especially, the stock market boom of the 1990s was historically unprecedented.) Memories were still fresh of the grim and potentially deadly **cold war,** which ended when the Communist regimes in the Soviet Union and East Central Europe imploded beginning in 1989. It looked as if international politics would be driven much more by global economic competition than by hard-edged national enmities.

Recent years have also witnessed a seeming flood of history-making events in the developing, or **Third World,** nations of Asia, Africa, and Latin America. (The use of the terms *developing* and *Third World* is discussed in Section 3 below.) China, for example, long one of the world's poorest countries, has become the world's most dynamic economy. The brutally racist apartheid regime in South Africa has been replaced, largely through the process of a nonviolent political revolution, by a multiracial democracy. Latin America has been transformed from a region dominated by harsh military regimes to one in which nearly every country is either a democracy or can be said to be moving toward democratization.

But we have also seen increased instability and conflict in the developing world. Freedom, peace, and a reasonable standard of living cannot be built on hopes alone. It is desperately hard to make such dreams a reality. In many developing countries, economic scarcity, widespread poverty, and extreme inequality make it especially hard to turn such dreams into reality. Toppling dictatorial regimes often proves less difficult than building new democracies. In some Third World nations, the rush to democracy awakens new and restless constituencies with demands that cannot easily be met by the government. Even in a relatively long-established Third World democracy like India, religious divisions frequently explode into communal violence that not only threatens the social order but also shakes the very foundations of the country's democratic political system.

An Uncertain World Order

Post–cold war political changes and the transformation of the global balance of power have produced new forms of international cooperation and competition, as well as new sources of international tension and violence. The grim but predictable bipolar world of superpower rivalry between the United States and the Soviet Union has been replaced by the uncertainties of a more fragmented map of global power. Increasing economic, religious, and ethnic divisions create tensions in every corner of the globe. We have witnessed a surge of brutal clashes between and within countries, along with a quieter dynamic of fierce competition and a rash of trade wars—and perpetual diplomatic combat—among professed allies. The very connectedness of the global economy means that the U.S. stock market is watched for signs of impending crisis today the way the power struggles in Moscow were watched during the heyday of the cold war.

These international changes have had a far-reaching effect on developing countries. During the cold war, the rivalry between the Soviet Union and the United States was often fought out and contained in the Third World at a safe distance from the superpowers, as in the Vietnam War and the conflicts in the Angola and Nicaragua. This situation was certainly politically destabilizing for and caused much human suffering in the Third World, but the superpower standoff also gave the developing nations some bargaining power when it came to securing economic or military aid as the Americans and Soviets wooed allies among the developing nations.

The end of the cold war has meant an end to such strategic leverage for the Third World. Indeed, the collapse of communism has diverted economic resources away from the Third World as the developed nations and international organizations channel more funds to help the struggling democracies and market economies of Russia and East Central Europe. Yet one reason that democracy has recently been able to spread throughout much of the Third World is that dictators can no longer rely on their superpower patrons to keep them in power for strategic reasons.

In short, both the national and international contexts of politics in the developing world changed profoundly in the last decades of the twentieth century. Yet (as we will discuss in more detail later) there remain very important continuities in the domestic and global situations of the developing nations of Asia, Africa, and Latin America that continue to distinguish them in major ways from the world's economically richer and politically more powerful countries.

Globalization and Comparative Politics of the Developing World

By 2000, although the post–cold war world order had not fully crystallized, a new lens for analyzing politics within and among—and behind the backs of—countries seemed to focus everyone's attention. The key new question that promised to dominate the political agenda of the early twenty-first century was whether the processes of **globalization**—the global diffusion of investment, trade, production, and extraordinary communication technologies—would promote a worldwide diffusion of opportunity and enhancement of human development, or would reinforce the comparative advantages of the more prosperous and powerful regions and peoples, undermine local cultures, and intensify regional conflicts.

These issues are very much with us today and they continue to frame the country studies in this book. Yet the terrorist attacks of September 11, 2001, on the United States and their aftermath have partially reframed our thinking about globalization. Until September 11, the economic aspects of globalization claimed major attention. Since September 11, political and military concerns have been at the forefront, involving how U.S. power will recast global alliances and affect both national politics and people's lives throughout the world. But these issues do not replace concerns about economic globalization. Instead, we are challenged to develop a more complex understanding of globalization and how it frames both politics and the study of politics in the developing world.

The terms *globalization* and *global era* are everywhere applied as a general catch phrase to identify the growing depth, extent, and diversity of cross-border connections that are a key characteristic of the contemporary world. Discussion of globalization begins with accounts of economic activities, including the reorganization of production and the global redistribution of the work force (the "global factory") and the increased extent and intensity of international trade, finance, and foreign direct investment. Globalization involves the movement of peoples due to migration, employment, business, and educational opportunities.

Globalization includes other profound changes that are less visible but equally significant. For example, new applications of information technology (such as the Internet and CNN) blur the traditional distinction between what is around the world and what is around the block, thereby instantly transforming cultures and eroding the boundaries between the local and global. These technologies make instantaneous communication possible and link producers and contractors, headquarters, branch plants, and suppliers in real time anywhere in the world. Employees may be rooted in time and place, but employers can take advantage of the ebb and flow of a global labor market. A secure job today is gone tomorrow. Globalization fosters insecurity in everyday life and presents extraordinary challenges to government, particularly in developing nations, which are often in a disadvantaged and vulnerable position in the international system.

Globalization forges new forms of international governance, from the Asian Pacific Economic Cooperation forum to the World Trade Organization. And as we all know, international terror networks can strike anywhere, from New York to Bali to Mobassa. In an attempt to regulate and stabilize the myriad international flows, an alphabet soup of international organizations—APEC, NATO, the UN, IMF, WTO, OECD, NAFTA, to name but a few—has been enlisted.

All of these processes complicate politics as they erode the ability of even the strongest countries to control their destinies. No state can secure economic and life cycle security for its citizens. None can preserve pristine national models of economic governance or distinctly national cultures, values, understandings of the world, or narratives that define a people and forge their unity.

It is clear that countries face a host of challenges simultaneously from above and below. The capacities of states to control domestic outcomes and assert sovereignty are compromised by regional and global technological and market forces, as well as growing security concerns. The very stability and viability of countries are simultaneously assaulted by ethnic, nationalist, and religious divisions that often involve both internal and external components. The bright line separating domestic and international politics has been rubbed out by the complex set of cross-border economic, cultural, technological, governance, and security processes, institutions, and relations that constitute the contemporary global order. And nowhere else are the challenges of globalization more monumental or its impacts more momentous than in the developing world.

Making Sense of Turbulent Times

It is not surprising that in the flash of newspaper headlines and television sound bites, the upheavals, rush of events, and sheer range and complexity of the cross-border phenomena of globalization tend to make politics look chaotic beyond comprehension. Although the study of comparative politics can help us understand current events in a rapidly changing world, it involves much more than snapshot analysis or Monday-morning quarterbacking. *Introduction to Politics of the Developing World* describes and analyzes in detail the government and politics of six countries (China, India, Mexico, Brazil, Nigeria, and Iran) and identifies common themes in their development that explain longer-term causes of both changes and continuities. The book provides cross-national comparisons and explanations based on four themes that we believe are central for understanding politics in the developing world:

- The pressures for more democracy and the challenges of democratization
- The interaction of states within the international order
- The role of the state in economic management
- The political impact of diverse attachments and sources of group identity, including class, gender, ethnicity, and religion

We also expect that these four themes will be useful for analyzing where the countries discussed in this book may be heading politically in the first decades of the twenty-first century. Moreover, the themes illustrate how comparative politics can serve as a valuable tool for making political sense of even the most tumultuous times. The contemporary period presents an extraordinary challenge to those who study politics in developing countries, but the study of comparative politics also provides a unique opportunity for understanding this part of the world in an uncertain era.

In order to appreciate the complexity of politics and political transitions in developing countries, we must look beyond any single national perspective. Today, business and trade, information technology, mass communications and culture, immigration and travel, as well as politics, forge deep connections among people worldwide. It is particularly urgent that we adopt a truly global perspective as we explore both the politics of different countries and their growing interdependence.

The developing world provides a fascinating laboratory for the study of comparative politics and gives unusual significance to the subject. We hope that you share our sense of excitement and join us in the challenging effort to understand the complex and ever-shifting terrain of politics in the developing world. We begin by exploring what comparative politics actually compares and how comparative study enhances our understanding of politics generally.

Section ❷ What—and How—Comparative Politics Compares

To compare and contrast is one of the most common human exercises, whether in the classroom study of literature or politics or animal behavior—or in selecting dorm rooms or listing favorite movies. In the observation of politics, the use of comparisons is very old, dating at least from Aristotle, the ancient Greek philosopher. Aristotle categorized Athenian city-states in the fifth century B.C. according to their form of political rule: rule by a single individual, rule by a few, or rule by all citizens. He added a normative dimension (a claim about how societies should be ruled) by distinguishing ("contrasting") good and corrupt versions of each type. The modern study of comparative politics refines and systematizes the age-old practice of evaluating some feature of X by comparing it to the same feature of Y in order to learn more about it than isolated study would permit.

The term **comparative politics** refers to a field within the academic study of politics (that is, political science), as well as to a method or approach to the study of politics.[1] The subject matter of comparative politics is the domestic politics of countries or peoples. This book focuses on the comparative study of several developing nations, whereas other comparative politics books might focus, for example, on the industrial democracies of Western Europe. Within the discipline of political science, comparative politics is one of four areas of specialization. In addition to comparative politics, most political science (or government) departments in U.S. colleges and universities include courses and academic specialists in three other fields: political theory, international relations, and American politics.

The comparative approach principally analyzes similarities and differences among countries by focusing on selected institutions and processes. As students of comparative politics (we call ourselves **comparativists**), we believe that we cannot make reliable statements about most political observations by looking at only one case. We often hear statements such as: "The United States has the best health care system in the world." Comparativists immediately wonder what kinds of health care systems exist in other countries, what they cost and how they are financed, who is covered by health insurance, and so on. Besides, what does "best" mean when it comes to health care systems? Is it the one that provides the widest access? The one that is the most technologically advanced? The one that is the most cost-effective? The one that produces the healthiest population? We would not announce the "best movie" or the "best car" without considering other alternatives or deciding what specific factors enter into our judgment.

Comparativists often analyze political institutions or processes by looking at two or more cases deliberately selected to isolate their common and contrasting features. The analysis involves comparing similar aspects of politics in more than one country. For example, a comparativist might ask what explains the vastly different political roles of the military in India and Nigeria (both former British colonies).[2] One of the strengths of democracy in India is that the military has never intervened in politics, whereas the Nigerian military has done so frequently and with disastrous political and economic consequences for the country. Other comparative political studies take a thematic approach and analyze broad issues, such as the causes and consequences of revolutions in different countries.[3]

Levels of Analysis

Comparisons can be very useful for political analysis at several different levels. Political scientists often compare developments in different cities, regions, provinces, or states. Comparative analysis can also focus on specific institutions and processes in different countries, such as the legislature, executive, political parties, social movements, or court systems. The organization of *Introduction to Politics of the Developing World* reflects our belief that the best way to begin the study of comparative politics is with **countries.** Countries, which are also sometimes referred to as **nation-states,** comprise distinct, politically defined territories that encompass political institutions, cultures, economies, and ethnic and other social identities.

Although often highly divided internally, countries have historically been the most important source of a people's collective political identity and are the major arena for organized political action in the modern world. Therefore, countries are the natural unit of analysis for most domestic political variables and processes:

- **political institutions:** the formal and informal rules and structured relationships that organize power and resources in society
- **political culture:** attitudes, beliefs, and symbols that influence political behavior
- **political development:** the stages of change in the structures of government.

Within a given country, the state is almost always the most powerful cluster of institutions. But just what is the state? The way the term is used in comparative politics is probably unfamiliar to many students. In the United States, it usually refers to the states in the federal system—Texas, California, and so on. But in comparative politics, the **state** refers to the key political institutions responsible for making, implementing, enforcing, and adjudicating important policies in a country. The most important state institutions are the national **executive**—usually, the president and/or prime minister and **cabinet**—but in some cases (such as China), it is the Communist Party leader, the head of a military government (as in Nigeria until 1999), or the supreme religious leader (as in the Islamic Republic of Iran). Other important state institutions are the military, police, and administrative **bureaucracy;** the legislature; and the courts. In many ways, the state is synonymous with what is often called "the government."

States claim, usually with considerable success, the right to issue rules—notably, laws, administrative regulations, and court decisions—that are binding for people within the country. Even democratic states, in which top officials are chosen by procedures that permit all citizens to participate, can survive only if they can preserve enforcement (or coercive) powers both internally and with regard to other states that may pose challenges. A number of countries have highly repressive states whose political survival depends largely on military and police powers. But even in such states, long-term stability requires that the ruling regime have some measure of political **legitimacy;** that is, a significant segment of the citizenry must believe that the state is entitled to command. Political legitimacy is greatly affected by the state's ability to "deliver the goods" through satisfactory economic performance and an acceptable distribution of economic resources. Moreover, in the contemporary period, legitimacy seems to require that states represent themselves as democratic in some fashion, even if they are not in fact. Thus, *Introduction to Politics of the Developing World* looks closely at both the state's role in governing the economy and the pressures exerted on states to develop and extend democratic participation.

The fact that states are the fundamental objects of analysis in comparative politics does not mean that all states are the same. Indeed, the organization of state institutions varies widely, and these differences have a powerful impact on political and social life. Hence, each country study in this book devotes considerable attention to variations in institutions of governance, participation, and representation and their political implications. Each country study begins with an analysis of how the institutional organization and political procedures of the state have evolved historically. This process of **state formation** fundamentally influences how and why states in the developing world differ politically.

Causal Theories

Because countries are the basic building blocks in politics and because states are the most significant political organizations and actors, these two are the critical units for comparative analysis. The comparativist looks at similarities and differences among countries or states. One influential approach in comparative politics involves developing causal theories—hypotheses that can be expressed formally in a causal mode: "If X happens, then Y will be the result." Such theories include factors (the independent variables, symbolized by X) that are believed to influence the outcome (the dependent variable, symbolized by Y) to be explained. For example, it is commonly argued that if a country's economic pie shrinks, conflict among groups for resources will intensify. This hypothesis suggests what is called an inverse correlation between variables: as X varies in one direction, Y varies in the opposite direction. As the total national economic product (X) decreases, then political and social conflict over economic shares (Y) increases. This was the case in Iran, for instance, when economic problems caused by sharply declining oil revenues fed the social discontent that led to the Islamic revolution of 1979.

Even when the explanation does not involve the explicit testing of hypotheses (and often it does not), comparativists try to identify similarities and differences among countries and significant patterns.

It is important to recognize the limits on just how "scientific" political science, and thus comparative politics, can be. Two important differences exist between the "hard" (or natural) sciences like physics and chemistry and the social sciences. First, social scientists study people who exercise free will. Because people have a margin for free choice, their choices, attitudes, and behavior cannot be fully explained by causal analysis. This does not mean that people choose in an arbitrary fashion. We choose within the context of material constraint, institutional dictates, and cultural prescriptions. Indeed, comparative politics analyzes how these and other factors orient political choices in systematic ways. But there will probably always be a wide gulf between the natural and social sciences because of their different objects of study.

A second difference between the natural and social sciences is that in the natural sciences, experimental techniques can be applied to isolate the contribution of distinct factors to a particular outcome. It is possible to change the value or magnitude of a factor—for example, the force applied to an object—and measure how the outcome has consequently changed. However, like other social scientists, political scientists and comparativists rarely have the opportunity to apply such experimental techniques.

In the real world of politics, unlike in a laboratory, variables cannot easily be isolated or manipulated. Statistical techniques can be used in an attempt to identify the specific causal weight of different variables in explaining variations in political outcomes. But it is difficult to measure precisely how, for example, a person's ethnicity, gender, or income influences her or his choice when casting a ballot. And we can never know for sure what exact mix of factors—conflicts among elites, popular ideological appeals, the weakness of the state, the organizational capacity of rebel leaders, or the discontent of the masses—precipitates a successful revolution. Indeed, different revolutions may result from different configurations of factors, such that one cannot develop a theory of revolution.

There is a lively debate about whether the social sciences should seek comparable scientific explanation to what prevails in the natural sciences, such as physics. Some claim that political scientists should seek to develop what has been called covering laws to explain political outcomes, that is, political phenomena should be explained by universal laws in a similar way to how physicists develop universally applicable laws to explain specific features of the physical world. Critics of this view claim that the social world is essentially different from the natural world. Some contend that the social sciences should seek to identify particular mechanisms that operate in different settings but that discerning recurrent mechanisms do not fully explain outcomes. Another group claims that the social scientist should focus on identifying unique configurations that coexist in a particular case but that, once again, the result will not be a full explanation or the development of covering laws.[4] And yet a fourth

group advocates what one practitioner described as "thick description," which seeks to convey the rich and subtle texture of any given historical situation, including the subjective and symbolic meaning of that situation for its participants. For the last group, and possibly the second and third groups as well, the aim is thus not to provide causal explanations of particular events.

Leaving aside the knotty issue of causality, most comparativists probably agree on the value of steering a middle course that avoids focusing exclusively on one country as well as combining all countries indiscriminately. If we study only individual countries without any comparative framework, then comparative politics would become merely the study of a series of isolated cases. It would be impossible to recognize what is most significant in the collage of political characteristics that we find in the world's many countries. As a result, the understanding of patterns of similarity and difference among countries would be lost, along with an important tool for evaluating what is and what is not unique about a country's political life.

If we go to the other extreme and try to make universal claims that something is always true in all countries, we would either have to stretch the truth or ignore the interesting differences and patterns of variation. The political world is incredibly complex, shaped by an extraordinary array of factors and an almost endless interplay of variables. Indeed, after a brief period in the 1950s and 1960s when many comparativists tried—and failed—to develop a "grand theory" that would apply to all countries, most comparativists now agree on the value of **middle-level theory,** that is, theories focusing on specific features of the political world, such as institutions, policies, or classes of similar events, such as revolutions or elections.

For example, comparativists have analyzed the process in which many countries with authoritarian forms of government, such as military **dictatorships** and one-party states, have developed more participatory and democratic regimes. In studying this process, termed *democratic transitions,* comparativists do not treat each national case as unique or try to construct a universal pattern that ignores all differences. Applying middle-level theory, we identify the influence on the new regime's political stability of specific variables, such as institutional legacies, political culture, levels of economic development, the nature of the regime before the transition, and the degree of ethnic conflict or homogeneity. Comparativists have been able to identify patterns in the emergence and consolidation of democratic regimes in southern Europe in the 1970s (Greece, Portugal, and Spain) and have compared them to developments in Latin America, Asia, and Africa since the 1980s and in Eastern and Central Europe since the revolutions of 1989.[5] In this book, we can study the transition from military rule to democracy in Brazil and Nigeria and progress toward deeper democratization in Mexico knowing that these cases fit within a broader comparative framework.

The study of comparative politics has many challenges, including the complexity of the subject matter, the fast pace of change in the contemporary world, and the impossibility of manipulating variables or replicating conditions. What can we expect when the whole political world is our laboratory? When we put the method of comparative politics to the test and develop a set of themes derived from middle-level theory, we discover that it is possible to find explanations and discern patterns that make sense of a vast range of political developments and link the experiences of states and citizens throughout the world. We believe that the comparative approach can be a very powerful tool for analyzing politics in the developing world.

Section ③ The Developing World in a World in Transition

Most textbooks and courses in comparative politics have traditionally been organized according to categories that distinguished between industrial (and primarily Western) democracies—the "First World"—Communist Party states as the "Second World," and the less developed countries of Asia, Africa, and Latin America as the "Third World." This categorization was based, in part, on distinctive economic features that helped characterize different political systems. Economic organization and performance both affected and reflected the realities of politics in these different political systems: the capitalist (or market) economies and high standard of living in North America, Western Europe, Japan, and a few other countries; the socialist (or planned) economies of countries ruled by a Communist party, such as the Soviet Union and China; and the low level of economic development and extensive poverty characteristic of the Third World.

Democracy was another dividing line in this way of looking at the nations of the world. The capitalist industrialized countries were not only wealthy but also stable and democratic; Communist systems were unquestionably dictatorial; and most Third World nations had personal despots, one-party rule, military regimes, or—at best—democracies marred by high levels of social conflict and political violence.

One of the consequences of the many profound changes of recent decades is that these economic and political differences among types of countries are no longer so obvious. For one thing, sharp differences in growth rates among developing countries in recent years make it difficult to generalize with confidence about the "Third World." For example, from 1990 to 2000, China's economy grew at an annual average per capita rate of 9.2 percent, whereas India's growth rate was less than half that (4.1 percent), and some developing countries, such as Burundi experienced negative growth during that period (-4.7 percent). Furthermore, scores of developing countries have become democratic, or moved in that direction, in the past two decades. From Argentina to Zambia, formerly undemocratic states have adopted democratic institutions.

Linked to the swelling of the ranks of democratic countries in the Third World has been the near-disappearance of the Communist countries in the Second World. Beginning in 1989, the collapse of communism in the former Soviet Union and Eastern and Central Europe set off a revolutionary change in world politics. Only a handful of countries—China, Cuba, Vietnam, Laos, and the Democratic People's Republic of Korea (North Korea)— are now ruled by Communist parties and declare an allegiance to Communist ideology. It follows that "Second World" is no longer a useful category to classify countries.

These recent trends have certainly challenged and complicated the way that comparativists categorize the world's countries. But we believe that despite major political and economic difference, the countries included in this book continue to share many distinct characteristics that allow us to group and study them together as part of the developing world.

Third World or Developing World?

The term *Third World* was coined by French authors in the 1950s to draw attention to the plight of the world's poorer nations, which they believed to be as important as the then headline-grabbing cold war and its superpower adversaries. To make their point, these authors adapted terminology from the French Revolution of the eighteenth century to dramatize the global inequalities of the mid-twentieth century: a long-neglected and oppressed *Third* World, they noted, was struggling against the *First* World (the industrial democracies) and the *Second* World (the Soviet Union and other Communist countries) for recognition and power just as the *Third* Estate of the common people in France had done against the privileged and powerful clergy (the *First* Estate) and the nobility (the *Second* Estate) in the 1780s.

Some people criticize the label as suggesting a numerical order in which the Third World ranks behind the First World and the Second World in a cultural sense. But its creators intended the term *Third World* to embody the struggle of poor nations for empowerment in the international system and a fairer share of global wealth. For many, the term *Third World* remains a powerful symbol of common purpose and determination and is still widely used to describe the developing countries of Asia, Africa, and Latin America.[6]

This book uses the terms *developing* and *Third World* interchangeably to refer to countries that are economically poorer ("less developed") than the industrial democracies. Many people also use the term *South* as a way of referring collectively to developing nations in contrast to the developed nations of the "North."[7] Like *Third World, South* has achieved a certain symbolic importance by conveying the fact that there are enormous differences between the richer and poorer nations of the world. Granted, *South* is geographically somewhat misleading since there are developed nations in the Southern Hemisphere (like Australia) and less developed nations in the northern part of the globe (like Afghanistan).

But, whatever term you prefer, it is very important to recognize that the developing countries (which contain about 85 percent of the world's population) are very diverse geographically, economically, politically, and culturally. Some observers have asserted that there is such enormous diversity among developing nations that they question whether it is still valid to use such a catch-all category as *Third World* because it implies too much similarity in the challenges facing the developing nations and too much unity in their international policies. They point to the huge differences in levels of economic development among countries usually considered part of the Third World. They question whether a country like Bangladesh with its extreme poverty ($362 average income) and overwhelmingly rural population (75 percent) has much in common with a much more prosperous ($9,762 average income) and highly urbanized (80 percent) **newly industrializing country (NIC),** such as the Republic of Korea (South Korea), which many still consider to be a developing nation. Others argue not for abandoning the categories like developing countries or Third World, but for taking account of the differences among developing countries by adding more nuanced distinctions such as "low income," "least developed," or even "Fourth World" to refer to the poorest countries.

This book acknowledges the rich diversity of the developing world. In fact, the countries examined here were chosen, in part, to reflect this variety, as well as to illustrate important issues in the study of comparative politics. Table 1 indicates some of the important differences that mark the developing nations that are covered in this text.

The Development Gap

If there are such extensive differences among developing nations, what gives coherence to the concept of the Third World? Simply put, Third World nations are poorer, their peoples have a lower standard of living, and their economies are not as modernized as the industrialized countries: in other words, they are less developed. A few examples should make the realities of this development gap between the Third World and the industrialized countries clearer.[8]

The World Bank, a major international organization that provides financial assistance to the Third World,

Table 1

Diversity in the Developing World			
Country	Location	Political System	Economy
Brazil	South America	Transitional democracy	Upper-middle income, low growth
China	East Asia	Communist party–state	Low-middle income, high growth
India	South Asia	Established democracy	Low income, moderate growth
Iran	Middle East	Islamic Republic; theocracy	Lower-middle income, moderate growth, heavily dependent on oil exports
Mexico	Northern Central America	Recent transition from one-party dominant to competitive democracy	Upper-middle income, negative growth
Nigeria	West Africa	Very early stages of transition from military rule to democracy	Low income, low growth, heavily dependent on oil exports

divides developing countries according to their annual **gross national income** (GNI) per capita (a broad measure of the total output of an economy divided by the total population) into three groups: low income ($745 or less), lower middle income ($746–2,975), and upper middle income ($2,976–9,205). The industrialized (high-income) countries are those with a GNI per capita above $9,206, but these countries have an average GNI per capita of about $27,000 per year.

Generally, a country's GNI per capita reflects both its level of modernization and its relative power in the international economic system. But it also tells us a lot about the capacity of a government or an economy to meet the material needs of the people of a country. Thus, low GNI per capita figures also reflect the low average standard of living and greater poverty that distinguish less developed from more developed nations.

The stark contrasts in the statistics used to measure a country's overall **physical quality of life (PQLI)** give some sense of what low GNI per capita means in terms of people's lives:

- **Life expectancy** in the low-income countries averages only fifty-nine years; in the middle-income developing countries, it is about sixty-nine, and in the high-income developed countries, a person can expect to live seventy-eight years on average. In the poorest countries, such as Afghanistan, life expectancy is only about forty-three; in Sierra Leone, it is thirty-nine.
- The **child mortality rate** (which measures how many children die between birth and age five) in low-income countries is 115 per 1,000 live births, and in the very poorest countries it reaches well over 250 per 1,000; in the middle-income countries, the average child mortality rate is 39 per 1,000; in the world's richest countries, the child mortality rate is only 7 per 1,000 live births.
- **Illiteracy** among adults (people over age fifteen who cannot read or write) averages 37 percent in the low-income countries (and up to 70 to 80 percent in some) and 14 percent in the middle-income countries. In the developed countries, almost all adults can read, although there is some debate about how functionally literate a sizable part of the population of these countries really is.

It is very important to recognize that there are vast differences in the PQLI statistics even among Third World countries that have roughly similar levels of GNI per capita. For example, China, India, and Nigeria are all in the World Bank's lowest two income-defined categories of countries. Yet China's life expectancy of seventy years is considerably higher than India's (sixty-three years) and Nigeria's (forty-seven years). China also has much lower levels of child mortality and illiteracy than do India and Nigeria. The case studies in this book analyze how such differences reveal important contrasts in the historical experiences and government policies of various developing nations.

We also need to be aware that national averages tend to mask class, gender, and racial inequalities *within* countries. Although this is true in all countries, developing or developed, the disparities are particularly acute in the Third World. For example, Pakistan has an overall adult literacy rate of 43 percent, but among women it is only 28 percent (for males, it is 57 percent). Some people have even suggested that poor women in the least developed "Fourth World" countries should be called the "Fifth World" because they are, indeed, the poorest of the poor.

Some developing nations have achieved significant progress over the past few decades. A few, such as China, have experienced tremendous economic growth, and child mortality rates in the developing world as a whole have dropped by nearly 50 percent since 1970. Similar positive trends are apparent in some of other figures that are used to measure poverty in the less developed countries.

Nevertheless, many developing countries still have very low and sometimes even negative economic growth rates, and for many of their citizens, the physical quality of life is hardly improving and may even be deteriorating. Other countries may be experiencing increases in production, but their swelling populations are swallowing up the gains of increased output, making real economic expansion impossible. The economy of Honduras, for example, grew by an average of 3.1 percent per year in the period 1990–2001; but its population grew by 2.7 percent per year during the same period. The result? Per capita income in Honduras hardly grew at all. Thus, the enormous development gap that separates most of the Third World and the industrialized nations (which have *very* low population growth rates) is at best closing very slowly—and, in some ways, is even widening—and remains one of the most important ways of categorizing the world's countries (see Figure 1).

Figure 1

The Development Gap

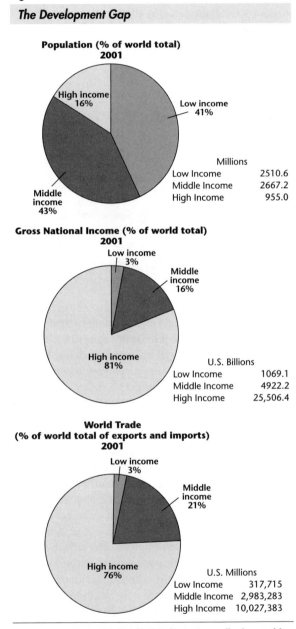

Population (% of world total) 2001

High income 16%
Low income 41%
Middle income 43%

	Millions
Low Income	2510.6
Middle Income	2667.2
High Income	955.0

Gross National Income (% of world total) 2001

Low income 3%
Middle income 16%
High income 81%

	U.S. Billions
Low Income	1069.1
Middle Income	4922.2
High Income	25,506.4

World Trade (% of world total of exports and imports) 2001

Low income 3%
Middle income 21%
High income 76%

	U.S. Millions
Low Income	317,715
Middle Income	2,983,283
High Income	10,027,383

These charts show graphically just how unequally the world's wealth is divided between the developed (high-income) and developing (middle- and low-income) countries. *Source:* World Development Report 2003.

Third World States

There are many types of political systems in the Third World. As Table 1 indicates, the countries presented in this book include an established, highly competitive democracy (India); a country that had been a single-party-dominant democracy for decades but has recently moved toward multiparty competition (Mexico); two nations that can be categorized as transitional democracies, but one of which (Brazil) is fairly far along in the transition from a military dictatorship, while the other (Nigeria) started on that path only in the very late 1990s; a communist party-state (China), and a theocracy (Iran) in which supreme political power is held by the religious elite. Analyzing the differences among such varied types of political systems is one of the most important and interesting tasks in the study of comparative politics. But it is also important to note some of the political characteristics shared by Third World states that distinguish them politically from the developed nations.

First, politics and government in most developing countries are shaped by the basic facts of scarce economic resources, extensive poverty and inequality, and a relatively weak position in the international system. Political leaders in less developed countries simply have fewer options available in resolving problems or responding to demands from various groups for a bigger piece of the national economic pie. Economic conflicts therefore are more likely to lead to violence or repression in Third World states; for example, peasants may rebel in their quest for more land, or the government may violently suppress labor unions striking for higher wages. Corruption, a recurrent theme in the case studies in this book, is a very serious problem in much of the Third World because public officials personally profit from the state's control over various kinds of economic transactions. Resistance to democratization in the Third World has often come—as it also did during earlier stages in the political development of Europe and North America—from elites who fear that greater popular control of the government will jeopardize their economic privileges as well as their political power.

Second, the political legitimacy of many Third World states is very weak. Citizens often lack faith in their political leaders or perhaps even in the very nature of the political system of their country. They may obey the law, and they may even vote. But they do not see the government as being very relevant to their lives or as being able to do anything about their most serious concerns; they may even regard the national government as having a negative impact on their lives. Membership in a religious or ethnic group is often a much more important source of political identity in the Third World than formal citizenship in a particular country. For example, many Tibetans feel only loosely (and perhaps negatively) connected to the Chinese government even though Tibet is formally part of the People's Republic of China.

There are various causes of weak state legitimacy in the Third World. The government may be seen as favoring one ethnic, religious, or economic group or even actively discriminating against some groups. Economic failure, political repression, extreme corruption, and military defeat may cause people to lose faith in the government. New democracies, which are now quite common in the developing world, simply have not had enough time to establish legitimacy in the eyes of their citizens. Whatever the cause, states with weak legitimacy are prone to political violence, radical and sudden changes (such as a military **coup d'état**), and government paralysis. And such chronic instability only further erodes the legitimacy of governments.

Third, the effective power of governments in the less developed countries is often very limited. The state may have little ability to exert its authority much beyond the capital city and a few large urban centers. In the rural areas and small towns where much or most of the population lives, political life is frequently based more on the relationship between powerful and usually wealthy individuals ("patrons") and those they control ("clients") by dispensing favors or instilling fear. In much of the Third World, the formal aspects of government such as laws, parties, and elections are less important than the nonformal **patron-client politics** and other types of personal relationships.

There are significant variations in how governments in the developing countries face the political struggle over scarce resources, weak legitimacy, and the influence of patron-client politics. But to one degree or another, they all experience these problems in ways that make the Third World state a distinctive and important entity in the study of comparative politics.

Section ④ Themes for Comparative Analysis

This section describes the four themes we use to organize the information on institutions and processes in the country chapters in *Introduction to Politics of the Developing World*. These themes help explain continuities and contrasts among the six countries included in this book and demonstrate what patterns apply to a group of countries and why, and what patterns are specific to a particular country. We also suggest a way that each theme highlights some puzzle in Third World politics.

Before we introduce the themes, a couple of warnings are necessary. First, our four themes cannot possibly capture the infinitely varied experience of politics throughout the developing world. Our framework is built on four core themes and provides a guide to understanding many political features of the contemporary Third World. But we urge students (and rely on instructors!) to challenge and expand on our interpretations. Second, we want to note that a textbook builds from existing theory but does not construct or test new hypotheses. That task is the goal of original scholarly studies. The themes are intended to distill some of the most significant findings in the field of contemporary comparative politics as they apply to developing countries.

Theme 1: The Democratic Idea

The spread of democracy throughout much of the world has, without doubt, been one of the most important and dramatic political developments of the late twentieth and early twenty-first centuries. At the close of 1981, there were 50 electoral democracies among the world's 123 independent nations; by the end of 2001, there were 121 democracies out of 192 nations.[9] Many of these new democracies are in Asia, Africa, and Latin America, a fact that has fundamentally transformed politics in the developing world.

What do we mean by democracy? For a regime to qualify as democratic, it must include the following characteristics:

- **Political accountability.** There must be formal procedures by which those who hold political power are chosen and held accountable to the people of the country. The key mechanism for such accountability is regular, free, and fair elections in which all citizens are eligible to cast ballots to elect candidates for office.
- **Political competition.** Political parties must be free to organize, present candidates for office, express their ideas, and compete in fair elections. The winning party must be allowed to take office, and the losing party must relinquish power through legal and peaceful means.
- **Political freedom.** All citizens must possess political rights and civil liberties. These include the right to participate in the political process, free of government reprisals; freedom of assembly, organization, and political expression (including the right to criticize the government); equality before the law; and protection against arbitrary state intrusion into citizens' private lives. A judiciary not subject to direct political control is a common institutional means for safeguarding these freedoms.
- **Political equality.** All citizens must be legally entitled to participate in politics (by voting, running for office, and joining an interest group), and their votes must have equal weight in the political process. Men and women of political, ethnic, religious, or other minority groups must have equal rights as citizens.

By these measures, the countries in this book fall in the following categories: established democracy (India), developing (or transitional) democracy (Brazil, Mexico, Nigeria), and nondemocracy (China, Iran). This is probably a fair approximation of the distribution of regime types in the developing world in general and reflects the trend toward democratization.

But our comparative case studies reveal a surprising level of complexity in the seemingly simple fact of the rapid increase in the number of Third World democracies. First, they show the strong appeal of the democratic idea, by which we mean the claim by citizens that they should in some way exercise substantial control over the decisions made by their states and governments. As authoritarian rulers have recently learned in the former Soviet Union, Brazil, Iran, South Africa, Nigeria, and China, once persistent and widespread pressures for democratic participation develop, they are hard (although not impossible) to resist. As the Nobel Prize–winning economist and comparative public policy analyst Amartya Sen puts it, "While democracy is not yet uniformly practiced, nor indeed uniformly accepted, in the general climate of world opinion, democratic governance has now achieved the status of being taken to be generally right."[10] A good indication of the near-universal appeal of the democratic idea is that even authoritarian regimes proclaim their attachment to democracy, usually asserting that they embody a superior form to that prevailing elsewhere. For example, leaders of the People's Republic of China claim that their brand of "socialist democracy" represents the interests of the vast majority of citizens more effectively than do the "bourgeois democracies" of capitalist societies.

Second, the case studies draw attention to diverse sources of support for democracy. Democracy has proved appealing throughout the developing world for many reasons. In some historical settings, it may represent a standoff or equilibrium among political contenders for power, in which no one group can gain sufficient strength to control outcomes alone.[11] Democracy may appeal to citizens in authoritarian settings because democratic regimes often rank among the world's most stable, affluent, and cohesive countries. Another important pressure for democracy is born of the human desire for dignity and equality. Even when dictatorial regimes appear to benefit their countries— for example, by promoting economic development or nationalist goals—citizens are still likely to demand democracy. Although authoritarian governments can suppress demands for democratic participation, the domestic and (in recent years) international costs of doing so are high.

Third, the country studies show that democracies in the Third World vary widely in concrete historical, institutional, and cultural dimensions. We pay close attention to different electoral and party systems, to the distinction between parliamentary and presidential systems, and to differences in the values and expectations that shape citizens' demands in different countries.

Fourth, many of the country studies illustrate the potential fragility of democratic transitions in the developing nations. The fact that popular movements or leaders of moderate factions often displace authoritarian regimes and then hold elections does not mean that democratic institutions will prevail or endure: a wide gulf exists between a transition to democracy and the consolidation of democracy. Historically, powerful groups have often opposed democratic institutions because they fear that democracy will threaten their privilege. On the other hand, disadvantaged groups may oppose the democratic process because they see it as unresponsive to their deeply felt grievances. As a result, reversals of democratic regimes have occurred in the past and will doubtless occur in the future. Our country studies do not support a philosophy of history or theory of political development that identifies a single (democratic) end point toward which all countries will eventually converge. One important work, published in the early phase of the most recent democratic wave, captured the tenuous process of democratization in its title: *Transitions from Authoritarian Rule: Tentative Conclusions About Uncertain Democracies*.[12] Some suggest that it is far easier for a country to hold its first democratic election than its second or third. Hence, the fact that the democratic idea is so powerful does not mean that all countries will adopt or preserve democratic institutions.

A puzzle: democracy and stability. Comparativists have intensely debated whether democratic institutions contribute to political stability or, on the contrary, to political disorder. On the one hand, democracy by its very nature permits political opposition: one of its defining characteristics is competition among those who aspire to gain high political office. Political life in democracies is turbulent and unpredictable. On the other hand, the fact that political opposition and competition are legitimate in democracies appears to deepen support for the state even among opponents of a particular government. History reveals far more cases of durable democratic regimes than durable authoritarian regimes in the modern world. In your country-by-country studies, look for the stabilizing and destabilizing consequences of recent democratic transitions in Brazil, Mexico, and Nigeria; the pressures (or lack of pressures) for democratization in China and Iran; and the challenges faced by even India's established democracy.

Theme 2: A World of States

The theme that we call a world of states reflects the fact that since the beginning of the modern era about 500 years ago, states have been the primary actors on the world stage. Although international organizations and private actors like transnational corporations play a crucial role, for the most part it is the rulers of states who send armies to conquer other states and territories. It is the legal codes of states that make it possible for businesses to operate within their borders and beyond. States provide for the social protection of citizens through the provision—in one way or another—of health care, old age pensions, aid to dependent children, and assistance to the unemployed. It is states that try to regulate the movement of people across borders through immigration law. And even the most influential contemporary international organizations in large part reflect the balance of power among member states. That said, there is no longer as sharp a distinction between courses in international relations that focus primarily on interaction among states or on cross-border processes and courses in comparative politics that analyze what goes on within a country's borders. Therefore, in *Introduction to Politics of the Developing World,* we emphasize the interactive effects of domestic politics and international forces.

No state, even the most powerful, such as the United States, is unaffected by influences originating outside its borders. Today, a host of processes associated with globalization underscore the heightened importance of various cross-national influences. A wide array of international organizations and treaties, including the United Nations, the European Union, the World Trade Organization, and the North American Free Trade Agreement, challenge the sovereign control of national governments. Transnational corporations, international banks, and currency traders in New York, London, Hong Kong, and Tokyo affect countries and people throughout the world. A country's political borders do not protect its citizens from global warming, environmental pollution, or infectious diseases that come from abroad. More broadly, developments linked to technology transfer, the growth of an international information society, immigration, and cultural diffusion have a varying but undeniable impact on the domestic politics of all countries. For example, as a result of the

global diffusion of radio, television, and the Internet, people in nearly every part of the world are remarkably informed about international developments. This knowledge may fuel popular local demands that governments intervene in faraway Kosovo, Rwanda, East Timor, or elsewhere. And heightened global awareness may make citizens readier to hold their own government to internationally recognized standards of human rights.

In the first decade of this new century, all nation-states are experiencing intense pressures from an expanding and increasingly complex mix of external influences. But international political and economic influences do not have the same impact in all countries, and all states do not equally shape the institutional form and policy of international organizations in which they participate. It is likely that the more advantaged a state is, as measured by its level of economic development, military power, and resource base, the more it will shape global influences. Conversely, the policies of less advantaged countries are more extensively molded by other states, international organizations, and broader international constraints. With the world of states theme, we emphasize one key feature of the international arena: the impact on the domestic political institutions and processes of developing states on its relative success or failure in competing economically and politically with other states, particularly those that are wealthier and more powerful. What sphere of maneuver is left to states in the developing world by imperious global economic and geopolitical forces? How do CNN, the Internet, McDonald's, television, and films (whether produced in Hollywood or in "Bollywood," that is, Bombay, by India's thriving film industry) shape local cultures and values, influence citizen perceptions of and demands of government, and affect political outcomes? Today, post 9/11 global security concerns influence both the domestic and international politics of Third World states. The events and aftermath of September 11 have also exerted a ripple effect on conflicts long predating the attacks on the United States, such as the Kashmir dispute that bitterly divides predominantly Hindu India and mostly Muslim Pakistan.

The theme we identify as a world of states includes a second important focus: similarities and contrasts among developing countries in state formation. Here we consider the effects of the global order long before the contemporary era of globalization. We study the ways that states have developed historically, the impact of international forces on state formation, diverse patterns in the organization of political institutions, the processes and limits of democratization, the ability of the state to control social groups and sustain power, and the state's economic management strategies and capacities. For example, why did China and India, both of which mark the formation of their modern state in the late 1940s, take such divergent paths, and what role did international forces play in that divergence? It is particularly important to note how the experiences of colonialism and imperialism shaped the formation of Third World states. In India, for example, the British established a professional civil service staffed by Indians to help run the colony, a legacy that greatly influenced the shape of independent India's government and has contributed to the durability of Indian democracy. By contrast, in Iran, Britain and the United States supported a despotic monarchy because it protected Western oil interests; the end result was the revolution that produced that country's contemporary Islamic Republic.

A puzzle: To what extent do states in the developing world still remain the basic building blocks of political life? Increasingly, the politics and policies of such states are shaped by diverse external factors often lumped together under the category of globalization. At the same time, many Third World states face increasingly restive constituencies who challenge the power and legitimacy of central governments. In reading our country case studies, try to assess what impact pressures from both above and below—outside and inside—have had on the role of the state in carrying out its basic functions and sustaining the political attachment of its citizens. Can weaker (in terms of economic and military power) states pursue and defend their interests in a world where some great powers, particularly the United States, are trying to define the global agenda in terms of its perceived national security needs? More broadly, is a significant degree of national autonomy and policy innovation for the states of the developing world compatible with globalization? For the countries in this book, try to assess their relative position in the international system, particularly their relationship with the more developed nations. How do you account for the similarities and differences in the ways various developing countries fit into the world of states in the early twenty-first century?

Theme 3: Governing the Economy

The success of all states in maintaining their authority and sovereign control is greatly affected by their ability to ensure that an adequate volume of goods and services is produced to satisfy the needs of their populations. Certainly, the inadequate performance of the Soviet economic system was an important reason for the rejection of communism and the disintegration of the Soviet Union. In contrast, the economic achievements of China's Communist Party are a major factor in explaining why Communist rule has survived in that country.

An important goal of all countries in the contemporary world is to achieve durable economic development. In fact, effective economic performance is near the top of every state's political agenda. The term **political economy** refers to how governments affect economic performance and how economic performance in turn affects a country's political processes. We accord great importance to political economy in *Introduction to Politics of the Developing World* because we believe that politics in all countries is deeply influenced by the relationship between government and the economy in both domestic and international dimensions. However, the term *economic performance* conveys the impression that there is a single standard by which to measure performance. In fact, the matter is far more complex. Should economic performance be measured solely by how rapidly a country's economy grows? By how equitably it distributes the fruits of economic growth? By the quality of life of its citizenry, as measured by such criteria as life expectancy, level of education, and unemployment rates? (For additional analysis of this point, see "Global Connection: How Is Development Measured?") We invite you to consider this question as you study the political economies of the six developing countries analyzed in this book.

How a country "governs the economy"—how it organizes production and intervenes to manage the economy—is one of the key elements in its overall pattern of political as well as economic development.[13] It is important to analyze, for example, how countries

Global Connection: *How Is Development Measured?*

Two frequently used measures of a country's level of economic development are its **gross domestic product** (GDP) and gross national income (GNI) per capita. These figures are slightly different ways to estimate a country's total economic output divided by its total population. Such estimates are made in a country's own currency, such as pesos in Mexico or rupees in India.

In order to make comparisons of GDP or GNI per capita across countries, it is necessary to convert the estimates to a common currency, usually the U.S. dollar. This is done using **official international currency exchange rates,** which, for example, would tell you how many pesos or rupees it takes to buy U.S.$1. But many economists believe that an estimate of GDP/GNI per capita in dollars based on such exchange rates does not give an accurate sense of the real standards of living in different countries because it does not tell what goods and services (such as housing, food, and transportation) people can actually buy with their local currencies.

An alternative and increasingly popular means of comparing levels of economic development across countries is to calculate exchange rates based on **purchasing power parity** (PPP). PPP-based exchange rates take into account the actual cost of living in a particular country by figuring what it costs to buy the same bundle of goods in different countries. For example, how many pesos does it take to buy a certain amount of food in Mexico or rupees to pay for housing in India? Many analysts think that PPP provides a more reliable (and revealing) tool for comparing standards of living among countries.

The data boxes at the start of each country chapter in this book show GDP per capita (the measure favored by the United Nations) at both the official exchange rates and purchasing power parity. As you will see, the differences between the two calculations can be quite dramatic. However, income comparisons based on either method do not provide a complete picture of a country's level of development, since these measurements do not necessarily capture what might be considered better ways of measuring the quality of life for the citizen of that country. As a result, the United Nations has introduced another concept that is useful in making socioeconomic comparisons among nations: the **Human Development Index** (HDI). Based on a formula that takes into account the three factors of longevity (life expectancy at birth), knowledge (literacy and average years of schooling), and income (according to PPP), the United Nations assigns each country of the world, for which there are enough data, an HDI decimal number between 0 and 1; the closer a country is to 1, the better is its level of human development.

Of 173 countries ranked according to HDI by the United Nations Development Programme in 2002, Norway (.942) was at the top and Sierra Leone (.275) was ranked last. Countries such as the United States (6), Japan (9), France (12), Britain (13), Israel (22), Singapore (25), and the Republic of (South) Korea (27) scored as having "high human development"; Mexico (54), Brazil (73), China (96), Iran (98), India (124), and Kenya (134) had "medium human development"; and Pakistan (138) and Nigeria (148) were ranked as having "low human development."

---

differ in the balance between agricultural and industrial production in their economies, how successful they are in competing with other countries that offer similar products in international markets, and the relative importance of market forces versus government control of the economy.

Most developing countries are taking steps to reduce the state's role in regulating the economy and

are increasing the nation's involvement in the international economy by expanding exports and seeking foreign investment. The collapse of communism and the discrediting of the socialist model of extensive government control of the economy have vastly increased the global economic influence of the world's great capitalist powers, including the United States, Japan, and Germany. Furthermore, the World Bank and the

International Monetary Fund (another major source of economic aid and advice for developing countries) are taking the lead—sometimes quite forcefully—in steering developing countries toward **economic liberalization.** Some observers see the emphasis on free markets and international competition that are at the heart of economic liberalization as a blueprint for development and modernization. Others see the pressures on developing countries to liberalize their economies as an example of **neo-imperialism,** in which the powerful capitalist countries are once again dictating policies to the Third World. In either case, the trend toward economic liberalization—which, in one way or another, affects every country included in this book—demonstrates how a state's approach to governing its economy is strongly shaped by its position in the world of states.

A puzzle: What is the relationship between economic development and political democracy?[14] There are several aspects of this puzzle that you should ponder while reading this book.

First, are democratic states more or less able to pursue effective developmental strategies? Although all economies, even the most powerful, experience ups and downs, the United States, Canada, and the countries of the European Union—all democracies—have been notable economic success stories. Yet until the East Asian economic crisis that began in 1997, several countries with authoritarian regimes had also achieved remarkable records of development. The Republic of Korea (South Korea), Taiwan, and Singapore surged economically in the 1960s and 1970s, and Malaysia and Thailand followed suit in the 1980s and 1990s. Much of East Asia remains in the throes of an economic downturn and loss of international confidence by investors and international financial organizations such as the International Monetary Fund, which question whether the nondemocratic elements of political regimes will allow them to reform institutions effectively and stabilize their economies. But Amartya Sen has argued recently, "There is no clear relation between economic growth and democracy in *either* direction."[15] Indeed, as the case of India shows, it is possible to have democracy without development—or at least with only very limited development. Democracy may give the poor a voice in government, but it can also allow the economic elite to use their political power to block needed changes (such as land reform or poverty alleviation). In contrast, China, an authoritarian communist party-state that has enjoyed the highest growth rate in the world since the early 1990s, provides a vivid example of development without democracy. As you read the country studies, think about how democracy may help or hinder the state in its task to govern the economy.

Second, what special burdens do the difficult economic conditions typical of the developing world impose on a country that is trying to establish or sustain democracy? Many social scientists have argued that for democracy to take root and flourish, a certain level of economic development—one characterized, for example, by a decent average standard of living, extensive urbanization, a large middle class, and high literacy rates—is necessary. Yet democratization has recently spread to some of the world's poorest countries (such as Mozambique and Nepal), which do not meet any of these socioeconomic prerequisites. What chance does democracy have to flourish in such circumstances? In this book, another very poor nation, Nigeria, is the clearest case of a country in the early stages of the transition from **authoritarianism** to democracy. Its struggle to establish democracy must be understood within the context of the special economic challenges it faces as a low-income developing nation. Do these challenges make it harder for Nigeria to build the kind of basic national consensus and spirit of compromise on which a healthy democracy depends? Economic failure was one of the principal causes of the collapse of many dictatorial regimes in recent decades. The political fate of the new democracies of the Third World will also depend largely on their economic records.

Third, in what ways, and with what effects, do economic development and modernization create pressures for further democratization in the Third World? Social scientists have also observed that as an economy and society become more modern and complex, as incomes and educational levels rise, and as a country becomes more connected economically and in other ways to the outside world, the pressures on a state to democratize tend to grow. These pressures may come from within the government itself, from the society below, or from abroad. In what ways has the modernizing economy and society influenced the process of democratization in countries such as Brazil and Mexico? How has successful economic development in China generated powerful pressures for political change that confront an authoritarian government with fundamental challenges?

Theme 4: The Politics of Collective Identity

How do individuals understand who they are in political terms, and on what basis do groups of people come together to advance common political aims? In other words, what are the sources of collective political identity? At one point, social scientists thought they knew the answer. Observers argued that the age-old loyalties of ethnicity, religious affiliation, race, gender, and locality were being dissolved and displaced by economic, political, and cultural modernization. Comparativists thought that **social class**—solidarities based on the shared experience of work or, more broadly, economic position—had become the most important source of collective identity. They believed that most of the time, groups would pragmatically pursue their interests in ways that were not politically destabilizing.[16] We now know that the formation of group attachments and the interplay of politically relevant collective identities are far more complex and uncertain.

In many industrial democracies, such as the United States and Canada, the importance of identities based on class membership has declined, although class and material sources of collective political identity remain significant in political competition and economic organization. But in much of the Third World, class remains a very potent source of identity and political conflict because of the extreme socioeconomic inequalities and barriers to social mobility that are found in these countries. By contrast, contrary to earlier predictions, in many developed and developing countries, nonclass identities have assumed growing, not diminishing, significance. These affiliations develop from a sense of belonging to particular groups based on language, region, religion, ethnicity, race, nationality, or gender. Conflict based on such affiliations is often particularly intense in postcolonial countries like Nigeria, where colonial authorities drew borders with little regard to preexisting collective identities. This process of state formation by the imposition of external power

sowed seeds for future ethnic conflict in Nigeria and elsewhere and threatens the prospects for democracy in many postcolonial countries.

The politics of collective political identity involves struggles to define which groups are full participants in the political community and which are marginalized or even ostracized. It also involves a constant tug of war over relative power and influence, both symbolic and substantive, among groups. And there are questions of representation: Who is included in an ethnic minority community, for example, or who speaks for the community or negotiates with a governmental authority on its behalf? One reason that conflict around these questions can be so intense is that political leaders in the state and in opposition movements often seek to mobilize support by exploiting ethnic, religious, racial, or regional rivalries and manipulating the issue of representation. Every country in this book is, in one way or another, challenged by intense and sometimes violent identity-based conflicts that involve issues of inclusion, political recognition, and priority.

A puzzle: collective identity and distributional politics. Once identity demands are placed on the political agenda, can governments resolve them by distributing political, economic, and other resources in ways that redress the grievances of the minority or politically weaker identity groups? Collective identities operate at the level of symbols, attitudes, values, and beliefs and at the level of material resources. However, the contrast between material- and nonmaterial-based identities and demands should not be exaggerated. In practice, most groups are animated by both feelings of attachment and solidarity and the desire to obtain material benefits and political influence for their members. But the analytical distinction between material and nonmaterial demands remains useful, and it is worth considering whether the nonmaterial aspects of the politics of collective identities make political disputes over ethnicity or religion or language or nationality especially divisive and difficult to resolve.

In a situation of extreme scarcity, as is found in much of the developing world, it may prove nearly impossible to reach any compromise among groups with conflicting material demands. But if an adequate level of material resources is available, such conflicts may be easier to resolve because groups can negotiate at least a minimally satisfying share of resources. This process of determining who gets what or how resources are distributed is called **distributional politics.** However, the demands of ethnic, religious, and nationalist movements may be difficult to satisfy by a distributional style of politics. The distributional style may be quite ineffective when, for example, a religious group demands that the government require all citizens to conform to its social practices, or a dominant linguistic group insists that a single language be used in education and government throughout the country. In such cases, political conflict tends to move from the distributive realm to the cultural realm, where compromises cannot be achieved by simply dividing the pie of material resources. The country studies examine a wide range of distributional conflicts involving collective identities. It will be interesting (and possibly troubling) to ponder whether and under what conditions they are subject to the normal give-and-take of political bargaining—and when, instead, they lead to the fury and blood of political violence.

These four themes provide our analytic scaffold. With an understanding of the method of comparative politics and the four themes in mind, we can now discuss how *Introduction to Politics of the Developing World* is organized for comparative analysis.

Section ⑤ Organization of the Text

The core of this book consists of six case studies selected for their significance in terms of our comparative themes and ability to provide a reasonable cross-section of types of political regimes and geographic regions in the developing world. Although each of the country studies makes important comparative references, the studies are primarily intended to provide detailed descriptions and analyses of the politics of individual countries. At the same time, the country studies have common section and subsection headings to help you make comparisons and explore similar themes across the various cases. Following are brief summaries of the main issues and questions covered in the country studies.

1: The Making of the Modern State

Section 1 in each chapter provides an overview of the forces that have shaped the particular character of the state. We believe that an understanding of the contemporary politics of any country requires some familiarity with the historical process by which its current political system was formed. "Politics in Action" uses a specific event to illustrate an important political moment in the country's recent history and to highlight some of the critical political issues it faces. "Geographic Setting" locates the country in its regional context and discusses the political implications of its geographic setting. "Critical Junctures" looks at some of the major stages and decisive turning points in state development. This discussion should give you an idea of how the country assumed its current political order and a sense of how relations between state and society have developed over time. "Themes and Implications" shows how the past pattern of state development continues to shape the country's current political agenda. "Historical Junctures and Political Themes" applies the text's core themes to the making of the modern state: How was the country's political development affected by its place in the world of states? What are the political implications of the state's approach to economic management? What has been the country's experience with the democratic idea? What are the important bases of collective identity in the country, and how do these relate to the people's image of themselves as citizens of the state? "Implications for Comparative Politics" discusses the broader significance of the country for the study of comparative politics.

2: Political Economy and Development

Section 2 in each chapter traces the country's recent and contemporary economic development. It explores the issues raised by the core theme of governing the economy and analyzes how economic development has affected political change. The placement of this section near the beginning of the country study reflects our belief that an understanding of an economic situation is essential for analyzing its politics. "State and Economy" discusses the basic organization of the country's economy, with an emphasis on the role of the state in managing economic life and on the relationship between the government and other economic actors. How do the dynamics and historical timing of the country's insertion into the world economy—and its current position and competitiveness within the globalized economy—affect domestic political arrangements and shape contemporary challenges? This section also analyzes the state's social welfare policies, such as health care, housing, and pension programs. "Society and Economy" examines the social and political implications of the country's economic situation. It asks who benefits from economic change and looks at how economic development creates or reinforces class, ethnic, gender, regional, or ideological cleavages in society. "The International Political Economy" considers the country's global role: How have patterns of trade and foreign investment changed over time? What is the country's relationship to regional and international organizations? To what degree has the country been able to influence multilateral policies? How have international economic issues affected the domestic political agenda?

3: Governance and Policy-Making

In Section 3, we describe the state's major policy-making institutions and procedures. "Organization of the State" lays out the fundamental principles—as reflected in the country's constitution, its official ideology, and its historical experience—on which the political system and the distribution of political power are based. It also sketches the basic structure of the state, including the relationship among different levels and branches of government. "The Executive" encompasses whatever key offices (for example, presidents, prime ministers, Communist Party leaders) are at the top of the political system, focusing on those who have the most power, how they are selected, and how they use their power to make policy. It looks at the national

bureaucracy and its relationship to the chief executive and the governing party and its role in policy-making. "Other State Institutions" generally looks at the military, the judiciary and the legal system, state-run corporations, and subnational government. "The Policy-Making Process" summarizes how public policy gets made and implemented. It describes the roles of formal institutions and procedures, as well as informal aspects of policy-making, such as patron-client relations and interest group activity.

4: Representation and Participation

The relationship between the state and the society it governs is the topic of Section 4. How do different groups in society organize to further their political interests, how do they participate and get represented in the political system, and how do they influence policy-making? Given the importance of the U.S. Congress in policy-making, American readers might expect to find the principal discussion of "The Legislature" in Section 3 ("Governance and Policy-Making") rather than Section 4. But the United States is rather exceptional in having a legislature that is very nearly a coequal branch of government with the executive in the policy process. In most other political systems, the executive dominates the policy process, even when it is ultimately responsible to the legislature, as in a parliamentary system. In most countries other than the United States, the legislature functions primarily to represent and provide a forum for the political expression of various interests in government; it is only secondarily (and in some cases, such as China, only marginally) a policy-making body. Therefore, although this section does describe and assess the legislature's role in policy-making, its primary focus is on how the legislature represents or fails to represent different interests in society. "Political Parties and the Party System" describes the overall organization of the party system and reviews the major parties. "Elections" discusses the election process and recent trends in electoral behavior. It also considers the significance of elections (or lack thereof) as a vehicle for citizen participation in politics and in bringing about changes in the government. "Political Culture, Citizenship, and Identity" examines how people perceive themselves as members of the political community: the nature and source of political values and attitudes, who is considered a citizen of the state, and how different groups in society understand their relationship to the state. The topics covered may include political aspects of the educational system, the media, religion, and ethnicity. How has globalization shaped collective identities and collective action? "Interests, Social Movements, and Protests" discusses how various groups pursue their political interests outside the party system. When do they use formal organizations (such as unions) or launch movements (such as religious or "green" environmental movements)? What is the relationship between the state and such organizations and movements? When and how do citizens engage in acts of protest? And how does the state respond to such protests?

5: Politics in Transition

In Section 5, each country study returns to the book's focus on the major challenges that are reshaping our world and the study of politics in the developing world. "Political Challenges and Changing Agendas" lays out the major unresolved issues facing the country and assesses which are most likely to dominate in the near future. "Politics in Comparative Perspective" returns to the four themes and highlights what this case study tells us about politics in other countries that have similar political systems or that face similar kinds of political challenges.

It is quite a challenge to understand the contemporary world of politics. We hope that the timely information and thematic focus of this book will both prepare and inspire you to explore further the endlessly fascinating and increasing important terrain of politics in the developing world.

Key Terms

cold war	political institutions
Third World	political culture
globalization	political development
comparative politics	state
comparativists	executive
countries	cabinet
nation-states	bureaucracy

legitimacy	political economy
state formation	gross domestic product (GDP)
middle-level theory	
dictatorship	official international currency exchange rates
newly industrializing countries (NICs)	purchasing power parity (PPP)
gross national income (GNI)	Human Development Index (HDI)
physical quality of life (PQLI)	economic liberalization
life expectancy	neo-imperialism
child mortality rate	authoritarianism
illiteracy	social class
coup d'état	distributional politics
patron-client politics	

Suggested Readings

Anderson, Benedict. *Imagined Communities: Reflections on the Origins and Spread of Nationalism.* Rev. ed. London: Verso, 1991.

Anderson, Lisa, ed. *Transitions to Democracy.* New York: Columbia University Press, 1999.

Annual Editions. *The Developing World.* Guilford, Conn.: Dushkin. Published annually.

Bates, Robert H. *Markets and States in Tropical Africa: The Political Basis of Agricultural Policies.* Berkeley: University of California Press, 1981.

Cammack, Paul, Pool, David, and William Tordoff. *Third World Politics: A Comparative Introduction.* 3rd ed. Baltimore, Md.: Johns Hopkins University Press, 2001.

Diamond, Larry. *Developing Democracy: Toward Consolidation.* Baltimore, Md.: Johns Hopkins University Press, 1999.

Isbister, John. *Promises Not Kept: The Betrayal of Social Change in the Third World.* 5th ed. West Hartford, Conn.: Kumarian Press, 2001.

Jameson, Kenneth P., and Wilber, Charles K. *The Political Economy of Development and Underdevelopment.* 6th ed. New York: McGraw-Hill, 1996.

Jim, Yong Kim, et al., eds. *Dying for Growth: Global Inequality and the Health of the Poor.* Monroe, Me.: Common Courage Press, 2000.

Klitgaard, Robert. *Tropical Gangsters: One Man's Experience with Development and Decadence in Deepest Africa.* New York: Basic Books, 1991.

Landes, David S. *The Wealth and Poverty of Nations: Why Some Are So Rich and Some So Poor?* New York: Norton, 1999.

Linz, Juan J., and Stepan, Alfred. *Problems of Democratic Transition and Consolidation: Southern Europe, South America, and Post-Communist Europe.* Baltimore, Md.: Johns Hopkins University Press, 1996.

Marx, Anthony. *Making Race and Nation: A Comparison of the United States, South Africa, and Brazil.* Cambridge: Cambridge University Press, 1998.

Mittelman, James. *The Globalization Syndrome: Transformation and Resistance.* Princeton, N.J.: Princeton University Press, 2001.

Nordquist, Joan. *Third World Women and Development: Bibliography.* Santa Cruz, Calif. : Reference and Research Services, 2001.

O'Donnell, Guillermo A., Schmitter, Philippe C., and Whitehead, Laurence, eds. *Transitions from Authoritarian Rule.* 4 vols. Baltimore, Md.: Johns Hopkins University Press, 1986.

Rapley, John. *Understanding Development: Theory and Practice in the Third World.* 2nd ed. Boulder, Colo.: Lynn Rienner, 2002.

Seligson Mitchell A,, and Passé-Smith, John T, eds. *Development and Underdevelopment: The Political Economy of Global Inequality.* 3rd ed. Boulder, Colo.: Lynn Reinner, 2003.

Sen, Amartya. *Development as Freedom.* New York: Random House, 1999.

Smith, B. C. *Understanding Third World Politics: Theories of Political Change and Development.* 2nd ed. Bloomington: Indiana University Press, 2003.

Woo-Cummings, Meredith, ed. *The Developmental State.* Ithaca, N.Y.: Cornell University Press, 1999.

Suggested Websites

CIA World Factbook
www.odci.gov/cia/publications/factbook/index.html
Development Gateway
www.developmentgateway.org/
United Nations Development Programme
www.undp.org
World Audit
www.worldaudit.org
World Bank
www.worldbank.org

Notes

[1]See Philippe Schmitter, "Comparative Politics," in Joel Krieger, ed., *The Oxford Companion to Politics of the World*, 2nd ed. (New York: Oxford University Press, 2001), 160–165. For a more extended discussion and different approach, see David D. Laitin, "Comparative Politics: The State of the Subdiscipline," in Ira Katznelson and Helen V. Milner, eds., *Political Science: The State of the Discipline* (New York: Norton, 2002), 630–659.

[2]Although not specifically on the Indian and Nigerian militaries, see David Schwam-Baird, "Ideologies and Military Institutions in Third World Politics: Five Models," *Journal of Third World Studies*, 17, no. 1 (Spring 2000): 105–132.

[3]See, for example, Theda Skocpol, *Social Revolutions in the Modern World* (Cambridge: Cambridge University Press, 1994).

[4]For diverse views, see Gary King, Robert O. Keohane, and Sidney Verba, *Designing Social Inquiry: Scientific Inference in Qualitative Research* (Princeton, N.J.: Princeton University Press, 1994); Mark Irving Lichbach and Alan S. Zuckerman, eds., *Comparative Politics: Rationality, Culture, and Structure* (Cambridge: Cambridge University Press, 1997); and Katznelson and Milner, eds., *Political Science.*

[5]For a fine example, see Juan J. Linz and Alfred Stepan, *Problems of Democratic Transition and Consolidation: Southern Europe, South America, and Post-Communist Europe* (Baltimore, Md.: Johns Hopkins University Press, 1996).

[6]See, for example, the academic journal *Third World Quarterly: Journal of the Emerging Areas* and the following recently published books: Rajagopal Balakrishnan, *International Law from Below: Development, Social Movements and Third World Resistance* (Cambridge: Cambridge University Press, 2003); Mike Davis, *Late Victorian Holocausts: El Niño Famines and the Making of the Third World* (London: Verso, 2002); and Lee Kuan Yew, *From Third World to First: The Singapore Story, 1965–2000* (New York: HarperCollins, 2000).

[7]See, for example, Focus on the Global South, at http://www. focusweb.org/, and South-North Development Monitor, at http://www.sunsonline.org/.

[8]Among the best sources for development statistics are the annual publications of the United Nations Development Program (*The Human Development Report*) and the World Bank (*The World Development Report*).

[9]See Adrian Karatnyck, "The 2001–2002 Freedom House Survey of Freedom: The Democracy Gap," at http://www. freedomhouse. org/research/freeworld/2002/essays.htm

[10]Amartya Sen, "Democracy as a Universal Value," *Journal of Democracy* 10, no. 3 (July 1999): 3–17, available at http:// muse.jhu.edu/demo/jod/10.3sen.html). Another influential study of this question reaches a similar conclusion: Adam Przeworski et al., *Democracy and Development: Political Institutions and Well-Being in the World, 1950–1990* (Cambridge: Cambridge University Press, 2000).

[11]This view has been developed well by Adam Przeworski, *Democracy and the Market: Political and Economic Reforms in Eastern Europe and Latin America* (Cambridge: Cambridge University Press, 1991).

[12]Guillermo O'Donnell and Philippe Schmitter, *Transitions from Authoritarian Rule: Tentative Conclusions About Uncertain Democracies* (Baltimore, Md.: Johns Hopkins University Press, 1986).

[13]The term "governs the economy" is borrowed from Peter A. Hall, *Governing the Economy: The Politics of State Intervention in Britain and France* (New York: Oxford University Press, 1986).

[14]For an excellent discussion of the relationship between democracy, economic growth, and human development, see United

Nations Development Programme, *Human Development Report 2002: Deepening Democracy in a Fragmented World* (New York: Oxford University Press, 2002).

[15]Sen, "Democracy as a Universal Value."

[16]For a survey of political science literature on this question, see Mark Kesselman, "The Conflictual Evolution of American Political Science: From Apologetic Pluralism to Trilateralism and Marxism," in J. David Greenstone, ed., *Public Values and Private Power in American Democracy* (Chicago: University of Chicago Press, 1982), 34–67.

CHAPTER 2

China

William A. Joseph

People's Republic of China

Land and People

Capital	Bejing
Total area (square miles)	3,696,100 (slightly larger than the U.S.)
Population	1.275 billion

Annual population growth rate (%)	1975–2000	1.3
	2000–2015 (projected)	0.7

Urban population (%)	36

Ethnic composition (% of total population)	Chinese (Han)	92
	Others	8

Major language(s)	Chinese (various dialects, including Mandarin and Cantonese)

Religious affiliation (%)	Atheist*	94–96
	Christian	3–4
	Muslim	1–2

*Although officially atheist, many people practice Buddhism and traditional folk and other religions, e.g., Daoism (Taoism)

Economy

Domestic currency	Renminbi ("People's Currency") CNY US$1: 8.28 CNY (2002 av.)
Total GDP (US$)	1.08 trillion
GDP per capita (US$)	866
Total GDP at purchasing power parity (US$)	5.02 trillion
GDP per capita at purchasing power parity (US$)	3,976

GDP annual growth rate (%)	1997	8.8
	2000	7.9
	2001	7.3

GDP per capita average annual growth rate (%)	1975–2000	8.1
	1990–2000	9.2

Inequality in income or consumption (1998) (%)	Share of poorest 10%	2.4
	Share of poorest 20%	5.9
	Share of richest 20%	46.6
	Share of richest 10%	30.4
	Gini Index (1995)	40.3

Structure of production (% of GDP)	Agriculture	50.9
	Industry	15.9
	Services	33.2

Labor force distribution (% of total)	Agriculture	50
	Industry	23
	Services	27

Exports as % of GDP	26
Imports as % of GDP	23

Society

Life expectancy at birth	70.5
Infant mortality per 1,000 live births	32

Adult literacy (%)	Male	91.7
	Female	76.3

Access to information and communications (per 1,000 population)	Telephone lines	112
	Mobile phones	66
	Radios	339
	Televisions	293
	Personal computers	15.9

Women in Government and the Economy

Women in the national legislature Lower house or single house (%)	21.8
Women at ministerial level (%)	5.1
Female economic activity rate (age 15 and above) (%)	72.7
Female labor force (% of total)	42

Estimated earned income (PPP US$)	Female	3,132
	Male	4,773

2002 Human Development Index Ranking (out of 173 countries)	96

Political Organization

Political System   Communist party-state; officially, a socialist state under the people's democratic dictatorship.

Regime History   Established in 1949 after the victory of the Chinese Communist Party (CCP) in the Chinese civil war.

Administrative Structure   Unitary system with 22 provinces, 5 autonomous regions, 4 centrally administered municipalities, and 2 Special Administrative Regions (Hong Kong and Macao).

Executive   Premier (head of government) and president (head of state) formally elected by legislature, but only with approval of CCP leadership; the head of the CCP, the general secretary, is in effect the country's chief executive.

Legislature   Unicameral National People's Congress; 2985 delegates elected indirectly from lower-level people's congresses for five-year terms. Largely a "rubber-stamp" body for Communist Party policies, although in recent years has become somewhat more assertive.

Judiciary   A nationwide system of people's courts, which is constitutionally independent but, in fact, largely under the control of the CCP; a Supreme People's Court supervises the country's judicial system and is formally responsible to the National People's Congress, which also elects the court's presidents.

Party System   A one-party system, although in addition to the ruling Chinese Communist Party, there are eight politically insignificant "democratic" parties.

Section **1** The Making of the Modern Chinese State

Politics in Action

When it was announced in July 2001 that Beijing had been chosen as the site of 2008 Summer Olympics, an estimated 200,000 Chinese citizens poured into Tiananmen ("Gate of Heavenly Peace") Square in the heart of China's capital to celebrate the honor that had been bestowed on their country. They saw the awarding of the games to Beijing by the International Olympics Committee (IOC) as overdue recognition of the remarkable modernization of the Chinese economy, the stunning successes of Chinese athletes in international sports competitions, and the emergence of the People's Republic of China (PRC) as major global power.

But there were also many voices that were extremely critical of the IOC's decision. Human rights organizations such as Amnesty International argued that the decision rewarded one of the world's most oppressive governments. Some compared the Beijing Games to those held in Berlin, Germany, in 1936, shortly after Hitler had come to power and which the Nazis used to gain international legitimacy. The Dalai Lama, the exiled spiritual leader of Tibet, which has been occupied by China since 1950, strongly objected to awarding the games to Beijing. As his spokesman noted, "This will put the stamp of international approval on Beijing's human rights abuses and will encourage China to escalate its repression."[1] Critics of the Beijing games also pointed out the irony that the Olympics celebrations in Tiananmen Square were held very near the place where, in 1989, China's Communist leaders ordered troops to crush a prodemocracy movement, which led to the killing of hundreds of civilians, many of them college students.

Others argued that hosting the Olympics could be a force for positive change in China. PRC leaders would not want to risk an international boycott of the Beijing Games by engaging in highly visible repression. This, in turn, could embolden China's democracy activists, who have been largely silent since the Tiananmen massacre. In this way, the 2008 Beijing Olympics might spur much-needed political reform, as did the 1988 Olympics in Seoul, an important impetus to South Korea's transition from a military dictatorship to a democracy.

The controversy over the Beijing Olympics reflects the fundamental contradictions that define contemporary Chinese politics. The People's Republic of China is one of only a few countries in the world that is still a **communist-party state** in which the ruling party claims an exclusive monopoly on political power and proclaims allegiance (at least officially) to the ideology of **Marxism-Leninism.** At the same time, the country has experienced dramatic economic and social liberalization—and even some political relaxation since the bloodshed in Tiananmen—and is more fully integrated into the world than at any other time in its history. But the Chinese Communist Party (CCP) rejects any meaningful movement toward democracy, and the rift between an oppressive political system and an increasingly modern and globalized society remains deep and ominous.

Geographic Setting

The PRC is located in the eastern part of mainland Asia at the heart of one of the world's most strategically important and volatile regions. It shares land borders with more than a dozen countries, including Russia, India, Pakistan, Vietnam, and the Democratic People's Republic of Korea (North Korea) and is a relatively short distance by sea from Japan, the Philippines, and Indonesia. China, which had largely assumed its present geographic identity by the eighteenth century, is slightly bigger than the United States in land area, making it the third largest country in the world, after Russia and Canada.

The PRC is bounded on all sides by imposing physical barriers: the sea to the east; mountains to the north, south, and west (including the world's largest, Mount Everest); deserts, vast grasslands, and dense forests in various parts of the north; and tropical rain forests to the south. In traditional times, these barriers isolated China from extensive contact with other peoples and contributed to the country's sense of itself as the "Middle Kingdom" (which is how the Chinese word

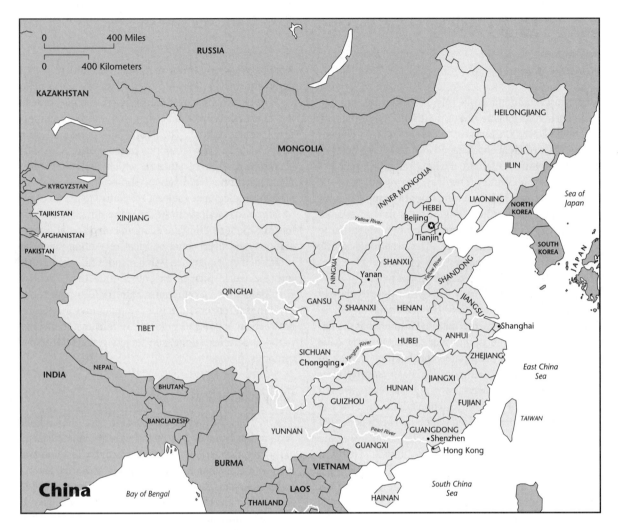

China

for China, *Zhongguo*, is translated) that lay not only at the physical but also at the political and moral center of its known world.

Administratively, the PRC is made up of twenty-two provinces, five **autonomous regions,** and four centrally administered cities (including the capital, Beijing), and two Special Administrative Regions (Hong Kong and Macao). The sparsely populated but territorially vast western part of the country is mostly mountains, deserts, and high plateaus. The northeast, which is much like the U.S. plains states in terms of weather and topography, is both a wheat-growing area and China's industrial heartland. Southern China has a much warmer, and in places even semitropical, climate, which allows year-round agriculture and inten-

sive rice cultivation. The country is very rich in natural resources, particularly coal and petroleum (including significant, but untapped onshore and offshore reserves), and is considered to have the world's greatest potential for hydroelectric power.

Although China and the United States are roughly equal in geographic size, China's population of about 1.3 billion—by far the world's largest—is five times greater. But only a relatively small part of China's land is usable for agriculture. China has a little over 20 percent of the world's population but only 10 percent of the world's arable land. The precarious balance between people and the land needed to feed them has been a dilemma for China for centuries and remains one of the government's major concerns.

Industrialization and urbanization have expanded significantly in recent years. The PRC now has more than thirty cities of 1 million or more, the three largest being Shanghai (16.7 million), Beijing (13.8 million), and Tianjin (10.0 million). In 1997, the former British colony of Hong Kong, one of the world's great commercial centers (population 6.8 million), became part of the PRC. Nevertheless, about 65 percent of China's people still live and work in rural areas. The countryside has played—and continues to play—a very important role in China's political development.

China's population is highly concentrated along the eastern seaboard and in the most agriculturally fertile areas around the country's three great rivers: the Yellow River, the Yangtze (Yangzi), and the Pearl River. The vast majority (92 percent) of China's citizens are ethnically Chinese (referred to as the Han people, after one of China's earliest dynasties). The remaining 8 percent is made up of more than fifty ethnic minorities, who differ from the Han in several major ways, including race, language, culture, and religion. Most of these minority peoples live in the country's geopolitically vital border regions, including Tibet. This makes the often uneasy and sometimes hostile relationship between China's minority peoples and the central government in Beijing a crucial and sensitive issue in Chinese politics today.

Critical Junctures

The PRC was founded in 1949. But understanding the critical junctures in the making of the modern Chinese state requires that we go back much further into China's political history. Broadly considered, that history can be divided into three periods: the imperial period (221 B.C.–1911 A.D), during which China was ruled by a series of dynasties and emperors; the relatively brief and unstable republican period (1912–1949), when a weak central government was plagued by civil war and foreign invasion; and the Communist period, from the founding of the People's Republic of China in 1949 to the present.

From Empire to Republic (221 B.C.–1911 A.D)

Modern China is heir to one of the world's oldest cultural and political traditions. The roots of Chinese culture date back more than 4,000 years, and the Chi-

nese empire first took political shape in 221 B.C., when a number of small kingdoms were unified under the Emperor Qin, who laid the foundation of an imperial system that lasted for more than twenty centuries until its overthrow in 1911. During those many centuries, China was ruled by more than a dozen different dynasties and experienced extensive geographic expansion and far-reaching political, economic, social, and cultural changes. Nevertheless, many of the core features of the imperial system remained remarkably consistent over time.

There are several reasons that the Chinese empire survived for such a long time. First, imperial China developed a sophisticated and effective system of national government long before the strong monarchical states of Europe took form in the seventeenth century. Second, the traditional Chinese economy was a source of great strength to the empire. Urbanization expanded in China much sooner than it did in Europe, and Westerners, like Marco Polo, who journeyed to China as early as the thirteenth century were amazed by the grandeur of the Middle Kingdom's cities.

Third, the structure of traditional Chinese society, especially in the million or more small villages that were its foundation, gave imperial China great staying power. The vast majority of the village population was made up of poor and relatively poor peasants. But life was dominated by landlords and other local elites who worked with the national government to maintain and sustain the system.

Fourth, the traditional order was supported by the enduring influence in Chinese society of Confucianism. This philosophy, based on the teachings of Confucius (c. 551–479 B.C.), stresses the importance of the group over the individual, deference to one's elders and superiors, and the need to maintain social harmony. Confucianism did contain a teaching, the "Mandate of Heaven," that the people could overthrow an unjust ruler. Nevertheless, Confucianism was basically a conservative philosophy that justified and preserved an autocratic state, a patriarchal culture, and a highly stratified society. Finally, the Chinese imperial system endured because, throughout most of its history, China was by far the dominant political, military, and cultural force in its known world.

In the late eighteenth and early nineteenth centuries, imperial China experienced a population explosion and economic stagnation, along with a significant rise in official corruption and exploitation of the peasants by both landlords and the government. Social unrest culminated in the Taiping Rebellion (1850–1864), a massive revolt that took 20 million lives and nearly toppled the ruling Qing dynasty.

In the meantime, the West, which had surged far ahead of China in industrial development and military technology, was pressing the country to open its markets to foreign trade. China showed little interest in such overtures and tried to limit the activities of Westerners in China. But Europe, most notably Britain, in the midst of its era of mercantile and colonial expansion, used its military supremacy to compel China to engage in "free" trade with the West. China's efforts to stop Britain from selling opium in China led to military conflict between the two countries. After suffering a humiliating defeat in the Opium War (1839–1842), China was literally forced to open its borders to foreign merchants, missionaries, and diplomats on terms dictated by Britain and other Western powers. China lost control of significant pieces of its territory to foreigners (including Hong Kong), and important sectors of the Chinese economy fell into foreign hands.

There were many efforts to revive or reform the dynasty in the late nineteenth and early twentieth centuries, but political power in China remained largely in the hands of staunch conservatives who resisted change. As a result, when change came, it was in the form of a revolution in 1911 that toppled the Qing dynasty and brought an end to the 2,000-year-old imperial system.

Warlords, Nationalists, and Communists (1912–1949)

The Republic of China was established on January 1, 1912, with Dr. Sun Yat-sen,* then China's best-known revolutionary, as president. However, the Western-educated Sun was not able to hold onto power, and China soon fell into a lengthy period of conflict and disintegration, with parts of the country run by rival warlords. Sun set about organizing another revolution to

---

*In China, the family name, or surname (e.g., *Sun*) comes before the personal, or given, name (e.g., *Yat-sen*). Therefore, Sun Yat-sen would be referred to as President Sun.

Critical Junctures in Modern China's Political Development

1911	Revolution led by Sun Yat-sen overthrows 2,000-year-old imperial system and establishes the Republic of China.
1912	Sun Yat-sen founds the Nationalist (*Guomindang*) Party to oppose warlords who have seized power in the new republic.
1921	Chinese Communist Party (CCP) founded.
1927	Civil war between Nationalists (now led by Chiang Kai-shek) and Communists begins.
1934	Mao Zedong becomes leader of the CCP.
1937	Japan invades China, marking the start of World War II in Asia.
1949	Chinese Communists win the civil war and establish the People's Republic of China.
1958–1960	Great Leap Forward.
1966–1976	Great Proletarian Cultural Revolution.
1976	Mao Zedong dies.
1978	Deng Xiaoping becomes China's paramount leader.
1989	Tiananmen massacre.
1997	Deng Xiaoping dies; Jiang Zemin becomes China's most powerful leader.
2002–2003	Hu Jintao succeeds Jiang as head of the CCP and president of the People's Republic of China.

defeat the warlords and reunify the country under his Nationalist Party (the *Guomindang*).

In 1921, the Chinese Communist Party (CCP) was established by a few intellectuals who had been inspired by the Communist revolution in Russia in 1917 and by the anti-imperialism of the newly founded Soviet Union to look for more radical solutions to China's problems. In 1924, the small Communist Party, acting on Soviet advice, joined with Sun Yat-sen's Nationalists to fight the warlords. After some initial successes, this alliance came to a tragic end in 1927 when Chiang Kai-shek, a military leader who had become the head of the Nationalist Party after Sun's death in 1925, turned against his coalition partners and ordered a bloody suppression that nearly wiped out the Communists. Chiang then proceeded to unify the Republic of China under his personal rule, largely by striking an accommodation with some of the country's most powerful remaining warlords who supported him in the civil war against the communists

Ironically, the defeat of the CCP created the conditions for the eventual triumph of the man who would lead the party to nationwide victory. Mao Zedong, who had been one of the junior founders of the Communist Party, strongly advocated paying more attention to China's suffering peasants as a potential source of support. "In a very short time," he wrote in 1927, "several hundred million peasants will rise like a mighty storm, like a hurricane, a force so swift and violent that no power, however great, will be able to hold it back."[2]

In 1934–1935, the party undertook its fabled Long March, an epic journey of 6,000 miles through some of China's roughest terrain, to escape attack by Chiang's forces. At the end of the Long March, the CCP established a base in Yanan, a remote rural area in northwestern China. In Yanan, Mao consolidated his political and ideological leadership of the CCP, sometimes through coercive means, and was elected party chairman in 1943, a position he held until his death in 1976.

Japan's invasion of China in 1937 pushed the Nationalist government deep into the country's southwest and effectively eliminated it as an active combatant against Japanese aggression. In contrast, the CCP base in Yanan was on the front line against Japan's troops in northern China, and Mao and the Communists successfully mobilized the peasants to use **guerrilla warfare** to fight the invaders. By the end of World War II in 1945, the CCP had vastly expanded its membership and controlled much of the countryside in north China. The Nationalists, on the other hand, were isolated and unpopular with many Chinese because of the corruption, political repression, and economic mismanagement of Chiang Kai-shek's regime.

After the Japanese surrender, Communist forces won decisively against the U.S.-backed Nationalists, who were forced to retreat to the island of Taiwan, 90 miles off the Chinese coast. (See "Global Connection: The Republic of China on Taiwan.") On October 1, 1949, Mao Zedong stood on a rostrum in Tiananmen near the entrance to the former imperial palace in Bei-jing and declared the founding of the People's Republic of China.

Mao in Power (1949–1976)

The CCP came to power on the crest of an enormous wave of popular support because of its reputation as being a party of social reformers and patriotic fighters. Chairman Mao and the CCP quickly turned their attention to some of the country's most glaring problems. For instance, a massive land reform campaign redistributed property from the rich to the poor and increased productivity in the countryside. Highly successful drives eliminated opium addiction and prostitution from the cities, and a national law greatly enhanced the legal status of women in the family and allowed many women to free themselves from unhappy arranged marriages. Although the CCP did not hesitate to use violence to achieve its objectives and silence opponents, the party gained considerable legitimacy because of its successful policies during these years.

Between 1953 and 1957, the PRC implemented a Soviet-style five-year economic plan. The complete nationalization of industry and **collectivization** of agriculture carried out as part of this plan were decisive steps away from the mixed state-private economy of the early 1950s and toward **socialism.** Although the plan achieved good economic results, Mao was troubled by the persistence of inequalities in China, especially those caused by the emphasis on industrial and urban development and relative neglect of the countryside. In response, he launched the **Great Leap Forward** (1958–1960), a utopian effort to accelerate the country's economic development by relying on the labor and willpower of the masses while also propelling China into a radically egalitarian era of true **communism.**

The Great Leap was a great flop and turned into "one of the most extreme, bizarre, and eventually catastrophic episodes in twentieth-century political history."[3] In the rural areas, irrational policies, wasted resources, poor management, and the lack of labor incentives combined with bad weather to produce a famine that claimed between 20 and 30 million lives. An industrial depression soon followed the collapse of agriculture, causing a terrible setback to China's economic development.

Global Connection: *The Republic of China on Taiwan*

Despite the victory of the Chinese Communist Party in the civil war and the founding of the People's Republic of China on the Chinese mainland in October 1949, the Republic of China (ROC) under Chiang Kai-shek and the Nationalist Party continued to function on Taiwan. The Chinese Communists would likely have taken over Taiwan at the end of the civil war if the United States had not intervened to protect the island. The U.S. government, alarmed by the outbreak of the Korean War in 1950, saw the defense of the Nationalist government on Taiwan as part of the effort to stop the further expansion of communism in Asia.

When Chiang Kai-shek and his supporters fled to Taiwan in 1949, the island was already firmly under the control of Nationalists, who had killed or arrested many of their opponents on Taiwan in the aftermath of a popular uprising in February 1947. The harsh dictatorship imposed by Chiang's Nationalists deepened the sharp divide between the "mainlanders," who had come over to escape the Communists, and the native Taiwanese majority, whose ancestors had settled on the island centuries before and who spoke a distinctive Chinese dialect.

Economically, Taiwan prospered under Chiang Kai-shek's rule. With large amounts of U.S. aid and advice, the Nationalist government sponsored a successful and peaceful program of land reform and rural development, attracted extensive foreign investment, and encouraged an export-led strategy of economic growth that made Taiwan a model newly industrializing country (NIC) by the 1970s. The government also invested heavily in the modernization of Taiwan's roads and ports, and it promoted policies that have given the island health and education levels that are among the best in the world and a standard of living that is one of the highest in Asia.

Political change, however, came more slowly to Taiwan. After his death in 1975, Chiang Kai-shek was succeeded as president by his son, Chiang Ching-kuo, whom most people expected to continue the authoritarian rule of his father. Instead, the younger Chiang permitted some opposition and dissent, and he gave important government and party positions previously dominated by mainlanders to Taiwanese. When he died in 1988, the presidency of the republic passed to the Taiwanese vice president, Lee Teng-hui, who also became head of the Nationalist Party.

Under President Lee, Taiwan made big strides toward democratization. Laws used to imprison dissidents were revoked, the media were freed of all censorship, and open multiparty elections were held for all local and island-wide positions. In presidential elections in 1996, Lee Teng-hui won 54 percent of the vote in a hotly contested four-way race, reflecting both the new openness of the political system and the credit that Taiwan's voters gave the Nationalist Party for the island's progress.

But in 2000, an opposition party candidate, Chen Shui-bian of the Democratic Progressive Party (DPP), won the presidency, which many observers saw as reflecting a further maturing of Taiwan's democracy. Chen's victory was due in part to a combination of the desire for change, especially in the light of a serious downturn in the island's economic growth and a split within the National Party.

The most contentious political issue in Taiwan, which is still formally called the Republic of China, is whether the island should continue to work, however slowly, toward reunification with the mainland, as was the Nationalists' policy under Lee Teng-hui, or declare formal independence. A big factor in Chen's election was the growing popularity of the DPP's position that Taiwan should seriously consider the independence option. Beijing still regards Taiwan as a renegade province and has threatened to use force if the island moves toward formal separation.

Taiwan and the PRC have developed extensive, if indirect, economic relations with each other, and millions of people from Taiwan have gone to the mainland to do business, visit relatives, or just sightsee. The PRC and ROC have engaged in some negotiations about possible reunification, but the two sides remain far apart because of their vastly differing political, economic, and social systems.

Taiwan

Land area (sq. miles)	13,895 (about one-third the size of Virginia)
Population	22.5 million
Ethnic composition	Taiwanese 84%, mainland Chinese 14%, aborigine 2%
GDP (purchasing power parity)	$386 billion
GDP per capita (purchasing power parity)	$17,200
GDP growth rate:	–2.2% (2001)
Life expectancy	Male, 74; Female, 80
Infant mortality (per 1,000 live births)	6
Literacy	94%

In the early 1960s, Mao took a less active role in day-to-day decision making. Two of China's other top leaders at the time, Liu Shaoqi and Deng Xiaoping, were put in charge of efforts to revive the economy and used a combination of careful planning and some market-oriented policies to stimulate production, particularly in agriculture.

This strategy did help the Chinese economy, but once again Mao found himself profoundly unhappy with the consequences of China's development. By the mid-1960s, the chairman had concluded that the policies of Liu and Deng had led to a resurgence of elitism and inequality that were threatening his revolutionary goals for China by setting the country on the road to capitalism.

The result of Mao's disquiet was the **Great Proletarian Cultural Revolution** (1966–1976), an ideological crusade designed to jolt China back toward his vision of socialism. Like the Great Leap Forward, the Cultural Revolution was a campaign of mass mobilization and utopian idealism, but its methods were much more violent, and its main objective was the political purification of the party and the nation through struggle against so-called class enemies, not accelerated economic development. Using his unmatched political clout and charisma, Mao put together a potent coalition of radical party leaders, loyal military officers, and student rebels (called Red Guards) to purge anyone thought to be guilty of **revisionism,** that is, betrayal of his version of Marxism-Leninism known as Mao Zedong Thought.

In the Cultural Revolution's first phase (1966–1969), 20 million or so Red Guards went on a rampage across the country, harassing, torturing, and killing people accused of being class enemies, particularly intellectuals and discredited party leaders. During the next phase (1969–1971), Mao used the People's Liberation Army (PLA) to restore political order, while the final phase (1972–1976) involved intense factional conflict over who would succeed the aging Mao as party chairman. Mao died in September 1976 at age eighty-two. A month later, the power struggle was settled when a coalition of the moderate leaders masterminded the arrest of their radical rivals, the so-called Gang of Four, who were led by Mao's wife, Jiang Qing. The arrest of the Gang (who were sentenced to long prison terms) marked the end of the Cultural Revolution, which had claimed at least a million lives and brought the nation to the brink of civil war.

Deng Xiaoping and the Transformation of Chinese Communism (1977–1997)

In order to help them repair the damage caused by the Cultural Revolution, China's new leaders restored to office many of the veteran officials who had been purged by Mao and the radicals, including Deng Xiaoping. By 1978, Deng had clearly become the most powerful member of the CCP leadership—though he preferred to install a loyal lieutenant in the formal position of party leader rather than take it for himself. He lost little time in putting China on a path of reform that dramatically transformed the nation.

Deng's policies were a profound break with the Maoist past. State control of the economy was significantly reduced, and market forces were allowed to play an increasingly important role in all aspects of production. Private enterprise was encouraged, and the economy was opened to unprecedented levels of foreign investment. On the cultural front, Chinese artists and writers saw the shackles of party dogma that had bound them for decades greatly loosened. Deng took major steps to revitalize China's government by bringing in younger, better-educated officials. The results of Deng's initiatives were, by any measure, astounding. After decades of stagnation, the Chinese economy experienced spectacular growth throughout the 1980s and beyond (see Figure 1).

Then came June 1989 and the massacre near Tiananmen Square. Discontent over inflation and official corruption, as well as a desire, especially among students and intellectuals, for more democracy, inspired large-scale demonstrations in Beijing and several other Chinese cities that spring. The demonstrations in Beijing grew through April and May, and at one point more than 1 million people from all walks of life gathered in and around Tiananmen. For several months, the CCP, constrained by internal divisions about how to handle the protests and intensive international media coverage, did little other than engage in some threatening rhetoric to dissuade the demonstrators. But China's leaders ran out of patience, and the army was ordered to clear the square during the very early morning hours of June 4. By the time dawn broke in Beijing,

Figure 1

The Economic Transformation of Post-Mao China

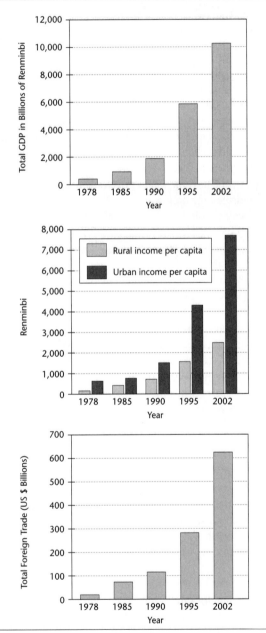

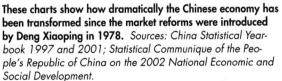

These charts show how dramatically the Chinese economy has been transformed since the market reforms were introduced by Deng Xiaoping in 1978. *Sources: China Statistical Yearbook 1997 and 2001; Statistical Communique of the People's Republic of China on the 2002 National Economic and Social Development.*

Tiananmen Square had indeed been cleared, but with a death toll that still has not been revealed.

Following the Tiananmen massacre, China went through a few years of intensified political repression and economic retrenchment. Then in early 1992, Deng Xiaoping took some bold steps to accelerate reform of the economy. He did so in large part because he hoped it would help the PRC avoid a collapse of the Communist system such as had occurred just the year before in the Soviet Union.

From Revolutionary Leaders to Technocrats (1997 to the Present)

Another important consequence of the 1989 Tiananmen crisis was the replacement as formal head of the CCP of one Deng protégé, Zhao Ziyang, by another, Jiang Zemin. Zhao was ousted by Deng because he was considered too sympathetic to the student demonstrators, and Jiang was promoted from his previous posts as mayor and CCP chief of Shanghai because of his firm but relatively bloodless handling of similar protests in that city. Although Deng remained the power behind the throne for several years, he gradually turned over greater authority to Jiang, who, in addition to his positions as head (general secretary) of the CCP and chair of the powerful Central Military Commission, became president of the PRC in 1993. When Deng Xiaoping died in February 1997, Jiang was secure in his position as China's top leader.

Jiang Zemin retired at age seventy-six as head of the Communist Party in late 2002 and as president of the PRC in early 2003. Under his leadership, China continued the process of economic reform and its record of remarkable economic growth. China became even more fully integrated into the global economy, as exemplified by its admission to the World Trade Organization (WTO) in 2001, and enhanced both its regional and international stature as a rising power. Overall, the country was politically stable during the Jiang era. But the CCP still ruthlessly repressed any individual or group perceived as challenging its authority and faced serious problems, including mounting unemployment, pervasive corruption, and widening gaps between the rich and the poor that threatened to disrupt the calm.

Jiang was succeeded as CCP general secretary in November 2002 and PRC president in March 2003 by

This cartoon captures the contradiction between economic reform and political repression that characterized China under the leadership of Deng Xiaoping. *Source:* © 1992, *The Boston Globe.* Distributed by Los Angeles Times Syndicate. Reprinted with permission.

Hu Jintao, who had previously served as China's vice president. At age sixty when he took these offices, Hu Jintao was considerably younger than most of China's recent leaders. But both Jiang and Hu represented a new kind of leader for the PRC. Mao Zedong and Deng Xiaoping were professional revolutionaries who had participated in the CCP's long struggle for power and were among the founders of the Communist regime when it was established in 1949. In contrast, Jiang and Hu were "technocrats," party officials with academic training (in their cases, as engineers) who worked their way up the political ladder by a combination of competence and loyalty.

The most significant aspect of the transfer of power from Jiang to Hu was how predictable and orderly it was. In fact, some observed that it was the first relatively tranquil top-level political succession in China in more than 200 years. Jiang had retired after two terms in office, as required by both party rules and the state constitution, and Hu had, for several years, been expected to succeed Jiang.

This smooth leadership transition, however, masked much that echoed the secretive and highly personalistic politics that has long characterized Chinese politics. First, Hu Jintao had been designated years before by Deng Xiaoping to be Jiang's successor. So Hu's "election" to the posts of CCP general secretary and PRC president was less the result of an institutionalized process than of personal and factional machinations.

Second, despite retiring from all party and government positions, Jiang Zemin retained considerable political power and influence. He was, in various ways, able to orchestrate his enshrinement as the successor to Mao and Deng as one of the great luminaries in party history. He also kept at least an ear in the inner sanctum of decision making through the placement of numerous close associates in the party's most powerful organizations. Most significant, Jiang did not relinquish his position as chair of the Military Commission, which meant that he was following in Deng's footsteps by keeping control of the country's armed forces even though he did not hold any of the country's top executive offices. Nevertheless, the coming to power of Jiang Zemin and then Hu Jintao did mark a critical juncture in that it reflected the passing of power from the revolutionary to the technocratic generation of Chinese Communist leaders.

Themes and Implications

Historical Junctures and Political Themes

The World of States. When the People's Republic was founded, China was in a weak position in the international system. For more than a century, its destiny had been shaped by incursions and influences from abroad that it could do little to control. Mao made many tragic and terrible blunders, but one of his great

Student demonstrators erected a statue called the "Goddess of Democracy" in Beijing's Tiannmen Square in late May 1989 to symbolize their demands for greater political freedom in China. In the background is an official portrait of former Chinese Communist Party leader, Mao Zedong. Chinese troops toppled and destroyed the statue after they occupied the square on June 4, 1989, a process that also resulted in the death of many protestors. *Source:* AP/Wide World Photos.

achievements was to build a strong state able to affirm and defend its sovereignty. China's international stature has increased as its economic and military strength have grown in recent decades. Although still a relatively poor country by many per capita measures, the sheer size of its economy makes the PRC an economic powerhouse whose import and export policies have an important impact on many other countries. China is a nuclear power with the world's largest conventional military force, and it is an active and influential member of nearly all international organizations, including the United Nations, where it sits as one of the five permanent members of the Security Council. Clearly, China has become one of the major players in the world of states

The making of the modern Chinese state has also been profoundly influenced at several critical points by China's encounters with other countries. The end of the Middle Kingdom's relative isolation from the non-Asian world and the conflict with the militarily superior West in the nineteenth century was a major factor in the collapse of the imperial system in 1911. Anger over European and U.S. treatment of China, admiration for the Russian Revolution, and the invasion of China by Japan in the 1930s all played a role in propelling the CCP to power in 1949.

American hostility to the new Communist regime in Beijing helped push the PRC into an alliance with the Soviet Union and follow the Soviet model of development in the early 1950s. But Mao's disapproval of the direction in which Soviet Communist leaders were taking their country greatly influenced his decisions to launch both the Great Leap Forward in 1958 and the Cultural Revolution in 1966. In the early 1970s, Mao supported the beginnings of détente with the United States in response to what he saw as a growing and more immediate threat to China from the Soviet Union. The relationship between China and the United States deepened throughout the 1970s and paved the way for the marketization and globalization of the Chinese economy under Deng Xiaoping.

Sino-American interaction (*sino* means "China," as derived from the Latin) is, arguably, the most important bilateral diplomatic relationship in the post–cold war world. There have been numerous ups and downs in that relationship since the two countries resumed ties in the 1970s. A particularly low point came after the 1989 Tiananmen massacre, when the United States cut back contacts with the Beijing regime. But shared economic and geopolitical interests have brought the United States and China closer since then, although issues such as human rights, arms control, and trade policies have sometimes caused serious friction. American presidential administrations have differed about whether the PRC should be seen as a rising power best dealt with by cooperation or containment.

The terrorist attacks of September 11, 2001, had a significant impact on Sino-American relations. The PRC became a key ally in the U.S.-led war on terrorism, which led to a downgrading of any and all outstanding disagreements between Beijing and Washington. When Presidents Bush and Jiang met in Texas in October 2002, their mutual interest in dealing with the terrorist threat was practically the only matter for discussion. This was after a period in which Sino-American ties had been strained by the accidental bombing of the PRC embassy in Belgrade, Yugoslavia, by U.S. aircraft during the Kosovo war in July 1999 and the collision of an American spy plane with a Chinese jet fighter off the coast of China in April 2001. Common ground in the war on terrorism has led to a distinct warming of U.S.-China relations as issues that had become contentious between the two nations, including human rights, the trade imbalance, and Chinese arms exports, were put on the diplomatic back burner. China's leaders were quite happy to have tensions with the United States off their already overly burdened agenda. Indeed, one observer concluded that "the country that has benefited most from 9-11 is China."[4]

Governing the Economy.   Economic issues were central to the revolutionary process that resulted in the founding of the People's Republic. The Western powers were primarily motivated by the lure of the China market in their aggressive policies toward the Chinese empire in the nineteenth century. Chiang Kai-shek's Nationalist government lost popular support partly because of its mismanagement of the economy and inability to control corruption. Mass poverty and terrible inequality fueled the Chinese revolution and led millions of peasants and workers to back the Communist Party in the civil war.

The history of the PRC is largely the story of experimentation with a series of very different economic systems: a Soviet-style planning system in the early 1950s, the radical egalitarianism of the Maoist model, and Deng Xiaoping's market-oriented policies. Ideological disputes within the CCP over which of these development strategies China should follow were the main cause of the ferocious political struggles, such as the Cultural Revolution, that have so often wracked

the country. Deng's bold reforms were, in large measure, motivated by his hope that improved living standards would restore the legitimacy of the CCP, which had been badly tarnished by the economic failings of the Maoist era. The remarkable successes of those reforms under Deng and his successors have helped sustain the CCP in power at a time when most other Communist regimes have disappeared. Continuing China's economic progress will be one of the most important challenges facing Hu Jintao and China's other leaders.

The Democratic Idea.   The CCP also faces major political challenges, especially the challenge of the democratic idea, which has had a troubled history in modern China. The revolution of 1911, which overthrew the imperial system and established the Republic of China under Sun Yat-sen, was the culmination of the first effort to establish a Chinese government in which citizens would have a greater voice. But the combination of warlordism, civil war, world war, and Chiang Kai-shek's sharp turn toward dictatorship undermined any real progress toward democracy. Any hope that the democratic idea might take root in the early years of Communist rule in China was violently dispelled by the building of a one-party Communist state and Mao's unrelenting campaigns against alleged enemies of his revolution. The Deng Xiaoping era brought much greater economic, social, and cultural freedom for the Chinese people, but time and again the CCP acted to strangle the stirrings of the democratic idea, most brutally near Tiananmen Square in 1989. Jiang Zemin has been a faithful disciple of Deng; he not only has vigorously championed economic reform in China, but also has also made sure that the CCP retains its firm grip on power. Although it is unlikely that Hu Jintao will act any differently, he could face increasing pressure for political change as Chinese society becomes more modernized, complex, and globalized. In fact, in his first months in power, Hu struck a number of populist themes in his speeches and travels that could portend an effort to establish a "close to the people" leadership style distinct from that of the more aloof Jiang.

The Politics of Collective Identity.   Because of its long history and high degree of cultural homogeneity, China has a very strong sense of national identity.

Memories of past humiliations and suffering at the hands of foreigners still influence the international relations of the PRC. For example, Beijing's insistence that Britain return Hong Kong to Chinese control in 1997 largely on its terms was shaped by the desire to redress what it saw as one of the most blatant injustices of China's defeat in the Opium War of the mid-nineteenth century. China also believes that Japan should apologize more fully for atrocities committed by the Japanese army during World War II before the two Asian powers can have completely cordial diplomatic relations. And as faith in communist ideology has weakened, party leaders have increasingly turned to nationalism as a means to rally the Chinese people behind their government, as reflected in the large-scale public celebrations that greeted Beijing's selection as the site for the 2008 Summer Olympics

China's cultural homogeneity has also spared it the kind of ethnic or religious violence that has plagued so many other countries in the modern world. The exception has been in the border regions of the country, where there is a large concentration of minority peoples, particularly in Tibet and the Muslim areas of China's northwest (see Section 4).

But China did experience a particularly vicious and destructive kind of identity politics during the Maoist era. Although landlords and capitalists had lost their private property and economic power by the mid-1950s, Mao continued to promote class struggle that pitted workers, peasants, and loyal party activists against "capitalist roaders" and other alleged counterrevolutionaries. When he took over in the late 1970s, Deng Xiaoping called for an end to such divisive class struggles and proclaimed an era of social harmony in which the whole nation could concentrate its energies on the overarching goal of economic development, a trend that was continued and deepened by his successor, Jiang Zemin. But economic reform has led to new (or renewed) cleavages in Chinese society, including glaring inequalities between those who have profited handsomely from the marketization of the economy and those who have done less well or even been disadvantaged by the changes. These inequalities could become the basis of class, regional, or other kinds of identity-based conflicts that severely test the economic and political management skills of China's leaders.

Implications for Comparative Politics

China is a particularly important and interesting case for the study of comparative politics. First, the PRC can be compared with other communist party-states with which it shares or has shared many political and ideological features. From this perspective, China raises intriguing questions: Why has China's communist party-state so far proved more durable than that of the Soviet Union and nearly all other similar regimes? By what combination of reform and repression has the CCP held onto power? What signs are there that it is likely to continue to be able to do so for the foreseeable future? What signs suggest that Communist rule in China may be weakening? Studying Chinese politics is important for understanding the past, present, and future of a type of political system, the communist party-state, that has had a major impact on the modern world.

China can also be fruitfully compared with other developing nations that face similar economic and political challenges. Although the PRC is part of the Third World as measured by the average standard of living of its population, its record of growth in the past several decades has been far better than almost all other developing countries. Furthermore, the educational and health levels of the Chinese people are quite good when compared with many other countries at a similar level of development, for example, India and Nigeria. How has China achieved such relative success in its quest for economic and social development? On the other hand, while much of the Third World has gone through a wave of democratization in recent decades, China remains a one-party dictatorship. How and why has China resisted this wave of democracy? What does the experience of other developing countries say about how economic modernization might influence the prospects for democracy in China?

Napoleon Bonaparte, emperor of France in the early nineteenth century, is said to have remarked, "Let China sleep. For when China wakes, it will shake the world."[5] No doubt China has awakened, and given the country's geographic size, vast resources, huge population, surging economy, and formidable military might, it will certainly be among the world's great powers in the near future. China should command the attention of all students of comparative politics.

Section ❷ Political Economy and Development

The growth of China's economy since reform began in the late 1970s has been called "one of the century's greatest economic miracles," which has led to "one of the biggest improvements in human welfare anywhere at any time."[6] Such superlatives seem justified in describing overall economic growth rates that averaged about 10 percent per year for nearly two decades while most of the world's other economies were growing much more slowly. China's gross domestic product (GDP), in dollar terms, is now the sixth largest in the world (about the same as that of France). In terms of purchasing power parity (which adjusts for price differences between countries), China has the second largest economy in the world after the United States and accounts for nearly 12 percent of global GDP. Between 1980 and 2000, the average income of the Chinese people increased more than fifteen-fold. Although there are still many very poor people in China, more than 200 million have been lifted from living in absolute poverty to a level where they have a minimally adequate supply of food, clothing, and shelter. China's economic miracle has involved much more than growth in GDP and personal income. There has also been a profound transformation of the basic nature of economic life in the PRC from what it had been during the Maoist era.

State and Economy

The Maoist Economy

When the CCP came to power in 1949, the Chinese economy was suffering from the devastating effects of more than a hundred years of rebellion, invasion, civil war, and bad government. The first urgent task of China's new Communist rulers was the stabilization and revival of the economy. Although a lot of property was seized from wealthy landowners, rich industrialists, and foreign companies, much private ownership and many aspects of capitalism were allowed to continue in order to gain support for the government and get the economy going again.

Once production had been restored, the party turned its attention to economic development by following the Soviet model of state socialism. The essence of this model was a **command economy,** in which the state owns or controls most economic resources, and economic activity is driven by government planning and commands rather than by market forces.

The command economy in China was at its height during the First Five-Year Plan of 1953–1957, when the government took control of the production and distribution of nearly all goods and services. The First Five-Year Plan yielded some impressive economic results, but it also created huge bureaucracies and new inequalities, especially between the heavily favored industrial cities and the investment-starved rural areas. Both the Great Leap Forward and the Cultural Revolution embodied a Maoist approach to economic development that was intended to be less bureaucratic and more egalitarian than the Soviet model.

For example, in the Great Leap, more than 1 million backyard furnaces were set up throughout the country to prove that steel could be produced by peasants in every village, not just in a few huge modern factories in the cities. In the Cultural Revolution, revolutionary committees, controlled by workers and party activists, replaced the Soviet-style system of letting managers run industrial enterprises. Both of these Maoist experiments were less than successful. The backyard furnaces yielded great quantities of useless steel and squandered precious resources, while the revolutionary committees led many factories to pay more attention to politics than production.

The economic legacy of Maoism is mixed. Under Mao, the PRC "did accomplish, in however flawed a fashion, the initial phase of industrialization of the Chinese economy, creating a substantial industrial and technological base that simply had not existed before."[7] In addition, by the end of the Maoist era, the people of China were much healthier and more literate than they had been in the early 1950s. But for all of its radical rhetoric, the Maoist strategy of development never broke decisively with the basic precepts of the command system. Political interference, poor management, and ill-conceived projects led to wasted resources of truly staggering proportions. Overall, China's economic growth rates, especially in agriculture, barely kept pace with population increases, and the standard of living changed little between the 1950s and Mao's death in 1976.

China Goes to Market

After he consolidated power in 1978, Deng Xiaoping took China in an economic direction far different from Mao's or from that which had ever been followed by a communist party-state anywhere. His pragmatic views on how to promote development were captured in his famous 1962 statement, "It doesn't matter whether a cat is white or black, as long as it catches mice."[8] Deng meant that China should not be overly concerned about whether a particular policy was socialist or capitalist if it in fact helped the economy. It was just such sentiment that got him in trouble with Mao and made Deng one of the principal victims of the Cultural Revolution.

Once he was in charge, Deng spearheaded a program of far-reaching reforms that remade the Chinese economy, touched nearly every aspect of life in the PRC, and redefined socialism in China. These reforms greatly reduced the role of government control while allowing market mechanisms, such as the profit motive, to operate in increasingly large areas of the economy. They also involved a significant degree of decentralization in the economy. Authority for making economic decisions passed from bureaucrats to individual families, factory managers, and private entrepreneurs, all of them presumably motivated by the desire to make more money.

Almost all prices are now set according to supply and demand, as in a capitalist economy, rather than by administrative decree, and in most sectors of the economy decisions about what to produce and how to produce it are no longer dictated by the state. The Chinese government also encourages private ownership of factories and businesses. According to some estimates, private and semiprivate enterprises, including those in industry, services, commerce, and agribusiness, now account for between 50 and 60 percent of China's GDP and employ nearly 200 million people.

In many areas of the economy, government monopolies have given way to fierce competition between state-owned and non-state-owned firms. For example, the government-run national airline, which was the country's only airline until 1985, now competes with dozens of foreign and domestic carriers. Several government-approved stock markets, which sell shares in enterprises to private individuals, have been established, and many more unauthorized ones have sprung up around the country.

A decade ago there were over 100,000 state-owned enterprises (SOEs) in China; now there are fewer than half that number. But these so-called economic dinosaurs still employ nearly 80 million workers, produce a significant share of China's total industrial output, and continue to dominate critical sectors of the economy, such as the production of steel and petroleum. Nevertheless, the role of the state sector is rapidly shrinking as private industries and so-called collective enterprises (which are usually run by combinations of local governments and private entrepreneurs) are expanding at a much faster rate (see Figure 2). Moreover, even SOEs must now be responsive to market forces. Those that are unable to turn a profit are forced to restructure or even threatened with bankruptcy. It is estimated that between 45 and 60 million SOE employees have been laid off in recent years. Many are too old or too unskilled to find good jobs in the modernized and marketized economy, and China has very little in the way of unemployment insurance or social security for its displaced workers.

Some SOEs have been privatized, but most of those that remain are vastly overstaffed and have outdated facilities and machinery, which make them very unattractive to potential foreign or domestic buyers. They remain a huge drain on the country's banking system and hinder modernization of key sectors of the Chinese economy. But the country's leaders are understandably concerned about the political and social consequences that would result from an even more massive layoff of industrial workers.

The economic results of China's move to the market have been phenomenal. The PRC has been the fastest-growing major economy in the world for more than two decades and even weathered, relatively unscathed, the severe financial crisis that struck the rest of East Asia in the late 1990s. China's GDP per capita (that is, the total output of the economy divided by the total population) grew at an average rate of 9.2 percent per year from 1990 to 2000. By way of comparison, the per capita GDP of the United States grew at 2.2 percent

Figure 2

China's Industrial Output by Ownership Type

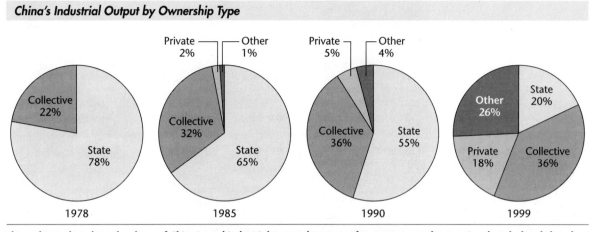

These charts show how the share of China's total industrial output that comes from state-owned enterprises has declined sharply since economic reforms began in 1978. The category "Collective" consists mostly of rural township and village enterprises (TVEs), which are owned by local governments, but operate according to the market rather than by state planning. "Private" refers to industries owned by individuals, and "Other" includes foreign-owned enterprises and various kinds of mixed ownership. *Source: China Statistical Yearbook 1998 and 2000.*

per year during the same period, India's at 4.1 percent, and Brazil's at 1.5 percent.

A booming economy and rapidly rising incomes have unleashed a consumer revolution in the PRC. To cite just one example, in the late 1970s, hardly anyone owned a television of any kind; now nearly every urban household has a color TV, and a large proportion of rural families have at least a black-and-white set.

The PRC says that it currently has a **socialist market economy.** Although this terminology may seem to be mere ideological window dressing to allow the introduction of capitalism into a country still ruled by a communist party, the phrase conveys the fact that China's economy now combines elements of both socialism and capitalism. In theory, the market remains subordinate to government planning and CCP leadership, which is supposed to prevent too much capitalist-like exploitation and inequality.

Despite these far-reaching changes, the Chinese economy is not fully marketized. Central planning, though greatly refined and reduced, has not been eliminated altogether, and national and local bureaucrats still exercise a great deal of control over the production and distribution of goods, resources, and services. The extent of private property is still restricted, and

unproductive state enterprises continue to exert a considerable drag on key economic sectors. Although the market reforms have gained substantial momentum that would be nearly impossible to reverse, the CCP still wields the power to decide the future direction of China's economy.

Remaking the Chinese Countryside

The economic transformation of China has been particularly striking in the countryside, where over 700 million people live and work.

One of the first major efforts launched by the CCP after it came to power in 1949 was a land reform campaign that confiscated the property of landlords and redistributed it as private holdings to the poorer peasants. But in the mid-1950s, as part of the transition to socialism, China's peasants were reorganized into collective farms made up of about 250 families each. The land then belonged to the collective, and production and labor were directed by local officials working in coordination with the state plan. Individuals were paid according to how much they worked on the collective land, while most crops and other farm products had to be sold to the state at low fixed prices. During

This picture, taken in Shanghai in the 1990s, graphically captures how the modern and the traditional exist side-by-side in China. It also shows how the market-style reforms introduced by Deng Xiaoping greatly increased disparities in wealth, a problem that could lead to growing social and political tensions in the future. *Source:* Dan Habib.

the Great Leap Forward, the collective farms were merged into gigantic **people's communes** with several thousand families. Although the size of the communes was scaled back following failure of the Leap, the commune system remained the foundation of the rural economy throughout the rest of the Maoist period. The system of collectivized agriculture proved to be one of the weakest links in China's command economy. Per capita agricultural production and rural living standards were essentially stagnant from 1957 to 1977.

The first changes in the organization of agriculture in post-Mao China came from the spontaneous actions of local leaders who were looking for ways to boost production. They moved to curtail the powers of the commune and allow peasants more leeway in planting and selling their crops. In the early 1980s, Deng Xiaoping used his newly won political power to support this trend and moved to "bury the Maoist model once and for all" in the countryside.[9] The communes were replaced by a **household responsibility system,** which remains in effect today. Under this system, farmland is contracted out to individual families, who take full charge of the production and marketing of crops. Families can sign contracts for thirty years or more, but there has been no move to privatize agriculture fully by selling the land to individuals. The freeing of the rural economy from the constraints of the communal system led to a sharp increase in agricultural productivity and income for farm families.

But nothing contributed more to the remaking of the Chinese countryside than the spread of a rural industrial and commercial revolution that, in speed and scope, was unprecedented in the history of the modern world. Although the foundations of rural industrialization were laid during the Maoist period, **township and village enterprises** (TVEs) expanded enormously under Deng Xiaoping's economic reforms. These rural factories and businesses, which vary greatly in size, are generally owned and run by local government and private entrepreneurs. Although they are called collective enterprises, TVEs operate outside the state plan, make their own decisions about all aspects of the business process, and are responsible for their profits and losses.

For much of the 1980s and 1990s, TVEs were the

fastest-growing sector of the Chinese economy, producing 80 percent of the nation's clothes and, by 1998, accounting for nearly 30 percent of China's total economic output. But the economic Darwinism of the market caught up with the rapid expansion of TVEs by the turn of the century, and many were forced out of business. Nevertheless, they can still be found in nearly every part of the country, except the poorest areas of the interior, and they employ tens of millions of people.

The transformation of the Chinese countryside has not been without serious problems, however. Local officials who run TVEs "often behave more like business tycoons than public servants" and pay more attention to making money for themselves than to their civic duties.[10] Peasant protests, which sometimes turn violent, against high taxes, corrupt local officials, and delays in payments for agricultural products purchased by the government have increased significantly in recent years.

There have also been concerns about China's ability to produce enough food to feed its big population. Now that the state no longer commands farmers to give priority to the production of grain (which dropped 9 percent in 2001) and other essential foods, they often choose to raise more lucrative cash crops, such as flowers and vegetables. In fact, China has recently had to import fairly large quantities of grain. And overall, the growth of agriculture has slowed considerably since the first burst of reform: it averaged a little over 4 percent per year in the 1990s and dropped to 2.4 percent in 2000 and 2.8 percent in 2001. It is likely that there needs to be more investment, particularly in technology, and deeper structural changes in the rural economy if agriculture is going to resume rapid growth.

The social services safety net provided for China's rural dwellers by the communes has all but disappeared with the return to household-based farming. Many rural clinics and schools closed once government financial support was eliminated. The availability of health care, educational opportunities, disability pay, and retirement funds now depends on the relative wealth of families and villages, which has led to very large gaps between the prosperous and the poor areas of the country. Economic factors, such as the need for larger families in situations where income is dependent on household labor, have also contributed to peasant efforts to circumvent China's controversial one-child popula-

tion control policy (see "Current Challenges: China's One-Child Policy").

The Political Impact of Economic Reform

Efforts to transform the economy through market-style policies have had an important impact on China's domestic politics. First, both Deng Xiaoping and then Jiang Zemin faced opposition from other party leaders who believe that China has moved too fast and too far toward a market economy. The critics of reform are worried about the spread of capitalist influences, including calls for more democracy, at home and from abroad. Deng was able to accommodate such challenges, and the emergence of Jiang and, more recently, Hu Jintao as Deng's successors has kept power in the hands of leaders strongly committed to continuing economic reform. But a major economic setback or widespread political turmoil could still lead to a resurgence of antireform elements in the party.

Second, the **decentralization** of economic decision making, which has been an important factor in the success of the market reforms, has also greatly increased the autonomy of subnational governments. Local governments often defy or ignore the central government by, for example, evading taxes or undertaking massive construction projects without consulting Beijing. Such seepage of economic and political power from the central to the local levels poses serious questions about the ability of the national government to maintain control in the country.

Finally, China's economic transformation has brought far-reaching social change to the country, creating new pressures on the political system and new challenges to the CCP. The party wants the Chinese people to believe that economic growth depends on the political stability that only its firm leadership can provide. CCP leaders hope that growing prosperity will leave most people satisfied with the party and reduce demands for political change. But economic reform has created many groups—entrepreneurs, professionals, middle-class consumers, the hundreds of thousands of Chinese students who have studied abroad—who cannot be repressed if the party wants to sustain the country's economic progress. In time, these and other emerging groups are likely to press their claims for a more independent political voice and confront the

Current Challenges: **China's One-Child Policy**

While he was in power, Mao Zedong did not see a reduction of China's population growth rate as an important national priority. On the contrary, he viewed vast amounts of human labor and the revolutionary enthusiasm of the masses as precious national resources. As a result, little was done to promote family planning in China during most of the Maoist era.

By the early 1970s, China's population had reached over 800 million, and because of greatly improved health conditions, it was growing at about 2.8 percent per year. This meant that the number of people in China would double in just twenty-five years, which would put a great strain on the country's resources. Cutting the birthrate came to be seen as major prerequisite to economic development. Since the 1980s, the Chinese government implemented a stringent population control policy that has used various means to encourage or even force couples to have only a single child. Intensive media campaigns have lauded the patriotic virtues and material benefits of small families. Positive incentives such as more land or preferred housing have been offered to couples with only one child, and fines or demotions have been meted out to those who violate the policy. In some places, contraceptive use and women's fertility cycles are monitored by workplace medics or local doctors, and a couple must have official permission to have a child. Defiance has sometimes led to forced abortion or sterilization.

The one-child campaign, the modernizing economy, and a comparatively strong record in improving educational and employment opportunities for women have all played a role in bringing China's population growth rate to under 0.9 percent per year. This figure is *very* low for a country at China's level of economic development. India, for example, has also had some success in promoting family planning, but its annual population growth rate is 1.5 percent, while Nigeria's is 2.5 percent. These might not seem like big differences, but consider this: at these respective growth rates, it will take seventy-seven years for China's population to double, whereas India's population will double in forty-seven years and Nigeria's in just twenty-eight years!

There have been some very serious problems with China's population policy. The compulsory, intrusive nature of the family planning program and the extensive use of abortion as one of the major means of birth control has led to some international criticism, which Beijing has rejected as interference in its domestic affairs.

Many farmers have evaded the one-child policy—for example, by not registering births—because the return to household-based agriculture has made the quantity of labor an important ingredient in family income. The still widespread belief that male children will contribute more economically to the family and that a male heir is necessary to carry on the family line causes some rural families to take drastic steps to make sure that they have a son. Female infanticide and the abandonment of female babies have increased dramatically, and the spread of ultrasound technology has led to large number of sex-selective abortions of female fetuses. As a result, China has an unusual gender balance among its young population: normally, 105 to 107 boys are born for every 100 girls, but China's last census, completed in 2000, showed a gender ratio of 116.9 boys for every 100 girls and as high as 135 to 100 in some regions. As a result, there are hundreds of thousands (perhaps millions) of "missing girls" in China's population under the age of thirty. One estimate suggests that there are 70 million more males in China than females, and some worry this has already led to "bride stealing" and other kinds of trafficking in women.

Partly in response to rural resistance and international pressure, the Chinese government has relaxed its population policies somewhat; forced abortion is now infrequent, though sex-selective abortion is not. Rural couples are now often allowed to have two children. In the cities, where there has been more voluntary compliance with the policy because of higher incomes and limited living space, the one-child policy is still basically in effect.

regime with some fundamental questions about the nature of Communist power in China.

Society and Economy

Market reform and globalization of the Chinese economy have created a much more diverse and open society. People are vastly freer to choose careers, travel about the country and internationally, practice their religious beliefs, buy private homes, join nonpolitical associations, and engage in a wide range of other activities that were prohibited or severely restricted during the Maoist era. But economic change has also caused grave social problems. There has been a sharp increase in crime, prostitution, and drug use; although such problems are still far less prevalent in China than in many other countries, they are serious enough to be a growing concern for national and local authorities.

Economic reform has also brought significant changes in China's basic system of social welfare. The Maoist economy was characterized by what was called the **iron rice bowl.** As in other state socialist economies such as the Soviet Union, this meant that employment, a certain standard of living (albeit, a low one), and basic cradle-to-grave benefits were guaranteed to most of the urban and rural labor force. In the cities, the workplace was more than just a place to work and earn a salary; it also provided its employees with housing, health care, day care, and other services.

China's economic reformers believe that such guarantees led to poor work motivation and excessive costs for the government and enterprises, and they have implemented policies designed to break the iron rice bowl. Income and employment are no longer guaranteed but are more directly tied to individual effort. Workers in the remaining state-owned enterprises still have rather generous health and pension plans, but employees in the rapidly expanding semiprivate and private sectors usually have few benefits.

The breaking of the iron rice bowl has increased productivity and motivated people to work harder in order to earn more money. But it has also led to a sharp increase in unemployment, which is estimated to be as high as 20 percent of the total urban labor force (the official number is about 4 percent). Labor unrest, including strikes, slowdowns, demonstrations, and sit-ins, has been rising, particularly in China's rust belt, where state-owned industries have been particularly hard-hit. In early 2002, 50,000 laid-off workers demonstrated in Daqing, a one-time model Maoist oil field in northeastern China, demanding unpaid benefits, and 30,000 workers in another northeastern city staged protests against official corruption and nonpayment of wages.

In the past, the CCP has not dealt gently with protesting workers: the army was ordered to crush the 1989 Tiananmen demonstrations partly because party leaders were alarmed by the large number of workers who had joined the protests under the banner of an unauthorized union. If inefficient state-owned firms are shut down or downsized as the current leadership has promised, another 30 million workers might lose their jobs. Unemployment and labor unrest could be a political time bomb for China's communist party-state.

Market reforms have also opened China's cities to a flood of rural migrants. After the agricultural communes were disbanded in the early 1980s, many of the peasants who were not needed in the fields found work in the rapidly expanding township and village enterprises. But many others, no longer constrained by the strict limits on internal population movement enforced in the Mao era, headed to the urban areas to look for jobs. The 80 to 120 million people who make up this so-called floating population are mostly employed in low-paying temporary jobs such as unskilled construction work—when they can find any work at all. These migrants are putting increased pressure on urban housing and social services, and their presence in Chinese cities could become politically destabilizing if they find their aspirations thwarted by a stalled economy or if they are treated too roughly or unfairly by local governments, which often see them as intruders.

China's economic boom has also created enormous opportunities for corruption. In a country in transition from a command to a market economy, officials still control many resources and retain power over many economic transactions from which large profits can be made. Bribes are common in this heavily bureaucratized and highly personalized system. Because the rule of law is often weaker than personal connections (called *guanxi* in Chinese), nepotism and cronyism are rampant. Recognizing the threat that corruption poses to its legitimacy, the government has repeatedly launched well-publicized campaigns against official graft, with severe punishment, including execution, for some serious offenders, but with little effect in curbing such nefarious practices.

The benefits of economic growth have spread throughout most of China. But there has also been a growth in inequality—a contradiction for a country led by a party that still claims to believe in socialist ideals. China's market reforms and economic boom have created sharp class differences, generally benefiting people who live in the cities much more than those in the countryside (see Figure 1), particularly since agricultural growth rates started to fall in the 1990s. There is also widening gap between the more developed coastal regions and the inland areas, though recent poverty alleviation programs, including a "Develop the West" campaign, have brought some economic progress to some of poorest parts of the country. Hu Jintao, China's new president and party leader, has also taken steps to portray himself as the champion of the poor, promising to place their plight at the top of his administration's agenda.

Gender inequalities also appear to have increased in some ways since the introduction of the market reforms. There is no doubt that the overall situation of women in China has improved enormously since 1949 in terms of social status, legal rights, employment, and education. Women have also benefited from rising living standards and expanded economic opportunities that the reforms have brought. But the trend toward marketization has not benefited men and women equally. In the countryside, it is almost always the case that only male heads of households may sign contracts for land, and therefore men dominate rural economic life. This is true despite the fact that farm labor has become increasingly feminized as many men move to jobs in rural industry or migrate to the cities. Economic and cultural pressures have also led to an alarming suicide rate (the world's highest) among rural women. Over 70 percent (about 120 million) of illiterate adults in China are female. Although China has one of the world's highest rates of female urban labor participation, the market reforms have "strengthened and in some cases reconstructed the sexual division of labor, keeping urban women in a transient, lower-paid, and subordinate position in the workforce."[11] Women

workers are the first to be laid off or are forced to retire early when a state-owned enterprise downsizes.

Finally, the momentous economic changes in China have had serious environmental consequences. As in the former Soviet Union and East-Central Europe, China's environment suffered greatly under the old state socialist system, but in some ways, ecological damage has gotten even worse in the profit-at-any-cost atmosphere of the market reforms. Industrial expansion is fueled primarily by the use of highly polluting coal, which has made the air in China's cities and even many rural areas among the dirtiest in the world. Soil erosion, the loss of arable land, and deforestation are serious problems for the countryside. The dumping of garbage and toxic wastes goes virtually unregulated, and it is estimated that 80 percent of China's rivers are badly polluted. One of the most serious problems is a critical water shortage in north China due to urbanization and industrialization. To meet this need, a $60 billion megaproject was begun in December 2002 to build a system of channels and pump stations to divert water from the central part of the country to the north. The government has also enacted some policies to protect the environment and increased environmental spending. However, "as is the case in most developing countries, the quest for economic development has superseded concern over environmental pollution."[12]

Dealing with some of the negative social consequences of China's market reforms and economic growth is one of the main challenges facing the government. The ability of labor, women's, or environmental movements to get these social issues on the political agenda remains limited by the party's tight control of political life and restrictions on the formation of autonomous interest groups in China (see Section 4).

China and the International Political Economy

Deng Xiaoping's program for transforming the Chinese economy rested on two pillars: the market-oriented reform of the domestic economy and the policy of opening China to the outside world. The extensive internationalization of the Chinese economy that has taken place in recent decades contrasts sharply with the semi-isolationist policy of economic self-reliance pursued by Mao Zedong.

China was not a major trading nation when Deng took power in 1978. Total foreign trade was about $20 billion (about 10 percent of GDP), and foreign investment in China was minuscule, as the stagnant economy, political instability, and heavy-handed bureaucracy were not attractive to potential investors from abroad.

In the early 1980s, China embarked on a strategy of using trade as a central component of its drive for economic development, following in some ways the model of export-led growth pioneered by Japan and **newly industrializing countries** (NICs) such as the Republic of Korea (South Korea). The essence of this model is to take advantage of low-wage domestic labor to produce goods that are in demand internationally and then to use the earnings from the sale of those goods to finance the modernization of the economy.

China's foreign trade totaled more than $620 billion in 2002 (about 50 percent of GDP), making the PRC the sixth largest trading nation in the world. Seventy percent of China's exports are garments, shoes, furniture, small electronic goods, and toys; the country manufactures 60 percent of the world's bicycles and 86 percent of those sold in the United States. The PRC imports mostly machinery, technology, and raw materials needed to support modernization. Despite having large domestic sources of petroleum and significant untapped reserves, China became a net importer of oil for the first time in 1993 because of the huge energy demands of its economic boom. And in 2002, in order to meet the voracious appetite for steel generated by a construction boom and surge in automobile production, China surpassed the United States as the world's largest importer of that commodity, even though it already produces more steel than the United States and Japan combined.

Much of China's trade is in East Asia, particularly with Japan, South Korea, Taiwan, and Hong Kong (which is now administratively part of the PRC but is a highly developed, capitalist economy; see "Global Connection: Hong Kong—From China to Britain and Back Again"). The financial crisis that hit that part of the world in the late 1990s caused a sharp drop in the rate of growth of Chinese exports (from 27 percent in 1997 to 0.5 percent in 1998). But China's export growth rate rebounded to about 6 percent in 2001 and to 22 percent in 2002. Nevertheless, there are still serious doubts about the long-run viability of an economic development strategy that is so heavily dependent on foreign trade.

The United States has also become one of the PRC's major trading partners and is now the biggest market for Chinese exports (over 20 percent of the total in 2001). In 2000, China surpassed Japan as the country with which the United States had the largest trade deficit by a small margin, but as Japan continued to be mired in a deep recession, the U.S. deficit with China in 2002 ($103 billion) far exceeded that with Japan ($70 billion). The growing trade imbalance was a source of some tension in U.S.-China relations, especially over the issue of restricted access to China's domestic market for American goods and the violation of U.S. copyrights by Chinese firms that produce compact discs, video recordings, and computer software. The United States and a number of China's other big trading partners hope that the PRC's accession to the WTO will help remedy some of these problems and open the Chinese market to more imported goods.

Foreign investment in China has also skyrocketed. From close to zero in 1978, by 2001, more than $700 billion in investments had been pledged (and over $400 billion actually used) in nearly 400,000 different enterprises, ranging from small factories producing toys and clothing for export to huge firms producing goods and services for the Chinese market, like Coca-Cola, Motorola, and General Motors. China is now the world's largest absorber of foreign direct investment, and more than 400 of the world's 500 top corporations have operations in the PRC. The low cost of labor in China is a major attraction to foreign firms: manufacturing wages average about 60 cents per hour.

Many of these foreign ventures are located in Special Economic Zones (SEZs) set aside by the government to attract overseas investors through incentives such as tax breaks, modern infrastructure, and the promise of less bureaucratic red tape. The SEZs are even more free-wheeling and faster growing than the Chinese economy as a whole and have also become hotbeds of speculation, corruption, and crime. The largest SEZ, Shenzhen (near Hong Kong), has been transformed in less than twenty years from a nondescript border town of 70,000 people into China's most modern city, with a population of about 7 million.

Global Connection: *Hong Kong: From China to Britain—and Back Again*

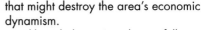

Hong Kong became a British colony in three stages during the nineteenth century as a result of what China calls the "unequal treaties" imposed under military and diplomatic pressure from the West. Two parts of Hong Kong were ceded permanently to Britain in 1842 and 1860, respectively, but the largest part of the tiny territory was given to Britain in 1898 with a ninety-nine-year lease. It was the anticipated expiration of that lease that set in motion negotiations between London and Beijing in the 1980s over the future status of Hong Kong. In December 1984, a joint declaration was signed by the two countries in which Britain agreed to return all of Hong Kong to Chinese sovereignty on July 1, 1997. On that date, Hong Kong became a Special Administrative Region (SAR) of the People's Republic of China.

Britain ruled Hong Kong in a traditional, if generally benevolent, colonial fashion. A governor sent from London presided over an administration in which foreigners rather than the local people exercised most of the power. There was a free press, a fair and effective legal system, and other important features of a democratic system. In the last years of British rule, there were efforts to appoint more Hong Kong Chinese to higher administrative positions and expand the scope of elections in choosing some members of the colony's executive and representative bodies. The British, who controlled Hong Kong for over a century, were criticized for taking steps toward democratization only on the eve of their departure from the colony. They allowed only a small number of Hong Kong residents to emigrate to the United Kingdom before the start of Chinese rule.

Hong Kong flourished economically under the free-market policies of the British and became one of the world's great centers of international trade and finance. Hong Kong has the highest standard of living in Asia outside of Japan and Singapore. At the same time, Hong Kong was and is characterized by extremes of wealth and poverty. When it took over Hong Kong in 1997, China pledged to preserve capitalism in the SAR for at least fifty years under the principle of "one country, two systems." Because of the extensive integration of the economies of Hong Kong and southern China, the PRC has a strong motivation not to do anything that might destroy the area's economic dynamism.

Although the PRC took over full control of Hong Kong's foreign policy and has stationed troops of the People's Liberation Army in Hong Kong, Beijing has generally fulfilled its promise that the SAR will have a high degree of political as well as economic autonomy. Civil liberties, the independence of the judiciary, and freedom of the press have largely been maintained.

The PRC nevertheless has made sure that it keeps a grip on political power in Hong Kong. The SAR is headed by a chief executive, Tung Chee-hwa, a wealthy businessman appointed by the PRC, and PRC-approved civil servants wield enormous authority in the government. Although democratic parties critical or at least skeptical of the Chinese Communist Party have a strong presence among the elected members of the SAR's legislature, a majority of seats are chosen by an indirect process that strongly favors pro-China candidates. Beginning in 2001, the Hong Kong government started to tighten rules on holding public demonstrations and banned visits by some prominent Chinese dissidents. And in late 2002, it took steps to implement a law that prohibited "any act of treason, secession, sedition, subversion against the Central People's Government, or theft of state secrets." Some residents and politicians who favor democracy in Hong Kong fear this antisedition law will pave the way for a clampdown on free speech and reinforces their worry that British colonialism has only been replaced by Chinese authoritarianism.

Hong Kong

Land area (sq. miles)	401.5 (about six times the size of Washington, D.C.)
Population	6.9 million
Ethnic composition	Chinese, 95%; other, 5%
GDP (US$)	$163 billion
GDP per capita (US$)	$25,153
GDP growth rate	0% (2001)
Human Development Index	23 (out of 173)
Life expectancy	Male, 77; female, 82
Infant mortality (per 1,000 live births)	5.73
Literacy	94%

The admission of the PRC to the WTO in December 2001 was a significant step in the country's integration into the global economy. The WTO is the major international organization that oversees and regulates commerce between nations, and membership in it is a great benefit to any country that engages in foreign trade. The United States and other highly developed countries agreed to let China in only once they felt that its economy was more "market" than "state" dominated and that China would play by the rules of free trade. The United States also was inclined to speed up approval of WTO membership for the PRC in late 2001 in order to encourage China's support for and participation in the post–September 11 war on terrorism.

In agreeing to the terms of joining the WTO, China had to promise to make some fundamental changes in its trade practices and domestic economic policies. Most important is the further opening of the Chinese economy to foreign investment and competition. Tariffs (i.e., taxes) on imported goods must be drastically cut, and sectors of the economy that have been largely closed to foreign companies, such as banking, insurance, and agriculture, will have to be unbarred. China's state-owned enterprises, government monopolies, and lagging rural economy will likely find this step toward deeper globalization particularly challenging, but the advantages to the PRC are an expected large increase in foreign trade and investment.

China has a major, but somewhat contradictory, position in the international economy. On the one hand, its relatively low level of economic and technological development compared to the industrialized countries makes it very much a part of the Third World. On the other hand, the total output and rapid growth of its economy, expanding trade, and vast resource base (including its population) make it a potential economic superpower among nations. In the years ahead, China is certain to become an even more active participant in the global economy. At the same time, international influences are likely to play an increasingly important role in China's economic and political development.

Section ❸ Governance and Policy-Making

The PRC is by far the most important of the world's few remaining communist party-states in terms of size and power. The basic political organization of the PRC, like that of the Soviet Union before its collapse in 1991, includes Communist Party domination of all government and social institutions, the existence of an official state ideology based on Marxism-Leninism, and the repression of any political opposition. The CCP, which had about 66 million members as of late 2002, claims that only it can govern in the best interests of the entire nation and therefore it has a right to exercise the leading role throughout Chinese society. Although China has moved sharply toward a market economy in recent decades, the CCP still asserts that it is building socialism with the ultimate objective of creating an egalitarian and classless communist society.

Organization of the State

"The force at the core leading our cause forward is the Chinese Communist Party," observed Mao Zedong in a speech given in 1954 at the opening session of China's legislature, the National People's Congress, which according to the constitution adopted at that meeting, was the "highest organ of state power" in the People's Republic.[13] Mao's statement was a blunt reminder that the party was in charge of the national legislature and all other government organizations. This same line was the very first entry in *The Little Red Book,* the bible of Mao quotes used by the Red Guards who ransacked the country in the name of ideological purity during the Cultural Revolution. Although many party members became targets of the Cultural Revolution, the prominence of this quotation reflected the fact that even at the height of the movement's near anarchy, Mao and his supporters did not intend to call into question the primacy of Communist rule in China. Even Deng Xiaoping, the architect of China's economic reforms, was unwavering in his view that the country should "never dispense with leadership by the party."[14] Despite the many fundamental changes that have taken place in recent decades, party leadership remains an unchallengeable principle of political life in China, and the nation's rulers still claim allegiance to communist ideology. Any analysis of governance and policy-making in China therefore must begin with a discussion of the ideology and power of the Communist Party.

Mao Zedong Thought is said to have made a fundamental contribution to communist ideology by adapting Marxism-Leninism to China's special circumstances, particularly its emphasis on the peasant-based revolution that brought the party to power. In 1997, the CCP added Deng Xiaoping Theory to its official ideology to reflect the late leader's role in justifying a self-proclaimed socialist country's use of market forces to promote the growth of the economy. And in 2002, even Jiang Zemin's ideas (the Three Represents) about expanding the CCP to incorporate all sectors of Chinese society, including private entrepreneurs, in the drive for modernization was enshrined in the party constitution when he retired as general secretary (see Section 4).

Although the focus of Chinese communism has shifted from an emphasis on revolutionary change to economic development, most people in China have lost faith in the ideology because of the CCP's erratic and repressive leadership over the past several decades, or they consider ideology largely irrelevant to their daily lives. Many of those who join the party now do so mainly for career advancement. There are numerous other sources of beliefs and values in society, such as the family and religion, that are more important to most people than the official ideology. But the latest Chinese communist variant of Marxism-Leninism still provides the framework for governance and policy-making and sets the boundaries for what, in the party's view, is permissible in politics.

The underlying organizing principles of China's political system are clearly laid out in the PRC constitution, which is a totally different document from the party (CCP) constitution.[15] The preamble makes repeated reference to the fact that the country is under "the leadership of the Communist Party of China." Article 1 defines the PRC as "a socialist state under the people's democratic dictatorship" and declares that "disruption of the socialist system by any organization or individual is prohibited." Such provisions imply that the Chinese "people"—implicitly defined as those who support socialism and the leadership of the party—enjoy democratic rights and privileges; but the Chinese

constitution also gives the CCP the authority to exercise dictatorship over any person or organization that it believes is opposed to socialism and the party.

Constitutional change (from amendments to total replacement) has reflected the shifting political winds in China. The character and content of the document in force at any given time bear the ideological stamp of the prevailing party leadership. For example, in 1993, the current PRC constitution (adopted in 1982) was amended to replace references to the superiority of central planning and state ownership with phrases more consistent with economic reform, including the statement (Article 15) that China "practices a socialist market economy."

The constitution of the People's Republic specifies the structures and powers of subnational levels of government, including the country's provinces, autonomous regions, and centrally administered cities. But China is not a federal system (like Brazil, Germany, India, Nigeria, and the United States), in which subnational governments have considerable policy-making autonomy. Provincial and local authorities operate "under the unified leadership of the central authorities" (Article 3), which makes China a unitary state (like France and Japan), in which the national government exercises a high degree of control over other levels of government.

The Executive

The PRC government is organizationally and functionally distinct from the Chinese Communist Party. For example, the PRC executive consists of both a premier (prime minister) and a president, whereas the CCP is headed by a general secretary. But there is no alternation of parties in power in China, and the Communist Party exercises direct or indirect control over all government organizations and personnel. Therefore, real executive power in the Chinese political system lies with the top leaders and organizations of the CCP (see Table 1). The government essentially acts as the administrative agency for carrying out and enforcing policies made by the party. Nevertheless, to fully understand governance and policy-making in China, it is necessary to look at both the Chinese Communist Party and the government of the People's Republic of China (the "state") and the relationship between the two.

Table 1

Who's Who In Beijing: China's Most Important Party and State Leaders Since 1949

Leader	Highest Positions Held	Comment
Mao Zedong (1893–1976)	CCP Chairman (1943–1976) PRC President (1949–1959) Military Commission Chair (1949–1976)	Became effective leader of the CCP in 1934–1935 during the Long March, although not elected Chairman until 1943.
Liu Shaoqi (1898–1969)	PRC President (1959–1966) CCP Vice Chairman (1949–1966)	Purged as a "capitalist roader" during the Cultural Revolution. Died in detention.
Zhou Enlai (1898–1976)	PRC Premier (1949–1976) PRC Foreign Minister (1949–1958) CCP Vice Chairman (1949–1969; 1973–1976)	Long-time Mao ally, but a moderating influence during the Cultural Revolution. Architect of détente with U.S. in early 1970s.
Lin Biao (1907–1971)	CCP Vice Chairman (1958–1971) PRC Vice Premier (1954–1971) PRC Defense Minister (1959–1971)	One of Mao's strongest supporters in the Cultural Revolution. Allegedly killed in plane crash after a failed coup attempt against Mao.
Jiang Qing (1914–1991)	Deputy Director, Cultural Revolution Group (1966–1969) Member, CCP Politburo (1969–1976)	Former movie actress who married Mao in 1939. One of the leaders of the Cultural Revolution. Arrested after Mao's death in 1976 and sentenced to life in prison, where she died.
Hua Guofeng (1920–)	CCP Chairman (1976–1981) PRC Premier (1976–1980) Military Commission Chair (1976–1981)	Became CCP chairman after Mao's death and purge of Jiang Qing and her radical followers. Removed from power by Deng Xiaoping, who saw him as too weak and a neo-Maoist.
Deng Xiaoping (1904–1997)	PRC Vice-Premier (1952–1966; 1973–1976; 1977–1980) CCP Vice-Chairman (1975–1976; 1977–1987) Military Commission Chair (1981–1989)	Purged twice during Cultural Revolution. Became China's most powerful leader in 1978 and remained so until shortly before his death.
Jiang Zemin (1926–)	CCP General Secretary[a] (1989–2002) PRC President (1993–2003) Military Commission Chair (1989–)	Former Shanghai mayor promoted by Deng as a safe choice to carry out his policies after Tiananmen crisis. Consolidated his own power after Deng's death in 1997.
Hu Jintao (1942–)	CCP General Secretary (2002–) PRC President (2003–)	Chosen by Deng Xiaoping before his death to succeed Jiang Zemin as head of the CCP. A relatively young technocrat.

[a]The position of CCP chairman was abolished in 1982 and replaced by the general secretary as the party's top position.

The Chinese Communist Party

The constitution of the CCP specifies local and national party structures and functions, the distribution of authority among party organizations, the requirements for joining, the behavior expected of members, and procedures for dealing with infractions of party rules. But such details do not negate the fact that individual power, factional maneuvering, and personal connections are ultimately more important than formal constitutional arrangements for understanding how the party works.

For example, Deng Xiaoping, who was indisputably the most powerful individual in China from 1978 until he became physically incapacitated a year or so before his death in 1997, never occupied any of the top executive offices in the party or the government. Even when he no longer played an active role in day-to-day governance, no major decision was made without his approval, and he was regularly referred to as China's "paramount leader." The sources of Deng's immense power came from informal factors, such as his seniority as one of the founding leaders of the regime and his long advocacy of now widely supported ideas about how China should develop into a strong and modern nation.

But by the late 1990s, most of the elderly men (including Deng) who had wielded great informal authority in post-Mao China were dead. Despite the persisting strong influence of personal ties in Chinese politics, the formal structures of power have assumed greater importance for understanding who has the power and how decisions are made.

According to the CCP constitution, the "highest leading bodies" of the party are the National Party Congress and the Central Committee (see Figure 3). But its infrequent, short meetings (for one week every five years) and large size (more than 2,100 delegates) mean that the role of the Congress in the party is more symbolic than substantive. The essential function of the National Party Congress is to approve decisions already made by the top leaders and provide a showcase for the party's current policies. For example, the party congress that convened in November 2002 was a highly orchestrated celebration of Jiang Zemin's leadership and installation of Hu Jintao as the new general secretary. There was little debate about policy and no contested voting of any consequence.

The Central Committee, which currently has 198 full and 158 alternate members, is the next level up in the pyramid of party power and consists of party leaders from around the country. It meets annually for about a week. It is elected by the National Party Congress by secret ballot, and there is limited choice of candidates. Contending party factions may jockey to win seats, but the overall composition of the Central Committee is closely controlled by the top leaders to ensure compliance with their policies. The Central Committee elected in late 2002 continued the trend toward promoting younger and better-educated party members who are strong supporters of economic reform.

The Central Committee directs party affairs when the National Party Congress is not in session, but its size and relatively short and infrequent meetings (called plenums) also greatly limit its effectiveness. However, Central Committee plenums and occasional informal work conferences do represent significant gatherings of the party elite, which can be a very important arena of political maneuvering and decision making.

The most powerful political organizations in the communist party-state are the two small executive bodies at the very top of the CCP's structure: the Politburo (or Political Bureau) and its even more exclusive Standing Committee. These bodies are elected by the Central Committee from among its own members under carefully controlled conditions. The Politburo elected in 2002 had twenty-four members (plus one alternate) and the Standing Committee, the formal apex of power in the CCP, had nine. People who study Chinese politics scrutinize the membership of the Politburo and Standing Committee for clues about leadership priorities, the balance of power among party factions, and the relative influence of different groups in policy-making.

The Politburo and Standing Committee are not responsible to the Central Committee or any other institution in any meaningful sense. The workings of these organizations are shrouded in secrecy. Most of their work goes on, and many of the top leaders live, in a high-security compound called Zhongnanhai ("Central and Southern Seas"), which is adjacent to the former imperial palace near Tiananmen Square.

Power in the CCP is highly concentrated in the hands of those who control the highest party organizations. Prior to 1982, the top position in the party was the

Figure 3

Organization of the Chinese Communist Party

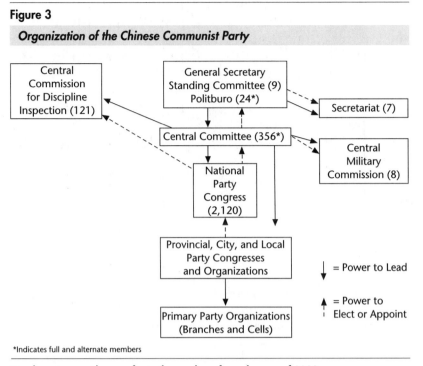

↓ = Power to Lead

↑ = Power to
    Elect or Appoint

*Indicates full and alternate members

Numbers in parentheses refer to the number of members as of 2003.

chairman of the Politburo's Standing Committee, which was occupied by Mao Zedong (hence *Chairman* Mao) for more than three decades until his death in 1976. The title of chairman was abolished in 1982 to symbolize a break with Mao's highly personalistic and often arbitrary style of leadership. Since then, the party's leader has been the general secretary, who presides over the Politburo and the Standing Committee, a position held from 1989 to 2002 by Jiang Zemin. Although Jiang clearly emerged as China's most powerful individual in the late 1990s, he did not have the personal clout or charisma of either Deng or Mao and therefore governed as part of a collective leadership that included his fellow members on the Standing Committee and Politburo. It will certainly be the same with Hu Jintao, who succeeded Jiang as general secretary.

Hu Jintao is said to be the core of the "fourth generation" of CCP leadership, while Jiang was the core of the "third generation." (Mao Zedong and Deng Xiaoping were, respectively, the core leaders of the first and second "generations.") The transition in power from the

Mao-Deng generations to the Jiang-Hu generations represents a shift from revolutionary to technocratic leadership. Indeed, both Jiang and Hu, as well as all nine members of the Politburo Standing Committee elected in 2002, were trained and worked as engineers before embarking on political careers.

Two other party organizations deserve brief mention. The Secretariat manages the day-to-day work of the Politburo and Standing Committee and coordinates the party's complex and far-flung structure with considerable authority in organizational and personnel matters. The Central Commission for Discipline Inspection is responsible for monitoring the compliance of party members with the CCP constitution and other rules. The commission has been used as a vehicle against thousands of party members accused of corruption. In a recent three-year period, more than 861,900 cases were filed by discipline organs at different levels across the country, resulting in 137,711 people being expelled from the party; 37,790 of them were also prosecuted in the courts. Many of those punished were

Former Chinese president and communist party leader, Jiang Zemin, confers with his successor, Hu Jintao, during a meeting of the National People's Congress in March 2003. *Source:* © Reuters NewMedia, Inc. / Corbis.

leading officials at the county provincial and ministry levels.

Below the national level, the CCP has a hierarchy of local party organizations in provinces, cities, and counties, each headed by a party committee. There are also more than 3 million primary party organizations, called branches and cells, which are found in workplaces, schools, urban neighborhoods, rural towns, villages, and army units. Local and primary organizations extend the party's reach throughout Chinese society and are designed to ensure the subordination of each level of party organization to the next-higher level and ultimately to the central party authorities in Beijing.

The Government of the PRC

Government (or state) authority in China is formally vested in a system of people's congresses that begins with the National People's Congress at the top and continues in hierarchically arranged levels down through provincial people's congresses, municipal people's congresses, rural township people's congresses, and so on (see Figure 4). In theory, these congresses (the legislative branch) are empowered to supervise the work of the "people's governments" (the executive branch) at the various levels of the system, but in reality, government executives (such as cabinet ministers, provincial governors, and mayors) are ultimately subject to party authority rather than to the people's congresses. Unlike the parallel system of party congresses, the people's

congresses are supposed to represent all of the citizens at the relevant level, not just the minority who are members of the CCP. Like the party congresses, the people's congresses play a politically limited, but symbolically important, role in policy-making.

The National People's Congress elects the president and vice president of China. But there is only one candidate, chosen by the Communist Party, for each office. The president's term is concurrent with that of the congress (five years), and there is a two-term limit. The position is largely ceremonial, although a senior party leader has always held it. As China's head of state, the president meets and negotiates with other world leaders. Jiang Zemin revived the practice that the leader of the CCP serve concurrently as PRC president, as Mao had done from 1949 to 1959. Hu Jintao followed Jiang's example and was elected president of China at the National People's Congress in March 2003.

The premier (prime minister) is the head of the government and has authority over the bureaucracy and policy implementation. The premier is formally appointed by the president with the approval of the National People's Congress. But in reality, the Communist Party decides who will serve as premier, and that post has always been held by a very high-ranking member of the CCP Standing Committee. Like the president, the premier may serve only two five-year terms. Wen Jiabao, a geologist and a former vice premier in charge of agriculture, the financial system,

Figure 4

Organization of the Government of the People's Republic of China

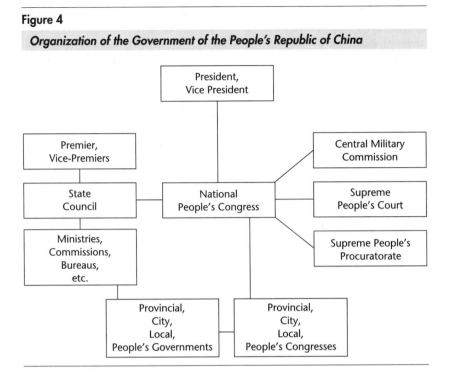

flood control, and poverty alleviation, was chosen as premier in March 2003.

The Bureaucracy

The premier directs the State Council, which is constitutionally "the highest organ of state administration" (Article 85) in the PRC. The State Council is formally appointed by the National People's Congress, though its membership is determined by the party leadership. It functions much like the cabinet in a parliamentary system and includes the premier, a few vice premiers, the heads of government ministries and commissions, and several other senior officials.

The size of the State Council varies as ministries and commissions are created, merged, or disbanded to meet changing policy needs. At the height of the state socialist planned economy, there were more than one hundred ministerial-level officials. In the 1990s, there were forty ministries and commissions, and in 2003 the number was cut to twenty-eight, reflecting the decreased role of central planning and the administrative

streamlining undertaken to make the government more efficient. The ministers run either functionally specific departments, such as the Ministry of Public Health, or organizations with more comprehensive responsibilities, such as the Science, Technology, and Industry Commission. Beneath the State Council is an array of support staffs, research offices, and other bureaucratic agencies charged with policy implementation.

The so-called central leading groups are important and flexible instruments of coordinated decision making in the PRC. These bodies are formed by the CCP and are made up of government officials who are also high-ranking party members. Current leading groups include those on national security, finance and economics, and information technology.

Government administration in the PRC is based on the principle of **dual rule,** which was adapted from the Soviet political system. Dual rule means that government organizations below the national level are under both the vertical supervision of the next higher level of government and the horizontal supervision of the Communist Party at their own level. For example, the organization in charge of education in one of China's provinces would be subject to both administrative supervision by the Ministry of Education in Beijing and political control by the province's CCP committee. Such a system leads to complex and sometimes conflicting lines of authority within the Chinese bureaucracy. It also reinforces two key aspects of governance and policy-making in the PRC: centralization and party domination. Nevertheless, since the 1980s, government administration in China has become increasingly decentralized as the role of central planning has been reduced and more power has been given to provincial and local authorities, particularly in economic matters. Efforts have also been made to reduce party interference in administrative work.

China's bureaucracy is immense in size and expansive in the scope of its reach throughout the country. The total number of **cadres**—people in positions of authority who are paid by the government or party—in the PRC is in the range of 40 million. A minority of these work directly for the government or the CCP. The remainder occupy key posts in economic enterprises (e.g., factory directors); schools (e.g., principals); and scientific, cultural, and other state-run institutions. Not all party members are cadres; in fact, most party members are ordinary workers, farmers, teachers, and so on. And most cadres (25 million) are not party members, though party cadres ultimately have power over nonparty cadres. In 2001, the government announced a plan to reduce the size of the bureaucracy by 10 percent, particularly at the city, county, and township levels, over the next five to ten years. There have also been substantive moves toward professionalizing the bureaucracy, particularly at the city level of government, by making more official positions subject to competition through civil service exams rather than the still-prevalent method of appointment from above.

One of the most significant administrative reforms of the post-Mao era—and one that is quite unprecedented in a communist party-state—has been the implementation of measures to limit how long officials can stay in their jobs. Depending on their position, both government and party cadres must now retire between the ages of sixty and seventy. A two-term limit has been set for all top cadres. In 1998, Premier Li Peng became the first central leader of the People's Republic to leave office at the end of a constitutionally specified term limit. But exceptions are still sometimes made for core leaders such as Jiang Zemin (born in 1926), who stayed on as CCP general secretary until he was seventy-six and as chair of the Central Military Commission even beyond that.

Other State Institutions

The Military and the Police

China's People's Liberation Army (PLA), which encompasses all of the country's ground, air, and naval armed services, is the world's largest military force, with about 2.5 million active personnel (down from nearly 4 million in 1989). The PLA also has a formal reserve of another 1 million or so and a backup people's militia of 12 to 15 million, which could be mobilized in the event of war, although the level of training and weaponry available to the militia are generally minimal. There is a draft in China, but serving in the PLA is considered a prestigious option for many young people, particularly for rural youth who might not have many other opportunities for upward mobility.

In recent years, China has increased its defense spending quite substantially (over 17 percent in both 2001 and 2002) in order to modernize its armed forces and raise the pay of its military personnel. But the Chinese military is quite small in relation to China's total population. In the late 1990s, the PRC had 1.9 military personnel per 1,000 population, considerably fewer than the U.S. ratio of 3.2 per 1,000. China said that it would spend $20 billion on defense in 2002, compared with $379 billion by the United States. Many analysts think that the PRC vastly understates its defense budget and estimate that it is really closer to three times the official figures; still, China devotes a much smaller part of its annual government spending to defense than does the United States.

The military has never held formal political power in the PRC, but it has been a very important influence on politics and policy. Ever since the days of the revolution and the civil war, there have been close ties between the political and military leaders of the CCP, with many top leaders (such as Mao and Deng) serving in both political and military capacities. One of the most famous quotes from Chairman Mao's writings, "Political power grows out of the barrel of a gun," conveyed his belief that the party needed strong military backing in order to win and keep power. However, the often overlooked second half of the quote, "Our principle is that the party commands the gun, and the gun must never be allowed to command the party," made the equally important point that the military had to be kept under civilian (that is, CCP) control.[16] Although there have been a few periods when the role of the military in Chinese politics appeared to be particularly strong (such as during the Cultural Revolution), the party has always been able to keep the "gun" under its firm command.

Nevertheless, the PLA continues to play an important, if muted, role in Chinese politics. Military support remains a crucial factor in the factional struggles that still figure prominently in inner-party politics. Deng Xiaoping's long-standing personal ties to many very senior PLA officers were critical to his success in defeating the efforts of conservative party leaders to slow economic reform. Jiang Zemin, who had no such ties and lacks any military experience, paid close attention to building political bridges to the PLA by supporting increased defense spending and promoting generals who are loyal to him. There are no military officers on the party's most elite body, the Standing Committee, but two of the twenty-four full members of the Politburo are generals, and PLA representatives make up about 20 percent of the full members of the Central Committee.

Chinese Communist leaders have long been divided over the issue of what kind of armed forces the PRC needed. Mao was a strong advocate of equality between rank-and-file soldiers and officers and the use of guerrilla tactics ("people's war") even in modern warfare. He also stressed the importance of ideological education within the military and the extensive use of the PLA in nonmilitary tasks such as the construction of public works projects and the training of citizen paramedics ("barefoot doctors"). Some of China's foremost military leaders believed just as strongly that the PLA ought to emphasize the discipline, professionalism, and modernization needed to defend the nation. In the post-Mao era, the military leadership has been able to keep politics and ideology in the armed forces to a minimum and focus on making the PLA an effective, modern fighting force. But the PLA is also an instrument for keeping the CCP in power. The party

extends its control of the PLA through a system of party committees and political officers who are attached to all military units.

The key organizations in charge of the Chinese armed forces are the CCP and PRC Central Military Commissions (CMC). On paper, these are two distinct organizations, but, in fact, they overlap entirely in membership and function. The chair of the state Military Commission is "elected" by the National People's Congress, but is always the same person as the chair of the party CMC. The CMC chair is, in effect, the commander in chief of China's armed forces. This position has almost always been held by the most powerful party leader, for example, by Deng Xiaoping from 1981 to 1989, or his protégé, as was the case when Jiang Zemin took over the chairmanship in 1989 under Deng's auspices. The fact that Jiang held onto the CMC chairmanship after retiring as CCP general secretary in November 2002 and as PRC president in March 2003 was seen as a reflection that he was retaining a lot of formal power as well as informal influence in Chinese politics.

Beginning in the 1980s, the PLA climbed on the economic reform bandwagon in order to supplement its official budget by converting a number of its military factories to the production of consumer goods such as refrigerators and motorcycles, running hotels and even discos, and opening up some of its formerly secret facilities to foreign tourists. At one point, it was estimated that the PLA was running more than 15,000 nonmilitary enterprises at home and abroad with over $10 billion in revenues. In 1998, the government, concerned about both corruption and the need for the military to concentrate on its defense responsibilities, ordered the PLA to sell off many of its commercial ventures.

China's internal security apparatus consists of several different organizations. The Ministry of State Security is responsible for combating espionage and gathering intelligence at home and abroad. A 1 million strong People's Armed Police (under the PLA) guards public officials and buildings, carries out some border patrol and protection, and is used to quell serious public disturbances, including worker or peasant unrest. The Ministry of Public Security is responsible for the maintenance of law and order, the investigation of crimes, and the surveillance of Chinese citizens and foreigners in China suspected of being a threat to the state. Local Public Security Bureaus are under the command of central ministry authorities in Beijing. In effect, then, China has a national police force stationed throughout the country. There are also local police forces, but they do little more than supervise traffic.

Public Security Bureaus have the authority to detain indefinitely people suspected of committing a crime without making a formal charge and can use administrative sanctions, that is, penalties imposed outside the court system, to levy fines or sentence detainees to up to three years. For people convicted of serious crimes, including political ones, the Ministry of Public Security maintains an extensive system of labor reform camps. These camps, noted for their harsh conditions and remote locations, are estimated to have millions of prisoners. They have, at times, become a contentious issue in U.S.-China relations because of claims that they use political prisoners as slave labor to produce millions of dollars worth of products (such as toys) that are then exported to U.S. and other foreign markets. China has agreed to curtail the export of prison-produced goods, but it maintains that productive work by prison inmates (common in many countries, including the United States) helps to rehabilitate prisoners and is a legitimate part of the penal system.

The Judiciary

China has a four-tiered "people's court" system reaching from a Supreme People's Court down through higher, intermediate, and basic people's courts. The Supreme People's Court supervises the work of lower courts and the application of the country's laws, but it hears few cases and does not exercise judicial review over government policies. A nationwide organization called the "people's procuratorate" serves in the courts as both public prosecutor and public defender and also has investigatory functions in criminal cases. Citizen mediation committees based in urban neighborhoods and rural villages play an important role in the judicial process by settling a large majority of civil cases out of court.

China's judicial system came under attack as a bastion of elitism and revisionism during the Cultural Revolution. The formal legal system pretty much ceased to operate during that period, and many of its functions were taken over by political or police organizations, which often acted arbitrarily in making arrests or administering punishments.

In recent decades, the legal system of the PRC has been revitalized. There are now more than 100,000 lawyers in China (by way of comparison, there are about 1 million lawyers in the United States), and legal advisory offices have been established throughout the country to provide citizens and organizations with legal assistance. Many laws and regulations have been enacted, including new criminal and civil codes, in the effort to regularize the legal system. In 1997, the government revoked a vaguely worded law against "counter-revolutionary crimes," which had given the authorities broad powers to detain political dissidents, but the government has found other ways to accomplish the same ends.

In recent years, there has been an enormous surge in the number of lawsuits filed (and often won) by people against businesses, local officials, and government agencies. Chinese courts can provide a real avenue of redress to the public for a wide range of nonpolitical grievances, including loss of property, consumer fraud, and even unjust detention by the police.

China's criminal justice system works swiftly and harshly. Great faith is placed in the ability of an official investigation to find the facts of a case, and the outcome of cases that actually do come to trial is pretty much predetermined: there is a conviction rate of 98 to 99 percent for all criminal cases. Prison terms are long and subject only to cursory appeal. A variety of offenses in addition to murder—including, in some cases, rape and particularly serious cases of embezzlement and other "economic crimes"—are subject to capital punishment, which is carried out within days of sentencing by a single bullet in the back of the convicted person's head. Particularly large numbers of people have been executed during the periodic government-sponsored anticrime "Strike Hard" campaigns. Between April and July 2001, an estimated 1,781 people were executed in China—more than the total number of people executed in the rest of the world in the previous three years. China has been harshly criticized by human rights organizations such as Amnesty International for its extensive use of the death penalty.

Although the Chinese constitution speaks of judicial independence, China's courts and other legal bodies remain under rigorous party control. The appointment of judicial personnel is subject to party approval, and the CCP can and does bend the law to serve its interests. Recent legal reforms in China have been undertaken because China's leaders are well aware that economic development requires detailed laws, professional lawyers and judicial personnel, predictable legal processes, and binding documents such as contracts. China has, by and large, become a country where there is rule by law, in which the CCP uses the law to carry out its policies and enforce its rule. But it is still far from having established the rule of law, in which everyone and every organization, including the CCP, is accountable and subject to the law.

Subnational Government

There are four main layers of state structure beneath the central government in China: provinces, cities, counties, and rural towns. There are also four so-called very large centrally administered cities (Beijing, Shanghai, Tianjin, and Chongqing) and five autonomous regions, which are areas of the country with large minority populations (such as Tibet and Mongolia). Each of these levels has a representative people's congress that meets infrequently and briefly and plays a limited role in managing affairs in the area under its jurisdiction.

Day-to-day administration at each subnational level is carried out by a people's government, which consists of an executive (for instance, a provincial governor or city mayor), various functional bureaus, and judicial organs. According to China's constitution, the work of a local government is to be supervised by the local people's congress. But, in fact, the principle of dual rule makes local officials accountable more to higher levels of state administration and party organizations than to the local congresses.

Economic reform has led to considerable decentralization of decision making. As a result, local governments are becoming more vigorous in pursuing their own interests, but they are also experiencing enormously increased financial pressures. The latter has led many local governments, particularly in rural towns, to impose largely arbitrary fees for all sorts of services; this in turn has fed popular resentment that has sometimes exploded in violent protest.

Despite decentralization, the central government still retains the power to intervene in local affairs when and where it wants. This power of the central authorities derives not only from their ability to set binding national priorities but also from their control over the military and the police, critical energy sources, resource allocation, and the construction of major infrastructure projects. A number of political scientists in China and abroad have suggested that the PRC, given its continental size and great regional diversity, would be better served by a federal system with a more balanced distribution of power between the national, provincial, and local levels of government, but such a move would be inconsistent with the highly centralized structure of a communist party-state.

Beneath the formal layers of state administration are China's 700,000 or so rural villages, which are home to the majority of the country's population. These villages are technically self-governing and are not formally responsible to a higher level of state authority. In recent years, village leaders and representative assemblies have been directly and competitively elected by local residents (see Section 4), which has brought an important degree of grass-roots democracy to village government. Nevertheless, the most powerful person in Chinese villages is still the local Communist Party leader (the party secretary).

The Policy-Making Process

At the height of Mao's power, many scholars described the policy process in China as a "Mao-in-command" system. Then the Cultural Revolution led many analysts to conclude that policy-making in China was best understood as a result of factional and ideological struggles within the Chinese political elite. More recently, emphasis has shifted to analyzing the importance of bureaucratic actors and institutions in the policy process. Rather than portraying policy-making as simply a matter of the top party leaders' issuing orders, a model of fragmented authoritarianism sees policy outcomes as the result of conflict, competition, and bargaining among party and government organizations at various levels of the system.[17] The national focus on economic development has also led to the growing influence of nonparty experts in the policy loop.

Nevertheless, policy-making at all levels is still ultimately under the control of the CCP. Public debate, media scrutiny, and the influence of truly independent interest groups play little, if any, role in the policy process in the communist party-state. The CCP uses a weblike system of organizational controls to make sure that the government bureaucracy complies with the party's will in policy implementation. Almost all key government officials are also party members and therefore subject to party discipline. The CCP also exercises control over the policy process through party organizations that parallel government agencies at all levels of the system. For example, each provincial government works under the watchful eye of a provincial party committee. In addition, through its committees, branches, cells, and "leading members groups," the CCP maintains an effective presence inside every government organization.

Another means by which the CCP exercises control over the policy process is through the use of a cadre list, or as it was known in the Soviet Union, the **nomenklatura** system. The cadre list covers millions of positions in the government and elsewhere (including newspapers, hospitals, banks, and trade unions). Any personnel decision involving appointment, promotion, transfer, or dismissal that affects a position on this list must be approved by the party organization department, whether or not the official involved is a party member. In recent years, the growth of nonstate sectors of the economy and administrative streamlining have led to a reduction in the number of positions directly subject to party approval. Nevertheless, the *nomenklatura* system remains one of the major instruments by which the CCP tries to "ensure that leading institutions throughout the country will exercise only the autonomy granted to them by the party."[18]

No account of the policy process in China is complete without noting the importance of *guanxi* ("connections"), the personal relationships and mutual obligations based on family, friendship, school, military, professional, or other ties. The notion of *guanxi* has its roots in Confucian culture and has long been an important part of political, social, and economic life in China. These connections are still a basic fact of life within the Chinese bureaucracy, where personal ties are often the key to getting things done. Depending on how they are used, *guanxi* can either help cut red tape and increase efficiency or bolster organizational rigidity and feed corruption.

Guanxi also count mightily in the highly personalized world of elite politics within the CCP, where key policy decisions are made. Much of the informal power that Jiang Zemin appeared to wield even after his term as head of the party ended in late 2002—and which led some observers to dub him China's "de-facto Number One leader"—derived from his close personal ties (often based on common roots in Shanghai) to fifteen of the twenty-four full members of the CCP Politburo and five of the nine members of its Standing Committee.

In sum, the power of the Communist Party, particularly the nearly unchecked power of the two dozen or so top leaders, is at the heart of governance and policy-making in China. Party domination, however, does not mean that the system "operates in a monolithic way"; in fact, the system "wriggles with politics" of many kinds, formal and informal.[19] In order to get a complete picture of the policy process in China, it is important to look at how various influences, including ideology, factional struggles, bureaucratic interests, and *guanxi* shape the decisions made by the Communist Party leadership.

Section ❹ Representation and Participation

The Chinese Communist Party describes the political system of the People's Republic as a **socialist democracy,** which it claims is superior to democracy in a capitalist country. Unlike the *social* democracy of Western European's center-left political parties, however, which is rooted in a commitment to competitive politics, China's *socialist* democracy is based on the unchallengeable leadership of the Chinese Communist Party.

Nevertheless, representation and participation do play important roles in the PRC political system. There are legislative bodies, elections, and organizations like labor unions and women's associations, all of which are meant to provide citizens with ways of influencing public policy-making and the selection of government leaders. But such mechanisms of popular input are strictly controlled and bounded by the party's continuing insistence that all politics and policies in the country be guided by the CCP.

The Legislature

The Chinese constitution grants the National People's Congress (NPC) the power to enact and amend the country's laws, approve and monitor the state budget, and declare and end war. The NPC is also empowered to elect (and recall) the president and vice president of the PRC, the chair of the state Central Military Commission, the head of China's Supreme Court, and the procurator-general (something like the U.S. attorney general). It also has final approval over the selection of the premier and members of the State Council. At least on paper, these powers make China's legislature the most powerful branch of the government, but in fact these powers are exercised only in the manner allowed by the Communist Party.

The NPC is a unicameral legislature. It is elected for a five-year term and meets annually for only about two weeks in March. Deputies to the NPC are not full-time legislators but remain in their regular jobs and home areas except for the brief time when the congress is in session. The precise size of the NPC is set by law prior to each five-year electoral cycle. The NPC that was elected in 2003 consisted of nearly 3,000 deputies. All the delegates, except those who represent the People's Liberation Army, are chosen on a geographic basis from China's provinces, autonomous regions, and major municipalities. About 73 percent of the deputies elected in 2003 were members of the CCP, while the others either belonged to one of China's few non-Communist (and powerless) political parties or had no party affiliation.

Workers and farmers made up about 18 percent of the deputies elected in 2003, intellectuals and professionals made up another 21 percent, government and party cadres accounted for a little under a third, 9 percent were from the military, and the remainder consisted of representatives of other occupational categories, such as entrepreneurs. Women made up 20 percent and ethnic minorities 14 percent of the deputies.

The annual sessions of the NPC are hailed with great fanfare in the Chinese press as an example of socialist democracy at work, but generally legislation is passed and state leaders are elected by an overwhelming majority. For instance, Hu Jintao was elected president of China in March 2003 by a vote of 2,937 for him, 4 against, and 3 abstentions. Nevertheless, some debate and dissent do occur. For example, in 1992, about a third of NPC deputies either voted against or abstained from voting on the construction of the hugely expensive ($70 billion) and ecologically controversial Three Gorges dam project now being built on the Yangtze River. And in 2003, nearly 10 percent of deputies opposed relecting the outgoing party leader and president Jiang Zemin as chair of the Central Military Commission. On very rare occasions, government legislative initiatives have even been defeated. But all NPC proceedings are subject to party scrutiny, and the congress never debates politically sensitive issues. The CCP also monitors the election process to make sure that no outright dissidents are elected as deputies.

Still, as economics has replaced ideology as the main priority of China's leaders, the NPC has become a much more important and lively part of the Chinese political system than it was during the Mao era. Many NPC deputies are now chosen because of their ability to contribute to China's modernization rather than simply on the basis of political loyalty, and some have become a bit more assertive in expressing their opinions on various issues.

Political Parties and the Party System

China is usually called a one-party system because the country's politics are so thoroughly dominated by the Chinese Communist Party. In fact, China has eight political parties in addition to the CCP, but these parties neither challenge the basic policies of the CCP nor play a significant part in running the government, although they do sometimes provide important advice in the policy-making process.

The Chinese Communist Party

At the time of the National Party Congress that met in November 2002, the Chinese Communist Party had about 66 million members. The party has grown steadily since it came to power in 1949, when it had just under 4.5 million members. Only during the Cultural Revolution was there a sharp drop in membership due to the purge of "capitalist roaders" from party ranks, and many of those purged were welcomed back into the CCP after the death of Mao.

The CCP is the largest political party in the world in terms of total formal membership. But as with all other former and current ruling communist parties, its members make up a small minority of the country's population. CCP members are now about 5 percent of China's population, or about 8 percent of those over eighteen, the minimum age for joining the party.

The social composition of the CCP's membership has changed considerably in recent decades. In the mid-1950s, peasants made up nearly 70 percent of party membership. In 2002, a generic category that included "industrial workers, laborers in township enterprises, farmers, herdsman, and fishermen" accounted for only 45 percent of the CCP even though the party constitution still claims that "Members of the Communist Party of China are vanguard fighters of the Chinese working class imbued with communist consciousness" (Article 2). The majority of CCP members are not manual laborers of any sort, but are government officials, enterprise managers, military personnel, professionals, and retirees. In mid-2001, in a major speech commemorating the eightieth anniversary of the CCP, Jiang Zemin proclaimed that in order to serve the cause of national economic development, the party must include "worthy people from all sectors of society," by which he specifically meant that private entrepreneurs (capitalists) would be welcomed as members.[20] This important policy change was certainly a recognition of the rapidly changing nature of economic life in China, including the growth of the private sector in industry, commerce, and services. But it will also likely change the social composition of the CCP and perhaps even lead to a gradual redefinition of the party's political role in China.

Women make up less than 20 percent of the CCP as a whole and only 2.5 percent of full members of Central Committee (and 14 percent of alternates) elected in 2002. There is one female member of the Politburo, Wu Yi, who is also a senior government official and former minister of foreign trade. There are no women on the party's most powerful organization, the Politburo Standing Committee.

Despite the party's tarnished image since Tiananmen and what many Chinese feel is the increasing irrelevance of communist ideology to their lives and the nation's future, the CCP still recruits about 1 million new members each year. Party membership provides unparalleled access to influence and resources, especially given the current quasi-market nature of China's economy, and being a party member is still a prerequisite for advancement in many careers in China, particularly in government.

China's Noncommunist Parties

The eight noncommunist political parties in the PRC are referred to as the "democratic parties," a designation meant to signify the role they play in representing different interests in the political process and to lend some credibility to China's claim that it is a socialist democracy. Each noncommunist party draws its membership from a particular group in Chinese society. For example, the China Democratic League consists mostly of intellectuals, whereas the Chinese Party for the Public Interest draws on returned overseas Chinese and experts with overseas connections.

The democratic parties, all of which were founded before the CCP came to power, have a total membership of fewer than 500,000. These parties do not contest for power or challenge CCP policy. Their function is to provide advice to the CCP and generate support within their particular constituencies for CCP policies. Individual members of the parties may assume important government positions. But organizationally these parties are relatively insignificant and function as little more than "a loyal non-opposition."[21]

Elections

Elections in the PRC are basically mechanisms to give the party-state greater legitimacy by allowing large numbers of citizens to participate in the political process under very controlled circumstances.

China has both direct and indirect elections. In direct elections, all eligible citizens vote for candidates for offices in a particular government body. For example, all the voters in a rural county would vote for the deputies to serve in the county-level people's congress. In indirect elections, higher-level bodies are elected by lower-level government bodies rather than by the voters at large. For example, deputies to the National People's Congress are elected by the provincial-level people's congresses, which have been elected by lower-level people's congresses. Most elections in China are indirect, and there are no direct elections at the provincial or national levels. Turnout for direct elections is heavy—usually over 90 percent of eligible voters.

For several decades after the founding of the PRC, only one candidate stood for each office, so the only choice facing voters was to approve or abstain. Since the early 1980s, many direct and indirect elections have had multiple candidates for each slot, with the winner chosen by secret ballot. The nomination process has also become more open. Any group of more than ten voters can nominate candidates for an election. Most candidates in direct elections are now nominated by the voters, and there have been a significant number of cases where independent candidates have defeated official nominees, though even independent candidates are basically approved by the CCP.

The most significant progress toward real democratic representation and participation in China has occurred in the rural villages. Laws implemented since the late 1980s have provided for directly elected village representative assemblies and the election, rather than the appointment from above, of village officials. These are, for the most part, multicandidate, secret-ballot elections, though still carried out under the watchful eye of the CCP. Outside observers have been split on whether such direct grass-roots elections in China represent the seeds of real democracy or are merely a facade designed by the Communist Party to appease international critics and give the rural population a way to express discontent with some officials without challenging the country's fundamental political organization.

Recent electoral reform has certainly increased popular representation and participation in China's government. But elections in the PRC still do not give citizens a means by which they can exercise effective control over the party officials and organizations that have the real power in China's political system. In a major speech in December 1998 marking twenty years of economic reform, President Jiang Zemin stated bluntly, "The model of the West's political system should not be copied." He vowed that China would adhere to a system of socialist democracy in which "the Communist Party, being the ruling party . . . leads and supports the people in controlling and exercising the power to manage the country." And in his political report to the Sixteenth Party Congress in November

2002, Jiang, the retiring general secretary of the CCP, repeatedly reminded the delegates that, while pursuing economic development and socialist democracy, China had to preserve the leadership of the Communist Party, which was, in his words, "the very foundation on which we build our country."[22] There is little reason to think that this bottom-line framework for political representation and participation in China will change much in the foreseeable future.

Political Culture, Citizenship, and Identity

From Communism to Consumerism

Since the PRC's founding in 1949, its official political culture has been based on communist ideology, and the party-state has made extensive efforts to get people's political attitudes and behavior to conform to the currently prevailing version of Marxism-Leninism. But this ideology has gone through such severe crises and profound changes during the turbulent decades of Communist rule that its future in China is seriously in doubt.

At the height of the Maoist era, Mao Zedong Thought was hailed as "an inexhaustible source of strength and a spiritual atom bomb of infinite power" that held the answer to all of China's problems in domestic and foreign policy.[23] By the mid-1970s, however, the debacles of the Mao years had greatly tarnished the appeal of communism in China.

After Deng Xiaoping came to power in 1978, he set about trying not only to restore the legitimacy of the Communist Party through economic reforms but also to revive communist ideology by linking it directly to China's development aspirations. Toward the end of 1997, the CCP amended the party constitution to add Deng Xiaoping Theory to its official ideology. One key part of Deng's theory, often referred to under the rubric of "Building Socialism with Chinese Characteristics," was a major departure from Maoism and emphasizes that China is a relatively poor country in the "primary stage of socialism" and therefore must use any means possible, even capitalist ones, to develop the economy. The other central component of Deng's ideology, and one fully consistent with Maoist theory and practice, is his so-called **Four Cardinal Principles:** upholding the socialist road, the people's democratic dictatorship, the leadership of the Communist Party, and Marxism-Leninism. In essence, then, Deng Xiaoping Theory is an ideological rationale for the combination of economic liberalization and party dictatorship that characterizes contemporary China.

In an effort to have himself placed on a historical pedestal equal to that of Deng and Mao as he neared semiretirement, Jiang Zemin offered his own variation on Chinese communism, the Three Represents, which was said to sum up his contribution to the party's ideology. According to the amended party constitution, the Three Represents depict the CCP as the faithful representative of the "development trend of China's advanced productive forces, the orientation of China's advanced culture, and the fundamental interests of the overwhelming majority of the Chinese people." In other words, the Communist Party (and Jiang) take the credit for the country's vastly improved economic fortunes.

The CCP tries to keep communist ideology—now officially called "Marxism-Leninism, Mao Zedong Thought, Deng Xiaoping Theory, and the Important Thought of the Three Represents"—viable and visible by continued efforts to influence public opinion and socialization—for instance, by controlling the media and overseeing the educational system. Although China's media are much livelier and more open than during the Maoist period, there is no true freedom of the press. Reduced political control of the media has, to a large extent, meant only the freedom to publish more entertainment news, human interest stories, local coverage, and some nonpolitical investigative journalism. The Chinese film industry has emerged as one of the best in the world, with many of its directors, stars, and, productions winning international acclaim, including a Best Film award at Cannes and an Oscar nomination in 1993 for *Farewell My Concubine*. But movie making in the PRC is subject to political controls, and some films made in China are not distributed in the country.

Internet access is growing extremely fast in the PRC, with more than 58 million users as of 2002 and wired cafés found in even some quite remote towns. The government, worried about the potential influence of email and electronic information it cannot control, has at times blocked access to certain foreign websites, shut down unlicensed cybercafés, which it likened to the opium dens of the past, and even arrested people it

has accused of disseminating subversive material over the Internet, including, in December 2002, the publisher of an online prodemocracy journal. Nevertheless, the party-state has found it very difficult to control these new technologies as tightly as it would like; indeed, in mid-2002, an outlawed spiritual group, the Falun Gong (see below), hacked into the state-run television network to briefly broadcast its own message. But in another sign of the times, both the government of the PRC and the CCP have set up numerous Internet sites of their own.

Schools are one of the main institutions through which all states instill political values in their citizens. Educational opportunities have expanded enormously in China since 1949. Although enrollment rates drop sharply at the secondary school level, primary school enrollment is close to 100 percent of the age-eligible population (ages six to eleven). In Maoist China, students at all levels spent a considerable amount of time studying politics and working in fields or factories, and teaching materials were often overlaid with a heavy dose of political propaganda. Today, political study (recently with an emphasis on learning the Three Represents) is a required but relatively minor part of the curriculum at all levels of education. Much greater attention is paid to urging students to gain the skills and knowledge they need to further their own careers and help China modernize.

Yet schools in China are by no means centers of critical or independent thinking, and teachers and students are still closely monitored for political reliability. More than 80 percent of China's youth between the ages of seven and fourteen belong to the Young Pioneers, an organization designed to promote good social behavior, patriotism, and loyalty to the party among school children.

The party's efforts to keep socialist values alive in China do not appear to be meeting with much success, and public confidence in the party and in communist ideology is very low. Alternative sources of socialization are growing in importance, although these do not often take expressly political forms because of the threat of repression. In the countryside, peasants have replaced portraits of Mao and other Communist heroes with statues of folk gods and ancestor worship tablets, and the influence of extended kinship groups such as clans often outweighs the formal authority of the party in the villages. In the cities, popular culture, including gigantic rock concerts, shapes youth attitudes much more profoundly than do party messages about the Three Represents. Throughout China, consumerism and the desire for economic gain rather than communist ideals of self-sacrifice and the common good provide the principal motivation for much personal and social behavior.

Religion, which was ferociously repressed during the Mao era, is attracting an increasing number of Chinese adherents. Buddhist temples, Christian churches, and other places of worship operate more freely than they have in decades. However, religious life is still strictly controlled and limited to officially approved organizations and venues. The Chinese Catholic Church is prohibited from recognizing the authority of the Vatican, and clergy of any religion who defy the authority of the party-state are still imprisoned. Clandestine Christian communities, called house churches, have sprung up in many areas of China among people who reject the government's control of religious life and are unable to worship in public. The regime has reacted with particular harshness toward this underground movement, arresting leaders and lay people alike and bulldozing the private homes where the services have been held.

Citizenship and National Identity

China in the early twenty-first century is going through a profound and uncertain transformation in its national identity. Party leaders realize that most citizens view communist ideology as irrelevant to their lives. Therefore, the CCP has turned increasingly to patriotic themes to rally the country by portraying itself as the best guardian of China's national interests. The official media put considerable emphasis on the greatness and antiquity of Chinese culture, with the not-so-subtle message that it is time for the Chinese nation to reclaim its rightful place in the world order—under the leadership of the CCP.

The party-state also does all it can to get political capital by touting its leading role in China's impressive economic achievements, winning the 2008 Summer Olympics for Beijing, and securing the return to China of territories like Hong Kong and Macao (a former Portuguese colony) that were lost long ago to Western imperialist powers. Some observers have expressed concern that such officially promoted nationalist sentiments could lead to a more aggressive foreign and military policy, particularly toward areas such as the potentially oil-rich South China Sea, where the PRC's historical territorial claims conflict with those of other countries like Vietnam and the Philippines.

China's Non-Chinese Citizens

The PRC calls itself a multinational state with fifty-six officially recognized ethnic groups, one of which is the majority Han people. The defining elements of a minority group in China involve some combination of language, culture (including religion), and race that distinguish them from the Han. The fifty-five minorities number a little more than 100 million, or about 8.5 percent of the total population of the PRC. These groups range in size from 16 million (the Zhuang of southwest China) to about 2,000 (the Lhoba in the far west of the country). Most of these minorities have come under Chinese rule over many centuries through territorial expansion rather than through migration into China.

China's minority peoples are highly concentrated in the five autonomous regions of Guangxi, Inner Mongolia, Ningxia, Tibet, and Xinjiang, although only in the last two do minority groups outnumber Han Chinese. These five regions are sparsely populated, yet they occupy about 60 percent of the total land area of the PRC. Some of these areas are resource rich, and all are located on strategically important borders of the country, including those with Vietnam, India, and Russia.

The Chinese constitution grants autonomous areas the right of self-government in certain matters, such as cultural affairs, but their autonomy is in fact very limited, and the minority regions are kept firmly under the control of the national party-state. Minority peoples are given some latitude to develop their local economies as they see fit, religious freedom is generally respected, and the use of minority languages in the media and literature is encouraged, as is bilingual education. In order to keep the already small minority populations from dwindling further, China's stringent family planning policy is applied much more loosely among minorities, who are often allowed to have two or more children per couple rather than the one-child prescribed limit for most Chinese.

There has also been a concerted effort to recruit and promote minority cadres to run local governments in autonomous areas. But the most powerful individual in minority areas, the head of the regional or local Communist Party, is likely to be Han Chinese: in 2002, the party secretary in all five autonomous regions was Han. Also despite significant progress in modernizing the economies of the minority regions, these areas remain among the poorest in China.

The most extensive ethnic conflict in China has occurred in Tibet, which has been under Chinese military occupation since the early 1950s. Hu Jintao, the newly elected general secretary of the CCP, served as the party chief in Tibet from 1988 to 1992. This gives him vastly more personal experience in this troubled part of the country than any previous national leader. Some see this experience as a cause for optimism, while others are critical of Hu's record of enforcing repressive Chinese control of the region (see "Current Challenges: Tibet and China").

According to official PRC statistics, there are about 20 million Muslims in China (though some outside observers put the number at several times that). China's Muslims live in many parts of the country and are spread among several different ethnic minorities, the largest of which are the Hui (9 million) and Uighur (7 million). The highest concentration of Muslims is in the far west of China in the Ningxia Hui and Xinjiang Uighur autonomous regions, the latter of which borders the Islamic nations of Afghanistan and Pakistan and the Central Asian states of the former Soviet Union.

In recent years, there has been growing unrest among Uighurs in Xinjiang (the more secular Hui are better integrated into Han Chinese society). The government has clashed with Uighur militants who want to create a separate Islamic state of "East Turkestan" and have sometimes used violence, including bombings and assassinations, to press their cause. One of the reasons that the PRC became an eager ally of the United States in the post–September 11 war on terrorism was that it allowed China to justify its crackdown on the Xinjiang-based East Turkestan Islamic Movement (ETIM), which Washington has included on its list of organizations connected to Osama bin Laden and al Qaeda.

China's minority population is relatively small and geographically isolated, and where ethnic unrest has occurred, it has been limited, sporadic, and easily quelled. Therefore, the PRC has not had the kind of intense identity-based conflict experienced by countries with more pervasive religious and ethnic cleavages, such as India and Nigeria. But it is very likely that in the future, both domestic and global forces will cause identity issues to become more visible and volatile on China's national political agenda.

Interests, Social Movements, and Protests

The formal structures of the Chinese political system are designed more to extend party-state control of political life than to facilitate citizen participation in politics. Therefore, people make extensive use of their personal connections (*guanxi*) based on kinship, friendship, and other ties to help ease their contacts with the bureaucrats and party officials who wield such enormous power over so many aspects of their lives. Patron-client politics is also pervasive at the local level in China, as it is in many other developing countries where ordinary people have little access to the official channels of power. For example, a village leader (the patron) may help farmers (the clients) avoid paying some taxes by reporting false production statistics in exchange for their support to keep him in office. Such clientelism can be an important way for local communities to resist state policies that they see as harmful to their interests.

Organized interest groups and social movements that are truly independent of party-state authority are not permitted to influence the political process in any significant way. Rather, the party-state tries to preempt the formation of autonomous groups and movements through the use of official "mass organizations." These organizations provide a means for interest groups to express their views on policy matters within strict limits.

China has numerous mass organizations formed around social or occupational categories, with a total membership in the hundreds of millions. Two of the most important mass organizations are the All-China Federation of Trade Unions, to which most Chinese factory workers belong, and the All-China Women's Federation, the only national organization representing the interests of women in general. Both federations are top-down, party-controlled organizations, and neither constitutes an independent political voice for the

Current Challenges: *Tibet and China*

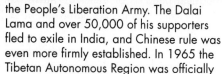

Tibet is located in the far west of China on the border with India, Burma, Nepal, and Bhutan. It is a large area (about 470,000 square miles, which is nearly 13 percent of China's total area) and is ringed by some of the world's highest mountains, including the Himalayas and Mt. Everest. Ninety-four percent of Tibet's 2.6 million people are Tibetans, who are ethnically, linguistically, and culturally distinct from the Chinese. Another 2.5 million ethnic Tibetans live elsewhere in China, mostly in provinces adjacent to Tibet.

In the thirteenth century, Tibet became a theocracy in which absolute power was held by a Buddhist priest, called the Dalai Lama, who ruled the country with the help of other clergy and the aristocracy. Traditional Tibetan society was sharply divided between the tiny ruling class and the common people, most of whom were serfs living and working under difficult and often brutal conditions.

Tibet became subordinate to China in the early eighteenth century, although the Dalai Lama and other Tibetan officials continued to govern the country. After the collapse of China's imperial system in 1911, Tibet achieved de facto independence. However, Britain, which saw Tibet in the context of its extensive colonial rule in South Asia, exercised considerable influence in Tibetan affairs.

Shortly after coming to power, the Chinese Communists made known their intention to end foreign intervention in Tibet, which they, like previous Chinese governments, considered to be part of China. In 1951 the Dalai Lama agreed to the peaceful incorporation of Tibet into the People's Republic of China rather than face a full-scale military assault. Although some Chinese troops and officials were sent to Tibet, the Dalai Lama remained in a position of symbolic authority for much of the 1950s. In 1959 a widespread revolt against Chinese rule led to the invasion of Tibet by the People's Liberation Army. The Dalai Lama and over 50,000 of his supporters fled to exile in India, and Chinese rule was even more firmly established. In 1965 the Tibetan Autonomous Region was officially formed, but Chinese political and military officials have kept a firm grip on power in Tibet.

During the Maoist era, traditional Tibetan culture was suppressed by the Chinese authorities. Since the late 1970s, Buddhist temples and monasteries have been allowed to reopen, and Tibetans have gained a significant degree of cultural freedom; the Chinese government has also significantly increased investment in Tibet's economic development. However, China still considers talk of Tibetan political independence to be treason, and Chinese troops have violently crushed several anti-China demonstrations in Lhasa, the capital of Tibet.

The Dalai Lama is very active internationally in promoting the cause of independence for Tibet. In 1989, he was awarded the Nobel Peace Prize. He has met with several U.S. presidents, addressed Congress, and spoken widely to universities and other audiences in the United States. In 1999, the U.S. State Department appointed a special coordinator for Tibetan issues. The Chinese government considers these events as proof of tacit American support for Tibetan independence.

There have been some tentative talks between the Dalai Lama's representatives and Chinese officials about the conditions under which the Dalai Lama might return to Tibet. In September 2002, a high-level delegation from the Dalai Lama's government-in-exile visited Beijing and Lhasa to further explore better relations. But the PRC insists that the Dalai Lama renounce independence as a goal for Tibet, and the two sides appear far from any agreement. Tensions between Tibetans and Chinese in Tibet also remain high and potentially explosive.

groups they are supposed to represent. But they do sometimes act as an effective lobby in promoting the nonpolitical interests of their constituencies. For example, the Trade Union Federation has pushed for legislation to reduce the standard work week from six to five days, and the Women's Federation has become a strong advocate for women on issues ranging from domestic violence to economic rights.

Since the late 1990s, there has been huge increase in the number of nongovernmental organizations (NGOs) less directly subordinate to the CCP than the traditional mass organizations. There is an enormous variety of national and local NGOs, including those that deal with the environment (e.g., the China Green Foundation), health (e.g., the China Foundation for the Prevention of STDs and AIDS), charitable work (e.g., the China Children and Teenagers Fund), and legal issues (e.g., the Beijing Center for Women's Law Services). These NGOs have considerable latitude to operate within their functional areas without direct party interference *if* they steer clear of politics and do not challenge official policies.

Although they remain subordinate to the CCP, the various government bodies and other organizations discussed in this section should not be dismissed. They do "provide important access points between the Party and the organized masses, which allow the voicing of special interests in ways that do not threaten Party hegemony and yet pressure the shaping of policy."[24]

Mechanisms of Social Control

While China has certainly loosened up politically since the days of Mao Zedong, the party-state's control mechanisms still penetrate to the basic levels of society and serve the CCP's aim of preventing the formation of groups or movements that could challenge its authority. In the rural areas, the small-scale, closely knit nature of the village facilitates control by the local party and security organizations. The major means of control used by the party-state in urban China, called the unit (or *danwei*) system, is more complex. In the cities, almost everyone belongs to a unit, usually their place of work, and the *danwei* is the center of economic, social, and political life for most urban residents.

The unit holds meetings to discuss the official line on important policies or events. The personnel departments of units also keep a political dossier on every employee. The dossier contains a detailed record of the political activities and attitudes of the employee and his or her immediate family members. If a person changes jobs, which often can be done only with the *danwei*'s approval, the dossier moves too. In these and other ways, the unit has acted as a check on political dissidents. Residents' committees are another instrument of control in urban China. These neighborhood-based citizen organizations, which are often staffed by retired persons, housewives, or others not attached to a work unit, combine service and surveillance and effectively extend the unofficial reach of the party-state down to the most basic level of urban society.

As Chinese society continues to change because of the impact of economic reform, these control mechanisms are weakening. The growth of private and semiprivate enterprises, increasing labor and residential mobility, and new forms of association (such as discos and coffeehouses) and communication (for example, cell phones, email, fax machines, and TV satellite dishes) are just some of the factors that are making it much harder for the party-state to monitor citizens as closely as it has in the past.

Protest and the Party-State

The Tiananmen massacre of 1989 showed the limits of protest in China. The leadership was particularly alarmed at signs that a number of grass-roots organizations, such as the Beijing Federation of Autonomous Student Unions and the Beijing Workers' Autonomous Union, were emerging from the demonstrations. The success of Solidarity, the independent Polish workers' movement, in challenging the power of the Communist Party in Poland in the 1980s was much in the minds of China's leaders as they watched the Tiananmen protests unfold. Massive repression was their way of letting it be known that the "Polish disease" would not be allowed to spread to China and that neither open political protest nor the formation of autonomous interest groups would be tolerated.

There have been no large-scale political demonstrations in China since 1989, and prodemocracy groups have been driven deep underground or abroad. Known dissidents are continuously watched, harassed, imprisoned, and, recently and more benevolently, expelled from the country, sometimes as a conciliatory diplomatic gesture. In late December 2002, one of China's leading democratic activists, Xu Wenli, was released and sent to the United States for medical care after spending sixteen of the previous twenty-one years in prison: he was most recently sentenced to a thirteen-year jail term in 1998 for his efforts to organize an independent political party.

But repression has by no means put an end to all forms of citizen protest in the PRC. Ethnic protests occur sporadically on China's periphery. The biggest and most continuous demonstrations against the party-state in recent years have been carried out by the Falun Gong (literally, Dharma Wheel Practice). Falun Gong (FLG) is a spiritual movement that combines philosophical and religious elements drawn from Buddhism and Taoism with traditional Chinese physical and meditative exercises (similar to *tai chi*). It was founded in the early 1990s by Li Hongzhi, a one-time low-level PRC government employee now living in the United States. The movement claims 70 million members in China and 30 million in more than forty other countries: these numbers may be exaggerated, but there is no doubt that the FLG has an enormous following. Its promise of inner tranquility and good health has proven very appealing to a wide cross-section of people in China as a reaction to some of the side effects of rapid modernization, including crass commercialism, economic insecurity, and the rising crime rate.

The Chinese authorities, reacting to the movement's growing popularity, began a crackdown on Falun Gong in 1999. Ten thousand FLG followers responded that April by holding a peaceful protest outside the gates of Zhongnanhai, the walled compound in the center of Beijing where China's top leaders live and work. The government then outlawed Falun Gong and deemed it an "evil cult" that spread lies, fooled people to the point that they rejected urgently needed medical care, encouraged suicides, and generally threatened social stability. It is not only the movement's size that alarms the Chinese party-state but also its ability to communicate with and mobilize its members and spread its message through both electronic means and by word of mouth.

The intense suppression of Falun Gong has included destruction of related books and tapes, jamming of websites, and the arrest of thousands of practitioners, many of whom, the movement claims, have been not only jailed but also beaten (sometimes to death) and sent to psychiatric hospitals or labor camps. But the movement is far from being crushed. Although there have been no more protests as large as that of April 1999, FLG followers have staged numerous public demonstrations, including several in Tiananmen Square, most of which are stopped by quick arrests, and one in January 2001 that involved self-immolation by five believers.

Labor unrest has been growing in China, with reports of thousands of strikes and other actions in recent years. There have been big demonstrations at state-owned factories by workers angry about the ending of the iron rice bowl system, layoffs, the nonpayment of pensions or severance packages, and the arrest of grass-roots labor leaders. Workers at some foreign-owned enterprises have gone on strike to protest unsafe working conditions or low wages. Most of these actions have remained limited in scope and duration, so the government has usually not cracked down on the protesters and has, on occasion, actually pressured the employers to meet the workers' demands.

The countryside has also seen a rising tide of protest, especially in the poorer areas of central China. Farmers have attacked local officials and rioted over exorbitant taxes and extralegal fees, corruption, and the government's failure to pay on time for agricultural products it has purchased. These protests have not spread beyond the locales where they started and have focused on farmers' immediate material concerns, not on grand-scale issues like democracy. They have usually been contained by the authorities through a combination of coercion and concessions to some of the farmers' demands. But if the countryside is left too far behind in the process of economic development, rural discontent could spread and translate into more generalized anger against the regime.

The political situation in China early in the twenty-first century presents a rather contradictory picture. Although people are freer in many ways than they have been in decades, repression can still be intense, and open political dissent is almost nonexistent. But there are many signs that the Chinese Communist Party is losing some of its ability to control the movements and associations of its citizens and can no longer easily limit access to information and ideas from abroad. Some forms of protest also appear to be increasing and in places may come to pose a serious challenge to the authority of the party-state.

Section ⑤ Chinese Politics in Transition

Political Challenges and Changing Agendas

Scenes from the Chinese Countryside

The economic and political circumstances of China's vast rural population differ dramatically depending on where in the countryside you look.[25]

Guanqiao, Hubei Province.   In many ways, this rural village looks like an American suburb: spacious roads lined with two-story townhouses, potted plants on doorsteps, green lawns, and luscious shade trees. Some homes have leather living room furniture, studies with computers, and exercise rooms. And the village is spotless: garbage is picked up house by house every morning. But the pigsties and chicken coops are a good clue that this is farm country, not suburbia.

Things were not always so prosperous in Guanqiao. In 1978, the average annual income was only about $80, and the state had to provide the village with grain relief most every year. Now a typical young couple might earn $6,000 annually—about ten times the income of the average rural household in China.

This transformation came about in stages beginning in the early 1980s when the Maoist communes were replaced with household-based farming and agricultural production was diversified by the planting of profitable tea trees. Then came the establishment of a few small-scale village enterprises, such as ice cream making and brick factories. Under the leadership of the savvy farmer-turned-entrepreneur who was the village leader, enough capital was accumulated to allow for expansion into more sophisticated industries in the 1990s, the most recent of which is the production of steel cables used in bridge construction. Guanqiao is doing so well that much of the cost of the modern townhouses was paid for out of village funds.

Meishu, Yunnan Province.   This rural village is located in one of the areas known as China's Third World, where persistent poverty rather than growing prosperity is still the common lot in life. There are no townhouses here; most families have a total income of less than $50 a year and live in one-room, mud-brick houses with no running water that they often share with pigs or other farm animals. There are no paved roads.

The children, dressed in grimy clothes and ragged cloth shoes, are not starving, but they do not seem to be flourishing either. Education, professional health care, and other social services are minimal or nonexistent. There is no industry, and the land barely supports those who work it. Tens of millions of Chinese peasants in villages like Meishu remain mired in poverty and have benefited little from the country's economic boom.

Daolin, Hunan Province.   A few years ago, thousands of angry farmers marched on the township government headquarters to protest excessive taxes and the gross corruption of local officials. One farmer was killed and dozens injured when the police used clubs and tear gas to disperse the crowd. Shortly afterward, nine people suspected of being ringleaders of the protests were arrested. The demonstrations had been spurred by a grass-roots organization called Volunteers for Publicity of Policies and Regulations, formed to bring attention to local violations of a national law that limits taxes on farmers to 5 percent of their income. In many parts of rural China, villagers are subject to a wide range of arbitrary fees: charges for slaughtering pigs, for sending children to school, for permits to get married or to have a baby, for registering land, and for outhouse renovations—to name just a few. As a result of such local fees, Daolin's farmers were paying double the legal tax rate, which for people with an annual per capita income of only $170 was quite a burden. People were even more furious because the extra fees often went to support the wining and dining of township bureaucrats rather than for worthy local projects.

Beiwang, Hebei Province.   This was one of the first villages in China to hold democratic elections for a representative assembly to supervise the work of local government officials. Among the first decisions made by the representatives was to reassign the contracts for tending the village's 3,000 pear trees. After the rural communes were disbanded in the 1980s, each of the five hundred or so families in the village was given six trees to look after under the new household responsibility system. The assembly, however, decided that it would be better to reassign the trees to a very small number of families who would care for them in a more efficient and productive manner. The local Communist Party branch objected on the grounds that the village might lose much of the revenue that it earned from signing contracts with many households, which was used to pay for various public works projects such as road maintenance. The party was probably also concerned about the ideological implications of a less egalitarian distribution of the village's trees and the income derived from them. Nevertheless, assembly representatives were able to generate strong support from their constituents for their proposal, and the party branch allowed the trees to be recontracted to just eleven households. In a short time, pear production zoomed. The new system proved to be economically beneficial not only to the few families who looked after the trees but also to the village as a whole because of the local government's share of the increased profits.

The scenes just described make several important points about Chinese politics today. First, they remind us of the central role that China's rural areas will play in the nation's future. Most Chinese still live in the countryside, and China's political and economic fate will be greatly influenced by what goes on there. These scenes also reflect the enormous diversity of the Chinese countryside: prosperity and poverty, mass protests and peaceful politics. It is very hard to generalize about such a vast and varied nation by looking at what is going on in only one small part of the country.

The scene from Beiwang reminds us that in China, as in other countries, not all politics involves matters of national or international significance. For many, perhaps most, Chinese, who looks after the village pear trees matters more than what goes on in the inner sanctums of the Communist Party or the outcomes of U.S.-China presidential summits. The victory of the Beiwang representative assembly on the pear tree issue shows that even in a one-party state, the people sometimes prevail against the those with power, and democracy works on the local level—as long as the basic principle of party leadership is not challenged.

The Guanqiao scene is just one example of the astonishing improvement in living standards in much of rural China brought about by decollectivization and industrialization. But huge pockets of severe poverty, like that in Meishu, still persist, especially in inland regions that are far removed from the more prosperous coastal regions. Most of rural China falls somewhere

between the affluence of Guanqiao and the extreme poverty of Meishu. And it is in these in-between areas, such as Daolin, where the combination of new hopes brought about by economic progress and the anger caused by blatant corruption, growing inequalities, stagnating incomes, and other frustrations may prove to be politically explosive.

Economic reform has yielded a better life and higher hopes for most of China's farmers. The CCP must now deal with the challenge of having to satisfy those hopes or risk the wrath of a social group that for decades has been the bedrock of the party's support.

Economic Management, Social Tension, and Political Legitimacy

The problems of China's rural areas are part of a larger challenge facing the country's leadership: how to sustain and effectively manage the economic growth on which the CCP's legitimacy as China's ruling party is now largely based. The party is gambling that continuing solid economic performance will literally buy it legitimacy in the eyes of the Chinese people and that most citizens will care little about democracy if their material lives continue to get better.

Despite the overall success of the reforms, the Chinese Communist Party faces a number of very serious challenges in governing the economy that will affect the party's political fortunes. Failure to keep inequality under control, especially between city and countryside, or to continue providing opportunities for advancement for the less well off could become a source of social instability and a liability for a political party that still espouses a commitment to socialist goals. One of the government's most formidable tasks will be to create enough new jobs for the millions of workers who are expected to be laid off by the closure or restructuring of state-owned enterprises. This situation will very likely be compounded by those displaced from industries that are no longer competitive in China's increasingly globalized economy.

The considerable autonomy gained by provinces and localities as a result of the decentralization of economic decision making has fostered a growing regionalism that poses a potentially serious threat to the political control of the central government. Corruption, which affects the lives of most people more directly than does political repression, has become so blatant and widespread that it is probably the single most corrosive force eating away at the legitimacy of the Chinese Communist Party.

An increasingly serious issue on China's national agenda, and one with the potential to turn into a major crisis, is the spread of AIDS. Recent surveys estimate the number of infected citizens to be between 850,000 and 1 million. Unless the current infection rate is slowed, predictions are that there could be 10 million AIDS victims in China by 2010.

AIDS first spread in China in the early 1990s among needle-sharing heroin users, mostly in the border regions of the west and southwest. It has since spread to all areas of the country through drug use and sexual activity. There was also an extensive outbreak of AIDS in several provinces among blood donors and their families. In these cases, poor farmers had sold their blood for cash at unscrupulous and unsafe collection stations run by local "entrepreneurs," doctors, and officials. Some villages in Henan Province have an HIV infection rate of over 60 percent of the population.

The government has recently taken active steps to deal with the situation, including increased funding for AIDS prevention, support for AIDS awareness campaigns, improved access to cheaper drugs, and punishment of some blood dealers, as well as new laws regulating the blood supply. But responding effectively to the problem will require concerted action on the local level and the involvement of nongovernmental organizations and experts best equipped to address the root causes of the looming epidemic.

It was not an encouraging sign that China's leading AIDS activist, Dr. Wan Yanhai, was detained by the authorities in mid-2002 for "revealing state secrets," a reference to his role in exposing the Henan blood scandal. Wan was released a month later, after he admitted his "mistake" in distributing a classified government report on AIDS through foreign journalists and websites. As one authoritative article observed, "There are few countries in the world with a comparable level of governmental infrastructure and control, or that have experienced such steady and dynamic economic growth. China must muster the political will and resources to prevent this progress from quickly unraveling as a result of AIDS."[26]

Clearly, the leaders of the PRC will have to make some difficult policy choices in deciding how to manage China's rapidly modernizing economy and respond to its radically changing society.

China and the Democratic Idea

China has evolved in recent decades toward a system of what has been called "market Leninism," a combination of increasing economic openness and continuing political rigidity under the leadership of a ruling party that adheres to a remodeled version of communist ideology.[27] The major political challenges now facing the CCP and the country emerge from the sharpening contradictions and tensions of this hybrid system.

In the short run, the CCP's gamble that the country's economic boom would divert the attention of most Chinese from politics to profits has paid off. However, as the people of China become more secure economically, better educated, and more aware of the outside world, they are likely to become politically less quiescent. The steadily expanding class of private entrepreneurs may want political clout to match their economic wealth. Scholars, scientists, and technology specialists may become more outspoken about the limits on intellectual freedom. And the many Chinese citizens who travel or study abroad may find the political gap between their party-state and the world's growing number of democracies to be increasingly intolerable.

There are reasons to be both optimistic and pessimistic about the future of the democratic idea in China.[28] On the negative side, China's long history of bureaucratic and authoritarian rule and the hierarchical values of still-influential Confucian culture seem to be mighty counterweights to democracy. And although its political legitimacy may be weak and some aspects of its social control have broken down, the coercive power of China's communist party-state remains formidable. The PRC's relatively low per capita standard of living, a largely rural population and vast areas of extreme poverty, and state-dominated media and means of communications also impose some impediments to democratization. Finally, many in China are rather apathetic about national politics (preferring to focus on their immediate economic concerns) or fearful of the violence and chaos that radical political change might unleash.

On the positive side, the impressive successes of democratization in Taiwan in the past decade, including free and fair multiparty elections from the local level up to the presidency, strongly suggest that the values, institutions, and process of democracy are not incompatible with Confucian culture. And though it is still a developing country, China has a higher literacy rate, more extensive industrialization and urbanization, a faster rate of economic growth, and less inequality (though there are some worrisome trends here) than most other countries at its level of economic development—conditions widely seen by social scientists as favorable to democracy.

Despite the CCP's continuing tight hold on power, there have been a number of significant political changes in China that could be planting the seeds of democracy: the decentralization of political and economic power to local governments; the setting of a mandatory retirement age and term limits for all officials; the coming to power of younger, better educated, and more worldly leaders; the increasingly important role of the National People's Congress in the policy-making process; the introduction of competitive elections in rural villages; the strengthening and partial depoliticization of the legal system; tolerance of a much wider range of artistic, cultural, and religious expression; and the important freedom (unheard of in the Mao era) for individuals to be apolitical.

Furthermore, the astounding spread of democracy around the globe has created a trend that will be increasingly difficult for China's leaders to resist. The PRC has become a major player in the world of states, and its government must be more responsive to international opinion in order to continue the country's deepening integration with the international economy and growing stature as a responsible and mature global power.

One of the most important political trends in China has been the resurgence of civil society, a sphere of independent public life and citizen association, which, if allowed to thrive and expand, could provide fertile soil for future democratization. The development of civil society among workers in Poland and intellectuals in Czechoslovakia, for example, played an important role in the collapse of communism in East-Central Europe in the late 1980s by weakening the critical underpinnings of party-state control.

The Tiananmen demonstrations of 1989 reflected the stirrings of civil society in post-Mao China. The brutal crushing of that movement showed the CCP's determination to thwart the growth of civil society before it could seriously challenge Communist authority. But as economic modernization and social liberalization have deepened in the PRC, civil society has begun to stir again. Some stirrings, like the Falun Gong movement, have met with vicious repression by the party-state. But others, such as the proliferation of semiautonomous nongovernmental organizations, have been encouraged by the authorities. Academic journals and conferences have recently had surprisingly open, if tentative discussions about future political options for China, including multiparty democracy.

At some point, the leaders of the CCP will face the fundamental dilemma of whether to accommodate or, as they have done so often in the past, repress organizations, individuals, and ideas that question the principle of party leadership. On the one hand, accommodation will require less party-state control and more meaningful citizen representation and participation. On the other hand, repression would likely derail the country's economic dynamism and could have terrible costs for China.

Chinese Politics in Comparative Perspective

As mentioned at the end of Section 1, students of comparative politics should find it particularly interesting to compare China with other nations from two perspectives. First, the People's Republic of China can be compared with other communist party-states with which it shares or has shared many political characteristics. Second, China can be compared with other developing nations that face similar economic and political challenges.

China as a Communist Party-State

Why has the Chinese communist party-state been more durable than other regimes of its type? The PRC's successful economic restructuring and the rapidly rising living standard of most of the people have saved the CCP from the kinds of economic crises that greatly weakened other Communist systems, including the Soviet Union. China's leaders believe that one of the biggest mistakes made by the last Soviet party chief, Mikhail Gorbachev, was that he went too far with political reform and not far enough with economic change, and they are convinced that their reverse formula is a key reason that they have not suffered the same fate.

The fact that the Chinese Communists won power through an indigenous revolution with widespread popular backing and did not depend on foreign military support for their victory also sets China apart from the situation of most of the now-deposed East-Central European communist parties. Therefore, although repression and corruption may be harming the popularity of the CCP, the party still has a deep reservoir of historical legitimacy among large segments of the population.

But China also has many things in common with other communist party-states, including the basic features of what has been often called its totalitarian political system. **Totalitarianism** (a term also applied to fascist regimes such as Nazi Germany) describes a system in which the ruling party prohibits all forms of meaningful political opposition and dissent, insists on obedience to a single state-determined ideology, and enforces its rule through coercion and terror. Such regimes also seek to bring all spheres of public activity (including the economy and culture) and even many parts of its citizens' private lives (including reproduction) under the total control of the party-state in the effort to modernize the country and, indeed, to transform human nature.

China offers an interesting comparative perspective on the nature of change in totalitarian systems. Partly because of their inflexibility, totalitarian regimes in Russia and East-Central Europe collapsed quickly and thoroughly, to be replaced by democracies in the 1990s. The CCP appears to be trying to save Communist rule in China by abandoning or at least moderating many, if not all, of its totalitarian features. In order to promote economic development, the CCP has relaxed its grip on many areas of life, and citizens are now free to pursue their interests without state interference as long as they steer clear of sensitive political issues.

In this sense, the PRC has evolved from Maoist totalitarianism toward a less intrusive, but still dictatorial, "consultative authoritarian regime" that "increasingly recognizes the need to obtain information, advice, and support from key sectors of the population, but insists on suppressing dissent . . . and maintaining ultimate political power in the hands of the Party."[29] Thus, China seems, at least for the moment, to be going through a type of post-totalitarian transition characterized by bold economic and social reform, but which also leads to another type of dictatorship rather than to democracy.

China as a Third World State

The record of Communist rule in China raises many issues about the role of the state in economic development. It also provides an interesting comparative perspective on the complex relationship between economic and political change in the Third World.

When the Chinese Communist Party came to power in 1949, China was a desperately poor country, with an economy devastated by a century of civil strife and world war. It was also in a weak and subordinate position in the post–World War II international order. Measured against this starting point, the PRC has made remarkable progress in improving the well-being of its citizens, building a strong state, and enhancing the country's global role.

Why has China been more successful than so many other nations in meeting some of major challenges of development? Third World governments have often served narrow class or foreign interests more than the national interest. Many political leaders in Africa, Asia, and Latin America have been a drain on development rather than a stimulus. The result is that Third World states have many times become defenders of a status quo built on extensive inequality and poverty rather than agents of needed change. In contrast, the PRC's recent rulers have been quite successful in creating what social scientists call a **developmental state** in which government power and public policy are used effectively to promote national economic growth.

Whereas much of the Third World seems to be heading toward democracy without development—or at best very slow development—China seems to be following the reverse course of very fast development without democracy. There is a sharp and disturbing contrast between the harsh political rule of the Chinese communist party-state and its remarkable accomplishments in improving the material lives of the Chinese people. This contrast is at the heart of what one journalist has called the "riddle of China" today, where the government "fights leprosy as aggressively as it attacks dissent. It inoculates infants with the same fervor with which it arrests its critics. Partly as a result, a baby born in Shanghai now has a longer life expectancy than a baby born in New York City."[30] This "riddle" makes it difficult to settle on a clear evaluation of the overall record of Communist rule in China, particularly in the post-Mao era. It also makes it hard to predict the future of the Chinese Communist Party, since the regime's economic achievements could provide it with the support, or at least compliance, it needs to stay in power despite its serious political shortcomings.

The CCP's tough stance on political reform is in part based on its desire for self-preservation. But in keeping firm control on political life while allowing the country to open up in other important ways, the Chinese Communist Party also believes it is wisely following the model of development pioneered by the newly industrializing countries (NICs) of East Asia such as South Korea, Taiwan, and Singapore.

The lesson that the CCP draws from the NIC experiences is that only a strong "neoauthoritarian" government can provide the political stability and social peace required for rapid economic growth. According to this view, democracy—with its open debates about national priorities, political parties contesting for power, and interest groups squabbling over how to divide the economic pie—is a recipe for chaos, particularly in a huge and relatively poor country. Chinese leaders point out that democracy has not often been conducive to successful economic development in the Third World. In India, for example, a democratic but weak government has been unable to respond effectively to internal ethnic strife and has been stymied by entrenched interests in its efforts to alleviate poverty.

But another of the lessons from the East Asian NICs—one that most Chinese leaders have been reluctant to acknowledge so far—is that economic development, social modernization, and global integration also create powerful pressures for political change from below and abroad. In both Taiwan and South Korea, authoritarian governments that had presided over economic miracles in the 1960s and 1970s gave way in the 1980s and 1990s to the democratic idea, largely in response to domestic pressures.

The dynamic expansion and transformation of the Chinese economy indicate that the PRC is in the early stages of a period of growth and modernization that will lead it to NIC status. However, in terms of the extent of industrialization, per capita income, and the strength of the middle and professional classes, China's economic development is still far below the level at which democracy succeeded in Taiwan and South Korea. It is important to remember that "authoritarian governments in East Asia pursued market-driven economic growth for decades without relaxing their hold on political power."[31]

Nevertheless, economic reform in China has already created groups and processes, interests and ideas that are likely to become sources of pressure for more and faster political change. And the experience of the NICs and other developing countries suggests that such pressures are likely to intensify as the economy and society continue to modernize. Therefore, at some point in the not-too-distant future, the Chinese Communist Party may again face the challenge of the democratic idea. How China's new generation of leaders responds to this challenge is perhaps the most important and uncertain question about Chinese politics in the early twenty-first century.

Key Terms

communist party-state
Marxism-Leninism
autonomous regions
guerrilla warfare
collectivization
socialism
Great Leap Forward
communism
Great Proletarian
  Cultural Revolution
revisionism
command economy
socialist market
  economy
people's communes
household responsibility
  system

township and village
  enterprises
decentralization
iron rice bowl
guanxi
newly industrializing
  countries
dual rule
cadres
nomenklatura
socialist democracy
Four Cardinal Principles
danwei
totalitarianism
developmental state

Suggested Readings

Bernstein, Thomas P., and Xiaobo Lü. *Taxation Without Representation in Contemporary Rural China.* Cambridge: Cambridge University Press, 2003.

Blecher, Marc J. *China Against the Tides: Restructuring Through Revolution, Radicalism, and Reform.* London: Pinter, 1997.

Chang, Jung. *Wild Swans: Three Daughters of China.* New York: Simon & Schuster, 1991.

Fairbank, John King, and Goldman, Merle. *China: A New History.* Cambridge, Mass.: Harvard University Press, 1998.

Gao Yuan. *Born Red: A Chronicle of the Cultural Revolution.* Stanford, Calif.: Stanford University Press, 1987.

Hutchings, Graham. *Modern China: A Guide to a Century of Change.* Cambridge, Mass.: Harvard University Press, 2001.

Judd, Ellen R. *The Chinese Women's Movement Between State and Market.* Stanford, Calif.: Stanford University Press, 2002.

Lampton, David M. *Same Bed, Different Dreams: Managing U.S.-China Relations, 1989–2000.* Berkeley: University of California Press, 2001.

Lardy, Nicholas R. *Integrating China into the Global Economy.* Washington, D.C.: Brookings Institution Press, 2002.

Li, Cheng. *China's Leaders: The New Generation.* Lanham, Md.: Rowman & Littlefield, 2001.

MacFarquhar, Roderick (ed.). *The Politics of China: The Eras of Mao and Deng.* 2nd ed. Cambridge: Cambridge University Press, 1998.

Ogden, Suzanne. *Inklings of Democracy in China.* Cambridge, Mass.: Harvard University Press, 2002.

Perry, Elizabeth J., and Selden, Mark (eds.). *Chinese Society: Change, Conflict and Resistance.* New York: Routledge, 2000.

Saich, Tony. *Governance and Politics of China.* New York: Palgrave Macmillan, 2001.

Solinger, Dorothy J. *Contesting Citizenship in Urban China: Peasant Migrants, the State, and the Logic of the Market.* Berkeley: University of California Press, 1999.

Spence, Jonathan. *Mao Zedong.* New York: Viking, 1999.

Spence, Jonathan D., and Annping Chin. *The Chinese Century: A Photographic History of the Last Hundred Years.* New York: Random House, 1996.

Starr, John Bryan. *Understanding China: A Guide to China's Economy, History, and Political Culture.* 2nd ed. New York: Hill and Wang, 2001.

Unger, Jonathan. *The Transformation of Rural China.* Armonk, N.Y.: M. E. Sharpe, 2002.

Zweig, David. *Internationalizing China: Domestic Interests and Global Linkages.* Ithaca, N.Y.: 2002.

Suggested Websites

China Links, Professor William A. Joseph, Wellesley College
www.wellesley.edu/Polisci/wj/China/chinalinks.html
Embassy of the People's Republic of China in the United States
www.china-embassy.org
Finding News About China
chinanews.bfn.org/
PRC China Internet Information Center

www.china.org.cn/english/index.htm
Washington Post.com: China
www.washingtonpost.com/wp-dyn/world/asia/eastasia/china

Notes

[1]"Beijing Win Divides World Opinion," CNN.com, http://www.cnn.com/2001/WORLD/asiapcf/east/07/13/beijing.win/.

[2]Mao Zedong, "Report on an Investigation of the Peasant Movement in Hunan," March 1927, in *Selected Readings from the Works of Mao Tsetung* (Beijing: Foreign Languages Press, 1971), 24.

[3]David Bachman, *Bureaucracy, Economy, and Leadership in China: The Institutional Origins of the Great Leap Forward* (Cambridge: Cambridge University Press, 1991), 2.

[4]Fareed Zakaria, "The Big Story Everyone Missed," *Newsweek,* December 30, 2002, 52.

[5]See, for example, "When China Wakes," *Economist,* November 28, 1992; and Nicholas D. Kristof and Sheryl WuDunn, *China Wakes: The Struggle for the Soul of a Rising Power* (New York: Time Books, 1994).

[6]"When China Wakes," 3, 15.

[7]Barry Naughton, "The Pattern and Legacy of Economic Growth in the Mao Era," in Kenneth Lieberthal et al. (eds.), *Perspectives on Modern China: Four Anniversaries* (Armonk, N.Y.: M. E. Sharpe, 1991), 250.

[8]Deng Xiaoping first expressed his "cat theory" in 1962 in a speech, "Restore Agricultural Production," in the aftermath of the failure and famine of the Great Leap Forward. In the original speech, he actually quoted an old peasant proverb that refers to a "yellow cat or a black cat," but it is most often rendered "white cat or black cat." See *Selected Works of Deng Xiaoping (1938–1965)* (Beijing: Foreign Languages Press, 1992), 293.

[9]Kathleen Hartford, "Socialist Agriculture Is Dead; Long Live Socialist Agriculture! Organizational Transformation in Rural China," in Elizabeth J. Perry and Christine P. W. Wong (eds.), *The Political Economy of Reform in Post-Mao China* (Cambridge, Mass.: Council on East Asian Studies, Harvard University, 1985), 55.

[10]Christine P. W. Wong, "China's Economy: The Limits of Gradualist Reform," in William A. Joseph (ed.), *China Briefing,1994* (Boulder, Colo.: Westview Press, 1994), 50.

[11]Emily Honig and Gail Herschatter, *Personal Voices: Chinese Women in the 1980s* (Stanford, Calif.: Stanford University Press, 1988), 337.

[12]Baruch Boxer, "China's Environment: Issues and Economic Implications," in Joint Economic Committee of Congress, *China's Economic Dilemmas in the 1990s: The Problems of Reform, Modernization, and Interdependence*, vol. 1 (Washington, D.C.: Government Printing Office, 1991), 306–307.

[13]Mao Zedong, "Strive to Build a Great Socialist Country," September 15, 1954, in *Selected Works of Mao Tsetung,* vol. 5 (Beijing: Foreign Languages Press, 1977), 149.

[14]Deng Xiaoping, "Uphold the Four Cardinal Principles," March 30, 1979, in *Selected Works of Deng Xiaoping (1977–1982),* (Beijing: Foreign Languages Press, 1984), 178.

[15]The constitution of the People's Republic of China can be found on line at the website of China's People's Daily, http://english.peopledaily.com.cn/constitution/constitution.html. The full text of the most recently amended version of the constitution of the Chinese Communist Party can be found at the website of the party's Sixteenth National Congress held in November 2002, http://www.16congress.org.cn/english/features/49109.htm.

[16]Mao Zedong, "Problems of War and Strategy," November 6, 1938, in *Selected Works of Mao Tsetung,* vol. 2 (Beijing: Foreign Languages Press, 1972), 224.

[17]Kenneth Lieberthal and David Michael Lampton (eds.), *Bureaucracy, Politics, and Decision-Making in Post-Mao China* (Berkeley: University of California Press, 1992).

[18]John P. Burns, *The Chinese Communist Party's Nomenklatura System: A Documentary Study of Party Control of Leadership Selection, 1979–1984* (Armonk, N.Y.: M. E. Sharpe, 1989), ix–x.

[19]Gordon White, *Riding the Tiger: The Politics of Economic Reform in Post-Mao China* (Palo Alto, Calif.: Stanford University Press, 1993), 20.

[20]Jiang Zemin, "Speech at the Meeting Celebrating the 80th Anniversary of the Founding of the Communist Party of China," July 1, 2001, http://www.china-un.ch/eng/14905.html.

[21]James D. Seymour, *China's Satellite Parties* (Armonk, N.Y.: M. E. Sharpe, 1987), 87.

[22]For Jiang's 1999 speech, see the People's Daily website, http://www.peopledaily.com.cn/english/50years/news/19991001A117.html). For the 2002 speech, see the official website of the Sixteenth Party Congress, http://www.16congress.org.cn/english/features/49007.htm.

[23]Lin Biao, "Foreword to the Second Edition," *Quotations from Chairman Mao Tse-tung* (Beijing: Foreign Languages Press, 1967), iii.

[24]James R. Townsend and Brantly Womack, *Politics in China,* 3d ed. (Boston: Little, Brown, 1986), 271.

[25]The following scenes are extrapolated from Wang Zhe, "Behind the Dream of a Village," *Beijing Review,* June 14, 2001, 13–16; Lu Xueyi, "The Peasants Are Suffering, the Villages Are Very Poor," *Dushu* (Readings), January 2001, in U.S. Embassy (Beijing, China), PRC Press Clippings, http://www.usembassy-china.org.cn/sandt/peasantsuffering.html); Erik Eckholm, "Heated Protests by Its Farmers Trouble Beijing," *New York Times,* February 1, 1999, A; Susan V. Lawrence, "Democracy, Chinese-Style: Village Representative Assemblies," *Australian Journal of Chinese Affairs,* no. 32 (July 1994): 61–68.

[26]Joan Kaufman and Jun Jing, "China and AIDS—The Time to Act Is Now," *Science,* June 28, 2002, 2340.

[27]Nicholas D. Kristof, "China Sees 'Market-Leninism' as Way to Future," *New York Times,* September 6, 1993, 1, 5.

[28]Many of the points in this section are based on Martin King Whyte, "Prospects for Democratization in China," *Problems of Communism* (May–June 1992): 58–69; Michel Oksenberg, "Will China Democratize? Confronting a Classic Dilemma," *Journal of Democracy* 9, no. 1 (January 1998): 27–34; and Minxin Pei, "Is China Democratizing?" *Foreign Affairs* 77, no. 1 (January–February 1998), 68–82.

[29]Harry Harding, *China's Second Revolution: Reform After Mao* (Washington, D.C.: Brookings Institution, 1987), 200.

[30]Nicholas D. Kristof, "Riddle of China: Repression as Standard of Living Soars," *New York Times,* September 7, 1993, A1, A10.

[31]Nicholas Lardy, "Is China Different? The Fate of Its Economic Reform," in Daniel Chirot (ed.), *The Crisis of Leninism and the Decline of the Left* (Seattle: University of Washington Press, 1991), 147.

CHAPTER 3

India

Atul Kohli and Amrita Basu

Republic of India

Land and People

Capital	New Delhi
Total area (square miles)	1,269,338 (slightly more than one-third the size of the U.S.)
Population (2001)	1.09 billion

Annual population growth rate (%)

1975–2000	1.9
2000–2015 (projected)	1.3

Urban population (%)	27.7

Major languages* (%)

Hindi	40
Telugu	8
Bengali	8
Marathi	7.3
Tamil	6.6
Gujarati	4
Urdu	5
Other	22

*Hindi is the main language, but English is the most important language for political, commercial, and other national-level communication.

Religious affiliation (%)

Hindu	81.3
Muslim	12
Christian	2.3
Sikh	1.9
Buddhist and other	2.5

Economy

Domestic currency

Rupee (INR)
US$1: 47.9 INR
(2002 average)

Total GDP (US$)	457 billion
GDP per capita (US$)	476
Total GDP at purchasing power parity (US$$)	2.4 trillion
GDP per capita at purchasing power parity (US$)	2,358

GDP annual growth rate (%)

1997	4.4
2000	3.9
2001	4.5

GDP per capita average annual growth rate (%)

1975–2000	3.2
1990–2000	4.1

Inequality in income consumption (1997) (%)

Share of poorest 10%	3.5
Share of poorest 20%	8.1
Share of richest 20%	46.1
Share of richest 10%	33.5
Gini index (1997)	37.8

Structure of production (% of GDP)

Agriculture	24.9
Industry	26.9
Services	48.2

Labor force distribution (% of total)

Agriculture	60
Industry	23
Services	17

Exports as % of GDP	14
Imports as % of GDP	17
Electricity consumption per capita (kwh)	448
Carbon dioxide emissions per capita (metric tons)	1

Society

Life expectancy

Female	63
Male	62.8

Doctors per 100,000 people	48
Infant mortality (per 1,000 live births)	69

Adult literacy (%)

Female	45.4
Male	68.4

Access to information and communications (per 1,000 people)

Telephone lines	32
Mobile phones	4
Radios	121
Televisions	78
Personal computers	4.5

Women in Government and Economy

Women in the national legislature

Lower house or single house (%)	8.8
Upper house (%)	9.1

Women at ministerial level (%)	10.1
Female economic activity rate (age 15 and above) (%)	50
Female labor force (% of total)	32

Estimated earned income (PPP US$)

Female	1,267
Male	3,383

2002 Human Development Index ranking
(out of 173 countries) — 124

Political Organization

Political System Parliamentary democracy and a federal republic.

Regime History Current government formed by the Bharatiya Janata Party (BJP), under the leadership of Atal Behari Vajpayee.

Administrative Structure Federal, with 28 state governments.

Executive Prime minister, leader of the party with the most seats in the parliament.

Legislature Bicameral, upper house elected indirectly and without much substantial power; lower house, the main house, with members elected from single-member districts, winner-take-all. Judiciary Independent constitutional court with appointed judges.

Party System Multiparty system. The Bharatiya Janata Party (BJP) is the dominant party; major opposition parties include the Congress Party, Janata Dal, and the Communist Party of India, Marxist (CPM).

Section ❶ The Making of the Modern Indian State

Politics in Action

On December 6, 1992, thousands of Hindus, encouraged by the Bharatiya Janata Party (BJP, Indian People's Party), stormed and destroyed a Muslim mosque in Ayodhya, India. In the accompanying riots, 1,700 people were killed.

In May 1998, the BJP-led coalition government proclaimed that India was a nuclear power, since it had successfully detonated five underground nuclear explosions.

*In late February and early March 2002, groups instigated by the **Hindu** nationalists attacked and killed well over 1,000 **Muslims** in the state of Gujarat, in apparent retaliation for an attack on a train bringing Hindu activists back from Ayodhya.*

The tense, tumultuous, bloody trek from Ayodhya to the nuclear bomb, back to Ayodhya, highlights the turbulent nature of Indian democracy in the early twenty-first century. It challenges images of an earlier era in which India exemplified principles of secularism, stability, and nonviolence. And yet, with it all, Indian democracy has endured and succeeded for well over half a century.

The Ayodhya incident was triggered by the electoral mobilization strategies of the BJP, a religious, nationalist party that had been courting the electoral and political support of Hindus, India's largest religious group at over 80 percent of the country's population. BJP leaders argued that the mosque at Ayodhya, a place of worship for India's Muslims, who constitute nearly 11 percent of India's population, had been built on the birthplace of the Hindu god Rama. They wanted to replace the mosque with a Hindu temple. The BJP mobilized Hindus, including unemployed youth and small traders, throughout India, in political protest. The political use of religious symbols touched a raw nerve in a multiethnic society in which religious conflict has a long history and memories of communal hostility and suspicion are ever present. After all, Indian independence in 1947 was achieved at the same time that the "jewel in the crown" of Britain's colonial empire was dismembered into mostly Hindu India and mostly Muslim Pakistan. The partition was achieved by vast migration between the two countries and widespread religious violence.

The BJP's successful use of religious divisions enabled it to emerge as India's ruling party in the 1998 parliamentary elections and again in general elections a year later. Shortly afterward, in fulfillment of one of

A crowd of Hindu nationalists listens to speeches by leaders around a disputed mosque in Ayodhya, a town in northern India, on December 6, 1992. The mosque was later torn down by belligerent volunteers, precipitating a major political crisis. *Source:* Bettmann/Corbis.

the BJP's electoral promises, the BJP-led coalition government gate-crashed the nuclear club, triggering a nuclear arms race in South Asia. Although the Indian government cited regional threats from China and Pakistan as the key reason, the decision to become a nuclear state can also be traced directly to the evolution of Indian democracy since the late 1980s. Electoral mobilization along ethnic lines (religious, language, or caste) in an atmosphere of economic turmoil and poverty prompted political parties to mobilize Indians' national pride, thereby deflecting attention from domestic economic and political problems. Within a few weeks, India's archenemy and neighbor, Pakistan, responded by testing its own bomb. Swift worldwide condemnation followed as many countries, including the United States, punished both countries with the imposition of economic and technology sanctions.

The riots in Gujarat in the spring of 2002 were among the worst that India has experienced in the postindependence period, compared even to the violence that accompanied the destruction of the mosque in Ayodhya. The catalyst for the violence was an attack on a trainload of pilgrims returning from Ayodhya, in which fifty-nine Hindus were killed. In the weeks that followed, Hindu groups engaged in a campaign of terror against the Muslim population of Gujarat. The rampage was a particularly grave challenge to democratic prin-

ciples because it was sanctioned by leading political officials of the BJP state government in Gujarat. Unlike riots of the past, which were an urban phenomenon, this one spread to the villages and gained the support of untouchables, the lowest caste in the Hindu caste hierarchy, and tribals, or indigenous peoples The violence often included sexual assaults on women. However, the tragedy far surpassed the immediate destruction of lives and property. With tacit support from the national government, the BJP government in Gujarat called for early elections in 2002 and won a landslide victory by capitalizing on the electoral support of the Hindus that it had mobilized during the riots.

These incidents capture three important themes in contemporary Indian politics. First, political struggles in a relatively poor, multicultural democracy are especially likely to be contentious. Many of these struggles readily become ethnic conflicts, broadly concerned with questions of religion, language, and caste. The most violent conflicts in India in the recent past have been religious and have often involved Hindus and Muslims. Protracted ethnic conflicts over territory have also acquired religious overtones, especially in Kashmir, a state in northern India in which Hindu-Muslim divisions are especially strong.

Second, although ethnic conflicts appear to be the products of primordial animosities, they are often

Indian nuclear test, May 1998.
Source: Baldev/Sygma.

instigated by political parties and the state. In recent years, the growing strength of the BJP, both in opposition and in office, has heavily contributed to religious polarization. As the development of the nuclear bomb and the riots suggest, the BJP's anti-Muslim stance has influenced both its domestic and foreign policy.

Although growing conflicts often push Indian democracy to the brink, the democratic system has managed to absorb the crises and muddle through for over half a century, albeit with strains. An important question for students of Indian politics, and comparative politics more generally, is how and why the second most populous country in the world, and one of the poorest, has maintained democratic institutions since it gained independence after World War II.

Geographic Setting

India is a big, populous, and geographically and culturally diverse country. Its large size, approximately 2,000 miles in both length and width, is rivaled in Asia only by China. Its rich geographic setting includes three diverse topographic zones (the mountainous northern zone, the basin formed by the Ganges River, and the peninsula of southern India) and a variety of climates (mountain climate in the northern mountain range; dry, hot weather in the arid, northern plateau; and subtropical climate in the south). Along with its neighbors Pakistan and Bangladesh, the region is physically isolated from the rest of Asia by the Himalayas to the north and the Indian Ocean to the east, south, and west. The northwest frontier is the only permeable frontier, and it is the route that successive invaders and migrants have used to enter this region.

India's population of over 1 billion people makes it the second largest country in the world, after its neighbor China. It is the world's largest democracy and the oldest democracy among the developing countries of Asia, Africa, and Latin America. India has functioned as a democracy with full adult suffrage since 1947, when it emerged as a sovereign nation-state following the end of British colonial rule. The durability of Indian democracy is especially intriguing considering the diversity of Indian society. Some fourteen major languages and numerous dialects are spoken. India contains many different ethnic groups, a host of regionally concentrated tribal groups, as well as adherents of virtually all the world's major religions. In addition to the majority Hindu population, India includes Muslims, **Sikhs,** Jains, Buddhists, Christians, and even several tiny Jewish communities. Furthermore, Indian society, especially Hindu society, is divided into myriad caste groupings. Although these are mainly based on occupation, they also tend to be closed social groups in the sense that people are born into, marry, and die within their caste. India is still largely an agrarian society; 73 percent of the population lives in far-flung villages in the rural areas. The major cities, Bombay, Calcutta, and New Delhi, the national capital, are densely populated.

Critical Junctures

India is among the most ancient civilizations of the world, dating back to the third millennium B.C. The Indian subcontinent, comprising Pakistan, India, and Bangladesh, has witnessed the rise and fall of many civilizations and empires. Only five of the most recent legacies that have shaped present-day politics are reviewed here.

The Colonial Legacy (1757–1947)

Motivated by a combination of economic and political interests, the British started making inroads into the Indian subcontinent in the late seventeenth and early eighteenth centuries. Since 1526, large sections of the subcontinent had been ruled by the Mughal dynasty, which hailed from Central Asia and was Muslim by religion. As the power of the Mughal emperors declined in the eighteenth century, lesser princely contenders vied with one another for supremacy. In this environment, the British East India Company, a large English trading organization with commercial interests in India and strong backing from the British Crown, was able to play off one Indian prince against another, forming alliances with some, subduing others, and thus strengthening its control through a policy of divide and rule.

This informal empire was replaced in the mid-nineteenth century with a more formal one. After a major revolt by an alliance of Indian princes against growing British power, known as the Sepoy Rebellion or the Mutiny of 1857, the British Crown assumed direct control of India. British rule over India from 1857 to

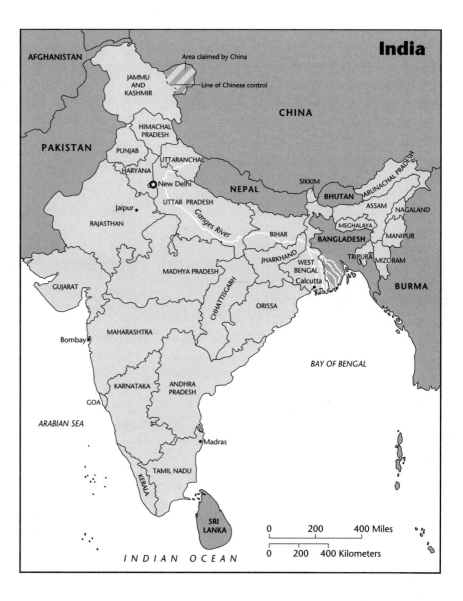

1947 left important legacies. Like other colonies, India contributed to Britain's Industrial Revolution because it was a source of cheap raw materials and provided an outlet for both British manufactured goods and investment. Colonial rule in India also provided a model for subsequent British colonial ventures.

In order to consolidate its political and economic hold over India, the British created three main varieties of ruling arrangements. First, numerous small- to medium-sized states, as many as five hundred covering an area equal to two-fifths of the subcontinent,

continued to be ruled throughout the colonial period by traditional Indian princes, the **Maharajas.** In exchange for accepting British rule, these Indian princes were allowed a relatively free hand within their realms. Second, in other parts of India, British indirect rule penetrated more deeply than in the princely states, for example, in the Bengal area (currently Bihar, West Bengal, and Bangladesh). In these regions, the British transformed traditional Indian elites, who controlled much agricultural land, into legal landlords, the *zamindars,* in exchange for periodic payments to the

Critical Junctures in Modern India's Development

1526	Mughal dynasty founded.
1612–1690	British East India Company establishes trading stations at Surat, Bombay, and Calcutta.
1757	Britain establishes informal colonial rule.
1857	Britain establishes formal colonial rule in response to Sepoy Rebellion.
1885	Indian National Congress is created.
1947	India achieves independence from Britain; India and Pakistan are partitioned; modern Indian state is founded.
1947–1964	Jawaharlal Nehru is prime minister.
1966–1984	Indira Gandhi is prime minister (except for a brief period from 1977 to 1980).
1990–Present	Rise of the Bharatiya Janata Party and India's emergence as a nuclear power.

colonial administration. Third, the British established direct rule in the remaining regions of India, for example, in Bombay and the Madras presidencies (large areas around the cities of the same name), where British civil servants were directly responsible for collecting land taxes and adjudicating law and order.

Whatever its particular forms, British rule seldom reached very deep into Indian society, especially in rural areas, which were organized into countless relatively self-sufficient villages. Social life within villages was further divided by religiously sanctioned caste groups. Typically, a few landowning castes dominated many other castes lower in the ritual, occupational, and income hierarchies.

The British sought to create a semblance of coherence in India through the creation of a central government that controlled and led these various territories and indigenous authority structures. Important instruments included the creation of an all-India civil service, police force, and army. Although at first only British nationals could serve in these institutions, with the introduction of modern educational institutions, some educated Indians were incorporated into government services. Unlike many other colonies, particularly in Africa, the British helped create a relatively effective state structure in India. When India emerged from

British rule in 1947, it inherited, maintained, and expanded colonial institutions. The civil administration, police, and armed services in contemporary India continue to be organized along the principles established by the British colonialists in the last century. Thus, there is close continuity between the modern Indian state and the British colonial tradition.

The Nationalist Movement (1885–1947)

With the growth of commerce, education, and urbanization, groups of urban, educated upper caste Indian elites emerged as the new Indian leaders. They both observed and closely interacted with their colonial rulers and often felt slighted by their treatment as second-class citizens. Even at this stage, a secular-religious divide was apparent. Some of them were Hindu nationalists who believed that a reformed Hinduism could provide a basis for a new, modern India. Others were attracted to British liberal ideas and invoked these to seek greater equality with the British.

Two centuries of British colonial rule witnessed growing intellectual and cultural ferment in India. The British colonial rulers and traditional Indian elites had become allies of sorts, squeezing from the poor Indian peasantry resources that were simultaneously used to maintain the colonial bureaucratic state and support the conspicuous lifestyles of a parasitic landlord class. It was not long before Indian nationalists opposed these arrangements through the Indian National Congress (INC), which was actually formed by an Englishman in 1885. Its aim was to right the racial, cultural, and political wrongs of colonial rule. In its early years, the INC was mainly a collection of Indian urban elites who periodically met and petitioned India's British rulers, invoking liberal principles of political equality and requesting greater Indian involvement in higher political offices. The British largely ignored these requests, and over time, the requests turned into demands, pushing some nationalists into militancy and others into nonviolent mass mobilization.

World War I was an important turning point for Indian nationalists. After the war, as great European empires disintegrated, creating new sovereign states in Europe and the Middle East, the principle of self-determination for people who considered themselves a nation gained international respectability. Indian nationalists were also inspired by the Russian revolution of 1917, which they viewed as a successful uprising against imperialism.

The man most responsible for helping to transform the INC from a narrow, elitist club to a mass nationalist movement was Mohandas Karamchand Gandhi, called Mahatma ("great soul") by his followers, one of the most influential and admirable leaders of the twentieth century. After becoming the leader of the INC in the 1920s, Gandhi successfully mobilized the middle classes, as well as a segment of the peasantry, into an anti-British movement that came to demand full sovereignty for India.

Three characteristics of the nationalist movement greatly influenced state building and democracy in India. First, the INC came to embody the principle of

Leaders: *Mahatma Gandhi*

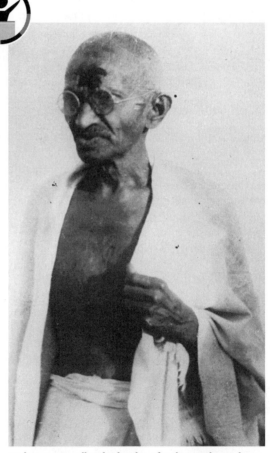

Born in 1869 in western India, Mohandas Gandhi studied law in London for two years and worked in Durban, South Africa, as a lawyer and an activist for twenty-one years before returning home to join the Indian nationalist movement. His work among the different communities in South Africa helped him to develop the political strategies of nonviolence, or *satyagraha* (grasp of truth). On his arrival in India in 1915, he set about transforming the Indian National Congress into a mass party by reaching out to the urban and rural poor, non-Hindu religious groups, and the scheduled castes, whom he called *Harijans,* or Children of God. Following the British massacre of unarmed civilians gathered in protest in the Punjab (at the Jallianwala Bagh, a location well-known in Indian history) in April 1919, Gandhi and Jawaharlal Nehru proposed a noncooperation movement. This required a boycott of British legal and educational institutions as well as British merchandise, for which were substituted indigenous, or *swadeshi,* varieties. (The image of Gandhi weaving his own cloth is familiar to many.) Gandhi believed that mass civil disobedience could succeed only if people were truly committed. The involvement of some Congress workers in a violent incident in 1922 greatly disturbed him, causing him to call off the noncooperation movement. Gandhi was strongly opposed to the partition of India along religious lines in 1947, but because he had resigned from the Congress in 1934, his protests went unheard. Nevertheless, he dominated India's nationalist movement for more than two decades until he was assassinated in January 1948, five months after India achieved its goal of self-rule, or *swaraj.* He is often referred to as the Mahatma, or "great soul."

Mahatma Gandhi, the leader of India's independence movement as he appeared at the head of a 200-mile march, staged in defiance of the statute establishing a government salt monopoly by the British colonial government in 1930. *Source:* UPI/Bettmann.

unity within diversity, which served India well in creating and maintaining a relatively stable political system. Because the INC became a powerful political organization committed to establishing an Indian nation, many conflicts could play themselves out within the INC without undermining its unity. Second, although a variety of Indians in their encounter with the British discovered what they had in common with each other, they also recognized their differences. The most serious conflict was between Hindus and Muslims. A segment of the Indian Muslim elite refused to accept the leadership of Gandhi and the INC, demanded separate political rights for Muslims, and called for an independent Muslim state when the INC refused.

The resulting division of the subcontinent into two sovereign states in 1947—the Muslim state of Pakistan and the secular state of India—was turbulent and bloody. Millions of Muslims fled from India to Pakistan, and millions of Hindus fled the other way; nearly 20 million people migrated, and up to 3 million may have died in communal violence. The euphoria of independence in India was thus tempered by the human tragedy that accompanied the subcontinent's partition.

Third, the nationalist movement laid the foundations for democracy in India. Although Gandhi pioneered the use of civil disobedience to challenge British laws that he regarded as unjust, he did so on the basis of profound ethical commitments and nonviolent means. Many of the INC's prominent leaders, like Jawaharlal Nehru, were educated in England and were committed democrats. Moreover, the INC participated in limited elections allowed by the British, ran democratic governments with limited powers in various British-controlled Indian provinces, and chose its own leaders through internal elections. These preindependence democratic tendencies were valuable assets to Indian democracy.

During the 1920s and 1930s, Gandhi, Nehru, and other leaders of the INC were increasingly successful in mobilizing Indians in an anti-British nationalist movement for India's independence. The more successful the movement became, the more the British either had to repress the INC or make concessions, and they tried both. However, World War II consumed Britain's energies, and the economic and symbolic costs of colonization became extremely onerous. In order to gain Indian support for its war efforts, the British promised Indians independence following the war. India became a sovereign state in August 1947, when the British, weakened from World War II, decided to withdraw from the subcontinent.

The Nehru Era (1947–1964)

Within India, Jawaharlal Nehru, who Gandhi favored, emerged as the leader of the new nation. Soon after, a militant member of the extremist anti-Muslim Hindu cultural organization, the *Rashtriya Swayam Sevak Sangh* (RSS), assassinated Gandhi, who had opposed partition and later ardently defended Muslims within India. Nehru became the uncontested leader of a new India, a position he maintained until his death in 1964. The years of Nehru's rule shaped the dominant patterns of India's future development.

Nehru's India inherited an ambiguous legacy from British rule: a relatively strong central government and a weak economy. Nehru, a committed nationalist and social democrat, sought to strengthen India's independence and national power and to improve its economy and the lives of the Indian poor. He used the governmental machinery that India had inherited to accomplish these tasks.

At independence, India was confronted with major political problems, including a massive inflow of refugees, war with Pakistan over the disputed state of Kashmir, situated between the two countries, and the need to consolidate numerous Indian princely states into a coherent national state. Concerned about India's capacity to deal with such problems, Nehru and other leaders depended on and further strengthened the civil, police, and armed services that were legacies of colonial rule.

After independence, India adopted a democratic constitution and established a British-style democracy with full adult suffrage. Because political power now required winning elections, the INC had to transform itself from an opposition movement into a political party, the Congress Party. It was highly successful in doing so, in part by establishing a nationwide patronage system. Another important change in the decade following independence was the linguistic reorganization of states. As in the United States, the Indian constitution defines India as a federal system. The contentious political issue in the 1950s was the criterion by which Indian political groups could demand a state within the federal union. With Indians divided by the languages they speak, an

Leaders: *The Nehru-Gandhi Dynasty*

Jawaharlal Nehru

Jawaharlal Nehru was a staunch believer in liberal democratic principles. Along with Gandhi and others, he was at the forefront of India's nationalist movement against the British. When India became independent in 1947, Nehru became prime minister as head of the Congress Party and retained that position until his death in 1964. During this period, he established India as a socialist, democratic, and secular state in theory, if not always in practice. On the international front, he helped found the nonaligned movement, a forum for expressing the interests and aspirations of developing countries that did not want to ally with the United States or the Soviet Union during the cold war. Nehru attempted to set India on a rapid road to industrialization by establishing heavy industry. His efforts to effect redistribution of wealth through land reform were combined with an equally strong commitment to democratic and individual rights, such as the right to private property. Upon his death, India inherited a stable polity, a functioning democracy, and an economy characterized by a large public sector and an intricate pattern of state control over the private sector.

Indira Gandhi

Indira Gandhi became prime minister shortly after the death of her father, Jawaharlal Nehru, and dominated the Indian political scene until her assassination in 1984. Her years in power strengthened India's international position, but her domestic policies weakened the organizational structure of the Congress Party. Her tendencies toward centralization and the personalization of authority within the Congress and the concomitant use of populist rhetoric in electoral campaigns contributed to the erosion of the Congress Party. By presenting the regional conflict in the Punjab and problems with Pakistan as Hindu-Sikh and Hindu-Muslim problems, respectively, she contributed to further erosion of the party's secular base and to rising religious factionalism. Her decision to send troops into the holiest of the holy Sikh temples in Amritsar deeply alienated Sikhs, a small but important religious group in India. The ensuing bloodshed culminated in her assassination by one of her Sikh bodyguards in 1984. Her assassination ushered in a new generation of the Nehru-Gandhi dynasty, as her son Rajiv Gandhi served as prime minister until 1989.

obvious basis for the federal system was to organize constituent units based on language groups. Hindi is the most widely spoken Indian language; however, most Hindi speakers are concentrated in the north-central part of the country. Indians living in the south, east, and parts of the west speak a variety of other languages. Concerned about domination by Hindi speakers, many of these non-Hindi groups demanded a reorganization of the Indian union into linguistically defined states. Initially, Nehru resisted this demand, worried that linguistic states within a federation might become secessionist and demand sovereignty. As demands for linguistic states mounted, especially from south Indian groups, Nehru compromised in 1956: the new Indian union was organized around fourteen linguistically defined states. Following subsequent changes, there are now twenty-eight major states within India.

Another legacy of the Nehru era is noteworthy. Jawaharlal Nehru was an internationalist who wanted India to play a global role. However, as he was consolidating power in India, the cold war was unfolding between the Soviet Union and the United States. Together with postcolonial leaders of Asia and Africa, Nehru initiated what became known as the nonaligned movement, which united those countries wishing to maintain a distance from the two superpowers. India and many other developing countries viewed both Western capitalism and Soviet communism with suspicion. Under Nehru, India played a leadership role among other nonaligned developing countries while pursuing mixed economic policies at home that were neither fully capitalist nor fully socialist (see Section 2).

Nehru's initiatives put India firmly on a stable, democratic road. However the strong, centralized state that

Nehru created also had some negative long-term consequences. The new Indian state came to resemble the old British Indian state that Nehru and others had so vociferously opposed. The colonial state's tendency to favor traditional Indian elites carried over into the Nehru era. Powerful groups in the society, including elite bureaucrats, wealthy landowners, entrepreneurs, and leaders of well-organized ethnic movements, enjoyed a favored position. While Nehru and the Congress Party continued to maintain a pro-poor, socialist rhetoric, they generally failed to deliver on their promises.

The Indira Gandhi Era (1966–1984)

When Nehru died in 1964, the Congress Party was divided over the choice of a successor and hurriedly selected mild-mannered Lal Bahadur Shastri to be prime minister. When he died of a heart attack in 1966 and rivalry again broke out over his successor, party elites found a compromise candidate in Nehru's daughter, Indira Gandhi. They chose her to capitalize on the fact that as Nehru's daughter, she would help the Congress Party garner the electoral support it needed to remain in power. They also calculated that she would be a weak woman who could be manipulated by competing factions within the party. They were right about the first point, but decisively wrong about the second.

As prime minister from 1966 to 1984, except for the brief period of 1977 to 1980, Indira Gandhi's rule had several long-term legacies for contemporary Indian democracy. First, Indian politics became more personalized, populist, and nationalist. To bolster her popularity, Indira Gandhi deliberately whipped up Indian nationalism. During the late 1960s, the Bengali-speaking eastern half of Pakistan, which was separated from its western half by nearly 1,000 miles of Indian territory, demanded sovereignty. As violence escalated within Pakistan and refugees from East Pakistan began pouring into India, Gandhi ordered Indian forces to intervene. This led to the creation of the sovereign state of Bangladesh. Because the United States sided with Pakistan in that conflict (and the Soviet Union backed India), Indira Gandhi was able to mobilize Indian nationalist sentiment against both Pakistan and the United States. This war-related victory added to her popularity. She soon consolidated her leadership over the Congress Party, forcing out leaders who opposed her and replacing them with loyal allies. The result was to create a new Congress Party in her own image. Subsequently, she portrayed the old Congress elite as defending the status quo and preventing her from helping the poor. Gandhi's populist rhetoric won her immense popularity among India's poor. From 1971 to 1984, she dominated Indian politics as much as Mahatma Gandhi or her father ever had.

A second legacy of Indira Gandhi's rule was to further centralize the Indian political system. During the Nehru era, local elites had helped select higher political officeholders, but in the 1970s, Indira Gandhi directly appointed officeholders at both the national and regional levels. Although this strategy enabled her to gain a firm grip over the party, it isolated her from broader political forces and eroded the legitimacy of local leaders.

A third important legacy of Indira Gandhi's rule was her failure to translate populist rhetoric into real gains for India's poor. She was unable to redistribute agricultural land from large landowners to those who worked the land or generate employment, provide welfare, or improve access by the poor to education and medical services. The reasons are complex and controversial. Some analysts argue that she was never sincere in her commitment to the poor and that her populism was mainly a strategy for gaining votes. Given the magnitude of India's poverty, however, even sincere efforts faced a monumental task.

Indian politics became more and more turbulent under Indira Gandhi, a fourth legacy of her rule. As her popularity soared, so did the opposition to her. The old Congress elite denounced her populist political style, arguing that her government was corrupt and that India needed to oust her from power and clean up the government. Led by a credible follower of Mahatma Gandhi, Jai Prakash Narain, they began organizing mass demonstrations and strikes to press their case. During 1974, the political situation in India became unstable, with the opposition organizing general strikes and Indira Gandhi threatening massive state repression. When Narain called on the Indian armed forces to mutiny, Gandhi declared a national **Emergency,** suspended many democratic rights, and arrested most opposition leaders. The Emergency lasted nearly two years, the only period since 1947 when India was not a democracy.

In 1977, Indira Gandhi rescinded the Emergency

and called for national elections, confidently expecting that she would win. To her surprise, she was soundly defeated, and for the first time since independence, a non-Congress government came to power. Various groups that had opposed Gandhi hastily joined together in a loosely organized party (the Janata Party) and won power. Indira Gandhi's authoritarian measures during the Emergency were so unpopular that the newly formed party was able to unite India's fragmented opposition groups and achieve electoral success. However, soon after the elections, Janata leaders became factionalized and the Janata government collapsed, providing a new opportunity for Indira Gandhi to regain power in the 1980 parliamentary elections.

Indira Gandhi's tenure in power between 1980 and 1984 resembled the preceding period, in that it was marked by a personal and populist political style, an increasingly centralized political system, failure to implement antipoverty policies, and growing political turbulence. However, she departed from her previous approach in two ways. The first was in the realm of the economy. During the 1970s, India's industrial establishment grew relatively slowly because the government spent too much on buying political support and too little on investment; incomes of the poor were not improving and therefore demand for new products was limited; and excessive rules and regulations were counterproductive, both for domestic entrepreneurs and for integrating India into the world economy. With few means to rechannel government spending or improve the spending capacity of the poor, Gandhi started liberalizing the rules that governed India's economy.

The second important change concerns the strategy Indira Gandhi employed to achieve electoral support. It was clear that continuing appeals to poverty alleviation would not provide a successful electoral strategy, because poverty had not diminished and would not without greater government intervention. Meanwhile government policy was tending toward liberalization. With the loss of populist promises as a strategy to win support, the prime minister needed to devise alternative appeals to socialism and secularism, which both she and her father had championed since the 1950s. In the early 1980s, Indira Gandhi began to use religious appeals to mobilize India's Hindu majority. By introducing religion into politics, the Congress Party sowed the seeds for the growth of the Hindu nationalist BJP and thereby accelerated its own demise.

Religious conflicts began to reenter Indian politics in the early 1980s, as illustrated by the growing conflict between the Sikh religious minority, based in the Punjab, and the national government. During the course of the conflict, Indian security forces invaded and extensively damaged the holiest Sikh shrine, the Golden Temple in the city of Amritsar, to attack Sikh militants besieged there. The resulting alienation of Sikhs from Gandhi peaked when she was assassinated in 1984 by one of her Sikh bodyguards.

Immediately after her assassination, rampaging mobs of Hindus brutally murdered Sikhs in New Delhi, Kanpur, and other north Indian cities. Most of the 3,700 Sikh victims were poor. Anti-Sikh violence was not spontaneous but orchestrated by some leading figures within the Congress Party. In this respect, it resembled the anti-Muslim violence organized by BJP party and state leaders in the following decade.

Indira's son, Rajiv Gandhi, won a landslide victory in the subsequent national elections as a result of the sympathy wave that his mother's assassination generated. He came to office promising clean government, a high-tech economy that would carry India into the next century, and reduced ethnic conflict. He was somewhat successful in ameliorating tensions in the state of Punjab, helped by the fact that the Sikh independence movement lost popular support and was repressed by the state. But Rajiv Gandhi inflamed tensions between Hindus and Muslims by sponsoring a law that placed Muslim women under the purview of the family. He left office in 1989 under a cloud after a scandal involving an arms deal with the Swedish Bofors company.

With Indira Gandhi's death, the tradition of powerful and populist prime ministers came to an end. India has since been facing a crisis of governance that began during the Indira Gandhi era. This was evident in increasing factionalism within the Congress Party, India's dominant party since independence. Moreover, other secular political parties proved unable to fill the vacuum in government caused by the Congress Party's disintegration. Since 1984, only two governments, both Congress led, have lasted their full terms: under Rajiv Gandhi (1984–1989) and under Narasimha Rao (1991–1996). Rao rode to victory on a sympathy vote for

Congress when Rajiv Gandhi was assassinated in 1991 while campaigning for election. However, the Congress Party split in 1995, further contributing to the fragmentation of the entire party system.

Coalition Governments and the Growth of the BJP (1989 to the Present)

In the five general elections since 1989, no single party has won a majority of seats in parliamentary elections. A succession of unstable coalition and minority governments ruled from 1989 to 1998. Since then, India has been led by BJP coalition governments, with Atal Behari Vajpayee as prime minister.

The tendency for Indian elections to produce unstable and short-lived coalitions at the national level has grown because no party has been able to fill the vacuum created by the Congress Party's decline. Coalition governments at the national level and in most states have generally been hurriedly arranged and poorly conceived. The cement that binds coalitions together has more often been negative than positive. For example, opposition to Congress brought governments to power in 1977 and 1989. By the early 1990s, when the Congress had crumbled and hence was not an attractive target to oppose, opposition to the BJP provided the major incentive for coalitional arrangements among regional and lower caste parties (see Table 1).

Politics in India today is characterized by governments of precarious coalitions, weakened political institutions, and considerable political activism along ethnic lines. These developments have generated policies that range from limited action on the economic front to nationalist outbursts on the military front. Whether any party or charismatic leader capable of unifying the country across the salient cleavages will emerge remains to be seen.

Themes and Implications
Historical Junctures and Political Themes

India in a World of States. India's domestic difficulties both reflect and influence its changing status in the world of states. In an increasingly interdependent global political and economic system, India's attainment of nuclear power signaled the dawn of a new era. As a

Table 1

Prime Ministers of India, 1947–Present

	Years in Office	Party
Jawaharlal Nehru	1947–1964	Congress
Lal Bahadur Shastri	1964–1966	Congress
Indira Gandhi	1966–1977	Congress
Morarji Desai	1977–1979	Janata
Charan Singh	1979–1980	Janata
Indira Gandhi	1980–1984	Congress
Rajiv Gandhi	1984–1989	Congress
V. P. Singh	1989–1990	Janata
Chandra Shekhar	1990–1991	Janata (Socialist)
Narasimha Rao	1991–1996	Congress
Atal Bihari Vajpayee	1996 (13 days)	BJP & allies
H. D. Deve Gowda	1996–1997	United Front
I. K. Gujral	1997–1998	United Front
Atal Bihari Vajpayee	1998–1999, 1999–	BJP & allies

result, simmering historical tensions over territories such as Kashmir will need to be managed very carefully. India now shares borders with two nuclear powers, China and Pakistan, and has engaged in wars and periodic border skirmishes with both. With the end of the cold war, managing regional tensions poses problems. India and Pakistan have fought three wars, and their politicians have exploited the tensions between them during domestic political crises. The challenge facing the Indian state is how to prevent domestic pressures from escalating into international belligerence.

Governing the Economy. Successful economic performance is necessary for India to fulfill its national and domestic ambitions. Indian policy-makers initially sought economic self-sufficiency through a policy of state-led industrialization focused on meeting the needs of its large internal market. This protectionist economic strategy had mixed results. Although it resulted in the development of some important basic industries, it also generated extensive inefficiencies and did little to alleviate the country's severe poverty. Like many other developing nations, India must adjust its economic strategy to meet the demands of increasingly competitive and interdependent global markets.

But in a global environment that requires making quick decisions and grasping ephemeral opportunities, the halting steps taken by Indian economic liberalizers have fallen short of expectations. How can India prevent its liberalization policy from being held hostage by entrenched elites? How can policy-makers simultaneously pursue economic reforms and provide for social benefits through well-aimed schemes that avoid clientalism and patronage? Will liberalization of India's state-controlled economy provide a basis for increased wealth in an extremely poor country? These are among the daunting challenges that face Indian leaders and observers concerned about the future of this continent-sized, poor democracy.

The Democratic Idea.   The democratic idea has been sustained in India for over half a century, barring a short period of authoritarianism between 1977 and 1979. India can boast of a vibrant and vigilant civil society, periodic elections, unfettered media, and relatively autonomous courts and bureaucracy. However, these institutions have been corroded over the years. For example, Indira Gandhi's radical posturing brought turbulence to Indian democracy, damaged the economy, and never provided real benefits to the poor. Since the late 1980s, political parties have deployed electoral strategies that have exacerbated ethnic tensions. The challenge that India faces is how to balance an increasingly divided society with the demands of social, economic, and political citizenship for all. Given the fact that the vast majority of India's citizens are Hindu, the danger is that political parties will be tempted to mobilize on the basis of Hindu religious identity and thereby marginalize India's religious minority communities. Indeed, this is precisely the scenario that brought the BJP to power in 1998.

Paradoxically, Indian democracy has become more democratic in some ways and less so in others. More groups with more diverse identities are participating in politics than ever before. They are joining a larger range of political parties from more diverse regions of the country. The Indian political class can no longer be identified with a single region, caste, and class. However, a key ingredient of democracy is the protection of minority rights, and on this count, India is less democratic than in the past. Sikhs, Christians, and above all Muslims have suffered brutal attacks since the mid-1980s. Muslims have been rendered especially vulnerable. Democracy and identity politics have become intricately linked, often in destructive fashion, in contemporary Indian politics.

The Politics of Collective Identity.   That there are intense conflicts around the issue of collective identity is not surprising in multicultural India. What is alarming is how mobilization of the electorate on ethnic grounds could corrode democratic values. Democracy is supposed to provide a level playing field for a tussle between different interests and identities. But the victory of the BJP, a Hindu nationalist party, has deepened regional and religious divisions and changed the nature of Indian democracy. India faces the challenge of reconciling domestic electoral strategies of ethnic mobilization to capture power with the demands of moderation demanded in the exercise of such power and the challenge of coping with demands of multiethnic and multiclass groups and sustaining economic growth.

Implications for Comparative Politics

There are exceptional political features of the Indian state that have great significance for the study of comparative politics. First, India is a poor yet vibrant democracy. Most Indians value their citizenship rights and exercise them vigorously, despite widespread poverty and illiteracy. Theories of modernization have usually posited that democracy and economic growth are conjoined, but India stands out as an exception. At independence, the country was struggling with problems of nation building, poverty, poor human development indicators, and managing a transition to democracy. Against all odds, India became and remains a thriving democracy, an achievement especially striking when compared to the authoritarian fate of other newly independent British colonies in Asia and Africa.

Second, unlike other multiethnic states such as Yugoslavia and the former Soviet Union, which disintegrated with the advent of democracy, the Indian state has managed to remain cohesive and stable—although this must be qualified by the severe turmoil at various times in the states of Assam, Punjab, Gujarat, and especially Kashmir. Indian politics thus offers a case study of the tempering influence of democracy on ethnic cleavages. Contrast the exclusionary rhetoric of

Hindu nationalism during the BJP's tenure as an opposition party with its rhetorical shift toward moderation as India's ruling party. In an attempt to stabilize a fractious multiparty coalition government, the BJP was forced to put contentious religious issues such as the temple in Ayodhya on a back burner.

Third, as home to 1 billion people with diverse cultural, religious, and linguistic ties, Indian democracy offers an arena for testing and studying various theories and dilemmas of comparative politics. For instance, one dilemma in comparative politics is how multiethnic democracies can develop a coherent institutional system that gives representation to diverse interests without degenerating into authoritarianism or total collapse. The history of the Congress Party until the Indira Gandhi era demonstrates how one party successfully managed to unite diverse and multiple ethnic identities under one umbrella.

Fourth, theorists dealing with recent transitions to democracy in Latin America and Eastern Europe have puzzled over the question of what constitutes a consolidated democracy and how one achieves such consolidation. Here, a comparison of India with Pakistan would help us evaluate the role of historical junctures, leaders, and their interaction with institutions. At independence, Pakistan adopted a centralized, authoritarian, system, while India created a federal, parliamentary state. These decisions had critical implications. India has functioned as a democracy for all but two years since 1947, whereas Pakistan has functioned as an authoritarian state for most of the same period. Moreover, the Indian experience with authoritarianism during the Emergency era in the late 1970s, and the resurgence of democratic norms when Indira Gandhi was voted out by an angry populace, shows the importance of elections. It also shows that the existence of democratic institutions and procedures leads to the diffusion of democratic norms throughout the society.

Fifth, comparativists have focused on the dilemma of whether democracy and social equity can be achieved simultaneously in poor countries. The case of Kerala, a state in southern India, suggests an affirmative answer. Although it is one of the poorer states in India, Kerala has achieved near total literacy, long life expectancy, low infant mortality, and high access to medical care. Kerala's development indicators compare favorably with the rest of India, other low-income countries, and even wealthy countries like the United States.

This discussion of critical junctures in Indian history highlights the central challenge of contemporary Indian politics: how to establish a coherent, legitimate government and use its power to facilitate economic growth and equitable distribution. The former requires forming durable electoral coalitions without exacerbating political passions and ethnic conflicts. The latter requires careful implementation of policies that simultaneously help entrepreneurs produce goods and ensure a fair distribution of the growth in production. The remainder of this chapter describes how India is coping with these challenges.

Section ❷ Political Economy and Development

At the time of independence, India was largely a poor, agricultural economy. Although it still has a very large agricultural sector and considerable poverty, India today also has a quite substantial industrial base and a vibrant middle class. Since the introduction of economic liberalization policies under Narasimha Rao's Congress government in 1991, all Indian governments have supported economic reform. Before discussing what liberalization entails, why it has become a priority, and what its implications are for Indian politics, we review the development of the Indian political economy historically.

State and Economy

The Economy Under British Rule

During the colonial period, the Indian economy was largely agricultural, with hundreds of millions of poor peasants living in thousands of small villages, tilling the land with primitive technology, and producing at a low level of efficiency. The British, along with Indian landlords, extracted extensive land revenues, land taxes, and tributes from Indian princes. However, they reinvested only a small portion of this surplus into improving agricultural production. Most resources were squandered through conspicuous consumption by Indian princes and landlords or used to finance the expensive colonial government. The result of this mismanagement of resources was that Indian agricultural productivity, that is, the amount of wheat, rice, and other products produced from one unit of land, mostly stagnated in the first half of the twentieth century. Agricultural productivity in India was considerably lower in 1950 than in Japan or even China.

Some industry developed under colonial rule, but its scope was limited. The British sold their own manufactured goods to India in exchange for Indian raw materials. Because the British economy was more advanced, it was difficult for Indians to compete successfully. Indigenous manufacturing, especially of textiles, and artisanal production were ruined by the forced opening of the Indian market to British goods. Thus, the Indian economy at independence in 1947 was relatively stagnant, especially in agriculture and industrial development.

The Economy After Independence

One of the central tasks facing Indian leaders after 1947 was to modernize the sluggish economy. During Nehru's rule, India adopted a model of development based largely on private property, although there was extensive government ownership of firms and government guidance to private economic activity. Nehru created a powerful planning commission that, following the Soviet model, made five-year plans for the Indian economy, outlining the activities in which government investment would be concentrated. Unlike the plans in communist party states, however, the Indian plans also indicated priority areas for private entrepreneurs, who remained a powerful force in the Indian economy.

The Indian government levied high tariffs on imports, arguing that new Indian industries, so long disadvantaged under colonial rule, required protection from foreign competitors. The government tightly regulated the start-up and expansion of private industries under the presumption that the government was a better safeguard of the public interest than private entrepreneurs. This government-planned private economy achieved mixed results. It helped India create an impressive industrial base but did little to help the poor, and its protected industries were quite inefficient by global standards.

Nationalist in temperament, Nehru and other Congress Party leaders were suspicious of involving foreign investors in India's economic development. The government thus undertook a series of coordinated economic activities on its own. It made significant public sector investments to create such heavy industries as steel and cement; protected Indian entrepreneurs from foreign competition; where possible, further subsidized these producers; and finally, created elaborate rules and regulations controlling the activities of private producers. As a result, India developed a substantial industrial base over the next few decades.

Congress leaders promised to redistribute land from landowners to tenants in order to weaken the former supporters of the colonial government and motivate the tillers of the land to increase production. Although some of the largest landowners were indeed eliminated in the early 1950s, poor tenants and agricultural laborers received very little land. Unlike the communist government in China, India's nationalist government had neither the will nor the capacity to undertake radical property redistribution. Instead, most of the land remained in the hands of medium- to large-sized landowners. Many became part of the Congress political machine in the countryside. This development further weakened the Congress Party's capacity to assist the rural poor and undermined its socialist commitments.

The failure of land reforms led to a new agricultural strategy in the late 1960s known as the **green revolution.** Instead of addressing land redistribution, the state sought to provide landowners with improved seeds and access to subsidized fertilizer. Because irrigation was essential for this strategy to succeed and because irrigation was assured only to larger farmers in some regions of India, the success of the green revolution was uneven. Production increased sharply in some areas, such as the Punjab, but other regions (and especially the poorer farmers in these regions) got left behind. Nevertheless, as a result of this strategy, India became self-sufficient in food (and even became a food exporter), thus avoiding the mass starvation and famines that had occurred in the past.

Between 1950 and 1980, the Indian government facilitated what has been described as **state-led economic development.** This development policy consisted of an expansion of the public sector, protection of the domestic sector from foreign competition, and rules and regulations to control private sector activity. Political leaders hoped to strengthen India's international position by promoting self-sufficient industrialization. To a great extent, the Indian government succeeded in achieving this goal. By 1980, India was a major industrial power able to produce its own steel, airplanes, automobiles, chemicals, military hardware, and many consumer goods. On the agricultural side, although land reforms failed, the revised agricultural strategy improved food production.

State-led development insulated the Indian economy from global influences while aligning the Indian state with business and landowning classes. The strategy resulted in modest economic growth—not as impressive as that of Brazil, Mexico, or the Republic of Korea but better than that of Nigeria. The main beneficiaries were business classes, medium and large landowning farmers, and political and bureaucratic elites. A substantial urban middle class also developed during this phase. However, state-led development was associated with a number of problems. First, given the lack of competition, much industry was inefficient by global standards. Second, the elaborate rules and regulations controlling private economic activity encouraged corruption, as entrepreneurs bribed bureaucrats to get around the rules. And third, the focus on heavy industry directed a substantial portion of new investment into buying machinery rather than creating jobs. As a result, 40 percent of India's population, primarily poor tenant farmers and landless laborers, did not share in the fruits of this growth. And because population growth continued, the number of desperately poor people increased substantially during these decades.

Economic Liberalization

A number of global and national changes moved India toward **economic liberalization** beginning in the 1980s and accelerating after 1991. Throughout the 1980s, socialist models of development came under attack. Within India, political and economic elites were increasingly dissatisfied with India's relatively sluggish economic performance, especially compared with dynamic East Asian economies. For example, during the 1970s, whereas India's economy grew at the rate of 3.4 percent per year, South Korea's grew at 9.6 percent. New elites coming to power in India, less nationalist

and socialist than their predecessors, interpreted the country's slow economic growth as a product of excessive governmental controls and of India's relative insulation from the global economy. India's business and industrial classes increasingly found government intervention in the economy more of a hindrance than a help. Realizing that the poverty of most Indians limited the possibility for expanding domestic markets, they increasingly sought to export their products.

India's economy did relatively well during the 1980s and 1990s, growing at nearly 5 percent per year, a record especially noteworthy when compared to the dismal performance of many debt-ridden Latin American and African economies, such as Brazil and Nigeria. Some of this improved performance resulted from economic liberalization that further integrated India into the global economy. Some resulted from public loans to small factory owners and farmers and public investments in their enterprises. However, a large part of economic growth in the 1980s was based on increased borrowing from abroad, which represented a shift from a fairly conservative fiscal policy. This expansionary fiscal policy, largely funded by foreign loans, was risky because India's exports to other countries did not grow very rapidly. For example, its exports during the 1980s grew at approximately 6 percent per year in comparison to 12 percent per year for both South Korea and China. As a result, the need to repay foreign loans put enormous pressure on the government toward the end of the decade. India was forced in the early 1990s to borrow even more from such international agencies as the International Monetary Fund (IMF) and World Bank. In return for fresh loans, these international organizations required the Indian government to reduce its deficit through such controversial measures as reducing subsidies to the poor and selling government shares in public enterprises to the private sector. Critics allege that the government sold many public enterprises at prices well below their market value.

Liberalization has both a domestic and an international component. The government has sought to dismantle controls over private sector economic activities, especially in industry. More recently, new industries have been created, including oil and natural gas, transportation infrastructure, telecommunications, and power generation. The government has provided a variety of incentives to industry, including tax breaks, eliminating customs duties on the import of equipment, and underwriting losses.

Over the years, the government has progressively increased the scope of stockholding by foreign enterprises and of foreign direct investment in key industries, including pharmaceuticals, and coal mining. For the first time, it allowed multinational investment in natural resources. The government invited bids from private and foreign companies to invest in twenty-five oil and gas exploration blocks in the country. The agreement provides for a seven-year tax holiday from the date of commencement of commercial production; no customs duty on imports required for petroleum operations; a 100 percent cost recovery on exploration, production, and development; and full recovery of all royalties paid to the Indian government for the oil or gas extracted.[1] Such arrangements would have been unthinkable until a few years ago.

Foreign investment has increased significantly, from $100 million a year between 1970 and 1991 to nearly $4 billion annually between 1992 and 1998. In 2000, the government authorized increased foreign direct investment in eight areas: pharmaceuticals, coal and lignite for power plants, tourism, mining, prospecting for gold and diamonds, advertising, pollution control machinery, and the film industry. However, the level of foreign direct investment in India—2 to 3 percent of the annual gross domestic product (GDP)—is relatively modest; China and Brazil receive several times that volume each year.[2] Furthermore, because foreign investment focuses on the domestic market, it has not always facilitated export promotion, which is potentially one of its major benefits in poor countries.

One high-tech sector in which India has excelled is computer software. Indian firms and multinational corporations with operations in India take ample advantage of India's highly skilled and poorly paid scientific and engineering talent to make India a world leader in the production of software. India can boast the equivalent of Silicon Valley in the boom area around Bangalore in southern India, home to a large number of software firms.

Considerable pressure is being brought to bear on the Indian government to liberalize banking, insurance, and other services as part of the World Trade Organization's (WTO) agreement on trade in services. Over forty foreign banks operate independently in India, and the government is now allowing foreign holdings in Indian banks. It has also opened up the insurance sector to private and foreign investment. Small borrowers in agriculture and small-scale industrialists have found their access to bank lending curtailed. Loans to rural areas and poorer regions have fallen. Foreign banks have focused on retail banking in profitable urban areas, ignoring less lucrative areas of lending.

Under the WTO regime, the Indian government has removed restrictions on the volume of imports. Three-fourths of India's tariffs now have a ceiling beyond which they cannot be raised. Import duties have also been reduced. From 35 percent in 1997–1998, they fell marginally to 32 percent in 2001–2002 and are scheduled to come down to 29 percent in 2002–2003. The government has announced that it will create a two-tier duty structure of 10 and 20 percent by 2004–2005.[3]

Alongside government reforms aimed at opening up and privatizing the economy have been policy moves to cut the work force in public enterprises in order to reduce public spending and deficits. The government has announced measures to reduce the size of the work force by not filling vacancies when employees retire. The goal is to reduce the labor force in public enterprises by 2 percent a year, or 10 percent over five years. In 2002, the government sponsored a voluntary retirement scheme for government employees, under which they could take early retirement.

The government has also been considering reducing workers' legal protections. Industrialists have demanded that the government revise a law requiring government authorization before firms can lay off workers or close factories that employ a minimum of a hundred workers; industry has demanded that the threshold be raised to a thousand. Industry has also sought easing restrictions on hiring temporary workers. In the face of this pressure, the government in 1999 appointed the Second Labor Commission to recommend reforming existing labor laws. The commission proposed replacing the forty-hour week with a sixty-four-hour week, abolishing employment security, enlarging possibilities for employing temporary workers, making government authorization of retrenchment and plant closures easier, and restricting workers' rights to form unions. Recent court decisions have also contributed to the hostility toward workers' organizing, striking, and defending traditional benefits.

Unions and workers have resisted these measures. In 2001, unions prevented the privatization of the Uttar Pradesh State Electricity Board. The privatization of some government enterprises has generated spirited resistance from workers who feared that their jobs were threatened. In 2002, in the largest action ever against the economic reforms, 10 million workers across the country went on strike opposing proposed changes to the labor laws and moves toward privatization.

There has also been opposition to economic liberalization from segments of Indian business. The BJP government that came to power in 1998 based much of its campaign on nationalist rhetoric. It gained support from powerful Indian businesses whose monopolies were threatened by imports and foreign investors. This reaction has slowed the liberalization process, especially when compared to countries in Latin America or Eastern Europe.

To summarize, India's economy during the 1990s grew at a relatively impressive annual growth rate, averaging between five and six percent (see Figure 1). While liberalizing economic policies might have contributed to this robust economic performance, their impact needs to be kept in perspective. Economic liberalization in India, especially external opening and privatization, has been relatively limited. Furthermore, liberalization policies have failed in their intentions of accelerating industrial growth. The significant growth of the Indian economy is most likely propelled by a number of other factors: the share of the slower growing agricultural economy in the overall economy continues to decline steadily, both the knowledge and the stock of modern technology continues to grow, and the closer relationship between government and business has increased the share of private investment in overall investment, thereby increasing production.

Reforms in Agriculture

India's agricultural production made steady and modest progress during the 1990s, helped by good rains during the decade. Weather patterns, especially the timeliness of seasonal rains (the monsoons), continue to have significant bearing on Indian agriculture. Drought hit large parts of the countryside and affected agricultural production and employment opportunities in 2002. Unable to find work or buy food, starvation, suicide, and

mass migration occurred in Rajasthan, Madhya Pradesh, and other states. The victims were invariably from the poorest, lowest-caste segments of the rural population.

The impact of economic liberalization on agriculture has been growing. With the goal of reducing subsidies, the central government excluded millions of impoverished families just above the poverty line from receiving publicly subsidized food supplies. Furthermore, the government linked the price of food sold under the public distribution system to costs incurred, resulting in a sharp increase in prices. Sixty million tons of food grain have been rotting in the storage centers of the Food Corporation of India because it is too costly for the poor to afford.[4]

The removal of restrictions on imports under the WTO has important implications for the agrarian sector. Agricultural producers, such as coffee farmers in south India, are being harmed by increased imports. At a time when prices of primary commodities are falling worldwide, and the United States and other industrialized countries are putting up trade barriers and subsidizing agriculture, India's agriculture economy is being opened up to global forces without safety nets in place.

There has been no unified response to the economic reforms from rural groups. Medium and small peasant farmers, who cultivate between five and thirty acres of land, are scattered across different regions of the country and are divided by language, culture, and caste. They do not constitute a unified political entity. The largest landowning peasant farmers in more affluent states like Punjab and Haryana are more of a political force. They have organized mass demonstration when the national government has removed fertilizer subsidies and implemented other policies that adversely affect their interests.

Economic reforms have had mixed results thus far. India's foreign exchange reserves are much higher than they were in the past. Some industries, such as information technology, have taken off. The service sector is expanding and contributing significantly to India's economic growth. However, as noted earlier, economic liberalization is only partly responsible for robust economic growth. A variety of other long-term factors such as closer relations between a right-wing nationalist government and Indian business also help explain larger and more efficient private investments and economic growth.

Source: World Bank, WDI Data Query, http://devdata.
worldbank.org/data-query/

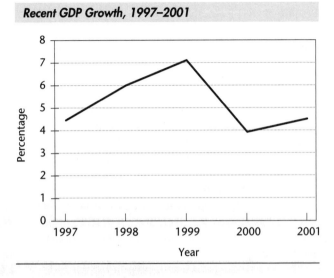

Figure 1

Recent GDP Growth, 1997–2001

If Indian economic growth has been moderately impressive, numerous other problems remain. Most significantly, the state's capacity to facilitate development directly remains rather limited because of its organizational limitations and the interests it represents. For example, the state has been unable to increase public revenues through improved tax collection but has provided tax relief to business groups. As a result, the state has not spent on such critical areas of development as infrastructure, education, and health. The focus on economic liberalization also detracts its attention away from the question of poverty. Whether economic growth is helping India's poor or not is a controversial question. What is clear is that India has an enormous number of poor people and their numbers grow each year.

Social Welfare Policy

India's poor are a diverse, heterogeneous, and enormous group constituting more than one-third of the population. Since independence, the percentage of the poor has been cut in half. However, because of India's rapid population growth, this advance has not been sufficient to reduce the absolute number of poor, which increased from around 200 million in the 1950s to about 350 million by the late 1990s. India has the sad distinction of having the largest concentration of poor people in the world. Nearly two-thirds of the Indian population and three-fourths of the poor live in rural areas. Although urban poverty accounts for only one-fourth of the poor population, the number of poor urban people, over 70 million, is staggering.

India's poorest people are illiterate women and children and untouchables and tribals. They are peasant farmers who own little land, agricultural tenants, landless laborers in villages, and those without regular jobs in cities who eke out a living on society's margins, often huddled into shantytowns that lack sanitary facilities and electricity or living on the streets of cities like Calcutta or Bombay.

Although most poor people are politically unorganized, their political weight is felt in several ways. First, their sizable numbers impel many Indian politicians to adopt populist or socialist electoral platforms. Second, because many of the poor share a lower-caste status (especially within specific states), their group identity and united electoral behavior can have a considerable impact on electoral outcomes. In some states, notably West Bengal and Kerala, there is a long history of radical politics; the poor in these states are well organized by communist or socialist parties and periodically help elect left-leaning governments. Third, the anger and frustration of the poor provide the raw material for many contemporary movements of rage within India.

Over the years, Indian governments have tried different programs aimed at poverty alleviation. Some have been partly successful, but most have not. Redistribution of agricultural land to the poor was mostly a failure compared to results in countries like China, where radical land redistribution was a key component of a successful assault on poverty. As a communist dictatorship, however, China used government coercion to implement property redistribution. In some Indian states, such as West Bengal and Kerala, elected communist governments have been somewhat successful in land redistribution. Overall, however, land reforms have proved to be nearly impossible in India's democracy.

India has very few Western-style welfare programs such as unemployment insurance, comprehensive public health programs, or guaranteed primary education. The size of the welfare problem is considerable and would tax the resources of any government. No Indian government has ever attempted to provide universal primary education, although there has been considerable pressure from both Western and Indian sources to do so.

The one set of welfare-enhancing programs that has had modest success in India are public employment programs. These programs enable the national and state governments to allocate a portion of the public budget to such projects as the construction of roads and bridges and the cleaning of agricultural waterways. Because the rural poor are unemployed for nearly half the year when agricultural jobs are not available, public employment programs become their off-season source of employment and income. Many surveys have demonstrated that such programs help the poor, though the impact merely improves living conditions in the short run and usually fail to reach the poorest. In the 1990s, however, under the impact of liberalization policies, government budgets came under considerable pressure, creating a squeeze on public investments, especially in such areas as public employment.

Many respected observers have repeatedly stated that development spending, public investment, and bank credit to the rural sector were crucial to economic growth in the 1980s and remain critical today. Food-for-work programs, however inefficient, leaky, and corrupt, not only deal with surplus stock but also help generate nonfarm employment, and consequently generate demand for local manufactures, stimulate industry, and hence help savings and investment.[5] Food-for-work spending was only US$170 million in 2001, and budgeted at $259 million for 2002–2003, whereas its food stocks are valued at $10.6 billion.

Society and Economy

Wealth and income present intense contrasts in Indian society. At the top are a small number of incredibly affluent people who have made their fortunes in basic business and industry. The personal fortunes of the wealthiest industrial families, for example, the Ambanis, Tatas, and Birlas, rival the wealth of the richest corporate tycoons in the world. Below them, a much larger group, nearly 100 million Indians (approximately 10 percent) are relatively well off and enjoy a standard of living comparable to that of the middle classes in many developed countries. India has a sophisticated, technologically developed industrial sector that produces a variety of consumer products, military technologies, nuclear energy, and computers. For instance, India's nuclear explosions were the product of indigenous scientific and technological research.

India's lower middle classes, about half of all Indians, are mainly small farmers or urban workers. Relatively poor by global standards, they barely eke out a living. Finally, at the bottom of the class structure, about a third of the population is extremely poor and is concentrated mostly in India's thousands of villages as landless laborers or as the urban unemployed in city slums. Low levels of literacy, poverty, and primitive technology characterize a good part of India's rural society.

India's large population continues to grow at a relatively rapid pace. India will surpass China as the world's largest country in a few years. Since India already has more labor than it can use productively, rapid population growth hinders economic growth. Simply put, the more people there are, the more mouths there are to feed, and the more food and economic products must be produced simply to maintain people's standard of living.

Why should India's population continue to grow at such a rapid pace? The comparison with China provides part of the explanation. The communist-led Chinese government has pursued strict birth control policies of one child per family since the late 1970s. In part, coercion was used to implement these policies. The result was to reduce birthrates dramatically. India's democratic government, by contrast, has found it difficult to implement population control policies.

Coercion is not the only means of reducing population growth rates. By 1995, the national rate of population growth was around 2 percent per year, while the rate in Kerala was 1.4 percent, close to that of China in the early 1990s. An important reason was that Kerala has one of the highest literacy rates, especially female literacy rates, in India. Whereas the average literacy rate in India is around 37 percent for females (and 65 percent for males), Kerala's female literacy rate is 87 percent. Literate women are more likely to marry later, have more options in the work force, have greater power in personal relationships, and practice birth control.

India is one of the few countries in the world that has a lower percentage of females than men: 52 percent of the population is male and 48 percent female. Indian society favors boys over girls, as evidenced by all social indicators, from lower female literacy and nutrition rates to lower survival of female versus male infants. The favoring of males over females is reinforced through such traditions as the dowry system (the Hindu custom of giving the groom and his family some assets, a dowry, at the time of a daughter's wedding). These traditions, deeply rooted and slow to change, confine the majority of Indian women, particularly poor women, to a life of fewer opportunities than those available to men.

India also has the world's largest population of child labor. Children are employed widely, not only in agricultural labor but also in such urban enterprises as match making and rug weaving and selling tea or sweets at train stations. Children usually work long hours at low wages and are unable to receive an education and consequently lose the chance for upward social mobility. The issue of child labor is closely related to India's failure to provide universal primary education (see Figure 2). If school-age children were required to be in school, they could not be readily employed as full-time laborers. Many Indian elites argue that in their poor country, compulsory primary education is an unaffordable luxury. However, this argument is not very persuasive; many poor African countries have higher rates of primary school enrollments than does India (and recall the example of Kerala, among India's poorer states). The more likely obstacle to universal primary education is poverty and caste inequality. Many upper-caste elites do not see lower-caste children as their equals and do not consider the issue of educating lower-caste children a priority. Child labor is directly linked to poverty and survival, since many poor families see larger numbers of children as a form of insurance. Yet for most poor families, a larger family also means not being able to invest in each child's education and depending on their children's labor for survival.

Caste issues pervade many other aspects of India's political and economic life (See "Institutional Intricacies: The Caste System"). First, by assigning people to specific occupations, it impedes the free movement of labor and talent. Although the link between caste and occupation has been weakening in India, especially in urban areas, it remains an important organizing principle

Figure 2

Educational Levels by Gender

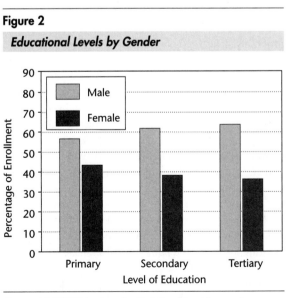

Source: UNESCO Institute for Statistics, http://www.uis.unesco.org/en/stats/stats

for employment Second, in the political arena, caste is a powerful force around which political groups and voting blocs coalesce. Because caste is usually organized at the local level, Indian politics often takes on a local and segmented quality. Related to this, caste cuts across class, making it difficult for labor, business, and other economic classes in India to act in a politically cohesive manner. Third, the Indian government often uses caste as a basis for **reservations,** the Indian version of affirmative action. The government reserves some jobs, admissions into universities, and similar privileges for members of specific underprivileged castes. This has become a highly contentious issue in Indian politics. And last, those who suffer the most in India's caste system are those at the bottom of the caste hierarchy: the untouchables. Nearly 10 percent of India's population, or some 90 million people, is categorized by the Indian census as belonging to the untouchables or scheduled castes, as they are officially known. Notwithstanding considerable government efforts, the social stigma that members of this group suffer runs deep in India.

India and the International Political Economy

After a prolonged colonial experience, nationalist India in the 1950s shunned economic links with the outside world. Although India pursued an active foreign policy as a leader of the **nonaligned bloc,** it was defensive in its economic contacts. A prolonged and successful nationalist movement help explain both India's urge to play a global political role and its desire to protect its economy from foreign influence. India's political and economic elites favored protectionism in trade and sought to limit foreign investment. Although three decades of this policy helped generate an industrial base and domestic capitalism, it gave rise to problems that led to economic liberalization, from which new problems arose.

During the decades of relatively autarkic development, powerful groups emerged that now have vested interests in maintaining the old order. Many bureaucrats abused the system of government controls over private economic activities by accepting bribes to issue government licenses to start private businesses. Indian industry

---

Institutional Intricacies: *The Caste System*

Originally derived from the Portuguese word *castas,* today the word *caste* inevitably evokes images of a rigid hierarchy that characterizes Indian society. In reality, however, castes are less immutable and timeless categories than suggested by the popular image.

Historically, the **caste system** compartmentalized and ranked the Hindu population of the Indian subcontinent through rules governing various aspects of daily life, such as eating, marriage, and prayer. Sanctioned by religion, the hierarchy of caste is based on a conception of the world as divided into realms of purity and impurity. Each hereditary and endogamous group (that is, a group into which one is born and within which one marries) constitutes a *jati,* which is itself organized by *varna,* or shades of color. The four main *varna* are the **Brahmin,** or priestly, caste; the Kshatriya, or warrior and royal, caste; the

Vaishyas, or trading, caste; and the Shudra, or artisan, caste. Each of these *varna* is divided into many *jatis* that often approximate occupational groups (such as potters, barbers, and carpenters). Those who were not considered members of organized Hindu society because they lived in forests and on hills rather than in towns and villages, or were involved in "unclean" occupations such as sweepers and leather workers were labeled **untouchables,** outcastes, or **scheduled castes.** Because each *jati* is often concentrated in a particular region, it is sometimes possible to change one's *varna* when one moves to a different part of the country by changing one's name and adopting the social customs of higher castes, for example, giving up eating meat. Some flexibility within the rigidity of the system has contributed to its survival across the centuries.

was often relatively inefficient because neither cheaper foreign goods nor foreign investors were readily allowed into India. Moreover, organized labor, especially in government-controlled factories, had a stake in maintaining inefficient factories because they offered a greater number of jobs. These well-entrenched groups resisted liberalization and threatened to throw their political weight behind opposition parties, making the ruling government hesitant to undertake any decisive policy shift.

The other significant component of India's performance in the international political economy concerns its regional context. India is a giant among the South Asian countries of Pakistan, Bangladesh, Sri Lanka, Nepal, and Bhutan, though its northern neighbor, China, is an even bigger and more powerful giant. Since 1947, India has periodically experienced regional conflict: a war with China in 1962; three wars with Pakistan, the last of which was fought in 1971 and precipitated the breakup of Pakistan into the two states of Pakistan and Bangladesh; a military intervention into strife-torn Sri Lanka in the 1980s; and on-and-off troubled relations with Nepal.

The net effect is that India has not developed extensive economic interactions with its neighbors. Figure 3 compares exports as a percentage of gross national product (GNP) for India and its major trading partners; India's export quantity and rate of growth are relatively low. As nations increasingly look to their neighbors

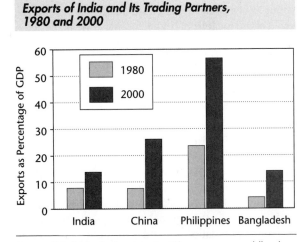

Figure 3

Exports of India and Its Trading Partners, 1980 and 2000

Source: World Bank Country at a Glance, www.worldbank.org/data/countrydata/countrydata.html

for trade and investment, the pressure on India and its neighbors to put aside their mutual conflicts for increased economic contact is likely to grow. Some movement in this direction was already evident in the first half of the 1990s, especially toward China, but there is still a long way to go before South Asia develops an integrated zone of economic activity.

Section ❸ Governance and Policy-Making

Organization of the State

India is a democratic republic with a parliamentary and federal system of government. The constitution adopted in 1950 created this system, and although there have been many profound changes since then in the distribution and use of power, the basic character of India's political system has remained unchanged. For much of this period, India has been a stable, democratic country with universal suffrage and periodic elections at local, state, and national levels. This continuity and democratic stability are remarkable among developing countries. To simplify a complex reality, Indian democracy has proved so resilient because its political institutions, while always under pressure, have been able to accommodate many new power challenges and to repress the most difficult ones.

India's constitution is lengthy. In contrast to the British constitution on which it is modeled, it is a written document that has been periodically amended by legislation. Among its special features, three are worth noting. First, unlike many other constitutions, the Indian constitution directs the government to promote social and economic equality and justice. The constitution thus goes beyond stipulating formal procedures of decision making and allocating powers among political institutions, and outlines policy goals. Although the impact of these constitutional provisions on government policies is limited, the provisions ensure that issues of welfare and social justice are not ignored. Second, the Indian constitution, similar to the U.S. Constitution, provides for freedom of religion and defines India as a secular state. This was an especially controversial issue in Indian politics during the late 1990s because the ruling BJP was committed to establishing Hinduism as a state-sanctioned religion. And third, the constitution allows for the temporary suspension of many democratic rights under conditions of emergency. These provisions were used, somewhat understandably, during wars with Pakistan or China. But they have also been invoked, more disturbingly, to deal with internal political threats, most dramatically during the national Emergency from 1975 to 1977, when a politically vulnerable Indira Gandhi suspended many democratic rights and imprisoned her leading political opponents.

India's federal system of twenty-eight states and several other special political units is relatively centralized. The central government controls the most essential government functions such as defense, foreign policy, taxation, public expenditures, and economic planning, especially industrial planning. State governments formally control such policy areas as agriculture, education, and law and order within the states. Because they are heavily dependent on the central government for funds in these policy areas, however, the power of the states is limited.

India is a parliamentary democracy designed on the British model. The Indian parliament, known as the **Lok Sabha,** or House of the People, is the most significant political institution. The leader of the political party with the most seats in the *Lok Sabha* becomes the prime minister, who nominates a cabinet, mostly from the ranks of other members of parliament belonging to the ruling coalition. The prime minister and the cabinet, along with permanent civil servants, control much of the government's daily functioning. The prime minister is the linchpin of the system because effective power is concentrated in that office, where most of the country's important policies originate. By contrast, the office of the president is largely ceremonial. In periodic national elections, 544 members of the *Lok Sabha,* the lower house of the bicameral parliament, are elected. The *Lok Sabha* is much more politically significant than the **Rajya Sabha,** the upper

house. The prime minister governs with the help of the cabinet, which periodically meets to discuss important issues, including any new legislation that is likely to be initiated. Individually, cabinet members are the heads of various ministries, for example, Foreign Affairs or Industry, that direct the daily work of the government and make up the permanent bureaucracy.

The Executive

The President and the Prime Minister

The president is the official head of the state and is elected indirectly every five years by an electoral college composed of elected representatives from the national and state governments. In most circumstances, the president acts on the advice of the prime minister and is thus not a very powerful political figure. The presidency is a ceremonial office, symbolizing the unity of the country, and it is supposedly above partisan politics. Under exceptional circumstances, however, especially when the selection of a prime minister becomes a complex issue, the president can play an important political role. For example, in the 1998 election, there was a hung parliament, with no party gaining a clear majority. The president then requested the party with the largest percentage of votes, the BJP, to show that it could muster enough allies to form a government.

The prime minister and other cabinet ministers are the most powerful political figures in India. Because they represent the majority party coalition in parliament, the passage of a bill is not as complicated a process as it can be in a presidential system, especially one with a divided government. The prime minister and the cabinet also head various ministries, so that after legislation is passed, they oversee its implementation. In practice, the permanent bureaucracy, especially the senior and middle-level bureaucrats, are responsible for policy implementation. Nevertheless, as in most other parliamentary systems, such as those in Britain, Germany, and Japan, there is considerable overlap in India between the executive and the legislative branches of the government, creating a greater degree of centralization of power than is initially evident. The duration of the prime minister's tenure in office has become steadily truncated over time. Between 1947 and 1984, except for a few brief interludes, India had only two prime ministers: Nehru and Indira Gandhi (see Table 1). This is nearly unique among democracies; it underlines the powerful hold that the Nehru-Gandhi family had on India's political imagination. Since then, there has been a more rapid turnover. Rajiv Gandhi, Indira Gandhi's son, succeeded his mother after her assassination in 1984. When he lost power four years later, there were short-lived governments under the leadership of V. P. Singh and Chandra Shekhar. Narasimha Rao lasted his full term in office. Atal Behari Vajpayee is serving an entire term since his election in 1999, unlike his previous truncated terms.

The method of selecting a prime minister in India is fairly complex. The original choice of Nehru was a natural one, given his prominent position in the nationalist movement and his relationship to founding father Mahatma Gandhi. The choice of Indira Gandhi was less obvious. She was chosen to head the Congress Party by a group of prominent second-tier party leaders, because of her national name, which they calculated would reap handsome electoral rewards. A similar logic prevailed when Rajiv Gandhi was chosen by party elites to succeed his mother. Rajiv Gandhi benefited from the wave of sympathy generated by his mother's assassination, and he led the Congress Party back to power in 1984 with a handsome electoral majority.

Following Rajiv Gandhi's assassination, the Nehru-Gandhi family line appeared to have reached an end, since Rajiv Gandhi's wife, Sonia Gandhi, was an Italian national and their children were too young to enter politics. In 1991, Narasimha Rao was brought back as an elder statesman, nonthreatening and acceptable to competing factions within the Congress Party. He was the first prime minister from south India; all the previous heads of state had been from the north. Both subsequent United Front prime ministers were compromise candidates who lacked the personality and power to manage their disparate coalitions. In 1998, the Congress Party attempted to resurrect its fortunes by choosing Sonia Gandhi to head their party, creating the possibility that the political rule of the Nehru-Gandhi family would continue. Despite criticisms that Sonia was not born in India, she has proved an able and popular politician.

The Cabinet

The prime minister chooses the cabinet, mostly from among the party's members elected to parliament. Seniority, competence, and personal loyalty are the main criteria that a prime minister takes into account when choosing cabinet ministers. Regional and caste representation at the highest level of government must also be considered. During Indira Gandhi's rule, personal loyalty was critical in the choice of senior ministers. Rajiv Gandhi, by contrast, put a high premium on competence, which unfortunately he equated with youth and technical skills, at the expense of political experience. Since Vajpayee was able to form a government only with the help of many smaller parties, the heads of these parties had to be accommodated, producing a vast, eclectic, and disparate cabinet.

The Bureaucracy

The prime minister and cabinet ministers run the government in close collaboration with senior civil servants. Each senior minister oversees what is often a sprawling bureaucracy, staffed by some very competent, overworked, senior civil servants and by many not-so-competent, underworked, lowly bureaucrats, well known for taking long tea breaks while they stare at stacks of unopened files.

The **Indian Administrative Service** (IAS), an elite corps of top bureaucrats, constitutes a critical but relatively thin layer at the top of India's bureaucracy. The competence of the IAS is a central reason that India is moderately well governed. Because political leaders come and go, whereas senior civil servants stay, many civil servants possess a storehouse of knowledge and expertise that makes them very powerful. Higher-level civil servants in India reach their positions after considerable experience within the government. They are named to the IAS at a relatively young age, usually in their early twenties, by passing a highly competitive entrance exam. Some of India's most talented young men and women were attracted to the IAS during the 1950s and 1960s, reflecting the prestige that service in national government used to enjoy in Indian society. The attraction of the IAS has declined, however, and many talented young people now go into engineering or business administration or leave the country for better opportunities abroad. Government service has become tainted as areas of corruption have developed and the level of professionalism within the IAS has eroded, mainly because politicians prefer loyalty over merit and seniority when making promotions. Nevertheless, the IAS continues to recruit very talented young people, many of whom become dedicated senior civil servants who still constitute the backbone of the Indian government.

Below the IAS, the level of talent and professionalism drops rather sharply. Within each ministry at the national level and in many parallel substructures at the state level, the bureaucracy in India is infamous for corruption and inefficiency. These problems contribute to the gap between good policies made at the top and their poor implementation at the local level.

Other State Institutions

The Military and the Police

Unlike the militaries in many other developing countries, say, Brazil and Nigeria, the Indian military has never intervened directly in politics. The Indian military, with more than 1 million well-trained and well-equipped members, is a highly professional organization. Over the years, the continuity of constitutional, electoral politics and a relatively apolitical military have come to reinforce and strengthen each other. Civilian politicians provide ample resources to the armed forces and, for the most part, let them function as a professional organization. The armed forces, in turn, obey the orders of democratically elected leaders, and although they lobby to preserve their own interests, they mostly stay out of the normal tumble of democratic politics.

Since the 1970s, two factors have weakened this well-institutionalized separation of politics and military. First, during Indira Gandhi's rule, loyalty to political leaders became the key criterion for securing top military jobs. This policy tended to politicize the military and narrow the separation between politics and military.

Second, there were growing regional and ethnic demands for secession (see Section 4). As these demands became more intense in some states, notably in Kashmir, and as militants began to resort to armed conflict,

occasionally with the help of India's often hostile neighbor Pakistan, the Indian government called in the armed forces. However, soldiers are not trained to resolve political problems; rather, they are trained to use force to secure compliance from reluctant political actors. As a result, not only have democratic norms and human rights been violated in India, but the distance between politics and the military has narrowed.

A similar trend toward politicization and de-professionalization has occurred in India's sprawling police services, but with a difference. The Indian police organization was never as professionalized as the armed forces, and the police services come under the jurisdiction of state governments, not the central government. Because state governments are generally less well run than the national government, the cumulative impact is that the Indian police are not apolitical civil servants. State-level politicians regularly interfere in police personnel issues, and police officers in turn regularly oblige the politicians who help them. The problem is especially serious at lower levels. The police are widely regarded as easily bribed and often allied with criminals or politicians. In some states, such as Bihar and Uttar Pradesh, police often take sides in local conflicts instead of acting as neutral arbiters or enforcers of laws. When they do, they tilt the power balance in favor of dominant social groups such as landowners or upper castes or the majority Hindu religious community.

In addition to the regular armed forces and the state-level police forces, paramilitary forces, controlled by the national government, number nearly half a million men. As Indian politics became more turbulent in the 1980s, paramilitary forces steadily expanded. Because the national government calls on the regular armed forces only as a last resort in the management of internal conflicts and because state-level police forces are not very reliable, paramilitary forces are viewed as a way to maintain order. A large, sprawling, and relatively ineffective police service remains a problematic presence in Indian society.

The Judiciary

An independent judiciary is another component of India's state system. But unlike Britain, where the judiciary's role is limited by parliamentary sovereignty, a fundamental contradiction is embedded in the Indian constitution between the principles of parliamentary sovereignty and judicial review. Over the years, the judiciary and the parliament have often clashed, with the former trying to preserve the constitution's basic structure and the latter asserting its right to amend the constitution (See "Institutional Intricacies: The Executive Versus the Judiciary"). The judiciary comprises an apex court, atop a series of national courts, high courts in states, and lower courts in districts.

The supreme judicial authority is the Supreme Court, comprising a chief justice and seventeen other judges, appointed by the president, but as in most other matters of political significance in India, only on the advice of the prime minister. Once appointed, judges cannot be removed from the bench until retirement at age sixty-five. The caseload on the Supreme Court, as on much of the rest of the Indian legal system, is extremely heavy, with a significant backlog.

The main political role of the Supreme Court is to ensure that legislation conforms with the intent of the constitution. Because the Indian constitution is very detailed, however, the need for interpretation is not as great as in many other countries. Nevertheless, there are real conflicts, both within the constitution and in India's political landscape, that often need to be adjudicated by the Supreme Court. For example, the constitution simultaneously protects private property and urges the government to pursue social justice. Indian leaders have often promulgated socialist legislation, for example, requiring the redistribution of agricultural land. Legislation of this nature is considered by the Supreme Court because it potentially violates the right to private property. Many Supreme Court cases have involved the conflict between socialistically inclined legislation and constitutional rights. Cases involving other politically significant issues, for instance, rights of religious minorities such as Muslims and the rights of women, also periodically reach the Supreme Court.

Like many other Indian political institutions, the Supreme Court lost much of its autonomy in the 1980s. The process began during Indira Gandhi's rule, when she argued that the court was too conservative and an obstacle to her socialist program. To remedy this shortcoming, she appointed many pliant judges, including the chief justice. The Supreme Court itself more or less complied with her wishes during the two years of Emergency (1975–1977), when the political and civil rights of many Indians were violated. No such dramatic instance of a politicized Supreme Court has recurred since the late 1970s.

The Supreme Court often functions as a bulwark for citizens against state invasiveness, as is evident from many landmark civil rights judgments. The Court introduced a system of public interest litigation that enabled bonded laborers, disenfranchised tribal people, the homeless, and indigent women to redress their claims. In recent years, the Supreme Court has defended environmental causes. To protect the Taj Mahal, India's most treasured national monument, from damage by air pollution, it ordered 212 nearby businesses that had chronically violated environmental regulations to close. It similarly shut down almost 200 polluters along the Ganges River. The Court enforced clean water and air laws in New Delhi in 1996–1997 by ordering that polluting cars and buses be removed from the roads and shutting down polluting enterprises. It required central and state governments to prevent starvation by releasing food stocks and to promote education by providing school lunches and day care facilities.

Subnational Government

Under India's federal system, the balance of power between the central and state governments varies by time and place. In general, the more powerful and popular the central government and prime minister are, the less likely states are to pursue an independent course. During the rule of Nehru and especially under Indira Gandhi, the states were often quite constrained. By contrast, a weaker central government, like the BJP-led alliance that took office in 1998, enlarges the room for state governments to maneuver. When state governments are run by political parties other than the national ruling party—and this is often true in contemporary India—there is considerable scope for center-state conflict. For example, a popular communist government in West Bengal has often disagreed with the national government in New Delhi, charging it with discriminatory treatment in the allocation of finances and other centrally controlled resources.

Institutional Intricacies: **The Executive Versus the Judiciary**

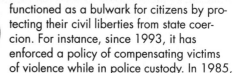

Over the years, the Supreme Court has clashed head-to-head with the parliament as a result of the contradiction between principles of parliamentary sovereignty and judicial review that is embedded in India's constitution. For instance, during the early years of independence, the courts overturned state government laws to redistribute land from landlords (*zamindars*), saying that the laws violated the *zamindars'* fundamental rights. In retaliation, the parliament passed the first of a series of amendments to the constitution to protect the executive's authority to promote land redistribution. But matters did not end there. The Supreme Court responded by passing a judgment stating that the parliament did not have the power to abrogate fundamental rights. In 1970, the court also invalidated the bank nationalization bill and a presidential order abolishing privy purses (including titles and privileges of former rulers of India's princely states). In retaliation, the parliament passed a series of amendments that undercut the Supreme Court's rulings, thus moving the power balance toward parliamentary sovereignty. The Supreme Court responded that the court still reserved for itself the discretion to reject any constitutional amendments passed by parliament on the grounds that the amendments could not change the constitution's basic structure. During the Emergency period, the parliament passed yet another amendment that limited the Supreme Court's judicial review to procedural issues. The Janata government in the post-Emergency era, however, reversed these changes, thus reintroducing the tension between the executive and judiciary.

Since the 1980s, the courts have increasingly functioned as a bulwark for citizens by protecting their civil liberties from state coercion. For instance, since 1993, it has enforced a policy of compensating victims of violence while in police custody. In 1985, the Supreme Court upheld a verdict finding two people guilty of murdering their wives on the grounds that the dowry was insufficient and sentenced them to life imprisonment. In the mid-1980s, the Supreme Court clashed with parliament on its interpretation of personal law over the Shah Bano case. In India, in keeping with a secular ethos, personal law falls under the purview of religion, although an individual can choose secular alternatives. However, this recourse is circumscribed: a woman married under religious law cannot seek divorce or alimony under secular law. Neither Muslim nor Hindu personal law entitles women to alimony. The British colonial government had passed a law entitling destitute divorced women to maintenance by their husbands. Shah Bano, a destitute seventy-five-year-old woman abandoned and later divorced by her husband, filed for maintenance under this law. The Supreme Court upheld Shah Bano's right to maintenance on the grounds that secular laws transcended personal law (religious law). The parliament, succumbing to pressures from religious leaders, passed a bill excluding Muslim women from the purview of secular laws.

The battle between the executive and the judiciary has taken a toll on the autonomy of the courts. The judiciary has been affected by the general malaise of institutional decay that has affected Indian politics over the years. The backlog of cases has grown phenomenally, while expeditious judgment of cases has declined dramatically.

While the political parties at the national and the state levels may differ, the formal structure of the twenty-eight state governments parallels that of the national government. The chief minister of each state heads the state government. The chief minister is the leader of the majority party (or the party with most seats) in the lower house of the state legislature. The chief minister appoints cabinet ministers who head various ministries staffed by a state-level, permanent bureaucracy. The quality of government below the national level is often poor, contributing to regional and ethnic conflicts.

In lieu of a president, each state has a governor, appointed by the national president. The governors, like the president, are supposed to serve on the advice of the chief minister, but in practice, they often become politically powerful, especially in states where the national government is at odds with the state government or where state governments are unstable. Governors can dismiss elected state governments and proclaim temporary presidential rule if they determine state governments to be ineffective. When this happens, the elected government is dissolved and the state is governed from New Delhi until fresh elections are called and a new government is elected. Although this provision is intended to be a sensible constitutional option, an intrusive national government has often used it for partisan purposes.

The power struggle between the central government and the states is ongoing. With many Indian states inhabited by people with distinctive traditions and cultures, including language, and with conflicting political parties in power at the national and state levels, central-state relations can be fueled by substantial political and ethnic conflicts.

In recent years, Indian politics has become increasingly regionalized. Three new states were formed in 2000 out of existing states. Furthermore states have become increasingly autonomous economically and politically. As a result of economic liberalization, states have acquired rights and opportunities to seek out investors independent of the national government. One consequence is that regional inequalities are widening as some states, for example, Haryana, Punjab, Maharashtra, Gujarat, Andhra Pradesh, Karnataka, and Tamil Nadu, have aggressively sought investments while some of the largest and poorest states in the north and east have fallen behind.

The twenty-eight states of India's federal system have also come to play an increasingly important role in national governance. In each of the national elections since 1989, parties based in a single state have been key to the success of coalition governments. According to the Election Commission's classification of parties, in the four national elections between 1991 and 1998, the vote share of national parties (those with a base in many states) dropped from 77 to 67 percent, and the proportion of seats they controlled slipped from 78 to 68 percent. By contrast, parties based in single states increased their percentage share of the votes from 17 to 27 percent and their seats from 16 to 29 percent. Since 1989, every coalition government has depended on regional parties for its survival. This development has double-edged implications for democracy. On the one hand, governing coalitions that are established by disparate parties with little ideological or programmatic cohesion are likely to be unstable. On the other hand, national governments are less likely than they were in the past to seek the dismissal of state governments because national governments are likely to be composed of regional political parties.

The **panchayats,** which function at the local, district, and state levels, represent the most important attempts at the devolution of power. The *panchayats* are a precolonial institution that was responsible historically for administering justice by abjudicating conflicts and presiding over community affairs in the rural areas. In 1959, the Indian government introduced a three-tier model of *panchayats,* linked together by indirect elections. However, it gave the *panchayats* meager resources, for members of Parliament and the Legislative Assembly saw them as potential rivals to their authority. By the mid-1960s, the *panchayats* were stagnating and declining.

Some states revived the *panchayats* on their own initiative. In 1978, the communist government of West Bengal overhauled the *panchayat* system by providing for direct elections and giving them additional resources and responsibilities. Other states followed suit. In 1992, the government amended the constitution to enable all states to strengthen the *panchayats*, although states were free to create their own models. It envisaged the *panchayats'* primary role as implementing development programs and encouraging greater local involvement in government. The amendment stipulated that *panchayat* elections would be held every five years and made provisions for reserving 33 percent of the seats for women and seats proportional to the population for scheduled castes and tribes. In the first elections held under the new framework (in 1993), 700,000 women were elected to office. Most states met and several exceeded the 33 percent women's reservations at all three levels.

The abilities of women who were elected to the *panchayats* varied widely. Women who had a prior history of political activism were most likely to use the *panchayats* to benefit women. Some were responsible for the *panchayats'* sponsoring important local development projects. Others sought *panchayat* action on behalf of women over issues like marriage, divorce, and alcoholism. However, most women elected to the *panchayats* had no prior history of activism and became tokens who were silenced, marginalized, and, in extreme situations, even harassed and attacked. Many women ran for election in order to represent the interests of powerful men. In some cases, when women threatened male candidates, they were often accused of sexual immorality. Women were often ignorant about the functions of the *panchayats* and relied on their husbands for advice. Female *panchayat* members were often inhibited from participating actively.

More generally, the resources and planning capabilities of the *panchayats* are relatively limited. State legislatures determine how much power and authority the *panchayats* can wield. Very few states have engaged in a serious devolution of the *panchayats'* development functions. Most *panchayats* are responsible for implementing rural development schemes but not devising them. Policy is made at the national and state levels. Although considerable resources pass through them, local governments seldom enjoy formal discretion over how these resources are allocated. Local political elites, bureaucrats, and others with influence often collude as they determine where projects will be located, who gets a contract, and who is hired on public projects. They often siphon off a healthy share of the public money. Thus, many local governments in India tend to be corrupt, ineffective, and wasteful. City streets are not kept clean, potholes are not repaired, irrigation canals are not properly maintained, and rural schools are so poorly built that they leak as soon as the monsoons start.

The Policy-Making Process

Major policies in India are made by the national government, in New Delhi. The prime minister and senior cabinet ministers are generally responsible for initiating policies. Behind the scenes, senior civil servants in each ministry, as well as in cross-ministry offices like the prime minister's secretariat and the planning commission, play a critical role in identifying problems, synthesizing data, and presenting to political leaders alternative solutions and their implications. After decisions have been made at the highest level, many require new legislation. Because the prime minister usually has a clear majority in parliament, passage of most legislation is ensured except in extremely controversial areas.

The real policy drama in India occurs early on, when major bills are under consideration, and during the process of implementation. Consider economic liberalization policies, which represented a major policy change. The new course was formulated at the highest level of government, involving only a handful of senior ministers and bureaucrats. To reach the decision, however, a fairly complex set of political activities took place. Decision makers consulted some of the most important interest groups, such as associations of Indian businessmen and representatives of international organizations like the World Bank and the IMF. Others, including those who might be adversely affected, were heard; organized labor, for example, might call a one-day general strike (it actually did) to warn the government that any attempt to privatize the public sector would meet considerable resistance. Newspapers, magazines, and intellectuals also expressed support or opposition. Political parties got into the act. Members of the ruling party, the Congress in this case, did not necessarily support the political thinking of their own leaders at the early stage; rather, they worried about the political implications of policies for intraparty power struggles and future elections. Opposition parties, in turn, worried about the interests of their constituents. These pressures modified the policy that the government eventually adopted.

After policies have been adopted, their implementation is far from assured. Continuing with the liberalization example, some aspects of the new policy package proved easier to implement than others. Changing the exchange rate (the value of the Indian rupee in relation to the U.S. dollar) was relatively easy to implement because both the policy decision and its implementation require the actions of only a handful of politicians and bureaucrats. By contrast, the attempts to simplify the procedures for Indian or foreign business executives to create new business enterprises proved far more complicated. Implementation of such policies involves layers of bureaucrats, most of whom benefit from the control they already exercise. When forced to relinquish power, many dragged their feet and, where possible, sabotaged the newly simplified procedures.

Another example is the policies aimed at improving

the standard of living for the Indian poor. Since the 1960s, the national government has attempted to redistribute agricultural land and create public works programs to help India's rural poor. The national government set the broad outlines for land reforms and allocated funds for public works programs but left refinement of these policies, as well as their implementation, to state governments. State governments vary in terms of social classes in the state, ruling party coalitions, and the quality of their bureaucracies. The result is that the implementation of antipoverty policies within India has been quite uneven.

Land redistribution involves taking land from well-off, powerful landlords and redistributing it to poor tenants or agricultural laborers. This is a highly controversial process, requiring some combination of forceful actions by state governments and the organization of the poor beneficiaries. Generally, attempts at land redistribution have been relatively unsuccessful in most Indian states because the interests of landowning classes are well represented, and state-level bureaucrats often have close links to these landowning groups. Partial exceptions to these trends are found in the states of Kerala and West Bengal, where communist state governments and the well-organized poor have made some progress in land reform.

Attempts to generate extra employment for the rural poor through public works projects (such as road construction and canal cleaning) have been somewhat more successful than land redistribution policies because they do not involve any direct confiscation of property. The main issues in the implementation of these policies are the quality of projects chosen, whether they target the poor, and how honestly they are completed. Because the quality of local governments in implementing national policies varies (although it is rarely very high), many of the funds spent on poverty alleviation programs have been wasted. Public works policies have been most effectively implemented in the states of Maharashtra and West Bengal, where there is considerable political pressure from caste or class politics, and in some southern states, where the local bureaucracy is more efficient.

To review, the policy-making process in India, though relatively centralized, takes into account various interests and frequently produces well-developed policies. By contrast, the process of implementation is quite decentralized and relatively ineffective. What often start out as sound policy ideas and positive intentions do not reach fruition because policies are diluted as they get redefined at the state level and because of lackluster implementation.

Section ❹ Representation and Participation

Over the years, India has become a participatory democracy, as previously excluded social groups such as the poor, the landless, and backward castes entered the political arena and used their influence to shape the political process. In the early years of independence, the Congress Party mobilized most groups. However, in recent years, there has been a proliferation of political parties that have appealed to the Indian masses on ethnic grounds (particularly caste and religion), a trend initiated by Indira Gandhi. Simultaneously, the adoption of the democratic idea in the institutional sphere led to an explosion of social movements in civil society. Poor women have marched on the streets of Andhra Pradesh demanding prohibition of the sale of liquor (because of the economic toll it inflicts and its role in domestic violence), while poor tribals in Maharashtra have protested their displacement by the construction

of large dams. The democratic idea is so deeply rooted that today thousands of nongovernmental organizations function in the country, representing causes ranging from welfare issues to the environment to human rights. Some social movements have transformed themselves into political parties, while others militantly oppose the established political system. Thus, ironically, while Indian democracy has become more truncated in some respects, as it has experienced institutional decline and decay, political participation through social movements and political parties has grown and flourished.

The Legislature

A good place to begin the discussion of representation and participation in a democracy is with the legislature. The Indian parliament is bicameral, consisting of the

Rajya Sabha and the *Lok Sabha*. Although the government dominates the parliament, election to the *Lok Sabha* is much sought after in India. First, the outcome of parliamentary elections determines which party coalition will control the government. Second, although members of parliament are unable to influence policies directly, they enjoy considerable status, personal access to resources, and influence over allocations of government monies and contracts within their constituencies.

Elections to the *Lok Sabha* must be held at least every five years, but, as in other parliamentary systems, the prime minister may choose to call elections earlier. India is divided into 544 electoral districts of roughly equal population, each of which elects and sends one representative to the national parliament. The major political parties nominate most candidates. Elections in India are won or lost mainly by parties, especially by party leaders, so most legislators are beholden to party leaders for securing a party ticket. Success in elections therefore does not depend on having an independent power base but on belonging to a party whose leader or whose programs are popular. Given the importance of the party label for nominations, members of parliament maintain strong voting discipline in the *Lok Sabha*. The main business of the *Lok Sabha* is to pass new legislation as well as to debate the pros and cons of government actions. Although members sometimes introduce bills, the government introduces most new legislation. After bills are introduced, they are assigned to parliamentary committees for detailed study and discussion. The committees report the bills back to the *Lok Sabha* for debate, possible amendment, and preliminary votes. They then go to the *Rajya Sabha,* the upper house, which is not a powerful chamber; it generally approves bills passed by the *Lok Sabha*. Most members of the *Rajya Sabha* are elected indirectly by state legislatures. After any final modifications by the *Rajya Sabha,* bills return to the *Lok Sabha* for a third reading, after which they are finally voted on in both houses and forwarded to the president for approval.

To understand why the *Lok Sabha* does not play a significant independent role in policy-making, keep in mind that (1) the government generally introduces new legislation; (2) most legislators, especially those belonging to the Congress Party, are politically beholden to party leaders; and (3) all parties use party whips to ensure voting along party lines. One implication of parliament's relative ineffectiveness is that routine changes in its social composition do not have significant policy consequences. Whether members of parliament are business executives or workers, men or women, members of upper or lower castes, is not likely to lead to dramatic policy shifts. Nevertheless, groups in society derive satisfaction from having one of their own in the parliament, and dramatic shifts in social composition are bound to influence policy.

The typical member of parliament is a male university graduate between forty and sixty years old. Over the years, there have been changes in the social composition along some criteria but not others. For example, legislators in the 1950s were likely to be urban men and were often lawyers and members of higher castes. Today, nearly half the members of parliament come from rural areas, and many have agricultural backgrounds. Members of the middle castes (the so-called backward castes) are also well represented today. These changes reflect some of the broad shifts in the distribution of power in Indian society. By contrast, the proportion of women and of poor, lower-caste individuals in the parliament remains low. The representation of women in parliament has not increased much from the 4.4 percent (or 22 women) in the first parliament (1952–1957) to 8.8 percent (48 women) who were elected in the 1998 elections, the largest number ever (see Figure 4).

Three successive governments since 1996 have supported a constitutional amendment guaranteeing at least 33 percent reserved seats for women in Parliament and the Legislative Assemblies. However although most political parties have endorsed the bill in their election manifestos, they have not supported its passage in Parliament. It was defeated most recently in December 2000, when a range of parties expressed either ambivalence or opposition to it. As a compromise measure, Home Minister L. K. Advani supported the chief election commissioner's proposal to require all political parties to reserve 33 percent of their nominations for women contestants. Critics fear that political parties will nominate women in unwinnable constituencies. Thus far, parties' records in nominating women candidates have been poor. In the 1996 parliamentary elections, for example, political parties allotted less than 15 percent of the total number of tickets to women. Women constitute only 10 to 12 percent of the membership of political parties.[6]

Figure 4

Women in Parliament

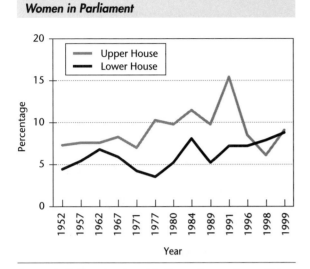

Source: India Together, http://indiatogether.org/manushi/issue116/Table-1.htm

There has been far more resistance to state and national reservations for women by political parties than by the broad public. A survey by *India Today* indicates that 75 percent of women and 79 percent of men favor the active participation of women in politics, and 75 percent of men and women favor reservations in legislative bodies. Opposition from parties has been both gendered and caste based. Parties that represent the lower middle castes have opposed the reform because it makes no provision for reservations on a caste basis.

Political Parties and the Party System

Political parties and elections are where much of the real drama of Indian politics occurs. Parties in control of a majority of seats in the national or state parliaments form the national or state governments and control government resources. Parties thus devote substantial political energy to contesting and winning elections. Since independence, the party system has evolved from being dominated by the Congress Party to one in which Congress is among the major parties but far from dominant (see Table 2). Thus, what began as virtually a one-party system has evolved into a real multiparty system, with three main political tendencies: centrist, center-left,

and center-right. Within this framework, there are at least four potentially significant national parties and many regional parties competing for power. The four parties with significant national presence are the Congress, the Janata Party, the BJP, and the Communist Party of India (Marxist; CPM). Whereas the CPM is a left-leaning party and the BJP is a religious, right-leaning one, both Congress and the Janata are more or less centrist parties. Furthermore, coalitions among these parties have occurred in the past. For example, the Janata Party joined forces with the CPM and other smaller parties in the 1996 elections to form the United Front and has been able to form two short-lived left-leaning governments.

The Congress Party

Congress was India's premier political party until the 1990s. Many aspects of this party have already been discussed because it is impossible to analyze Indian politics without referring to its role. To summarize briefly, the Congress Party built its electoral network by creating patrons who would mobilize electoral support for the party during elections. Once in power, the Congress Party would channel government resources to these people, further enhancing their local position and ensuring their support.

This patronage system (some call it machine politics) worked quite well for the Congress Party for nearly two decades. Nevertheless, even when the party was electorally successful, this strategy generated internal contradictions. The pro-poor Congress Party of India, with a socialist shell, came to be internally dominated by high-caste, wealthy Indians.

By the early 1950s, with Nehru at its helm, Congress was the unquestioned ruling party of India. Over the years, especially since the mid-1960s, this hegemony came to be challenged. By the time Indira Gandhi assumed power in 1966, the old Congress Party had begun to lose its political sway, and anticolonial nationalism was fading. The spread of democratic politics mobilized many poor, lower-caste citizens who depended less and less on village big men for political guidance. As a result, numerous regional parties started challenging Congress's monopoly on power. Weather-related food shortages in the mid-1960s also hurt the Congress Party in the 1967 elections.

Table 2

Major Party Election Results

	1991 %	1991 Seats	1996 %	1996 Seats	1998 %	1998 Seats	1999 %	1999 Seats
Congress (I)	37.3	225	29	143	25.4	140	28.4	112
BJP & Allies	19.9	119	24	193	36.2	250	41.3	296
Janata	10.8	55	Joined with UF		Joined with UF		1	1
United Front	—	—	31	180	20.9	98	—	—
Communists[a]	—	48	Joined with UF		Joined with UF		5.4	32
Others							23.9	107

[a]Includes both the CPM and the CPI.

Source: India Today, July 15, 1991, March 16, 1998; *Economic Times* website http://economictimes.indiatimes.com.

Indira Gandhi sought to reverse the decline in the Congress's electoral popularity through mobilizing India's vast majority, the poor, by promising poverty alleviation as the core of her political program. This promise struck a popular chord, propelling Indira Gandhi to the top of India's political pyramid. Her personal success, however, came at a cost to the party. The old Congress split into two parties, with one branch, the Congress (O), becoming moribund and leaving the other, Congress (I) (the "I" stands for Indira) to inherit the position of the old undivided Congress. Nevertheless, the Congress Party formed all governments from independence to 1989, with just one interlude, when the Janata Party formed the government, (1977–1980). Since 1989, however, Congress headed the government only from 1991 to 1996.

Prior to Indira Gandhi's prime ministership, rank-and-file party members elected the lowest-level Congress Party officers, who in turn elected officers at higher levels of the party organization, up to the position of the party leader, who was the prime minister during the long period when the Congress formed the government. Indira Gandhi reversed this bottom-up party structure by creating a top-down party in which leaders appointed party officers. With some modifications, including some limited internal party elections, this is basically how the contemporary Congress Party is organized. The top-down structure enables the leaders to control the party, but it is a major liability when grassroots support is necessary. As the nation's oldest party, the Congress continues to attract substantial

electoral support. If this support ever declined sharply, most likely the party rank-and-file would demand its reorganization.

Whereas Congress during the 1970s had a left-of-center, pro-poor political platform, beginning in 1984 it moved toward the ideological center under Rajiv Gandhi (see Section 2 for the reasons behind this shift). Today, the Congress Party tilts right-of-center, championing issues of economic efficiency, business interests, and limited government spending over the rights of the poor and the working people and over social questions of health, education, and welfare.

As a nationalist party, the Congress Party is intimately associated with the stability of the Indian nation and the state in Indian political culture. Regardless of its economic program, therefore, the Congress has always attracted support from diverse social groups: rich and poor, upper and lower castes, Hindus and Muslims, northerners and southerners. Nevertheless, elections in the 1990s indicate that Congress has lost some of its traditional constituencies among the poor, lower castes, and Muslims.

The Janata Party

The Janata Party, India's other centrist party, formed short-lived national governments in 1977, 1989, and together with other parties through the United Front in 1996 and 1997. The Janata Party, however, is not so much a political party as an umbrella for various parties and factions that change with the political circumstances. The Janata Party was created in 1977 when several small parties that opposed Indira Gandhi's Emergency hurriedly united to contest her and, much to their own surprise, won the national elections. This loose coalition lasted only a little over two years, when conflicting leadership ambitions tore it apart.

During the late 1980s, the Janata Party enjoyed another brief term as a national government under the leadership of a breakaway Congress leader, V. P. Singh. With these appeals, the party won enough seats in the national parliament to form a minority government in 1989. Once again, factionalism overwhelmed any attempt at a stable government, and this second attempt with a non-Congress-led government collapsed after a little over two years. Since then, the Janata Party has been able to survive only under the umbrella of the United Front, which is a collection of smaller parties, including the CPM.

The Janata Party has a very weak organizational structure and lacks a distinctive, coherent political platform. To distinguish itself from Congress, it claims that it is more Gandhian, a reference to Mahatma Gandhi's vision that modern India should be more decentralized and village oriented, and less pro-Brahmin. Although most of its efforts at political self-definition have not been very successful, V. P. Singh undertook one major policy initiative while in power that identified the Janata Party with a progressive cause. This was the acceptance of the Mandal Commission's recommendation that India's **"Other Backward Classes,"** generally, the middle, rural castes that constitute a near majority in the Indian countryside, be provided substantial reservations (or reserved access) to government jobs and educational institutions. The government's acceptance of this recommendation produced a nationwide outburst of riots and violence, led by upper castes, who felt threatened. The uproar eventually contributed to the downfall of V. P. Singh's government. Nevertheless, Singh's acceptance of what has been called "Mandal" associated the Janata Party with the interests of the backward castes. How strongly backward castes will continue to identify with this party in the future is unknown. For now, the Janata Party is viewed, especially in north-central India, as a party of small, rural agriculturalists who generally fall somewhere in the middle of the rigid caste hierarchy between Brahmins and untouchables.

The Bharatiya Janata Party (BJP)

The BJP, the major political party in contemporary India, is a direct descendant of the Jana Sangh Party, which entered the Indian political scene in 1951. The Jana Sangh joined the Janata Party government in 1977 but then split off and formed the BJP in 1980. The BJP is a right-leaning, Hindu-nationalist party, the first major party to mobilize explicitly on the basis of religious identity and to often adopt an anti-Muslim stance. In comparison to both the Congress and the Janata, the BJP is better organized; it has disciplined party members, who after a prolonged apprenticeship become party cadres, and the authority lines within the party are relatively clear and well respected.

The party is closely affiliated with many related organizations, the most significant of which is the RSS. Most BJP leaders were at one-time members of the RSS, which recruits young people (especially educated youth in urban areas) and involves them in a fairly disciplined set of cultural activities, including the study of a chauvinistic reinterpretation of India's "great Hindu past." These young people, uniformed in khaki shorts and shirts, can often be seen in Indian cities doing group exercises in the mornings and evenings and singing songs glorifying India's Sanskritic civilization (Sanskrit is the classical language in which some of the ancient Hindu scriptures are written). Recalling the pursuits of right-wing fascist groups of interwar Europe, the activities of these youth groups, seemingly no more than an appeal to cultural pride, dismay many non-Hindu minorities and Indian liberals, who fear the havoc that cultural pride can produce, as it did in Nazi Germany.

Those traditionally attracted to the Jana Sangh and the BJP were mainly urban, lower-middle-class groups, especially small traders and commercial groups. As long as this was its main source of support, the BJP remained a minor actor on the Indian political scene. Since the mid-1980s, however, the BJP has widened its base of support appreciably by appealing to Hindu nationalism, especially in north-central India. The decline in the Congress Party's popularity created a vacuum that the BJP was well positioned to fill. Moreover, the BJP found in Indian Muslims a convenient scapegoat for the frustrations of various social groups and successfully mobilized Hindus in an attempt to create a religiously oriented political force where none had existed before. The electoral success of the BJP in 1989 and 1991 and its formation of the government in 1999 underscore the party's rapid rise to power. The BJP's early efforts resulted in its ruling four states from 1991 to 1993, though it lost power in three of the four in 1993. During the 1999 parliamentary elections, the BJP scored a major success and formed the national government.

The growth of the BJP in recent years represents a break with past traditions. In the aftermath of independence, the RSS and its affiliated organizations were widely regarded as divisive, anti-Muslim organizations. The BJP's predecessor, the *Bharatiya Jana Sangh,* responded to its stigmatization by adopting a relatively moderate, centrist position through the 1984 elections, when it won only two seats in parliament. Its fortunes began to rise after the 1989 elections, when it emerged as the third largest party after the Congress and Janata parties. In 1991, the BJP held the second largest number of seats in parliament. To capitalize on the Hindu support it had been mobilizing, the BJP acquiesced in the demolition of the Babri Masjid (a Muslim mosque) in Ayodhya in 1992.

Six years later, as a result of the failures of other parties to lead effective governments, the BJP formed a governing coalition, the National Democratic Alliance, led by Prime Minister Atal Behari Vajpayee. However, its mismanagement of the economy soon generated a popular backlash against the BJP. The BJP performed very badly in four state government assembly elections in 1998, losing to the Congress Party in three states and to a regional party in the fourth state. The BJP government collapsed in 1999, just thirteen months after taking power.

The BJP formed a new electoral coalition, the National Democratic Alliance government, headed by Atal Behari Vajpayee, which was elected in 1999. It was more broadly based than previous BJP-led coalition governments because it attracted the support of regionally based political parties in various states. The result not only strengthened the BJP's hold on power but also strengthened trends toward the regionalization of Indian politics.

Another reason for the greater strength of the BJP-led government in 1999 was its cultivation of a more moderate, centrist stance. In 1996, most political parties shunned an alliance with the BJP, for it was tainted by its militant identity. Even in 1998, the BJP put together a governing coalition with great difficulty. In 1999, the BJP went to great lengths to project Atal Behari Vajpayee as a moderate, centrist leader. Moreover, the National Democratic Alliance platform shelved contentious issues that identified it with the interests of Hindus over and against those of religious minorities.

The BJP has not fully swung to the political center or abdicated its militance. It continues to retain strong ties to the RSS and periodically demonstrates its commitment to constructing a temple in Ayodhya. Its handling of the Gujarat riots in 2002 revealed its reluctance to act decisively to bring the guilty to trial either during the riots or in their aftermath for fear of alienating hard-line supporters.

A number of factors have prevented the BJP from moving in a wholly centrist direction. The first and most important concerns its close ties to the RSS and the Hindu religious organization, the *Visva Hindu Parishad* (VHP). Since its formation in 1964, the VHP has sought to strengthen Hindu identity in a chauvinist and exclusionary fashion. In the 1960s, its activities centered on converting Muslims, who, it claimed, had been forcibly converted to Hinduism. Since the 1980s, it has been active around the construction of the temple in Ayodhya.

There are clearly some important differences in the orientation of these organizations. The RSS is committed to economic nationalism, the BJP to liberalization. The VHP has been implicated in violence, whereas the BJP has promised stability. Despite these differences, the BJP has maintained a close relationship to the RSS and the VHP. The RSS has intervened to mend rifts within the party in various states. It has helped ensure that the BJP, unlike most Indian political parties, has never split. Moreover, it is hard to imagine a complete severance between the two organizations when the highest-ranking BJP members are of RSS backgrounds, and many of them have continuing ties to the RSS. The BJP's relationship to the VHP, though conflictual at times when the BJP is in office, has also been salutary. RSS and VHP activists have regularly participated in the electoral campaigns of the BJP in state and general elections. Moreover, the riots that the VHP has engineered have polarized the electorate along Hindu-Muslim lines and expanded the BJP's electoral fortunes.

The BJP's continuing commitment to privileging the interests of the Hindu majority, evident in response to the Gujarat riots, the temple construction in Ayodhya, and policies in Kashmir, has increased the vulnerability of the Muslim community. Although the BJP has consistently proclaimed its attachment to secular principles, it has taken steps to undermine the conditions under which secularism flourishes. Its promises of providing clean, honest governance have been marred in recent years by disclosures of corruption by high-ranking officials, for example, in the discriminatory distribution of relief after a massive earthquake in Gujarat in 2001, in charges that the army had engaged in corruption after a border clash with Pakistan in 1999, and in patterns of bribery in defense procurement in 2001.

The Communist Party of India (CPM)

The CPM is an offshoot of the Communist Party of India, which was formed during the colonial period and has existed nearly as long as the Congress Party. Although the contemporary CPM has a national presence in that it nearly always elects representatives to the *Lok Sabha,* its political base is concentrated in two of India's states, West Bengal and Kerala. These states have often been ruled by the CPM, and they often elect *Lok Sabha* members who run on a CPM ticket.

The CPM is a disciplined party, with party cadres and a hierarchical authority structure. Other than its name and internal organization, however, there is nothing communist about the CPM; rather, it is a social democratic party like the British Labour Party or the German Social Democratic Party. The CPM accepts the framework of democracy, regularly participates in elections, and often wins them in West Bengal and Kerala. In these two states, the CPM enjoys the support of the lower-middle and lower classes, both factory workers and poorer peasants. Within the national parliament, CPM members often strongly criticize government policies that are likely to hurt the poor. On occasion, the CPM joins with other parties against the BJP, as it did in the 1996 elections by joining the United Front. Where the CPM runs state governments, for example, in West Bengal and Kerala, it has provided a relatively honest and stable administration. It has also pursued a moderate but effective reform program,

ensuring the rights of agricultural tenants (such as preventing their evictions), providing services to those living in shanty towns, and encouraging public investments in rural areas.

Elections

Elections in India are a colossal event. Nearly 500 million people are eligible to vote, and close to 300 million do so. The turnout rate in the 1990s was over 60 percent, considerably higher than in the United States. The level of technology used in both campaigning and the conduct of elections is fairly low. Television plays an increasingly important role, but much campaigning still involves face-to-face contact between politicians and the electorate. Senior leaders fly around the country, making speeches to millions of potential supporters at political rallies held in tiny villages and district towns. Lesser politicians and thousands of their party supporters travel the dusty streets, blaring music and political messages from loudspeakers mounted on their vehicles.

Given the high rate of illiteracy, pictures of party symbols are critical: a hand for the Congress (I); a lotus for the BJP; a hammer and sickle for the CPM. Illiterate voters signify their vote for a candidate in the polling booth by putting thumb marks on one of these symbols. During the campaign, therefore, party representatives work very hard to associate certain individuals and election platforms with specific symbols. A typical election slogan is, "Vote for the hammer and sickle because they stand for the rights of the working people."

India's electoral system, like the British system, is a first-past-the-post system. A number of candidates compete in an electoral district; the candidate who has the most votes wins. For example, if the Congress candidate wins the most votes, say 35 percent of the vote from a district, and the candidates of other parties split the remaining votes, the Congress candidate is victorious. This system privileges the major political parties. It also generates considerable pressure for opposition parties to collaborate as a single voice against the government. In practice, however, given the differences between opposition parties and the considerable clash of leadership ambitions, many parties compete, enabling the candidates of the larger party to squeeze by as winners.

Village women wait in line to get voting slips at a polling station in a village in India's Orissa state, March 7, 1995. *Source:* Bettmann/Corbis.

One of the pillars of Indian democracy is its system of free and fair elections. Credit for this goes in part to the Election Commission, a constitutionally mandated central body that functions independently of the executive. Particularly since 1991, with the appointment of an honest and respected chief, the Election Commission has defended free and fair elections.

Political Culture, Citizenship, and Identity

The only generalization that can be made about Indian political culture is that in such a large and culturally diverse country, no single set of cultural traits is shared by the entire population. Nevertheless, three important tendencies or habits of mind are worth noting. These political cultural traits reflect India's hybrid political style, as a rigid, hierarchical, and village-oriented old civilization adapts itself to modern socioeconomic changes, especially to democratic politics.

One important tendency is that India's political and public spheres are not sharply divided from personal and private spheres of activity. The idea that public office is not a legitimate means for personal enrichment or for furthering the interests of family members or of personal associates is not yet fully accepted in India. As a result, there is fairly widespread misuse of public resources for personal gain, that is, widespread corruption in political life.

Second, the Indian elite is highly factionalized. The roots of such behavior are complex, reflecting India's fragmented social structure. Although some important exceptions exist, generally the personal political ambitions of Indian leaders prevent them from pursuing such collective goals as forming cohesive political parties, running a stable government, or focusing on problems of national development. In contrast to many East Asian countries, where the norms of consensus are powerful and political negotiation is often conducted behind closed doors, politics in India veers toward the other extreme, and open disagreements and conflicts are the norm.

The third, and possibly most important, political cultural tendency that deserves mention concerns the fragmentation of political life in India. Indian society is highly segmented. Different regions have different languages and cultures; within regions, villages are poorly connected with each other; and within villages, different castes often live in isolation from one another. Politics is often fragmented along caste lines, but even caste grievances tend to remain local rather than accumulate nationally or even regionally. Some observers of India find this segmented quality of Indian politics a blessing because it localizes problems, facilitating political stability, but others find it a curse because it stymies the possibility of national reforms to improve the lot of the poorest members of society.

Democracy is relatively well established in India. Most Indians value their citizenship rights and, in spite of poverty and illiteracy, exercise them with vigor. However, the spread of democratic politics can simultaneously fuel political conflicts. The spread of democracy is undermining many of India's political givens, including some of the most rigid hierarchies, and has begun to produce new political patterns.

The most significant of these recent developments concerns identity politics, whereby the dynamics of democratic politics mobilizes social identities in the service of political conflicts. Region, language, religion, and caste all help Indians define who they are. Such differences have generated political cleavages in India, underlining the importance and yet the malleability of collective identities, for example, the Hindu-Muslim conflict at the time of independence. Some of these identity conflicts remained dormant when Nehru's secular nationalism and Indira Gandhi's poor-versus-rich cleavage defined the core political issues. In the 1980s and 1990s, however, with the relative decline of the Congress Party and with developments in telecommunications and transportation that have made people more aware of each other's differences, identity-based political conflicts have mushroomed in India.

Two of the more significant conflicts deserve mention. First, caste conflicts, though usually confined to local and regional politics, have taken on a national dimension in recent years, for example, former prime minister V. P. Singh's acceptance of the Mandal Commission recommendations. These recommendations were meant to benefit India's backward castes, who are numerically significant and tend to be rural agriculturalists by occupation and somewhere in the middle of the caste hierarchy. Groups of backward castes had made a political mark in many states, but prior to Mandal, they were seldom a cohesive factor in national politics. In all probability, V. P. Singh hoped to create a powerful support base out of these disparate groups. However, the move backfired. The threatened upper castes reacted sharply with demonstrations, riots, and political violence. Not only did this disruption contribute to the downfall of Singh's government, but it also converted the conflict between castes from a local and regional issue to a divisive national issue.

The second identity-based political conflict that has reemerged has pitched Hindus and Muslims against each other. Tensions between these religious communities go back several centuries, when Muslim rulers from Central Asia established the Moghul dynasty in India. Stories and memories of the relative greatness of one community over the other, or of atrocities and injustices unleashed on one community by the other, abound in India's popular culture. For the most part, these legends fan low-level hostilities that do not prevent peaceful coexistence. However, political circumstances, especially political machinations by ambitious leaders, can inflame these tendencies and instigate overt conflict. This is what has happened since the mid-1980s, as the BJP has whipped up anti-Muslim

sentiments in an effort to unite disparate Hindu groups into a political force. The resulting victimization of Muslims in acts of political violence, including destruction of life, property, and places of worship, illustrates the dangers of identity-based political passions.

There are many poor or otherwise frustrated social groups in India whose anger is available for political mobilization. Whether the BJP will succeed in tapping this anger in the longer term cannot be predicted. What can be said is that democracy and large pockets of social frustration provide a combustible mix that will continue to generate unexpected outcomes in Indian politics.

Interests, Social Movements, and Protest

India has a vibrant tradition of political activism that has both enriched and complicated the workings of democracy. Social movements, nongovernmental organizations (NGOs), and trade unions have put pressure on the state to be attentive to the interests and needs of underprivileged groups and have checked its authoritarian tendencies.

Among the groups that are politically active, labor has played a significant but not leading role. Labor unions are politically fragmented, particularly at the national level. Instead of the familiar model of one factory/one union, several political parties often organize within a single factory. Above the factory level, several labor organizations compete for labor's support. The government generally stays out of labor-management conflicts. India's industrial relations are thus closer to the pluralist model practiced in Anglo-American countries than to the corporatist model of, say, Mexico. The political energies of unions are channeled into frequent local battles involving strikes, demonstrations, and a peculiarly Indian protest technique called *gherao,* which entails workers' encircling and holding executives of the firm hostage until their demands are met.

Social movements, the most important form of civil society activism, date back to the mid-1970s. During the period of the national Emergency (1975–1977) when the government imprisoned members of the opposition, activists began to come together to form political parties and social movements, often with close ties to one another. In 1977, the Gandhian Socialist leader Jai Prakash Narain organized the movement for total democracy that ultimately brought about the downfall of Congress and the election of the Janata Party. A decade later, V. P. Singh resigned from Congress and formed the *Jan Morcha* (Peoples' Front), an avowedly nonpolitical movement that brought new groups into politics and helped bring the National Front to power in 1989.

Social movements continued to grow and assume new organizational forms in the 1980s. Some engaged in grassroots activism, and others worked more closely with the state. The number of NGOs also expanded. Until the early 1980s, when Indira Gandhi was prime minister, the state was distrustful of what is commonly known in India as the voluntary sector and sought to restrict its activities. When Rajiv Gandhi came to power, he attempted to cultivate a closer relationship with NGOs, for he recognized their potential for taking over some of the development work that the state had traditionally performed. Over the years, financial support for NGOs from the national government has steadily increased. During the seventh five-year plan (1985–1990), the federal government spent about US$11 million each year through NGOs; by 2002 this had increased to over $44 million annually. Today there are 20,000 voluntary organizations listed with the Ministry of Home Affairs, and the actual number is much higher. The most significant social movements organized around either distinctive themes or identities include the women's movement, the environmental movement, and the *dalit* (a term of pride used by untouchables) movement. In recent years, there has also been the growth of antinuclear, civil liberties activism. The extraordinarily large number and extensive activities of social movements make India quite distinctive among developing countries.

The environment movement is organized by educated urban activists and some of India's poorest and most marginal groups. Their activism has been spurred by the magnitude of the country's environmental crisis and the ineffectiveness of its environmental laws. India suffers from severe air pollution in large cities and contaminated lakes and rivers. The shortage of drinking water is worsened by salinization, water overuse, and groundwater depletion. The emission of carbon dioxide has contributed to the greenhouse effect, leading to an increase in temperature, a rise in the sea level, and the destruction of coastal crop lands and fisheries.

Commercial logging, fuel wood depletion, and urbanization have caused serious problems of deforestation, which is associated with droughts, floods, and cyclones.

Successive governments have chosen to promote increased production at the expense of environmental protection. Effective enforcement of environmental laws and policies would put many firms out of business and slow economic growth. Moreover, it would be very time-consuming and difficult for the government to monitor and control all small-scale industries. Although the Congress Party sponsored most of India's environmental laws, it also catered to the interest of big business at the expense of environmental protection. The United Front parties have been strong supporters of environmental issues but have tended to target only big business rather than small businesses. The Bharatiya Janata Party has explicitly placed business interests over environmental concerns. Thus, the major sources of support for environmental protection have been social movements and NGOs.

The Chipko movement against deforestation in the Himalayas, which emerged in the early 1970s, has been one of the longest-lasting movements against deforestation and has influenced similar forms of activism in other regions of the country. Large-scale protest at the 1984 Union Carbide disaster in Bhopal demanded greater compensation for victims of the gas leak, as well as more environmental regulations to prevent similar disasters in the future. This resulted in the creation of the Central Pollution Control Board in 1986 and a series of environmental statutes, regulations, and protocols.

The largest and most significant environmental movement in India has protested the construction of the Sardar Sarvodaya Dam in western India. The Narmada Bachao Andolan (NBA), led by a woman named Medha Pathkar, has organized opposition to the construction of the dam on grounds that it will benefit already prosperous regions to the detriment of poor regions, lead to the large-scale displacement of people, and put in place vastly inadequate resettlement schemes. A large proportion of those who would be displaced are tribals who do not possess land titles. The movement has galvanized tens of thousands of people to engage in nonviolent protest to oppose the construction of the dam. The protest caused the World Bank to rescind promised loans, but the Indian government is still pursuing the project.

Women and questions of gender inequality have been at the forefront of environmental struggles like the Chipko and Narmada movements. The 1980s also witnessed the formation of a number of autonomous urban women's organizations. They campaigned around rape in police custody, dowry murders, *sati* (the immolation of widows on their husbands' funeral pyres), female feticide (through the use of amniocentesis), misrepresentation of women in the media, protest against harmful contraception dissemination, coercive population policies, and, most recently, the adverse impact of the economic reforms.

The *dalit* movement looks back to Dr. Ambedkar, the *dalit* author of the Indian constitution, as the founding father of the movement. He was responsible for the creation of the Republican Party in the late 1960s The disintegration of the party gave rise to the emergence of a radical youth movement that called itself the Dalit Panthers. The movement organized *dalits* to demand to be treated with dignity, to be provided better educational opportunities, and to become more politically active. Today, the *dalit* movement reflects dalits' growing aspirations for electoral power and public office.

Kanshi Ram formed the Bahujan Samaj Party (BSP) in 1989 with the goal of achieving political power for the *dalits*. The BSP experienced significant growth in the 1990s. With a share of 4.7 percent of the national vote in 1998 and 4.2 percent in 1999, it is almost as strong as the CPM (5.4 percent). However, its strength is mainly confined to Uttar Pradesh. Other small lower-caste parties have been active in Maharashtra and Tamil Nadu. However, none of these parties is able to play a national role other than participating in and influencing electoral alliances. Moreover, these parties have confined themselves to seeking political power for *dalits* and lack a broader vision of social transformation. Tensions have emerged within the *dalit* community. Some of the poorer and lower-status *dalits* feel that the better-off, higher-status *dalits* have benefited from reservations at their expense. Radical sections within the *dalit* movement argue that *dalits* ought not to depend entirely on reservations or the state, but should initiate a mass movement of their own that highlights issues of employment, education, and landlessness.

Three important developments have influenced the character and trajectory of social movements in recent years. First, many social movements have been drawn into a closer relationship to the state and to electoral politics. In the past, social movements tended to be community based and issue specific. Once they had achieved some success, around, say, the felling of forest trees, the construction of a dam, or higher prices for agricultural subsidies, the movement would subside. Although many social movements continue to be confined by their focus, duration, and geographic reach, some of them have sought to overcome these difficulties by engaging in electoral politics. The *dalit* movement and Hindu nationalism are two of the most important examples. Participation in electoral politics has in turn shaped and influenced these movements' goals. Other movements have sought to work with particular branches of the state. The women's movement, for example, has worked closely with the bureaucracy and the courts. In part because of the closer relationship between social movements and the state, an enduring broad left-wing formation consisting of left-wing parties and social movements has not emerged. By contrast, Hindu nationalists, particularly under the auspice of the VHP, have sustained their strong connections to the BJP.

Second, the growth of the religious right has confronted left-wing social movements with a serious challenge and dilemma. Unlike some other regions of the world where the religious right and the secular left disagree on most issues, the situation in India is more complex. Segments of the religious right, like parts of the left, oppose economic liberalization and globalization. For example, both feminists and Hindu nationalists oppose the commodification of women's bodies that occurs in international beauty pageants. Similarly, the women's movement has put on the back burner its demand for a uniform civil code that would provide equal treatment of men and women of all religious communities under the law because the BJP has made this very demand, albeit for very different reasons.

A third important development has been that many NGOs and social movements have developed extensive transnational connections. The consequences for social movements have been double-edged. On the positive side, funding from foreign sources has been vital to the survival of NGOs and social movements. India lacks a tradition of donating to secular-philanthropic causes, and corporate funding is limited and tightly controlled. However, organizations receiving foreign funding are often viewed with suspicion and have difficulty establishing their legitimacy. Moreover, foreign funding has created a sharp division between activists with and without access to foreign donors.

If these developments have complicated the agendas of social movements, there is also a strong potential for NGOs and social movements to grow stronger. There are greater opportunities than ever before for social movement and NGO activists to take advantage of the resources that the state is making available to the local level. Some groups have already done this by putting candidates up for elections at the local level, as we have seen in the case of the *panchayats.*

To review, political participation over the years in India has broadened in scope and deepened in intensity. A single-party system dominated by the Congress Party has slowly been supplanted by a multiparty system of parties on the left and the right. Similarly, old hierarchies of caste have eroded in Indian society, and upper castes cannot readily control the political behavior of those below them. The result is that many groups in society increasingly feel empowered and hope to translate this new consciousness and sense of efficacy into material gains by influencing government policies.

Section ⑤ Indian Politics in Transition

Political Challenges and Changing Agendas

As a large country with a legitimate government and sizable armed forces, India has not readily been influenced by external forces. For example, India tested nuclear bombs in 1998 and successfully withstood international condemnation and sanctions. However, in an increasingly interdependent global economic context, India has become far more vulnerable to global pressures. The changing geopolitical environment in the aftermath of the September 11 terrorist attacks has drawn India into closer relations with the United States. India today must confront major challenges at home and abroad if it is to preserve and strengthen its democratic institutions and improve its economic performance.

Kashmir Within a World of States

Of all the challenges that India has faced since independence, among the most enduring and intractable is its relationship to Kashmir, the state located in northern India on the border with Pakistan. The roots of conflict within Kashmir have often been attributed to the ethnic and religious diversity of the state, which is roughly 65 percent Muslim and 35 percent Hindus and other minorities. The non-Muslim minorities—Hindus, Sikhs, and Buddhists, who are concentrated in the areas of the state called Jammu and Ladakh—largely wish to live under Indian sovereignty. The Kashmir Valley, which is predominantly Sunni Muslim, is mostly in favor of Kashmir's becoming an independent country or part of Pakistan. However, separatist sentiments cannot be explained primarily by ethnic differences. Rather, one must ask what led many Kashmiri Muslims to become progressively radicalized against India.

Heightened separatist, fundamentalist, and terrorist activities have resulted from the frustrations many Kashmiris have experienced as a result of the central government's actions. At independence, Nehru promised that a referendum would be held in Kashmir to decide the status of the region. However, the Indian government never honored this pledge, mainly because it has feared a pro-independence vote. With the partial exceptions of 1947–1953 and 1977–1984, Kashmir has been directly ruled from New Delhi. This has retarded democratic participation and institutional development in the state. As demands for independence grew, so too did the repressive actions of the Indian state, leading to spiraling cycles of insurgent militance and state-sanctioned violence. Pakistan also contributed significantly to the insurgency by training and supporting the militants. Whether the fate of Kashmiris can be resolved today through democratic means is an open question.

More than any other conflict, the Kashmir dispute is triggered and sustained by the international context. The timing of Indian independence and simultaneous partition of the subcontinent into India and Partition fueled tensions in Kashmir and created uncertainty over its status within the Indian union. Superpower rivalry in the cold war deterred India and Pakistan from reaching an agreement on the status of Kashmir that would be acceptable to India, Pakistan, and the population of Kashmir itself.

Kashmir represents an important case study of the pitfalls and possibilities of democratic governance in India. It reveals the limits of democracy, for the national government has ruled Kashmir more undemocratically than any other state in India, through a combination of repression, direct control, and intervention to uphold unrepresentative governments. The constant rigging of elections has prevented the development of free and autonomous competition among political parties. While elections were held in most parts of the country from 1952 onward, in Kashmir elections to the Legislative Assembly were held in only 1962 and to the Parliament only in 1967. Most elections in Jammu and Kashmir were fraudulent. The most recent elections in 2002 are a partial exception to this. Although these elections witnessed the police and army forcing people to vote, in part in response to the separatists' support for an electoral boycott, they were more open and inclusive than previous elections. The National Conference, which had been in power for over two decades and had become an ally of the BJP government at the national level, lost heavily. The BJP, which had previously had a strong presence in the Hindu-dominated Jammu region, faced an even bigger setback. After strenuous negotiations, the People's Democratic Party (PDP) and the Congress Party formed a coalition government with PDP's Mufti Mohammad Sayeed as chief minister. The new government proclaimed that it would not implement the undemocratic Prevention of Terrorism Act. It also released several prominent political prisoners. Both policies have already led to friction with the national BJP government.

In addition to ethnic conflict within Kashmir, the other serious impediment to resolving the Kashmiri dispute is continuing tensions between India and Pakistan. These tensions are one of the important reasons for the two countries' high military expenditures (see Figure 5). As recently as the summer of 1999, Pakistani units infiltrated the Indian border and launched a massive air and land campaign. After six weeks of fighting in May and June 1999, Pakistan's prime minister, Musharaf, agreed to withdraw Pakistani troops. Frosty relations between India and Pakistan began to thaw

only a year later. In November 2000, Prime Minister Vajpayee proclaimed a cease-fire, and firing along the Line of Control, the border between India and Pakistan, almost came to a halt. However, the gains of the cease-fire were partial. Within Kashmir, violence by the Indian army and militants continued. Vajpayee and Musharaf held a summit in Agra in July 2001, where the two sides made some progress on numerous secondary issues dividing the two countries, including peace and security, terrorism, drug trafficking, and economic and commercial cooperation. But they failed to make progress on resolving the status of Kashmir, which remains the fundamental cause of tensions between the two countries. Indeed, following the attacks in the United States of September 11, 2001, relations became even more fraught. Understanding why requires putting the aftermath of September 11 in a wider context.

The Effects of September 11

The terrorist attacks of September 11 had important implications for India's relations with its neighbors and with the United States. Prior to September 11, the

Figure 5

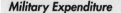

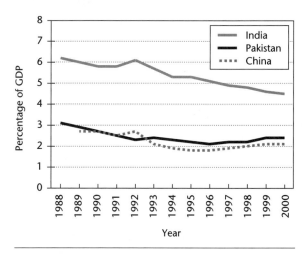

Source: Information from the Stockholm International Peace Research Institute (SIPRI), Military Expenditure Database, http://first.sipri.org/non_first/result/milex.php

Pakistani regime had been a major supporter of the Taliban government. With the overthrow of the Taliban and the establishment of the Hamid Karzai government, the new Afghan government established close diplomatic, civil, and commercial ties to India.

In the aftermath of September 11, India began to depict opposition forces in Kashmir as part of international Islamic militancy and demanded that one front in the global U.S. war against terror was militant groups operating from Pakistan to destabilize Kashmir. As a result, tensions increased between India and Pakistan. Soon after September 11, there was an exchange of fire on the border between the two countries. Relations plummeted further with an attack on the Jammu and Kashmir Legislative Assembly in early 2001 and, far more serious, following an attack on the Indian parliament later that year. India charged that the attacks on a key political institution were orchestrated by Pakistan. Following the attack on parliament, India prepared for war with Pakistan by recalling its high commissioner from Islamabad, the Pakistani capital, terminating train and bus service between the two countries, and, most alarming, massing most of its 1.2 million troops near the Pakistani border. Pakistan responded in kind, and for several weeks, nuclear conflagration seemed a distinct possibility. Intense intervention by the United States helped to defuse the situation, and Pakistan and India withdrew most of their troops from the border. However, relations between the two countries remain tense.

Relations between India and the United States became much closer after September 11. Abandoning its previous policy of nonalignment, India allowed the United States to establish a military presence in the country. The United States has been more involved than ever before in negotiating Indo-Pakistan tensions over Kashmir, in the conflict in Sri Lanka over a separate Tamil state, and in Nepal, which has experienced bitter conflict between the monarchy and Maoist militants for over six years.

Nuclear Power Status

One major political challenge for India is how to negotiate with the rest of the world, particularly the United States, on its emergence as a nuclear weapons state. Following India's nuclear tests of May 1998, the focus of international, and particularly U.S., diplomacy sought

to enforce a universal nonproliferation agreement. The Vajpayee and the Clinton administrations engaged in several rounds of delicate arms control talks in which Clinton tried to persuade India to sign the Comprehensive Test Ban Treaty (CTBT) and the Nuclear Non-Proliferation Treaty (NPT) in exchange for completely lifting U.S. sanctions. India opposed the NPT on the grounds that it was unfair to nonnuclear countries because it did not establish a procedure for eventual phase-out of nuclear weapons by the nuclear powers. The United States urged India to exercise restraint on its nuclear weapons and missiles programs, while New Delhi insisted on its right to minimum nuclear deterrence. In late 1998, India announced its intention to sign the CTBT if talks with the United States ended successfully and also signaled its willingness to join other nuclear control groups. In February 1999, during a historic visit to Pakistan by the Indian prime minister, both countries agreed to continue their declared nuclear moratoriums on further nuclear tests.

Can India combine its new nuclear power status with responsible use of such weapons? Can it negotiate with its nuclear neighbors, Pakistan and China, to ensure that South Asia does not set off a nuclear disaster? How India confronts challenges on the nuclear front is closely tied to its success in several other areas, including resolution of the Kashmir dispute, the management of increasing ethnic tensions, and its economic performance.

Civil Liberties

Compared to other comparably large, multiethnic democracies, India has generally shown great respect for the pillars of civil rights: a free and lively press, legal protections for citizens' rights, and an independent judiciary. India's media, especially its newspapers and magazines, are as free as any in the world. They represent a wide variety of viewpoints, engage in vigorous investigative reporting and analysis, and maintain pressure for public action. The combination of a vocal intellectual stratum and a free press is a cherished element in India's democracy.

Nevertheless, India's tradition of a strong, interventionist state has enabled the state to violate civil liberties, and the trend since the mid-1980s has been troubling. Global events conjoined with national ones resulted in a restriction of civil liberties in the aftermath of the September 11. The BJP-led government used the war against terrorism as justification for depicting pro-independence groups in Kashmir and Muslim groups throughout India as terrorist.

Soon after September 11, the Indian government banned the Students Islamic Movement of India (SIMI), the students' wing of the radical Islamic political party, the Jamaat-e-Islami, in Pakistan. However, the government did not ban the Bajrang Dal, the militant organization with ties to the VHP that has repeatedly organized anti Muslim violence, most recently in Gujarat in 2002.

After September 11, the Indian government issued the Prevention of Terrorism Ordinance (POTO), later enacted into law by parliament. Its definition of terrorism is extremely vague, and a citizen need not have committed a specific act to be charged under POTO: conspiring, attempting to commit, advocating, abetting, advising, or inciting such acts are punishable, with penalties ranging from stiff prison sentences to death. Membership in a terrorist organization is punishable with life imprisonment. Confessions made to police officers are admissible as evidence in courts, contrary to ordinary law, and confessions are brutally extracted in Indian police stations. The right to bail is severely restricted. An accused person can be kept in police custody for one month and in jail for six months without even being charged.[7] In certain regions, merely possessing arms is punishable with life imprisonment.

Predictably, POTO has been used mostly against Muslims and political dissidents. The largest number of arrests took place in India's newest state, Jharkhand, where members and supporters of Marxist-Leninist groups have been taken into custody under POTO. Marxist-Leninist parties such as CPI (ML)–People's War Group, and the Maoist Communist Center have been banned. By 2002, twenty-three organizations had been banned under POTO.

The Challenge of Ethnic Diversity

The future of Indian democracy is closely bound up with how the country confronts the growing political impact of ethnic identities. Mobilized ethnic groups seeking access to state power and state-controlled economic resources are a basic component of the contemporary Indian political scene. Caste, language, and religion all provide identities around which political mobilization can be galvanized. Identification with a group is heightened by the democratic context, in which parties and leaders freely choose to manipulate such symbols. When studying Indian politics, it is difficult to separate interest- and identity-based politics. For example, caste struggles in India are simultaneously struggles for identity, power, and wealth. Identity politics in India is likely to be characterized by two trends: considerable political ferment, with a variety of dissatisfied groups making demands on parties and governments, and pressure on political parties to broaden their electoral appeal to disadvantaged groups, especially those belonging to the middle and lower strata, many of whom are very poor. India's political leaders will thus continue to experience pressures to expand their support base by promising economic improvements or manipulating nationalist symbols. Under what conditions will such political forces engage in constructive rather than destructive actions? Will democracy succeed in merely tempering the effect of such forces, or will it in the long run promote a positive channeling of identity politics? A factor that will affect an answer to these questions is India's economic performance.

Economic Performance

Comparativists debate how well an economy is governed. India's economic experience is neither a clear success nor a clear failure. If many African countries have done poorly economically and many East Asian countries (prior to 1997) have had dramatic successes, India falls somewhere in the middle. Three conditions may explain this outcome. The first is the nature and the quality of the government for promoting economic growth. In this, India has been fortunate to have enjoyed relatively good government since independence: its democratic system is mostly open and stable, its most powerful political leaders are public spirited, and its upper bureaucracy is well trained and competent. These positive attributes stand out in comparison with many African countries, such as Nigeria.

The second condition concerns India's strategy for economic development. India in the 1950s chose to insulate its economy from global forces, limiting the role of trade and foreign investment and emphasizing the role of government in promoting self-sufficiency in heavy industry and agriculture. The positive impact of this strategy was that India now produces enough food to feed its large and growing population while it simultaneously produces a vast range of industrial goods. This strategy, however, was not without costs. Most of India's manufactured goods are produced rather inefficiently by global standards. India sacrificed the additional economic growth that might have come from competing effectively in the global markets and by selling its products abroad. It also gave up another area of potential economic growth by discouraging foreign investment. And last, during the phase of protective industrialization, India did little to alleviate its staggering poverty: land redistribution failed, job creation by heavy industries was minimal, and investment in the education and health of the poor was minuscule in relation to the magnitude of the problem. The poor also became a drag on economic growth because they were unable to buy goods and stimulate demand for increased production and because an uneducated and unhealthy labor force is not a productive labor force.

A stable government and an emphasis on self-sufficiency have promoted modest economic growth in India; higher growth rates, however, have been difficult to achieve without greater links to the outside world and the alleviation of poverty. This leads to the third condition regarding India's middling political economy. India's continuing economic weakness has made it more vulnerable to global forces. The country's economic crisis in the early 1990s during the Gulf War exposed its vulnerability and prompted a shift toward a more open economy. This shift was associated with improved economic growth in the 1990s. However, the continuation of staggering levels of poverty in India is disturbing. If India is to sustain high levels of growth, the Indian government must address the issues of literacy, health, and welfare for the poor, enabling them to join the economy as truly productive participants. The challenge that Indian politicians face is to reconcile the demands of promoting an efficient economy with those of winning elections. The latter involves encouraging an expansion of government programs and subsidies to discontented groups, while the former calls for austerity. Restricting government's role conflicts with

implementing distributive or populist programs; opening the national economy to foreign economic actors and products is likely to aggravate nationalist sentiments.

Indian Politics in Comparative Perspective

Given its large size, diversity, and vibrant social and political system, India is an exceptionally good case study for analyzing themes of general significance in comparative politics. In this concluding section, we first examine the implications of the study of India for comparative politics and then assess how Indian politics and its economy will influence developments in a regional and global context.

Some comparative scholars suggest that citizens' widespread desire to exercise some control over their government is a potent force encouraging democracy. This assumption is clearly illustrated in India. Although democracy was introduced to India by its elites, it has established firm roots within society. A clear example is when Indira Gandhi declared Emergency rule (1975–1977) and curtailed democratic freedoms. In the next election, in 1977, Indian citizens decisively voted Indira Gandhi out of power, registering their preference for democratic rule. Most Indians value democracy and use its institutions to advance their claims.

Comparativists debate whether democracy or authoritarianism is better for economic growth. In the past, India did not compare well with the success stories of East Asian and Chinese authoritarian-led countries. The collapse in the late 1990s of several East Asian economies and the subsequent rise of instability within those societies makes a study of Indian democracy more relevant to understanding the institutional and cultural factors underpinning economic stability in the long run.

Another theme has been to assess the implications of establishing democracy in multiethnic societies. The rising tide of nationalism and the breakup of the Soviet Union and Yugoslavia, among others, have prompted closer examination of how and why India continues to exist as a cohesive entity. By studying India's history, particularly the post-1947 period, comparativists could explore questions of how cleavages of caste, religion, and language in India balance one another and cancel the most destructive elements in each. Comparativists have also puzzled about the conditions under which multiple and contradictory interests could be harnessed within a democratic setup to generate positive economic and distributional outcomes. Here, the variable performance of different regions in India can serve as a laboratory. For instance, two communist-ruled states, Kerala and West Bengal, have (to a certain extent) engaged in land redistribution policies. An examination of factors such as the role of the mobilizing parties and the interaction between the landless poor and the entrenched landed elite could provide answers. The main elements of the Kerala model are a land reform initiative that abolished tenancy and landlord exploitation, effective public food distribution that provides subsidized rice to low-income households, protective laws for agricultural workers, pensions for retired agricultural laborers, and a high rate of government employment for members of low-caste communities.

Another question engaging comparativists is whether success in providing education and welfare inevitably leads to success in the economic sphere. Again, the case of Kerala provides pointers for further research. Kerala scores high on human development indicators such as literacy and health, but paradoxically has not performed well in terms of achieving economic growth.

What are the international and domestic challenges that India faces at the dawn of the twenty-first century? How will it cope with its new-found status as a nuclear power? How can it prevent further escalation of conflict in the region that could end in a nuclear conflagration? A worst-case scenario would be a conventional war with Pakistan that could escalate into a nuclear war. Domestically, both countries are wracked with ethnic tensions, one with a military dictatorship and the other with an elected coalition government. In an attempt to hold on to power, the leaders of each country could try to divert attention toward a national security threat from its neighbor, a ploy that has been used effectively in the past by politicians in both countries. The history of three wars between India and Pakistan, the simmering tensions over Kashmir, and both countries' possession of nuclear arms could prompt a nuclear war. The challenge for India is to establish a stable relationship with its nuclear neighbors, Pakistan and China, that would eschew proliferation of their nuclear and ballistic missiles arsenals and engage in constructive diplomatic and economic cooperation. India's history of wars with both countries is not an encouraging starting point, but the

engagement of Western powers in generating a dialogue between these countries is a portent for the future. The visit to Pakistan by the Indian prime minister in 1999, the first visit in ten years and only the third ever, provides grounds for optimism. Whether such overtures will result in fruitful negotiations on Kashmir and on economic cooperation in the region remains to be seen. Answers to these questions depend at least in part on developments in the sphere of domestic politics.

Fifty years of democracy in India have been a double-edged sword. Winning elections involves attracting votes. While avoiding authoritarianism, the practice of democracy, particularly electoral politics, has worsened ethnic relations between Hindus and Muslims, upper and lower castes, and north and south. With the spread of democracy, many dissatisfied groups are finding their voices and becoming politically mobilized. The challenge for Indian politics is how to repair the divide within a democratic framework. Current voter emphasis on good governance and sound economic management rather than on religious or nationalistic issues might transform electoral platforms in the twenty-first century. In any case, on this score Indian politics will continue to tread a shaky path, as witnessed by the intensification of communal tensions marked by the macabre killing of a Christian missionary and his two young sons in Orissa in January 1999 by Hindu nationalists, as well as other attacks on Christians in scattered regions. Will India be able to manage its domestic tensions and enlarge social, political, and economic rights for its citizens?

Another challenge for India is how to combine its global ambitions of becoming a strong power with its program for economic liberalization. The increasing interdependence of global economies as manifested in global effects of the 1997 East Asian crisis and the dependence of developing countries on investor confidence and external aid should not be underestimated. While India was protected from the East Asian debacle because of the partially closed nature of its economy, the country nevertheless suffered economic blows in the aftermath of becoming nuclear in the form of frozen aid programs worth billions. In addition, a decrease in foreign direct investment followed from the loss of investor confidence as a result of the downgrading of India's credit rating. The economic woes engendered by the sanctions were accentuated by the BJP government's lack of progress on the economic liberalization front. The Indian case embodies the tensions inherent in combining democracy with economic liberalization. Political parties in India face pressures to expand their support base by promoting contradictory economic improvements or by manipulating nationalist symbols. But simultaneously, these promises clash with the task of economic liberalization. The challenge faced by Indian governments is how to combine the task of economic liberalization with the conflicting demands of electoral politics. If the economic problems are not addressed swiftly and effectively, the world will be confronted by an India that is poor, ethnically mobilized, and controlling a formidable nuclear arsenal. This would compromise both regional and global security.

How India reconciles its national political ambitions, domestic political demands for greater economic redistribution, and global pressures for an efficient economy will affect its influence on regional and global trends. Will India be able to capitalize on some of its positive achievements, such as the long-standing democratic ethos framed by functioning institutions, a vibrant civil society and media, and a growing middle class imbued with the desire to succeed economically? Or will it be crippled by ethnic hostility resulting in inaction at best and total disintegration of the country at worst? If the Congress Party is able to remobilize its old umbrella party constituency (such as Muslims and backward castes) under Sonia Gandhi, we might see a return to the era of one-party rule in India. However, if current trends are any indication, the stage seems set for a scenario of two-party rule, with either a BJP-led or a Congress-led coalition ruling at the center. There also seems to be some room for optimism with regard to voter needs and interests on the international and domestic fronts. For instance, during Vajpayee's February 1999 visit to Pakistan, public opinion polls showed that an overwhelming number of people in India and Pakistan wanted improved relations between the two countries. On the domestic side, the preoccupation of voters with economic management, law and order, and other governance issues was evident from the results of the 1998 assembly elections. Of course, balancing the demands of simultaneously achieving equity and efficiency generates its own problems. The understanding of evolving political trends in India will remain matters of continuing significance.

Key Terms

Hindu
Muslims
Sikhs
Maharajas
zamindars
Emergency
green revolution
state-led economic development
economic liberalization
reservations
nonaligned bloc

caste system
Brahmin
untouchables
scheduled castes
Lok Sabha
Rajya Sabha
Indian Administrative Service
panchayats
"Other Backward Classes"

Suggested Readings

Bardhan, Pranab. *The Political Economy of Development in India.* New Delhi: Oxford University Press, 1984.
Basu, Amrita. *Two Faces of Protest: Contrasting Modes of Women's Activism in India.* Berkeley: University of California Press, 1992.
———, and Kohli, Atul, eds. *Community Conflicts and the State in India.* New Delhi: Oxford University Press, 1998.
Bayly, C. A. *The New Cambridge History of India: Indian Society and the Making of the British Empire.* Vol. 2, no. 1. Cambridge: Cambridge University Press, 1988.
Brass, Paul R. *The New Cambridge History of India: The Politics of India Since Independence.* Vol. 4, no. 1. Cambridge: Cambridge University Press, 1990.
———. *The Theft of an Idol.* Princeton, N.J.: Princeton University Press, 1997
Carras, Mary C. *Indira Gandhi: In the Crucible of Leadership.* Boston: Beacon Press, 1979.
Chatterjee, Partha, ed. *State Politics in India.* New Delhi: Oxford University Press, 1997.
Cohen, Stephen P. *The Indian Army: Its Contribution to the Development of a Nation.* Berkeley: University of California Press, 1971.
Dreze, Jean, and Amartya, Sen, eds. *Economic Development and Social Opportunity.* New Delhi: Oxford University Press, 1995.
Frankel, Francine. *India's Political Economy, 1947–1977.* Princeton, N.J.: Princeton University Press, 1978.
Gopal, Sarvepalli. *Jawaharlal Nehru: A Biography.* Vols. 2 and 3. New Delhi: Oxford University Press, 1984.
Graham, Bruce. *Hindu Nationalism and Indian Politics.* Cambridge: Cambridge University Press, 1990.
Hardgrave, Robert L., Jr., and Kochanek, Stanley A. *India: Government and Politics in a Developing Nation.* 4th ed. New York: Harcourt Brace Jovanovich, 1986.
Hasan, Zoya. *Quest for Power: Oppositional Movements and Post-Congress Politics in Uttar Pradesh.* Delhi: Oxford University Press, 1998.

Jaffrelot, Christophe. *The Hindu Nationalist Movement and Indian Politics, 1925 to the 1990s: Strategies on Identity Building, Implantation and Mobilization.* New York: Columbia University Press, 1996.

Jalal, Ayesha. *Democracy and Authoritarianism in South Asia.* Cambridge: Cambridge University Press, 1995.

Jalan, Bimal. *India's Economic Crisis: The Way Ahead.* New Delhi: Oxford University Press, 1991.

Kohli, Atul. *Democracy and Discontent: India's Growing Crisis of Governability.* Cambridge: Cambridge University Press, 1991.

———, ed. *The State and Poverty in India: The Politics of Reform.* Cambridge: Cambridge University Press, 1987.

———. *The Success of India's Democracy.* Cambridge: Cambridge University Press, 2001.

Misra, B. B. *Government and Bureaucracy in India: 1947–1976.* New Delhi: Oxford University Press, 1986.

Nayar, Baldev Raj. *India's Mixed Economy.* Bombay: Popular Prakashan, 1989.

Rothermund, Dietmar. *An Economic History of India: From Pre-Colonial Times to 1986.* London: Croom Helm, 1988.

Rudolph, Lloyd, and Rudolph, Susanne. *In Pursuit of Lakshmi: The Political Economy of the Indian State.* Chicago: University of Chicago Press, 1987.

Sarkar, Sumit. *Modern India: 1885 to 1947.* Madras: Macmillan, 1983.

Varshney, Ashutosh. *Ethnic Conflict and Civic Life: Hindus and Muslims in India.* New Haven, Conn.: Yale University Press, 2002.

Weiner, Myron. *The Child and the State in India.* Princeton, N.J.: Princeton University Press, 1992.

———. *The Indian Paradox: Essays in Indian Politics.* New Delhi: Sage, 1989.

Suggested Websites

BJP Party
www.bjp.org
Economic and Political Weekly, a good source of information on Indian politics
www.epw.org
Frontline, a magazine with coverage of Indian politics
www.flonnet.com
Hindu, an English daily paper in India
www.hinduonnet.com
Hindustan Times
www.hindustantimes.com
Indian government
www.nic.in
Sabrang Communications, providing coverage of human rights issues in India
www.sabrang.com

Notes

[1]Sudha Mahalingam, "Petroleum Sector: An Ambitious Roadshow," *Frontline,* March 3–16, 2001, pp. 99–100.

[2]*Times of India,* September 7, 2002.

[3]C. P. Chandrashekhar, "FDI and the Balance of Payments in the 1990s," www.macroscan.com, June 2000.

[4]Madhura Swaminathan, "Food Security: No Panacea?" *Frontline,* October 14–27, 2000; Jayati Ghosh, "Wasted Food, Wasted Opportunities?" *Frontline*, September 30–October 13, 2000.

[5]Prabhat Patnaik, "Budget 2002: The Poverty of Economic Policy?" *Frontline,* March 16–29, 2002.

[6]Shirin M. Rai, "Gender and Representation: Women MPs in the Indian Parliament," in Anne Marie Goetz, ed., *Getting Institutions Right for Women and Development* (London: Zed Books, 1997), p. 105.

[7]People's Union for Democratic Rights, Resisting POTO, People's Union for Democratic Rights, "No Vakeel, No Daleel, No Appeal," *Delhi,* November 2001. pp. 5–9; also see V. Venkatesan, "Terror Through Ordinance," *Frontline,* November 23, 2001, pp. 26–29, and Gautam Navlakha, "POTO: Taking the Lawless Road," *Economic and Political Weekly,* December 8, 2001, pp. 4520–4522.

CHAPTER 4

Mexico

Merilee S. Grindle

United Mexican States

Land and People

Capital	Mexico City
Total area (square miles)	756,066 (about 3 times the size of Texas)
Population	98.6 million
Annual population growth rate (%)	1975–2000 2.1
	2000–2015 (projected) 1.2
Urban population (%)	74.4
Major language(s) (%)	Spanish 94.1
	Mayan, Nahuatl, and other indigenous languages 5.9
Religious affiliation (%)	Roman Catholic 89
	Protestant 6
	Other 5

Economy

Domestic currency	Peso (MXN) US$1: 9.66 MXN (2002 av.)
Total GDP (US$)	574.5 billion
GDP per capita (US$)	5,805
Total GDP at purchasing power parity (US$	884.0 billion
GDP per capita at purchasing power parity (US$)	9,023
GDP annual growth rate (%)	1997 6.8
	2000 6.6
	2001 −0.3
GDP per capita average annual growth rate (%)	1975–2000 0.9
	1990–2000 1.4
Inequality in income or consumption (1995) (%)	Share of poorest 10% 1.4
	Share of poorest 20% 3.6
	Share of richest 20% 58.2
	Share of richest 10% 42.8
	Gini Index (1995) 53.7
Structure of production (% of GDP)	Agriculture 4.1
	Industry 27.9
	Services 68.0
Labor force distribution (% of total)	Agriculture 20
	Industry 24
	Services 56
Exports as % of GDP	31
Imports as % of GDP	33

Society

Life expectancy at birth	72.6
Infant mortality per 1,000 live births	25

Adult literacy (%)	Male	93.4
	Female	89.5
Access to information and communications (per 1,000 population)	Telephone lines	125
	Mobile phones	142
	Radios	320
	Televisions	283
	Personal computers	50.6

Women in Government and the Economy

Women in the national legislature	
Lower house or single house (%)	16.0
Upper house (%)	15.6
Women at ministerial level (%)	10.1
Female economic activity rate (age 15 and above) (%)	50
Female labor force (% of total)	32
Estimated earned income (PPP US$) Female	4,978
Male	13,152
2002 Human Development Index Ranking (out of 173 countries)	54

Political Organization

Political System   Federal republic.

Regime History   Current form of government since 1917.

Administrative Structure   Federal with 31 states and a federal district.

Executive   President, elected by direct election with a six-year term of office; reelection not permitted.

Legislature   Bicameral Congress. Senate (upper house) and Chamber of Deputies (lower house) elections held every three years. There are 128 senators, 3 from each of the 31 states, 3 from the federal (capital) district, and 32 elected nationally by proportional representation. The 500 members of the Chamber of Deputies are elected from 300 electoral districts, 300 by simple majority vote and 200 by proportional representation.

Judiciary   Independent federal and state court system headed by a Supreme Court with 11 justices appointed by the president and approved by the Senate.

Party System   Multiparty system. One-party dominant (Institutional Revolutionary Party) system from 1929 until 2000. Major parties: National Action Party, Institutional Revolutionary Party, and the Democratic Revolutionary Party.

Section ❶ The Making of the Modern Mexican State

Politics in Action

On December 1, 2000, Vicente Fox Quesada became president of Mexico. Although most of the inauguration ceremony followed long-established tradition for the transfer of power from one administration to the next, the event was historic. For the first time in seventy-one years, the president of Mexico did not represent the Institutional Revolutionary Party (PRI, pronounced "pree"), which had governed the country without interruption since 1929. Fox assumed the presidency under the banner of the National Action Party (PAN, pronounced "pahn"), a center-right party that had long opposed the PRI. He won the election largely because the old civil-authoritarian system could no longer ensure political stability, economic progress, and responsiveness to the demands of a society that was increasingly characterized by inequality.

The inauguration of Fox signaled a new stage in Mexico's quest for democracy. Under the PRI, political conflict had been largely limited to internal struggles within the party, and those who questioned its monopoly of power were usually co-opted into quiescence with promises and benefits or quietly but effectively repressed. The regime was sometimes called "the perfect dictatorship." For several decades, this system produced political stability and economic growth. Yet, increasingly during the 1980s and 1990s, Mexicans began to question the right of the PRI to monopolize political power. They organized to press for fairer elections and more responsive public officials. They demanded the right of opposition parties to compete for power on an equal basis with the PRI. They argued that the president had too much power and that the PRI was riddled with corruption. By 2000, a significant number of the country's 100 million citizens wanted political change.

Mexicans from every walk of life watched Fox's inauguration with trepidation. Just six years before, in 1994, despite widespread disillusionment with the political system, PRI candidate Ernesto Zedillo had easily won the presidency. At that time, many voters feared that political change might bring violence and instability more than they feared politics as usual under the continuation of a PRI government. And having spent all their lives under the PRI, some citizens remembered the party's triumphs of decades past and supported it. By 2000, however, a majority of the voters had had enough. Yet it was natural that they should be concerned about what government under the PAN would bring. Along with trepidations about change, many were expecting a great deal from the new government—more open political debate, more open government, more capacity to influence public policies, more economic growth, improved public services. President Fox had his job cut out for him.

In the two decades leading up to this historic change of administrations, the government had introduced major policy changes that affected virtually every aspect of the country's economy. Reformers of the 1980s and 1990s wanted Mexico to have a market-oriented economic system to replace one in which the state played a major role in guiding the process of development. They wanted to see the country's industry and agriculture thrive in a competitive global market. However, the new policies, together with a series of economic crises, affected many people adversely. Incomes fell, businesses went bankrupt, jobs were lost, and government services were cut back. Inequalities grew, and many blamed free-market policies and globalization for the plight of the country's poor and dispossessed. Despite growing disillusion with the reforms, the Fox government was committed to maintaining them and to seeking greater integration into the global marketplace.

Today, Mexicans are proud that their country has demonstrated its ability to move toward more democratic politics. Yet political and economic dissatisfaction continues to characterize the country. Regime change did not bring much evidence of improved capacity to respond to the needs of many. For elites, the opportunities of globalization have provided unprecedented wealth and cosmopolitan lifestyles. Yet indicators of increased poverty are everywhere. At least four of every ten Mexicans live on less than two dollars a day. The public education and health systems struggle with minimal resources to meet overwhelming demand. In the countryside, the peasant population faces destitution. Indigenous groups challenge government to end historical injustices and show respect for their cultures. In urban areas, the poor are forced to find meager sources of income however they can.

Thus, the advent of the Fox administration drew attention to ongoing and interrelated challenges of Mexico's development:

- Would a country with a long tradition of authoritarian government be able to sustain a democratic political system in the face of increasing demands and high expectations?
- Would a country that had long sought economic development through government activism and the domestic market be able to compete effectively in a competitive and market-driven global economy?
- Would a country long noted for severe inequalities between the rich and the poor be capable of providing better living standards for its growing population?

Geographic Setting

Mexico is one of the most geographically diverse countries in the world, encompassing snow-capped volcanoes, coastal plains, high plateaus, fertile valleys, rain forests, and deserts within an area slightly less than three times the size of Texas. To the north, it shares a 2,000-mile-long border with the United States, to the south, a 600-mile-long border with Guatemala and a 160-mile-long border with Belize. Two imposing mountain ranges run the length of Mexico: the Sierra Madre Occidental to the west and the Sierra Madre Oriental to the east. As a result, the country is noted for peaks, plateaus, and valleys that produce an astonishing number of microclimates and a rich diversity of plants and animals. Mexico's varied geography has historically made communication and transportation between regions difficult and infrastructure expensive. The mountainous areas tend to limit large-scale commercial agriculture to irrigated fields in the northern part of the country, while the central and southern regions produce a wide variety of crops on small farms. Soil erosion and desertification are major problems because of the steep terrain and unpredictable rainfall in many areas. The country is rich in oil, silver, and other natural resources but has long struggled to manage those resources wisely.

The human landscape is equally dramatic. With some 100 million inhabitants, Mexico is among the world's ten most populated countries—the second-largest nation in Latin America after Portuguese-speaking Brazil and the largest Spanish-speaking nation in the world. Sixty percent of the population is *mestizo,* or people of mixed **Amerindian** and Spanish descent. About 30 percent of the population claims indigenous (Amerindian) descent, although only about 6 percent of population speaks an indigenous language rather than Spanish. The rest of the population is Caucasian or people with other backgrounds. The largest **indigenous groups** are the Maya in the south and the Náhuatl in the central regions, with well over 1 million speakers each. Other important groups like the Zapotec, Mixtec, Otomí, Purépecha, and the Tarahumara number in the tens of thousands. There are also dozens and perhaps hundreds of smaller linguistic and social groups throughout the country. Although Mexicans pride themselves on their Amerindian heritage, problems of racism and classism run deep, and there is a great deal of ambivalence about issues of "Indianness."

Mexico was transformed from a largely rural to a largely urban country in the second half of the twentieth century, with over 74 percent of the population now living in urban areas. Mexico City has become one of the world's largest cities, with about 20 million inhabitants.[1] Population growth has slowed to about 1.5 percent, but society continues to adjust to the baby boom of the 1970s and early 1980s as these fifteen to thirty year olds seek jobs and form families. Migration both within and beyond Mexico's borders has become a major issue. Greater economic opportunities in the industrial cities of the north lead many men and women to seek work there in the *maquiladoras,* or assembly industries. Border cities like Tijuana and Ciudad Juárez have experienced tremendous growth in the past twenty years. Many job seekers continue on to the United States, lured by a larger job market and higher wages. The problem repeats itself in reverse on Mexico's southern border, with many thousands of Central Americans looking for better prospects in Mexico and beyond.

Critical Junctures

Mexicans are deeply affected by the legacies of their collective past, including centuries of colonialism and decades of political instability that followed Spanish rule. The legacies of the distant past are still felt, but the most formative event in the country's modern history was the Revolution of 1910. Mexico experienced

Mexico

the first great social revolution of the twentieth century, a conflict that lasted for more than a decade and claimed the lives of as many as 2 million people. Some died in violent confrontations, but the majority lost their lives through the massive destruction, dislocation, and famine caused by the shifting and sporadic nature of the conflict. The revolution was fought by a variety of forces for a variety of reasons, which made the consolidation of power that followed as significant as the revolution itself. The institutions and symbols of the current political regime emerged from these complex conflicts.

Independence and Instability (1810–1876)

Spain ruled Mexico for three centuries, administering a vast economic, political, and religious empire in the interests of the imperial country, its kings, and its representatives in North America (see "Global Connec-

tion: Conquest or Encounter?"). Colonial policy was designed to extract wealth from New Spain and to limit the possibilities for Spaniards in the New World to benefit from agriculture, commerce, or industry without at the same time benefiting Spain. It was also designed to ensure commitment to the Roman Catholic religion and the subordination of the Amerindian population.

In 1810, a parish priest in central Mexico named Miguel Hidalgo issued a rallying cry to a group assembled in a church in the town of Dolores. He called for an end to Spanish misrule. At the head of a motley band of rebels, he began the first of a series of wars of independence that pitted rebels against the Spanish Crown for eleven years. Although independence was gained in 1821, Mexico struggled to create a stable and legitimate government for decades after. Liberals and conservatives, federalists and centralists, those who sought to expand the power of the church and those

---

Critical Junctures in Mexico's Political Development

1810–1821 War of independence from Spain.

1876–1911 Dictatorship of Porfirio Díaz.

1910–1921 Mexican Revolution.

    1917 Mexican Constitution.

    1929 Plutarco Elías Calles founds PRI.

1934–1940 Presidency of Lázaro Cárdenas; entrenchment of corporatist state.

    1968 Massacre of Tlaltelolco; 200 students killed.

1978–1982 State-led development reaches peak with petroleum boom and bust.

    1982 Market reformers come to power in PRI.

    1988 Carlos Salinas elected amid charges of fraud.

    1989 First governorship won by an opposition party.

    1994 NAFTA goes into effect; uprising in Chiapas; Colosio assassinated.

    1996 Four largest political parties agree on electoral reform.

    1997 Opposition parties advance nationwide; PRI loses absolute majority in congress for first time in its history.

    2000 PRI loses presidency; Vicente Fox of PAN becomes president, but without majority support in congress.

---

who sought to curtail it, and those who wanted a republic and those who wanted a monarchy were all engaged in the battle for Mexico's soul during the nineteenth century. Between 1833 and 1855, thirty-six presidential administrations came to power.

Adding insult to injury during this disorganized period, Mexico lost half its territory to the United States. Its northern territory of Texas proclaimed and then won independence in a war ending in 1836. Then the Lone Star Republic was annexed to the United States by the U.S. Congress in 1845, and claims on Mexican territory north of the Rio Grande were increasingly heard from Washington. On the basis of a dubious claim that Mexico had invaded U.S. territory, the United States declared war on its southern neighbor. The war was first fought along what was later to become the border between the two countries, and then, in 1847, the U.S. army invaded the port city of Veracruz. With considerable loss of civilian lives, U.S. forces marched toward Mexico City, where they engaged in the final battle of the war at Chapultepec Castle. An 1848 treaty gave the United States title to what later became the states of Texas, New Mexico, Utah, Nevada, Arizona, California, and part of Colorado for about $18 million, leaving a legacy of deep resentment toward the United States, the "Colossus of the North."

The loss of this war did not make it any easier to govern Mexico. Liberals and conservatives continued their struggle to resolve issues of political and economic order and, in particular, the power of the Catholic Church. The constitution of 1857 incorporated many of the goals of the liberals, such as republican government, a bill of rights, abolition of slavery, and limitations on the economic and political power of the church. The constitution did not guarantee stability, however. In 1861, Spain, Great Britain, and France occupied Veracruz to collect customs claims from the government, and the French army marched on Mexico City, subdued the weak government, and established the rule of Emperor Maximilian and Empress Carlota (1864–1867). Conservatives and Catholic loyalists welcomed this respite from the liberals. Benito Juárez, who occupied the presidency on three separate occasions, was back in office in 1867, spearheading reforms in economic, social, and political arenas, as well as building up the institutions of a new national government. He continues to be revered in Mexico as an early proponent of open and republican government.

The Porfiriato (1876–1911)

Over the next few years, a popular retired general named Porfirio Díaz became increasingly dissatisfied with what he thought was a "lot of politics" and "little action." After several failed attempts to win and then take the presidency, he finally succeeded in 1876. His dictatorship lasted thirty-four years and was at first welcomed by many because it brought sustained stability to the country.

Díaz imposed a highly centralized authoritarian

Global Connection: *Conquest or Encounter?*

The year 1519, when the Spanish conqueror Hernán Cortés arrived on the shores of the Yucatán Peninsula, is often considered the starting point of Mexican political history. But the Spanish explorers did not come to an uninhabited land waiting to be excavated for gold and silver. Instead, the land that was to become New Spain and then Mexico was home to extensive and complex indigenous civilizations that were advanced in agriculture, architecture, and political and economic organization—civilizations that were already over a thousand years old. The Mayans of the Yucatán and the Toltecs of the central highlands had reached high levels of development long before the arrival of the Europeans. By 1519, diverse groups had fallen under the power of the militaristic Aztec Empire, which extended throughout what is today central and southern Mexico.

The encounter between the Europeans and these indigenous civilizations was marked by bloodshed and violence. The great Aztec city of Tenochtitlán—the site of Mexico City today—was captured and largely destroyed by the Spanish conquerors in 1521. Cortés and the colonial masters who came after him subjected indigenous groups to forced labor, robbed them of gold, silver, and land, and introduced flora and fauna from Europe that destroyed long-existing aqueducts and irrigation systems. They also brought alien forms of property rights and authority relationships, a religion that viewed indigenous practices as the devil's work, and an economy based on mining and cattle—all of which soon overwhelmed existing structures of social and economic organization. Within a century, wars, savage exploitation at the hands of the Spaniards, and the introduction of European diseases reduced the indigenous population from an estimated 25 million to 1 million or fewer. The Indian population took three hundred years just to stop decreasing after the disaster of the conquest.

Even so, the Spanish never constituted more than a small percentage of the total population, and massive racial mixing between the Indians, Europeans, and to a lesser extent Africans produced a new *raza*, or *mestizo* race. This unique process remains at once a source of pride and conflict for Mexicans today. What does it mean to be Mexican? Is one the conquered or the conqueror? While celebrating Amerindian achievements in food, culture, the arts, and ancient civilization, middle-class Mexico has the contradictory sense that to be "Indian" nowadays is to be backward. Many Amerindians are stigmatized by mainstream society if they speak a native dialect. But perhaps the situation is changing, with the upsurge of indigenous movements from both the grass roots and the international level striving to promote ethnic pride, defend rights, and foster the teaching of Indian languages.

The collision of two worlds resonates in current national philosophical and political debates. Is Mexico a Western society? Is it colonial or modern? Third or First World? South or North? Is the United States an ally or a conqueror? Perhaps most important, many Mexicans at once welcome and fear full integration into the global economy, asking themselves: Is globalization the new conquest?

---

system to create political order and economic progress. In time, he relied increasingly on a small clique of advisers, known as *científicos* (scientists), who wanted to adopt European technologies and values to modernize the country, forcefully if necessary. Deeply disdainful of the vast majority of the country's population, Díaz and the *científicos* encouraged foreign investment and amassed huge fortunes, which they used to support lavish lifestyles and copy the latest European styles. During this period, known as the Porfiriato, this small elite group monopolized political power and reserved lucrative economic investments for itself and its allies. Economic and political opportunities were closed off for new generations of middle- and upper-class Mexicans, who became increasingly sensitive to the greed of the Porfirians and their own lack of opportunities.

The Revolution of 1910 and the Sonoran Dynasty (1910–1934)

In 1910, conflict broke out as reformers sought to end the dictatorship. Díaz had pledged himself to an open election for president, and in 1910, Francisco I. Madero, a landowner from the northern state of Coahuila, presented himself as a candidate. The slogan "Effective Suffrage, No Reelection" summed up the reformers' goals in creating opportunities for a new class of politically ambitious citizens to move into positions of power. When this opposition swelled, Díaz cancelled the election and tried to repress growing dissent. But it was too late. The clamor for change forced Díaz into exile. Madero was elected in 1911, but he was soon using the military to put down revolts from reformers and reactionaries alike. When Madero was assassinated, political order in the country virtually collapsed.

At the same time that middle-class reformers struggled to displace Díaz, a peasant revolt that focused on land claims erupted in the central and southern states of the country. This revolt had roots in legislation that made it easy for wealthy landowners and ranchers to claim the lands of peasant villagers. Encouraged by the weakening of the old regime and driven to desperation by increasing landlessness, villagers armed themselves and joined forces under a variety of local leaders. The most famous of these was Emiliano Zapata, who amassed a peasant army from Morelos, a state in southern Mexico. Peasant battalions swept through the countryside and grew in numbers; women as well as men flocked to fight under Zapata and other revolutionary leaders. Zapata's Plan de Ayala, first announced in 1911 and agreed to at a national meeting of revolutionary leaders in 1915, became the cornerstone of the radical agrarian reform that would be incorporated into the Constitution of 1917.

In the northern part of the country, Francisco (Pancho) Villa rallied his own army of workers, small farmers, and ranch hands. He presented a major challenge to the national army, now under the leadership of Venustiano Carranza, who had inherited Madero's middle-class reformist movement and eventually became president. Villa's forces recognized no law but that of their chief and combined military maneuvers with banditry, looting, and warlordism in the territories under their control. In 1916, troops from the United States entered Mexico to punish Villa for an attack on U.S. territory. Although this military operation was badly planned and poorly executed and Villa was never located by the U.S. forces, Mexican hostility toward the United States, already running high because of an invasion of Veracruz in 1914, increased.

The Constitution of 1917 was forged out of this diverse and often conflicting set of interests. It established a formal set of political institutions and guaranteed a range of progressive social and economic rights to citizens: agrarian reform, social security, the right to organize in unions, a minimum wage, an eight-hour workday, profit sharing for workers, universal secular education, and adult male suffrage. Despite these socially advanced provisions, the constitution did not provide suffrage for women, who had to wait until 1953 to vote in local elections and 1958 to vote in national elections. In an effort to limit the power of foreign investors, the constitution declared that only Mexican citizens or the government could own land or rights to water and other natural resources. It also contained numerous articles that severely limited the power of the Roman Catholic Church, long a target of liberals who wanted Mexico to be a secular state. The signing of the docu-

In 1914, Pancho Villa (right) met with Emiliano Zapata in Mexico City to discuss the revolution and their separate goals for its outcome. *Source:* Robert Freck/Odyssey/Chicago.

ment signaled the formal end of the revolution and the intent of the contending parties to form a new political regime. Despite such noble sentiments, violence continued as competing leaders sought to assert power and displace their rivals. By 1920 a modicum of stability had emerged, but not before many of the revolutionary leaders—Zapata, Villa, and Presidents Carranza and Obregon—had been assassinated in struggles over power and policy. There were, however, occasional outbreaks of violence among local warlords during this decade.

Despite this violence, power was gradually consolidated in the hands of a group of revolutionary leaders from the north of the country. Known as the Sonoran Dynasty, after their home state of Sonora, these leaders were committed to a capitalist model of economic development. During the 1920s, they skillfully outmaneuvered those who wished to see a socialist economy rise from the ashes of civil war. Eventually, one of the Sonorans, Plutarco Elías Calles, emerged as the *jefe máximo*, or supreme leader. Elected president in 1924, Calles managed to select and dominate his presidential successors from 1929 to 1934. The consolidation of power under his control was accompanied by extreme **anticlericalism,** which eventually resulted in warfare between conservative leaders of the Catholic Church and their followers, and the government.

In 1929, Calles brought together many of the most powerful contenders for leadership, including many regional warlords, to create a political party. The bargain he offered was simple: contenders for power would accommodate each others' interests in the expectation that without political violence, the country would prosper and they would be able to reap the benefits of even greater power and economic spoils. They created a political party, whose name was changed in 1939 and again in 1946, to consolidate their power, and for the next seven decades, Calles's bargain was effective in ensuring nonviolent conflict resolution among elites and the uninterrupted rule of the PRI in national politics.

Although the revolution was complex and the interests contending for power in its aftermath were numerous, there were five clear results of this protracted conflict. First, the power of traditional rural landowners was undercut. In the years after the revolution, wealthy elites would again emerge in rural areas, but they would never again be so powerful in national politics or their power so unchecked in local areas. Second, the power of the Catholic Church was strongly

curtailed. Although the church remained important in many parts of the country, it no longer participated openly in national political debates. Third, the power of foreign investors was severely limited; prior to the revolution, foreign investors owned much of the country's land as well as many of its railroads, mines, and factories. Henceforth, Mexican nationalism would shape economic policy-making. Fourth, a new political elite consolidated power and agreed to resolve conflicts through accommodation and bargaining rather than through violence. And fifth, the new constitution and the new party laid the basis for a strong central government that could assert its power over the agricultural, industrial, and social development of the country.

Lázaro Cárdenas, Agrarian Reform, and the Workers (1934–1940)

In 1934, Plutarco Calles handpicked Lázaro Cárdenas, a revolutionary general and state governor, as his successor to the presidency. He fully anticipated that Cárdenas would go along with Calles's behind-the-scenes management of the country and continue the economic policies of the postrevolutionary coalition. To his great surprise, Cárdenas executed a virtual coup that established his own supremacy and sent Calles packing to the United States for an "extended vacation."[2] Even more unexpectedly, Cárdenas mobilized peasants and workers in pursuit of the more radical goals of the 1910 revolution. He encouraged peasant syndicates to petition for land and claim rights promised in the Constitution of 1917. During his administration, more than 17 million hectares of land were distributed (1 hectare is 2.471 acres). Most of these lands were distributed in the form of *ejidos* (collective land grants) to peasant groups. *Ejidatarios* (those who acquired *ejido* lands) became one of the most enduring bases of support for the government. Cárdenas also encouraged workers to form unions and demand higher wages and better working conditions. He established his nationalist credentials in 1938 when he wrested the petroleum industry from U.S. and British investors and placed it under government control.

During the Cárdenas years (1934–1940), the bulk of the Mexican population was incorporated into the political system. Organizations of peasants, workers, middle-class groups, and the military were added to the party, and the voices of the poor majority were heard within the councils of government, reducing the risk that they would become radicalized outside them. In addition, the Cárdenas years witnessed a great expansion of the role of the state as the government encouraged investment in industrialization, provided credit to agriculture, and created infrastructure.

Lázaro Cárdenas continues to be a national hero to Mexicans, who look back on his presidency as a period when government was clearly committed to improving the welfare of the country's poor. His other legacy was to institutionalize patterns of political succession and presidential behavior that continue to set standards for Mexico's leaders. He campaigned extensively, and his campaign travel took him to remote villages and regions, where he listened to the demands and complaints of humble people. Cárdenas served a single six-year term, called a *sexenio,* and relinquished full political power to the new president, Manuel Avila Camacho. Cárdenas's conduct in office created hallowed traditions of presidential style and succession that all subsequent national leaders have observed.

The Politics of Rapid Development (1940–1982)

Although Cárdenas had directed a radical reshuffling of political power in the country, his successors were able to use the institutions he created to counteract his reforms. Ambitious local and regional party leaders and leaders of peasants' and workers' groups began to use their organizations as pawns in exchange for political favors. Gradually, the PRI developed a huge patronage machine, providing union and *ejido* leaders with jobs, opportunities for corruption, land, and other benefits in return for delivering their followers' political support. Extensive chains of personal relationships based on the exchange of favors allowed the party to amass far-reaching political control and limit opportunities for organizing independent of the PRI. These exchange relationships, known as **clientelism,** became the cement that built loyalty to the PRI and the political system.

This kind of political control translated into the capacity of post-Cárdenas presidents to reorient the country's development away from the egalitarian social goals of the 1930s toward a development strategy in which the state actively encouraged industrialization and the accumulation of wealth. Initially, industrialization created jobs and made available a wide range of basic consumer goods to Mexico's burgeoning population. Growth rates were high during the 1940s, 1950s, and 1960s, and Mexicans flocked to the cities to take advantage of the jobs created in the manufacturing and construction industries. By the 1970s, however,

Mexican presidential candidates are expected to campaign hard, traveling to remote locations, making rousing campaign speeches, and meeting with citizens of humble origins. Here, presidential candidate Vicente Fox Quesada is on the campaign trail. *Source:* R. Kwiotek/Zeitenspiegel/Corbis/Sygma.

industrial development policies were no longer generating rapid growth and could not keep pace with the rapidly rising demand for jobs.

The country's economy was in deep crisis by the mid-1970s. Just as policy-makers began to take actions to correct the problems, vast new amounts of oil were discovered in the Gulf of Mexico. Soon, rapid economic growth was refueled by extensive public investment programs in virtually every sector of the economy. Based on the promise of petroleum wealth, the government and private businesses borrowed huge amounts of capital from foreign lenders, who were eager to do business with a country that had so much oil. Unfortunately for Mexico, international petroleum prices plunged sharply in the early 1980s. Almost overnight, there was no more credit to be had and much less money from petroleum to pay for economic expansion or the interest on the debts incurred in preceding years. Mexico plunged into a deep economic crisis that affected many other countries around the world.

Crisis and Reform (1982 to the Present)

This economic crisis helped two presidents, Miguel de la Madrid (1982–1988) and Carlos Salinas (1988–1994), introduce the first major reversal of the country's development strategy since the 1940s. New policies were put in place to limit the government's role in the economy and to make it easier for Mexican producers to export their goods. This period clearly marked the beginning of a new effort to become more important in international economic affairs. In 1993, by signing the **North American Free Trade Agreement** (NAFTA), which committed Mexico, the United States, and Canada to eliminating trade barriers among them, Mexico's policy-makers signaled the extent to which they envisioned the future prosperity of their country to be tied to that of its two neighbors to the north. Efforts to increase trade and investment to Latin American, European, and Asian countries also emphasized Mexico's new commitment to competitiveness in a global economy.

The economic reforms of the 1980s and 1990s were a turning point for the country's development and meant that Mexico's future development would be closely tied to conditions in the international economy. A major economic crisis at the end of 1994, in which billions of

dollars of foreign investment fled the country, was indicative of this new international vulnerability. The peso lost half of its value against the dollar within a few days, and the government lacked the funds to pay its obligations. Suddenly, Mexico's status among nations seemed dubious once more, and the country felt betrayed by outgoing President Salinas, convinced that he had patched together a shaky house of cards only long enough to get himself out of office. The economy shrank by 6.2 percent in 1995, inflation soared, taxes rose while wages were frozen, and the bank system collapsed. The United States orchestrated a $50 billion bailout, $20 billion of which came directly from the U.S. Treasury. Faced with limited options, the administration of Ernesto Zedillo (1994–2000) implemented a severe and unpopular economic austerity program, which restored financial stability over the next two years. The actions taken to meet that crisis helped shield Mexico from the impact of the Asian financial crisis of 1997 and 1998. It was also helped by its increasing interconnection with the United States, whose economy was growing during this period.

Economic crisis was exacerbated by political concerns. On January 1, 1994, a guerrilla movement, the Ejército Zapatista National Liberation Front (EZLN), seized four towns in the southern state of Chiapas. The group demanded land, democracy, indigenous rights, and an immediate repeal of NAFTA. Many citizens throughout the country openly supported the aims of the rebels, pointing out that the movement brought to light the reality of two different Mexicos: those who enjoyed the fruits of wealth and influence and those who were getting left behind because of poverty and repression. The government and the military were criticized for inaction and human rights abuses in the state (See "Citizen Action: Rebellion in Chiapas"). A second guerrilla movement, the Popular Revolutionary Army (EPR), also challenged the government. This movement was far more mysterious, less ideological, and more committed to violence than the Zapatistas. Considered terrorist by the government, it claimed to have operatives throughout the country and took responsibility for several destructive actions.

Following close on the heels of rebellion came the assassination of the PRI's presidential candidate, Luis Donaldo Colosio, on March 23, 1994, in the northern border city of Tijuana. The assassination shocked all

Citizen Action: *Rebellion in Chiapas*

In the months after January 1994, indigenous women set out daily for the tourist zones of central Mexico City to sell handmade dolls. These dolls, dressed in brightly colored costumes, also sported black ski masks. They represented a symbolic connection to the rebels of the Ejército Zapatista National Liberation Front (EZLN) in the southern state of Chiapas, who wore ski masks to avoid identification by the government. Images of the ideological leader and public spokesman of the Zapatista movement, Subcomandante Marcos, also appeared throughout the country, and people of diverse ethnic, class, and political backgrounds began expressing support for the goals of the rebels.

The rebellion by some 2,000 members of the EZLN broke out on January 1, 1994, the day that NAFTA went into effect. The Zapatista army captured four towns in the state of Chiapas, including the city of San Cristobal de las Casas, a popular tourist destination. The EZLN demanded "jobs, land, housing, food, health, education, independence, freedom, democracy, justice and peace."[1] The peasant army also called on the government to repeal NAFTA. These demands and the progress of the rebellion were immediately transmitted throughout Mexico and around the globe by domestic and international media as camera crews and reporters flocked to this remote, poverty-stricken state.

The EZLN's call for an end to exploitation at the hands of voracious landowners and corrupt bosses of the PRI, as well as for social services and citizenship rights, resonated deeply throughout the country. Soon, a broad spectrum of local, regional, professional, and human rights groups took up the banner of the Chiapas rebels and called on the government to open the political system to more just and democratic elections, decision-making processes, and policies. By calling in the army to suppress armed peasants, most of whom were Mayan Indians, and to retake the four towns by force, the government only increased sympathy for the marginalized, impoverished indigenous groups. The Chiapas rebellion symbolized for many the reality of Mexico's political, economic, and social inequalities.

The Zapatistas were not seeking to overthrow the Mexican political system. They believed, however, that the system created and maintained by the PRI had become very much like the dictatorship of Porfirio Díaz, toppled in the Revolution of 1910. They were united in their demand that indigenous groups throughout Mexico be granted fair treatment and the means to escape their poverty and powerlessness.

They resorted to violence because they believed the government would not otherwise pay attention to their demands.

The Zapatista rebellion presented a major challenge to Mexico's image of political stability. It had a profound effect on the election of 1994, as competing political parties and candidates sought to identify with rebel demands for indigenous rights, economic justice, and honest elections. The rebels rejected a peace treaty that would have promoted the electoral fortunes of the PRI, arguing instead for increased space for political debate and dialogue. The government spent over $200 million on social programs and infrastructure projects in the state in the months leading up to the election, a 44 percent increase over what had been budgeted. Just weeks before the elections, however, the EZLN hosted a National Democratic Convention of a large number of groups committed to pressuring the government for fundamental political reform. The rebels insisted that economic assistance alone would not solve the problems in the southern part of the country. They pointed to the deeper causes of injustice: concentration of wealth in the hands of a brutal local elite and monopolization of power by a government that valued stability and compromise with local elites above all else.

In the aftermath of the rebellion, Mexican officials sought to erase the impression that the insurgency was an Indian uprising. They pointed out that many indigenous groups rejected the EZLN. Yet major indigenous organizations across Mexico and elsewhere in Latin America expressed solidarity with the Chiapas rebels and the decision to take up arms. While some argued that the Chiapas rebellion was a local phenomenon and an isolated set of incidents, others predicted the spread of the Mexican example of armed uprisings by indigenous groups. The roots of such insurrections are in economic and social exploitation, they argued, not in specific ethnic identities. A stalemate continued: talks broke down, foreign observers were expelled, and accusations of human rights violations by the government were on the rise. President Fox attempted to resolve the impasse by granting greater autonomy to indigenous communities, but congress altered his proposal and the EZLN rejected it.

---

[1]As cited in Neil Harvey, *Rebellion in Chiapas: Rural Reforms, Campesino Radicalism, and the Limits to Salinismo* (San Diego: Center for U.S.-Mexican Studies, University of California, 1994), 1.

citizens and shook the political elite deeply. Not since 1923, when a military revolt threatened presidential elections, had there been such uncertainty about who would lead the government for the next six years. Not since 1928, when president-elect Alvaro Obregón was assassinated, had a politician bound for the highest office met with violent death. Not since 1929, when the PRI was founded, had there been such fear that the political elite was so divided that overt violence, not accommodation and compromise, might be used to resolve disputes. The murder opened wide rifts within the PRI and unleashed a flood of speculation and distrust among the citizenry. Many Mexicans were convinced that the assassination was part of a conspiracy of party "dinosaurs," political hard-liners who opposed any kind of democratic transformation.[3] Fear of violence helped provide the PRI with strong support in the August 1994 elections, although the secretary-general of the PRI, José Francisco Ruiz Massieu, was assassinated the following month. In 1996, Raúl Salinas, brother of the former president, was indicted on charges of masterminding the murder of Ruiz Massieu as well as illicit enrichment and money laundering.

These shocks provoked widespread disillusionment and frustration with the political system. Many citizens, especially in urban areas, decided that there was no longer any reason to support the PRI. Buoyed by a 1996 electoral reform, important gains were made by the opposition in the legislative elections. For the first time in modern Mexican history, the PRI lost its absolute majority in the Chamber of Deputies. Since then, the congress has shown increasing dynamism as a counterbalance to the presidency, blocking executive decisions, demanding unrestricted information, and initiating new legislation. In addition, opposition parties have won important governorships and mayorships. The election of Vicente Fox was the culmination of this electoral revolution.

Themes and Implications

Historical Junctures and Political Themes

The modern Mexican state emerged out of a popular revolution that proclaimed goals of democratic government, social justice, and nationalism. In the chaotic years after the revolution, the state created conditions for political and social peace. By incorporating peasants and workers into party and government institutions and providing benefits to low-income groups during the 1930s, it became widely accepted as legitimate. In encouraging considerable economic growth in the years after 1940, it also created belief in its ability to provide material improvements in the quality of life for large portions of the population. These factors worked together to create a strong state capable of guiding economic and political life in the country. Only in the 1980s did this system begin to crumble.

In its external relations, Mexico has always prided itself on ideological independence from the world's great powers. For many decades, its large population, cultural richness, political stability, and front-line position regarding the United States prompted Mexico to consider itself a natural leader of Latin America and the developing world in general. After the early 1980s, however, the government rejected this position in favor of rapid integration into a global economy. The country aspired to the status of newly industrialized countries of the world, such as South Korea, Malaysia, and Taiwan. While the reforms of the 1980s and 1990s, and especially NAFTA, have advanced this goal, many citizens are concerned that the government has accepted a position of political, cultural, and economic subordination to the United States.

Mexico enjoyed considerable economic advancement after the 1940s, but economic and political crises after 1980 shook confidence in its ability to achieve its economic goals and highlighted conflict between a market-oriented development strategy and the country's philosophical tradition of a strong and protective state. The larger questions of whether a new development strategy can generate growth, whether Mexican products can find profitable markets overseas, whether investors can create extensive job opportunities for millions of unemployed and part-time workers, and whether the country can maintain the confidence of those investors over the longer term continue to challenge the country.

Politically, after the Revolution of 1910, the country opted not for true democracy but for representation through government-mediated organizations within a **corporatist state,** in which interest groups became an institutionalized part of state structure. This increased state power in relation to civil society. The state took the lead in defining goals for the country's development and, through the school system, the party, and the media, inculcated a broad sense of its legitimate right to set such goals. In addition, the state had extensive resources at its disposal to control or co-opt dissent and purchase political loyalty. The PRI was an essential channel through which material goods, jobs, the distribution of land, and the allocation of development projects flowed to increase popular support for the system or to buy off opposition to it.

This does not mean that Mexican society was unorganized or passive. Indeed, many Mexicans were actively involved in local community organizations, religious activities, unions, and public interest groups. But traditionally, the scope for challenging the government, insisting on basic civil rights, or demanding an open and responsive government was very limited. At the same time, Mexico's strong state did not become openly repressive except when directly challenged. On the contrary, officials in the government and the party generally worked hard to find ways to resolve conflicts peacefully and to use behind-the-scenes accommodation to bring conflicting interests into accord. In this conflict resolution system, the power of the PRI could not be successfully challenged, and the emergence of an effective democracy was curtailed for decades.

By the 1980s, cracks began to appear in the traditional ways in which Mexican citizens interacted with the government. As the PRI began to lose its capacity to control political activities and civic groups increasingly insisted on their right to remain independent from the PRI and the government, the terms of the state-society relationship were clearly in need of redefinition. Ethnic groups, religious organizations, community movements, private business, and regionalism all emerged to pressure government to be more responsive, fair, democratic, and effective. The administration of President Zedillo signaled its willingness to cede political power to successful opposition parties in fair elections, and electoral reform in 1996 and elections in 1997 were significant steps that led to the defeat of the PRI in 2000. Mexico's future stability depends on how well a more democratic government can accommodate conflicting interests while at the same time providing economic opportunities to a largely poor population.

Implications for Comparative Politics

The Mexican political system is unique among developing countries in the extent to which it managed to institutionalize and maintain civilian political authority for a very long time. In a world of developing nations wracked by political turmoil, military coups, and regime changes, the PRI regime established enduring institutions of governance and conditions for political stability. Other countries have sought to emulate the Mexican model of stability based on an alliance between a dominant party and a strong development-oriented state, but no other government has been able to create a system that had widespread legitimacy for so long. The regime's revolutionary heritage, as well as its ability to maintain a sense of national identity, were important factors in accounting for its political continuity.

Currently, Mexico represents a nation undergoing significant political change without widespread violence, transforming itself from a corporatist state to a democratic one for the first time in its long history. At the same time, it struggles to resolve the conflicts of development through integration with its North American neighbors. Mexico has been categorized as a middle-income developing country, and its per capita income is comparable to countries such as Estonia, Malaysia, Poland, South Africa, and Uruguay.[4] It has made significant strides in industrialization, which accounts for about 28.4 percent of the country's gross domestic product (GDP). Agriculture contributes about 4.4 percent to GDP, and services contribute some 67.3 percent.[5] This structure is very similar to the economic profiles of Argentina, Brazil, Poland, and Hungary. But unlike those countries, Mexico is oil rich. The government-owned petroleum industry is a ready source of revenue and foreign exchange, but this commodity also makes the economy extremely vulnerable to changes in international oil prices.

Mexico's industrial and petroleum-based economy means a higher per capita income than in most other developing countries. If income were spread evenly among all Mexicans, each would receive $4,400 annually—far more than the per capita incomes of India ($450),

China ($780), and Nigeria ($310) but considerably less than those of Britain ($22,640), France ($23,480), and Germany ($25,350).[6] Of course, income is not spread evenly. Mexico suffers from great inequalities in how wealth is distributed, and poverty continues to be a grim reality for millions of Mexicans. The way the country promoted economic growth and industrialization is important in explaining why widespread poverty has persisted and why political power is not more equitably distributed.

Section ② Political Economy and Development

State and Economy

During the years of the Porfiriato (1876–1911), Mexico began to produce some textiles, footwear, glassware, paper, beer, tiles, furniture, and other simple products. At that time, however, policy-makers were convinced that Mexico could grow rich by exporting its raw materials to more economically advanced countries. Their efforts to attract domestic and international investment encouraged a major boom in the production and export of products such as henequin (for making rope), coffee, cacao (cocoa beans), cattle, silver, and gold. Soon, the country had become so attractive to foreign investors that large amounts of land, the country's petroleum, its railroad network, and its mining wealth were largely controlled by foreigners. Nationalist reaction against the power of these foreign interests played a significant role in the tensions that produced the Revolution of 1910.

In the postrevolutionary Mexican state, this nationalism combined with a sense of social justice inspired by popular revolutionary leaders such as Zapata. Mexicans widely shared the idea that the state had the responsibility to generate wealth for all its citizens. In addition, it was thought that only the state was powerful enough to mobilize the resources and stimulate the development necessary to overcome the destruction of the revolution. As a result, the country adopted a strategy in which the government guided the process of industrial and agricultural development and set the political conditions for its success.

Often referred to as **state capitalism,** this development strategy relied heavily on government actions to encourage private investment and lower risks for private entrepreneurs. In the twenty years following the revolution, many of those concerned about the country's

development became convinced that economic growth would not occur unless Mexico could industrialize more fully. They argued that reliance on exports of agricultural products, minerals, and petroleum— called the agro-export model of development—forced the country to import manufactured goods, which, over the long term, would always cost more than what was earned from exports. Critics of the agro-export model also argued that prices of primary products shifted greatly from one year to the next. Countries that produced them were doomed to repeat boom-and-bust cycles as their domestic economies reflected sharp fluctuations in international prices for the goods they exported. Mexico, they believed, should begin to manufacture the goods that it was currently importing.

Import Substitution and Its Consequences

Between 1940 and 1982, Mexico pursued a form of state capitalism and a model of industrialization known as import substitution, or **import substituting industrialization** (ISI). Like Brazil and other Latin American countries during the same period, the government promoted the development of industries to supply the domestic market by encouraging domestic and international investment, providing credit and tax incentives to industrialists, maintaining low rates of inflation, and keeping wage demands low through subsidized food, transportation, housing, and health care for workers. It also fostered industrialization by establishing state-owned steel mills, electric power generators, ports, and petroleum production and by using tariffs and import licenses to protect Mexican industries from foreign competition. Between 1940 and 1970, over 40 percent of all fixed capital investment came from the government. These policies had considerable success. Initially, the country produced mainly simple products like shoes, clothing, and processed foods. But by the 1960s and 1970s, it was also producing consumer durables (refrigerators, automobiles, trucks), intermediate goods (steel, petrochemicals, and other products used in the manufacturing process), and capital goods (heavy machinery to produce manufactures).

Mexican agriculture was also affected by this drive to industrialize. With the massive agrarian reform of the 1930s (see Section 1), the *ejido* had become an important structure in the rural economy, accounting for half the cultivated area of the country and 51 percent of the value of agricultural production by 1940. After President Cárdenas left office, however, government policy-makers moved rapidly away from the economic development of the *ejidos*. They became committed instead to developing a strong, entrepreneurial private sector in agriculture. For them, "the development of private agriculture would be the 'foundation of industrial greatness.'"[7] They wanted this sector to provide foodstuffs for the growing cities, raw materials for industry, and foreign exchange from exports. To encourage these goals, the government invested in transportation networks, irrigation projects, and agricultural storage facilities. It provided extension services and invested in research. It encouraged imports of technology to improve output and mechanize production. Since policy-makers believed that modern commercial farmers would respond more to these investments and services than would peasants on small plots of land, the government provided most of its assistance to large landowners.

The government's encouragement of industry and agriculture set the country on a three-decade path of sustained growth. Between 1940 and 1950, GDP grew at an annual average of 6.7 percent, while manufacturing increased at an average of 8.1 percent. In the following two decades, GDP growth rates remained impressive, and manufacturing growth continued to outpace overall growth in the economy. In the 1950s, manufacturing achieved an average of 7.3 percent growth annually and in the 1960s, 10.1 percent annually. Agricultural production grew rapidly as new areas were brought under cultivation and green revolution technology (scientifically improved seeds, fertilizers, and pesticides) was extensively adopted on large farms. These were years of great optimism as foreign investment increased,

the middle class grew larger, and indicators for health and welfare steadily improved. Between 1940 and 1970, Mexico City grew from a modest-sized city of 1.5 million people to a major metropolis of over 8 million inhabitants. Even the poorest Mexicans believed that their lives were improving. Table 1 presents data that summarize a number of advancements during this period. So impressive was Mexico's economic performance that it was referred to internationally as the Mexican Miracle.

U.S. private investment was an important source of capital for the country's effort to industrialize. In the twenty years after 1950, it grew at an average of over 11 percent a year. In 1962, the United States accounted for 85 percent of all foreign investment in Mexico. Moreover, two-thirds of Mexico's imports typically came from the United States, while it regularly sent two-thirds of its exports there. Mexican policy-makers increasingly saw the closeness and size of the U.S. economy as a significant threat, and many policy initiatives—restricting foreign investment in industries considered important to national development and seeking to diversify trade relationships with other countries, for example—were undertaken to lessen the country's dependence on the United States.

While the government took the lead in encouraging industrialization, it was not long before a group of domestic entrepreneurs developed a special relationship with the state. Government policies protected their products through high tariffs or special licensing requirements, limiting imports of competing goods. Business elites in Mexico received subsidized credit to invest in equipment and plants; they benefited from cheap, subsidized energy; and they rarely had to pay taxes. Additionally, inflation was kept in check, and the government helped ensure a supply of cheap labor by providing workers' housing, transportation, and medical coverage and ensuring that low cost staple foods were available in urban areas.

Through the impact of such policies, an elite of protected businesses emerged as powerful players in national politics. In the 1940s and 1950s, they strengthened a set of industry-related interest groups that worked to promote and sustain favorable policies. With this organizational base, groups like the chambers of industry, commerce, and banking began to play increasingly important roles in government policy-making. They

Table 1

Mexican Development, 1940–2000

	1940	1950	1960	1970	1980	1990	2000[a]
Population (thousands)	19,815	26,282	38,020	52,771	70,416	88,598	96,585
Life expectancy (years)[b]	—	51.6	58.6	62.6	67.4	68.9	71.35
Infant mortality (per 1,000 live births)[b]	—	—	86.3	70.9	49.9	42.6	32.6
Illiteracy (% of population age 15 and over)	—	42.5	34.5	25.0	16.0	12.7	8.9
Urban population (% of total)	—	—	50.7	59.0	66.4	72.6	74.2
Economically active population in agriculture (% of total)	—	58.3	55.1	44.0	36.6	22.0	21.0

	1940– 1950	1950– 1960	1960– 1970	1970– 1980	1980– 1990	1990– 2000
GDP growth rate (average annual percent)	6.7	5.8	7.6	6.7	1.6	3.3
Per capita GDP growth rate	—	—	3.7	3.7	–0.7	1.0[c]

[a]Except where noted, 2000 indicators are from *World Development Indicators 2002*.

[b]Five-year average.

[c]*Human Development Report 2001*. New York: Oxford University Press, 2001.

Sources: Statistical Abstract for Latin America (New York: United Nations, Economic Commission for Latin America, various years; Roger Hansen, *The Politics of Mexican Development* (Baltimore, Md.: Johns Hopkins University Press, 1971); *Statistical Bulletin of the OAS*. For 2000: *World Development Indicators 2002*, CD-ROM, and *Human Development Report 2001*, www.undp.org/hdr2001/.

were able to veto efforts by the government to cut back on their benefits and lobby for even more advantages. The government remained the source of most policy initiatives, but generally it was not able to move far in the face of opposition from those who benefited most from its policies. Perhaps just as important, business elites became adept at sidestepping government regulations; paying bribes to acquire licenses, credit, permits, and exemptions; and working out individual deals with officials.

Workers also became more important players in national politics. As mentioned in Section 1, widespread unionization occurred under President Cárdenas, and workers won many rights that had been promised in the Constitution of 1917. Cárdenas organized the unions into the National Confederation of Workers (CTM), which became the most powerful official voice of organized labor within the PRI. The policy changes

initiated in the 1940s, however, made the unions more dependent on the government for benefits and protection; the government also limited the right to strike. Wage standards were set through active annual negotiation between the CTM and the government, with employer groups largely sitting on the sidelines. Despite the fact that unions were closely controlled, organized workers continued to be an elite within the country's working classes. Union membership meant job security and important benefits such as housing subsidies and health care. These factors helped compensate for the lack of democracy within the labor movement. Moreover, labor leaders had privileged access to the country's political leadership and benefited personally from their control over jobs, contracts, and working conditions. In return, they guaranteed labor peace.[8]

In agriculture, those who benefited from government policies and services were primarily farmers who had enough land and economic resources to irrigate and mechanize and the capacity to make technological improvements in their farming methods and crops. By the 1950s, a group of large, commercially oriented farmers had emerged to dominate the agricultural economy.[9] They, like their urban counterparts in business, became rich and powerful. Industrialization also created a powerful class of government officials. Many abused their power to dispense jobs, licenses, and permits for a variety of activities, public works projects, and government investments by selling such favors in return for *mordidas* (bites, or bribes) or political support. They also became firm supporters of the continuation of government policies that provided them with special advantages.

There were significant costs to this pattern of economic and political development. Most important, government policies eventually limited the potential for further growth.[10] Industrialists who received extensive subsidies and benefits from government had few incentives to produce efficiently. High tariffs kept out foreign competition, further reducing reasons for efficiency or quality in production. Importing technology to support industrialization eventually became a drain on the country's foreign exchange. In addition, the costs of providing benefits to workers increased beyond the capacity of the government to generate revenue, especially because tax rates were kept low as a further incentive to investors. Mexico's tax rates, in fact, were among the lowest in the world, and opportunities to avoid payment were extensive. Eventually, the ISI strategy became less effective in generating new jobs as industrialists moved from investing in labor-intensive industries such as processed foods and textiles to capital-intensive industries such as automobiles, refrigerators, and heavy equipment.

But as the economy grew, and with it the power of industrial, agricultural, and urban interests, many were left behind. The ranks of the urban poor grew steadily, particularly from the 1960s on. Mexico developed a sizable **informal sector**—workers who produced and sold goods and services at the margin of the economic system and faced extreme insecurity. By 1970, a large proportion of Mexico City's population was living in inner-city tenements or squatter settlements surrounding the city.[11]

Also left behind in the country's development after 1940 were peasant farmers. Their lands were often the least fertile, plot sizes were minuscule, and access to markets was impeded by poor transportation and exploitive middlemen who trucked products to markets for exorbitant fees. The 1940s and 1950s were important years for increasing the gap between commercial agriculture, largely centered in the north and northwestern regions of the country, where much of Mexico's political elite originated, and subsistence agriculture, largely made up of small private farmers and *ejidatarios* who lived in central and southern parts of the country. Farming in the *ejido* communities, where land was held communally, was particularly difficult. Because *ejido* land could not be sold or (until the early 1980s) rented, *ejidatarios* could not borrow money from private banks because they had nothing to pledge as collateral if they defaulted on their payments. Government banks provided credit, but usually only to those who had political connections. The government invested little in small infrastructure projects throughout the 1960s, and agricultural research and extension focused on the large-farm sector. Moreover, because prices for basic foodstuffs were controlled, the *ejidatarios* saw little advantage to investing in farming. Not surprisingly, the *ejido* sector consistently reported low productivity.

Increasing disparities in rural and urban incomes, coupled with high population growth rates, contributed to the emergence of rural guerrilla movements and student protests in the mid- and late 1960s. The government was particularly alarmed in 1968, when a student movement openly challenged the government on the eve of the Olympic Games being hosted in Mexico City. Moreover, by the early 1970s, it was becoming evident that the size of the population, growing at a rate of some 3.5 percent a year, and the structure of income distribution were impeding further industrial development. The domestic market was limited by poverty; many Mexicans could not afford the sophisticated manufactured products the country would need to produce in order to keep growing under the import substitution model.

The Mexican government had hoped that industrialization would free the economy from excessive dependence on the industrialized world, and particularly on the United States, making the country less subject to abrupt swings in prices for primary commodities.

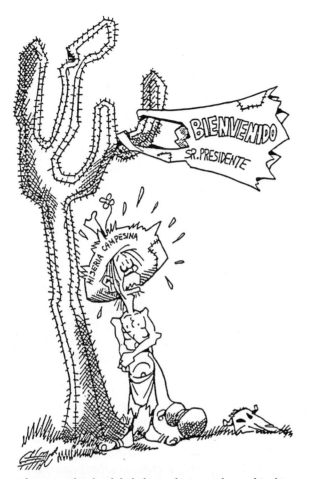

A farmer with a hat labeled "rural misery" hangs his shirt on a cactus: "Welcome, Mr. President." Among those who have benefited least from the government's development policies are the rural poor. *Source: Ausencias y Presencias Gente de Ayer y Hoy en su Tinta: Problematica Politica, Social, Vista por un Cartoonista Potosino by Luis Chessal, Unversidad Autonoma de San Luis Potosi, Mexico, 1984.*

Industrialization, however, highlighted new vulnerabilities. Advanced manufacturing processes required ever more foreign investment and imported technology. Concern grew about powerful multinational companies, which had invested heavily in the country in the 1960s and about purchasing foreign technology with scarce foreign exchange. By the late 1960s, the country was no longer able to meet domestic demand for basic foodstuffs and was forced to import increas-ingly large quantities of food, costing the government foreign exchange that it could have used for better purposes. By the 1970s, some policy-makers had become convinced that industrialization had actually increased the country's dependence on advanced industrial countries and particularly on the United States.

Sowing the Oil and Reaping a Crisis

In the early 1970s, Mexico faced the threat of social crisis brought on by rural poverty, chaotic urbanization, high population growth, and the questioning of political legitimacy. The government responded by increasing investment in infrastructure and public industries, regulating the flow of foreign capital, and increasing social spending. It was spending much more than it generated, causing the public internal debt to grow rapidly and requiring heavy borrowing abroad. Between 1971 and 1976, inflation rose from an annual average of 5.3 percent to almost 16 percent, and the foreign debt more than tripled. In response to mounting evidence that current policies could not be sustained, the government devalued the peso in 1976 and signed a stabilization agreement with the International Monetary Fund (IMF) to reduce government spending, increase tax collection, and control inflation. Little progress was made in changing existing policies, however, because just as the seriousness of the economic situation was being recognized, vast new finds of oil came to the rescue.

Between 1978 and 1982, Mexico was transformed into a major oil exporter. As international oil prices rose rapidly, from $13.30 per barrel in 1978 to $33.20 per barrel in 1981, so did the country's fortunes, along with those of other oil-rich countries such as Nigeria, Iran, Indonesia, and Venezuela. The administration of President José López Portillo (1976–1982) embarked on a policy to "sow the oil" in the economy and "administer the abundance" with vast investment projects in virtually all sectors and major new initiatives to reduce poverty and deal with declining agricultural productivity. Oil revenues paid for much of this expansion, but the foreign debt also mounted as both public and private sectors borrowed heavily to finance investments and lavish consumer spending.

By 1982, Mexico's foreign debt was $86 billion, and the exchange rate was seriously overvalued, making the peso and Mexican products more expensive on the world market. Oil accounted for 77.2 percent of the country's exports, causing the economy to be extremely vulnerable to changes in oil prices. And change they did. Global overproduction brought the international price for Mexican petroleum down to $26.30 a barrel. Revenues from exports declined dramatically. At the same time, the United States tightened its monetary policy, and access to foreign credit dried up. Wealthy Mexicans responded by sending vast amounts of capital out of the country just as the country's international creditors were demanding repayment on their loans. In August 1982, the government announced that the country could not pay the interest on its foreign debt, triggering a crisis that reverberated around the world.

The impact of these conditions on the Mexican economy was devastating. GDP growth in 1982 was −0.6 percent and fell to −4.2 percent the following year. New policy measures were put in place by the administration of Miguel de la Madrid (1982–1988) to deal with the economic crisis, but policy-makers were repeatedly overtaken by escalating inflation, financial sector panic, depleted foreign reserves, severe trade imbalances, and debt renegotiations. In 1986, petroleum prices dropped to $12 a barrel, exacerbating an already desperate situation.

The economic crisis had several important implications for structures of power and privilege in Mexico. First, faith in the import substitution policy was destroyed. The crisis convinced even the most diehard believers that import substitution created inefficiencies in production, failed to generate sufficient employment, cost the government far too much in subsidies, and increased dependency on industrialized countries. In addition, the power of interest groups and their ability to influence government policy declined. Prolonged economic crisis hit the business sector particularly hard. When the economy stagnated, declined, and failed to recover rapidly, private debts could not be repaid, inflation and unemployment reduced demand, government subsidies were repeatedly cut back, and most public investment plans were put on hold. The inevitable result was the failure of many Mexican companies. Bankruptcy and recession exacted their toll on the fortunes of even large entrepreneurs. As economic hardship affected their members, traditional business organizations lost their ability to put strong pressure on the government.

Similarly, the country's relatively privileged unions lost much of their bargaining power with government over issues of wages and protection. Union leaders loyal to the PRI emphasized the need for peace and order to help the nation get through tough times, while inflation and job loss focused many of the country's workers on putting food on the table. A shift in employment from the formal to the informal sector further fragmented what had once been the most powerful sector of the party. Cuts in government subsidies for public transportation, food, electricity, and gasoline created new hardships for workers. The combination of these factors weakened the capacity of labor to resist policy changes that affected the benefits they received.

In addition, new voices emerged to demand that the government respond to the crisis. During the recession years of the 1980s, wages lost between 40 and 50 percent of their value, increasingly large numbers of people became unemployed, inflation cut deeply into middle-class incomes, and budgets for health and education services were severely cut back. A wide variety of interests began to organize outside the PRI to demand that government do something about the situation. Massive earthquakes in Mexico City in September 1985 proved to be a watershed for Mexican society. Severely disappointed by the government's failure to respond to the problems created by death, destruction, disorientation, and homelessness, hundreds of communities organized rescue efforts, soup kitchens, shelters, and rehabilitation initiatives. A surging sense of political empowerment developed, as groups long accustomed to dependence on government learned that they could solve their problems better without government than with it.[12]

In addition, the PRI was challenged by the increased popularity of opposition political parties, one of them headed by Cuauhtémoc Cárdenas, the son of the country's most revered president, Lázaro Cárdenas. The elections of 1988 became a focus for protest against the economic dislocation caused by the crisis and the political powerlessness that most citizens felt. Carlos Salinas, the PRI candidate, received a bare majority of 50.7 percent, and opposition parties claimed widespread electoral fraud.

New Strategies and Democratic Institutions

Demands on the Salinas administration to deal with the economic and political crisis were extensive. At the same time, the weakening of the old centers of political power provided the government with a major opportunity to reorient the country's strategy for economic development. Between 1988 and 1994, the dependent relationship between industry and government was weakened when new free-market policies were put in place. Decreasing regulation was an important part of this restructuring of state-economy relationships. Deregulation gave the private sector more freedom to pursue economic activities and less reason to seek special favors from government. A number of large government industries, such as the telephone company, the banking sector, the national airlines, and steel and sugar mills, were reorganized and sold to private investors. A constitutional revision made it possible for *ejidatarios* to become owners of individual plots of land; this made them less dependent on government but more vulnerable to losing their land. In addition, financial sector reform that changed laws about banking and established a stock exchange encouraged the emergence of new banks and brokerage and insurance firms.

Salinas pursued, and Zedillo continued, an overhaul of the federal system and the way government agencies worked together. Called the New Federalism, it was an attempt to give power and budgetary responsibilities to state and local governments, which had been historically very weak in Mexico. Beginning with education and health, the presidents hoped decentralization would make government more efficient and effective. In addition, federal agencies began to be broken down into regional bureaus to work more closely with lower levels of government. This was a major change from the highly centralized government of the past. Additionally, the central bank became independent from the government in 1994, though exchange rates are still determined by the finance ministry.

Among the most far-reaching initiatives was NAFTA. This agreement with Canada and the United States created the basis for gradual introduction of free trade among the three countries. These changes were a major reversal of import substitution and economic intervention that had marked government policies in the past. However, the liberalization of the Mexican economy and opening up its markets to foreign competition increased the vulnerability of the country to changes in international economic conditions. These factors, as well as mismanaged economic policies, led to a major economic crisis for the country at the end of 1994 and profound recession in 1995. NAFTA has meant that the fate of the Mexican economy is increasingly linked to the health of the U.S. economy, sheltering it from the contagion of the 1997–1998 financial crisis in Asia and putting it at risk in the cool-down of the U.S. system in the early 2000s.

New economic institutions were followed by the emergence of more democratic structures. In 1996, an independent election board composed of private citizens helped ensure fairer and more competitive elections. Constitutional amendments helped ensure more fairness for political parties during campaigns. Now, election funds are mostly public, with private expenditures limited. Changes also introduced procedures for auditing the political parties. By 1997, it became much more possible for opposition parties to win elections from the PRI. In that year, the party of the old regime lost its majority in congress. Numerous governors and mayors were elected from the opposition. In 2000, the PRI lost the presidency.

Society and Economy

Mexico's economic development has had a significant impact on social conditions in the country. Overall, the standard of living improved markedly after the 1940s. Rates of infant mortality, literacy, and life expectancy have steadily improved. Provision of health and education services expanded until government cutbacks on social expenditures in the early 1980s. Among the most important consequences of economic growth was the development of a large middle class, most of whom live in Mexico's numerous large cities. By the 1980s, a third or more of Mexican households could claim a middle-class lifestyle: a steady income, secure food and shelter, access to decent education and health services, a car, some disposable income and savings, and some security that their children would be able to experience happy and healthy lives.

These achievements reflect well on the ability of the economy to increase social well-being in the country. However, the impressive economic growth through the early 1970s and between 1978 and 1982 could have produced greater social progress. In terms of standard indicators of social development—infant mortality, literacy, and life expectancy—Mexico fell behind a number of Latin American countries that grew less rapidly but provided more effectively for their populations. Costa Rica, Colombia, Argentina, Chile, and Uruguay had lower overall growth but greater social development in the period after 1940. These countries paid more attention to the distribution of the benefits of growth than did Mexico. Moreover, in its pursuit of rapid industrialization, Mexico City has become one of the most congested and polluted cities in the world. In some rural areas, oil exploitation left devastating environmental damage, destroying the lifestyles and opportunities of *ejidatarios* and small farmers.

Mexico's economic development also resulted in a widening gap between the wealthy and the poor and among different regions in the country. Although the poor are better off than they were in the early days of the country's drive toward industrialization, they are worse off when compared to middle- and upper-income groups. In 1950, the bottom 40 percent of the country's households accounted for about 14 percent of total personal income, while the top 30 percent had 60 percent of total income.[13] In 1995, it is estimated, the bottom 40 percent accounted for about 11 percent of income, while the top 40 percent shared 77.4 percent.[14] As in the United States, as the rich grew richer, the gap between the rich and the poor increased.

Among the poorest are those in rural areas who have little or no access to productive land and those in urban areas who do not have steady jobs. Harsh conditions in the countryside have fueled a half-century of migration to the cities. Nevertheless, some 25 million Mexicans continue to live in rural areas, many of them in deep poverty. Many of them work for substandard wages and migrate seasonally to search for jobs in order to sustain their families. Traditionally, those who, legally and illegally, crossed the border to the United States in search of jobs came from depressed rural areas. Increasingly, however, they come from urban areas.

Among rural inhabitants with access to land, almost half have five hectares or less. This land is usually not irrigated and depends on erratic rainfall. It is often leached of nutrients as a result of centuries of cultivation, population pressure, and erosion. The crops grown on such farms, primarily corn and beans, do not bring high prices in the markets. To improve production, peasant farmers would have to buy fertilizer, improved seeds, and insecticides, and they would have to find ways to irrigate their plots. But they generally have no money to purchase these supplies or invest in irrigation. In many areas, farm production provides as few as twenty to one hundred days of employment each year. Not surprisingly, underemployment is high in rural Mexico, as are rates of seasonal migration. The incidence of disease, malnutrition, and illiteracy is much higher in Mexico's rural areas than in urban areas. When the rebels in Chiapas called for jobs, land, education, and health facilities, they were clearly reflecting the realities of life in much of the country.

Poverty has a regional dimension in Mexico. The northern areas of the country are significantly better off than the southern and central areas. In the north, large commercial farms using modern technologies grow fruits, vegetables, and grains for export. The U.S. border, the principal destination of agricultural products, is close at hand, and transportation networks are extensive and generally in good condition. Moreover, industrial cities such as Monterrey and Tijuana provide steady jobs for skilled and unskilled labor. Along the border, a band of manufacturing and assembly plants, called *maquiladoras*, provides many jobs, particularly for young women who are seeking some escape from the burdens of rural life or the constraints of traditional family life.

In the southern and central regions of the country, the population is denser, the land poorer, and the number of *ejidatarios* eking out subsistence greater. Transportation is often difficult, and during parts of the year, some areas may be inaccessible because of heavy rains and flooding. Most of Mexico's remaining indigenous groups live in the southern regions, often in remote areas where they have been forgotten by government programs and exploited by regional bosses for generations. The conditions that spurred the Chiapas rebellion are found throughout the southern states.

The economic crisis of the 1980s had an impact on social conditions in the country as well. Wages declined by about half, and unemployment soared as businesses collapsed and the government laid off workers in public offices and privatized industries. The informal sector expanded rapidly. Here, people eked out a living by hawking chewing gum, umbrellas, sponges, candy, shoelaces, mirrors, and a variety of other items in the street; jumping in front of cars at stoplights to wash windshields and sell newspapers; producing and repairing cheap consumer goods such as shoes and clothing; and selling services on a daily or hourly basis. While the informal sector provides important goods and services, conditions of work are often dangerous, and insecurity about where the next peso will come from is endemic.

The economic crisis of the 1980s also reduced the quality and availability of social services. Expenditures on education and health declined after 1982 as the government imposed austerity measures. Salaries of primary school teachers declined by 34 percent between 1983 and 1988, and many teachers worked second and even third jobs in order to make ends meet. Per capita health expenditures declined from a high of about $19 in 1980 to about $11 in 1990. Hospitals, clinics, and schools were left in disrepair, and obtaining equipment and supplies became almost impossible. Although indicators of mortality did not rise during this troubled decade, the incidence of diseases associated with poverty—malnutrition, cholera, anemia, and dysentery—increased. The diet of most Mexicans became less rich in protein as they ate less meat and drank less milk. The crisis began to ease in the early 1990s, however, and many came to believe that conditions would improve for the poor. The government began investing in social services. When a new economic crisis occurred, however, unemployment surged, and austerity measures severely limited investments. Despite considerable recovery in the late 1990s, wages remain low for the majority of workers while taxes have increased. Subsidies on basic goods like tortillas, water, and gas have been lowered or eliminated, making the cost of living rise steeply for the poor and the working class.

Mexico and the International Political Economy

The crisis that began in 1982 altered Mexico's international policies. In response to that crisis, the government relaxed restrictions on the ability of foreigners to own property, reduced and eliminated tariffs, and did away with most import licenses. Foreign investment was courted in the hope of increasing the manufacture of goods for export. The government also introduced a series of incentives to encourage the private sector to produce goods for export. In 1986, Mexico joined the General Agreement on Tariffs and Trade (GATT), a multilateral agreement that seeks to promote freer trade among countries.

The government's effort to pursue a more outward-oriented development strategy culminated in the ratification of NAFTA in 1993, with gradual implementation beginning on January 1, 1994. This agreement is important to Mexico. In 2000, 89 percent of the country's exports were sent to the United States, and 74 percent of its imports came from that country. The next most active trading country with Mexico was Canada, which received only 2 percent of its exports and accounted for only 2.3 percent of its imports.[15] Access to the U.S. market is thus essential to Mexico and to domestic and foreign investors. NAFTA signaled a new period in U.S.-Mexican relations by making closer integration of the two economies a certainty. To date, trade among Mexico, Canada, and the United States has increased along with foreign direct investment. Additionally, NAFTA contains two parallel agreements regarding the environment and labor that were negotiated in order to pass the treaty in the U.S. Congress. These documents created trinational institutions to cooperate and mediate on these issues to prevent potentially damaging side effects from free trade. The new institutions have not been very active, however, and it is unknown what positive effect, if any, they are having. (See "Global Connection: NAFTA and Beyond.")

NAFTA also entails risks for Mexico. Domestic producers worry about competition from U.S. firms. Farmers worry that Mexican crops cannot compete effectively with those grown in the United States; for example, peasant producers of corn and beans have been hard hit by lower-priced U.S.-grown grains. In addition, many believe that embracing free trade with Canada and the United States indicates a loss of sovereignty. Certainly Mexico's economic situation is now more vulnerable to the ebb and flow of economic conditions in the U.S. economy. Some are also concerned with increasing evidence of "cultural imperialism" as

Global Connection: **NAFTA and Beyond**

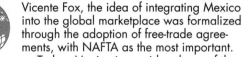

On January 1, 1994, the North America Free Trade Agreement (NAFTA) between Mexico, Canada, and the United States went into effect. The day chosen for the EZLN's action was no coincidence: besides demanding social justice for indigenous groups, the rebels called on Carlos Salinas de Gortari's administration to revoke NAFTA. Since that time, Mexico has been both a subject of deep criticism for its evident failure to integrate those who have been gradually excluded by its development strategy, and respect for being able to negotiate—on a fairly equal basis—a major trade pact with the world's strongest economy. The coincidence of the Chiapas rebellion and the beginning of NAFTA was symbolic of the difficulty of at least one of the many "Mexicos" to catch up with the high-speed train of the country's aspirations to become a key player in the new international economy.

Almost a decade later, the debate surrounding free trade and its tangible benefits to the vast majority of Mexicans remains. While Mexico has achieved some successes in advancing economic development in the context of NAFTA and other trade agreements, economic growth has not only not contributed to poverty reduction but also has steadily increased income disparities, benefiting the better off at the expense of the poorest sectors. Mexico is the twelfth biggest economy in the world, but 42.5 percent of its more than 100 million inhabitants live on less than $2 a day and 17.9 percent on less than $1 a day. The Gini index for Mexico, a measure of inequality, was 53.7 in 2000. The United States and Canada had indexes of 40.8 and 31.5, respectively (the higher the number, the greater the inequality).

NAFTA was conceived as a mechanism through which Mexico's historical economic and political ties to the United States could become institutionalized on both sides of the border. NAFTA was perceived as the "seal of gold" to technocrats' efforts to pursue an outward-oriented development strategy. Since the mid-1980s and in a clear response to the negative traits associated with the protectionist model that culminated in the 1982 crisis, Mexico began a series of dramatic changes in its economic, fiscal, and monetary policies and legal and institutional frameworks, emphasizing the need to develop export platforms and liberalize trade. Beginning with President Miguel de la Madrid and followed by Presidents Carlos Salinas de Gortari, Ernesto Zedillo, and Vicente Fox, the idea of integrating Mexico into the global marketplace was formalized through the adoption of free-trade agreements, with NAFTA as the most important.

Today, Mexico is considered one of the most prolific signers of free-trade agreements in the world. Besides the United States and Canada, Mexico has signed trade accords with Argentina, Bolivia, Brazil, Chile, Colombia, Costa Rica, El Salvador, the European Union (Austria, Belgium, Denmark, Finland, France, Germany, Greece, Ireland, Italy, Luxembourg, the Netherlands, Portugal, Spain, Sweden, and the United Kingdom), the European Free-Trade Association (Norway, Switzerland, and Liechtenstein), Guatemala, Honduras, Israel, Nicaragua, and Venezuela. Formal negotiations continue with Ecuador, Japan, MERCOSUR (a free-trade area in southern Latin America), Panama, Peru, Singapore, Trinidad and Tobago, and the Free-Trade Area of the Americas. And while this list might seem comprehensive in proving Mexico's attempts to diversify its economic relationships with the rest of the world, Mexican-U.S. trade and political ties are stronger than ever before: currently the United States accounts for about 80 percent of Mexico's foreign trade.

Without any doubt, NAFTA signaled a new period in Mexican-U.S. relations. Mexico's foreign policy shift from historical commitment to nonintervention to one that is more proactive and assertive in international affairs, for example, has been considered a direct consequence of the strategic position gained through the new relationship with the United States. Also, further economic and political transformation has been undertaken to fulfill NAFTA requirements. Alas, NAFTA has also added more issues to an already complex and difficult relationship. In the years since it went into effect, the two countries have locked horns in various trade disputes, such as antidumping regulations to cross-border trucking provisions, and social and political sectors in the United States and Mexico continue to hold each other responsible for their respective misfortunes, particularly as electoral opportunities arise. In addition, antinarcotics efforts and undocumented immigration continue to fuel intense debate on both sides over the costs and benefits of managing economic integration.

Written by Bertha Angulo Curiel, Harvard University. Reprinted with permission.

U.S. movies, music, fashions, and lifestyles increasingly influence consumers.

In addition, the incorporation of Mexico into NAFTA has political ramifications. During negotiations for this agreement, new international political alliances developed. Environmental groups from the United States sought support in Mexico and Canada for fighting the agreement, and labor groups also looked across both borders for allies in opposing new trade relations. Environmental and labor groups united around concerns that Mexico would not enforce environmental protection and fair labor legislation. Some business interests allied across countries in supporting the agreement, anticipating opportunities for larger markets, cheaper labor, or richer sources of raw materials. For Mexico, which has traditionally feared the power of the United States in its domestic affairs, internationalization of political and economic relationships poses particularly difficult problems of adjustment.

On the other hand, the United States, newly aware of the importance of the Mexican economy to its own economic growth and concerned about instability on its southern border, hammered together a $50 billion economic assistance program composed of U.S., European, and IMF commitments to support its neighbor when crisis struck in 1994. The Mexican government imposed a new stabilization package that contained austerity measures, higher interest rates, and limits on wages. Remarkably, by 1998, Mexico had paid off all of its obligations to the United States.

Globalization is also stripping Mexico of some of the secrecy that traditionally surrounded government decision making, electoral processes, and efforts to deal with political dissent. International attention increasingly focuses on the country. Investors want clear and up-to-date information on what is occurring in the economy. The Internet and email, along with lower international telephone rates, are increasing information flow across borders. The government can no longer respond to events such as the peasant rebellion in Chiapas, alleged electoral fraud, or the management of exchange rates without considering how such actions will be perceived in Tokyo, Frankfurt, Ottawa, London, or Washington.

Section ❸ Governance and Policy-Making

Mexico is a federal republic, although until the 1990s, state and local governments had few resources and a limited sphere of action when compared with the national level. Under the PRI, the executive branch concentrated almost all power, while the legislative and judiciary branches followed the executive's lead and were considered rubber-stamp bodies. During the seventy-one years of PRI hegemony, the government was civilian, authoritarian, and corporatist. Currently, it has multiparty competitive elections, and power is less concentrated in the executive branch and the national government. Since the mid-1980s, great efforts have been made to reinvigorate the nation's laws and institutions and make the country more democratic.

Organization of the State

According to the supreme law of the land, the Constitution of 1917, Mexico's political institutions resemble those of the United States. There are three branches of government, and a set of checks and balances limits the power of each. The congress is composed of the Senate and the Chamber of Deputies. One hundred twenty-eight senators are elected, three from each of the country's thirty-one states and an additional three from the federal district (capital), Mexico City, and another thirty-two elected nationally by proportional representation. Five hundred deputies are elected from 300 electoral districts—300 by simple majority vote and 200 by proportional representation. States and local governments are also elected. The president, governors, and senators are elected for six years, and deputies (representatives in the lower house) and municipal officials are elected for three.

In practice, the Mexican system is very different from that of the United States. The constitution is a very long document that is easily amended, especially when compared to that of the United States. It lays out the structure of government and guarantees a wide range of human rights, including familiar ones such as freedom of speech and protection of the law, but also economic and social rights such as the right to a job and the right to health care. Economic and social rights are acknowledged but in practice do not reach all of the population. Although there has been some decentralization of power, the political system is still much more centralized than that of the United States. Congress is now more active as a decision-making arena and as a check on presidential power, but the executive remains central to initiating policy and managing political conflict.

The Executive

The President and the Cabinet

The Mexican presidency is the central institution of governance and policy-making. Until the 1990s, the incumbent PRI president always selected who would run as the party's next presidential candidate, appointed officials to all positions of power in the government and the PRI, and often named the candidates, who almost automatically won elections as governors, senators, deputies, and local officials. Even with a non-PRI incumbent, the president continues to set the broad outlines of policy for the administration and has numerous resources to ensure that those policy preferences are adopted. Until the mid-1970s, Mexican presidents were considered above criticism in national politics and revered as symbols of national progress and well-being. While economic and political events of the 1980s and 1990s diminished presidential prestige, the extent of presidential power remains a legacy of the long period of PRI ascendance.

Mexican presidents have a set of formal powers that allows them to initiate legislation, lead in foreign policy, create government agencies, make policy by decree or through administrative regulations and procedures, and appoint a wide range of public officials. More important, informal powers provide them with the capacity to exert considerable control. The president manages a vast patronage machine for filling positions in government and initiates legislation and policies that were, until recently, routinely approved by the congress. When Vicente Fox became president in 2000, he promised many fewer personnel changes in government than under previous incumbents. He promised more open government and greater diversity

among his cabinet and other appointees. His powers have been curtailed to some degree by a more forceful congress and his administration's lack of experience in governing.

Under the PRI, presidents were always male and almost always members of the outgoing president's cabinet. Several had served as ministers of the interior, the person responsible for maintaining law and order in the country. This was true of Miguel Alemán (1946–1952), Adolfo Ruiz Cortines (1952–1958), Gustavo Díaz Ordaz (1964–1970), and Luis Echeverría (1970–1976). With the expansion of the government's role in economic development, candidates in the 1970s and 1980s were selected from the ministries that managed the economy. José López Portillo (1976–1982) had been minister of finance, and Miguel de la Madrid (1982–1988) and Carlos Salinas (1988–1994) had served as ministers of planning and budgeting. The selection of Luis Donaldo Colosio, who had been minister of social development and welfare, was thought by political observers to signal renewed concern with problems of social development. When Colosio was assassinated in 1994, the selection of Ernesto Zedillo, who had first been minister of planning and budgeting and then minister of education, was interpreted as an ongoing concern with national social problems and as an effort to maintain the policies of economic liberalization that Salinas had introduced. With the victory of the PAN in 2000, this long tradition came to an end. Prior to running for president, Vicente Fox had been in business and had served as the governor of the state of Guanajuato (see "Leaders: Vicente Fox Quesada").

Candidates since the mid-1970s have had impressive educational credentials and have tended to be trained in economics and management rather than in the traditional field of law. Presidents since López Portillo have had postgraduate training at elite institutions in the United States. Miguel de la Madrid held a master's degree in public administration from Harvard; Carlos Salinas received a Ph.D. degree in political economy and government from Harvard; Luis Colosio studied for a Ph.D. degree in economics from the University of Pennsylvania; Ernesto Zedillo had a Ph.D. degree in economics from Yale; and Vicente Fox holds a certificate from the prestigious Advanced Management Program at the Harvard Business School. By the 1980s, a topic of great debate in political circles was

Leaders: *Vicente Fox Quesada*

When Vicente Fox Quesada was governor of the small but prosperous state of Guanajuato, he embarked on a major political gamble. In 1998, he declared himself a candidate for the presidency, even before gaining the backing of his political party, the National Action Party (PAN). He was not only gambling on the nomination of the party, by no means assured because he was not considered an insider by party leaders, but also on being able to campaign effectively for the presidency. For seven decades, the dominant party, the PRI, had controlled Mexico's presidency. In the fall of 1999, the conservative, probusiness PAN reluctantly gave the nomination to Fox, and he began active campaigning. His first major national test came in a presidential debate in April 2000, and most analysts declared him the winner. By May, he was leading in public opinion polls. On July 2, 2000, he won the election, and on December 1, he assumed the presidency. He had won his gamble. Mexicans were intrigued by their new president, the one who had upset the PRI after seventy-one years. Who was he? What were his plans for the country?

Vicente Fox was born on July 2, 1942, one of nine children. When he was a child, the family moved to a small town in Guanajuato, where he became familiar with rural life and the challenges of agriculture in a country that was rapidly industrializing. He also saw firsthand the poverty that afflicted many of those who lived in rural areas. He is reported to have said, "I grew up in an *ejido* with the children of peasants and the only difference between me and my childhood friends were the opportunities I had."[1] He attended the Iberoamerican University in Mexico City, where he majored in business administration. He also earned a certificate in advanced management from Harvard Business School. He became the father of four children, although his marriage dissolved in divorce some years later. In 1964, he became a route director for Coca-Cola in Mexico and gradually rose to become the president of Coca-Cola for Mexico and Latin America. He returned to Guanajuato to pursue interests in business and politics, becoming president of the Fox Group of farming, livestock, agro-industrial, shoe, and boot companies.

In the 1980s, Fox became a member of the PAN, which had long been tied to business interests in the north of the country and had long opposed the central government in Mexico City. He was elected to congress as a deputy in 1988, ran for governor and lost in 1991, and then won the gubernatorial election of 1995. His administration was recognized for its promotion of "good government," including greater efficiency and effectiveness in carrying out public policies and programs.

His path to the presidency was not smooth, however. PAN leaders, among them those who wanted to run for this important position, considered Fox to be a newcomer to the party, one who had not fully demonstrated his commitment to it. They recognized his growing reputation and popularity and tried to use party rules to keep him from gaining greater power. Fox, recognizing the uphill battle he would encounter with the PAN, organized his own electoral machine, the "Friends of Fox," to finance and lead his campaign. Eventually, the party was forced to recognize his candidacy, but the main vehicle for the election continued to be the Friends of Fox. When he became president, the tension between the candidate and the party continued, and Fox could not count on the support of the PAN when he sent legislation to congress.

As president, Fox committed himself to greater transparency in government decision making and continued efforts to liberalize the economy and encourage its global integration. He promised that citizens would have more information and that there would be greater responsiveness in public services. He had a difficult time delivering on these promises, however, as the PAN did not have a majority in congress and he did not have many experienced people to plan policy and manage government activities. Moreover, he made a number of widely broadcast political mistakes—spending lavishly on refurbishing the presidential residence, for example, and pursuing what was viewed as an improper relationship with his spokesperson, Martha Sahagun (they were married in 2001)—and at times seemed uncertain about the direction of his presidency. In a system that had always depended on the president to generate and promote a vision of government every six years, many Mexicans came to the conclusion that he lacked decisiveness. Nevertheless, the first president from an opposition party since 1929 earned high marks for bringing democratic change to Mexico and supporting a more open political system.

---

[1]www.presidencia.gob.mx.

the extent to which a divide between *políticos* (politicians) and *técnicos* (**technocrats**) had emerged within the national political elite. Among the old guard of the PRI, there was open skepticism about the ability of young technocrats like Carlos Salinas and Ernesto Zedillo to manage political conditions in the country. During the presidential campaign of 1994, considerable efforts were made to stress the more humble beginnings of Colosio and Zedillo and the fact that they had had to work hard to get an education. Under Fox, the ties of the president to business elites raised similar fears that the government would not respond to the concerns of everyday citizens.

Once elected, the president moves quickly to name a cabinet. Under the PRI, he usually selected those with whom he had worked over the years as he rose to political prominence. He also used cabinet posts to ensure a broad coalition of support; he might, for example, appoint people with close ties to the labor movement, business interests, or some of the regional strongholds of the party. Only in rare exceptions were cabinet officials not active members of the PRI. When the PAN assumed the presidency, the selection of a cabinet and close advisers was more difficult. Until then, the party had elected officials only to state and local governments and to congress. As a consequence, the range of people with executive experience whom Fox could turn to was limited. He appointed U.S.-trained economists for his economic team and business executives for many other important posts. Few of these appointees had close ties to the PAN, and few had prior experience in government. Over the years, few women have been selected for ministry-level posts—there are a handful of examples in recent administrations—and thus far only in those agencies that have limited influence over decision making, like Tourism, Ecology, and Foreign Relations.

The president has the authority to fill numerous other high-level positions, which allows him to provide policy direction and keep tabs on what is occurring throughout the government. Such appointments provide the president with the capacity to build a team of like-minded officials in government and ensure their loyalty to him. In turn, high-level appointees fill many jobs in their organizations. Like the president, they use this patronage power to put together loyal teams of officials whose career advancement is tied to their own

political fate. These officials, in turn, build their own teams, and so on down through middle levels in the bureaucracy. This system traditionally served the interests of presidents and the PRI well; under the PAN, given the limited number of its partisans who have experience at national levels, the system has not guaranteed the president as much power over the workings of the executive branch. In addition, when he assumed power, President Fox committed himself to retaining qualified people in their positions and making many fewer changes than customary.

Given the range of appointments that a president can make, the beginning of each administration is characterized by extensive turnover of positions, although under the PRI, many of the newly appointed officials served in other positions in prior administrations. While the PRI held power, little happened in government in the year prior to an election as officials bided their time or jockeyed for positions in the next administration. Even under alternative parties, little is likely to happen in the year following an election as newly appointed officials learn the ropes and assemble their teams. Nevertheless, when a president has set clear goals and expects high performance from his personally chosen officials, these people in turn must expect good performance from their staffs if they are to produce for the president. In many situations, then, the patronage system results in the potential for increased presidential leadership and effective performance, at least at high levels in government. Under the PRI, delivering for "the boss" might even result in a position in the next administration, if one's boss happened to be chosen as the presidential candidate or one of his ministers. Just as frequently, however, appointments to government service can mean opportunities to amass personal wealth, take bribes, and use insider information for personal benefit. Under more democratic conditions today, there is mounting pressure for a less politicized and more professional civil service.

Mexican presidents, though powerful, are not omnipotent. They, must, for example, abide by a deeply held constitutional norm, fully adhered to since 1940, to step down at the end of their term, and they must honor the political norm to step out of the political limelight to allow the successor to assume full presidential leadership. All presidents, regardless of party, must demonstrate their loyalty to the myths and symbols of Mexican nationalism, such as the indigenous roots of much of its culture, the agrarian origins of the revolution, and rhetorical commitment to social justice and sovereignty in international affairs. In addition, several factors tend to limit the extent of presidential discretion. PRI presidents were always creatures of the system, selected because they proved themselves adept at understanding and playing by the existing rules. Through their careers in politics or government, they became familiar with the range of interest groups in the country and demonstrated a willingness to compromise on policy and political issues so that these interests would not unduly challenge the government. They also proved themselves to be skillful in the fierce bureaucratic politics that surround career advancement and in guessing about whom the next PRI candidate for president was likely to be. Under more democratic conditions since 2000, presidential backgrounds and career trajectories can no longer be predicted. Indeed, Vicente Fox, although the standard-bearer of the PAN, was not close to the party apparatus and did not ascend through its ranks. This meant that he could not necessarily count on party support in the congress or its unconditional loyalty as launched new initiatives or sought to mobilize public support for his actions.

In the 1990s, President Zedillo relinquished a number of the traditional powers of the presidency. He announced, for example, that he would not select his PRI successor but would leave it up to the party to determine its candidate. In doing so, however, he created considerable conflict and tension as the PRI had to take on unaccustomed roles and as politicians sought to fill the void left by the "abandonment" of presidential power. President Fox inherited a system in which he was expected to set the policies and determine the priorities for a very wide range of government activity. Without a strong party in congress or many experienced people in government, he was often unable to deliver. In the absence of strong presidential leadership, government often seemed to flounder.

The Bureaucracy

Mexico's executive branch is large and powerful. Almost 1.5 million people work in the federal bureaucracy, most of them in Mexico City. An additional 1 million work for the large number of state-owned industries and semiautonomous agencies of the government. State and local governments employ over 1.5 million people. Pay scales are usually low, and in the past, the number of people filling lower-level positions such as drivers, messengers, secretaries, and maintenance people far exceeded the demand for them. In the 1980s, austerity measures cut down on some of this overstaffing.

Officials at lower levels in the bureaucracy are unionized and protected by legislation that gives them job security and a range of benefits. At middle and upper levels, most officials are called "confidence employees"; they serve as long as their bosses have confidence in them. These are the officials who are personally appointed by their superiors at the outset of an administration. Their modest salaries are compensated for by the significant power that they can have over public events. For aspiring young professionals, a career in government is often attractive because of the challenge of dealing with important problems on a daily basis and being part of the process of finding solutions to them. Some employees also benefit from opportunities to take bribes or use other means to promote their personal interests.

The Para-Statal Sector

The **para-statal** sector—composed of semiautonomous or autonomous government agencies, many of which produce goods and services—was extremely large and powerful in Mexico. Because the government provided significant support for the development of the economy as part of its post-1940 development strategy, it engaged in numerous activities that in other countries are carried out by the private sector. Thus, until the Salinas administration, the country's largest steel mill was state owned, as were the largest fertilizer producer, sugar mills, and airlines. In addition, the national electricity board still produces energy and supplies it at subsidized prices to industries. The petroleum company, PEMEX, grew to enormous proportions in the 1970s and 1980s under the impact of the oil boom. NAFIN, a state investment corporation, provides a considerable amount of investment capital for the country. At one point, a state marketing board called CONASUPO was responsible for the importation and purchase of the country's basic food supplies, and in the

1970s, it played a major role in distributing food, credit, and farm implements in rural areas.

This large para-statal sector was significantly trimmed by the economic policy reforms of the 1980s and 1990s. In 1970, there were 391 para-statal organizations in Mexico. By 1982, their number had grown to 1,155, in part because of the expansion of government activities under presidents Echeverría and López Portillo and in part because of the nationalization of private banks in 1982. In the 1980s and 1990s, concerted efforts were made to privatize many of these industries, including the telephone company, the national airline, and the nationalized banks. By 1994, only 215 state-owned industries remained, and efforts continued to sell or liquidate many of them. The Fox government, a partisan of the private sector, raised the possibility of privatizing PEMEX and the electricity board, but quickly retreated to very partial measures in the face of extensive opposition to private ownership of the "national patrimony."

Other State Institutions

The Military

Mexico is one of only a few countries in the developing world to have successfully marginalized the military from centers of political power. Much of the credit for this process belongs to Plutarco Calles, Lázaro Cárdenas, and subsequent presidents who introduced the rotation of regional commands so that generals could not build up regional bases of power. In addition, postrevolutionary leaders made an implicit bargain with the military leaders by providing them with opportunities to engage in business so that they did not look to political power as a way of gaining economic power. After 1946, the military no longer had institutional representation within the PRI and became clearly subordinate to civilian control.

This does not mean that the military has existed outside politics. It has been called in from time to time to deal with domestic unrest: in rural areas in the 1960s, in Mexico City and other cities to repress student protest movements in 1968, in 1988 in the arrest of a powerful labor leader, in 1989 to break a labor strike, in 1990 to deal with protest over electoral fraud, in Chiapas beginning in late 1994, and to manage the

Mexico City police in 1997. The military was also called in to deal with the aftermath of the earthquake in Mexico City in 1985, but its inadequate response to the emergency did little to enhance its reputation in the eyes of the public. In recent years, the military has been heavily involved in efforts to combat drug trafficking, and rumors abound about deals struck between military officials and drug barons. Such fears were confirmed when General Jesús Gutierrez Rebollo, the head of the antidrug task force, was arrested in February 1997 on accusations of protecting a drug lord. When the PAN government made it possible for citizens to gain greater access to government information, it was discovered that the military had been involved in political repression, torture, and killing in the 1970s and 1980s. The scandal created by such revelations further lowered its reputation.

Whenever the military is called in to resolve domestic conflicts, some Mexicans become concerned that the institution is becoming politicized and may come to play a larger role in political decision making. From time to time, rumors of preparations for a coup are heard, as during financial panics in the 1980s and in the aftermath of Colosio's assassination. Thus far, such fears have not been realized, and many believe that as long as civilian administrations are able to maintain the country's tradition of stability, the military will not intervene directly in politics. The fact that the country successfully observed the transfer of power from the PRI to the PAN also has increased a sense that the military will remain subordinate to civilian control.

The Judiciary

Unlike Anglo-American legal systems, Mexico's law derives from the Roman and Napoleonic tradition and is highly formalized and explicit. The Constitution of 1917 is a lengthy document that has been amended many times and contains references to a wide range of civil rights, including items as broad as the right to a healthy environment. As in other countries, regulatory agencies can also create rules and regulations, known as administrative law, regarding material under their jurisdiction. Because Mexican law tends to be very explicit and because there are no punitive damages, there are fewer lawsuits than in the United States. One important exception to this is the *amparo*, whereby citizens may ask for a writ of protection claiming that their constitutional rights have been violated by specific government actions or laws. Each citizen who wants an *amparo* must present a separate case.

There are federal and state courts in Mexico. The federal system is composed of the Supreme Court, which decides the most important cases in the country; circuit courts, which take cases on appeal; and district courts, where all cases enter the system. As in the United States, Supreme Court justices are nominated by the president and approved by the Senate. Since most of the important laws in Mexico are federal, state courts have played a subordinate role. However, this is changing. As Mexican states become more independent from the federal government, state law has been experiencing tremendous growth. In addition, there are many important specialized federal courts, such as labor courts, military courts, and electoral courts.

Like other political institutions in Mexico, the judiciary was for many decades politically, though not constitutionally, subordinate to the executive. The courts occasionally slowed the actions of government by issuing *amparos*; however, in almost every case in which the power of government or the president was at stake, the courts ruled on the side of the government. The administration of Ernesto Zedillo tried to change this by emphasizing the rule of law over that of powerful individuals. Increasing interest in human rights issues by citizens' groups and the media has added pressure to the courts to play a stronger role in protecting basic freedoms. Citizens and the government are increasingly resorting to the courts as a primary weapon against sticky problems like corruption and police abuse. President Zedillo's refusal to interfere with the courts' judgments also strengthened the judiciary. This trajectory continued under President Fox. Nevertheless, the judicial system remains the weakest branch of government.

Subnational Government

As with many other aspects of the Mexican political system, regional and local government in Mexico is quite different from what is described in the constitution. Mexico has a federal system, and each state has its own constitution, executive, unicameral legislature, and judiciary. Municipalities (equivalent to U.S. coun-

ties) are governed by popularly elected mayors and councils. But most state and municipal governments are poor. Most of the funds they command are transferred to them from the central government, and they have little legal or administrative capacity to raise their own revenue. States and localities also suffer greatly from the lack of well-trained and well-paid public officials. As at the national level, many jobs are distributed as political patronage, but even officials who are motivated to be responsive to local needs are generally ill equipped to do so. Since the early 1990s, the government has made several serious efforts to decentralize and devolve more power on state and local governments. At times, governors and mayors have resisted such initiatives because they meant that regional and local governments would have to manage much more complex activities and be the focus of demands from public sector workers and their unions. They were also worried that they would be unable to acquire the budgetary resources necessary to carry out their new responsibilities.

There are exceptions to this picture of regional and local government impoverishment and lack of capacity. State governments in the north of the country, such as Nuevo León, have been more responsive to local needs and better able to administer public services. In such states, local municipalities have become famous for the extent to which they differ from the norm in most of Mexico. Monterrey, in Nuevo León, for example, has a reputation for efficient and forward-looking city government. Much of this local capacity can be credited to a regional political tradition that has stressed independence from—and even hostility to—Mexico City and the PRI. In addition, states and localities that have stronger governments and a tradition of better service tend to be areas of greater wealth, largely in the north of the country. In these cases, entrepreneurial groups and private citizens have often invested time and resources in state and local government.

Until 1988, all governors were from the PRI, although many believe that only electoral fraud kept two governorships out of the hands of an opposition party in 1986. Finally, in 1989, a non-PRI governor assumed power in Baja California Norte, an important first. After the 2000 election, twelve states and the Federal District of Mexico City were governed by parties other than the PRI. By 2002, the number had grown to fourteen states and the Federal District. Also, municipalities have increasingly been the focus of authentic party competition. As opposition parties came to control these levels of government, they were challenged to improve services such as police protection, garbage collection, sanitation, and education. PRI-dominated governments have also tried to improve their performance because they are now more threatened by the possibility of losing elections.

The Policy-Making Process

The Mexican system is very dependent on the quality of its leadership and presidential understanding of how economic and social policies can affect the development of the country. As indicated throughout this chapter, the six-year term of office, the *sexenio*, is an extremely important fact of political life in Mexico. New presidents can introduce extensive change in positions within the government. They are able to bring in "their" people, who build teams of "their" people within ministries, agencies, and party networks. This generally provides the president with a group of high- and middle-level officials who share a general orientation toward public policy and are motivated to carry out his goals. When the PRI was the dominant party, these officials believed that in following presidential leadership, they enhanced their chances for upward political mobility. In such a context, even under a single party, it was likely that changes in public policies could be introduced every six years, creating innovation or discontinuity, or both. As indicated, the limited experience of the PAN in executive office and the increasing role of congress in policy-making meant that the influence of the president on government was less strong. Nevertheless, Mexicans continue to look to the president and the executive for policy leadership.

Together with the bureaucracy, the president is the focal point of policy formulation and political management. Until 1997, the legislature always had a PRI majority and acted as a rubber stamp for presidentially sponsored legislation. Since then, the congress has proven to be a more active policy-maker, blocking and forcing the negotiation of legislation, and even introducing its own bills. The president's skills in negotiating, managing the opposition, using the media to acquire public support, and maneuvering within the bureaucracy can be important for ensuring that his program is fully endorsed.

Significant limits on presidential power occur when policy is being implemented. In fact, in areas as diverse as the regulation of working conditions, antipollution laws, tax collection, election monitoring, and health care in remote rural areas, Mexico has extremely advanced legislation on the books. Yet the persistence of unsafe factory conditions, pollution in Mexico City, tax evasion, election fraud, and poor health care suggests that legislation is not always translated into practice. At times, policies are not implemented because public officials at the lower levels disagree with them or make deals with affected interests in order to benefit personally. This is the case, for example, with taxes that remain uncollected because individuals or corporations bribe officials to overlook them. In other cases, lower-level officials may lack the capacity or skills to implement some policies, such as those directed toward improving education or rural development services. For whatever reasons, Mexican presidents cannot always deliver on their intentions. Traditionally, they have been above criticism when this has occurred because of the willingness of Mexican citizens to blame lower-level officials for such slippage. However, exempting the president from responsibility for what does or does not occur during his watch became much less common after the 1970s.

Section ❹ Representation and Participation

How do citizen interests get represented in Mexican politics, given the high degree of centralization, presidentialism, and, until recently, PRI domination? Is it possible for ordinary citizens to make demands on government and influence public policy? In fact, Mexico

has had a relatively peaceful history since the revolution in part because the political system offers some channels for representation and participation. Through this long history, the political system emphasized compromise among contending elites, behind-the-scenes conflict resolution, and distribution of political rewards to those willing to play by the formal and informal rules of the game. It also responded, if reluctantly and defensively, to demands for change.

Often, citizens are best able to interact with the government through a variety of informal means rather than through the formal processes of elections, campaigns, and interest group lobbying. Interacting with government through the personal and informal mechanisms of clientelism usually means that the government retains the upper hand in deciding which interests to respond to and which to ignore. For many interests, this has meant "incorporation without power."[16] Increasingly, however, Mexican citizens are organizing to alter this situation, and the advent of truly competitive elections has increased the possibility that citizens who organize can gain some response from government.

The Legislature

Students in the United States are frequently asked to study complex charts explaining how a bill becomes a law, because the formal process of lawmaking affects the content of legislation. Under the old reign of the PRI in Mexico, while there were formal rules that prescribed such a process, studying them would not have been useful for understanding how the legislature worked. Because of the overwhelming presence of this political party, opposition to presidential initiatives by Mexico's two-chamber legislature, the Senate and the Chamber of Deputies, was rarely heard. To the extent that representatives did not agree with policies they were asked to approve, they counted on the fact that policy implementation was flexible and allowed for after-the-fact bending of the rules or disregard of measures that were harmful to important interests.

Members of congress are elected through a dual system of "first past the post" and proportional representation. Each state elects three senators. Two of them are determined by majority vote, and the third is determined by whichever party receives the second highest number of votes. In addition, thirty-two senators are determined nationally through a system of proportional representation that awards seats based on the number of votes cast for each party. The same system works in the Chamber of Deputies, with 300 selected on the basis of majority vote and 200 additional representatives

chosen by proportional representation. Representation in congress has become somewhat more diverse since the end of the 1980s. In 2001, women held 15.6 percent of seats in the Senate and 16 percent in the Chamber of Deputies. Some representatives also emerged from the ranks of community activists who had participated in activities such as urban popular movements.

The PRI's grip on the legislature was broken in 1988. The growing strength of opposition parties, combined with legislation that provided for greater representation of minority parties in the congress, led to the election of 240 opposition deputies (out of 500) that year, giving the PRI less than the two-thirds majority it needed for major pieces of legislation or constitutional amendments. After that, when presidential legislation was sent to the chamber, the opposition challenged the tradition of legislative passivity and insisted on real debate about issues. The two-thirds PRI majority was returned in 1991—amid allegations of voter fraud— and presidentialism was reasserted. Nevertheless, the strong presence of opposition parties continued to encourage debate as PRI delegates were challenged to defend proposed legislation. The 1994 elections returned a clear PRI majority of 300 deputies and 64 senators, but in 1997, the PRI lost this majority when 261 deputies and 51 senators (of 128) were elected from opposition parties. For the first time in its history, the PRI did not have an absolute majority in the Chamber of Deputies. The party composition of the Chamber of Deputies and the Senate after the elections of 2000 is shown in Figure 1.

Since that time, the role of congress in the policy process has been strengthened considerably.[17] The cost of greater sharing of powers between the executive and the legislature, however, has been to stall the policy process. Several important pieces of legislation, including efforts to manage private debts and approve the budget, were stalled under President Zedillo. Even PRI legislators became more willing to slow or alter presidential initiatives. Under the Fox administration, relations with congress have been even more confrontational. The president lacks a party majority and had a difficult time promoting his investment plan, labor code reform, and the liberalization of the energy sector. In a first-ever use of congressional power, the senate denied President Fox permission to go to the United States and Canada, greatly embarrassing him. As a

Figure 1

Congressional Representation by Party, 2000

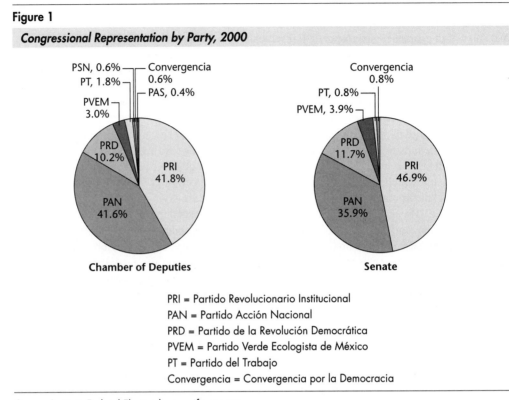

PRI = Partido Revolucionario Institucional
PAN = Partido Acción Nacional
PRD = Partido de la Revolución Democrática
PVEM = Partido Verde Ecologista de México
PT = Partido del Trabajo
Convergencia = Convergencia por la Democracia

Source: Instituto Federal Electoral, www.ife.org.mx.

consequence of this kind of muscle flexing, congressional committees that once were important only for their control over patronage have acquired new relevance, and committee members and chairs are becoming somewhat more like their U.S. counterparts in terms of the power they can wield. Party caucuses have also emerged as centers of power in the legislature. In addition, interest groups, which before 1997 had scant interest in lobbying for legislative action because this body did not make important decisions, have increased their lobbying activities in congress. Thus, as a genuine multiparty system emerged, the Mexican congress became a more important forum for a variety of political voices and points of view. PRI candidates now have to participate in competitive elections in many locales, and the number of safe seats for party stalwarts is declining.

Political Parties and the Party System

Mexico has a multiparty system. Even under the long reign of the PRI, a number of political parties existed. By the mid-1980s, some of them were attracting more political support, a trend that continued into the 1990s and 2000s. Electoral reforms introduced by the López Portillo, de la Madrid, Salinas, and Zedillo administrations made it easier for opposition parties to contest elections and win seats in the legislature. In 1990, an electoral commission was created to regulate campaigns and elections, and in 1996 it became fully independent of the government. Now all parties receive funding from the government and have access to the media. In addition to the PRI, two other political parties have demonstrated the capacity to acquire substantial support in elections.

The PRI

Mexico's Institutional Revolutionary Party—Partido Revolucionario Institucional—(PRI) was founded by a coalition of political elites who agreed that it was preferable to work out their conflicts within an overarching structure of compromise than to continue to resort to violence. In the 1930s, the PRI incorporated a wide array of interests, becoming a mass-based party that drew support from all classes in the population. Over seven decades, its principal activities were to generate support for the government, organize the electorate to vote for its candidates, and distribute jobs and development resources in return for loyalty to the system.

Until the 1990s, party organization was based largely on the corporate representation of class interests. Labor was represented within party councils by the National Confederation of Labor (CTM), which includes industry-based unions at local, regional, and national levels. Peasants were represented by the National Confederation of Peasants (CNC), an organization of *ejido* and peasant unions and regional syndicates. The so-called popular sector, comprising small businesses, community-based groups, and public employees, had less internal cohesion but was represented by the National Confederation of Popular Organizations (CNOP). Of the three, the CTM was consistently the best organized and most powerful. Traditionally, the PRI's strongest support came from the countryside, where *ejidatarios* and independent small farmers were grateful for and dependent on rewards of land or jobs. As the country became more urbanized, the support base provided by rural communities remained important to the PRI, but produced many fewer votes than were necessary to keep the party in power.

Within its corporate structures, the PRI functioned through extended networks that distributed public resources—particularly jobs, land, development projects, and access to public services—to lower-level activists who controlled votes at the local level. This informal clientelist organization formed multiple chains of patron-client interaction that culminated at the highest level of political decision making within the PRI and the office of the president. In this system, those with ambitions to public office or to positions within the PRI put together networks of supporters from above (patrons), to whom they delivered votes, and supporters from below (clients), who traded allegiance for access to public resources. For well over half a century, this system worked extremely well. PRI candidates won by overwhelming majorities until the 1980s (see Figure 2). Of course, electoral fraud and the ability to distribute government largesse are central explanations for these numbers, but they also attest to an extremely well-organized party. Although the PRI became much weaker in the 1980s and 1990s, it was still the only political party that could boast a network of constituency organizations in virtually every village and urban community in the country. Its vast political machinery also allowed it to monitor events, even in remote areas.

Within the PRI, power was centralized, and the sector organizations (the CTM, the CNC, and the CNOP) responded primarily to elites at the top of the political pyramid rather than to member interests. Over time, the corporate interest group organizations, particularly the CTM and the CNC, became widely identified with corruption, bossism, centralized control, and lack of effective participation. By the 1980s, new generations of voters were less beholden to patronage-style politics and much more willing to question the party's dominance. When the administrations of de la Madrid, Salinas, and Zedillo imposed harsh austerity measures, the PRI was held responsible for the resulting losses in incomes and benefits. Simultaneously, as the government cut back sharply on public sector jobs and services, the PRI had far fewer resources to distribute to maintain its traditional bases of support. Moreover, it began to suffer from increasing internal dissension between the old guard—the so-called dinosaurs—and the "modernizers" who wanted to reform the party.

Until the elections of 1988, there was no question that the PRI candidate would be elected president. Victories recording 85 to 95 percent of the total vote for the PRI were the norm (see Table 2). After 1988, however, PRI candidates were challenged by parties to the right and left, and outcomes were hotly contested by the opposition, which claimed fraudulent electoral practices. In 1994, Zedillo won primarily because the opposition was not well organized and failed to present a program other than its opposition to the PRI. Presidents Salinas and Zedillo also distanced themselves from the party during their administrations, giving the first clear signals in PRI history that there was a distinction between the party and the government.

Figure 2

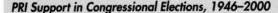

PRI Support in Congressional Elections, 1946–2000

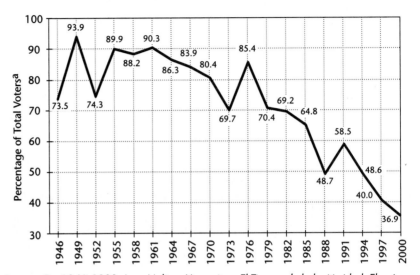

Sources: For 1946–1988: Juan Molinar Horcasitas, *El Tiempo de la legitimidad: Elecciones, autoritarismo y democracia en México* (México, D.F.: Cal y Arena, 1991). For 1991: Secretaría Nacional de Estudios, Partido Acción Nacional, *Análisis del Proceso Federal Electoral 1994, 1995.* For 1994: Instituto Federal Electoral, *Estadística de las Elecciones Federales de 1994, Compendio de Resultados* (Mexico, D.F., 1995). For 1997: www.ife.org.mx/ww-worge/tablas/mrent.htm. For 2000: Instituto Federal Electoral, www.ife.org.mx.

As the PRI faced greater competition from other parties and continued to suffer from declining popularity, efforts were made to restructure and reform it. The CNOP was replaced by an organization that sought to incorporate a wide array of non-class-based citizen and neighborhood movements. In 1990, membership rules were altered to allow individuals and groups not identified with its corporate sector organizations to join. In addition, regional party organizations gained representation at the national level. Party conventions were introduced in an effort to democratize the internal workings of the party, and some states and localities began to hold primaries to select PRI candidates, a significant departure from the old system of selection by party bosses.

The PRI continues to face a difficult future. The Mexican electorate is now predominantly urban. Voters are younger, better educated, and more middle class than in the days of the PRI's greatest success—the 1940s, 1950s, and 1960s. The 1988 elections demonstrated the relevance of changing demographic conditions when only 27.3 percent of the population of Mexico City voted for the PRI candidate and only 34.3 percent of the population in other urban areas supported him. In 2000, Mexico City gave only 22.7 percent of its vote to the PRI. Most important, the election of 2000 demonstrated to everyone that the PRI could lose the pinnacle of power in the country, the presidency. Many analysts believe that opposition party campaigns tapped into a deep well of resentment against evidence of corruption and mismanagement in the PRI.

The PAN

The National Action Party—Partido Acción Nacional—(PAN) was founded in 1939 to represent interests opposed to the centralization and anticlericalism of the PRI. It was founded by those who believed that the country needed more than one strong political party and

Table 2

Voting in Presidential Elections, 1934–2000

Year	Votes for PRI Candidate[a]	Votes for PAN Candidate	Votes for All Others[b]	Turnout (% Voters Among Eligible Adults)[c]
1934	98.2%	—	1.8%	53.6%
1940	93.9	—	6.1	57.5
1946	77.9	—	22.1	42.6
1952	74.3	7.8%	17.9	57.9
1958	90.4	9.4	0.2	49.4
1964	88.8	11.1	0.1	54.1
1970	83.3	13.9	1.4	63.9
1976[d]	93.6	—	1.2	29.6
1982	71.0	15.7	9.4	66.1
1988	50.7	16.8	32.5[e]	49.4[f]
1994	50.1	26.7	23.2	77.16
2000	36.1	42.5[g]	19.2[h]	64.0

[a]From 1958 through 1982, includes votes cast for the Partido Popular Socialista (PPS) and the Partido Auténtico de la Revolución Mexicana (PARM), both of which regularly endorsed the PRI's presidential candidate. In 1988, they supported opposition candidate Cuauhtémoc Cárdenas.

[b]Excludes annulled votes; includes votes for candidates of nonregistered parties.

[c]Eligible population base for 1934 through 1952 includes all males ages 20 and over (legal voting age: 21 years). Both men and women ages 20 and over are included in the base for 1958 and 1964 (women received the franchise in 1958). The base for 1970–1988 includes all males and females ages 18 and over (the legal voting age was lowered to 18, effective 1970).

[d]The PRI candidate, José Lopez Portillo, ran virtually unopposed because the PAN failed to nominate a candidate. The only other significant candidate was Valentín Campa, representing the Communist Party, which was not legally registered to participate in the 1976 election. More than 5 percent of the votes were annulled.

[e]Includes 31.1 percent officially tabulated for Cuauhtémoc Cárdenas.

[f]Estimated using data from the Federal Electoral Commission. However, the commission itself has released two different figures for the number of eligible voters in 1988. Using the commission's larger estimate of eligible population, the turnout would be 44.9 percent.

[g]Votes cast for Alianza por el Cambio, formed by the Partido Acción Nacional (PAN) and the Partido Verde Ecologista de Mexico (PVEM).

[h]Includes votes cast for Alianza por México, formed by the Partido de la Revolución Democrática (PRD), the Partido del Trabajo (PT), Convergencia por la Democracia, the Partido Alianza Social (PAS), and the Partido de la Sociedad Nacionalista (PSN).

Sources: From *Comparative Politics Today: A World View,* 4th ed. by Gabriel Almond and G. Bingham Powell, Jr. Copyright ©1988. Reprinted by permission of Addison-Wesley Educational Publishers, Inc. For 1994: Instituto Federal Electoral, *Estadística de las Elecciones Federales de 1994, Compendio de Resultados* (Mexico, D.F., 1995). For 2000: Instituto Federal Electoral, www.ife.org.mx.

that opposition parties should oppose the PRI through legal and constitutional actions. Historically, this party has been strongest in northern states, where the tradition of resistance to Mexico City is also strongest. It has also been primarily an urban party of the middle class and is closely identified with the private sector. The PAN has traditionally campaigned on a platform endorsing greater regional autonomy, less government intervention in the economy, reduced regulation of business, clean and fair elections, rapprochement with the Catholic Church, and support for private and religious education. When PRI governments of the 1980s and 1990s moved toward market-friendly and export-oriented policies, the policy differences between the two parties were significantly reduced. Nevertheless, a major difference of perspectives about religion continued to characterize the two parties. The PAN has always favored a closer relationship with the Catholic Church, and President Fox's public protestations of faith, including kissing the pope's ring when the pontiff visited Mexico in 2002, raised many an eyebrow in a system long noted for its commitment to secularism.

For many years, the PAN was able to elect 9 to 10 percent of all deputies to the national congress and capture control of a few municipal governments. Then, in the early 1980s, and especially after President López Portillo nationalized the banks, opposition to centralism and statism grew more popular. The PAN began to develop greater capacity to contest elections at higher levels of government. In particular, the party gained popularity among urban middle-class voters, won elections in several provincial cities, and came close to winning governorships in two states. In 1988, it captured 16.8 percent of the vote for president, 101 Chamber of Deputies seats, and one Senate seat. The following year, it won the governorship of the state of Baja California Norte. In the 1994 elections, PAN's candidate, Diego Fernández de Cevallos, garnered 26 percent of the presidential vote, and the party won 25 seats in the senate and 119 in the Chamber of Deputies. This number increased to 33 senate seats and 121 chamber seats in 1997. In 2000, the party elected 53 senators and 224 deputies and by 2002 controlled the governorships in ten states. And, of course, it won the presidency with 42.7 percent of the total vote. In these elections, the party ran in an electoral alliance, called the Alliance for Change, with the small Green Ecologist Party of Mexico (PVEM). The Fox campaign attracted many younger and well-educated voters.

The PAN has traditionally set relatively high standards for activism among its party members; as a consequence, the membership of the party has remained small, even as its capacity to attract votes has grown. In their efforts to control the development of the party, its leaders have had a difficult relationship with the PAN standard bearer, Vicente Fox. As Fox's political profile expanded while serving as the governor of the

state of Guanajuato, leaders of the party became concerned that he would emerge as a favorite for the presidency. They worked to limit his opportunities to run for office, forcing him to look for other sources of financing his campaign. In 1997, the Friends of Fox organization began to raise funds and promote his candidacy for president, and at the same time, the traditional leaders of the party were weakened significantly in electoral contests when the PAN made a poor showing. Fox gained in popularity throughout the country, and in 1999, the party had little option but to nominate him as its candidate. The Friends of Fox continued to provide the most important source of campaign support, however, and when Fox won the presidential election, the PAN organization was weak and not at all united in backing him. Further, although it made a very good showing in elections for the Chamber of Deputies and the Senate, it did not have a majority in either chamber.

The PRD

Another significant challenge to the PRI has come from the Democratic Revolutionary Party—Partido de la Revolucion Democrática—(PRD), a populist and nationalist alternative to the PRI, whose policies are left of center. Its candidate in the 1988 and 1994 elections was Cuauhtémoc Cárdenas, the son of Mexico's most famous and revered president. He was a PRI insider until party leaders virtually ejected him for demanding internal reform of the party and a platform emphasizing social justice. In the 1988 elections, Cárdenas was officially credited with winning 31.1 percent of the vote, and the party captured 139 seats in the Chamber of Deputies. He benefited from massive political defection from the PRI and garnered support from workers disaffected with the boss-dominated unions as well as peasants who remembered his father's concern for agrarian reform and investment in the poor. Mexico City gave him 50.4 percent of the vote, which also represented some middle-class support.

Even while the votes were being counted, the party began to denounce widespread electoral fraud and claim that Cárdenas would have won if the election had been honest. The PRD challenged a number of vote counts in the courts and walked out of Salinas's inaugural speech. Considerable public opinion supported the party's challenge. In the aftermath of the 1988 elections, then, it seemed that the PRD was a strong contender to become Mexico's second most powerful party. It was expected to have a real chance in future years to challenge the PRI's "right" to the presidency.

However, in the aftermath of these elections, the party was plagued by internal divisions over its platform, leadership, organizational structure, and election strategy. By 1994, it still lagged far behind the PRI and the PAN in establishing and maintaining the local constituency organizations needed to mobilize votes and monitor the election process. In addition, the PRD found it difficult to define an appropriate left-of-center alternative to the market-oriented policies carried out by the government. While the claims that such policies ignored the need for social justice were popular, policies to respond to poverty that did not imply a return to unpopular government intervention were difficult to devise. In the aftermath of the Colosio assassination, citizens also became more alarmed about violence, and some were concerned that the level of political rivalry represented by the PRD threatened the country's long-term political stability. In the 1994 elections, Cárdenas won only 17 percent of the votes, although the PRD elected seventy-one deputies and eight senators.

Thanks to the government's continued unpopular economic policies and the leadership of a successful grassroots mobilizer named Andrés Manuel López Obrador, who was elected to head the party in 1996, the PRD began to stage a remarkable turnaround. Factional bickering was controlled, and organizational discipline increased. In addition, the PRD proved successful in moving beyond its regional stronghold and established itself as a truly national party. In 1997, the party increased its share of seats to 125 in the Chamber of Deputies and 16 in the Senate. Most important, Cárdenas became the first popularly elected mayor of Mexico City. This provided him and the party with a critically important opportunity to demonstrate their ability to govern, not to mention a potential platform for the presidential elections of 2000. By this time, the PRD had managed to shed some of its reputation as a "one-horse show" and had won two governorships, with the PRI under question for fraud in a third. In 2000, López Obrador was elected mayor of Mexico City with 39.5 percent of the vote, signaling again the political importance of the capital city. In the presidential race,

Cárdenas ran again, but even in alliance with several small parties, the Alliance for Mexico, he was able to garner only 16.5 percent of the vote. Its performance in the legislative race was equally disappointing. The PRD alliance retained 16 seats in the senate, but lost 58 in the Chamber of Deputies, retaining only 67 seats. In 2000, three state governors represented the party, and by 2002, four were governed by the PRD, in addition to the Federal District of Mexico City.

Other Parties

There are a number of smaller parties that contest elections in Mexico. Some of them have always allied themselves with the PRI, supporting its candidates for president and other positions. Newer parties have also emerged to contest more democratic elections. In 2000, the Social Democracy Party—Partido Democrácia Social—(PDS) won 1.6 percent of the votes for president, and the Democratic Center Party—Partido de Centro Democrático—(PCD) won 0.6 percent. The PDS won 1.8 percent of votes for the Senate and 1.9 percent for the Chamber of Deputies, and the PCD won 1.1 percent each of votes for Senate and the Chamber of Deputies. This very poor performance raises questions about whether either party would survive. National law requires that parties must receive 2.5 percent of the vote in order to remain registered as political parties.

Elections

Each of the three main political parties draws voters from a wide and overlapping spectrum of the electorate. Nevertheless, a typical voter for the PRI is likely to be from a rural area or small town, to have less education, and to be older and poorer than voters for the other parties. A typical voter for the PAN is likely to be from a northern state, to live in an urban area, to be a middle-class professional, to have a comfortable lifestyle, and to have a high school or even a university education. A typical voter for the PRD is likely to be young, to be a political activist, to have an elementary or high school education, to live in one of the central states, and to live in a small town or an urban area. As we have seen, the support base for the PRI is the most vulnerable to economic and demographic changes in the country. Voting for opposition parties is an urban phenomenon, and Mexico continues to urbanize at the rate of 3 percent per year. This means that in order to stay competitive, the PRI will have to garner more support from urban areas. It must also be able to appeal to younger voters, especially the large numbers who are attracted to the PRD and the PAN.

Elections are becoming more competitive and fairer in Mexico. Electoral reforms introduced by the López Portillo, de la Madrid, Salinas, and Zedillo administrations made it easier for opposition parties to contest elections and win seats in the legislature. In 1990, an electoral commission was created to regulate campaigns and elections, and in 1996 it became fully independent from the government. Now all parties receive government funding and have ensured access to the media. These and other laws that limit campaign spending and campaign contributions were a response to demands that the government level the playing field between the PRI and the other parties. Voter registration was reformed to ensure that fraud would be more detectable. Election monitoring was also strengthened, and another reform increased the chances for opposition parties to win representation in the Senate. Beginning in 1994, elections have been much fairer, and subsequent congressional, state, and municipal elections reinforced the impression that electoral fraud is on the wane in many areas. PAN's victory in 2000 substantially increased this impression. Some state and local elections continue to be questioned, especially in rural areas in the south, where local PRI bosses remain powerful. For example, many citizens did not believe that the PRI had fairly swept the 1997 congressional elections in the state of Chiapas, where opposition to the government was strong.

Political Culture, Citizenship, and Identity

Most citizens in Mexico demonstrate overall commitment to the political system while expressing considerable criticism—and often cynicism—about how it works and how equitable it is. A survey of almost any *ejido*, for example, will uncover lengthy local histories of how *ejidatarios* have been mistreated, given the runaround by bureaucratic organizations, and cheated by local, regional, and national leaders of the CNC, the PRI, and government agencies. The survey will reveal deep commitment to the country's heroes and the institutions of government along with anger, distrust, frustration, and biting jokes told at the expense of the rich and powerful. Currently, many citizens criticize corruption in government and the PRI, but remain proud that their country has become more democratic.

Most Mexicans have a deep familiarity with how the political system works and the ways in which they might be able to extract benefits from it. They understand the informal rules of the game in Mexican politics that have helped maintain political stability despite extensive inequalities in economic and political power. Clientelism has long been a form of participation in the sense that through their connections, many people, even the poorest, are able to interact with public officials and get something out of the political system. This kind of participation emphasizes how limited resources, such as access to health care, can be distributed in a way that provides maximum political payoff. This informal system is a fundamental reason that many Mexicans continued to vote for the PRI for so long.

However, new ways of interacting with government are emerging, and they coexist along with the clientelistic style of the past. An increasing number of citizens are seeking to negotiate with the government on the basis of citizenship rights, not personal relationships. The movements that emerged in the 1980s sought to form broad but loose coalitions with other organizations and attempted to identify and work with reform-oriented public officials. Their suspicion of traditional political organizations such as the PRI or the CNC and the CTM also carried over to suspicion of close alliances with the PAN and the PRD.

As politics and elections became more open and competitive, the roles of public opinion and the mass media have become more important. In the past, public opinion polling was often contaminated by the dominance of the PRI, and some polling organizations were even subsidized by the party or the government. Increasingly, however, even the PRI and the government are interested in objective information and analysis of public opinion. These data have influenced the content and timing of government decisions and the development of strategies in election campaigns. In 1994 and 2000, politicians, citizens, and political activists closely followed the popularity polls of the three major candidates for president, and party officials monitored how the image of their contender could be molded to capture higher voter approval ratings. Because extensive public opinion polling is comparatively new in Mexico, it is difficult to assess how attitudes toward government have changed over time. Surveys taken in the 1980s and 1990s indicate that confidence fell extensively during the 1980s but rebounded somewhat in the 1990s. Fewer Mexicans claim a party preference today than in the past, and the percentage of citizens who identify with the PRI has fallen sharply.

Today, the media play an important role in public opinion formation. In the past, it was not easy for newspapers, magazines, or radio and television stations to be openly opposed to the government. For many years, the government used access to newsprint, which it controlled, to reward sympathetic news coverage and penalize coverage it considered hostile. In addition, the government subsidized the salaries of some reporters, and politically ambitious public and PRI officials paid stipends to those who covered their activities sympathetically. A considerable amount of the revenue of newspapers and other media organizations came from advertising placed by the government. Each of these mechanisms was used to encourage positive reporting of government activities, strong endorsement of presidential initiatives, and quashing of stories that reflected ill on the party or the government, all without resorting to outright government control of the media.

As with other aspects of Mexican politics, the media began to become more independent in the 1980s, enjoying a "spring" of greater independence and diversity of opinion.[18] There are currently several major television networks in the country, and many citizens have access to CNN and other global networks. The number of newspapers is expanding, as is their circulation, and several news magazines play the same role in Mexico that *Time* and *Newsweek* do in the United States. Citizens in Mexico today clearly hear a much wider range of opinion and much greater reporting of debates about public policy and criticism of government than at any time previously.

Interests, Social Movements, and Protests

The Mexican system has long responded to groups of citizens through pragmatic **accommodation** to their interests. This is one important reason that political tensions among major interests have rarely escalated into the kind of serious conflict that can threaten stability. Where open conflict has occurred, it has generally been met with efforts to find some kind of compromise solution. Accommodation has been particularly apparent in response to the interests of business. Mexico's development strategy encouraged the growth of wealthy elites in commerce, finance, industry, and agriculture (see Section 2). Although these elites were the primary beneficiaries of the country's development, they were never incorporated into the PRI. Instead, they represent themselves through a set of business-focused interest groups and personal relationships with influential officials. Through these networks, business organizations and individuals seek policies favorable to their interests.

Labor has been similarly accommodated within the system. Wage levels for unionized workers grew fairly consistently between 1940 and 1982, when the economic crisis caused a significant drop in wages. At the same time, labor interests were attended to in terms of concrete benefits and limitations on the rights of employers to discipline or dismiss workers. Labor union leaders controlled their rank and file in the interest of their own power to negotiate with government, but at the same time, they sought benefits for workers who continued to provide support for the PRI. The power of the union bosses has declined, in part because the unions are weaker than in the past, in part because union members are demanding greater democratization, and in part because the PRI no longer monopolizes political power.

Under the PRI, accommodation was often coupled with **co-optation** as a means of incorporating dissidents into the system so that they did not threaten its continuity. In 1968, for example, students protesting against authoritarianism, poverty, and inequity challenged the government just prior to the opening of the Olympic Games. The government responded with force—in one instance killing several hundred students in Mexico City—sparking even greater animosity. When Luis Echeverría became president in 1970, he recruited large numbers of the student activists into his administration. He also dramatically increased spending on social services, putting many of the young people to work in expanding antipoverty programs in the countryside and in urban slums. Through these actions, a generation of political and social activists was incorporated into the system, and there was some accommodation to their concerns. We also know now that his government allowed the military to kidnap, arrest, torture, and kill some political dissidents.

Despite the strong and controlling role of the PRI in Mexico's political history, the country also has a tradition of civic organizations that operate at community and local levels with considerable independence from politics. Local village improvement societies, religious organizations, and sports clubs are widespread. Many of their activities are not explicitly political, although they may have political implications in that they encourage individuals to work together to find solutions to problems or organize around common interests. Other organizational experiences are more explicitly political. The student movement of 1968 provided evidence that civil society in Mexico had the potential to contest the power of the state. The emergence of independent unionism in the 1970s was another indication of renewed willingness to question the right of the state to stifle the voices of dissent and the emergence of demands for greater equity and participation. The elections of 2000 were an announcement that the old system of accommodation, co-optation, and repression was no longer working.

The economic crisis of 1982 combined with this civic tradition to heighten demands for assistance from the government. In October 1983, as many as 2 million people participated in a civic strike to call attention to the crisis and demand a forceful government response. A less successful strike in June 1984 made the same point to the government. In urban areas, citizen groups demanded land rights in squatter settlements, as well as housing, infrastructure, and urban services, as rights of citizenship rather than as a reward for loyalty to the PRI.[19] In the aftermath of the 1985 earthquake, citizen groups became especially dynamic in demanding that government respond to the needs of citizens without reference to their history of party loyalty. Residents of Mexico City demanded that the government let them decide how to rebuild and relocate their neighborhoods and choose who would serve as mayor and represent them.[20] Many also became active in groups that share concerns about quality-of-life issues such as clean air

and safe neighborhoods. See "Citizen Action: Urban Popular Movements."

In rural areas, peasant organizations also demanded greater independence from government and the leaders of the PRI and the CNC in the 1980s.[21] In addition to greater access to land, they demanded better prices for the crops they produced, access to markets and credit, development of better infrastructure, and the provision of better education and health services. They began to form alliances with other groups. For example, in the Yucatán peninsula, PEMEX's exploration and production of oil caused massive ecological damage and was carried out with complete disregard for the rights of local *ejidatarios*. By the late 1970s, environmental groups had joined peasant organizations and student activists in protesting against PEMEX. Since 1994, the rebels in Chiapas have become a focal point for broad alliances of those concerned about the rights of indigenous groups (ethnic minorities) and rural poverty. Indigenous groups have also emerged to demand that government be responsive to their needs and respectful of their traditions.

A variety of groups have also organized around middle-class and urban issues. In Mexico City, community groups and broader citizen alliances have been active in calling attention to the disastrous levels of air,

Mexicans demonstrate for better housing in Mexico City's central plaza. *Source:* Robert Freck/Odyssey/Chicago.

Citizen Action: *Urban Popular Movements*

In October 1968, hundreds of students and working-class people took to the streets of Mexico City to protest high unemployment and the authoritarianism of the government. What began as a peaceful rally in Tlaltelolco Plaza ended in a tragedy when government troops opened fire on the crowd and killed more than two hundred people. The political activism of the students heralded the birth of urban popular movements in Mexico. The massacre in Tlaltelolco became a symbol of a government that was unwilling or unable to respond to citizen demands for economic and political equity. The protest movements sparked by the events of 1968 sought to transcend class boundaries and unite voices around a range of urban issues, from housing shortages to inadequate urban services to lack of land to centralized decision making. Such social movements forged new channels for poor and middle-class urban residents to express their needs. They also generated forums for demanding democratic government that the traditional political system was not providing. In May 1980, the first national congress of urban movements was held in Monterrey in northern Mexico.

Urban popular movements, referring to activities of low- and modest-income (popular) groups, gained renewed vitality in the 1980s. When the economic crisis resulted in drastic reductions of social welfare spending and city services, working- and middle-class neighborhoods forged new coalitions and greatly expanded the national discussion of urban problems. The Mexico City earthquake of 1985 encouraged the formation of unprecedented numbers of grass-roots movements in response to the slow and poorly managed relief efforts of the government. Turning to each other, earthquake victims organized to provide shelter, food, and relocation. The elections of 1988 and 1994 provided these groups with significant opportunities to press parties and candidates to respond to their needs. They insisted on their rights to organize and protest without fear of repression or co-optation by the government or the PRI. As the opposition parties expanded rapidly, some leaders of urban movements enrolled as candidates for public office.

Urban popular movements bring citizens together around needs and ideals that cut across class boundaries. Neighborhood improvement, the environment, local self-government, economic development, feminism, and professional identity have been among the factors that have forged links among these groups. As such identities have been strengthened, the need of the political system to negotiate and bargain with a more independent citizenry has increased. Urban popular movements have helped to transform political culture on the most local level, one reason the PAN was able to garner so many votes in the 2000 election.

water, and noise pollution in the capital. Women, with a strong cultural role as caretakers of the home, have begun to mobilize in urban areas around demands for community services, equal pay, legal equality, and opportunities in business traditionally denied them.[22] Religious groups, both Catholic and Protestant, have begun to demand greater government attention to problems of poverty and inequity, as well as more government tolerance of religious education and religious practices. In the early 1990s, the government's social development program, which many critics claim was a ploy by President Salinas to win back respect for his

government after the flawed elections of 1988, helped organize thousands of grassroots organizations and possibly contributed to a trend in broader mobilization independent of PRI clientelist networks.[23] In 1997 and 2000, unprecedented numbers of citizens volunteered their time to civic associations that observed the vote to ensure, ballot box by ballot box, that the votes were counted accurately. Where this occurred, mostly in urban areas, there were few accusations of fraud. Overall, then, civil society in Mexico is becoming more pluralist and less easily controlled and there is broader scope for legitimate protest, opposition, and dissent.

Section ⑤ Mexican Politics in Transition

Political Challenges and Changing Agendas

Mexico confronts a world of increasing interdependence among countries. For all countries, economic integration raises issues of national sovereignty and identity. Mexicans define themselves in part through a set of historical events, symbols, and myths that focus on the country's troubled relationship with the United States. Among numerous national heroes and martyrs are those who distinguished themselves in confrontations with the United States. The myths of the Revolution of 1910 emphasize the uniqueness of the country in terms of its opposition to the capitalists and militarists of the northern country. In the 1970s, Mexicans were encouraged to see themselves as leading Third World countries arguing for increased bargaining positions in relation to the industrialized countries of the north. This view stands in strong contrast to more recent perspectives touting the benefits of an internationally oriented economy and the undeniable reality of information, culture, money, and people flowing back and forth across borders. Mexicans see NAFTA as the beginning of closer integration with trading partners in Latin America, Asia, and Europe.

The country's sense of national identity is affected by international migration. Of particular importance in the Mexican case is labor migration. Every year, large numbers of Mexicans enter the United States as workers. Many return to their towns and villages with new values and new views of the world. Many stay in the United States, where Hispanics have become the largest ethnic population in the country. Most continue to believe that Mexican culture is preferable to American culture, which they see as excessively materialistic and violent. Although they believe that Mexico is a better place to nurture strong family life and values, they are nevertheless strongly influenced by U.S. mass culture, including popular music, movies, television programs, fast food, and consumer goods.

The inability of the Mexican economy to create enough jobs pushes additional Mexicans to seek work in the United States. Extensive migration to the United States has been occurring since the 1880s, when Mexican workers were recruited to help build railroads. In the 1920s and between 1942 and 1964, Mexico and the United States concluded a number of bilateral agreements to provide workers to help the United States meet labor shortages. When such programs ended, a greater proportion of the labor migrants crossed the border into the United States illegally. Differences in wage levels and the jobs lost during the Mexican economic crisis added to the number of workers seeking employment in the United States. The U.S. Congress passed stiff legislation to contain illegal immigration in 1986, but it has been largely ineffective. The difference in wages between the two countries will persist for a long time, which implies that migration will also persist. In fact, the militarization of the border and the increasing danger of crossing lead more illegal immigrants to settle permanently in the United States rather than risk continued trips back and forth across the border. Remittances sent back to Mexico from those working abroad contribute over $6 billion to Mexico's economy each year.

There is disagreement about how to respond to the economic challenges the country faces. Much of the debate surrounds the question of what integration into a competitive international economy really means. For some, it represents the final abandonment of Mexico's sovereignty. For others, it is the basis on which future prosperity must be built. Those who are critical of the market-based, outward-oriented development strategy are concerned about its impact on workers, peasants, and national identities. They argue that the state has abandoned its responsibilities to protect the poor from shortcomings of the market and to provide for their basic needs. They believe that U.S. and Canadian investors have come to Mexico only to find low-wage labor for industrial empires located elsewhere. They see little benefit in further industrial development based on importation of foreign-made parts, their assembly in Mexico, and their export to other markets. This kind of development, they argue, has been prevalent in the *maquiladoras*, or assembly industries, many of which are located along the U.S.-Mexico border. Those who favor closer integration with Canada and the United States acknowledge that some foreign investment does not promote technological advances or move the work force into higher-paying and more skilled jobs. They emphasize, however, that most investment will occur because the country has a relatively well-educated population, the capacity to absorb modern technology, and a large internal market for industrial goods.

In addition to the economic challenges it faces, Mexico provides a testing ground for the democratic idea in a state with a long history of authoritarian institutions. The democratic ideas of citizen rights to free speech and assembly, free and fair elections, and responsive government are major reasons that the power of the PRI came under so much attack. Currently, Mexico is struggling with opening up its political institutions to become more democratic. Vicente Fox, for example, promised to make information about government activities much more widely available to the population, and extensive files about violent military and police repression of political dissent in the past have been made available to citizens. The government also created the independent National Human Rights Commission, which has been active in protecting citizens' rights. (See "Current Challenges: Human Rights in Mexico.") Yet many citizens remain ill informed about government procedures and decision making and are trying to find ways to make their voices heard more effectively in politics. Meanwhile, when Fox demonstrated little capacity to set priorities and communicate a vision for his government, many government agencies found it difficult to act, given a long history of dependence on presidential leadership. This has left many citizens with questions about the effectiveness of more democratic institutions.

Centralization of power and decision making is another legacy that Mexico is trying to revise. Countries around the globe increasingly recognize that the solutions to many policy problems lie at regional and local levels. Issues such as how to ensure that children are receiving a high-quality education, how to relieve chronic and massive traffic congestion, how to dispose of garbage in ways that do not threaten public health, and how to reduce air and water pollution require state and municipal governments that have money, authority, and capable public officials—precisely the conditions that only a very few regional and local governments in Mexico have had. While the government has introduced the decentralization of a number of activities and services, state and municipal governments are struggling to meet the demands of citizens who want competence, responsiveness, and accountability from their local and regional public officials.

The complexity of contemporary problems and the inability of national governments to deal with them all at once make the politics of collective identities more important. The pressure for change in Mexico and many other countries is accelerating as modern technology increases the extent to which people in one country are aware of what is occurring in others and the degree to which citizens are able to communicate their concerns and interests among themselves and to government. The formation of a strong civil society capable of articulating its interests and ensuring that government is responsive to its needs is the other side of political reform.

Human and social development in a country make such a functioning civil society more possible. Improving social conditions is an important challenge for Mexico. While elites enjoy the benefits of sumptuous lifestyles, education at the best U.S. universities for their children, and luxury travel throughout the world, large numbers of Mexicans remain ill educated, poorly served with health care, and distant from the security of knowing that their basic needs for food, shelter, and employment can be met. The Chiapas rebellion of 1994 made the social agenda a topic of everyday conversation by reminding Mexicans that some people lived in appalling conditions with little hope for the future.

What to do about these conditions is debated. As in the United States, some argue that economic growth and expanded employment will resolve the major problems of poverty in the country. They believe that prosperity, tied to Mexico's economic future internationally, will benefit everyone in the long run. For this to occur, however, they insist that education will have to be improved and made more appropriate for developing a well-educated work force. They also believe that improved education will come about when local communities have more control over schools and curriculum and when parents have more choice between public and private education for their children. From their perspective, the solution to poverty and injustice is fairly clear: more and better jobs and improved education.

For those critical of the development path on which Mexico embarked in the 1980s and 1990s, the problems of poverty and inequity are more complex. Solutions involve understanding the diverse causes of

Current Challenges: **Human Rights in Mexico**

The government of Vicente Fox (2000–2006) committed itself to opening up government and improving the state of human rights in Mexico. In the past, the government had been able to limit knowledge of its repressive actions, use the court system to maintain the political peace, and intimidate those who objected to its actions. The president appointed human rights activists to his cabinet and ordered that secret police and military files be opened to public scrutiny. He instructed government ministries to supply more information about their activities and the rights that citizens have to various kinds of services. He also invited the United Nations to open a human rights office in Mexico. He encouraged the ratification of the Inter-American Convention on Enforced Disappearance of Persons. The government also sought to protect the rights of Mexicans abroad, and the United States and Mexico have established a working group to improve human rights conditions for migrants.

The results of these actions have been dramatic. For the first time, Mexicans learned of cases of hundreds of people who had "disappeared" as a result of police and military actions. In addition, citizens have come forward to announce other disappearances, ones they were unwilling to report earlier because they feared reprisals. In 2002, former president Luis Echvererría was brought before prosecutors and questioned about government actions against political dissent in 1968 and 1971, a kind of accountability unheard of in the past. The National Human Rights Commission has been active in efforts to hold government officials accountable and to protect citizens nationally and abroad from repetitions of the abuses of the past.

Yet challenges to human rights accountability remain. Opening up files and setting up systems for prosecuting abusers need to be followed by actions to impose penalties on abusers. The judicial system is weak and has little experience in human rights cases. In addition, action on reports of disappearances, torture, and imprisonment has been slowed by contention about civil and military jurisdictions. In an embarrassing revelation to the government, Amnesty International reported several cases of disappearances that occurred after Fox assumed leadership of the country. There were also reports of arbitrary detentions and extrajudicial executions. In October 2001, Digna Ochoa, a prominent human rights lawyer, was shot. In the aftermath of this assassination, the government was accused of not doing enough to protect her, even when it was widely known that she had been targeted by those opposed to her work. Human rights activists claimed that police and military personnel, in particular, still had impunity to the laws. The strength of the Fox administration was tested in these events, and although human rights were much more likely to be protected than in the past, the government continued to have a long way to go in safeguarding the rights of indigenous people, political dissidents, migrants, gays and lesbians, and poor people whose ability to use the judicial system is limited by poverty and lack of information.

---

poverty, including not only lack of jobs and poor education but also exploitation, geographic isolation, discriminatory laws and practices, and families disrupted by migration, urbanization, and the tensions of modern life. In the past, Mexicans looked to government for social welfare benefits, but their provision was deeply flawed by inefficiency and political manipulation. The government consistently used access to social services as a means to increase its political control and limit the capacity of citizens to demand equitable treatment. Thus, although many continue to believe that it is the responsibility of government to ensure that citizens are well educated, healthy, and able to make the most of their potential, the populace is deeply suspicious of the government's capacity to provide such conditions fairly and efficiently.

Finally, Mexico is confronting major challenges of adapting newly democratic institutions to reflect ethnic and religious diversity and provide equity for women in economic and political affairs. The past decade has witnessed the emergence of more organized and politically independent ethnic groups demanding justice and equality from government. These groups claim that they suffered for 300 years under colonial rule, for almost 200 years under an independent government, and for 70 years under the PRI and that they are no longer willing to accept poverty and marginality as their lot. The Roman Catholic Church, still the largest organized religion in the country, is losing members to Protestant sects that appeal particularly to the everyday concerns of poor Mexicans. Women, who make up 27 percent of the formal labor force but 40 percent of professional and technical workers, are becoming more organized, but they still have a long way to go before their wages equal those of men or they have equal voice in political and economic decisions.

Mexican Politics in Comparative Perspective

Mexico faces many of the same challenges that beset other countries: creating equitable and effective democratic government, becoming integrated into a global economy, responding to complex social problems, and supporting increasing diversity without losing national identity. Indeed, these were precisely the challenges that the United States faced at the millennium, as did India, Nigeria, China, Japan, Germany, and others. Mexico confronts these challenges within the context of a unique historical and institutional evolution. The legacies of its past, the tensions of the present, and the innovations of the future will no doubt evolve in ways that continue to be uniquely Mexican.

What will the future bring? How much will the pressures for change and the potential loss of national identity affect the nature of the political system? In 1980, few people could have predicted the extensive economic policy reforms and pressures for democracy that Mexico faced in the next two decades. Few would have predicted the outcome of the elections of 2000. In considering the future of the country, it is important to remember that Mexico has a long tradition of relatively strong institutions. It is not a country that will easily slip into sustained political instability. A tradition of constitutional government, a strong presidency, a political system that has incorporated a wide range of interests, a weak tradition of military involvement in politics, and a strong sense of national identity: these

are among the factors that need to be considered in predicting the political consequences of democratization, economic integration, and greater social equality.

Mexico represents a pivotal case for the Northern Hemisphere. If it can successfully bridge the gap between its past and its future and move from centralization to effective local governance, from regional vulnerability to global interdependence, and from the control of the few to the participation of the many, it will set a model for other developing countries that face the same kind of challenges.

Key Terms

mestizo	corporatist state
Amerindian	state capitalism
indigenous groups	import substituting
maquiladoras	industrialization
anticlericalism	informal sector
ejidos	technocrats
ejidatarios	para-statal
sexenio	accommodation
clientelism	co-optation
North American Free	
Trade Agreement	

Suggested Readings

Babb, Sarah L. *Managing Mexico: Economists from Nationalism to Neoliberalism.* Princeton, N.J.: Princeton University Press, 2001.

Chand, Vickram K. *Mexico's Political Awakening.* Notre Dame, Ind.: University of Notre Dame Press, 2001.

Collier, Ruth Berins. *The Contradictory Alliance: State-Labor Relations and Regime Change in Mexico.* Berkeley: University of California Press, 1992.

Cook, Maria Lorena, Middlebrook, Kevin J., and Molinar, Juan (eds.). *The Politics of Economic Restructuring in Mexico.* San Diego: Center for U.S.-Mexican Studies, University of California, 1994.

Cornelius, Wayne A. "Nation-Building, Participation, and Distribution: The Politics of Social Reform Under Cárdenas." In Gabriel A. Almond, Scott Flanagan, and Robert J. Mundt (eds.), *Crisis, Choice, and Change: Historical Studies of Political Development.* Boston: Little, Brown, 1973.

Cornelius, Wayne A., Craig, Ann L., and Fox, Jonathan (eds.). *Transforming State-Society Relations in Mexico: The National Solidarity Strategy.* San Diego: Center for U.S.-Mexican Studies, University of California, 1994.

Cornelius, Wayne A., Eisenstadt, Todd A., and Hindley, Jane (eds.). *Subnational Politics and Democratization in Mexico.*

San Diego: Center for U.S.-Mexican Studies, University of California, 1999.

Domínguez, Jorge I., and McCann, James A. *Democratizing Mexico: Public Opinion and Electoral Choices.* Baltimore, Md.: Johns Hopkins University Press, 1996.

Eckstein, Susan (ed.). *Power and Popular Protest: Latin American Social Movements.* Berkeley: University of California Press, 1989.

Foweraker, Joe, and Craig, Ann L. (eds.). *Popular Movements and Political Change in Mexico.* Boulder, Colo.: Lynne Rienner, 1990.

Gonzales, Michael J. *The Mexican Revolution, 1910–1940.* Albuquerque: University of New Mexico Press, 2002.

Grindle, Merilee S. *Challenging the State: Crisis and Innovation in Latin America and Africa.* Cambridge: Cambridge University Press, 1995.

Hansen, Roger. *The Politics of Mexican Development.* Baltimore, Md.: Johns Hopkins University Press, 1971.

Harvey, Neil. *The Chiapas Rebellion: The Struggle for Land and Democracy.* Durham, N.C.: Duke University Press, 1998.

Lawson, Chappell H. *Building the Fourth Estate: Democratization and the Rise of a Free Press in Mexico.* Berkeley: University of California, 2002.

Levy, Daniel C., and Bruhn, Kathleen. *Mexico: The Struggle for Democratic Development.* Berkeley: University of California Press, 2001.

Lustig, Nora. *Mexico: The Remaking of an Economy.* 2nd ed. Washington, D.C.: Brookings Institution, 1998.

Meyer, Michael C., and Sherman, William L. *The Course of Mexican History.* 5th ed. New York: Oxford University Press, 1995.

Paz, Octavio. *The Labyrinth of Solitude: Life and Thought in Mexico.* New York: Grove Press, 1961.

Suárez-Orozco, Marcelo (ed.). *Crossings: Mexican Immigration in Interdisciplinary Perspective.* Cambridge, Mass.: Harvard University Press, 1998.

Ugalde, Luis Carlos. *The Mexican Congress: Old Player, New Power.* Washington, D.C.: Center for Strategic and International Studies, 2000.

Ward, Peter. *Mexico City.* New York: Wiley, 1998.

Womack, John, Jr. *Zapata and the Mexican Revolution.* New York: Vintage Books, 1968.

———, (ed.). *Rebellion in Chiapas: An Historical Reader.* New York: New Press, 1999.

Suggested Websites

Bank of Mexico (in English and Spanish)
www.banxico.org.mx
Economist Intelligence Unit (registration required)
www.eiu.com
Mexico (search engine for Mexican web sites)
www.Mexico.com (in English and Spanish)
New York Times
www.nytimes.com/pages/world/americas/index.html

Office of the President (in English and Spanish)
www.presidencia.gob.mx
Treasury ministry (in English and Spanish)
www.shop.gob.mex
Washington Post
www.washingtonpost.com/wp-dyn/world/americas/northamerica/mexico/
Public Broadcasting System
www.pbs.org/newshour/bb/latin_america/mexico_index.html
Government of Mexico
www.precisa.gob.mx (in Spanish only)

Notes

Bertha Angulo Curiel of Harvard University assisted in the preparation of this chapter.

[1]This figure represents an estimate of the metropolitan area of Mexico City, which extends beyond the official boundaries of the city.

[2]An excellent history of this event is presented in Wayne A. Cornelius, "Nation-Building, Participation, and Distribution: The Politics of Social Reform Under Cárdenas," in Gabriel A. Almond, Scott Flanagan, and Robert J. Mundt (eds.), *Crisis, Choice and Change: Historical Studies of Political Development* (Boston: Little, Brown, 1973).

[3]Although the self-confessed "lone gunman" was jailed, the ensuing investigation raised concerns about a possible conspiracy involving party and law enforcement officials as well as drug cartels. Rumors circulated about a cover-up scandal. Eventually, skepticism about the integrity of the inquiry was so great that President Salinas called for a new investigation. At this point, little remains known about what exactly happened in Tijuana and why.

[4]United Nations Development Programme, *Human Development Report* (2001), http//www.undp.org/hdr2001/back.pdf.

[5]World Bank, *World Development Indicators 2002*, CD-ROM.

[6]World Bank, *World Development Report, 2001* (New York: Oxford University Press, 2001).

[7]Merilee S. Grindle, *State and Countryside: Development Policy and Agrarian Politics in Latin America* (Baltimore, Md.: Johns Hopkins University Press, 1986), 63, quoting President Avila Camacho (1940–1946).

[8]Kevin J. Middlebrook (ed.), *Unions, Workers, and the State in Mexico* (San Diego: Center for U.S.-Mexican Studies, University of California, 1991).

[9]Grindle, *State and Countryside*, 79–111.

[10]For a description of this process, see Carlos Bazdresch and Santiago Levy, "Populism and Economic Policy in Mexico," in Rudiger Dornbusch and Sebastian Edwards (eds.), *The Macroeconomics of Populism in Latin America* (Chicago: University of Chicago Press, 1991), 72.

[11]For an assessment of the mounting problems of Mexico City and efforts to deal with them, see Diane E. Davis, *Urban Leviathan: Mexico City in the Twentieth Century* (Philadelphia: Temple University Press, 1994).

[12]Joe Foweraker and Ann L. Craig (eds.), *Popular Movements and Political Change in Mexico* (Boulder, Colo.: Lynne Rienner, 1989).

[13]Roger Hansen, *The Politics of Mexican Development* (Baltimore, Md.: Johns Hopkins University Press, 1971), 75.

[14]World Bank, *World Development Report, 2001*, 283.

[15]Economist Intelligence Unit, *Country Commerce, Mexico* (London: EIU, September 2001), 43.

[16]Daniel Levy and Gabriel Székely, *Mexico: Paradoxes of Stability and Change* (Boulder, Colo.: Westview Press, 1983), 100.

[17]See Luis Carlos Ugalde, *The Mexican Congress: Old Player, New Power* (Washington, D.C.: Center for International and Strategic Studies, 2000).

[18]See Chapell H. Lawson, *Building the Fourth Estate: Democratization and the Rise of a Free Press in Mexico* (Berkeley: University of California Press, 2002).

[19]Susan Eckstein (ed.), *Power and Popular Protest: Latin American Social Movements* (Berkeley: University of California Press, 1989).

[20]Wayne A. Cornelius and Ann L. Craig, "Politics in Mexico," in Gabriel Almond and G. Bingham Powell (eds.), *Comparative Politics Today*, 5th ed. (Boston: Scott Foresman, 1992), 502.

[21]Jonathan Fox and Gustavo Gordillo, "Between State and Market: The Campesinos' Quest for Autonomy," in Wayne A. Cornelius, Judith Gentleman, and Peter H. Smith (eds.), *Mexico's Alternative Political Futures* (San Diego: Center for U.S.-Mexican Studies, University of California, 1989).

[22]Foweraker and Craig, *Popular Movements and Political Change in Mexico.*

[23]Wayne A. Cornelius, Ann L. Craig, and Jonathan Fox (eds.), *Transforming State-Society Relations in Mexico: The National Solidarity Strategy* (San Diego: Center for U.S.-Mexican Studies, University of California, 1994).

CHAPTER 5

Brazil

Alfred P. Montero

Federative Republic of Brazil

Land and People

Capital	Brasilia	
Total area (square miles)	3,286,500 (Slightly smaller than the United States)	
Population	170.4 million	
Annual population growth rate (%)	1975–2000	1.8
	2000–2015 (projected)	1.1
Urban population (% of total)		81.2
Ethnic composition (% of total)	White (includes Portuguese, German, Italian, Spanish, Polish)	55
	Mixed white and black	38
	Black	6
	Other (includes Japanese, Arab, Amerindian)	1
Major language(s)	Portuguese	
Religious affiliation (%)	Roman Catholic (nominal)	80

Economy

Domestic currency	Cruzeiro real	
Total GDP (US$)	595.5 billion	
GDP per capita (US$)	3484	
Total GDP at purchasing power parity (US$)	1299.4 billion	
GDP per capita at purchasing power parity (US$)	7625	
GDP annual growth rate (%)	1997	3.3
	2000	4.5
	2001	1.0
GDP per capita average annual growth rate (%)	1975–2000	0.8
	1990–2000	1.5
Inequality in income or consumption (1998)	Share of poorest 10%	0.7
	Share of poorest 20%	2.2
	Share of richest 20%	64.4
	Share of richest 10%	48.1
	Gini Index	60.7
Structure of production (% of GDP)	Agriculture	9.0
	Industry	32.0
	Services	59
Labor force distribution (% of total)	Agriculture	23
	Industry	24
	Services	53
Exports as % of GDP	12	
Imports as % of GDP	11	

Society

Life expectancy	67.7
Infant mortality per 1000 live births	32
Adult literacy (%)	Female	85.4
	Male	85.1
Access to information and communications (per 1000 population)	Telephone lines	182
	Mobile phones	136
	Radios	433
	Televisions	343
	Personal computers	44.1

Women in Government and the Economy

Women in the National Legislature		
Lower house or single house (%)		6.8
Upper house (%)		6.3
Women at ministerial level		0
Female economic activity rate (age 15 and above)		43.8
Female labor force (% of total)		36
Estimated earned income (PPP US$)	Female	4557
	Male	10,769
2002 Human Development Index Ranking (out of 173)		73

Political Organization

Political System   Federal republic, presidential with separation of powers.

Regime History   Democratic since 1946 with periods of military autoritarianism, especially 1964–1985.

Administrative Structure   Federal, with 26 states plus the Federal District, which also functions as a state. Subnational legislatures are unicameral. State governments have multiple secretariats, the major ones commonly being economy, planning, and infrastructure. The states are divided into municipalities (over 5,500), with mayors and councillors directly elected.

Executive   President, vice president, and cabinet. The president and vice president are directly elected by universal suffrage in a two-round runoff election for four-year terms.

Legislature   Bicameral: The Senate is made up of three senators from each state and from the Federal District, elected by plurality vote for an eight-year term; the Chamber of Deputies consists of representatives from each state and from the Federal District, elected by proprotional vote for a four-year term.

Judiciary   Supreme Court, High Tribunal of Justice, regional courts, labor courts, electoral courts, military courts, and state courts. Judiciary has financial and administrative autonomy. Most judges are elected for life.

Party System   Multiparty system including several parties of the right, center-left, and left. Elections are by open-list proportional representation. There is no restriction on the creation and merging of political parties.

Section ❶ The Making of the Modern Brazilian State

Politics in Action

In May 1997, thousands of Brazilians gathered outside the stock exchange in Rio de Janeiro while hundreds more collected inside the building. All were waiting for the beginning of an auction of *Companhia Vale do Rio Doce* (CVRD), a mining conglomerate that was Brazil's largest public firm. The sale of Vale, as the company is known, was the latest in a series of **privatization** moves that began in the early 1990s with the sale of Brazil's steel mills, fertilizer firms, and utility companies. Fifty-two state enterprises had already been sold, and now it was Vale's turn. For the Brazilians gathered outside the stock exchange, this event meant much more than a sale: a cherished piece of Brazil's past was being lost to the faceless market. Vale represented memories of the Brazilian economy that blossomed in the post–World War II era with ambitious industrialization projects led by large public firms. Now, all of that was under attack by "greedy capitalists" intent on exploiting the patrimony of the Brazilian people for personal gain. For the students, workers, and professionals who joined to protest the sale of the mining giant, it was too much to take. Minutes before the auction gavel fell, tempers flared. The angry crowd pushed against police barricades. Some threw punches; others were hurled to the floor and trampled; many would leave with bloodied faces. Everyone felt the painful defeat. The old Brazil was dead.

For those inside the stock exchange, the sale of Vale meant the birth of a new Brazil. By agreeing to privatize one of the most recognizable symbols of Brazilian industry, the country's leaders were embracing the importance of the market in modernizing Brazil. Despite its past successes, the state could no longer guarantee Vale or any other industrial firm the resources needed to become competitive in global markets. By putting Vale up for sale, Brazil's political leadership was guaranteeing that the firm would have a future. The new owners of Vale were young Brazilian industrialists and bankers as well as international investors, including U.S. firms such as NationsBank and the financier George Soros. Unlike most other Brazilian firms, which are family owned, the new Vale would be owned by share-holders and operated by professional administrators, much as major U.S. and European multinational firms are. Nothing less would befit the world's largest exporter of iron ore. The new Vale was emblematic of the new Brazil: modern, competitive, and linked to global markets.

Although opponents were thwarted in their attempts to stop the sale, the opposition to the auctioning of Vale revealed aspects of the new Brazil. Only a week before the sale, opponents had filed 135 separate lawsuits in state courts to halt the privatization. In response, squads of lawyers for the National Development Bank, the federal agency responsible for organizing the sale of Vale, had traveled to the far corners of Brazil to defeat each and every lawsuit. Yet the absence of a centralized and hierarchical system for adjudicating the dispute highlighted both the weakness of democratic institutions in Brazil and the difficulty of ruling over such a large, decentralized political order. The new Brazil is a relatively young democracy, and like Russia and India, it is big and complicated.

Geographic Setting

Brazil's size is only the most obvious characteristic of this country of 170 million people. In land surface, Brazil is larger than the continental United States and occupies two-thirds of South America. It borders all the other countries of South America except Ecuador and Chile. Because of the expansion of the coffee economy in São Paulo state during the nineteenth century and the growth of an industrial economy during the twentieth century, Brazil's largest cities are concentrated in the southern and southeastern regions. More than 15 million inhabitants live in Greater São Paulo alone. This density contrasts with the northern, sparsely populated rain forest regions of the Amazon. Generally, however, Brazil's 18.2 inhabitants per square kilometer means that the country is more underpopulated than the United States.

The physical geography of Brazil is impressively diverse, including thick rain forest in the Amazon valley, large lowland swamps known as the *pantanal* in the central western states, and vast expanses of badlands

known as the *sertão* in the north and northeast. The country is rich in natural resources and arable land. The Amazon has an abundance of tropical fruit and minerals; the central and southern regions provide most of the country's iron ore and coal; offshore and onshore sources of petroleum in Rio de Janeiro and the northeast coastline are also significant. Brazil's farmlands are particularly fertile, including large soy-producing areas in the central savannas called the *cerrados,* coffee areas of the Paraíba Valley near Rio de Janeiro and in São Paulo, and sugar and other agriculture along the narrow stretch off the northeast coast called the *litoral.* The Amazon's climate is wet, the *sertão* is dry, and the agricultural areas of the central, southeastern, and southern regions are temperate.

Centuries of voluntary and involuntary immigration of Europeans and Africans have contributed to the emergence of an ethnically mixed society. Combinations of Europeans, Africans, and Indians produced hundreds of distinct colors of people. Although this complexity makes any classification scheme precarious, the National Brazilian Institute of Geography and Statistics (IBGE) claims that 57 percent of the population is white, 37 percent is *pardo* (brown or mulatto), 6 percent is black, and 0.6 percent is Asian.[1] These numbers probably ignore people of mixed race, from indigenous and white parents, who are known as *mestizos* but are sometimes classified erroneously as being white or *pardo.* The indigenous people, who live in the vast Amazon basin and once numbered in the millions, were largely decimated by colonization and modernization; their number is usually estimated at 250,000. They occupy over 8.5 million square kilometers, 11 percent of the total area of Brazil.[2] The Asian population is dominated by people of Japanese descent who immigrated to the southeastern states and particularly São Paulo after 1925. Numbering over 2 million, São Paulo's community of Japanese descendants is the largest such grouping outside Japan.

Like other ethnically plural societies such as India, Mexico, Nigeria, Russia, Iran, and the United States, Brazil is a unique blend of distinct cultural influences. Unlike the people of India, Iran, and Nigeria, however, Brazilians are not greatly divided over religious differences. Roman Catholicism was imposed by Portuguese colonial rule, then reinforced by immigration from Catholic Italy, Spain, and Portugal at the end of the nineteenth century. In recent years, evangelical Protestants have made inroads and now compose about 11 percent of the population. Afro-Brazilian religions represent an older, and far more difficult to measure, tendency with religious practices that often mix Catholic and African traditions but are sometimes practiced independently. Indigenous religions and traditions are also part of the cultural landscape. More than religion, the dominance of Portuguese as the language of the land has served to keep this large country united.

Because of its size, large population, large internal market for foreign and domestic industry, and dominance over a majority of the rain forests in the Amazon (the so-called green lung of our planet), Brazil possesses resources that could make it a global superpower. Yet Brazil is a poor country that struggles to provide for its own people out of its impressive abundance of natural resources. Addressing the immense social problems of this big country requires administering its considerable resources with foresight. Unfortunately, Brazil's potential has often fallen victim to the political baggage from its past.

Critical Junctures

The Brazilian Empire (1822–1889)

Europeans first arrived in Brazil in 1500 with an expedition led by the Portuguese explorer Pedro Alvares Cabral. Unlike the other countries of Latin America, Brazil was a Portuguese colony, not a Spanish one. As a result, Brazil was spared the devastatingly violent wars of independence that afflicted other Latin American states, including Mexico. Violence, however, played

Critical Junctures in Brazil's Political Development

1822   Dom Pedro I declares himself emperor of Brazil, peacefully ending three hundred years of Portuguese colonial rule.

1824   Constitution drafted.

1888   Abolition of slavery.

1889   Dom Pedro II, who assumed throne in 1840, is forced into exile; landowning elites establish an oligarchical republic.

1891   A new constitution establishes a directly elected president.

1930   Getúlio Vargas gains power after a coup led by military and political leaders. His period of dictatorship (1937–1945) is known as the New State.

1945   Vargas calls for general elections. General Eurico Dutra of the Social Democratic Party wins.

1950   Vargas is elected president. Scandals precipitate his suicide in 1954.

1956   Juscelino Kubitschek becomes president.

1960   Jânio Quadros becomes president.

1961   Quadros resigns. João Goulart gains presidency despite an attempted military coup.

1964   A military coup places power in the hands of successive authoritarian regimes.

1985   *Diretas Já!* a mass mobilization campaign, calls for direct elections.

1985   Vice-presidential candidate José Sarney becomes president on the sudden death of elected president Tancredo Neves.

1988   A new constitution grants new social and political rights.

1989   Fernando Collor is elected president.

1992   Collor is impeached; Vice President Itamar Franco assumes presidency.

1994   Fernando Henrique Cardoso is elected president after his Real Plan controls inflation.

1998   Cardoso is reelected.

1999   The Real Plan weathers a financial crisis.

2002   Lula da Silva is elected president.

a prominent role in Brazil's conquest and development as indigenous peoples, and African slaves were mistreated and killed or died of disease.

In 1808, when Napoleon Bonaparte invaded Spain and Portugal, the Portuguese king, João VI, and his court escaped to Brazil. After the defeat of Napoleon, Dom João returned to Portugal to reclaim his throne, but he left his son, Dom Pedro, behind in Rio de Janeiro as prince regent. In September 1822, Dom Pedro declared Brazil independent and took the new title of emperor of Brazil. In 1824, a constitution was drafted, making Brazil the only constitutional monarchy in the Americas. In 1840, Dom Pedro I's son, Dom Pedro II, assumed the throne.

The Brazilian empire's chief concern was keeping control of the country's large, mostly unexplored territory. Complicating this task was the divisive issue of slavery, on which Brazil's plantation economy depended. The solution was to centralize authority in the emperor, who acted as a **moderating power** (*poder moderador*), mediating conflicts among the executive, legislative, and judicial branches of government and powerful landowning elites, known as the landed **oligarchy.** This centralization of authority provided a contrast with the other postcolonial Latin American states, which suffered numerous conflicts among territorially dispersed strongmen called *caudillos*. Brazil avoided the rise of figures such as Mexico's arch-strongman, Porfirio Díaz.

The constitutional empire marked the birth of Brazilian liberal institutions. In contrast with its neighbors, the country enjoyed several features of a functioning representative democracy: regularity of elections, the alternation of parties in power, and scrupulous observation of the constitution. In substance, however, liberal institutions only regulated political competition among the rural, oligarchical elites, reflecting the interests of a privileged minority and not the larger Brazilian population.

The Old Republic (1889–1930)

The next critical juncture in Brazilian history occurred in 1889 with the peaceful demise of the empire, the exile of Dom Pedro II, and the emergence of a republic ruled by the landowning oligarchy (the Old Republic). Many causes led to the end of the empire. The institutions of slavery and the monarchy were topics of heated debate among landowners, politicians, and commercial elites. The international pressures of abolitionists to end slavery resulted in the freeing of slaves over sixty years of age and unborn children of slaves. Socioeconomic changes also paved the way for abolition. The dynamic coffee economy, concentrated in the state of São Paulo, had grown impressively since the 1830s. Unlike the plantation sugar economy of the northeast, coffee did not require the use of slave labor, which was prohibitively expensive. Under sustained pressure by the coffee elite, all slaves were freed in 1888. By this time, too, liberal political values in opposition to the centralization of political authority had taken root among the coffee oligarchy.

The Old Republic (1889–1930) consolidated the political rise of the coffee oligarchy and a small urban industrial class and commercial elite linked to the coffee trade. By the end of the nineteenth century, coffee had become the main economic commodity, with Brazil supplying most of the world's demand. The economic importance of coffee only added to the rapidly growing political influence of the southern coffee oligarchy.

The constitution of 1891, which was inspired by the U.S. model, established a directly elected president as the head of government, guaranteed the separation of church and state, and expanded the franchise to include all literate males (about 3.5 percent of the population before 1930). The **legitimacy** of the republican political system was established on governing principles that were limited to a privileged few, but no longer determined by the hereditary rights of the emperor. Power was decentralized to the states, which gained greater authority to formulate policy, spend money, levy taxes, and maintain their own militias.

Although the republican elite went further than the empire's elite in expressing liberal ideas in the constitution, republican liberalism was a sham to the majority of Brazilians. Most Brazilians continued to reside in rural areas where the landed oligarchy vigorously suppressed dissent. As in the southern United States and in Mexico, landed elites manipulated local political activity. The colonels, as these elites were called in Brazil, assumed extensive extralegal authority to gather their poor workers and "vote them" (use their votes to guarantee the election of officials favored by the local colonels). This process became widely known as *coronelismo*.

The ties that developed between the patron (the landowner) and the client (the peasant) during the Old Republic became the basis of modern Brazilian politics. In return for protection and occasional favors, the client did the bidding of the patron. As urbanization and the growth of the state's administrative and bureaucratic agencies proceeded, the process of trading favors and demanding action was transformed and became known as **clientelism.** *Coronelismo* in rural areas and clientelism in urban areas were extended to the politics of the national state. In this way, the state was dominated by **patrimonialism**—the injection of private interests into public policy-making. Pervasive corruption, graft, and outright bribery developed as means of reinforcing patrimonialism.

In contrast to the centralization of power during the empire, the Old Republic consecrated the power of local elites. Perhaps at no other time in Brazilian political history was the **politics of the governors** as blatant as it was during the years of the Old Republic. Regional elites, mainly from the coffee and cattle regions, dominated national politics. Three states in particular emerged as key players: São Paulo (coffee), Minas Gerais (coffee and ranching), and Rio Grande do Sul (ranching). These states profoundly influenced economic policy-making and the choice of presidential candidates. The presidency alternated almost on a regular basis between São Paulo and Minas Gerais. The pattern was so obvious that this period of Brazilian political history is popularly referred to as the rule of *café com leite* ("coffee with milk"), reflecting the dominance of the São Paulo coffee and Minas Gerais cattle elites.

The 1930 Revolution

The Great Depression of the 1930s upset the economic and political base of the Old Republic. As world demand for coffee plummeted, the coffee and ranch elites faced their worst crisis. Worker demonstrations and a resurgent Brazilian Communist Party challenged the legitimacy of the Old Republic. Among the ranks of discontented political elites, a figure emerged who would change the shape of Brazilian politics for the rest of the century: Getúlio Vargas (see "Leaders: Getúlio Dornelles Vargas").

After a disputed presidential campaign in 1930, Vargas came to power as the head of what he called a new "revolutionary government." He moved swiftly to crush middle-class and popular dissent and built a political coalition around a new economic project of industrialization led by the central government and based on central state resources. In contrast to the Old Republic, Vargas insisted on controlling the regional governments by replacing all governors (except in Minas Gerais) with hand-picked allies (*interventores*). Once again, the center of gravity of Brazilian politics swung back to the national state.

Under the Old Republic, calls for rights by workers and middle-class professionals had been treated as issues for the police to resolve with force. By contrast, Vargas believed he could win the support of these groups by answering their demands in a controlled way. They would be allowed to participate in the new political order, but only if they mobilized within state-created and state-regulated unions and associations.

This model of government was **state corporatism.** State corporatism refers to a method of organizing societal actors in state-sponsored associations. It rejects the idea of competition among social groups by having the state arbitrate all conflicts. For instance, when workers requested increases in their wages, state agencies would determine to what extent such demands were answered and how business would pay for them.[3]

By 1937, Vargas had achieved a position of virtually uncontested power. From such a vantage point, he implemented a series of reforms whose influence is still felt. During the next eight years, Vargas consolidated his state corporatist paradigm with labor codes, the establishment of public firms to produce strategic commodities such as steel and oil, and paternalistic social policies. Packaged with nationalist fervor, these policies were collectively called the **New State** (*Estado Novo*).

The New State was decidedly authoritarian. Vargas, who was called *pai do povo* (father of the people), could not be upstaged by competing political images and organizations. Parties and congressional politicians became mere onlookers. Brazilian society would be linked directly to the state and to Vargas as the state's primary agent. Although the New State's constitution had fascist overtones, Vargas's policies were as much inspired by the New Deal of U.S. President Franklin D. Roosevelt as by fascist Italy or Nazi Germany.[4] The new regime expanded the existing rudimentary social

Leaders: *Getúlio Dornelles Vargas*

Getúlio Dornelles Vargas (1883–1954) came from a wealthy family in the cattle-rich southernmost state of Rio Grande do Sul. Vargas's youth was marked by political divisions within his family between federalists and republicans, conflicts that separated Brazilians during the Old Republic and particularly in Rio Grande do Sul, which had a strong regional identity. Political violence, which was common in the state's history, also affected Vargas's upbringing. His two brothers were each accused of killing rivals, one at the military school in Minas Gerais that Getúlio attended with one of his older siblings. After a brief stint in the military, Vargas attended law school in Porto Alegre, where he excelled as an orator. Like many others in his generation, his university education was incomplete. He supplemented his studies by reading many books published in other countries.

After graduating in 1907, he began his political career as a district attorney. Later, he served as majority leader in the state senate. In 1923, Vargas was elected federal deputy for Rio Grande do Sul, and in 1924 he became leader of his state's delegation in the Chamber of Deputies. In 1926, he made another political career change when he was named finance minister for the Washington Luis administration (1926–1930). He served for a year before winning the governorship of his home state. Never an ideologue, Vargas embraced a highly pragmatic style of governing that made him one of Brazil's most popular politicians by the end of the 1920s.

Vargas's powerful political position as governor of Rio Grande do Sul catapulted him into national prominence in 1929. The international economic crisis compelled several regional economic oligarchies to unite in opposition to the coffee and financial policies of the government. The states, including the state of São Paulo, divided their support between two candidates for the presidency: Julio Prestes, who was supported by President Luis, and Vargas, head of the opposition. The two states of Minas Gerais and Rio Grande do Sul voted as a bloc in favor of Vargas, but he lost the 1930 election. Immediately after this loss, a conspiracy among discontented military and political leaders led to the coup of October 1930, which installed Vargas in power.

No other figure in Brazilian political history has ever affected the country as much as Getúlio Vargas. His New State launched a series of reforms that established the terms on which Brazilian society would be linked to the state for decades. Even today, his political legacy continues in the form of state agencies and laws protecting workers.

Getúlio Vargas as president in 1952. *Source:* Hulton/Getty Archive by Getty Images.

Source: For more on Vargas's life, see Robert M. Levine, *Father of the Poor? Vargas and His Era* (New York: Cambridge University Press, 1998).

insurance and pension programs into a broad welfare and health care system for urban workers. Although unemployment insurance was not envisaged by the new laws, workers were provided with insurance against occupational accidents, illness, and death. Vargas created a Ministry of Labor and labor courts to regulate and solve conflicts between employers and labor.

In the New State, the military became an ever more important institution in politics. The armed forces experienced marked improvements in armament production and recruitment. Professional standards of promotion, conduct, and the use of force were codified in the establishment of the Superior War College (*Escola Superior de Guerra*). The military even developed new doctrines to justify the use of public funds to own and operate industries seen as essential to the nation's security. The ideology of the military regimes that dominated Brazil from 1964 to 1985 emerged directly from these earlier experiences.[5]

The Populist Republic (1945–1964)

The ever-growing mobilization of segments of the working and middle classes as well as U.S. diplomatic pressure forced Vargas, in 1943, to call for full democratic elections to be held in December 1945. Three political parties emerged to contest the election: the Social Democratic Party (PSD), the Brazilian Labor Party (PTB), and the National Democratic Union (UDN). The PSD was a collection of *Estado Novo* supporters and members of clientelist political machines across the country. The PTB was created by Vargas to mobilize members of the official labor unions. The PSD and the PTB, which operated in alliance, were both dependent on the state. The UDN brought together the various regional, anti-Vargas forces, which advocated a return to the liberal constitutionalism of the Old Republic. The UDN continued to support the role of the state in promoting economic development, however. By October 1945, the bitterness of the campaign led the military to force Vargas's resignation, two months before the general election.

The turn to democracy in 1945 fell far short of breaking with the past. The new president, Eurico Dutra of the PSD, was one of the architects of the New State. Although the new 1946 constitution provided for periodic elections, state corporatism continued in full force.

The most important economic and social policies of the country were still decided by Brazil's far-flung state bureaucracy, not by the national legislature.

Populism, not democracy, became the defining characteristic of the new political order. In Brazil, the terms *populist* and *populism* refer to politicians, programs, or movements that seek to expand citizenship to previously disenfranchised sectors of society in return for political support. Populist governments tend to grant benefits to guarantee support, but they discourage lower-class groups from creating autonomous organizations. Populist leaders, around whom personality cults often form, were successful in Brazil and other Latin American countries in generating mass support among urban working and middle classes (and sometimes rural groups) through the provision of social insurance, health care, and higher wages. Yet in no way were these leaders directly representative of or accountable to their constituencies.

Populism was Vargas's most important tool after his elected return to the presidency in 1950 with PSD and PTB support. Brazilian workers supported his return because he promised to increase the minimum wage, improve the social insurance system, and provide subsidies for public transportation and basic foodstuffs. However, many of these promises were threatened by economic problems in the early 1950s as inflation increased and wages eroded. Opposition politicians charged that Vargas was no longer able to ensure Brazil's development and that if he were given a chance, he would impose another dictatorship on the country.[6] Already politically vulnerable, Vargas was soon swept up in a bizarre scandal involving the attempted assassination of a popular journalist. The crisis drove Vargas to take his own life on August 24, 1954.

Under Vargas's democratic successor, Juscelino Kubitschek (in office from 1956 to 1960), the economic picture improved. Brazilian industry expanded tremendously in the 1950s. Kubitschek was a master of political symbolism and **nationalism.** His administration promoted images of a new and bigger Brazil, capable of generating "fifty years of development in five." Chief among these symbols of the new Brazil was Kubitschek's decision to move the country's capital from Rio de Janeiro to a planned city called Brasília. The building of this utopian city served to divert attention from the country's economic and social problems. It also

Brazil's capital, Brasília. The planned city was designed by the world-famous Brazilian architect Oscar Niemeyer.
Source: Georges Holton/Photo Researchers.

acted as a political symbol to rally support among Brazil's business class for Kubitschek's developmentalist policies.

The weak point in Brazil's political economic order was the country's incoherent party system. After Kubitschek's term ended, a populist antiparty maverick, Jânio Quadros, won the presidency in 1960 because of fragmented party identities and unstable partisan alliances.[7] Economic bad times returned as inflation soared and growth slowed. Then, without much explanation, Quadros resigned, elevating João Goulart, Vargas's former minister of labor and Quadros's acting vice president, to the presidency.

Goulart embarked on an ill-fated campaign for structural reforms, mainly of the educational system and the federal administration, and a progressive agrarian

policy. Meanwhile, Brazilian politics were becoming more polarized into right and left. New political actors burst onto the scene: peasant league movements, students, and professional organizations. Protests, strikes, and illegal seizures of land by poor Brazilians heightened ideological tensions. Goulart was severely hindered in responding to these problems by a congress that was almost perpetually stalemated in partisan bickering. Finally, industrial and landowning elites came down firmly against Goulart's reforms. Right-wing organizations flooded the streets of the main capital with anti-Goulart demonstrators. Convinced that the situation was out of control and that Goulart would soon resort to extraconstitutional measures, the military intervened in 1964, putting an end to Brazil's experiment with democratic populism.

The Rise of Bureaucratic Authoritarianism (1964–1985)

The military government that came to power in 1964 installed what the Argentine sociologist Guillermo O'Donnell has termed **bureaucratic authoritarianism** (BA).[8] These authoritarian regimes emerge in response to severe economic crises and are led by the armed forces and key civilian allies, most notably professional economists, engineers, and administrators. Repression in Brazilian BA varied from combinations of mild forms that constricted civil rights and other political freedoms and harsher forms that included wholesale censorship of the press through institutional acts, torture of civilians, and imprisonment without trial. The first and the last two military rulers, Castelo Branco (1964–1967), Ernesto Geisel (1974–1979), and João Figueiredo (1979–1985) presented less violent forms of authoritarianism, whereas the rule of Artur Costa e Silva (1967–1969) and of Emilio Médici (1969–1974) encompassed the worst forms of physical repression.

Initially, the military government envisioned a quick return to civilian rule and even allowed the continuation of democratic institutions, though in a limited form. Although purged in 1964 of perceived enemies of the military, the national congress continued to function afterward, and direct elections for federal legislators and most mayors (but not the president or state governors) were held at regular intervals. In November 1965, the military abolished all existing political parties and replaced them with only two: the National Renovation Alliance, or ARENA, and the Brazilian Democratic Movement, or MDB. ARENA was the military government's party, and MDB was the "official" party of the opposition. Although previous party labels were discarded, former members of the three major parties joined one of the two new parties. The most important party affiliations in ARENA belonged to former UDN and PSD members, while many PTB members flocked to MDB. Although the two parties did not operate until Castelo Branco left office in March 1967, the military hoped that the reform would give the BA regime a level of democratic legitimacy.[9]

Although these democratic institutions were more than pro forma, their powers were severely limited. The military government used institutional decrees to legislate the most important matters, thereby stopping the

congress from having an important voice. Few civilian politicians could speak out directly against the military for fear of being removed from office.

In economic policy, the military reinforced the previous pattern of state interventionism. The government actively promoted **state-led development** by creating hundreds of state corporations and investing millions in established public firms such as Vale. Under military leadership, Brazil implemented one of the most successful economic development programs in the Third World. Often called the Brazilian miracle, these programs demonstrated that, like France, Germany, and Japan in earlier periods, a developing country could create its own economic miracle.

The Transition to Democracy and the First Civilian Governments (1974–2002)

After the oil crisis of 1973 set off a wave of inflation around the world, the economy began to falter. Increasing criticism from Brazilian business led Geisel and Figueiredo to embrace a gradual process of democratization.[10] Initially, these leaders envisioned only a liberalizing, or opening (*abertura*), of the regime that would allow civilian politicians to contest for political office. As was the case with Gorbachev's *glasnost* in the Soviet Union, however, control over the process of liberalization gradually slipped from their hands and was captured by organizations within civil society. In 1974 the opposition party, the MDB, stunned the military government by increasing its representation in the Senate from 18 to 30 percent and in the Chamber of Deputies from 22 to 44 percent. These numbers did not give it a majority, but the party did capture a majority in both chambers of the state legislatures in the most important industrialized southern and southeastern states.[11]

Abertura accelerated in the following years. The opposition made successive electoral gains and used them to get concessions from the government. The most important of these concessions was the reestablishment of direct elections for governors in 1982, political amnesty for dissidents, the elimination of the government's power to oust legislators from political office, and the restoration of political rights to those who had previously lost them. The gubernatorial elections of November 1982 sealed the fate of promilitary candidates. Opposition gubernatorial candidates won landslide victories, capturing the most developed states: Minas Gerais, São Paulo, and Rio de Janeiro. The process of liberalizing the authoritarian regime was now irreversible.

The military, which wanted to maintain as much control over the succession process as possible, preferred to have the next president selected within a restricted electoral college. In 1983, mass mobilization campaigns seeking the right to elect the next president directly got off the ground. The *Diretas Já!* ("Direct Elections Now!") movement, comprising an array of social movements, opposition politicians, and labor unions, expanded in size and influence in 1984.[12] Their rallies exerted tremendous pressure on the military at a moment when the question of who would succeed General Figueiredo was not clear. The military's fight to keep the 1984 elections indirect alienated civilian supporters of the generals, many of whom broke with the regime and backed an alliance (the Liberal Front) with Tancredo Neves, the candidate of the opposition PMDB, or Party of the MDB. Neves's victory in 1984, however, was short-lived. His sudden death on the eve of his inauguration meant that Vice President José Sarney became the first civilian president of Brazil since 1964.

The sequence of events that led to Sarney's presidency was a keen disappointment to those who had hoped for a clean break with the authoritarian past. Most of the politicians who gained positions of power in the new democracy hailed from the former ARENA or its misleadingly named successor, the Democratic Social Party (PDS). Most of these soon joined Sarney's own PMDB or its alliance partner, the Party of the Liberal Front (PFL).[13] Labor unions in particular distrusted Sarney as a former political hack of the military. His administration failed to reform the old authoritarian modes of policy-making, including corporatist institutions and military prerogatives over civilian government.

A chance for fundamental change appeared in 1987 when the national Constituent Assembly met to draft a new constitution. Given the earlier success of the opposition governors in 1982, state political machines became important players in the game of constitution writing. The state governments petitioned for the devolution of new authority to tax and spend. Labor groups also exerted influence through their lobbying organization. Workers demanded constitutional protection of their right to strike and called for an extension of the right to public employees, who were heretofore

prohibited from engaging in such activism. The constitution also granted workers the right to create their own unions without authorization from the Ministry of Labor.[14] As a whole, the constitution guaranteed a rich array of social and political rights, yet it also left vestiges from the corporatist past, including protection of public firms in petroleum and telecommunications from foreign investment and privatization.

The other primary issue of the day was inflation. Soon after Sarney's rise to power, annual rates of inflation began to skyrocket. The government invoked several stabilization plans to stop the explosion of prices, but to no avail. By the presidential elections of 1989, the first since the 1960s to be held as direct elections for that post, Brazilian society was calling for a political leader who would remedy runaway inflation and remove corrupt and authoritarian politicians from positions of power.

Rising from political obscurity, an ex-governor from Alagoas, a small state in the poor northeast, Fernando Collor de Mello, became president. Collor and his small party, the Party of National Reconstruction (PRN), had fought a grueling campaign against the popular left-wing labor leader and head of the Workers' Party (*Partido dos Trabalhadores,* or PT), Luiz Inácio "Lula" da Silva (see "Citizen Action: The Workers' Party" in the "Political Parties and the Party System" section later in this chapter). To counteract Lula's appeal among the Brazilian people, Collor's campaign rhetoric appealed to the poor, known as the *descamisados* ("shirtless ones"), who were attracted by his attacks against politicians and the social problems caused by bureaucratic inefficiency. A skillful campaigner on television, Collor convinced Brazilians that he could "kill inflation with one shot" and get rid of the "maharajahs"— corrupt public servants who collected massive salaries but did little work.

The Collor presidency was a critical juncture as the government's economic team began the privatization of state enterprises, deregulation of the economy, and the reversal of decades of policies that had kept Brazil's markets closed to the rest of the world. Yet Collor failed to solve the nagging problem of inflation and, ironically, was soon accused of bribery and influence peddling and was impeached in September 1992, an ignominious end for the first directly elected president since the 1960s.

Collor's impeachment brought to the presidency

Itamar Franco, a well-known politician in Minas Gerais who was less well known at the national level as Collor's vice president. Despite a high level of uncertainty during Franco's first year, including rumors of a military coup that was allegedly in the works in 1993, his government provided an important stabilizing role. Perhaps his most important decision was to support his minister of finance, Fernando Henrique Cardoso, a sociologist and senator from São Paulo, in a plan to conquer inflation. In July 1994, Cardoso implemented a plan to fight inflation, the Real Plan, which succeeded. By creating a new currency, the real, the government hoped to wipe away the populace's memories of its weak and unstable predecessors, cruzeiros and cruzados. The result was that monthly inflation fell from 26 percent to 2.82 percent in October 1994 (see Section 2).

Cardoso rode the success of the Real Plan to the Brazilian presidency, beating out Lula of the PT in 1994 and again in 1998 to become the first Brazilian president since the Vargas dictatorship to be reelected. After his inauguration in January 1995, Cardoso proved adept at keeping inflation low and consolidating some of the structural reforms of the economy. As the tale of Vale suggests, privatization moved forward. Other reforms, however, remained stuck in congress, including crucial reforms of the tax system. Brazil's budget and trade deficits increased, requiring the government to finance the shortfall with short- and medium-term debt. As in Mexico in 1994, these conditions caused foreign investors to abandon the Brazilian market, leading to billions of dollars in capital flight. Financial crisis in Asia and Russia worsened the crisis in 1998 and early 1999. Even Cardoso's reelection in October 1998 could not stop Brazil from becoming the latest casualty in a widening global financial crisis as the real crashed in January 1999. Yet the months following the crisis showed how resilient Brazilian democracy and the economic reform process could be. The real soon stabilized, hyperinflation did not return, and the country weathered the financial calamity of the Argentine economy's meltdown after December 2001 without turning back on any of the structural reforms implemented during the 1990s.

Following the October 2002 elections, the country experienced the first regular transfer of the presidential sash from one directly elected chief executive to his successor, Lula da Silva. Despite international financial uncertainty in response to Lula's rise to power, this fourth presidential election in twelve years reflected the maturity and stability of Brazilian democracy.

Themes and Implications

Historical Junctures and Political Themes

The state has played a central role in the story of modern Brazilian politics. In the world of states, both international and domestic factors have influenced the Brazilian state's structure, capacity, and relations with society. During the days of the empire, international opposition to slavery forced powerful oligarchs to turn to the state for protection. The coffee and ranch economies that provided the material base for the power of the Old Republic were intricately tied to Brazil's economic role in the world. Even the *Estado Novo,* with its drive to organize society, was affected by events outside Brazil. The defeat of fascism in Europe helped turn the New State's authoritarian project into a populist-democratic one. The return to democracy during the 1980s was also part of a larger global experience, as authoritarian regimes gave way all over Latin America, eastern Europe, southern Europe, and the Soviet Union.

Within Brazil, the state adjusted to changes in the distribution of power, the rise of new, politically active social classes, and the requirements of development. In the federal state, power shifted regularly between the central and subnational governments. From the centralizing, moderating power of the Brazilian emperor Dom Pedro II and the state corporatist *Estado Novo* of Getúlio Vargas, to the decentralized, power-sharing exchange of *café com leite,* the swings of the pendulum between center and local punctuated many of the critical junctures of Brazilian politics. In recent decades, the pendulum has swung between the centralization of political power required by bureaucratic authoritarianism and the liberalization (and decentralization) of power involved in the transition to democracy.

The inclusion of new political actors such as the working and middle classes reshaped the Brazilian state during the twentieth century. The state corporatism of Vargas's New State provided mechanisms for mobilizing and organizing workers and professionals. Populist democracy later provided these social segments protection from unsafe working environments, the effects of eroding wages, and the prohibitive expense of health care. Public firms such as Vale employed hundreds of thousands of Brazilians and dramatically altered the development possibilities of the country. These policies have now come under attack by reformists both within the government and in the international financial institutions who believe their reform requires another round of state restructuring, this time with a generous dose of market-oriented criteria. Privatization, deregulation, economic liberalization, and the reform of public employment and pension programs are dramatically altering the role of the Brazilian state and its relations with society.

As for Brazil's distinctive approach to governing the economy, no one should discount the legacies of state-led development in the country's history. During the twentieth century, Brazil was transformed from a predominantly agrarian economy into an industrialized economy. To some extent, markets and foreign investment played key roles in this process, but the state also provided crucial financial, technical, and political support that made this great transformation possible. As a result, Brazil's position in the global system of production and exchange was fundamentally guided by politics.

Nonetheless, the growth produced by state-led development was poorly distributed. Social problems that emerged from this unequal model of development are at the heart of the country's ongoing struggles with democracy. For many Brazilians living in poverty, it was not clear what benefits the return to democracy had produced.

Regarding the democratic idea, Brazil certainly has the institutions of a democracy, but in many ways, the decades of patrimonialism, populism, and corporatism undermine these institutions. Brazilian politicians typically cultivate personal votes (they are known as *personalist politicians*) and avoid following the rule of parties or alliances. Many switch parties several times in a political career. As a result, Brazilian political parties are extremely weak. Personalism in Brazilian politics persists because it is well rewarded. Once elected, politicians can remain in power through frequent use of clientelist relations, favoritism, nepotism, and outright bribery.

Yet even with these enduring shortcomings in democracy, Brazilians continue to prefer this form of government. The appeal of democracy is based in part on their negative memories of the repression they suffered under the authoritarian regime and the military's poor management of the economy. More important, Brazilians impute positive values to the improved access to decision-making processes that democracy gives them. Thousands of new political groups, social movements, civic networks, and economic associations have emerged in recent years. The Brazilian state is highly decentralized into twenty-six states, a federal district, and over 5,500 municipalities. Each of these centers of power has become a locus of demand-making by citizens and policy-making by elites. Under these circumstances, centralized rule following the model of the New State or the bureaucratic authoritarian period is impossible today and, in any case, seems undesirable to most Brazilians.

Collective identities remain uncertain in Brazil, although Brazilians are now more commonly linked through their place in the democratic order. Who are the Brazilians? has always been a vexing question, no less so now that Brazil's borders are becoming obsolete in a world of heavy flows of international commerce, finance, and ideas. One common response to the question is that the symbols of the Brazilian nation continue to tie Brazilians together: carnival, soccer, samba, and bossa nova. Yet even as these symbols have become more prevalent, they have also lost some of their meaning because of commercialization and export as part of a tourist-attracting image of Brazil. Catholicism is a less unifying force today as Pentecostalism and evangelism have eaten into the Church's membership. Women have improved both their social position and their political awareness as gender-based organizations have become a more important resource of civil society. Yet even here, Brazil remains an extremely patriarchal society: women are expected to balance motherhood and other traditional roles in the household while they are pressured by economic need to produce income.

Perhaps race, more than any other form of identity, remains the most difficult issue to understand in Brazilian politics and society. Racial identity continues to divide Brazilians, but not in the clear-cut manner it does blacks and whites in the United States. These categories are more fluid in Brazil. Racial mixing has been the basis for easier integration. But it has also undercut the political mobilization of blacks by weakening the kind of stark, black–white segregation that helped blacks in the United States coalesce around the civil rights movement.

Like race, class continues to separate Brazilians. Economic reforms and the erosion of populist redistribution have caused social gaps to widen further, making Brazil a highly fragmented society. Although it is one of the world's ten wealthiest economies, with a gross domestic product over US$588 billion, that wealth is poorly distributed. Like India, Brazil's social indicators such as income distribution, infant mortality, and nutrition consistently rank near the bottom in the world of states. Income disparities mirror racial differences, as the poor are represented by mostly blacks and mulattos, and the rich are almost invariably white. The poverty of the north and northeast also contrasts with the more industrialized and prosperous southeastern and southern states.

Implications for Comparative Politics

As a large, politically decentralized, and socially fragmented polity, Brazil presents several extraordinary challenges to the study of comparative politics. First, the Brazilian state is an anomaly. It has been both highly centralized and decentralized during different periods of its history. In each of these periods, the state produced lasting political legacies that have both strengthened and weakened its capacity for promoting development, democracy, and social distribution. Although political centralization has been an important factor in making the French state strong, decentralized states such as the U.S. and German federations have also proven to be successful formulas for government. The Brazilian case is a laboratory for evaluating which

approach is likely to be more successful in other large, highly decentralized states in the developing world, such as Russia, China, and India.

While the complexity of the Brazilian state represents one problem area, the weakness of the country's democratic institutions suggests another, and perhaps more troubling, concern. Along with Russia, Brazil demonstrates how the lack of coherent party systems and electoral institutions can endanger democracy. In contrast to the highly organized polity of Germany and the strength of parties in parliamentary democracies like the United Kingdom and Japan, Brazil's experience highlights how anemic representative institutions can weaken democracy.

Paradoxically, as Brazil developed economically and made its way back to democracy in the 1980s, it also became a more socially unequal country. Established democracies like India and transitional democracies like Mexico and Russia have also experienced the reality that democratization does not improve the distribution of wealth. Yet the longest established democracies in our study—the United States, Britain, France, Germany, and Japan—are also the richest and, by and large, the countries where wealth is most equally distributed. Brazil and India therefore are a bit of a puzzle: If democracy and social development are intricately linked, shouldn't the distribution of wealth be getting better, not worse, in these two countries?

Finally, the complex divisions afflicting Brazilians' collective identities challenge all attempts to address the country's problems. Yet even today, Brazilians and outside observers continue to treat the country as a singular unit. In this regard, Brazil presents a puzzle for theories about collective identities: How has such a socially fragmented society remained a coherent whole for so long?

Section ❷ Political Economy and Development

Like most other countries in the developing world, Brazilian politics has always been shaped by the country's quest for economic and social development. Two processes in particular have left enduring legacies: the pattern of state intervention in the domestic market and the effects of external economic change. Historically these two factors have influenced each other. External

economic crises—world depressions, fluctuations in the price of exported goods such as coffee, upsurges in the prices of imported goods—have compelled the Brazilian state to intervene in the domestic economy through protection, subsidies, and even the production of goods that it previously imported. In turn, policies aimed at promoting the industrial growth of the country have made Brazil one of the newly industrialized countries of the world, alongside states such as Mexico, Taiwan, South Korea, and Malaysia.

In order to clarify how political and economic development have been intertwined in Brazil, this section explores the state-led model of development, considers how the domestic effects of the state-led model and its reform generated enormous social costs, and discusses the international capitalist forces that shaped domestic economic policy and society.

State and Economy

Like its Latin American neighbors, Brazil's early economic development was based on **export-led growth,** that is, on the export of agricultural products such as sugar, cotton, coffee, and, for a short time in the early 1900s, rubber. In the nineteenth century, coffee emerged as the engine of growth in the Brazilian economy. By the time of the Old Republic, a strong demand for Brazilian coffee in Europe and North America gave the country a virtual monopoly in the global market. Cotton, sugar, and cereals continued to be important export products too, but they were secondary to coffee. By 1919, coffee composed 56 percent of Brazil's total exports. Only five years later, that figure had jumped to 75 percent.[15]

The dominance of coffee ensured that the Old Republic would keep Brazil active in the world market. That meant that the state had only a minimal role in promoting the export-led economy, which functioned so well that money generated by coffee provided a reservoir of capital to build railroads, power stations, and other infrastructure. These investments, in turn, spurred the growth of some light industries, mostly in textiles, footwear, and clothing.

The Brazilian state's role in the economy became far more **interventionist** during the 1930s when the Great Depression caused international demand for coffee to decline. As exports fell, imports of manufactured goods also declined. The coffee export sector had created demand for these goods among the urban population in the decades before the Great Depression. Therefore, as the coffee economy declined, incentives to boost domestic industrial production to substitute for previously imported manufactures increased.

During the 1930s, Brazil's economy pursued **import substitution industrialization** (ISI), a model of development that promoted domestic industrial production of previously imported manufactured goods. By 1937, this policy, which relied heavily on state intervention, became a major pillar of Vargas's New State. At first, large doses of state intervention were not necessary. The initial phase of ISI—the so-called light, or easy, phase—focused on manufactured products that required little capital or sophisticated technology. Most of these industries, such as textiles and food processing, were labor intensive and therefore created jobs. Although these conditions did not require large infusions of state capital, the New State provided limited subsidies and tariff protection to nascent ISI sectors.

At the end of World War II, new ideas about Third World development came to be adopted by various international agencies. The new goal was to "deepen" the ISI model by promoting heavy industry and capital-intensive production. In Brazil, as in Argentina, Mexico, and India, a new generation of **state technocrats**—experts in economic development—took an active role in designing new policies. Inspired by the texts of the United Nations Economic Commission for Latin America (ECLA), these technocrats targeted particular industrial sectors as strategic.[16] Then, through the use of industrial policies including planning, subsidies, and financial support, state agencies promoted the quick growth of these sectors.

Brazil was the epitome of ECLA-style **developmentalism,** the ideology and practice of state-sponsored growth, during the 1950s in Latin America. More than any other Latin American state, the Brazilian state was organizationally capable of implementing industrial policies to deepen ISI. New bureaucratic structures, such as a national development bank and national public firms, were created during the first and second Vargas governments. Petrobrás, the state oil firm, quickly became a model of what the Brazilian state wanted to become: a state that could produce as well as regulate. The producer state promoted private investment by extracting and distributing raw materials for domestic industries at prices well below the international market level. These lower prices were in effect subsidies to domestic industry. In this way, subsidized steel and subsidized credit from the national development bank fueled domestic industrialization. Other firms linked to sectors of the economy receiving these supports would benefit in a chain reaction.

Although growth rates achieved impressive levels during the 1950s and early 1960s and even higher levels in the 1970s (see Table 1), it was during this period that the first serious contradictions of ISI emerged.[17] Protection fostered noncompetitive, inefficient production because it removed incentives for competition. Although industries grew, they did so by depending too heavily on public subsidies. ISI also became import intensive. Businesses used subsidized finance to import technology and machinery. The government helped these firms by overvaluing the currency to make import prices cheaper. This overvaluation of the currency hurt export earnings, which were necessary to pay for imports. As a result, the export sector could not supply the state with much-needed revenues to sustain growth, prompting the government to print money, which in turn led to inflation. Under the Goulart government (1961–1964), the economy's capacity to import and export dwindled, and stagnation set in. The economic crisis that soon followed contributed to the coup of 1964 and Goulart's fall.

The failures of ISI during the 1960s inspired new thinking, at least in Brazilian and Latin American academe, on development. The so-called dependency school, whose adherents were known as *dependencistas*,

emerged in the social sciences around the idea that underdeveloped or "peripheral" countries faced tremendous obstacles to achieving sustained levels of industrialization and growth in a world dominated by "core" economies in North America and western Europe. ISI's failures, the *dependencistas* argued, were due to the ill-fated attempt to adjust marginally the inherently exploitative structure of world markets. Core economies had created a global capitalist structure that would always favor their interests and lead to the extraction of wealth from poor countries. This early attack on what we today call globalization inspired a new generation of progressive thinkers, among them the sociologist and future president Fernando Henrique Cardoso, who became one of the preeminent proponents of a variant of the dependency argument. The fall of Brazilian democracy, however, would provide little opportunity for these groups to take their ideas out of the universities and implement them as policy.

The rise of the military governments in 1964 led to reform but eventually to an attempt to deepen ISI through state-led development methods. From 1964 to 1985, the state continued to promote industrialization, especially the production of consumer durable goods such as automobiles, televisions, refrigerators, and machinery for the domestic market. Domestic entrepreneurs relied on the transfer of technology from foreign investors, particularly after 1970, when they collaborated with multinational firms to produce pharmaceuticals and later computers. Table 2 highlights the important contribution of industry to the Brazilian gross domestic product.

Para-statals, also known as public or state firms, played an important role in the military's development model. Large-scale projects in shipbuilding, mining, steel, oil, bauxite, and aluminum were financed and managed by bureaucratic agencies and state firms. These projects often operated in conjunction with larger development plans designed to attract domestic and foreign entrepreneurs. Peter Evans, an American political economist, insightfully characterized these complex relations among the state, foreign investors, and domestic capitalists as a "triple alliance."[18] The state, however, remained the dominant partner.

In the 1970s, Brazil's military leaders realized that the deepening of ISI could not rely on domestic capital

Table 1

Governing the Economy: GDP Growth Rates, 1940–2000	
Year	GDP Growth Rate
1940–1949	5.6%
1950–1959	6.1
1960–1969	5.4
1970–1979	12.4
1980–1989	1.5
1990–1996	2.1
1997–2000	0.8

Source: Brazilian Institute of Geography and Statistics (IBGE), *Anuario Estatístico Brasileiro* (Rio de Janeiro: IBGE, various years).

Table 2

**Governing the Economy:
Sector Composition of the GDP, 1970–2000**

Year	Agriculture	Industry	Services
1970	11.55%	35.87%	52.59%
1980	10.16	40.99	48.84
1990	9.26	34.20	56.54
2000	9.00	29.00	62.00

Source: IBGE and Werner Baer, *The Brazilian Economy:
Growth and Development,* 4th ed. (New York: Praeger,
1994), 382–383. Copyright © 1995 by Werner Baer.
Reprinted by permission of Greenwood Publishing Group,
Inc. All rights reserved.

alone. In order to finance the huge public expenditures of national industrial policy, the military turned to international financial markets, particularly private investment markets in North America and Europe. The military also began to emphasize primary exports such as coffee, iron ore, cereals, and other agricultural products. Policies designed to increase agricultural productivity and technological modernization that had already been implemented in the first years of military rule were expanded. Agriculture began to be integrated with industrial production.

The export of agricultural surplus and the sale of food products in the internal market were facilitated by a growing agribusiness sector. Spurred on by state subsidies, agribusiness supplied new resources and management for previously inefficient agricultural subsectors. Agricultural production in the agribusiness sector employed heavy machinery and advanced technologies that increased the size of the average yield. One of the most unusual agribusiness ventures occurred in the 1970s, when the military government introduced a plan to use sugarcane alcohol as a fuel source. Northeast agribusiness boomed during these years as the sugar economy became tied to the dynamic industrial economy of the southern and southeastern regions.

The Environmental Costs of State-Led Growth

The impressive growth of industry and agriculture was concentrated in the central and southern regions of Brazil. Centers of growth in the states of São Paulo,

Minas Gerais, Rio de Janeiro, and Rio Grande do Sul became the locomotives of the country's development and sites of environmental degradation. As capital-intensive industries became more common in Brazil, ecologically destructive technologies were used without much regulation. Before the mid-1970s, Brazilian policy-makers were unconcerned with the emission of toxic waste into the ground at major industrial zones, air pollution in overgrown urban areas, or pesticide and chemical fertilizer use in agricultural regions. Industrial growth was simply more important than these environmental factors.

The environmental costs of these attitudes became clear in the 1970s. Guanabara Bay and the Paraiba do Sul River basin, both in Rio de Janeiro state, were brought to the brink of biological death. Urban pollution in São Paulo devastated the Tietê River, which runs through the city, making it no better than a toxic waste dump in some areas and threatening the health of millions. By far the worst tragedy was in Cubatão, an industrial city 60 kilometers east of metropolitan São Paulo. There, petrochemical industries and steel mills wreaked havoc on the environment, pumping 1 million kilograms of pollutants into the surrounding ecological system each day. The conditions in the residential area of Cubatão became so bad that by 1981, one city council member reported that he had not seen a star in twenty years.[19] Thousands reported becoming afflicted with tuberculosis, pneumonia, bronchitis, emphysema, asthma, and cancer. Forty of every one thousand babies in Cubatão were stillborn.

Big development projects reached the forests of the Amazon River basin in the 1970s with Vale do Rio Doce's Carajás mining work in the eastern Amazon. This and other industrial projects threatened the tropical forests, as did cattle ranching, timber extraction, and slash-and-burn agriculture by poor farmers, a practice that allowed frequent rains to leech nutrients from the soil and prevent the return of tropical habitats. By the 1980s, it was clear that the primary result of these practices was the deforestation of the Amazon.

Brazil's worsening environmental problems received official attention after 1972, when the United Nations held its Conference on the Human Environment. Soon afterward, Brazil created an environmental secretariat, and in 1981 the government established the National Environmental Council (CONAMA), which included officials from national and state government and representatives from business, professional, and environmental groups. State governments also established their own environmental agencies and passed important legislation.[20] In 1975, São Paulo passed a comprehensive antipollution law. The cleanup of Cubatão began in 1983.

Partly as a result of the return to democracy in 1984, new environmental movements within and outside Brazil began to influence official and public opinion on the costs of resource degradation. Much attention was brought to these problems when the Brazilian government successfully persuaded the United Nations to hold its Conference on the Environment, a follow-up to the 1972 conference, in Rio de Janeiro in 1992. Thousands of delegates and hundreds of **nongovernmental organizations** gathered in Rio to discuss global environmental problems that were virtually all present in Brazil. By that time, numerous environmental organizations were already active in Brazilian politics.[21]

Despite the attention the Rio conference brought to the issue, rates of deforestation, pollution, and resource degradation fell only briefly after 1992 and have since returned to historically high levels. Brazilian business has shown only passing interest in the use of clean technologies because of their expense. In the third international UN conference on the environment, held in Kyoto, Japan, in 1997, Brazil was joined by the rest of the developing world in deflecting the finger of blame for ecological problems. However, it did play an important diplomatic role toward the end of the conference by supporting a U.S.-backed clean development fund. Nevertheless, Brazil lags behind its neighbor Argentina, which in November 1998 became the first developing country to adopt binding targets for controlling emissions of industrial waste gases.

The Fiscal System

In developed countries such as the United States, Germany, France, and Britain, governments can use tax policy to punish polluters. In Brazil, however, tax collection has been notoriously weak, making this a less useful instrument to regulate business or individuals. Tax evasion has been a chronic problem. The military governments attempted to change that through a constitutional reform in 1967 that created new taxes, made

the federal government better able to collect taxes, and centralized fiscal policy and the control of revenues. However, because one of the military's primary objectives was to stimulate private savings and to increase capital formation, the new tax systems allowed for numerous costly exemptions and transfers of budgetary resources to private firms and to the upper and middle classes. As a result, the Brazilian tax system became more regressive by shifting the tax burden onto the middle and working classes.

As the Brazilian economy became more complex, new opportunities for evading taxes emerged. An **informal economy** of small firms, domestic enterprises, street vendors, and unregistered employees proliferated, virtually outside the domain of the taxable economy. In some cases, these enterprises acquired substantial size, accounting for the distribution of everything from artisans' goods to professional services. Legally registered companies began to subcontract unregistered professionals to render services beyond the reach of the tax system. Although reliable information is lacking, economists estimate that the informal economy represents close to half of Brazil's gross domestic product, or GDP (about US$300 billion) and employs about 30 million to 45 million people. More reliable figures on tax evasion in both the formal and informal sectors estimate that federal coffers lose over $95 billion a year.

Other problems developed for the tax system after the transition to democracy. The new constitution of 1988 decentralized the fiscal structure by allowing the states and municipalities to expand their collection of taxes and receive larger transfers of funds from Brasília. Significant gaps emerged in tax collection responsibilities and public spending as a result of these changes. Although the central state spent less than it collected in taxes between 1960 and 1994, Brazil's 5,500 municipal governments spent several times more than they collected. Subnational governments also gained more discretion over spending. More than 90 percent of funds transferred from the federal government to the states went unearmarked, so state governments could use these monies for their own purposes.

New reforms during the Collor administration began to reverse some of the adverse effects of fiscal decentralization and the weak tax system. In the 1980s, the state governments, which held almost half of Brazil's total debt, continued to roll over their debt with federal outlays and failed to cut expenditures. In the early 1990s, federal threats to cut off debt servicing and close down profligate regional banks owned by the state governments put an end to this unsustainable practice. Other reforms shifted some of the tax burden onto business, which helped to increase tax receipts to 25 percent of GDP.[22]

The Cardoso administration had some success in recovering federal tax revenues and reducing the fiscal distortions produced by Brazil's federal structure. Tax evasion was slowed as the federal tax collection agency was expanded and its surveillance powers enhanced. Legislation in 1994 and 1998 allowed the federal government to employ more discretion over transfers of funds constitutionally earmarked for the state and municipal governments and to cap the states' ability to acquire debt. That allowed the federal government to exert some leverage on state governments to control their spending. Brasília also shifted more spending responsibilities in health care, housing, and social policy to subnational governments. That has allowed the federal government to reduce its own spending and control how the states spend their resources. The most important reform in this area, the Fiscal Responsibility Law, which was passed in 2000, set strict limits on federal, state, and municipal expenditures, but its enforcement is still in doubt. Given still large civil service payrolls (often these constitute more than 70 percent of state and municipal revenues), governments are hard-pressed to implement the law. The National Confederation of Municipalities estimates that 80 percent of Brazil's mayors and sixteen of twenty-seven states are not in compliance with the law's strict requirements. These problems are at the center of Brazil's mounting public debt, which now hovers over 60 percent of GDP, and they have played a role in the country's recent financial crises.

The Problem of Inflation

Inflation deserves special mention in Brazil, for in no other country, with the possible exception of Germany, has this phenomenon had such a lasting impact on a country's politics. In Brazil, inflation accompanied state-led development, especially after 1974. Through various types of controls, the Brazilian state, business, and unions all attempted to govern prices, interest rates, and wages. Such manipulation distorted the value of goods and services, and facilitated inflation. With the return to democracy after 1985, successive governments attempted to control inflation. All of these "stabilization" packages failed as "hyperinflation" (four-digit inflation) returned repeatedly. Figure 1 illustrates this terrible track record.

The Sarney, Collor, and Franco governments sought to control the growth in prices by setting the price of some basic products and freezing wages while the government reduced spending. The plans failed for a mixture of reasons, but usually because one of these conditions could not be sustained. Once fixed prices could not be maintained or government spending could not be restrained or wages were increased in accordance with monthly inflation rates, the inflationary spiral would heat up.

Only Cardoso's Real Plan proved successful in reining in inflation. The Real Plan attempted to anchor the real, the new currency, in a unit of real value, which was itself indexed to the U.S. dollar. Unlike a similar plan in Argentina, the Real Plan did not fix the real to the dollar strictly but allowed it to float within bands, thus achieving more flexibility in the exchange rate.

Figure 1

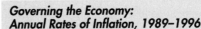

Governing the Economy:
Annual Rates of Inflation, 1989–1996

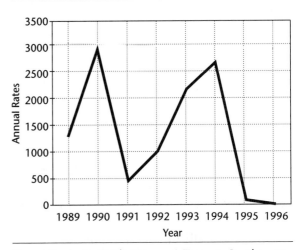

Source: Fundação Getúlio Vargas, *A Economia Brasileira em Gráficos* (Rio de Janeiro: FGV, 1996), 24.

This is one of the main reasons that the real was able to weather the kind of financial turmoil that led the Argentine economy to ruin in 2001–2002.

Paradoxically, the Real Plan's formula for success proved to be a source of weakness. Soon after the Mexican peso crisis of December 1994, Central Bank managers in Brasília became convinced that the real was overvalued, just as the peso had been before its crash. Overvaluation made exports more expensive abroad, raised the costs of production, and made imports cheaper. Brazil's trade deficit rose by more than 140 percent after 1995, threatening to scare away foreign investors. Despite dire predictions, though, Brazil's large foreign reserves (US$75 billion in mid-1998) kept investors confident in the economy, although turmoil in Asian financial markets led to the bleeding of these foreign reserves at $1 billion a day during October 1998. Improvements in tax collection, an influx of foreign investment, modest growth, and repeated attempts by the Cardoso administration to close the trade deficit by limiting imports and removing taxes on exports helped to keep the real's value stable. Yet high interest rates, escalating public debt, the inability to rein in spending, and monetary instability in Asia and Russia continued to threaten the real's stability. Signs of hope emerged in November 1998 when the International Monetary Fund (IMF) negotiated a US$42 billion bailout agreement with Brazil in order to keep the economy from sinking further into financial upheaval. These efforts proved unsuccessful. In January 1999, Itamar Franco, the ex-president and the newly elected governor of Minas Gerais, threatened his former minister of finance with a moratorium on the state government's debt to Brasília. The threat led to an upsurge in capital flight (US$6 billion in the first fourteen days of 1999) as investors lost confidence in Cardoso's government. Central Bank president Gustavo Franco, one of the Real Plan's chief defenders, resigned abruptly. The new president, Francisco Lopes, announced a "controlled" devaluation of 8 percent. Within just two days, pressures on the real forced the government to abandon the Real Plan's exchange rate regime altogether. The currency was forced to float, causing it to decline in value by more than 50 percent against the dollar. The devaluation generated renewed fears of inflation and refocused attention on the need to contain public sector spending. But hyperinflation did not return, and the government was successful in moderating the growth in public spending through reforms such as the Law of Fiscal Responsibility. Nevertheless, the massive public debt continued to grow to $245 billion by 2002, continuing to threaten the stability of the currency (see Figure 2).

Society and Economy

Brazil's astounding levels of industrialization during the 1950s, 1960s, and 1970s had lasting effects on the urban population. In 1950, 35 percent of the population lived in urban areas. By 1980, that number had increased to 68 percent. During the same period, employment in industry jumped from 14 percent to 24 percent, while employment in agriculture declined from 60 percent to 30 percent. Import substitution had created these jobs by expanding the domestic market. ISI led to a jump in the size of both the working and the middle classes. Service sector professionals like lawyers, doctors, and private teachers soon found clients as the domestic consumer market grew along with the working class.

Nevertheless, the number of jobs created in the industrial sector did not begin to absorb the huge number of unemployed Brazilians. Many of the new jobs required skilled and semiskilled specialized labor. Metallurgy, automobile production, and mining did not

Figure 2

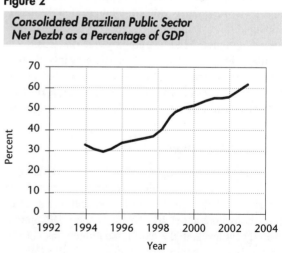

Consolidated Brazilian Public Sector Net Dezbt as a Percentage of GDP

Source: Based on numbers produced by the Central Bank of Brazil.

provide many opportunities for the large numbers of unskilled workers in the Brazilian labor market. In the late 1980s and 1990s, even skilled workers faced losing their jobs because of intense industrial restructuring. From 1990 to 1996, manufacturing jobs fell by 38.1 percent, and unemployment in metropolitan areas rose above 18 percent. Service sector employment increased, but not enough to make up for industrial job losses. These jobs also paid less and offered fewer protections from arbitrary dismissal.

Industrialization also failed to eradicate the racial inequalities inherited from slavery. Despite the impressive industrial development of Brazil, Afro-Brazilians continued to make less than their white colleagues and had fewer opportunities for upward mobility. According to one study, nonwhite men and women in Brazil have made real gains in their income because of improvements in education and occupation, but the gap separating nonwhite income from white income remains significant.[23] On average, blacks make 41 percent and mulattos make 47 percent of what whites make.

Women constitute 28 percent of the economically active population in Brazil and continue to enter the labor market in record numbers. Working women typically have more years of schooling than men and are better prepared to meet the demands of an increasingly technological economy. Despite such developments, women receive lower salaries than men employed at the same job. Women make 57 percent of what men make. Afro-Brazilian women, who are doubly disadvantaged by race and gender, are in a particularly precarious situation. Many are employed in underpaid and menial jobs, particularly as domestic servants, 90 percent of whom are black women. Mulatto women receive 46 percent of what white men make, and black women take in only 40 percent of what white men make.

The Welfare System

In a country of startling social inequalities, welfare policy plays a remarkably minor role in the lives of most Brazilians. Although welfare and education expenditures constitute about 11 percent of the GDP, among the highest levels in the world, the money has not improved Brazil's mediocre welfare state. Unlike the systems in Britain, France, Germany, and Japan, Brazil's welfare system has not reduced the high level of poverty or helped the majority of the poor. Vast sectors of the population, deprived of access to bank finance, higher education, and jobs, remain totally outside the reach of welfare services.

Brazil supports a public school system as well as a health, retirement, and social assistance system that includes funds for unemployment relief. Salaried workers are entitled to benefits such as health care, worker's compensation, retirement pensions, paid vacations, and overtime pay, yet only an estimated 15 percent of the Brazilian population qualify for these benefits. Workers in the informal sector, who are normally undocumented, cannot collect welfare since technically the federal government does not consider them employed. Corruption, clientelism, and outright waste make the welfare system incapable of delivering benefits to the people who need them the most.[24]

Part of the problem is that more people need welfare than actually contribute to the welfare state. Today, only half of the 70 million people who are economically active contribute to the welfare system. Between 1990 and 2000, while the population doubled, the number of retired people multiplied elevenfold, adding to the roster of those depending on public welfare spending. In 1995, the welfare system received US$3.5 billion less than was needed to pay the retirement pensions of the 15.2 million inactive workers and 3 million new beneficiaries. The shortfall was covered by public debt, thus adding to Brazil's fiscal problems. During the military period, changes to the welfare system produced additional distortions. Since the days of the New State, workers employed by a firm for ten years or more were guaranteed generous severance benefits. The military replaced these guarantees with a social insurance fund that prorated inferior benefits to the years of employment. The military expanded protection to several sectors of employment that previously had been outside the welfare system: rural workers, domestic workers, and professionals. But the chief beneficiaries of the new system continued to be public employees (including politicians and members of the military). Compared to total benefit payments of US$35.2 billion to 15 million inactive workers in the private sector, inactive public sector workers, who number 404,000, received $10.5 billion during the 1990s. That means that the average retired or unemployed civil servant received $2,188 monthly as compared to an average of $194 for private workers.

As in Margaret Thatcher's Britain, fundamental welfare reform in Brazil came with the rise of a new political figure. Fernando Collor began to dismantle the welfare system soon after his election to the presidency. The funding and quality of welfare services deteriorated to levels never seen in contemporary Brazilian history. Federal funds for health care fell 50 percent. In 1988, the federal welfare system devoted 25 percent of its revenues to health care; in 1990, that number was only 15 percent. In 1993, no funds were allocated. At present, the subnational governments have been left to take up the slack, with differing results throughout Brazil.

The combination of distortions in the distribution of welfare benefits and unavoidable social pressure to expand outlays to the poor caused the Cardoso administration to step up efforts to reduce tax evasion and reform the public pension system. Private employers and state companies (among the worst offenders) were increasingly obligated by federal authorities to pay their share of social welfare contributions. As in the United States, France, and all other countries in South America, the debate over welfare has begun to revolve around the issue of completely or partly privatizing the system. The experiences these other countries have with such ideas may influence Brazil's choices, but the final response will depend on whether state agencies and political parties can refrain from employing welfare as a means of clientelism.

Agrarian Reform

The restructuring of the rural economy in the 1960s and 1970s altered the rural social structure. The growing role of agribusiness created jobs for some segments of the rural working class while it crowded out small landowners. After 1964, various state welfare programs were launched in the agricultural sector: retirement policies for low-income producers, pension plans for rural workers, and financial support to community rural associations. These policies played a prominent role in breaking landowners' political and economic control of the rural population. During the 1970s and 1980s, rural workers were organized into rural unions that received welfare transfers from the state—medical plans, job security, and protection of wages against inflation.

Landownership in Brazil remains concentrated in the hands of only 1 percent of the landowning class. The arable land held by this small group of owners (about 58,000) is equal to the size of Venezuela and Colombia combined. Over 3 million other farmers survive on only 2 percent of the country's land. An additional 4.5 million Brazilians are farm laborers or squatters who own no land. In the 1980s and 1990s, several landless peasant movements grabbed headlines by sanctioning illegal land invasions and coming to blows with rural landowners and police. Among the most important of these groups, the Landless Workers' Movement (*Movimento dos Sem-Terra,* or MST) attracted the most attention by seizing some 1.38 million acres of land.

The Cardoso administration responded to these problems by expropriating some unproductive estates and settling 186,000 families on them. Substantial sums were set aside to provide financial support and the placement of additional rural families. However, these efforts fell far short of providing a lasting solution to rural poverty. Brazil continues to lack true agrarian reform.

Any serious effort to address rural poverty will affect urban poverty. Through rural-to-urban migration, the landless poor have swelled the rings of poverty that surround Brazil's major cities. During the 1950s and 1960s, the growth of industry in the south and southeast enticed millions to migrate to the states of São Paulo, Minas Gerais, and Rio de Janeiro in the hopes of finding new economic opportunities. The rapidity of rural-to-urban migration was striking. In the 1960s, over 13.8 million people (about 36 percent of the rural population in 1960) migrated to the cities of the south and southeast. In 1970, 17 million (approximately 42.2 percent of the rural population in 1970) moved from the countryside to the city. It took migrations in the United States eight decades to reach the same level of migrants as went from rural to urban areas in Brazil during the 1960s and 1970s. By the early 1980s, 68 percent of Brazil's population was living in urban areas. Between 1960 and 1980, rural-to-urban migration accounted for 58 percent of urban population growth.

The flood of migrants to urban areas and the growth of urban populations created terrible social problems. The pressures on Brazilian cities for basic services such as sanitation, education, and transportation soon overwhelmed the budgets of municipalities and state governments. Poor people were left to their own devices. Squatters soon took government land, settling on the outskirts of the major cities. Millions of these *descamisados* ("shirtless ones") built shelter out of cardboard, wood from dumps, and blocks of mortar and brick. Huge shantytowns called *favelas* sprang up around cities like Rio and São Paulo.

Regional disparities in income worsened during this period. The military governments addressed this problem by transferring revenues from the industrialized south and southeast to the poor north and northeast, where many of their supporters were based. The federal government subsidized communication and transportation in the poorer regions and created new state agencies to implement regional developmental projects. These policies had mixed results. The contribution of poor regions to GDP increased. The growth rate of the central and western regions was spurred on by agribusiness activities, mineral exploration, and financial services. The economic gap between regions narrowed, but social and income disparities within the underdeveloped regions increased.[25] Industrialization in the poorer regions was capital intensive and therefore labor saving but did not create jobs. Only the most skilled workers in these regions benefited from these changes. Poor agricultural management, ecological destruction, the murder of native Brazilians due to the need to expropriate land for mining and agriculture, and corruption all weakened the distributive effect of these policies.

Today, the northern and northeastern regions remain much poorer than those in the south and southeast. Whereas 15 percent of the population in the southeast subsist under the poverty line, more than 50 percent of the inhabitants of the northeast are below that marker. The life expectancy of a northeasterner—fifty-eight years—is nine years below that of a resident of São Paulo state (sixty-seven years) and fifteen years below that of a resident of Rio Grande do Sul (seventy-three years).[26]

The shrinking labor market for unskilled workers, the rapidity of rural-to-urban migration, and the regional disparities that add to poverty have all worked against the equalization of income distribution in Brazil. Compared with other developing countries, including Mexico and India, Brazil has the worst structure of income distribution in the world (see Table 3).

Brazil and the International Political Economy

As the financing needs of state-led industrialization outstripped the resources of the national development bank and domestic bankers, the deepening of ISI required Brazil to pursue international sources of credit. During the late 1960s and the 1970s, private lenders were eager to provide loans to Brazil and other fast-growing countries. As a result, Brazil became the largest single debtor country in the developing world.

External events had a hand in creating and then managing Brazil's external debt. By the end of the 1970s, the world economy had been hit with two oil

***Favelas* in Rio de Janeiro.** *Source:* © Marc Valdecantos.

Table 3

Governing the Economy: Brazilian Income Distribution in Comparative Perspective

Country	Year	Percentage of Total Income Received			
		10% Richest	20% Richest	40% Poorest	20% Poorest
Peru	1994	34.3%	50.4%	14.1%	4.9%
China	1995	30.9	47.5	15.3	5.5
United States	1994	28.5	45.2	15.3	4.8
India	1994	25.0	39.3	22.2	4.1
France	1989	24.9	40.1	19.9	7.2
Britain	1986	24.7	39.8	19.9	7.1
Brazil	1995	47.9	64.2	8.2	2.5
Chile	1994	46.1	61.0	10.1	3.5
Mexico	1992	39.2	55.3	11.9	4.1
Germany	1989	22.6	37.1	22.5	9.0
Poland	1992	22.1	36.6	23.1	9.3

Source: World Bank, *World Development Report 1998/99* (Washington, D.C.: World Bank, 1998), 198–199.

price shocks that sent inflation rates soaring in the United States and other industrialized countries. Many of these countries also held Brazilian debt. As the central banks in Europe and the Federal Reserve in the United States ratcheted interest rates upward to force prices back down, Brazil's interest payments soared.[27]

After Mexico declared a moratorium on interest payments in 1982, private investors began to shun Brazil and other Latin American debtors. During the 1980s, the so-called Lost Decade of slow growth and debt crisis, the IMF and the World Bank became important suppliers of badly needed credit. But only debtors who promised to take concrete steps to reduce inflation, open their domestic markets to foreign competition, promote exports, and privatize state industries were eligible for help.

Brazil, along with Argentina and Peru, rejected these conditions. The Sarney government refused to implement the free-market policies demanded by the international financial institutions. In 1987, his government took the ultimate gamble in resisting creditors by declaring a moratorium on debt repayment, a move that sent a signal to investors that Brazil would control its own reform agenda on its own terms. The moratorium, however, did not last. It was lifted a few months later under intense pressure from the international

financial community. Opposition to the moratorium within the country was also great among the business community, which feared that such aggressive action would scare off foreign investors and ruin the country's already tattered credit rating.

Collor reversed course. Partly in response to pressure from international creditors and partly in recognition that Sarney's alternative policies had failed, he agreed to put Brazil on the path of free-market policies. The Collor administration invoked both macroeconomic reforms to bring down inflation and reduce balance-of-payments deficits and structural adjustment policies to liberalize the domestic market, privatize state enterprises, and deregulate the economy. Although Collor's anti-inflation plans failed, his structural reforms provided a crucial catalyst for freeing up the economy from layers of bureaucratic red tape and inefficiency. These domestic changes were reflected externally as Collor began to normalize relations between Brazil and the multilateral agencies, especially the IMF.

The liberalization of markets opened Brazilian industry to higher degrees of foreign competition. As a result, the competitiveness of domestic firms has emerged as a core problem. Brazilian industrial productivity reached its lowest levels in 1992, when, on a list of fifty countries, Brazil was ranked forty-ninth, just ahead of Pakistan. One 1997 study showed that the overall productivity of Brazilian industry runs at only 27 percent of the U.S. level.[28] Although productivity levels improved by 7 percent after 1992, inherent inefficiencies caused by poor infrastructure, untrained labor, and lack of access to technology and capital continue to create obstacles to higher growth. The average Brazilian worker has only six years of schooling, half as much as the average worker in Japan or the United States. These problems undermine the rationale of IMF-style free-market policies, since they suggest that free markets alone cannot guarantee the country's growth.

How Brazil will fare in an increasingly interconnected and competitive global marketplace will also depend on its external political relations. During the 1980s, Brazil engaged in numerous conflicts with the United States over steel exports (one of Brazil's most export-competitive industries), computer hardware, and patent protection for multinational companies operating in Brazil. Washington threatened to slap protective tariffs on Brazilian products in retaliation. The political climate changed during the administrations of George H. W. Bush and Bill Clinton, when international free-trade accords, such as the North American Free Trade Agreement (NAFTA), received the support of both Washington and most Latin American governments. During the Summit of the Americas in Miami in December 1994, the leaders of the United States, Central America, the Caribbean (except Cuba), and South America agreed to form a Free Trade Area of the Americas (FTAA) by the year 2005. Several years later, Cardoso's skepticism about the schedule for FTAA's implementation and the nature of the agreement became apparent. At the Quebec summit of FTAA signatories in 2001, Brazil criticized growing U.S. protectionism, a view that was confirmed in 2002 when President George W. Bush imposed sweeping tariffs on steel, a major Brazilian export to the United States. Brazil is also more committed to its own subhemispheric group, the Market of the South (MERCOSUL), although enthusiasm for this common market was tempered by the

collapse in 2001–2002 of the Argentine economy, Brazil's key trade partner in MERCOSUL. (See "Global Connection: Governing the Economy in a World of States: MERCOSUL.")

Brazil's degree of commitment to the international free-trade system will depend on the endurance of the country's domestic reform agenda. If inflation threatens to return, Brazil's leaders have already shown that they would be willing to sacrifice MERCOSUL and other commitments to free trade. For example, an attempt to stave off growing trade deficits that threatened the Real Plan in 1995 forced Brazilian policy-makers to increase tariffs on imported automobiles from 32 percent to 70 percent, an act that immediately angered Argentina. Although such disagreements are regularly resolved through MERCOSUL's dispute resolution mechanisms, a larger crisis could push Brazil to sacrifice these commitments on the altar of inflation control.

Domestic and international opposition to globalization are also factors to consider. When delegates from the advanced capitalist countries and largest global firms convened the World Economic Forum in Davos, Switzerland, in 2000, globalization opponents, led by Lula da Silva and including famous activists such as the French farm leader Jose Bové, gathered in Porto Alegre, Rio Grande do Sul, for the World Social Forum. The instability of developing country economies and Brazil's own persistent problems of growing external debt and the need to periodically negotiate bailouts with the IMF fueled the attacks on "unbridled globalization" at Porto Alegre. Cardoso and other leaders were burned in effigy as delegates accused them of betraying progressive ideas, abandoning social redistribution, and embracing neoliberalism, a label commonly used to refer to reforms meant to reduce the intervention of the state in the market. Moreover, Cardoso seemed to symbolize all of these attributes as a former intellectual in the "dependency school" now turned neoliberal reformer. It is still an open question whether Cardoso's successor in the presidency will embrace the ideas of Davos or Porto Alegre.

Global Connection: *Governing the Economy in a World of States: MERCOSUL*

After several years of negotiating the Treaty of Asunción, Brazil, Argentina, Paraguay, and Uruguay inaugurated MERCOSUL, a regional common market group, in January 1995. Under MERCOSUL (Mercosur in Spanish), Brazil and its trade partners agreed to reduce tariffs on imports from signatories gradually until 2006, when the 10,000 items that make up the tariff listings of all four countries must conform to a common external tariff (CET) regime.

During the negotiations over the Treaty of Asunción between March 26, 1991, and MERCOSUL's inauguration, trade among the partners increased from 8 to 20 percent, making the case for a subhemispheric common market stronger. After a rough start due to the Mexican peso crisis, the signatories reaffirmed their commitment to forge the common market. Efforts to remove gradually tariff protections and nontariff protections such as regulations that slow the flow of trade, proceeded with few disruptions.

At the center of MERCOSUL's evolution is the long list of products that the CET targets. However, the signatories are allowed to exclude up to 300 items (399 in Paraguay) as exceptions to the CET. The partners also agreed to numerous dispute-resolution mechanisms to avoid conflicts that might threaten the free-trade group.

MERCOSUL is only the latest in a list of common market schemes in Latin America. In 1960, the Latin American Association of Free Trade (ALALC) initiated a process for forming a common market in twelve years. Although this goal was unfulfilled because of persistent differences among the group's members, intraregional trade increased from 7.7 percent in 1960 to 13.8 percent in 1980. Subhemispheric common market groups unconnected to ALALC also emerged as the Andean Group in 1969 (Bolivia, Colombia, Ecuador, and Venezuela) and the Central American Common Market in 1960 (Costa Rica, Guatemala, El Salvador, Honduras, and Nicaragua). ALALC was replaced in 1980 with the Latin American Integration Association (ALADI). Unlike ALALC's mission of forming a common market, ALADI's goal was to foster the formation of preferential trade agreements among subhemispheric groups. These efforts received their most important boost soon after the administration of George H. W. Bush delivered its Enterprise for the Americas Initiative (EAI) in 1990, a plan of lofty goals for hemispheric economic integration, which are being implemented now through the Free Trade Area of the Americas (FTAA). Soon after the EAI was announced, the existing

regional groups and a new wave of other groups formed preferential organizations. Besides MERCOSUL, the most important of these was the North American Free Trade Agreement (NAFTA), initiated on January 1, 1994.

MERCOSUL differs from NAFTA in several ways. First, it is designed to be a common market among developing countries and not, as NAFTA is, a tripartite free-trade area organized to reduce tariffs primarily across the U.S.-Mexico border. Second, MERCOSUL can evolve in ways unimagined in NAFTA, such as the creation of a common currency. Finally, MERCOSUL can and has negotiated free-trade agreements with other global blocks such as the European Union (EU). This gives these four developing countries more leverage on the international level. Mexico's interests as a developing country are arguably not given the same priority by its trade partners in NAFTA.

MERCOSUL also differs markedly from the EU. Because the EU is a supranational organization, its members shift important sovereign areas of policy such as commercial, competition, increasingly justice and home affairs, and for the members of the euro zone, monetary policy to Brussels. The signatories of MERCOSUL do not envision more than a commercial and perhaps monetary agreement, and all this is negotiated multilaterally. MERCOSUL does not have an executive body such as the EU Commission that regulates the behavior of members. It has dispute resolution mechanisms, but nothing like the European Court of Justice whose decisions are binding on EU members.

Like its predecessors, MERCOSUL was a product and a cause of increased commercial integration among its signatories. Since its creation, MERCOSUL has contributed to a threefold increase in trade among its members. The common market, however, is in dire straits now in the wake of the Argentine financial crisis and continued economic instability in Brazil, Uruguay, and Paraguay. MERCOSUL is also at a crossroads regarding the role it will play in the continuing FTAA process. President Lula da Silva will likely attempt to use Brazil's leadership within MERCOSUL to extract concessions from Washington on the type and pacing of trade liberalization in the hemisphere.

Source: Lia Valls Pereira, "Tratado de Assunção: Resultados e Perspectivas," in Antônio Salazar P. Brandão and Lia Valls Pereira, eds., *Mercosul: Perspectivas da Integração* (Rio de Janeiro: Fundação Getúlio Vargas, 1996), 11.

Section ❸ Governance and Policy-Making

Organization of the State

The institutions of the Brazilian state have changed significantly since independence. Even so, a number of institutional legacies have endured and continue to shape Brazilian politics. The most important is the centralization of state authority in the executive. Paradoxically, a second legacy is the decentralized federal structure of the Brazilian state. The constitution of 1988 attempted to construct a new democratic order but left these contradictory tendencies in place. The president retained the authority to legislate on social and economic matters, but new powers governing the implementation of these policies were devolved to the state and municipal governments.

As a result, the 1988 constitution was simultaneously the focus of much hope and intense attack. It was to be the governing document for the new democracy, but it became an instrument used to confound political and economic reform. As a product of political horse-trading, it failed to provide a coherent vision of how institutions should be structured and what functions they should have. The separation of powers remains ill-defined in Brazil. Instead, ad hoc and stopgap arrangements continue to determine the boundaries of official authority, while informal relations and understandings play a major role in the interpretation of law.

Some generalizations about the organization of the Brazilian state can be made. First, the church and state are officially separated. The Catholic Church never controlled any portion of the state apparatus or directly influenced national politics as it did in other Catholic countries, including Spain. This does not mean, however, that the Catholic Church plays no role in Brazilian politics (see Section 4).

Second, Brazil has a presidential system of government. The directly elected president is the head of state, head of government, and commander in chief of the armed forces. The Brazilian state has traditionally placed vast power in the hands of the executive. Although the executive is one of three branches of government (the legislature and the judiciary being the other two), Brazilian presidents have traditionally been less bound by judicial and legislative constraints than their European or North American counterparts. Brazilian constitutions have granted the executive more discretion than the other branches in enforcing laws or in making policy. The legislature and the judiciary historically have played secondary roles.

The Brazilian state does not have the checks and balances of the U.S. government system. It differs also from the semipresidentialism of France, in which the president, although dominant over the legislature and judiciary, faces broader constraints in the possibility of having to work with a hostile parliamentary majority. Although the French prime minister is appointed by the executive and is not elected by the legislature as in other parliamentary systems, he or she is chosen from the party with the majority of elected representatives in parliament, which is not necessarily the president's party. Moreover, the French party system is more organized and less fragmented than its counterpart in Brazil, making the legislature more efficient and capable of checking executive actions.

Brazil's executive and the bureaucracy manage most of the policy-making and implementation functions of government. Both the federal legislature and the state governments look to the president and, in economic matters, to the minister of the economy for leadership on policy. The heads of the key agencies of the economic bureaucracy—the ministers of the economy and of planning, the president of the Central Bank, and the head of the national development bank—have more discretion over the details of policy than the president does. Although some Brazilian presidents have delegated less to bureaucratic agencies, recent presidents have had little choice but to delegate, given the growing complexity of economic and social policy. Ultimate authority nevertheless remains in the hands of the president, who may replace his ministers.

Although the Brazilian president is the dominant player among the three branches of government, the powers of the legislature and the judiciary are becoming stronger. Since the transition to democratic rule in 1985, these institutions have become critical to democracy. The 1988 constitution gave many oversight functions to the legislature and judiciary, so that much presidential discretion in economic and social policy is now subject to approval by either the legislature or the judiciary, or both. This gives these branches of government some independence and leverage over the presidency, although this power is not often employed effectively. Centralizing traditions are still strong in Brazil, making the obstacles to the deconcentration of executive power enormous.

A third generalization that may be offered on the Brazilian state is that it is decentralized. Like Germany, India, and the United States, the Brazilian state has a federal structure. The country's twenty-six states are divided into 5,500 municipal governments. Most of the country's presidents have relied on subnational bases of power to stay in office. The presidents of the Old Republic and even Getúlio Vargas counted on the support of local clientelist political machines led by self-interested governors and mayors.

With the transition to democracy, these "barons of the federation," as one study calls them, became a crucial source of political support for legislators as well as presidents.[29] By controlling indispensable reservoirs of patronage through their powers of appointment and spending, governors and even some mayors can wield extraordinary influence. In recent years, some of the harsher elements of reform legislation have been jettisoned to mollify this subnational constituency.

Seen as a whole, political decentralization, which was accelerated with the constitution of 1988, has further fragmented the Brazilian polity. At the same time, some subnational governments have become an important source of innovative policy-making.[30] Average Brazilian citizens have more access to their municipal and state governments than they do to their federal representatives, which suggests that decentralization may eventually strengthen democracy by making political elites more accountable to their local constituencies.

The Executive

A majority of delegates to the 1987 National Constituent Assembly that drafted the new democratic constitution favored the creation of a parliamentary system. President Sarney, who did not want to see his powers reduced, used his support among the governors to lobby against the parliamentary option. The best he could do was force the members of the assembly to defer the issue to a plebiscite in 1993. Yet the plebiscite, envisioned by the constitution's framers as the climactic event that would determine Brazil's political structure, ended by giving a stamp of approval to the existing presidential system. With virtually no experience in parliamentary politics, Brazilians opted for presidentialism.

Why is there no parliamentarism in Brazil? For many Brazilians, governmental effectiveness has historically been identified with presidential supremacy. For the poor and for organized sectors such as workers and professionals, the presidency has always been the focus of their demands for improvements in living conditions and wages. As for the armed forces, few generals could imagine being led by a prime minister and a legislature. Although not a constitutional requirement, all Brazilian presidents, and most elected officials, have been men.

In 1993, widespread suspicion of legislative politics was fanned by the argument of the campaign to retain presidentialism that the parliamentary option was little more than a trick to "take the right to vote away from the people." The concept of a parliamentary system that would allow a prime minister to be elected by legislative elites and not directly by the citizenry seemed contrary to what Brazilians had fought for during the long struggle for democracy. Brazilians did not want to lose the ultimate check on the presidency: direct elections by voters every four years. This principle has become even more important as the Cardoso presidency gained the constitutional right to allow the president to run for a second term. Popular elections will now present a crucial test for presidents wishing to pursue their agendas for another four years.

If parliamentary government seemed a far-off goal, rules designed to rein in the power of the federal executive still found their way into the 1988 constitution. In part as a reaction to the extreme centralization of executive authority during military rule, the delegates restored some of the congressional prerogatives that had existed prior to 1964 and granted new ones. The congress gained oversight over economic policy and the right of consultation on executive appointments. Executive decrees, which allowed the president to legislate directly, were abolished. In their place "provisional measures" (also known as "emergency measures") were established, which preserved the president's power to legislate for thirty days, at the end of which congress can pass, reject, or allow the provisional law to expire.

President Sarney and his successors got around this restriction by reissuing their "provisional measures" indefinitely, yet to become law, they would need to survive a two-thirds vote of both houses of the congress. Finally, the 1988 constitution limited the president to a single term, a provision common to Latin American constitutions. In 1997, however, Cardoso succeeded in passing a constitutional amendment through congress that removed the no-reelect rule, allowing him and twenty-two governors to run again in 1998. This expansion of presidential power was later met with a restriction on the power to reissue provisional measures, which both houses of congress passed in 2001.

Despite these new constraints, Brazilian presidents were still able to use emergency measures with considerable success because of the sorry state of the economy. Given such crisis conditions, how could congress deny the president the right to railroad through much-needed reform legislation? Some presidents articulated such arguments with great frequency. Collor, for example, severely abused these powers. In his first year in office, Collor handed down 150 emergency measures. Technically, this meant that the country experienced a crisis situation every forty-eight hours.[31] Worse still, the Supreme Tribunal, the highest court in Brazil, did little to curb this obvious abuse of constitutional authority by the president. The use of presidential discretionary power has only reinforced the powers of the executive to legislate.[32] Even with the restrictions passed in 2001, over 80 percent of all legislation originates in the executive branch.

The president also retains extremely valuable powers of appointment over the huge Brazilian bureaucracy, particularly at the ministerial level. Among them are broad powers to select and dismiss close associates and select ministers for the armed forces according to the merit system prevailing in their respective branches. For most other positions, the president usually appoints ministers from groups of his long-time cronies and collaborators or from any of the existing parties. Although these appointees are not as cohesive a group as the presidential *camarillas* in Mexico, the close-knit and often personal networks binding the Mexican president and his chief ministers and advisors, this comparison serves to illustrate the importance of personal ties to the president in Brazil. Under the 1988 constitution, the president must negotiate with congress

and some powerful groups (e.g., business associations, labor unions, bar associations) over certain positions in the cabinet, mainly those responsible for economic policy-making. Even so, the power of appointments in Brazil continues to be a source of great influence.

Among the chief cabinet posts, the ministries of Economy (also called Finance during certain administrations) and Planning have had extraordinary influence. Since the beginning of the military governments, the Ministry of Economy has had more authority than any other executive agency of the state. These powers were heightened as a result of the economic problems of the 1980s and the reform agenda of the 1990s. As a result of their control of the federal budget and the details of economic policy, recent ministers of the economy have had levels of authority typical of a prime minister in a parliamentary system. The success of Cardoso in the 1994 presidential campaign was due in large part to his effective performance as Itamar Franco's minister of economy.

The Bureaucracy: State and Semipublic Firms

Bureaucratic agencies and public firms have played key roles in Brazilian economic and political development during the twentieth century. After 1940, the state created a large number of new agencies and public enterprises. Many of these entities were allowed to accumulate their own debt and plan development projects without undue influence from the central ministries or politicians. Public firms became a key part of the triple alliance of state, foreign, and domestic capital that governed the state-led model of development. Yet it was the state that dominated this alliance. By 1981, ten of the top twenty-five enterprises in Brazil were owned by the federal government, and eight others were owned by state governments. Public expenditures as a share of GDP increased from 16 percent in 1947 to more than 32 percent in 1969, far higher than in any other Latin American country except socialist Cuba.[33]

Much of this spending (and the huge debt that financed it) was concentrated on development projects, many of gigantic proportions. Key examples include the world's largest hydroelectric plant, Itaipú; Petrobrás's petroleum processing centers; and steel mills such as the gargantuan National Steel Company in Volta Redonda, Rio de Janeiro; and Vale do Rio Doce, a public firm with interests in sectors as diverse as mining, transport, paper, and textiles. Under the past three military governments (Médici, Geisel, and Figueiredo), dozens of other projects were completed, including the trans-Amazonian highway, the Tucuruí hydroelectric plants, the Açominas metallurgy park, and the National Nuclear Reactor Program. These and hundreds of more modest projects accounted for much of the country's industrial production. On the eve of the debt crisis in 1982, the top thirty-three projects, including those just listed, absorbed US$88 billion in external debt, employed 1.5 million people, and added $47 billion to the GDP.

Managing the planning and finance of these projects required enormous skill. Several public agencies were responsible, but the National Bank for Economic and Social Development (*Banco Nacional de Desenvolvimento Economico e Social,* or BNDES) stands out as an important coordinator. Founded by Vargas in the early 1950s, the BNDES played a key role in channeling public funds to industrial projects. Among the bank's greatest achievements was the creation of an automobile sector based on subsidized public steel; foreign assemblers such as Ford, General Motors, and Volkswagen; and domestic suppliers of parts and labor. Under President Juscelino Kubitschek, the BNDES implemented an industrial policy in automobiles called the Plan of Goals (*Plano de Metas*), which coordinated domestic and international resources to create the largest automobile industry in Latin America.[34]

The experience of the BNDES demonstrated that despite Brazil's clientelist legacies, the Brazilian bureaucracy could function effectively. Meritocratic advancement and professional recruitment granted these agencies some autonomy from political manipulation. Such agencies were considered islands of efficiency in a state apparatus characterized by patronage and corruption.[35]

Other state and semipublic firms, however, were rife with clientelism. Civilian and military leaders often appointed their supporters as the heads of these enterprises, positions with quite generous salary and retirement packages. Many public firm managers took advantage of their positions to dole out government contracts to associates and even to their own companies in the private sector.

The fiscal crisis of the 1980s had put severe strains on the entire economic bureaucracy, but some things failed to change. The 1988 constitution did not alter significantly the concentration of power in the economic bureaucracy that made developmentalism with clientelism possible. In fact, the new constitution reinforced certain bureaucratic monopolies by codifying them as rights. For example, the state's control over petroleum, natural gas, the exploration of minerals, nuclear energy, and telecommunications was protected constitutionally. These sectors could not be privatized, much less sold to foreign governments or multinational companies.

What the writers of the new constitution did do in response to the fiscal crisis was place new restraints on the activity of state-directed industries. The fiscal independence of state firms was curtailed with restrictions on the amount of debt they could incur. The constitution imposed additional obstacles to the creation of public firms, including the requirement that congress approve any new state enterprises proposed by the executive branch.

Some of the constitutional protections of the public firms lasted only a few years. After his election in 1989, Fernando Collor began a sweeping reform of Brazil's public bureaucracy, beginning with the privatization of large public firms in steel, chemicals, and mining. In 1990, his government launched the National Destatization Program (*Programa Nacional de Destatização,* PND). Under the PND, more than US$20 billion in public firms were sold ($8.5 billion in the steel sector alone). Although the program slowed under the Franco administration, the selloffs of the steel firms were completed. The Cardoso administration went even further. The government convinced the congress to amend the constitution to remove the public monopoly on petroleum refining, telecommunications, and infrastructure, making these sectors available for auction. Electricity distribution, cellular phone bands, and the octopus-like structure of Vale were put up for privatization. In 1998, much of the public telecommunication sector was privatized, bringing in about $25 billion.

Paradoxically, the agency at the center of the privatization process in Brazil is the BNDES, which is also the agency most responsible for developmentalism. Faced with the fiscal crisis of the 1980s, BNDES managers adopted a new perspective on the state's role in the economy. Instead of targeting industries and spending large sums to promote them, its new mission was to provide financing to productivity-enhancing investments such as new technology and labor retraining, outlays that promise to make firms soon to be privatized and already privatized more competitive in international markets.[36] As a result, the economic bureaucracy in Brazil continues to play a crucial role in the country's development.

The Military and the Police

The military is another significant arm of the state. Like many other South American militaries, the Brazilian armed forces retain substantial independence from civilian presidents and legislators. Brazil has suffered numerous coups; those in 1930 and 1964 were critical junctures, while others brought in caretaker governments that eventually ceded to civilian rule. Although the military's grip on power was never as tight as in Nigeria during the Abacha regime (1993–1998), the generals have maintained influence in Brazilian politics, blocking policies they do not like and lobbying on behalf of those they favor.

The military's participation in Brazilian politics became more defined following the transition to democracy. Several laws governing areas of policy-making affecting the armed forces gave the military broad prerogatives to "guarantee internal order" and to play a "tutelary role" in civilian government. During the Sarney administration, members of the armed forces retained cabinet-level rank in areas of importance to the military, such as the ministries of the armed forces and the nuclear program. Military officers also kept middle- and lower-level positions in public firms and bureaucratic agencies. Most important, the armed forces were successful in obtaining amnesty for human rights abuses committed during the preceding authoritarian regime.

In an effort to professionalize the armed forces and keep them in the barracks, the Collor government slashed the military budget and replaced the top generals with officers who had few or no connections to the authoritarian regime and were committed to civilian leadership. Collor's reforms were helped by the decline of the country's arms industry, which lost key markets for ordnance, tanks, and guns in the Middle East during the 1980s. These industries had previously supplied capital and armaments to the Brazilian armed forces, keeping them autonomous from civilian control. The collapse and, in some cases, privatization of these military industries gave civilians more control over the generals.[37] One recent test of civilian authority was the successful removal of the commandant of the Brazilian Air Force, Brigadier Walter Werner Braüer, for alleged involvement in drug trafficking, money laundering, and organized crime activities. Despite public demonstrations by air force officers supporting Braüer, congressional investigations continued, and the general was dismissed at the end of 1999.

Police enforcement primarily falls into the domain of the state governments. The state police consists of two forces: the civil police force, which acts as an investigative unit and is not completely uniformed, and the uniformed military police force, which maintains order. The military police are not formally under the command of the military; the constitution stipulates that in the event of a national emergency, they can be called to perform active military service. Like the military, the military police are governed by a separate judicial system.

During the 1990s, urban crime became one of the most important political issues facing the country. Perhaps the most telling indicator of the rising level of violence is the fact that over fifty mayors were assassinated in Brazil between 1990 and 2000. Murders, kidnappings, rapes, and violent robberies are the talk of nightly news programs, and these subjects often dominate citizens' lists of chief concerns.

The specter of criminal violence has shocked Brazilians into voting for politicians who promise them better police security. Yet as more attention has focused on the use of police resources, Brazilians have learned that these forces themselves are often part of the problem. Despite official oversight of police authorities, in practice the military and civil police forces in many cities of the northeast, in São Paulo, and in Rio de Janeiro often act extrajudicially. Cases of arbitrary detention, torture, corruption, and systematic killings by Brazilian police have received much international attention. Human rights investigations have found that off-duty police officers are regularly hired by merchants and assorted thugs to kill street urchins whom they accuse of thievery. One study in Rio de Janeiro between 1993 and 1996 showed that police officers preferred the use of deadly force, shooting to kill rather than to disable.[38] The majority of victims were shot in the shoulders or the head; in 40 of the 697 cases, the victims were shot in the back of the head in gangland execution style. The victims were mostly young black men and boys and had no criminal records whatsoever. Other studies have shown that at least 10 percent of the homicides in Rio de Janeiro are committed by the police. In São Paulo, police violence is just as bad. In 1992 alone, the São Paulo police killed 1,470 people, accounting for one-third of all homicides in the state.[39]

The federal police force is a small unit of approximately 3,000 people. It operates as a combined U.S. Federal Bureau of Investigation, Secret Service, Drug Enforcement Agency, and Immigration and Naturalization Service. Under the authority of the executive, the federal police are responsible for providing security to public officials, cracking down on drug rings, administering customs regulations, and investigating federal crimes. The demands placed on this single agency have caused some Brazilian politicians to propose that the federal police be split up into more specialized units, as in the U.S. system.

Other State Institutions

The Judiciary

The Brazilian judiciary is composed of a network of state courts, which has jurisdiction over state matters, and a federal court system, not unlike the one in the United States, which maintains jurisdiction over federal crimes. A supreme court (the Supreme Federal Tribunal), similar in jurisdiction to the U.S. Supreme Court but lacking authority over the other branches of government, acts as the final arbiter of court cases. The eleven justices are appointed by the president and confirmed by an absolute majority of the Senate. The Superior Court of Justice, with thirty-three sitting justices, operates under the Supreme Federal Tribunal as an appeals court. Matters requiring interpretation of the constitution go to the Supreme Federal Tribunal. The military maintains its own court system. Most judges in the Brazilian judicial system serve for life.

The judiciary is designed to adjudicate political conflicts as well as civil and social conflicts. The Electoral Supreme Tribunal (*Tribunal Supremo Electoral,* TSE) has exclusive responsibility for the organization and oversight of all issues related to voting. The seven-member TSE is composed of three justices elected from the members of the Supreme Federal Tribunal, two from the Superior Court of Justice, and two nominated by the president from a group of six attorneys of notable quality that are selected by the Supreme Federal Tribunal. The seven justices on the TSE serve for two years and they have the power to investigate charges of political bias by public employees, file criminal charges against persons violating electoral laws, and scrutinize and validate electoral results. In addition to these constitutional provisions, under electoral law and its own regulations, the TSE monitors the legal compliance of electoral campaigns and executive neutrality in campaigns. The integrity of the tribunal in the conduct of elections has remained very high, making fraud relatively rare in national elections. The TSE is assisted in this process by a system of regional electoral courts that oversee local elections.

As in the rest of Latin America, penal codes established by legislation govern the powers of judges. This makes the judiciary less flexible than its North American counterparts, which operate on case law, but it provides a more effective barrier against judicial activism—the tendency of the courts to render broad interpretations of the law.

Since the 1940s the judicial branch of government in Brazil in theory has been highly independent from the executive. In practice, especially under authoritarian rule, the judiciary has been dictated to by the executive branch. President Collor exercised sweeping executive powers without much judicial review. The Supreme Federal Tribunal was viewed as ceding significant extraconstitutional authority by not challenging Collor's rule by fiat. A year after Collor's anti-inflation asset freeze, some of the country's most renowned jurists decided to oppose further blockage of financial assets on the grounds that it was unconstitutional. Although their opposition came late, it began a national debate that continues to this day about the president's "emergency measures."

In recent years, the judiciary has been severely criticized for its perceived unresponsiveness to Brazil's social problems and the persistent corruption in the lower courts. These problems are particularly apparent in rural areas, where impoverished defendants are often denied the right to a fair trial by powerful landowners, who have undue influence over judges and procedures. Children are especially victimized; courts have refused to hear cases prosecuting those who profit from child prostitution, pornography, and murder of street urchins.

Official corruption in the judiciary became an important and high-profile issue in 2000 when a federal judge, Nicolau dos Santos, who was accused of embezzling US$90 million from official coffers, remained a fugitive for 227 days until he turned himself in. The ongoing investigation revealed a network of official corruption leading up to the ministerial level in some cases.

A more everyday indicator of systemic corruption is the difficulty citizens face in prosecuting the police. In the state of Rio de Janeiro, between January 1996 and July 1997, 68 percent of cases in military court involving the police were retired without a hearing because of insufficient evidence (which is often destroyed by the police) or because of the police's favorite excuse: that the defendant was injured or killed "while resisting arrest." Although federal legislation in 1996 granted civil courts jurisdiction over such matters, paradoxically the power to investigate these crimes was left in the hands of the police.

The Supreme Tribunal's reluctance to act on these matters leaves little hope for change in the short term. Judicial reform has thus far focused on speeding up the Supreme Tribunal's judicial review functions, avoiding the more difficult question of restructuring the judiciary to eliminate corruption.

Restructuring of the judiciary will continue to get attention as the 1988 constitution is revised. Proposals for reform include subjecting judges to external control through periodic elections. Members of the judiciary deeply resent and fear such a prospect. They argue that it would push the institution into the kind of partisanship that has marred policy debates on key social and political issues. Others view the structure of the judiciary and its approach to interpreting and implementing laws as the central obstacles to accomplishing policy goals. Like the Brazilian bureaucracy, the judiciary has a complex structure, with multiple jurisdictions at different levels of government. The problems inherent in this complex network of adjudication were made clear during the privatization of Vale, when opposition groups in different states and jurisdictions

were able to use the local courts to create numerous obstacles to the sale.

Subnational Government

The structure of subnational politics in Brazil is not unlike that of other federal systems throughout the world. Each state government consists of a governor; his chief advisers, who also usually lead key secretariats such as economy and planning; and a unicameral legislature, which is often dominated by the supporters of the governor. Governors are elected to four-year terms and, under the 1997 amendment of the 1988 constitution, may run for another term.

State and municipal governments wield tremendous influence in Brazilian politics. Since the days of the Old Republic, governors and mayors have been essential sources of support for presidents and federal legislators. This "politics of the governors" expanded with the transition to democracy. The fact that the 1982 elections created the first opportunity since the inauguration of the military regime for Brazilians to elect their governors directly made these subnational politicians crucial standard-bearers of the transition. It lent legitimacy to the governors' campaign to decentralize fiscal resources in the form of taxes and federal transfers.

The 1988 constitution provided much of what the governors and mayors wanted. First, the states and municipalities were promised a larger share of tax revenues. At the same time, however, the governors and mayors were successful in deflecting Brasília's attempts to devolve additional spending responsibilities to subnational government, particularly in the areas of education, health, and infrastructure. The governors also proved successful in protecting state banks from a major overhaul, which was greatly needed given that these financial institutions continued to fund irresponsible subnational spending by accumulating huge debts that the federal government agreed to roll over.

During the Collor administration, the federal government began to regain much of the fiscal authority it had lost to the states and municipalities. The Central Bank made good on its threats to intervene in bankrupt state banks and privatize them. The federal government also refused to roll over state debt without a promise of reform, including the privatization of money-losing utility companies. The Cardoso administration required states and municipalities to finance a larger share of social spending, including education and health care. At the same time, new legislation empowered Brasília to claim more discretionary authority over fiscal transfers and tax revenues that had previously devolved to subnational governments.

Despite these efforts, Brazilian presidents must continue to negotiate the terms of reform with governors as much as with the congress. Because they can now run for reelection, the governors and their political machines will represent an even more consistent element in national politics. The October 1998 elections proved the staying power of incumbent governors: fifteen of the twenty-two incumbents who ran were reelected, a turnover rate well below the high levels in the legislature (see Section 4).

Although most subnational politics are still preoccupied with the distribution of political favors in return for fiscal rewards, certain governors and mayors have devised innovative solutions to Brazil's social and economic problems. One recent study of the state of Ceará in the poor northern region has demonstrated that even the most underdeveloped subnational governments can produce important policies to promote industrial investment, employment, and social services.[40] Such an example is a useful reminder that not all states and municipalities are the same in a federal system. Much depends on the interests and quality of political and bureaucratic leadership.

The Policy-Making Process

Although policy-making continues to be fluid and ambiguous in Brazil, certain domains of policy are clearly demarcated. Foreign policy, for example, is exclusively within the purview of the executive branch. Political parties and the congress in general still have only inconsistent power over investment policies. Because most legislation originates in the executive branch, bureaucratic agencies have retained command over the details of social and economic policies.

The process of making policy in Brazil can be characterized by one common quality: the tendency of clientelism to inject itself at every stage, from formulation and decision making to implementation. Even when policies are formulated without the undue influence of societal and political actors, implementation is often obstructed or distorted by clientelism. Again, as noted, exceptions exist, but they are only that: exceptions.[41]

Complex formal and informal networks linking the political executive, key agencies of the bureaucracy, and private interests tend to be the chief players in clientelist circles. One of Cardoso's contributions to sociology before he became involved in Brazilian politics was his characterization of these clientelistic networks as **bureaucratic rings.** For Cardoso, the Brazilian state is highly permeable, fragmented, and therefore easily colonized by private interests that make alliances with midlevel bureaucratic officers. By shaping public policy to benefit these interests, bureaucrats gain the promise of future employment in the private sector. While in positions of responsibility, bureaucratic rings are ardent defenders of their own interests. Because they are entrenched and well connected throughout the Brazilian bureaucracy, few policies can be implemented without the resources and support of the most powerful bureaucratic rings.

One example of the role of bureaucratic rings is the creation of large development projects. The politics surrounding these decisions were often intense. Governors and mayors wanted lucrative public projects to be placed in their jurisdiction; private contractors yearned for the state's business; and politicians positioned themselves for all the attendant kickbacks, political and pecuniary.[42] Although the days of huge development projects are over, the public sector still formulates policy and allocates resources under the influence of bureaucratic rings.

Among the key sources of influence external to the state is organized business. Unlike business associations in some Asian and West European countries, Brazilian business groups have remained independent of corporatist ties to the state. There is no Brazilian version of the French agricultural association *Fédération Nationale des Syndicats d'Exploitants Agricoles* (FNSEA) or the para-public institutions of the Federal Republic of Germany. Business associations have also remained aloof from political parties. Brazil has nothing akin to Mexico's National Action Party (*Partido Acción Nacional,* or PAN), a party that claims to represent a large portion of the business class. That does not mean, however, that Brazilian business interests are not organized. Lobbying by Brazilian entrepreneurs is common, and their participation in bureaucratic rings is legendary. Few major economic policies are passed without the input of the Federation of São Paulo Industries (*Federação das Industrias do Estado de São Paulo,* or FIESP). Other business groups, some that have broken off from FIESP, continue to defend their interests energetically as Brazil reforms its economy.

The country's labor confederations and unions have had less consistent access to policy-making. Although unions were once directly organized and manipulated by the corporatist state, they gained autonomy in the late 1970s and the 1980s. From then on, they sought leverage over policy-making through outside channels, such as the link between the *Central Única dos Trabalhadores* (CUT, Workers' Singular Peak Association) and Lula da Silva's Workers' Party. Attempts to bring labor formally into direct negotiations with business and the state have failed. Shortly after assuming power, Sarney initiated talks among business, government, and representatives of the major labor federations. These talks quickly broke down. Widening cleavages within the Brazilian union movement tended to split sectors of organized labor, causing some segments to refuse to be bound by any

agreement. Later, during the Collor administration, a second attempt at tripartite negotiation, called the "sectoral chambers," took place in the São Paulo automotive sector. These talks produced some noteworthy accords, but the chambers did not last because of opposition from the Ministry of Economy and other agencies. These experiences contrast sharply with the legacy of codetermination in Germany and other formulas for maintaining collective bargaining with state mediation in West European countries.

Policy implementation is also highly politicized. Debate and lobbying do not stop in Brazil once laws are enacted. Policy implementation is a subject of perpetual bargaining. One popular phrase, *o jeito brasileiro* ("the Brazilian way"), captures this aspect of Brazilian politics.[43] The Brazilian way is to scoff at the law and find a way around it. If one wants to get something without really paying for it, one asks for a *jeito*. Paradoxically, *jeito* can be the source of great efficiency in Brazilian society, but it carries a heavy price in that the rule of law is not respected. Therefore, reform of the policy-making process will require more than restrictions on clientelism and legislative and judicial oversight of suspected bureaucratic rings. It will require a shift in thinking about the role of law in Brazilian society.

Section ❹ Representation and Participation

Because of urbanization and economic modernization, the Brazilian electorate grew impressively after 1945. Improved literacy and efforts by political parties to expand voter registration helped to increase the number of citizens eligible to vote. Voting rights were granted in 1981 to anyone eighteen or older (but not illiterates) and in 1988 to anyone over age sixteen. As a result of these changes, the percentage of the total population eligible to vote increased from 16.2 percent in 1945 to 60 percent in 1994. The Brazilian electorate stands at 106 million and regularly votes (for example, turnout in the October 2002 presidential vote was 82.2 percent in the first round and 79.5 percent in the second round).

The expansion of the Brazilian electorate coincided with the proliferation of political organizations

and movements dedicated to marshaling popular support. Mass appeal became an important element in campaigns and political alliances. With the return to democracy in the 1980s, newly independent labor unions and special-interest organizations emerged, making new alliances in civil society possible.

Nevertheless, the richness of political organization was restrained by the legacies of state-centered structures of social control. Despite the transition to democracy, state corporatism continued to govern important segments of the Brazilian polity. Some political parties and many of the new social movements and political organizations that helped end the military government lacked staying power. Clientelism continued to fragment the legislature and weaken other democratic institutions.

The Legislature

The 594-member national legislature is bicameral, consisting of an upper house, the Senate with 81 members, and a lower house, the Chamber of Deputies with 513 members. Each state and the federal district elects 3 senators, for a total of 81. Senators are elected by simple majority. Senators serve for eight-year terms and may be reelected without limits. Two-thirds of the Senate is elected at one time, and the remaining one-third is elected four years later. For example, in the elections of 1994, two-thirds of the Senate was renewed. In 1998, the remaining one-third was renewed. Senatorial elections are held concurrently with those for the Chamber of Deputies, which places all of its seats up for election after each four-year cycle. Federal deputies may be reelected without limits. The number of members in the Chamber of Deputies is, in theory, proportional to the population of each state and the federal district. Each state is allowed a minimum of 8 and a maximum of 70 deputies, regardless of population.

Both houses of the legislature have equal authority to make laws. In all cases, one chamber acts as a reviser of legislation passed by the other. Bills go back and forth between houses without going through a conference committee of the two chambers, as is the case in the United States. Once the bill is passed by both houses, the president may sign it into law, reject it as a whole, or reject it in part. The legislature can override a presidential veto with a majority of the vote in both houses during a joint session. Constitutional amendments must survive two three-fifths votes in each house of congress. Amendments may also be passed with an absolute majority in a special unicameral constituent assembly proposed by the president and created by both houses of congress. The Senate retains authority to try the president and other top officials, including the vice president and key ministers and justices, for impeachable offenses. It also has the power to approve appointments to high offices, including justices of the high courts, heads of diplomatic missions, and the directors of the Central Bank.

The formula for determining the proportionality of population to representatives is distorted by complex constitutional rules that favor the most sparsely populated states. Because these states are the most numerous in the federal system, they tend to be overrepresented in the legislature. For example, between 1990 and 1994, the northern region had 4.85 percent of the voters but elected 11.33 percent of the deputies, while the southeastern region had 46 percent of the electorate but only 33.59 percent of the seats. Only 40 percent of the population elects a majority of the Chamber of Deputies. The least populated states are also the poorest and most rural in Brazil. Typically, they have been political bases for conservative landowning interests and, more recently, agribusiness. After 1964 the military cultivated support among conservative rural groups by granting statehood to sparsely populated territories in the north and northeast, reinforcing their overrepresentation in the Chamber. These precedents continued into the democratic period and largely explain why conservative landowners and agribusiness elites maintain positions of great influence in the Brazilian congress.

In contrast to the presidency, the Brazilian legislature has rarely played a dominant role in the country's politics. In part, that is due to the ability of the president to impose policy through corporatism and populism. However, the congress must accept some of the blame. Many senators and deputies are more interested in cultivating and dispensing patronage than in representing and being accountable to the voters. As a result, representatives have never organized their parties or large segments of the population in support of national policy. Only the rarest of exceptions exist to this rule of Brazilian congressional politics.

Legislators view their service primarily as a means to enhance their own income with generous public pensions and through kickbacks earned in the dispensing of political favors. Election to the federal legislature is often used as a steppingstone to even more lucrative, especially executive, posts.[44] After the presidency, the governorships of the industrialized states are the most coveted positions. Appointment to head any of the premier ministries and state firms also ranks high, since these are choice positions from which to distribute and receive favors. Although many members of congress are independently wealthy, most come from the middle or upper middle classes and therefore have much to gain in the economics of public administration.

The congress has largely failed to use the expanded powers granted by the 1988 constitution. Lack of a quorum to vote is a frequent problem, and recently acquired powers have provided greater opportunities for some legislators to practice corruption and backroom dealing, conditions that have helped to break down party loyalties and reinforce the self-serving nature of congressional politics. The many deficiencies of the Brazilian legislature were magnified in recent years by several corruption scandals. In the most serious case, a handful of senators and deputies were accused of embezzling from regional development projects or directly from the national treasury.

One response to legislative corruption has been the use of parliamentary commissions of inquiry to review cases of malfeasance by elected officials. Although these temporary committees have demonstrated some influence, most notably the parliamentary commission of inquiry that investigated Collor and recommended his impeachment, they have not always produced results. The temporary committees work alongside sixteen permanent legislative committees that treat issues as diverse as taxation and human rights. These committees, however, are not nearly as strong as the major committees in the U.S. Congress. Due to the self-interested focus of Brazilian politicians and the related weakness of political parties, legislative committees, both temporary and permanent, often fail to get to the end of an investigation or find solutions to persistent dilemmas in policy.

Political Parties and the Party System

The Brazilian political party system is one of the most mercurial in the world. Party names, party affiliations, and the structure of party alliances are constantly in flux. This is nothing new in Brazilian political history. Like many of the country's current problems, party instability stretches back to the New State of Getúlio Vargas and the centralization of politics in the Brazilian state. State corporatism and populism were hostile to the development of independent party organizations. Political parties, when they did emerge, were created by state managers. Populist redistribution reinforced these tendencies, as workers and the middle class became accustomed to asking what they would receive from a politician in return for support. Except for members of the Communist Party and other extreme organizations, Brazilian voters did not develop a strong sense of political identity linked to established parties.

Personalist loyalties and the distribution of goods and services were more important.

Many of the traditional weaknesses of the party system were reinforced after the transition to democracy, making parties even more anemic. The rules governing the party system made it easier for politicians to switch parties, virtually at will. One of the most important observers of Brazilian democracy, Scott Mainwaring, found that the 559 representatives of the 1987–1991 legislature had belonged to an average of over three parties per politician.[45] Politicians switched parties to increase their access to patronage. Other rules of the electoral system created incentives for politicians to ignore the importance of party labels. Brazil's experience with **proportional representation** (PR), which is used to elect federal and state deputies, is particularly important in this regard. (See "Institutional Intricacies: Proportional Representation.")

Brazil's mix of presidentialism and multiparty democracy creates other problems for the country's system of representation. Given the political fragmentation of the legislature and the weakness of the party system, presidents are unable to maintain majority alliances in congress, a requirement for stability in a multiparty system. In parliamentary systems, the party in power has an absolute majority or stands at the head of an alliance of parties that compose a majority. As a result, the ruling party or alliance can implement a programmatic approach to legislation. By contrast, in Brazil, the president has never been able to maintain a supraparty alliance in congress. More often, Brazilian presidents have attempted to govern above parties, dispensing favors to key congressional politicians to get legislation approved. Alternatively, presidents have not been shy about railroading reform through congress by using their discretionary authorities. As Timothy Power, a scholar of presidential authority in Brazil, has noted, "The [presidential] pen is mightier than the congress."[46]

In the midst of Brazil's confusing party system, a number of political organizations have emerged over the last few years. These parties can be defined ideologically, although discrete categories are often not possible (see Table 4). Brazilian political parties are internally eclectic.

Political parties on the right currently defend neoliberal economic policies designed to shrink the size of the public sector. They support the reduction and

Institutional Intricacies: *Proportional Representation*

Proportional representation was introduced in Brazil in 1932 and was later reaffirmed by the military governments. Unlike Mexico, Britain, and the United States, but like many of the European parliamentary democracies, Brazil is divided into electoral districts that choose more than one representative. The ability to choose more than one representative means that a broader range of voices may be heard in elected offices.

Minority parties can make alliances to pass the threshold of votes needed to achieve representation. Proportional representation may be based on either a closed-list or an open-list system. In a closed-list PR, the party selects the order of politicians, and voters cannot cross party lines. Because voters are effectively choosing the party that best represents them, this system encourages party loyalty among both the electorate and individual politicians. In an open-list PR system, the voters have more discretion and can cross party lines. Brazil's PR system is open-list. Voters cast single ballots for either a party label, which adds to the party's total for determining representation, or for individuals. No names appear on Brazilian ballots, so voters must write in their choices.

Electoral districts for the election of state and federal deputies are entire states in Brazil. In any given election, there may be between six and seventy federal deputies and from twelve to eighty-four state deputies running for office. With few limits on how many individuals and parties may run in the same electoral district, crowded fields discourage party loyalty and emphasize the personal qualities of candidates, who must stand out in the minds of voters. Party affiliations do little to reduce the confusion of the average Brazilian voter as he or she is confronted with dozens of names for each position. Worse still, the open-list

PR system creates incentives for politicians to ignore party labels, because voters can cross party lines with ease. That even leads to politicians from the same party running against each other for the same position within a district.

Open-list proportional representation explains why there are so many parties in Brazil. With so much emphasis on the personal qualities of politicians, ambitious individuals can ignore the established party hierarchies while achieving elected office. They need only create their own parties or form alliances to get on the ballot and gain enough votes to qualify for representation. As a result, Brazil has the most fragmented party system in Latin America and one of the most fragmented in the world.

As if the open-list PR system were not distorting enough, Brazilian electoral law also allows incumbents to keep their party affiliation and remain on the ballot for the next election. This provision strips political parties of any control over their members: an incumbent may ignore the party's interests while in office but still must be kept on the ballot during the next contest.

Brazil's electoral system differs from other open-list proportional representation systems in that state, not national, parties select legislative candidates. In most cases, Brazilian governors exert tremendous influence over who can be elected. This further weakens national party leaders, who remain beholden to governors who can reward them with supportive nominees or rivals.

Source: Scott Mainwaring, "Brazil: Weak Parties, Feckless Democracy," in Scott Mainwaring and Timothy R. Scully, eds., *Building Democratic Institutions: Party Systems in Latin America* (Stanford, Calif., Stanford University Press, 1995), 375.

---

partial privatization of the welfare state. A majority advocate a liberal trade policy and MERCOSUL, but a substantial minority press for protectionism and the continuation of subsidies, particularly in agriculture. No party of the right has yet emerged as a solid

defender of neoliberal restructuring of the economy, although scholars have detected a significant trend in favor of these policies among the parties on the right. On constitutional reform, right-wing parties are fairly united in favor of curtailing the number and range of

Table 4

The Democratic Idea: The Major Parties in Brazil

Conservative/Right-Wing Parties

PFL: *Partido da Frente Liberal* (Party of the Liberal Front)

PL: *Partido Liberal* (Liberal Party)

PPB: *Partido Progressista Brasileiro* (Brazilian Progressive Party)

Centrist Parties

PMDB: *Partido do Movimento Democrático Brasileiro* (Party of the Brazilian Democratic Movement)

PSDB: *Partido da Social Democracia Brasileira* (Party of Brazilian Social Democracy)

PTB: Partido Trabalhista Brasileiro (Brazilian Labor Party)

Populist/Leftist Parties

PT: Partido dos Trabalhadores (Workers' Party)

PSB: *Partido Socialista Brasileiro* (Brazilian Socialist Party)

PCdoB: *Partido Comunista do Brasil* (Communist Party of Brazil)

PDT: Partido Democrático Trabalhista (Democratic Labor Party)

PPS: Partido Popular Socialista (ex-Partido Comunista Brasileiro) (Popular Socialist Party)

social rights protecting welfare entitlements and workers; they also advocate electoral reform—specifically, the establishment of a majority or mixed, rather than purely proportional, district voting system, although this is contentious within the rightist cohort.

A loose set of conservative parties currently struggles for the mantle of the right. In front of the pack is the PFL (Party of the Liberal Front), one of the largest parties in the Senate and the Chamber. Many wild card parties, with low to moderate levels of representation in congress, ally themselves with right-wing and center-right parties or advocate right-wing issues; the Brazilian Labor Party (PTB), the Brazilian Progressive Party (PPB), and the evangelistic Liberal Party (PL) are examples.

The two other large parties in congress are the PMDB (Party of the Brazilian Democratic Movement, a descendant of the old MDB) and the PSDB (the Party of Brazilian Social Democracy, originally an offshoot of the PMDB; Cardoso's party). These parties, while having disparate leftist and rightist elements, tend to

dominate the center and center-left segment of the ideological spectrum. Along with the PFL, these have been the key governing parties during the democratic era. Some scholars argue that these parties have formed a disciplined pro-reform bulwark in congress for Cardoso especially; hence, they are "government parties."[47] Other scholars argue that although these parties seem to vote coherently in favor of reform, these votes are infrequent and, more important, they are the product of the president's dispensing large amounts of patronage to particular politicians to manufacture a coherent vote.[48] Yet there is agreement that these parties have become ideologically more coherent in favor of neoliberal reform, and hence they can be characterized as being on the right or center-right.[49]

Political parties on the left advocate reducing deficits and inflation, but also maintaining the public sector in public hands and improving the welfare state. Left-oriented parties want to expand the state's role in promoting and protecting domestic industry. On constitutional reform, they support the social rights guaranteed by the 1988 constitution.

On the left, the most important party continues to be the Workers' Party (PT). (See "Citizen Action: The Workers' Party.") Since 1985 the PT has occupied much of the left's political space, marginalizing already peripheral parties such as the Brazilian Socialist Party (PSB), the Brazilian Communist Party (PCB—renamed the Popular Socialist Party, or PPS, in 1992), and the Communist Party of Brazil (PC do B). The Democratic Labor Party (PDT), a populist organization led by Leonel Brizola, the ex-governor of Rio de Janeiro, advocates Vargas-era nationalism and state-led development. In the elections of October 1998, this party formed an alliance with the PT at the national level. The PPS is led by Ciro Gomes, a former finance minister under the Itamar Franco presidency and a former governor of Ceará. Gomes ran for president in 1998 and 2002 but did not make it to the second round in either contest.

As might be expected, the proliferation of political parties has only added to the incoherence of legislative politics. Currently, no party has more than 24 percent of the seats in either house of congress (see Figures 3 and 4). Cardoso's multiparty alliance of the PSDB-PFL-PTB-PPB controlled 57 percent of the vote in the lower house and 48 percent in the upper house. Lula's alliance of his PT, the PL, and some of the leftist and

Citizen Action: *The Workers' Party*

The creation of the Workers' Party (PT) in the early 1980s was a remarkable development in Brazilian history. The PT was founded by workers who had defied the military government and engaged in strikes in São Paulo's metalworking and automobile industries in 1978 and 1979. Although the PT began with a working-class message and leftist platform, its identity broadened during the 1980s and early 1990s. The party and its leader, Luiz Inácio "Lula" da Silva, increasingly campaigned for the support of the middle class, the rural and urban poor, and even segments of business and the upper classes. Unlike previous populist parties in Brazil, the PT aimed both to bring previously excluded groups into the political arena and to change the status quo substantively.

Lula da Silva ran for the presidency four times: in 1989, 1994, 1998, and 2002. In 1989, he qualified for, but lost, the runoff to Collor. In 1994 and 1998, he was beaten during the first round by Cardoso. In 1998, the PT forged an electoral alliance with Leonel Brizola's left-populist PDT, as well as with other leftist parties, including the PSB, PC do B, and the PCB. Despite a unified leftist ticket, da Silva captured 31.7 percent of the vote to Fernando Henrique Cardoso's 53.1 percent. Lula did much better in 2002, beating Cardoso's designated successor, José Serra, in the second round with 61.3 percent, the largest share for any presidential winner in the democratic period. The party's electoral success is a product of its demonstrated capacity for clean and effective government at all levels in Brazil's federal system.

As Margaret Keck, an American scholar of the PT, argues, the party was a novel development because it sought to represent the interests of workers and the poor. This had never before been attempted by a political organization that operated independently from the state. The PT also tries to be an internally democratic party. Its leaders

Luiz Inácio "Lula" da Silva, founder of the Workers' Party and Brazilian President (2002–2006). *Source:* © Jornal do Brasil, August 19, 1998, Alexandre Sassaki.

respect the views of grassroots organizers and ensure that their voices are heard in the party's decision making.

———————

Source: Margaret Keck, *The Workers' Party and Democratization in Brazil* (New Haven, Conn.: Yale University Press, 1992), 219–220.

center-left parties might provide a "governing coalition" similar in size to Cardoso's. But because of party switching, merging, and clientelism, the loyalty of these "progovernment" parties to the administration remains remarkably soft. Consistency of support is difficult to maintain as turnover in the Chamber is high, with 50 to 60 percent of the members being replaced with each election. This reality has reinforced the common claim of the executive to be the only source of political order in the Brazilian democratic system.

Figure 3

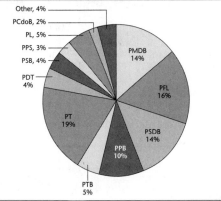

Share of Seats of the Major Parties in the Chamber of Deputies, February 2003 Congress

Source: Data from final TSE numbers.

The results of the October 1998 elections produced mounting recriminations among the leftist parties that a divided opposition was ineffectual. Conservative parties remained suspicious of Cardoso's social reform agenda, while center-left forces considered alternatives to right-wing support. Discussions have focused on the possibility of consolidating Brazil's political parties into a three- or four-party left-center-right structure. Yet the 2002 campaign produced no such major alliances. The right offered several candidates, including

Figure 4

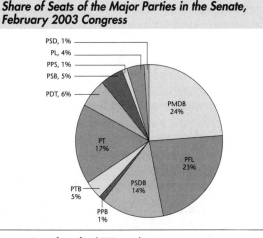

Share of Seats of the Major Parties in the Senate, February 2003 Congress

Source: Data from final TSE numbers.

the surprising Roseana Sarney, the PFL governor of Maranhão state and former president José Sarney's daughter, who dropped out of the race after being implicated in a widening embezzlement scandal. José Serra, Cardoso's PSDB health minister, quickly became the center-right's candidate to beat Lula, but opposition to Cardoso's government within the center and by populists such as Itamar Franco (PMDB) undercut his electoral standing prior to the second round of the presidential vote in October 2002. Lula, not needing any alliances with Brizola's PDT or Gomes's PPS (but forging a somewhat opportunistic tie to the Liberal Party, a probusiness, strongly evangelical party), proved that the PT could be successful at the presidential level. Yet without the support of the large conservative parties in congress and lacking a viable alliance of leftist parties, Lula's presidency will have great difficulty passing meaningful social and economic reform.

Elections

Contests for public office in Brazil are dominated by the rules of proportional representation (PR). Everything, from federal legislative to municipal council positions, is distributed on the basis of several mathematical calculations to ensure proportionality among political parties. Generally, the number of seats each party obtains is determined by multiplying the ratio between party and total votes by the total number of seats.

In addition to its effects on the party system, open-list PR (see "Institutional Intricacies: Proportional Representation") rules distort democratic representation in other ways. Given the multiplicity of parties, the unbalanced apportionment of seats among the states, and the sheer size of some electoral districts, candidates often have few incentives to be accountable to their constituency. In states with hundreds of candidates running in oversized electoral districts, the votes obtained by successful candidates are often scattered, limiting the accountability of those elected. In less populated states, there are more seats and parties per voter; the electoral and party quotients are lower. As a result, candidates often alter their legal place of residence immediately before an election in order to run for a safer seat, compounding the lack of accountability. Electoral laws are highly permissive regarding the candidate's change of residence. For example, ex-president Sarney, realizing that he would not be eligible to run for a Senate seat in his home state, successfully changed his residence only a few months before the 1990 elections.

As in all other modern nations, the media play a key role in Brazilian political campaigns. With the *abertura,* political parties gained the right to air electoral propaganda on radio and television. All radio stations and TV channels are required to broadcast, at no charge, two hours of party programming each day during a campaign season. The parties are entitled to an amount of time on the air proportional to their number of votes in the previous election. Some candidates have no more than a few seconds to present themselves and their platform to the public.

In recent years, elections, particularly presidential contests, have become touchstones of the country's progress in building democracy. Although the president was elected indirectly in 1984 and the eventual president, José Sarney (PMDB and PFL), had not been selected to be president in the first place, this first election set Brazil on the path to democracy. More important was the 1989 contest, which gave Brazilians their first opportunity to elect the president directly. Collor's (PRN) selection became an important precedent that further strengthened Brazilian democracy. Ironically, his impeachment two years later also promoted democracy, because it reinforced the rule of law and enhanced the oversight functions of the congress. Fernando Henrique Cardoso's election in 1994 and reelection in 1998 repeated and reinforced the 1989 precedent of direct elections for the presidency. Although elections cannot guarantee democracy, recent contests have shown how far Brazilian democracy has come in little over a decade.

Seen from the perspective of average Brazilians, however, the situation is a bit more complex. Although most Brazilians are suspicious of authoritarianism and wary of the return of the military or any other form of dictatorship, they seem to be disappointed with the results of democracy. The weakness of political parties, coupled with the persistence of clientelism, has discouraged average Brazilians with their country's politics. According to opinion polls, support for democracy as a viable system of government is under 50 percent nationwide. Brazilians vote, but they disparage politics and politicians regularly. For example, in the October 2002 presidential elections, 9.7 million voters turned in blank or spoiled ballots, a common indicator of voter discontent in Brazil. Electronic voting machines have reduced voter error in recent years making blank

and null voting statistics even stronger indicators of the discontent of the electorate.

Political Culture, Citizenship, and Identity

The notion of national identity describes a sense of national community that goes beyond mere allegiance to a state, a set of economic interests, regional loyalties, or kinship affiliations. The cultivation of a national identity occurs through a process of nation building during which a set of national symbols, cultural terms and images, and shared myths consolidates around historical experiences that define the loyalties of a group of people.

Several developments made Brazilian nation building possible. Unlike nation formation in culturally, linguistically, and geographically diverse western Europe, Africa, and Asia, Brazil enjoyed a homogeneous linguistic and colonial experience. As a result, Brazilian history largely avoided the ethnic conflicts that have become obstacles to nation building in eastern Europe, Nigeria, and India. Immigrants added their ideas and value systems at the turn of the century, but they brought no compelling identities that could substitute for an overarching national consciousness. Regional secessionist movements were uncommon in Brazilian history and were short-lived experiences when they did emerge in the twentieth century.

Despite Brazil's rich ethnic makeup, racial identities in Brazil have seldom been the basis for political action. In part, this was the result of the historical myth that the country was racially mixed. Therefore, a singular racial consciousness emerged around the spurious idea that Brazil was a racial democracy. Even in the face of severe economic and political oppression of native peoples, Afro-Brazilians, and Asians, the myth of racial democracy has endured in the national consciousness. As a result, the unique contributions of different ethnic groups were not appreciated.

Brazilian literature, political discourse, and history textbooks reinforced the myth of racial democracy. For example, the famous Brazilian historian Gilberto Freyre, in his book *The Masters and the Slaves,* described the evolution of social relations among blacks and whites since colonial times, but he treated the underlying reality of racial conflict as an issue of secondary importance.[50] For such intellectuals, miscegenation had diminished racial differences and made conflict unlikely.

Carnival in Brazil, the world's largest floor show, is also an insightful exhibition of allegories and popular myths about the country, its people, and their culture.
Source: Bettmann/ Corbis.

This thinking buttressed the false belief that prejudice and discrimination were lacking among whites, blacks, indigenous peoples, and mulattos.

Like the myth of racial democracy, the major collective political identities in Brazilian history have sought to hide or negate the real conflicts in society. For example, the symbols and images of political nationalism tended to boost the quasi-utopian visions of the country's future development. Developmentalists under democratic leaders such as Kubitschek and the military governments espoused optimism that "Brazil is the country of the future." In the face of severe fiscal, social, and political problems, Brazilians continue to have faith in their country, even when their confidence in their politicians and democratic institutions has been shaken.

Both the persistence of optimistic myths about the country and an almost angry disengagement from politics are reflections of a weak system of political socialization. Given the dominance of corporatism and populism in twentieth-century Brazilian politics and the current crisis in these forms of mobilizing popular support, Brazilians lack avenues for becoming more involved in politics. The weakness of political parties is one problem. But an underfunded primary and secondary educational system and a largely uncritical media leave most Brazilians without the resources to become more politically aware. Brazil's illiteracy rate of 16.7 percent remains one of the highest in Latin America and is a key obstacle to mobilizing the electorate. The frenetic nature of political change in Brazil has confused the citizenry, further breaking down whatever continuous political identities might emerge. Perhaps the ultimate reflection of these distressing tendencies is the cynical joke among Brazilians that "Brazil is the country of the future and *will always be.*"

The political sentiments of Brazilian society are actually quite static because most Brazilians feel powerless to change their fates. Brazilians have always considered liberal democratic institutions, particularly individual rights, as artificial or irrelevant. Although this view may appear cynical, it is a deeply ingrained notion in Brazilian political culture. Since the end of the nineteenth century, Brazilians have made a distinction between the "legal" Brazil—that is, the formal laws of the country—and the "real" Brazil—what actually occurs. A prime example was the turn-of-the-twentieth-century liberal democracy, which concealed the patronage-ridden interior of Brazilian politics. Brazilian intellectuals developed the phrase *para ingles ver* ("for the English to see") to describe the notion that liberal democracy had been implanted to impress foreign observers, hiding the fact that real politics would be conducted behind the scenes. As Brazil struggles to balance the interests of foreign investors with those of its own people, many Brazilians continue to believe that much of the politics they observe is really "for the English to see."

One of the key outcomes of the sense of powerlessness among the majority of Brazilians was the belief that the state should organize society. This idea helped to justify both the Vargas dictatorship in 1937 and the military rule that followed the coup of 1964. The primacy of the state manifested itself in Brazilian political culture. The notion that the state had a duty to provide for its citizens' welfare placed the state at the center of the Brazilian polity and the president at the center of the state. It should be clear, based on this analysis, that both society and the state in Brazil developed a set of core ideas that favored the establishment of a strong central government with an overbearing presidentialism. These ideas were not just imposed on Brazilians by savvy politicians; they were the product of many decades of social and political conflict.

During the redemocratization process, new trends in Brazilian political culture emerged. Most segments of Brazilian society came to embrace "modernization with democracy," even if they would later raise doubts about its benefits. The Catholic Church played an important role in promoting democracy. During the transition, a number of Catholic political organizations and movements aided by the Church organized popular opposition to the military governments. After the transition, archbishops of the Catholic Church helped assemble testimonials of torture victims. The publication of these depositions in the book *Nunca Mais* (*Never Again*) fueled condemnation of the authoritarian past. In this way, an establishment that previously had been associated with social conservatism and political oppression became a mobilizer of popular opposition to authoritarianism.

Another trend that developed during and after the transition to democracy was the growth of a profound distrust of the state. Brazilians began to doubt the ability of the state to find solutions to the country's economic and social problems. Business groups assailed the failures of state-led development, while labor unions claimed that corporatist management of industrial relations could not satisfy the interests of workers. As a result, Brazilians became increasingly receptive to fringe voices that promised to eradicate the previous economic-political order. By 1989, most Brazilians were willing to trust a little-known politician, Fernando Collor, who told the electorate what they wanted to hear. Collor swore to go to war against indolent state employees, corrupt politicians, and inefficient state enterprises. The results were, at least in part, disastrous. By ceding their authority to an untested figure like Collor, Brazilians failed one of the most important tests of democracy: ensuring that elected officials will be accountable to the electorate. In the end, antistatism proved hostile to democracy.

A third trend in Brazilian political culture can be seen among the most elite segments of society. Soon after the transition to democracy, many journalists, economists, politicians, intellectuals, and entrepreneurs began to embrace the notion that national institutions could be adjusted incrementally to strengthen democracy and promote economic growth. Constitutional, administrative, and economic reform became priorities of politicians such as Fernando Henrique Cardoso.

For average Brazilians, the dynamics of institutional tinkering are virtually unintelligible. The electorate must feel substantial change, primarily in their pocketbooks. Cardoso was able to deliver in 1994 when his Real Plan reduced inflation and increased the buying power of most Brazilians. That success gave him the popular support he needed to become president and launch an array of institutional reforms. In 1998, facing another presidential contest, Cardoso struggled to convince voters that his government of technocrats had the answers to the country's problems. With his reforms stuck in congress, Cardoso had difficulty backing up his claim to deserve a second term. Economic growth began to stall, raising fears that Cardoso's reforms had run their course and were beginning to erode. Despite these problems, he was reelected, but he continued to struggle with congress on the reform agenda, as his successor surely will.

The task of selling even the most complex sets of

policies to a population with weak political socialization and poor general education has become central to gaining and maintaining political power in Brazil. That has placed a premium on the adept management of the media, particularly radio and television. The Brazilian media are free to criticize the government, and most of the broadcast businesses are privately owned. Although there is significant government influence over the resources necessary for media production and the advertising revenue from government campaigns, there is no overt government censorship, and freedom of the press is widely and constitutionally proclaimed. Government officials must engage in a complex dance of symbols and words to attract the attention of the private media and cast the most appealing image to a distrustful electorate.

The largest media organizations are owned by a small group of conglomerates. The Globo network is Brazil's preeminent media empire and one of the five largest television networks in the world. It has been formidable in shaping public opinion; some believe it played a prominent role in Collor's election in 1989. Conglomerates like Globo have played favorites in the past and no doubt will continue to do so. In return, the media giants expect licensing concessions from their political friends.

Media independence from government interference varies. The print media are generally less restrained than the broadcast media in criticizing politicians and governments. Though television newscasts, which attract millions of viewers, continuously cover events embarrassing to the government or criticize government policies, the majority of viewers hear woefully little information on how and why political decisions are made, why one policy is favored over another, and the ultimate results. Domestic broadcast news coverage in Brazil is often merely the broadcasting of official government versions.

Interests, Social Movements, and Protest

Despite the growing disengagement of most Brazilians from politics and the country's legacy of state corporatism, autonomous collective interests have been able to take positions of importance in the political landscape. The role of business lobbies, rural protest movements, and labor unions, particularly those linked

to the Workers' Party, are all examples of how Brazilian civil society has been able to break through the vise of state corporatism and social control.

As noted, the Catholic Church was actively engaged in organizing grass-roots movements during and after the transition to democracy. After the profound changes in Catholic doctrine brought about by the Second Vatican Council in the early 1960s, the Church in Brazil became more active in advocating social and political reform. The Brazilian church, through the National Conference of Brazilian Bishops (CNBB), produced an array of projects to improve literacy, stimulate political awareness, and improve the working and living conditions of the poor. Although some conservative segments of the Brazilian church reacted violently against the Church's "messing in politics," the CNBB pressed on.

One well-known outcome of these changes was the development of liberation theology, a doctrine that argued that religion had to free people from both their sins and social injustice at the same time. In Brazil this thinking was associated with the Franciscan theologian Leonardo Boff. During the *abertura,* this doctrinal shift sought to relate theology to Brazilian reality by having priests become directly involved in improving the lot of poor Brazilians by defending their social and political needs.[51] By organizing community-based movements to press for improved sanitation, clean water, basic education, and, most important, freedom from oppression, Catholic groups mobilized millions of citizens. Among the Brazilian church's most notable accomplishments was the development of an agrarian reform council in the 1970s, the Pastoral Land Commission. The commission called for the extension of land tenure to poor peasants. The Brazilian Church also created ecclesiastical community movements to improve conditions in the *favelas.*

In the mid-1970s, Brazil witnessed a historic awakening of social and political organization: grassroots popular movements; new forms of trade unionism; neighborhood movements; professional associations of doctors, lawyers, and journalists; entrepreneurial associations; and middle-class organizations. At the same time, a host of nongovernmental organizations (NGOs) became more active in Brazil; among them were Amnesty International, Greenpeace, and native Brazilian rights groups. Domestic groups active in these areas increasingly turned to the NGOs for resources and information, adding an international dimension to what was previously an issue of domestic politics.

Women's organizations played a significant role in popular urban social movements during the 1970s. By the 1980s, women were participating in and leading popular initiatives on a wide variety of issues related to employment and the provision of basic services. Many of these organizations enlisted the support of political parties and trade unions in battles over women's wages, birth control, rape, and violence in the home. Although practically absent in employers' organizations, women are highly active in urban unions. Out of the country's 5,324 urban unions, 14.8 percent have elected women directors. Fewer women are leaders of rural unions (6.6 percent), but they compose 78 percent of active membership. In recent years, Brazilian women have created over 3,000 organizations to address their issues. Included in this total are special police stations (*delegacias de defesa da mulher,* DDMs) dedicated to addressing crimes against women. The DDMs have emerged in major Brazilian cities, and particularly in São Paulo, where their performance has been highly rated.

Women's groups have seen their power increase as more women have joined the work force: 39 percent of women now work outside the home. That figure is higher than in Mexico (22 percent) and Argentina (33 percent). More than 20 percent of Brazilian families are supported exclusively by women. The share of domestic servants in the female work force has declined from 32 percent to 20 percent over the past ten years, suggesting that traditional roles for women have not absorbed the increase in the female work force.

Women have also made great strides in representative politics and key administrative appointments. In March 2000, Teresa Grossi was confirmed as the first woman to occupy the directorship of the Central Bank. Judge Ellen Gracie Northfleet became the first woman to occupy a seat on the STF, Brazil's Supreme Court, and Marta Suplicy became mayor of São Paulo. Roseanna Sarney's startling, yet ill-fated, performance during the presidential campaign of 2002 suggests that Brazilians are prepared to consider a women for president. The number of women with seats in congress nearly doubled following the election of October 2002.

Despite women's improved economic, social, and political importance, progress on women's issues is slow. On average, women earn only 57 percent of what men make. Only 7 percent of women with university degrees earn more than twenty times the minimum wage (about $75 per month), as compared to 28 percent of men. Thirty-four percent of illiterate women earn the minimum wage or less versus 5 percent of illiterate males.

In contrast to the progress of women's movements, a politically significant organization to address racial discrimination has not emerged. This fact is especially surprising because Brazil is one of the world's most racially mixed countries. Only during the 1940s did some public officials and academics acknowledge that prejudice existed against blacks. At that time, the problems of race were equated with the problems of class. Given the absence of legally sanctioned discrimination since the abolition of slavery in 1888, prejudice came to be viewed as class based, not race based. Attacking class inequality was thus considered a way to address prejudice against blacks. This belief seemed plausible because most poor Brazilians are either *pardo* (mulatto) or black. But it might be just as logical to suggest that they are poor because they are black. In any case, the relationship between race and class in Brazil is just as ambiguous as it is in the United States and other multiethnic societies.

Some analysts believe that a gradual and peaceful evolution of race relations is possible. Others argue that as a consequence of white domination, blacks lack the collective identity and political organization necessary to put race relations on the political agenda. Both sides seem to agree, however, that although poverty and color are significantly correlated, overt confrontation among races is uncommon. Ironically, this may explain why no serious national discussion of race relations has ever emerged in Brazil.

The rights of Brazil's indigenous peoples, the Indians of the Amazon, remain at the center of the debate on the country's most pressing social problems. Over the past half-century, the development of the Amazon has threatened the cultures and lives of Indians. For example, members of the Ianomami, a tribe with one of the largest reserves in Brazil, are frequently murdered by miners so they can gain access to mines in Indian territory. Many such massacres have occurred in territories legally provided by the central state to the Ianomami. During the military government, the national

Indian agency, FUNAI, turned a blind eye to such abuses with its claim that indigenous cultures represented "ethnic cysts to be excised from the body politic."[52] With the *abertura,* many environmental NGOs defended the human rights of indigenous people as part of their campaign to defend the Amazon and its people. The end of military rule and the economic crisis of the 1980s slowed exploitation of the Amazon.

The 1988 constitution recognized the rights of indigenous peoples for the first time, creating large reserves for tribes like the Ianomami. Yet these protections were eroded when President Cardoso, under pressure by landowning conservative allies from the northeast, implemented a policy to allow private interests to make claims on over half of all indigenous lands. Miners, loggers, and land developers invade native lands, often with destructive consequences for the ecology and indigenous people. Allied against these interests are members of the Workers' Party, a coalition of indigenous groups known as COIAB, and church-based missionary organizations. The Kayapó and their resistance to large-scale development projects in the Amazon are a key example of how environmental, labor, and indigenous issues are melding together to form a powerful grass-roots campaign. Members of the Kayapó tribe have been successful in politically disrupting damming and mining projects through mass media campaigns.[53] Their struggle continues, but without more federal protection Amazonian Indians will continue to be threatened.

The sprouting of movements, associations, and interest groups may seem impressive, but they represent specific constituencies. Most Brazilians do not bother to participate in parties, movements, and unions because the basic functions of government such as security, justice, education, and health care simply do not reach them. When confronted with immediate deprivations, many Brazilians avoid organized and peaceful political action, often taking to the streets in sporadic riots. Such events demonstrate that many Brazilians feel they have only two choices in the face of unresponsive political and state organizations: violent protest or passivity.

Section ❺ Brazilian Politics in Transition

Political Challenges and Changing Agendas

As the financial and monetary crisis that began in Asia in late 1997 continued to scare foreign investors throughout the developing world, Fernando Henrique Cardoso appeared on a Cable News Network (CNN) business show in December. The Brazilian president proclaimed his country a safe place for foreign money, a stable and growth-oriented economy sure to remain immune from the economic difficulties afflicting Asia. To scholars of Brazil, Cardoso's CNN appearance seemed paradoxical. Here was an avowed social democrat, an old theorist of leftist sociology, a former *dependencista*, pitching his country to international investors. They noted that Cardoso made no mention of his country's worsening social problems, its disparities in income, land tenure, and access to basic social and educational services. For many Brazilians on the left, Cardoso's comments were a ruthless betrayal of shared principles.

From a comparative perspective, we might interpret Cardoso's CNN interview in very different terms. Cardoso's remarks become more understandable when we consider the dilemmas connected to our theme of governing the economy. Much like other leaders of developing countries, Cardoso needs to preserve a stable domestic economy attractive to foreign investors, who are likely to turn to other countries at the first signs of instability. Not surprisingly, then, on CNN the president talked up his economic policy and downplayed the political and social negatives of investing money in Brazil. Rather than a betrayal of his social democratic principles, Cardoso's pitch could be seen as a pragmatic attempt to turn a necessity into a virtue. Five years later, the same paradox faces Brazil's new president, Lula da Silva. During the presidential campaign, Lula repeatedly stated his commitment to preserve the real and to avoid an Argentine-style default on Brazil's ever-expanding public debt. By his efforts to court business interests inside and outside Brazil, the suit-and-tie Lula (not the blue-collar labor party leader) opted for the same strategy as his predecessor.

At the same time, there are serious costs to the presidential strategy of reforming the Brazilian political and economic structure in order to become more competitive in global markets. The Brazilian president has had to embrace the very mechanisms of clientelism to curry center-right support that are at the heart of many of the inefficiencies that create a deadlock on the country's democratic institutions. Given a weak party system and constitutional requirements that all amendments survive two majority votes of 60 percent in both houses of congress, clientelism has become the presidency's most powerful mechanism for cultivating support. Only with the support of conservative and probusiness groups, which maintain a majority of votes in both houses of congress, will any Brazilian president have the support to implement the constitutional, administrative, and social security reforms needed to restructure the economy.

This strategy has created serious paradoxes for the Brazilian president. Rather than strengthen Brazil's weak political parties and fragmented legislature, these tactics have reinforced the factors that make the country's democratic institutions anemic. By kowtowing to clientelistic interests, Cardoso's administration put on hold reforms to the electoral and party system. In the process, members of his own party, the Brazilian Social Democratic Party (PSDB), rebuked the president for cultivating support from other parties, particularly the conservative Party of the Liberal Front (PFL), and sometimes hurting his own social democrats in congressional and gubernatorial contests. By wooing many conservative interests, mostly in the north and northeast regions, Cardoso strengthened groups that oppose significant agrarian reform, income distribution, and improvements in social services. Most important, his strategy depended on increased spending, financed with public debt at high interest. The result has been a soaring deficit and public debt. Despite Lula's strong leftist credentials, his presidency will face similar strategic choices and structural constraints. Systemic reforms will require legislative coalitions with centrist and even right-wing parties, especially in the Senate, and Lula will be under even greater pressure from a leftist partisan base if he strays too far from his promises to address social inequalities.

Despite the heady rhetoric of Cardoso's 1994 presidential campaign and the rising expectations of long-frustrated social democrats inside and outside Brazil, his administration offered little in the way of changing Brazilian politics for the long haul. Cardoso made only token progress on the country's persisting social inequalities. The Real Plan reduced the eroding effect of mega-inflation on the incomes of the poor, boosting consumption for millions of Brazilians. But other policies were less effective. Economic liberalization caused thousands of Brazilian firms to shave their labor costs, putting hundreds of thousands out of work. Privatization, for example, put an estimated 546,000 out of work as sold-off firms downsized to become viable market actors. As urban unemployment has increased, so have urban violence and crime. The government distributed more land to poor people in rural areas, but these efforts failed to make a dent in Brazil's concentrated system of land tenure. Some innovation in health reform and education emerged regarding improving the availability of anti-HIV drugs and state-level experiments, respectively, but wider reforms received only lip-service from the administration. Lula's presidency will certainly try to do more for the poor, but against the backdrop of Brazil's mounting debt and the nervousness of international investors, he might not be able to produce the kind of systemic change many of his voters would like to see.

Both the fiscal and the environmental limits to Brazil's economic development have been stretched almost to their breaking points. Even without a significant downturn in the global economy, the fate of the Brazilian economy is being threatened by the state's burgeoning indebtedness, the inability to cut public spending, and the social and ecological costs of the maldistribution of income and the abuse of natural resources. The tendency to see solutions to Brazil's economic problems in terms of promoting exports and enlarging the economy deepens these problems. Considering that many of Brazil's exports are still extractive (e.g., iron ore, lumber), these recommendations place ever more pressure on the country's ecology. The quality of life of most Brazilians can only suffer as a result.

The challenges facing Brazil and the way that the country's political leaders have chosen to deal with them are similar to experiences elsewhere. The Brazilian state lacks the resources to promote development as it did during the days of Vargas, Kubitschek, and military rule. As the needs of the Brazilian citizenry grow, the state appears less capable, and political leaders less willing, to respond. With the advent of the Real Plan, the priorities have been to attract foreign capital, boost export earnings, and favor the highest bidders in the privatization of public firms. The developmentalist state lives on only in some BNDES policies. Like former state-led industrializers India, Mexico, and France, Brazil has turned in the neoliberal direction, limiting the state's role in the economy. This shift in the state's organization reminds us of the importance of our theme of highlighting critical junctures in state formation.

In contrast to the corporatist and populist role of the state, the moderating power in Brazilian history, the central state has become a far more passive agent in society. Brazilian workers no longer negotiate labor issues with state mediation, as they still do in Germany. Instead, labor unions, when they are capable, negotiate directly with business. In most cases, given high urban unemployment, the interests of business usually prevail. Urban workers receive little or no compensation from the state when they suffer layoffs or reductions in their salaries and workplace benefits. Most rural workers, the millions in the informal sector, and minorities are in an even more precarious position, as they lack the few benefits and protections enjoyed by salaried urban workers. The weakness of the judiciary, the abusive use of police authority, and the tendency to vigilantism and class conflict in poor, rural areas reinforce the anemia of a civil society that increasingly discounts its role in politics.

In this context, Brazilian democracy has suffered greatly, the importance of which we highlighted in our theme of the democratic challenge. The poor feel doubly divorced from politics, both socially and politically disenfranchised from a process they view as unresponsive to their needs. Over time, this sense of disengagement has turned into open doubt about the utility of democracy itself. Stories of official corruption and the popular assumption that a politician's priority is his or her own pocketbook reinforce the idea that representatives are unaccountable to their constituencies. The weakness of political party loyalties and the fragmentation of interests compound the problem of

accountability. By contrast, much stronger democracies such as Germany, the United States, France, and Britain rely on well-defined rules that force political leaders to be accountable to other branches of government and to their own constituencies. Brazil's example has shown how difficult it is to embrace the democratic idea without these structures.

While some of Brazil's problems are unique, many take the same form they do elsewhere. Like all other major economies in the world, Brazil's is well integrated into the global economy. Despite the country's current problems with monetary stability and debt, Brazil is one of the world's key platforms for agricultural production and manufacturing. Brazil's share of the world market in iron ore, textiles, footwear, steel, machine parts, and autos makes it an important hub in the multinational production of several industrial products. It is a crucial supplier of raw materials as well as a large market for multinational producers. As such, it has advantages few other developing countries enjoy. That also means, however, that Brazilian firms and workers (not to mention the public sector itself) must be able to adapt to greater competition from abroad and the needs of foreign capital. Given the speed with which technology outpaces itself, the pressure to train workers, boost productivity, and enhance research and development has grown tremendously. Brazil is struggling just to keep pace with globalization.

As globalization and democratization have made Brazilian politics less predictable, older questions about what it means to be Brazilian have reemerged. Brazil highlights the point made in the discussion of our theme on political identities in the Introduction that political identities are often reshaped in changed circumstances. What it means to be Brazilian has become a more complex question given the way that Brazil, like the rest of the world, has been bombarded by foreign consumer images. Democracy has given ordinary Brazilians more of a voice, and they have used it to forge their own understandings, but mostly on local issues, not at the national level. Women, nongovernmental organizations, Catholics, Pentecostals, blacks, landless peasants, and residents of *favelas* have all organized in recent years around social and cultural issues. On the one hand, these movements have placed additional pressure on an already weakened state to deliver goods and services. On the other hand, these groups have supplied alternatives to the state by providing their own systems of social and cultural support. As the domain of the state in other countries is constrained by the need to compete in the global economy, space is created for nonstate actors to provide goods and services that were previously produced by the state. What is missing in all of this is a sense of the "national question." How are all these disparate groups linked? Do they have a common, national interest? If they are increasingly disconnected, then the proliferation of social movements and organizations is only a symptom of the wider disengagement from the state and political society already being practiced by most Brazilians.

Brazilian Politics in Comparative Perspective

The most important lesson that Brazil offers for the broader study of comparative politics is that fragmented polities threaten democracy, social development, and nation building. The Brazilian political order is fragmented on several levels. The central state is fragmented by conflicts between the executive and the legislature, divided alliances and self-interested politicians in the congress, decentralized government, and an indecisive judiciary with a complicated structure and an uncertain mission. Political parties are fragmented by clientelism and electoral rules that create incentives for politicians and voters to ignore party labels. Finally, civil society itself is fragmented into numerous, often conflictual, organizations, interest groups, professional associations, social movements, churches, and, most important, social classes and ethnic identities.

In some societies that are similarly fragmented, such as the United States and India, institutions have been successful in bridging the gaps between individualistic pursuits and the demand of the people for good government. Rich systems of social organization and reciprocity that are linked to the state through political parties, parliaments, and even informal associations help to strengthen democracy in these countries. Where these systems are faulty, as they are in Brazil, fragmentation reinforces the weakness of the state and the society.

Recent Brazilian politics shows that a weak state deepens the citizenry's sense that all politics is corrupt. Although corruption is present in all polities to some degree, it does not by itself produce the angry disengagement from politics that has emerged in Brazil. Much more is wrong with the Brazilian political order. Police brutality, judicial incompetence, and the inability of bureaucratic agencies to respond to social demands have just as powerful an effect in legitimizing civil disengagement.

This only reinforces the importance of creating systems of accountability to reduce the corruption, police abuse, and bureaucratic incompetence that have given rise to these doubts. Unfortunately, the English word *accountability* has no counterpart in either Portuguese or Spanish. Given Brazil's (and Latin America's) long history of oligarchical rule and social exclusion, the notion of making elites accountable to the people is so alien that the languages of the region lack the required vocabulary. Systems of accountability must be built from the ground up; they must be nurtured in local government and in community organizations and then in the governments of states and the central state. The judiciary, political parties, the media, and civil societal organizations must be able to play enforcement and watchdog roles. These are the building blocks of accountability, and the accountability of political elites is the fulcrum of democracy.

Without a system of elite accountability, representation of the citizenry is impossible. The 60 percent of the Brazilian population that is classified as poor or close to that status has few autonomous organizations to pressure government. More than business, labor, or professional groups, the poor depend on their elected officials to find solutions to their problems. Brazilian politicians have shown that through demagoguery and personalism, they can be elected. But being elected is not the same as guaranteeing a constituency its right to be represented. For this to occur, institutions must make political elites accountable to the people who elected them. When that condition is met, genuine representation of citizens' interests becomes possible.

Political fragmentation can also have a virulent effect on a country's sense of national purpose. Collective identities, by definition, require mechanisms that forge mutual understandings among groups of people. Fractured societies turn to age-old ethnic identities that, as the India-Pakistan and Nigerian experiences demonstrate, can produce destructive, internecine conflict. In Brazil, such extreme conflict has been avoided, but the divisive effects of a fragmented polity on collective identities are serious nonetheless. Divided by class, poor Brazilians continue to feel that politics holds no solutions for them, so they fail to mobilize for their rights. Blacks, women, and Indians share some of the same interests because they are paid less than white men are for the same kind of work. Yet few national organizations have been able to unite a coalition of interest groups to change business practices in this regard. Finally, all Brazilians should be concerned with the clearing of rain forests, the pollution of rivers and lakes, and the destruction of species, yet the major political parties and the congress seem incapable of addressing these issues on behalf of future generations. Such national concerns continuously take a back seat to the self-interests of politicians in Brazil.

Perhaps the most serious effect of political fragmentation on Brazil has involved the struggle to achieve the country's interests in an increasingly competitive, global marketplace. While globalization forces all countries, and particularly developing countries, to adapt to new technology, ideas, and economic interests, it also lets states take advantage of the opportunity to attract investment. Given the weakness of the Brazilian state, the social dislocation produced by industrial restructuring (e.g., unemployment), and the currently unstable nature of the international investment climate, Brazil maintains only an ambiguous vision of its role in the global capitalist order. Although Brazilian business, some unions, and key political leaders speak of the need to defend Brazil's interests in the international political economy, the country has few coherent strategies. Such questions are inherently complex and politically difficult, perhaps no less so in Brazil than in France. But dealing with these issues requires a somewhat consistent policy created by a political leadership with clear ideas about the interests of the country. In Brazil's fragmented polity, developing such unambiguous strategies is difficult.

Acting now on behalf of Brazil's interests in the world of states must be a priority of Cardoso's successor. In the post–September 11 world, issues of security are quickly outpacing matters of equity and development, a concern that Cardoso himself voiced in various summits with world leaders in 2002. Brazil is solidly in the antiterrorist camp, yet Brazilians care more about their security against crime, malnutrition, and ecological disaster than they do about fanatical political violence.

Finally, Brazil's experience with economic restructuring and democratization will continue to influence countries undergoing similar transformations in Latin America and the rest of the developing world. As a large and resource-rich country, Brazil presents a useful example for other big developing countries such as Mexico, Russia, India, and China. Its evolving federal structure as well as its efforts to manage its resources while dealing with environmental costs can inform similar processes in these countries.

As a transitional democracy, Brazil can provide insights into which governance systems work better than others. As a negative example, Brazil's ongoing experiment with presidentialism, multiparty democracy, and open-list PR might well confirm the superiority of alternative parliamentary systems in India and Germany or presidentialism in France and the United States. As a positive example, Brazil's experiences with keeping a diverse country united through trying economic times will have much to teach Russia and Nigeria, as these countries are weighed down by the dual challenges of economic reform and nation building.

Within Latin America, Brazil continues to consolidate its position as the preeminent economy of the region. Through MERCOSUL, Brazil exerts authority on commercial questions, and with its continued dominance of the Amazon basin, the country's political elite retains the world's attention when they speak on environmental issues in the developing world. Brazil's experiences with balancing the exigencies of neoliberal economic adjustment with the sociopolitical realities of poverty will keep it on center stage as the World Bank and the IMF and the region's political, economic, and academic leaders discuss the possibilities for a new model of development.

Brazil may not be "the country of the future," but it is a country with a future. None of the maladies of Brazilian politics and social development is immune to improvement. If political reform is consolidated in the next few years, the groundwork will have been laid for transforming Brazil into a country that deserves the respect of the world.

Key Terms

privatization

moderating power

oligarchy

legitimacy

clientelism

patrimonialism

politics of the governors

interventores

state corporatism

New State

populism

nationalism

bureaucratic
authoritarianism

state-led development

abertura

personalist politicians

export-led growth

interventionist

import substitution
industrialization

state technocrats

developmentalism

para-statals

nongovernmental
organizations

informal economy

favelas

bureaucratic rings

proportional representation

Suggested Readings

Alvarez, Sonia. *Engendering Democracy in Brazil.* Princeton, N.J.: Princeton University Press, 1990.

Ames, Barry. *The Deadlock of Democracy in Brazil: Interests, Identities, and Institutions in Comparative Politics.* Ann Arbor: University of Michigan Press, 2001.

Baer, Werner, ed. *The Brazilian Economy: Growth and Development.* 4th ed. New York: Praeger, 1995.

Dean, Warren. *With Broadax and Firebrand: The Destruction of the Brazilian Atlantic Forest.* Berkeley: University of California Press, 1995.

Evans, Peter B. *Dependent Development: The Alliance of Multinational, State, and Local Capital in Brazil.* Princeton, N.J.: Princeton University Press, 1979.

Furtado, Celso. *The Economic Growth of Brazil: A Survey from Colonial to Modern Times.* Berkeley: University of California Press, 1963.

Keck, Margaret. *The Workers' Party and Democratization in Brazil.* New Haven, Conn.: Yale University Press, 1992.

Kingstone, Peter R., and Power, Timothy J., eds. *Democratic Brazil: Actors, Institutions, and Processes.* Pittsburgh: University of Pittsburgh Press, 2000.

Lamounier, Bolivar. "Brazil Towards Parliamentarism?" In Juan Linz and Valenzuela Arturo, eds., *The Failure of Presidential Democracy.* Baltimore: Johns Hopkins University Press, 1994.

Mainwaring, Scott. *Rethinking Party Systems in the Third Wave of Democratization: The Case of Brazil.* Stanford: Stanford University Press, 1999.

Matta, Roberto da. *Carnivals, Rogues, and Heroes: An Interpretation of the Brazilian Dilemma.* Notre Dame, Ind.: University of Notre Dame Press, 1991.

Roett, Riordan. *Brazil: Politics in a Patrimonial Society.* 4th ed. New York: Praeger, 1992.

Scheper-Hughes, Nancy. *Death Without Weeping: The Violence of Everyday Life in Brazil.* Berkeley: University of California Press, 1992.

Schneider, Ben Ross. *Politics Within the State: Elite Bureaucrats and Industrial Policy in Authoritarian Brazil.* Pittsburgh: University of Pittsburgh Press, 1991.

Skidmore, Thomas E. *Black into White: Race and Nationality in Brazilian Thought.* Durham, N.C.: Duke University Press, 1993.

———. *The Politics of Military Rule in Brazil, 1964—85.* New York: Oxford University Press, 1988.

Stepan, Alfred. *Rethinking Military Politics: Brazil and the Southern Cone.* Princeton, N.J.: Princeton University Press, 1988.

———, ed. *Democratizing Brazil: Problems of Transition and Consolidation.* New York: Oxford University Press, 1989.

Tendler, Judith. *Good Government in the Tropics.* Baltimore: Johns Hopkins University Press, 1997.

Weyland, Kurt. *Democracy Without Equity: Failures of Reform in Brazil.* Pittsburgh: University of Pittsburgh Press, 1996.

Suggested Websites

LANIC database, University of Texas-Austin, Brazil Resource page
lanic.utexas.edu/la/brazil/

U.S. Library of Congress Country Study Page for Brazil
lcweb2.loc.gov/frd/cs/brtoc.html

Political Resources for Brazil, Political Database of the Americas, Georgetown University
cfdev.georgetown.edu/pdba/Countries/countries.cfm?ID=43

SciELO Brazil, Searchable Database of Full-Text Articles on Brazil
www.scielo.br/

National Development Bank of Brazil, Searchable Database of Documents on Brazilian Economy and Development (many in English)
www.bndes.gov.br

Notes

[1]IBGE (Instituto Brasileiro de Geografia e Estatística), *PNAD–Síntese do Indicadores da Pesquisa Básica da PNAD de 1981 a 1989* (Rio de Janeiro: IBGE, 1990). For more on Brazil's multiclassification system, see George Reid Andrews, *Blacks and Whites in São Paulo, Brazil, 1888–1988* (Madison: University of Wisconsin Press, 1991).

[2]See Bertha K. Becker and Claudio A. G. Egler, *Brazil: A New Regional Power in the World Economy: A Regional Geography* (New York: Cambridge University Press, 1992), 5, and Terence Turner, "Brazil: Indigenous Rights vs. Neoliberalism," *Dissent* (Summer 1996): 67.

[3]For a complete treatment of state corporatism in Brazil during this period, see Ruth Berins Collier and David Collier, *Shaping*

the Political Arena: Critical Junctures, the Labor Movement, and Regime Dynamics in Latin America (Princeton, N.J.: Princeton University Press, 1991), 169–195.

[4]Robert M. Levine, *Father of the Poor? Vargas and His Era* (New York: Cambridge University Press, 1998), 8–9.

[5]For an analysis of this "new professionalism," see Alfred Stepan, *The Military in Politics: Changing Patterns in Brazil* (Princeton, N.J.: Princeton University Press, 1971).

[6]Thomas E. Skidmore, *Politics in Brazil, 1930–1964: An Experiment in Democracy* (New York: Oxford University Press, 1967), 101.

[7]Maria do Carmo Campello de Souza, *Estado e Partidos Políticos no Brasil (1930 a 1964)* (São Paulo: Editora Alfa-Omega, 1975).

[8]Guillermo O'Donnell, *Modernization and Bureaucratic-Authoritarianism: Studies in South American Politics* (Berkeley: Institute of International Studies, University of California, 1973).

[9]Thomas E. Skidmore, *The Politics of Military Rule in Brazil, 1964–85* (New York: Oxford University Press, 1988), 49.

[10]Leigh A. Payne, *Brazilian Industrialists and Democratic Change* (Baltimore: Johns Hopkins University Press, 1994), chap. 4.

[11]For an analysis of these critical elections, see Bolivar Lamounier, "Authoritarian Brazil Revisited: The Impact of Elections on the Abertura," in Alfred Stepan, ed., *Democratizing Brazil: Problems of Transition and Consolidation* (New York: Oxford University Press, 1989).

[12]Margaret Keck, *The Workers' Party and Democratization in Brazil* (New Haven, Conn.: Yale University Press, 1992), 219–220.

[13]Timothy J. Power, *The Political Right in Postauthoritarian Brazil: Elites, Institutions, and Democratization* (University Park: Pennsylvania State University Press, 2000).

[14]Margaret Keck, "The New Unionism in the Brazilian Transition," in Stepan, *Democratizing Brazil,* 284.

[15]See Celso Furtado, *The Economic Growth of Brazil: A Survey from Colonial to Modern Times* (Berkeley: University of California Press, 1963).

[16]For a more complete treatment of how developmentalist ideas cultivated in ECLA affected policy choices in Brazil, see Kathryn Sikkink, *Ideas and Institutions: Developmentalism in Brazil and Argentina* (Ithaca, N.Y.: Cornell University Press, 1991).

[17]More complete treatment of the ISI experience can be found in Albert O. Hirschman, *A Bias for Hope: Essays on Development and Latin America* (New Haven, Conn.: Yale University Press, 1971).

[18]Peter B. Evans, *Dependent Development: The Alliance of Multinational, State, and Local Capital in Brazil* (Princeton, N.J.: Princeton University Press, 1979).

[19]These and other examples of ecological destruction are analyzed in Werner Baer and Charles C. Mueller, "Environmental Aspects of Brazil's Development," in Werner Baer, ed., *The Brazilian Economy: Growth and Development*, 4th ed. (New York: Praeger, 1995).

[20]For more on state environmental efforts, see Barry Ames and Margaret E. Keck, "The Politics of Sustainable Development: Environmental Policy Making in Four Brazilian States," *Journal of Interamerican Studies and World Affairs* 39, no. 4 (Winter 1998), 1–40.

[21]Kathryn Hochstetler, "The Evolution of the Brazilian Environmental Movement and Its Political Roles," in Douglas Chalmers, Carlos M. Vilas, Katherine R. Hite, Scott B. Martin, Kerianne Piester, and Monique Segarra, eds., *The New Politics of Inequality in Latin America: Rethinking Participation and Representation* (New York: Oxford University Press, 1997).

[22]Alfred P. Montero, "Devolving Democracy? Political Decentralization and the New Brazilian Federalism," in Peter R. Kingstone and Timothy J. Power, eds., *Democratic Brazil: Actors, Institutions, and Processes* (Pittsburgh: University of Pittsburgh Press, 2000).

[23]Peggy A. Lovell, "Race, Gender, and Development in Brazil," *Latin American Research Review* 29, no. 3 (1994), 7–35.

[24]Kurt Weyland, *Democracy Without Equity: Failures of Reform in Brazil* (Pittsburgh: University of Pittsburgh Press, 1996).

[25]Wilson Cano, "Concentración, desconcentración y descentralización en Brasil," in José Luis Curbelo, Francisco Alburquerque, Carlos A. de Mattos, and Juan Ramón Cuadrado, eds., *Territorios en Transformación: Análisis y Propuestas* (Madrid: Fondo Europeo de Desarrollo Regional, 1994).

[26]Leonardo Guimarães Neto, "Desigualdades Regionais e Federalismo," in Rui de Britto Álvares Affonso and Pedro Luiz Barros Silva, eds., *Desigualdades Regionais e Desenvolvimento* (São Paulo: FUNDAP, 1995).

[27]Jeffry A. Frieden, *Debt, Development, and Democracy: Modern Political Economy and Latin America, 1965–1985* (Princeton, N.J.: Princeton University Press, 1991), 54–65.

[28]Diana Jean Schemo, "The ABC's of Business in Brazil," *New York Times*, July 16, 1998, B1, 7.

[29]Fernando Luiz Abrúcio, *Os Barões da Federação: O Poder dos Governadores no Brasil Pós-Autoritário* (São Paulo: Editora HUCITECU, 1998).

[30]Alfred P. Montero, *Shifting States in Global Markets: Subnational Industrial Policy in Contemporary Brazil and Spain* (University Park: Pennsylvania State University Press, 2002).

[31]Timothy J. Power, "Politicized Democracy: Competition, Institutions, and 'Civic Fatigue' in Brazil," *Journal of Interamerican Studies and World Affairs* 33, no. 3 (Fall 1991), 75–112.

[32]Argelina Figueiredo and Fernando Limongi, "O Congresso e as Medidas Provisórias: Abdicação ou Delegação?" *Novos Estudos CEBRAP* 47 (1997): 127–154.

[33]Thomas J. Trebat, *Brazil's State-Owned Enterprises: A Case Study of the State as Entrepreneur* (New York: Cambridge University Press, 1983).

[34]Helen Shapiro, *Engines of Growth: The State and Transnational Auto Companies in Brazil* (New York: Cambridge University Press, 1994).

[35]Peter B. Evans, "Predatory, Developmental, and Other Apparatuses: A Comparative Political Economy Perspective on the Third World State," *Sociological Forum* 4, no. 4 (1989), 561–587.

[36]Alfred P. Montero, "State Interests and the New Industrial Policy in Brazil: The Case of the Privatization of Steel, 1990–1994," *Journal of Interamerican Studies and World Affairs* 40, no. 3 (Fall 1998), 27–62.

[37]Wendy Hunter, *Eroding Military Influence in Brazil: Politicians Against Soldiers* (Chapel Hill: University of North Carolina Press, 1997).

[38]Paulo Sérgio Pinheiro, "Popular Responses to State-Sponsored Violence in Brazil," in Chalmers et al., eds., *The New Politics of Inequality in Latin America.*

[39]Human Rights Watch, *Police Brutality in Urban Brazil* (New York: Human Rights Watch, 1997), 13.

[40]Judith Tendler, *Good Government in the Tropics* (Baltimore: Johns Hopkins University Press, 1997).

[41]For a study of how these exceptions have emerged in Brazil, see Barbara Geddes, *Politician's Dilemma: Building State Capacity in Latin America* (Berkeley: University of California Press, 1994).

[42]Ben Ross Schneider, *Politics Within the State: Elite Bureaucrats and Industrial Policy in Authoritarian Brazil* (Pittsburgh: University of Pittsburgh Press, 1991).

[43]Lívia Neves de H. Barbosa, "The Brazilian Jeitinho: An Exercise in National Identity," in David J. Hess and Roberto A. DaMatta, eds., *The Brazilian Puzzle: Culture on the Borderlands of the Western World* (New York: Columbia University Press, 1995).

[44]Barry Ames, *The Deadlock of Democracy in Brazil: Interests, Identities, and Institutions in Comparative Politics* (Ann Arbor: University of Michigan Press, 2001).

[45]Scott Mainwaring, "Brazilian Party Underdevelopment in Comparative Perspective," *Political Science Quarterly* 107 (1993).

[46]Timothy J. Power, "The Pen Is Mightier Than the Congress: Presidential Decree Power in Brazil," in John M. Carey and Mathew S. Shugart, eds., *Executive Decree Authority: Calling Out the Tanks or Just Filling Out the Forms* (New York: Cambridge University Press, 1998).

[47]See Argelina C. Figueiredo and Fernando Limongi, "Presidential Power, Legislative Organization, and Party Behavior in Brazil," *Comparative Politics* 32 (January 2000): 151–170.

[48]See Ames, *Deadlock of Democracy.*

[49]See Power, *The Political Right in Postauthoritarian Brazil.*

[50]See especially Gilberto Freyre, *The Mansions and the Shanties: The Making of Modern Brazil* (New York: Knopf, 1963), chap. 12.

[51]Ralph Della Cava, "The 'People's Church,' the Vatican, and Abertura," in Stepan, *Democratizing Brazil.*

[52]Turner, "Brazil: Indigenous Rights vs. Neoliberalism," 67.

[53]William H. Fisher, "Megadevelopment, Environmentalism, and Resistance: The Institutional Context of Kayapó Indigenous Politics in Central Brazil," *Human Organization* 53, no. 3 (1994), 220–232.

CHAPTER 6

Nigeria

Darren Kew and Peter Lewis

Federal Republic of Nigeria

Land and People

Capital	Abuja
Total area (square miles)	356,669 (more than twice the size of California)
Population	130 million

Annual population growth rate (%)		
	1975–2000	2.9
	2000–2015 (projected)	2.7

Urban population (%)	38	
Ethnolinguistic composition (% of population)	Hausa-Fulani	32
	Yoruba	21
	Igbo	18
	Ibibio	6
	Various dialects	14
	Other	8
Official Language	English	
Religious affiliation (%)	Muslim	50
	Christian	45
	Indigenous	5

Economy

Domestic currency	Naira (NGN) US$1: 135 NGN (2003 av.)	
Total GDP (US$)	44 billion (2002)	
GDP per capita (US$)	363 (2002)	
Total GDP at purchasing power parity (US$)	113.7 billion	
GDP per capita at purchasing power parity (US$)	896	
GDP annual growth rate (%)	1997	2.7
	2000	3.8
	2001	4.0
	2002	3.4
GDP per capita average annual growth rate (%)	1975–2000	-0.7
	1990–2000	-0.4
Inequality in income or consumption (1996–1997) (%)	Share of poorest 10%	1.6
	Share of poorest 20%	4.4
	Share of richest 20%	55.7
	Share of richest 10%	40.8
	Gini Index (1996–1997)	50.6
Structure of production (% of GDP)	Agriculture	41
	Industry	32
	Services	27
Labor force distribution (% of total)	Agriculture	60
	Industry	8
	Services	32
Exports as % of GDP	52	
Imports as % of GDP	41	

Society

Life expectancy at birth	52.7	
Infant mortality per 1,000 live births	110	
Adult literacy (%)	Male	72.4
	Female	55.7

Access to information and communications (per 1,000 population)	Telephone lines	4
	Mobile phones	1
	Radios	200
	Televisions	68
	Personal computers	6.6

Women in Government and Economy

Women in the national legislature		
Lower house or single house (%)		3.4
Upper house (%)		2.8
Women at ministerial level (%)		22.6
Female economic activity rate (age 15 and above) (%)		47.6
Female labor force (% of total)		36
Estimated earned income (PPP US$)	Female	532
	Male	1,254
2002 Human Development Index Ranking (out of 173 countries)		148

Political Organization

Political System   Democracy.

Regime History   Democratic government took office in May 1999, after 16 years of military rule. The most recent elections were held in 2003.

Administrative Structure   Power is centralized largely under the presidency and the governors. Nigeria is a federation 36 states, plus the Federal Capital Territory (FCT) in Abuja.

Executive   U.S.-style presidential system, under Olusegun Obasanjo.

Legislature   A bicameral civilian legislature was elected in April 2003. The 109 senators are elected on the basis of equal representation: three from each state, and one from the FCT. The 360 members of the House of Representatives are elected from single-member districts.

Judiciary   The Nigerian judicial system resembles that of the United States with a network of local and district courts as well as state-level courts. The state-level judiciaries are subordinate to the Federal Court of Appeal and the Supreme Court of Nigeria, which consists of 15 appointed associate justices and the chief justice. Every state of the federation can also opt to establish a system of Islamic law (shari'a) courts for cases involving only Muslims in customary disputes (divorce, property, etc.); the secular courts, however, retain supreme jurisdiction at the federal level if any conflict arises over which system to use. Most Nigerian states feature such courts, which share a Federal Shari'a Court of Appeal in Abuja. Twelve Northern states since 1999 have also instituted the shari'a criminal code, which allows for cutting off hands for stealing, stoning to death for adultery, and other extreme sentences. This aspect of the shari'a remains contentious, however, and may soon be challenged at the Supreme Court, which is likely to dismantle it.

Party System   Three parties were registered by the Nigerian electoral commission in December 1998: the Alliance for Democracy (AD), All People's Party (APP—now the All Nigerian People's Party, ANPP), and People's Democratic Party (PDP). PDP won the presidency, majorities in both houses of the National Assembly, and control of many of the governorships, state assemblies, and local governments. 27 more parties were registered in 2002.

Section ❶ The Making of the Modern Nigerian State

Politics in Action

Olusegun Obasanjo took office as president in May 1999 amid tremendous domestic and international goodwill as Nigeria's first elected civilian leader in nearly twenty years. Flanked by Nelson Mandela and other global dignitaries, Obasanjo boldly stated his intentions to reform the corrupt Nigerian state, reverse its economic decline, and restore the nation to greatness. A succession of oppressive, thieving military leaders in the 1980s and 1990s had stolen billions from the national coffers, leaving this oil-rich nation in tremendous debt and making it an international pariah; 120 million Nigerians looked to Obasanjo to rectify the political sins of the past and pull them out of impoverishment. The president promised to do both, and in 1999 he set out with an ambitious political agenda.

Three years later, the National Assembly set out to impeach him. Members of Obasanjo's own party, including the Speaker of the House, sponsored the resolution to instigate impeachment proceedings. The legislators spoke in public of the president's unconstitutional behavior, but in private they were more outraged by his heavy-handed methods—and by the fact that he refused to disburse their personal allowances for the year.

President Obasanjo's struggles with the National Assembly are symptomatic of the larger obstacles his government faces in trying to revive the dysfunctional Nigerian state. His ambitious agenda has run aground on the many contradictions in governance left by years of military rule, such as a disproportionately powerful presidency married to an inexperienced legislature in search of power and relevance. In addition, the young democracy faces the challenge of managing the country's incredible diversity. Colonialism left Nigerians with a project as complex as the construction of the European Union, trying to build a single political structure out of many nations yet without the high levels of political and economic development that the Europeans enjoy. Furthermore, years of economic decline and political corruption have left most Nigerians with little patience to wait for Obasanjo's fragile, self-conflicted government to deliver significant progress.

The military left power in 1999 as a discredited institution, but it is slowly rebuilding, and the clock is ticking against the civilians: Will public frustrations with the slow pace of reform hold off long enough for democracy to consolidate sufficiently to meet minimal public expectations?

Although Nigeria has developed well beyond the point in the 1950s when its leaders saw it as a mere geographic expression, the development of national consciousness and character has progressed, often in spite of the nation's political direction. Many Nigerians intermarry across ethnic and religious lines, share common traditions like chewing kola nuts with friends, work (often their whole lives) and invest in cities outside their ethnic homelands, and unite in support of their national sports teams. Yet when talk turns to politics, southern Nigerians will complain of northern domination of the government, Igbos will claim that Yorubas cannot be trusted for their "betrayal" of Biafra during the civil war, Christians will complain that Muslims want an Islamic fundamentalist state, and so on.

Nigeria offers, within a single case, characteristics that identify Africa. These opposing forces are rooted in the constant struggle in Nigeria between **authoritarian** and democratic governance, the push for development and the persistence of underdevelopment, the burden of public corruption and the pressure for accountability. Nigeria, like all other African countries, has sought to create a viable nation-state out of the social incoherence created by its colonial borders. Over 250 competing nationalities—or ethnic groups, largely defined by language differences—in Nigeria have repeatedly clashed over economic and political resources. All of these factors combine to produce the political entity known as Nigeria with a low level of popular **legitimacy** and **accountability** and a persistent inability to meet the most basic needs of its citizens. The country therefore provides a crucible in which to examine questions of democracy and authoritarianism, the pressures and management of ethnic conflict, and economic underdevelopment brought about by both colonial oppression and independent Nigeria's mismanagement of its vast resources.

Much about Nigeria is contentious. Since gaining

independence from British colonial rule in 1960, Nigeria has undergone several political transitions, from democratic governments to autocratic regimes, both military and civilian, and from one military regime to another. After nearly four decades as an independent nation, Nigeria has yet to witness an orderly and constitutional transition from one democratic regime to another, although it will try once again to do so in 2003. It has experienced six successful coups (most recently in November 1993) and many unsuccessful attempted coups, and it was torn by three years of civil war that claimed over 100,000 military and over 1 million civilian casualties. Against this background, Nigeria today remains essentially an **unfinished state** characterized by instabilities and uncertainties.

Nigeria reached another critical turning point in 1999 when a military government transferred power to civilians for the second time since the British left in 1960. The civilians held their own elections in 2003 for the first time since 1983, which were so flawed then that the public welcomed a military coup. The 2003 elections also showed evidence of tampering. Will Nigeria return to the discredited path of authoritarianism and greater underdevelopment, or will the civilian leadership rise to achieve a consolidated democracy and sustainable growth?

Geographic Setting

Nigeria, with 130 million people inhabiting 356,669 square miles, ranks as the most populous nation in Africa and among the ten largest in the world. A center of West African regional trade, culture, and military strength, Nigeria is bordered by four countries—Benin, Niger, Chad, and Cameroon, all of them Francophone—and by the Gulf of Guinea in the Atlantic Ocean to the south. The modern country of Nigeria, however, like nearly all the other contemporary states in Africa, is not even a century old.

Nigeria was a British colony from 1914 until its independence on October 1, 1960, although foreign domination of much of the territory had begun in the mid-nineteenth century. Nigeria's boundaries had little to do with the borders of the precolonial African nations in the territory that the British conquered. Instead, these boundaries merely marked the point where British influence ended and France's began. Britain ruled northern and southern Nigeria as two separate colonies until 1914, when it amalgamated its Northern and Southern Protectorates. In short, Nigeria was essentially an arbitrary creation reflecting British colonial interests. The consequences of this forced union of a myriad of formerly independent African nations under one political roof remain a central feature of Nigerian political life today.

Nigeria's location in West Africa, its size, and its oil-producing status have made it a hub of regional activity. Demographically, it overwhelms the other fifteen countries in West Africa, with a population that is nearly 60 percent of the region's total. Moreover, Nigeria's gross domestic product (GDP) typically represents more than half of the total GDP for the entire subregion.

Nigeria's ethnic map can be divided into six inexact areas or "zones." The northwest (or "core North") is dominated by Nigeria's largest ethnic group, the Hausa-Fulani, two formerly separate groups that over the past century have largely merged. The northeast is a minority region, the largest of whom are the Kanuri. Both regions in the north are predominantly Muslim. A large swath of territory stretching across the center of the country, called the Middle Belt, is also home to a wide range of minority groups of both Muslim and Christian identification. The southwest (referred to as the Western Region in the First Republic) is dominated by the country's second largest ethnic group, the Yoruba, who are approximately 40 percent Muslim, 40 percent Christian (primarily Protestant), and 20 percent practitioners of Yoruba traditional beliefs. The southeast (which formed the hub of the First Republic's Eastern Region) is the Igbo homeland, Nigeria's third largest group, who are primarily Christian, and where Protestant evangelical movements have become popular. Between the Yoruba and Igbo regions of the south is the southern minority zone, which stretches across the Niger Delta areas and east along the coast as far as Cameroon.

Critical Junctures

A number of critical junctures helped shape the character of the Nigerian state and illustrate the difficult path that the country has taken during the past century. This path features influences from the precolonial period,

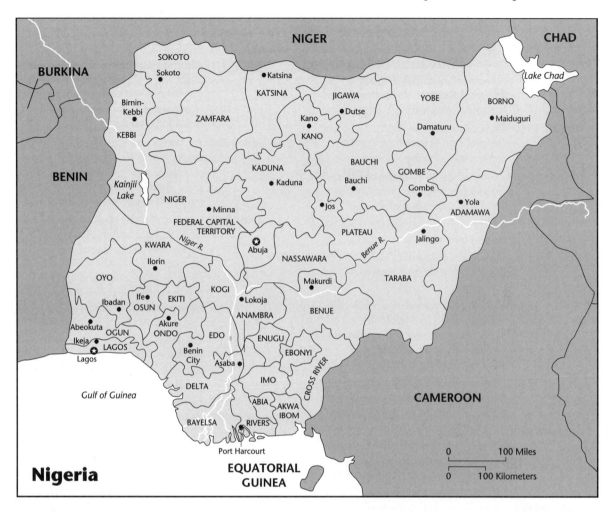

British colonialism, the alternation of military and civilian rule after independence, and the post-1980 economic collapse, precipitated by Nigeria's political corruption and overreliance on its petroleum industry.

The Precolonial Period (800–1900)

Much of Nigeria's precolonial history before 1000 has been reconstructed from oral histories because, with few exceptions, literate cultures evolved much later. In contrast to the peoples of the forest belt to the south, the more open terrain in the north, with its need for irrigation, encouraged the early growth of centralized states. Such states from the eighth century included Kanem-Bornu in the northeast and the Hausa states in the northwest. Another attempt at state formation led to the emergence of a Jukun kingdom; however, by the end of the seventeenth century, the Jukun became a tributary state of the Bornu empire.

A major element that shaped the course of events in the savanna areas of the north was trade across the Sahara Desert with northern Africa. Trade brought material benefits as well as Arabic education and Islam, which gradually replaced traditional spiritual, political, and social practices. In 1808, the Fulani, who came from lands west of modern Nigeria through a holy war (*jihad*) led by Uthman dan Fodio, established an Islamic empire, the Sokoto Caliphate. Portions of the region to the south, the present day Middle Belt, were able to repel the *jihad* and preserve their independence

Critical Junctures in Modern Nigerian Political Development

1960 Independence. Nigeria consists of three regions under a Westminster parliamentary model. **Abubakar Tafawa Balewa,** a Northerner, is the first prime minister.

January 1966 Civilian government deposed in coup. **General Aguiyi Ironsi,** an Igbo, becomes head of state.

July 1966 Countercoup led by **General Yakubu Gowon** (an Anga, from the "Middle Belt") with aid from northern groups.

1967–1970 Biafran civil war.

July 1975 Military coup deposes Gowon; led by **General Murtala Muhammed,** a northerner.

February 1976 Murtala Muhammed assassinated in failed coup led by Middle Belt minorities. Muhammed's second-in-command, **General Olusegun Obasanjo,** a Yoruba, assumes power.

September 1978 New constitution completed, marking the adoption of the U.S. presidential model in a federation with 19 states.

October 1979 Elections held. A majority in both houses is won by NPN, led by Northern/Hausa-Fulani groups. **Alhaji Shehu Shagari** is elected Nigeria's first executive president.

December 1983 Military coup led by **General Muhammadu Buhari,** a northerner.

August 1985 Buhari is overthrown by **General Ibrahim B. Babangida**, a Middle Belt Muslim, in a palace coup. Babangida promises a return to democracy by 1990, a date he delays five times before being forced from office.

June 12, 1993 **Moshood Abiola** wins presidential elections, but Babangida annuls the election 11 days later.

August 1993 Babangida installs **Ernest Shonekan** as "interim civilian president" until new presidential elections could be held later that autumn.

November 1993 Defense Minister **General Sani Abacha** seizes power in a coup. Two years later he announces a three-year transition to civilian rule, which he manipulates to have himself nominated for president in 1998.

July–Sept. 1994 Pro-democracy strike by the major oil union, NUPENG, cuts Nigeria's oil production by an estimated 25 percent. Sympathy strikes ensue, followed by arrests of political and civic leaders.

June 1998 General Abacha dies; succeeded by General **Abdulsalami Abubakar**, a Middle Belt Muslim from Babangida's hometown. Abubakar releases nearly all political prisoners and installs a new transition program. Parties are allowed to form unhindered.

1999 Former head of state **Olusegun Obasanjo** and his party, the PDP, sweep the Presidential and National Assembly elections, adding to their majority control of state and local government seats. The federation now contains 36 states.

November 1999 Zamfara state in the North is the first of 12 to institute the *shari'a* criminal code. That same month, President Obasanjo sends the army to the Niger Delta town of Odi to root out local militias, leveling the town in the process.

2000 Communal conflicts erupt in Lagos, Benue, Kaduna, and Kano states at different times over localized issues.

Spring 2002 The Supreme Court passes several landmark judgments, overturning a PDP-biased 2001 electoral law, and ruling on the control of offshore oil and gas resources. In November the Court opens the legal door for more parties to be registered.

August 2002 The National Assembly begins impeachment proceedings against President Obasanjo over budgetary issues. The matter ends by November, with the president apologizing.

and religious diversity. The Sokoto Caliphate used Islam and a common language, Hausa, to forge unity out of the disparate groups in the north. The Fulani empire held sway until British colonial authority was imposed on northern Nigeria by 1900.

Toward the southern edge of the savanna lived such groups as the Tiv, whose political organizations seldom extended beyond the village level. Within such societies, politics was generally conducted along kinship lines, and the fundamental political unit was the extended family. Political authority was diffused rather than centralized, such that later Western contacts described them as "stateless," or **acephalous societies.** Because they lacked complex political hierarchies, these societies escaped much of the upheaval experienced under colonialism by the centralized states, and they retained much of their autonomy.

The development of collective identities in southern Nigeria was equally complex. Groups included the highly centralized Yoruba empires and kingdoms of Oyo and Ife; the Edo kingdom of Benin in the midwest; the fragmentary, acephalous societies of the Igbo to the east; and the trading city-states of the Niger Delta and its hinterland, peopled by a wide range of ethnicities.

Several precolonial societies had democratic elements that scholars speculate might have led to more open and participatory polities had they not been interrupted by colonialism. Governance in the Yoruba and Igbo communities involved principles of accountability: rulers could not disregard the views and interests of the governed or they would risk revocation of consent and loss of their positions. Another element was representation, defined less in terms of formal procedures for selecting leaders, and more in terms of assurances that rulers adhered to culturally mandated principles and obligations that forced them to seek out and protect the interests of their subjects.

Among the Islamic communities of the north, political society was highly structured, reflecting local interpretations of Qur'anic principles. Leadership structures

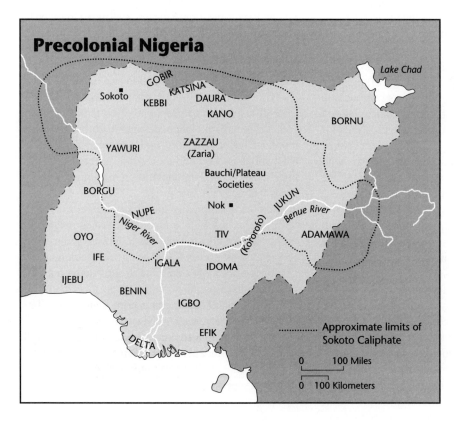

Precolonial Polities and Societies. *Source:* K. Michael Barbour, Julius Oguntoyinbo, J.O.C. Onyemelukwe, and James C. Nwafor, *Nigeria in Maps* (New York: Africana Publishing Company, 1982), 37.

Map: Precolonial Nigeria — Sokoto, Gobir, Katsina, Kebbi, Daura, Kano, Bornu, Lake Chad, Yawuri, Zazzau (Zaria), Bauchi/Plateau Societies, Nok, Borgu, Nupe, Niger River, Jukun (Kororofa), Benue River, Oyo, Ife, Tiv, Adamawa, Igala, Idoma, Ijebu, Benin, Igbo, Efik, Delta. Approximate limits of Sokoto Caliphate. 0–100 Miles, 0–100 Kilometers.

were considerably more hierarchical than those of the south, dominated by a few educated elites in positions of authority. In addition (although some of the pre-Islamic indigenous beliefs showed deference to important women spirit leaders), women were consigned to a subordinate position in systems of governance. The Islamic Fulani empire was a confederation in which the rulers, **emirs,** owed allegiance to the sultan, who was the temporal and spiritual head of the empire. The sultan's powers, in turn, were circumscribed by the obligation to observe the principles of Islam in fulfilling his duties.

Colonial Rule and Its Impact (1860–1945)

Competition for trade and empire drove the European imperial powers into Africa after 1860. During the colonial period, Nigeria's resources were extracted and its people exploited as cheap labor to further the growth of British society and defray administrative costs of the British Empire. Colonialism left its imprint on all aspects of Nigeria's existence, bequeathing a political system that was inappropriate in many respects.

Where centralized monarchies existed, particularly in the north, the British ruled through a policy known as **indirect rule,** which allowed traditional structures to persist as subordinates to the British governor and a small administrative apparatus. Where more democratic and acephalous societies existed, particularly among the Igbo and other groups in the southeast, the colonizers either strengthened the authority of traditional chiefs and kings or appointed **warrant chiefs** (who ruled by warrant of the British Crown), weakening the previous practices of accountability and participation.

The British played off ethnic and social divisions to keep Nigerians from developing organized political resistance to colonial rule, and where resistance did develop, the colonizers were not afraid to employ repressive tactics, even as late as the 1940s. They instilled two sets of rules: one for political leaders and another for the citizenry. Yet the British also promoted the foundations of a democratic political system before they left in 1960. This dual standard left a conflicted democratic idea: formal democratic institutions yet an authoritarian political culture. Colonialism also strengthened the collective identities of Nigeria's mul-

tiple ethnic groups by fostering political competition among them, primarily among the three largest: the Hausa-Fulani, Yoruba, and Igbo.

Divisive Identities: Ethnic Politics Under Colonialism (1945–1960)

Based on the British example, leaders of the anticolonial movement came to regard the state as an exploitative instrument, and its control as an opportunity to pursue personal and group interests rather than broad national interests. Thus, once the British in the 1940s announced their intention to negotiate the terms of their gradual exit from Nigeria, whatever semblance of unity had existed among the anticolonial leaders soon evaporated, and political competition became increasingly fierce.

Nigerian leaders quickly turned to ethnicity as the preferred vehicle to pursue this competition and mobilize public support. The three largest ethnic groups—the Hausa-Fulani, Igbo, and Yoruba, which together comprise approximately 65 percent of Nigeria's population—have dominated the political process since the 1940s. By pitting ethnic groups against each other for purposes of "divide and rule" and by structuring the administrative units of Nigeria based on ethnic groups, the British ensured that ethnicity would be the primary element in political identification and mobilization.

Nigerian ethnic groups, championed by educated local elites, began to propound tales of origin and to create standardized languages and histories to foster a more exclusivist identity and heritage. They rallied followers based on common ethnic identity and challenged the colonial administration in competition with rivals from other ethnic groups.

The early ethnically based associations were initially concerned with nonpolitical issues: promoting mutual aid for housing and education, as well as sponsoring cultural events. With the encouragement of ambitious leaders, however, these groups took on a more political character. Nigeria's first political party, the National Council of Nigeria and the Cameroons (later the National Convention of Nigerian Citizens, NCNC), initially drew supporters from across Nigeria. As the prospects for independence increased, however, indigenous elites began to divide along ethnic lines to mobilize support for their differing political agendas.

Recognizing the multiethnic character of their colony, the British divided Nigeria into a federation of three regions with elected governments in 1954. Each of the federated units soon fell under the domination of one of the three largest ethnic groups and their respective parties. The Northern Region came under the control of the Northern Peoples Congress (NPC), associated with and dominated by Hausa-Fulani elites. In the southern half of the country, the Western Region was controlled by the Action Group (AG), which was controlled by the elites of the Yoruba group. The Igbo, the numerically dominant group in the Eastern Region, were closely associated with the NCNC, which became the ruling party there. Thus, the distinctive and often divisive ethnic and regional characteristics of modern Nigeria were reinforced during the transition to independence.[1]

Chief Obafemi Awolowo, leader of the AG, caught the sentiment of the times when he wrote in 1947 that "Nigeria is not a nation. It is a mere geographical expression. There are no 'Nigerians' in the same sense as there are 'English,' 'Welsh,' or 'French.' The word 'Nigerian' is merely a distinctive appellation to distinguish those who live within the boundaries of Nigeria from those who do not."[2]

The First Republic (1960–1966)

The British granted Nigeria independence in 1960 to a civilian parliamentary government. Nigerians adopted the British Westminster model at the federal and regional levels, in which the chief executive, the prime minister, was chosen by the majority party. Northerners came to dominate the federal government by virtue of their greater population, based on the 1952–1953 census. The ruling coalition for the first two years quickly turned into a northern-only coalition when the NPC achieved an outright majority in the legislature. Having benefited less from the economic, educational, and infrastructural benefits of colonialism, the northerners who dominated the First Republic set out to redistribute resources in their own direction. This NPC policy of northernization brought them into direct conflict with their southern counterparts, particularly the Yoruba-based AG and later the Igbo-dominated NCNC.

When an AG internal conflict led to a political crisis in the Western regional assembly in 1962, the NPC-led national government seized the opportunity to subdivide the Western (largely Yoruba) Region in two, diluting Yoruba political power. Violence escalated among the Yoruba factions in the West as the

Nigeria in 1955: Divided into Three Federated Regions. The administrative division of Nigeria into three regions later became the basis for ethnoregional conflicts. (Note: At the time of independence, the southeastern part of the country, which had been governed as a trust territory, opted to become part of independent Cameroon; two northern trust territories opted to become part of independent Nigeria.)   Source: K. Michael Barbour, Julius Oguntoyinbo, J.O.C. Onyemelukwe, and James C. Nwafor, *Nigeria in Maps* (New York: Africana Publishing Company, 1982), 39.

NPC-dominated government engaged in extensive political corruption. A fraudulent census, falsified ballots, widespread violence, and intimidation of supporters and candidates alike ensured the NPC a tarnished victory in 1965.

Rivalries intensified as the NPC sat atop an absolute majority in the federal parliament with no need for its former coalition partner, the NCNC. NCNC leader Nnamdi Azikiwe, who was also president in the First Republic (then a largely symbolic position), and Tafawa Balewa, the NPC prime minister, separately approached the military to ensure that if it came to conflict, they could count on its loyalty. Thus, "in the struggle for personal survival both men, perhaps inadvertently, made the armed forces aware that they had a political role to play."[3]

Civil War and Military Rule (1966–1979)

With significant encouragement from contending civilian leaders, a group of largely Igbo officers seized power in January 1966. Aguiyi Ironsi, also an Igbo, became head of state by dint of being the highest-ranking officer rather than a coup plotter. His announced aim was to end violence in the Western Region and to stop political corruption and abuses by the northern-dominated government by centralizing the state apparatus, thereby replacing the federation with a unitary state. Although Ironsi claimed to be ethnically plural in his outlook, other Nigerians, particularly northerners, were deeply suspicious of his revocation of federalism. A second coup in July 1966 killed General Ironsi and brought Yakubu Gowon, a Middle Belt Christian, to power as a consensus head of state among the non-Igbo coup plotters.[4]

Because many northern officials had been killed in the initial coup, a tremendous backlash against Igbos flared in several parts of the country during 1966, especially after the second coup. Igbo migrant laborers were persecuted in the north, and many fled to their home region in the east. By 1967, the predominantly Igbo population of eastern Nigeria attempted to secede and form its own independent nation, called Biafra. The secessionists wanted to break free from Nigeria, believing that the north, by virtue of its greater numbers, would permanently lock the other regions out of power. General Gowon built a military-led government of national unity in what remained of Nigeria (the North and West) and, after a bloody three-year war of attrition and starvation tactics, defeated Biafra by January 1970. The conflict exacted a heavy toll on Nigeria's populace, including at least a million deaths.

After the war, Gowon presided over a policy of national reconciliation, which proceeded fairly smoothly with the aid of growing oil revenues. In order to dilute the power of the "big three" ethnic groups, he broke the four-state federation into twelve states, later increased to nineteen by his successor. He also oversaw an increase in the armed forces from about 10,000 men in 1966 to nearly 250,000 by 1970. Senior officers reaped the benefits of the global oil boom in 1973–1974, and corruption was widespread. Influenced by the unwillingness of the military elite to relinquish power and the spoils of office, Gowon opted to postpone a return to civilian rule, which he had pledged originally to complete by 1976. He was overthrown in 1975 by Murtala Muhammed, who promptly reactivated the transition program.

Muhammed was committed to the restoration of democracy, but he was assassinated in 1976. General Olusegun Obasanjo, Muhammed's second-in-command who took power after the assassination, peacefully ceded power to an elected civilian government in 1979, which became known as the Second Republic. Obasanjo retired but would later reemerge as a civilian president in 1999.

The Second and Third Republics, and Predatory Military Rule (1979–1999)

The president of the 1979–1983 Second Republic, Shehu Shagari, and his ruling National Party of Nigeria (NPN, the successor party to the First Republic's northern-dominated NPC), did little to assuage the mistrust between the various parts of the federation, or to stem rampant corruption. After the NPN "won" its 1983 reelection through massive fraud, the military, led by Major General Muhammadu Buhari, seized power within months.

When General Buhari refused to pledge a rapid return to democratic rule and failed to revive a plummeting economy, his popular support wavered, and in August 1985 General Ibrahim Babangida seized power. Although Babangida announced a program of transition

General Olusegun Obasanjo was the Nigerian head of state who supervised the transition to civilian rule from 1976 to 1979. In 1995 he was arrested and convicted in a secret trial in connection with an alleged attempt to overthrow the regime of General Abacha. After his release, he won the presidency in 1999 as a candidate for the PDP. *Source:* Bettmann/Corbis.

to democratic rule as one of his first acts as the new head of state, he and his cohort engaged in an elaborate set of stalling tactics in order to extend their tenure in office. What promised to be the dawn of a Third Republic ended in betrayal when Babangida annulled the presidential election of June 12, 1993, which should have preceded a full withdrawal of the military from the political scene. In stark contrast to all prior elections since independence, the 1993 election was widely acclaimed as fair (despite military restrictions on the scope of competition), and was evidently won by Yoruba

businessman Chief Moshood Abiola. The annulment provoked an angry reaction from a population weary of postponed transitions, military rule, and deception. Babangida could not resist the pressure to resign, but he did manage to handpick his successor, Ernest Shonekan, and a civilian caretaker government.

Following the pattern set by his predecessors, General Sani Abacha seized power in November 1993 from Shonekan. Shonekan's government, never regarded as legitimate after Babangida installed it in August 1993, was vulnerable to increasing agitation from both civilian and military ranks, providing an opportunity for Abacha to remove it. As head of state, General Abacha prolonged the now established tradition of military dominance and combined increased repression with frequent public commitments to restore constitutional democracy. Like Babangida, Abacha announced a new program of transition to civilian rule and regularly delayed the steps in its implementation. Only Abacha's sudden death in June 1998 saved the country from certain crisis, as his scheme to orchestrate the outcome of the transition to produce his own "election" as president became clearer. General Abdulsalami Abubakar, Abacha's successor, announced in his first broadcast to the nation his intention to return power to civilians. Within two months, Abubakar had established a new transition program and promptly handed over to an elected civilian government led by President Olusegun Obasanjo and the People's Democratic Party (PDP) in May 1999.

The Fourth Republic (1999 to the Present)

Obasanjo was called out of retirement by the leaders of the PDP to run for president for several reasons. First, many Yoruba people, particularly leaders, felt that their group had long been cheated out of the presidency by northern elites, especially when Moshood Abiola's election victory was annulled in 1993. Yet most northern leaders did not trust the prominent Yoruba politicians. Obasanjo, although he is Yoruba, as military head of state in 1979 had handed power to the northerner Shehu Shagari at the dawn of the Second Republic. The northern political establishment that dominated the PDP, when faced with the real prospect that the Yoruba might rebel if they did not win the presidency in 1999, concluded that the "detribalized"

General Sani Abacha, a prominent member of Nigerian military regimes since December 1983, took over the government in November 1993, disbanded all elective institutions, and suppressed opposition forces. His death in June 1998 was celebrated in the streets; he and his close supporters looted billions of U.S. dollars from the nation's coffers. *Source:* AP/Wide World Photos.

Obasanjo was the only Yoruba candidate they could trust. In addition, it was thought that, as an ex-military leader, Obasanjo could better manage the thorny task of keeping the military in the barracks once they left power.

Yet precisely because Obasanjo had handed power to Shagari in 1979, he was widely unpopular among his own Yoruba people, and he assumed the presidency in 1999 with few Yoruba votes, in an election marred by irregularities at the polls. Nonetheless, Obasanjo claimed a broad mandate from the Nigerian people to arrest the nation's decline by reforming the state and economy. Within weeks, he electrified the nation by retiring all the military officers who had held positions of political power under the previous military governments, seeing them as the most likely plotters of future coups.

Obasanjo then turned to the economy. The critical oil sector was targeted for new management, while the president lobbied foreign governments to forgive Nigeria's massive debts. The minimum wage was raised dramatically, a "truth and reconciliation" commission and an anticorruption commission were set up to address past and future offenses, and a special commission was created to channel an increased portion of oil revenues back to the impoverished and environmentally degraded Niger Delta region, where the oil is extracted. Civil society groups thrived on renewed political freedoms, and the media grew bold in exposing corrupt practices in government, forcing a Speaker of the House of Representatives and two Senate presidents to resign.

Despite his ambitions for reform, Obasanjo felt obliged to appoint the powerful leaders of his PDP party to ministerial positions in government. Consequently, his first cabinet included some of the same corrupt politicians who had brought down the nation's previous republics and had colluded with Generals Babangida and Abacha in the 1980s and 1990s. They and similarly corrupt politicians in the legislature, state governments, and local governments grew increasingly bold in lining their own pockets with public funds. With President Obasanjo's decision to run for reelection in 2003, however, he needed many of these same politicians to deliver their home states' support, rendering the president's anticorruption machinery largely dormant in his first term.

Having surrounded himself with politicians whom he did not particularly trust, Obasanjo largely kept his own counsel on matters of state. When it came to the National Assembly, members of which he referred to as "small boys," Obasanjo was openly disdainful. In the light of rampant corruption in the legislature, his views were not altogether without merit. When Obasanjo refused to pay half of funds allocated by the Assembly in the 2002 budget on account of a sharp drop in oil revenues, members of his own party in the legislature joined in motions to impeach him. After weeks of tense negotiations, including some legislative concessions and an apology by the president (and persistent rumors of money changing hands), the impeachment drive relented, marking an important victory for the National Assembly.

Themes and Implications

Historical Junctures and Political Themes

Nigeria's adoption of a federal democracy has been a strategy to ensure "unity in diversity" (the national motto) by building a coherent nation-state out of over 250 different ethnic groups and blending traditional democratic values with modern, accountable government. In reality, as a consequence of many years of colonial and military rule, a unitary system emerged in a federal guise: a system with an all-powerful central government surrounded by weak and economically insolvent states.

Another consequence of military rule is the relative overdevelopment of the executive arm at all levels of government—federal, state, and local—at the expense of weak legislative and judicial institutions. Executive superiority was a key feature of the colonial era and has been strengthened by each period of military rule in the postcolonial era. The current civilian government works under a military-authored constitution, which again placed tremendous powers in the presidency. Unchecked executive power under the military, and a dominant executive under the civilians, has encouraged the arbitrary exercise of authority, accompanied by patronage politics, which sap the economy of its vitality, prevent accountability, and undermine the rule of law.

Since the return of democratic rule in 1999, the state governments, the National Assembly, and the judiciary have been whittling away at the powers of the national executive. The president, however, remains the dominant figure in Nigerian politics.

Nigeria in the World of States: Oil Dependence and Decline. Although Nigeria enjoys economic and military power within the West African region, on a global level, it has become increasingly marginalized and vulnerable. Nigeria, with its natural riches, has long been regarded as a potential political and economic giant of Africa. Yet the World Bank lists it among the poorest 20 percent of the countries of the world, with a GDP per capita of just $300. Instead of independent growth, today Nigeria depends on unpredictable oil revenues, sparse external loans, and aid, a victim of its leaders' bad policies and poor management. Owing to underinvestment in and neglect of agriculture, Nigeria moved from self-sufficiency in the production of basic foodstuffs in the mid-1960s to heavy dependence on imports of those goods less than twenty years later. Manufacturing activities, after a surge of investment by government and foreign firms in the 1970s, suffered from inefficiency and disinvestment in subsequent decades, sagging to levels not seen since independence.

Nigeria's economy remains dependent on oil, and its heavy indebtedness gives foreign creditors and the International Monetary Fund (IMF) tremendous influence over its macroeconomic policies. Years of predatory military rule made Nigeria a political and economic pariah in the 1990s, and its declining political institutions have made the country a way station for international drug trafficking to the United States and international commercial fraud.

The installation of a democratic government in 1999 ended the nation's political isolation, but its economy remains subject to the vicissitudes of the international oil market. For most of its independent history, Nigeria has aligned itself with the United States, and President Obasanjo has given strong public support to the U.S. war on terrorism in the wake of the September 11, 2001, attacks. Partly in response to this support, the Bush administration is seeking to rely more on Nigerian oil and less on that from the Middle East.

Governing Nigeria's Economy. Nigeria's oil dependency is a symptom of deeper structural problems.

The very concept of the state was introduced into the colony in large part to restructure and subordinate the local economy to European capitalism. The Nigerian colonial state was conceived and fashioned as **interventionist,** with broad license to intrude into major sectors of the economy and society. The principal goals of the British colonial enterprise were to control the Nigerian economy and to marshal the flow of resources from the colonies to the metropole. A secondary concern was the creation of an economy hospitable to free markets and private enterprise. Nigeria's interventionist state extended its management of the economy, including broad administrative controls and significant ownership positions in areas as diverse as agriculture, banking, commerce, manufacturing, transportation, mining, education, health, employment, and, eventually, oil and natural gas.

After independence in 1960, Nigeria's civilian and military rulers alike expanded the interventionist state, which came to dominate all facets of the nation's economic life. Successive governments began in the late 1980s to reverse this trend, but privatization and economic reform have been piecemeal at best. By 2000, President Obasanjo promised to sell off government interests in the telephone, power, and oil sectors, though the state remains by far the largest source of economic activity.

Democratic Ideas Amid Colonialism and Military Rule. Colonialism introduced a cultural dualism— a clash of customs, values, and political systems— between the traditions of social accountability in precolonial society, and emerging Western ideas of individualism. These pressures weakened indigenous bases for the accountability of rulers and responsibility to the governed, along with age-old checks on abuses of office. Although the colonial rulers left Nigeria with the machinery of parliamentary democracy, they largely socialized the local population to be passive subjects rather than responsive participants. Even as colonial rule sought to implant democracy in principle, in practice it bequeathed an authoritarian legacy to independent Nigeria. Military rule continued this pattern from 1966 to 1979 and again from 1983 to 1999, as juntas promised democratization yet governed with increasing severity.

This dualism promoted two public realms to which individuals belonged: the communal realm, in which people identified by ethnic or subethnic groups (Igbo, Tiv, Yoruba, and others), and the civic realm under the colonial administration and its successors in which citizenship was universal.[5] Both realms fed on each other, though the communal realm was often stronger in certain respects than the civic realm. Thus, Nigerians faced a regular dilemma of loyalty and citizenship. Does one govern or serve the interests of one's ethnic group or those of a greater Nigeria? Viewing the colonial state and its "civic" realm as an alien, exploitative force, Nigerians came to view the state as the realm from which rights must be extracted, duties and taxes withheld, and resources plundered (see Section 4). This view was encouraged by the style of rule under military regimes in the post-colonial era.

The British policy of indirect rule had profoundly different effects on the northern and southern regions. The south experienced both the benefits and burdens of colonial occupation. The proximity of Lagos, Calabar, and their regions to the Atlantic Ocean made them important hubs for trade and shipping activity, around which the British built the necessary infrastructure— schools (promoting Christianity and Western education), roads, ports, and the like—and a large African civil service to facilitate colonialism. In northern Nigeria, where more developed hierarchical political structures were already present, the British used indigenous structures and left intact the emirate authorities and Islamic institutions of the region. The north consequently received few infrastructural benefits and little Christian missionary activity, and its traditional administration was largely preserved.

A pattern of uneven development resulted, with the south enjoying the basis for a modern economy and exposure to democratic institutions and the north remaining largely agricultural and monarchical. These disparities between northern and southern Nigeria propelled northern leaders in the First and Second Republics to secure control of the federal government in order to redistribute resources to the north, while military rulers pursued their own goals by selectively colluding with and manipulating northern fears and southern resentments.

Nigeria's Fragile Collective Identity. This division between north and south is overlaid with hundreds of ethnic divisions across the nation, which military governments and civilians alike have been prone to manipulate for selfish ends. Over three decades after the Biafran civil war, Nigeria often seems as divided as it was in the prelude to that conflict. Fears of another civil war rose during the mid-1990s.

These many cultural divisions have been continually exacerbated by the triple threats of **clientelism,** corruption, and unstable authoritarian governing structures, which together foster ethnic group competition and hinder economic potential.[6] Clientelism is the practice by which a particular group receives disproportionate policy benefits or political favors from a political patron, usually at the expense of the larger society. In Nigeria, patrons are often linked to clients by ethnic, religious, or other cultural ties, and these ties have generally benefited only a small elite. By fostering political competition along cultural lines, clientelism tends to undermine social trust and political stability, which are necessary conditions for economic growth. Clientelism thus reduces the state to an arena of struggle over distribution of the "national cake" among primarily ethnic clients rather than serving as a framework of governance.

Despite the prevalence of ethnicity as the primary form of political identity and the accompanying scourge of ethnic-based clientelism, the idea of Nigeria has taken root among the country's ethnic groups over forty years of independence. Most public discourse does not question the idea of a single cohesive country, but instead revolves around finding an equitable balance among different ethnic groups within the context of a united Nigeria. This can be seen in recent calls from some organizations for a national conference to restructure the federation. Most Nigerians enjoy many personal connections across ethnic and religious lines, and elites in both the north and the south hold significant business investments throughout the country. Nevertheless, ethnicity remains a critical flashpoint that has led to localized ethnic violence on many occasions, and politicians continue to use ethnic identification to forward their political objectives, often divisively.

Implications for Comparative Politics

The saying that "as Nigeria goes, so goes the rest of sub-Saharan Africa" may again be relevant. With a population of 130 million, Nigeria is by far the largest country in Africa and among the ten most populous countries in the world. One out of every five black Africans are Nigerians. Unlike most other countries on the continent, Nigeria has the human and material resources to overcome the vicious cycle of poverty and **autocracy.** Hopes for this breakthrough, however, have been regularly frustrated over four decades of independent rule. If Nigeria, with its vast resources, cannot succeed in breaking this cycle, what does that mean for the rest of sub-Saharan Africa?

Nigeria remains the oldest surviving federation in Africa. At a time when other federations are dissolving, whether peacefully, as in the former Czechoslovakia, or violently, as in the former Yugoslavia, Nigeria manages to maintain its fragile unity. That unity has come under increasing stress, and a major challenge is to ensure that Nigeria does not go the way of Yugoslavia. One fact is certain: Nigeria's multiethnic, multireligious, multiclass, and multiregional nature makes it an especially valuable case for the study of social cleavages in conflict and cooperation. Even the United States, which is nearing a demographic transition from a white majority, can learn from Nigeria's efforts to find unity amid cultural diversity.

Nigeria's past failures to sustain democracy and economic development also render it an important case for the study of resource competition and the perils of corruption, and its experience demonstrates the interrelationship between democracy and development. Democracy and development depend on other factors, including leadership, political culture, institutional autonomy, and the external economic climate. Nigeria has much to teach us on all these topics.

At this stage, it is uncertain whether Nigeria will return to the path of autocracy, underdevelopment, and fragmentation or shift to a course of democratic renewal and national construction. In the following sections, we will explore these issues and evaluate how they may shape Nigerian politics in the years ahead.

Section **2** Political Economy and Development

We have seen how colonialism bequeathed Nigeria an interventionist state and how governments in the post-independence period continued this pattern. The state became the central fixture in the Nigerian economy, stunting the private sector and encumbering industry and commerce. As the state began to unravel in the late 1980s and 1990s, leaders grew more predatory, plundering the one major revenue-generating sector remaining, oil, and keeping the nation's vast economic potential largely unrealized.

State and Economy

Through direct ownership of industry and services or through regulation and administrative control, the Nigerian state plays the central role in making decisions about the extraction, deployment, and allocation of scarce economic resources. Any major economic activity involves the state in some way, whether through licenses, taxes, contracts, legal provisions, trade and investment policy, or direct involvement of government agencies. The state's premier role in the economy arises from control of the most productive sectors, particularly the oil industry. Most of the nation's revenues, and nearly all of its hard currency, are channeled through the government. The discretion of leaders in spending those earnings, known as **rents,** forms the main path for channeling money through the economy. Consequently, winning government contracts—for supplies, construction, services, and myriad functions connected to the state—becomes a central economic activity, and control of the state makes its occupants the gatekeepers of contracting, licenses, and other areas of economic attainment.[7]

As individuals, groups, and communities jostled for state control or access, economic and social life became thoroughly politicized and consumed by **rent-seeking** behavior. The state has evolved beyond the role of regulator and manager, as seen in a less interventionist environment like Hong Kong. In most societies, access to the state and its leadership confers some economic advantages, but it can literally be a matter of life and death in impoverished countries like Nigeria.

Perhaps 70 percent of Nigerians struggle along without such access, surviving on petty trade and subsistence agriculture—the so-called informal sector of the economy—where taxes and regulation rarely reach. A number of analysts estimate that the Nigerian informal sector can be valued at approximately 20 percent of the entire Nigerian GDP, much of it earned through cross-border trade.

Origins of Economic Decline

In the colonial and immediate postcolonial periods, Nigeria's economy was centered on agricultural production for domestic consumption as well as for export. Peasant producers were induced by the colonial state to produce primary export commodities—cocoa in the west, palm oil in the east, and groundnuts and cotton in the north—through direct taxation, forced cultivation, and the presence of European agricultural firms. Despite the emphasis on exports, Nigeria was self-sufficient in food production at the time of independence. Vital to this effort was small-scale local production of sorghum and maize in the north and cassava and yams in the south. Some rice and wheat were also produced. It was not until later in the 1960s that emphasis shifted to the development of nonfood export crops through large-scale enterprises.

The nearly exclusive state attention to large-scale, nonfood production meant that small farmers were left out and received scant government support. Predictably, food production suffered, and food imports were stepped up to meet the needs of a burgeoning population. Despite government neglect, agriculture was the central component of the national economy in the First Republic. Michael Watts points to a combination of three factors that effectively undermined the Nigerian agricultural sector. The first was the Biafran War (1967–1970), which drastically reduced palm oil production in the east, where the war was concentrated. Second, severe drought in 1969 produced a famine from 1972 through 1974. Finally, the development of the petroleum industry caused a total shift in economic focus from agriculture (in terms of both labor and capital investment) to petroleum production. Agricultural export production plummeted from 80 percent of exports in 1960 to just 2 percent by 1980. To compensate for widening food shortfalls, food imports surged by 700 percent between 1970 and 1978.[8]

With the 1970s boom in revenues from oil, Nigeria greatly increased its expenditures on education, defense, and infrastructure. The university system was expanded, roads and ports were built, and industrial and office buildings were constructed. Imports of capital goods and raw materials required to support this expansion rose more than seven-fold between 1971 and 1979. Similarly, imports of consumer goods rose dramatically (600 percent) in the same period as an increasingly wealthy Nigerian elite developed a taste for expensive imported goods.[9] By 1978, the Nigerian government had outspent its revenues and could no longer finance many of its ambitious projects; consequently, the government was forced to borrow money to make up the deficit, causing external debt to skyrocket.

The acceleration in oil wealth was mirrored by a corresponding increase in corruption. Many public officials became very wealthy by setting up joint ventures with foreign oil companies. Other officials simply stole public funds for their own benefit. The economic downturn of the 1980s created even greater incentives for government corruption, and the Babangida and Abacha administrations became infamous for avarice. A Nigerian government commission reported that some $12.2 billion had been diverted to special off-budget accounts between 1988 and 1993. These funds were supposedly earmarked for national security and infrastructure, but they were never audited and their expenditure remains entirely unaccounted.[10] Within three years of seizing power, General Abacha allowed all of Nigeria's oil refineries to collapse, forcing this giant oil-exporting country into the absurd situation of having to import refined petroleum. Shamelessly, Abacha's family members and friends, who essentially served as fronts for him, monopolized the contracts to import this fuel in 1997. Small-time scam artists meanwhile proliferated, such that by 2002, Internet scams had become one of Nigeria's top five industries, earning over $100 million annually.

In sum, the oil boom was a double-edged sword for Nigeria. On one hand, it has generated tremendous income; on the other, it has become a source of external dependence and has badly skewed the Nigerian econ-omy. Since the early 1970s, Nigeria has relied on oil for over 90 percent of its export earnings and about three-quarters of government revenues, as shown in Table 1. Hasty, ill-managed industrial and infrastructural expansion under both military and civilian regimes, combined with the neglect of the agricultural sector, further weakened the Nigerian economy. As a result, the economy was unable to offset the sharp fall in world oil prices after 1981 and descended into crisis.

From 1985 to the Present: Deepening Economic Crisis and the Search for Solutions

Structural Adjustment. The year 1985 marked a turning point for the Nigerian state and economy. It ushered in Ibrahim Babangida's eight-year rule and revealed the economy's precarious condition. Within a year of wresting power from General Buhari in August 1985, the Babangida regime developed an economic **structural adjustment program (SAP)** with the active support of the World Bank and the IMF (also referred to as the **international financial institutions,** or **IFIs**). The decision to embark on the SAP was made against a background of increasing economic constraints arising from a combination of factors: the continued dependence of the economy on waning oil revenues, a growing debt burden, **balance of payments** difficulties, and lack of fiscal discipline.[11] (See "Global Connection: Structural Adjustment Programs.")

The large revenues arising from the oil windfall enabled the state to increase its involvement in direct production. Beginning in the 1970s, the government created a number of para-statals (state-owned enterprises; see Section 3) including large shares in major banks and other financial institutions, manufacturing, construction, agriculture, public utilities, and various services. This practice has ensured that the state remains the biggest employer as well as the most important source of revenue, even for the private sector. By the 1980s, the public bureaucracy in Nigeria had swollen to over 3 million employees (most employed by the federal and state governments), representing more than 60 percent of employment in the modern, formal sector of the economy.

Conversely, the share of the private sector in the economy fell from 45 percent in the 1960s to as little as 15 percent in the 1980s The stated goal of Nigerian

Table 1

Oil Sector Statistics, 1970–2003

	Annual Output (million barrels)	Average Price Index	Oil Exports as Percent of Total Exports	Government Oil Revenue (Naira millions)	Percent of Total Revenue
1970	396	37	58	166	26
1971	559	43	74	510	44
1972	643	40	82	767	54
1973	750	39	83	1,016	60
1974	823	162	93	3,726	82
1975	651	109	93	4,271	77
1976	756	115	94	5,365	79
1977	761	115	93	6,081	76
1978	692	100	89	4,556	62
1979	840	237	93	8,881	81
1980	753	220	96	12,353	81
1981	525	225	97	8,563	70
1982	470	212	99	7,814	66
1983	451	200	96	7,253	69
1984	508	190	97	8,268	74
1985	544	180	97	10,915	75
1986	534	75	94	8,107	66
1987	464	90	93	19,027	76
1988	507	60	91	20,934	77
1989	614	87	95	41,334	82
1990	–	125	–	–	–
1991	–	80	–	–	–
1992	714	79	98	164,078	86
1993	720	62	91	162,102	84
1994	733	70	85	160,192	79
1995	705	65	95	244,902	53
1996	783	95	95	266,000	51
1997	803	85	95	250,000	80
1998	700	62	90	248,500	70
1999	1950	–	–	–	76
2000	2040	–	–	–	65
2001	2083	–	98	1,668,000	79
2002	2068	–	94	1,884,000	80
2003*	2291	–	91	2,194,000	78

*Projected.

Sources: Output is from *Petroleum Economist* (1970–1989); price index and exports are from IMF, *International Financial Statistics* (1970–1984) and from Central Bank of Nigeria, *Annual Reports* (1985–1989); revenues are from Central Bank of Nigeria, *Annual Reports* (various years). From Tom Forrest, *Politics and Economic Development in Nigeria.* (Boulder: Westview Press, 1993), 134. 1990s statistics are from the Nigerian Federal Office of Statistics, *Annual Abstract of Statistics: 1997 Edition*, from the 1998 IMF *Annual Report*, and from Vision 2010, *Report of the Vision 2010 Committee: Main Report* (Abuja: Federal Government of Nigeria, September 1997). Nigerian Economic Summit Group, *Economic Indicators* (Vol. 8, no. 2, April–June 2002). Compilation and some calculations by Darren Kew.

Global Connection: *Structural Adjustment Programs*

The solutions to Nigeria's economic woes depend, in the first instance, on its own people and government, but assistance must also come from outside its borders. In addition to bilateral (country-to-country) assistance, multilateral economic institutions are a key source of loans, grants, and other forms of development aid. Two multilateral institutions that have become familiar players on the African economic scene are the International Monetary Fund (IMF) and the World Bank. These international financial institutions (IFIs) were established following World War II to provide short-term credit facilities to encourage growth and expansion of trade and longer-term financing packages, respectively, to rebuild the countries of war-torn Europe. Today, the functions of the IFIs have adapted and expanded to meet contemporary needs, including efforts to stabilize and restructure faltering economies. One area of emphasis by the IFIs, particularly among African countries, is the structural adjustment program (SAP).

Assistance from the World Bank and the IMF comes with many strings attached. These rigorous programs, which are intended to reduce government intervention and develop free markets, call for immediate austerity measures by recipient governments. SAPs generally begin with currency devaluation and tariff reductions. These actions are followed by measures aimed at reducing budget deficits, restructuring of the public sector (particularly employment practices), privatizing state-owned enterprises, agricultural reform (especially raising producer prices), and the reduction of consumer subsidies on staple foods. The social and economic hardships of these programs, particularly in the short term, can be severe. SAPs result in considerable economic, and frequently social, dislocation; dramatic price increases in foodstuffs

and fuel, plus rising unemployment, are seldom popular with the general population.

At Babangida's insistence, Nigeria's SAP was developed and deployed in 1986 independent of the IMF and the World Bank. The program was, however, endorsed by the IFIs, making Nigeria eligible to receive disbursements of funds from the IMF and the World Bank and to reschedule $33 billion of external debt with the Paris and London clubs of lenders. Ironically, Nigeria's SAP was in many regards more rigorous than an initial program designed by the IMF. Like SAPs elsewhere, the Nigerian program was designed to encourage economic liberalization and promote private enterprise in place of a reliance on state-owned enterprises and public intervention. The logic was that competition leads to more efficient products and markets. Recovery among Africa's struggling economies has, however, been limited. Africa's economic problems are deeply entrenched; although an economy may be stabilized relatively quickly, comprehensive structural adjustment takes considerably longer. Thus far, Nigeria's SAP—in part because of the popular reaction to austerity measures, continued corruption in its implementation, and the complicating factor of unstable military rule—has failed to revitalize the economy. The final years of the Babangida administration (1985–1993) saw a marked slippage in the reform program, and the Abacha regime continued that trend. Abacha did enact a number of economic policies in 1995 and 1996 that lowered inflation, stabilized the exchange rate, and fostered mild GDP growth, but by 1997, these achievements had been squandered. President Obasanjo has sought to uphold the overall policies of SAP without calling it such, including attempts to end subsidies on fuel and to finish the privatization of the major government para-statals.

governments since the mid-1980s has been to reduce unproductive investments in the public sector, improve the sector's efficiency, and promote the growth of the private sector. **Privatization,** which is central to Nigeria's adjustment program, means that state-owned businesses would be sold to private (nonstate) investors,

domestic or foreign. Privatization is intended to generate revenue, reduce state expenditures for loss-making operations, and improve efficiency. However, privatization also typically results in the loss of jobs. President Obasanjo entered office with a renewed commitment to privatization, beginning most prominently with the telecommunications network. There is also discussion of selling the jewel in the economic crown, the government's share of oil industry, sometime after the elections of 2003.

Expectations that privatization would encourage Nigerian and foreign investment in manufacturing have been largely disappointed. On a domestic level, Nigerian entrepreneurs have found that trading, government contracting, and currency speculation offer more reliable yields than manufacturing. Potential foreign investors remain hesitant to risk significant capital in an environment characterized by political and social instability, unpredictable economic policies, and endemic corruption. Only a few attractive areas such as telecommunications, utilities, and oil and gas are likely to draw significant foreign capital.

Economic Planning. Beginning in 1946, when the colonial administration announced the ten-year Plan for Development and Welfare, national plans have been prepared by ministries of finance, economic development, and planning. Five-year plans were the norm from 1962 through 1985, when their scope was extended to fifteen years. The national plan, however, has not been an effective management tool. The reasons are the absence of an effective database for planning and a great lack of discipline in plan implementation. The state strives to dictate the pace and direction of economic development, but lacks the tools and political will to deliver on its obligations.

Nigerian and foreign business leaders revived dialogue with government on economic direction with the 1994 establishment of the annual Nigerian Economic Summit (NES). This differed from previous planning efforts in that it was based on the coequal participation of government and private sector representatives. Two years later, General Abacha initiated the Vision 2010 process (see "Current Challenges: Vision 2010"). Participants in Vision 2010 advocated reductions in government's excessive role in the economy with the goals of increasing market efficiency and reducing competition for control of the state. The Obasanjo administration accepted much of the Vision 2010 agenda, although it did not say so publicly because of the plan's association with General Abacha's predatory regime. Many of the private sector participants in Vision 2010 continue to meet regularly through the Economic Sum-

mit. Advice from the NES continues to influence the economic policies of both the Obasanjo administration and the National Assembly.

Although the Economic Summit and Vision 2010 provide a basis for reform, many problems must still be overcome in the economy: low investment, low capacity utilization, unreliable distribution, stifling corruption, and overregulation. Average annual GDP growth rates were negative from 1981 through 1987 and have risen only mildly above the rate of population growth since Obasanjo took office in 1999. Consumption and investment have also recorded negative growth (see Table 2).

Nigeria's heavy foreign debt exacerbates the nation's economic stagnation (see Table 3). President Obasanjo made debt relief one of his highest priorities on taking office in 1999 and promptly undertook numerous visits to the capitals of Europe, Asia, and the United States to urge the governments of those countries to forgive most of Nigeria's obligations. His pleas fell largely on deaf ears, however, as Nigeria's National Assembly showed little inclination to spend within the nation's means. Obasanjo's government also showed a weak commitment to fiscal discipline, wastefully spending on such expensive prestige projects as a new football stadium in Abuja. Nigeria, once considered a country likely to achieve self-sustaining growth, now ranks among the more debt-distressed countries in the developing world. It cannot earn enough from the export of goods to service its foreign debt and also meet the basic needs of the population.

Social Welfare. Given the continued decline in its economic performance since the early 1980s, it is not surprising that Nigeria's social welfare has suffered greatly as well. Since 1986, there has been a marked deterioration in the quantity and quality of social services, complicated by a marked decline in household incomes (see Table 4). The SAP program and subsequent austerity measures emphasizing the reduction of state expenditures, have forced cutbacks in spending on social welfare.

Budgetary austerity and economic stagnation have hurt vulnerable groups such as the urban and rural poor, women, the young, and the elderly. Indeed, Nigeria performs poorly in meeting basic needs: life expectancy is barely above fifty years, and infant mortality is estimated at more than 80 deaths per 1,000 live births.

Current Challenges: *Vision 2010*

In the early 1990s, concerned with the nation's economic decline, a number of the larger Nigerian businesses and key multinational corporations decided to pursue new initiatives. With the August 1993 appointment of Ernest Shonekan, the former chairman of West Africa's largest local corporation, UAC, as head of state, these businesses sensed an opportunity to alter the course of Nigeria's economic policies. With Shonekan's involvement, they arranged the first Economic Summit, a high-profile conference that advocated numerous policies to move Nigeria toward becoming an "emerging market" that could attract foreign investment along the lines of the high-performing states in Asia.

Shortly after the first Economic Summit, however, General Abacha took control and continued the ruinous economic approach of Babangida's later years. The Economic Summit meanwhile continued to meet annually. After his flawed 1994 budget sent the Nigerian economy into a tailspin, Abacha was ready to listen to the summit participants. He accepted several of their recommendations, and by 1996 the economy began to make modest gains. Therefore, when key members of the summit proposed Vision 2010, General Abacha seized the opportunity presented and endorsed it in September 1996. Chief Shonekan was named the chair.

Vision 2010 relies on a model of strategic planning that begins with a visioning process to identify key corporate goals and the paths of action to realize these goals. The process brings together key stakeholders and implementers, who are expected to bring goals to fruition. Malaysia and other developing countries successfully employed this model in the 1980s to devise blueprints for development. As part of the visioning process, the government adopts a package of business-promoting economic reforms, while business pledges to work toward certain growth targets consistent with governmental priorities in employment, taxation, community investment, and the like. General Abacha's estimation of the poten-

tial of Vision 2010 was so great that he quickly increased its scope beyond its initial economic intentions. Committees were set up to develop plans for Nigeria's sports teams, interethnic relations, media development, and even for civil-military relations under the expected democratic rule. Along with government and business leaders, key figures were invited to participate from nearly all sectors of society, including the press, nongovernmental organizations, youth groups, market women's associations, and others. Government-owned media followed Vision 2010's pronouncements with great fanfare, while the private media reviewed them with a healthy dose of skepticism regarding Abacha's intentions and the elitist nature of the exercise.

In September 1997, on schedule, the Vision 2010 executive committee presented its final report. Its four volumes painted a surprisingly candid picture of where Nigeria stood and recommended how the country could transform itself into a strong emerging-market democracy by 2010. The recommendations called for, in part, restoring democratic rule, restructuring and professionalizing the military, lowering the population growth rate, rebuilding education, meaningful privatization, diversifying the export base beyond oil, supporting intellectual property rights, and central bank autonomy.

Whatever its merits, Vision 2010 was imperiled because of its association with Abacha. When the new Obasanjo administration took office in 1999 lacking a comprehensive economic plan of its own, however, it quietly approached Shonekan for the detailed recommendations and data produced by Vision 2010. Consequently, the general economic strategy and objectives of Vision 2010 are largely echoed in those of the current government. The Economic Summit, meanwhile, continues to provide annual assessments of the Nigerian economy and critical economic advice to policy-makers.

Source: Vision 2010 Final Report, *September 1997.*

Table 2

Selected Economic Indicators, 1980–1998

	Real GDP (Naira billions) (1993 = 100)	GDP (% Growth)	Manufacturing Capacity Utilization (%)*	Inflation Rate (%)
1980	96.2	5.5	70.1	9.9
1985	68.9	9.4	37.1	5.5
1990	90.3	8.1	40.3	7.4
1991	94.6	4.8	42.0	13.0
1992	97.4	3.0	41.8	44.6
1993	100.0	2.7	37.2	57.2
1994	101.0	1.3	30.4	57.0
1995	103.5	2.2	29.3	72.8
1996	106.9	3.3	32.5	29.3
1997	111.1	3.9	–	8.5
1998	113.3	2.0	–	9.0
1999	114.4	1.0	–	6.7
2000	118.8	3.8	–	6.9
2001	123.5	4.0	–	18.9
2002	127.7	3.4	–	16.9
2003	133.1	4.2	–	13.5

GDP % Growth

1976–1986	–1.3
1987–1997	1.6

*Manufacturing capacity utilization is the average (across the economy) percentage of full production capabilities at which manufacturers are producing.

Sources: Vision 2010. *Report of the Vision 2010 Committee: Main Report.* Abuja: Federal Government of Nigeria, September 1997; World Bank, "Nigeria at a Glance," 1998 (www.worldbank.org) the 1998 IMF *Annual Report.* Nigerian Economic Summit Group, *Economic Indicators* (Vol. 8, no. 2, April–June 2002).

Table 3

Nigeria's Total External Debt (millions of US$; current prices and exchange rates)

1975–1979	1980	1981	1982	1983
3,304	8,934	12,136	12,954	18,540
1984	**1985**	**1986**	**1987**	**1988**
18,537	19,551	24,043	31,193	31,947
1989	**1994**	**1995**	**1996**	**1997**
32,832	34,000	35,010	33,442	32,906
1999	**2000**	**2001**	**2002**	**2003**
29,358	34,134	33,766	33,723	33,740

Nigeria's Debt Compared to its Earnings:

	1976	1986	1996	1997	1999
Total Debt/GDP	3.7	109.9	72.0	63.1	83.8
Total Debt Service/ Exports	3.7	28.4	15.2	15.9	204

	2000	2001	2002	2003
Total Debt/GDP	97.3	86.9	76.5	72.6
Total Debt Service/ Exports	147.6	147	177.5	159.5

Sources: UNDP, World Bank, *African Development Indicators* (Washington, D.C.: World Bank, 1992), 159; UNDP *1998 Human Development Report;* World Bank, "Nigeria at a Glance," 1998 (www.worldbank.org). Nigerian Economic Summit Group, *Economic Indicators* (Vol. 8, no. 2, April–June 2002).

Nigeria's provision of basic education is also inadequate. Moreover, Nigeria has failed to develop a national social security system, with much of the gap filled by family-based networks of mutual aid. President Obasanjo took an important step in meeting basic needs when he raised the minimum wage nearly tenfold in 1999. Since wage levels had hardly been raised in years despite the inflation of the previous decade, the gains for workers with formal sector jobs were more meager than the increase suggests.

The provision of health care and other social services—water, education, food, and shelter—remains woefully inadequate in both urban and rural areas. Beyond the needless loss of countless lives to preventable and curable maladies, Nigeria's neglect of the health and social net will likely bear more bitter fruit. The nation stands on the verge of an AIDS epidemic of catastrophic proportions. The United Nations estimates—conservatively—that HIV infection rates are at approximately 6 percent of the population and are likely to spread to 10 percent by the end of the decade, dooming perhaps 15 million Nigerians to the slow death of that disease without access to the medications or treatment that can delay HIV's effects. The government has made AIDS a secondary priority, leaving much of the initiative to a small group of courageous but underfunded nongovernmental organizations.

Table 4

Index of Real Household Incomes of Key Groups 1980/81–1986/87, 1996, 2001
(Rural self-employed in 1980/81 = 100)

	1980/81	1981/82	1982/83	1983/84	1984/85	1985/86	1986/87	1996*	2001*
Rural self-employed	100	103	95	86	73	74	65	27	32
Rural wage earners	178	160	147	135	92	95	84	48	57
All rural households	105	107	99	89	74	84	74	28	33
Urban self-employed	150	124	106	94	69	69	61	41	48
Urban wage earners	203	177	164	140	101	101	90	55	65
All urban households	166	142	129	109	80	80	71	45	53

*Estimated, based on 1980/81 figures adjusted for a 73 percent drop in per capita GDP from 1980 to 1996, and an 18 percent increase in per capita GDP from 1996 to 2001. The FOS lists annual household incomes for 1996 as $75 (N 6,349) for urban households and $57 (N 4,820) for rural households, suggesting that the gap between urban and rural households is actually 19 percent closer than our estimate.

Sources: National Integrated Survey of Households (NISH), Federal Office of Statistics (FOS) consumer price data, and World Bank estimates. As found in Paul Collier, *An Analysis of the Nigerian Labour Market,* Development Economics Department Discussion Paper (Washington, D.C.: World Bank, 1986). From Tom Forrest, *Politics and Economic Development in Nigeria* (Boulder: Westview Press, 1993), 214. 1996 data from FOS *Annual Abstract of Statistics: 1997 Edition,* p. 80.

Society and Economy

Because the central government in Nigeria controls access to most resources and economic opportunities, the state has become the major focus for competition among ethnic, regional, religious, and class groups. In such an environment, elite members of these groups become conflict generators rather than conflict managers.[12] A partial explanation for the failure of economic strategies can be found within Nigerian society itself— a complex mix of contending ethnic, religious, and regional constituencies.

Ethnic and Religious Cleavages

Nigeria's ethnic relations have generated tensions that sap the country's economy of much needed vitality.[13] Competition among the largest groups is centered on access to national economic and political resources. The dominance of the Hausa-Fulani, Igbo, and Yoruba in the country's national life and the conflicts among political elites from these groups bias economic affairs. Religious cleavages have also affected economic and social stability. Some of the federation's states in the far north are populated mainly by Muslims, whereas others, particularly in the middle

and eastern parts of the south, are predominantly Christian.

A combination of government ineptitude—or outright manipulation—and growing Islamic and Christian assertion, have heightened conflicts between adherents.[14] Christians have perceived past northern-dominated governments as being pro-Muslim in their management and distribution of scarce resources as well as in their policy decisions, some of which jeopardized the secular nature of the state. These fears have increased since 1999, when several northern states instituted expanded versions of the Islamic legal code, the *shari'a*. For their part, Muslims now fear that President Obasanjo, a born-again Christian, is tilting the balance of power and thus the distribution of economic benefits against the north.

The decline in the Nigerian economy also contributed to the rise of Christian and Muslim fundamentalism, which have spread among unemployed youths and others in a society suffering under economic collapse. In northern Nigeria, disputes over economic and political issues have sometimes escalated into physical attacks on Christians and members of southern ethnic groups residing in the north. A demonstration led by Islamist groups in Kano against U.S. intervention in Afghanistan after the September 11, 2001, terrorist attacks, for instance, degenerated into a Muslim-Christian conflict when gangs of youths used the occasion to loot some Christian neighborhoods. Occasionally, religious revivalism among the various Christian sects has provoked violent protests by Muslims.

Evangelical Christian churches swept across the south and Middle Belt in the 1990s, growing with the general rise in poverty and social dislocation. Offering music, dancing, community, and even instant miracles (especially in regard to fertility, relationships, and finances), these churches have sprouted in nearly every neighborhood where Christians are to be found. The evangelical churches augment the more established denominations, including Anglicans, Catholics, and Methodists.

Northern-led governments after independence, fearing a "southern tyranny of skills,"[15] sought to use the political clout of their numerical majority to keep the south in check and to redistribute resources to the north. Early military governments (1966–1979) tried to maintain some measure of ethnic and religious balance, but the Babangida regime in the 1980s became increasingly northern dominated and more willing than any of its predecessors to manipulate Nigeria's ethnic divisions. General Abacha's Provisional Ruling Council (PRC) tilted overwhelmingly in favor of northerners, specifically Hausa-Fulani, in its membership. Numerous attacks were perpetrated against prominent southern civilians, particularly Yoruba, often using Abacha's secret hit squads. His regime also closed universities and detained a number of activists, particularly in the south.

Yoruba groups were not the only ones adversely affected by Abacha's rule. The Ogoni, Ijaw, and other southern minorities of the oil-producing regions were brutalized by military and police forces when they protested the scant oil revenues remitted to the region, as well as the environmental degradation from the irresponsible oil industry. The Ogoni in particular were organized through the Movement for the Survival of the Ogoni People (MOSOP), under the leadership of internationally renowned writer and environmentalist Ken Saro-Wiwa. The military's abrupt hanging of Saro-Wiwa and eight Ogoni compatriots in 1995 following a kangaroo trial was widely criticized as "judicial murder" by human rights groups, and led to Nigeria's suspension from the Commonwealth (an international

organization composed of Britain and its former colonies). A subsequent UN mission of inquiry declared the executions illegal under both Nigerian and international law.

MOSOP under Saro-Wiwa effectively blended claims for **self-determination,** which in this case meant increased local political autonomy and national political representation, with concerns over oil industry pollution in the Niger Delta, primarily on the part of global oil giant Royal Dutch/Shell, as a platform to forge alliances with international environmental and human rights organizations. Many other Niger Delta minority groups have subsequently followed MOSOP's lead in pushing a combination of self-determination, political rights, environmental concerns, and demands for greater control over the oil pumped from their lands.

Since the return of democracy in 1999, many ethnic-based and religious movements have taken advantage of restored political freedoms to mobilize and press the federal government to address their grievances. Some mobilization has been peaceful, but many armed groups have also formed, at times with the encouragement or complicity of the mainstream political movements.

Youths from the Niger Delta minorities, primarily the Ijaw, have occupied Shell and Chevron facilities on several occasions to protest their economic marginalization. One spectacular incident on an offshore oil platform in 2002 saw a group of local women stage a peaceful takeover using a traditional form of protest: disrobing in order to shame the oil companies and local authorities. Most of the protests have ended peacefully, although a large-scale upheaval in the Warri region in 2003 caused the deaths of several policemen, soldiers, and oil workers. The Obasanjo government has periodically responded to these incidents and other disturbances with excessive force. After Ijaw militias killed several policemen in the village of Odi in late 1999, the army was ordered to track down the perpetrators. The military subsequently flattened the village, raping and killing many innocent people in the process. Army units committed similar retaliatory atrocities in 2001 among villages in the Middle Belt state of Benue, when ethnic militias apparently killed several soldiers engaged in a peacekeeping mission during an interethnic dispute. In the Niger Delta, the struggle of the minority communities with the federal government and multinational oil corporations has been complicated by clashes among the minority groups themselves over control of land and access to government rents. Fighting among the Ijaws and the Itsekiris near Warri in 2003 claimed more than 100 lives. Ethnic-based mobilization has increased across Nigeria in general since 1999, including ethnic vigilantes. Political leaders unfortunately have built alliances with these groups and are increasingly using them to harass and even kill political opponents. Nigerian political and business elites have also demonstrated a propensity toward accentuating sectional cleavages. Culture or ethnicity is used to fragment rather than to integrate the country, with grave consequences for the economy and society.

These divisive practices overshadow certain positive aspects of sectional identities. For example, associations based on ethnic and religious affinities often serve as vehicles for mobilizing savings, investment, and production, such as informal credit associations. In addition, professional associations—comprising lawyers, doctors, journalists, business and trade groups, academics, trade unions, or students' organizations—played a prominent role in the anticolonial struggle. These groups, which form the core of civil society, have continued to provide a vehicle for political expression while also reflecting the divisive pressures of Nigeria's cultural pluralism.

Gender Differences

Although the Land Use Act of 1978 stated that all land in Nigeria is ultimately owned by the government, land tenure in Nigeria is still governed by traditional practice, which is largely patriarchal. Despite the fact that women, especially from the south and Middle Belt areas, have traditionally dominated agricultural production and form the bulk of agricultural producers, they are generally prevented from owning land, which remains the major means of production. Trading, in which women feature prominently, is also controlled in many areas by traditional chiefs and local government councilors, who are overwhelmingly male.

Women have not succeeded in transforming their economic importance into political clout, but important strides are being made in this direction. Their past inability and current struggle to achieve direct access to state power is a reflection of several factors. Women's associations in the past tended to be elitist, urban based, and mainly concerned with issues of trade, chil-

dren, welfare, and religion. The few that did have a more political orientation have been largely token appendages of the male-dominated political parties or instruments of the government. An example of the latter was the Better Life Program, directed by the wife of Babangida, and its successor, the Family Support Program, directed by Abacha's wife. Women are grossly underrepresented at all levels of the governmental system; only eight (of 469) national legislators are women.[16]

Reflecting the historical economic and educational advantages of the south, women's interest organizations sprouted in southern Nigeria earlier than in the north. Although these groups initially focused generally on nonpolitical issues surrounding women's health and children, organizations like Women in Nigeria began to form in the 1980s with explicit political goals, such as getting more women into government and increasing funds available for education.

By the 1990s, northern women had become nearly as active as southerners in founding nongovernmental organizations (NGOs). As in the south, northern women's NGOs at first focused on less politicized issues, but by the end of the decade, explicitly political organizations such as the 100 Women Groups, which sought to elect 100 women to every level of government, emerged. Northern groups also showed tremendous creativity in using Islam to support their activities, which was very important considering that tenets of the religion have been regularly used by Nigerian men to justify women's subordinate status. Women's groups in general have been much more dynamic than male-dominated NGOs, nearly all of which are entirely dependent on foreign or government funding, in developing income-generating projects to make their organizations and the women they assist increasingly self-reliant.

Nigeria and the International Political Economy

At the international level, the state has remained weak and dependent on Western industrial and financial interests four decades after Nigeria became a full-fledged member of the world community. The country suffers from an acute debt burden. In addition, Nigeria is reliant on the developed industrial economies for finance capital, production and information technologies, basic consumer items, and raw materials. Nigeria strives to provide leadership at the continental (African) and subregional (West African) levels. Most of its policy and intellectual elites support this self-image.

In recent years, Nigeria has played a major role in reorienting the focus of the Nonaligned Movement toward issues of economic development and cooperation. In bodies such as the Organization of African Unity (OAU) and the UN, Nigeria generally took firm positions to promote decolonization and the development of the Third World and against the apartheid regime in South Africa. Unfortunately, much of this international goodwill was largely squandered by the Babangida and Abacha regimes. Since taking office in 1999, President Obasanjo has made over 100 foreign visits, seeking to restore Nigerian credibility and status. Debt relief, or outright cancellation, has been an important goal of these trips. This has been such a central focus, in fact, that some of his critics charge that he is more interested in traveling abroad than addressing the problems at home.

Nigeria and the Regional Political Economy

Nigeria has aspired to be a regional leader in Africa. These aspirations have not been dampened by its declining position in the global political economy. Nigeria was a major actor in the formation in 1975 of the **Economic Community of West African States (ECOWAS)** and has carried a disproportionately high financial and administrative burden for keeping the organization afloat. Under President Obasanjo's initiative, ECOWAS voted to create a parliament and a single currency for the region as the next step toward a European Union–style integration. These lofty goals will take several years of concerted efforts from the region's troubled governments to become a reality, and the lackluster results of past integration efforts do not bode well for success.

Nigeria has also been the largest contributor of troops to the West African peacekeeping force, the ECOWAS Monitoring Group (known as ECOMOG). Under Nigerian direction, the ECOWAS countries dispatched ECOMOG troops to Liberia from 1990 to 1997 to restore order and prevent the Liberian civil war from destabilizing the subregion. Ironically, despite military dictatorship at home, Nigerian ECOMOG forces invaded Sierra Leone in May 1997 to restore its

democratically elected government, a move generally endorsed by the international community. The United Nations assumed leadership of the operation in 1999, but Nigeria continues to contribute troops. Nigeria under President Obasanjo has also sought to mediate crises in Guinea-Bissau and Ivory Coast, and in Congo and Zimbabwe outside the ECOWAS region.

Because it is the largest economy in the West African subregion, Nigeria has at times been a magnet for immigration. At the height of the 1970s oil boom, many West African laborers, most of them Ghanaians, migrated to Nigeria in search of employment. When the oil-based expansion ceased and jobs became scarce, Nigeria sought to protect its own workers by expelling hundreds of thousands of West Africans in 1983 and 1985. Many Nigerians now flock to the high-flying Ghanaian economy for work and to countries across the continent, including far-off South Africa.

Nigeria and the Political Economy of the West

Nigeria's global influence peaked in the 1970s at the height of the oil boom. Shortly after the 1973–1974 global oil crisis, Nigeria's oil wealth was perceived by the Nigerian elite largely as a source of strength. In 1975, for example, Nigeria was selling about 30 percent of its oil to the United States and was able to apply pressure to the administration of President Gerald Ford in a dispute over Angola.[17] By the 1980s, however, the global oil market had become a buyers' market. Thereafter, it became clear that Nigeria's dependence on oil was a source of weakness, not strength. The depth of Nigeria's international weakness became more evident with the adoption of structural adjustment in the mid-1980s. Given the enormity of the economic crisis, Nigeria was compelled to seek IMF/ World Bank support to improve its balance of payments and facilitate economic restructuring and debt rescheduling, and it has had to accept direction from foreign agencies ever since.

In addition to its dependence on oil revenues, Nigeria remains dependent on Western technology and Western industrial expertise for exploration and extraction of its oil reserves. Nevertheless, oil can be an important political resource. For example, after General Babangida cancelled presidential elections in 1993, pressure on their home governments by U.S. and

European oil companies, along with a few well-paid Abacha lobbyists, ensured that severe economic sanctions on Nigeria were never imposed. The United States is now turning toward Nigerian oil to diversify its supply base beyond the Middle East, which should improve Nigerian government revenues but may not significantly alter the overall dependency of the economy.

In the end, although oil creates dependencies, it also provides advantages: Nigeria's global leverage stems directly from oil. Nigeria remains a highly visible and influential member of the Organization of Petroleum Exporting Countries (OPEC), selling on the average 2 million barrels of petroleum daily and contributing approximately 8 percent of U.S. oil imports. Britain, France, and Germany each has over $1 billion in investments. Nigeria's oil wealth and its great economic potential have tempered the resolve of Western nations in combating human rights and other

abuses, notably during the Abacha period from 1993 to 1998.

With the end of the ruinous Abacha years, President Obasanjo enjoyed much goodwill among Western governments when he assumed office in 1999. They were, however, hesitant to forgive much of Nigeria's enormous debt without some evidence of fiscal responsibility. By the end of his first term in 2003, Obasanjo had little to show for his international persuasion efforts, because neither his administration nor the National Assembly succeeded in reining in Nigeria's budget or checking rampant public sector corruption.

The West has nevertheless been strongly supportive of the return of Nigeria's leadership across Africa at large under the president. Together with President Thabo Mbeki of South Africa, Obasanjo was instrumental in 2002 in convincing the continent's leaders to transform the OAU into the African Union (AU),

Despite being sub-Saharan Africa's largest crude oil exporter, Nigeria faces chronic fuel shortages. General Abacha allowed the nation's four refineries to collapse, forcing the country into the absurd situation of importing fuel—through middlemen who gave enormous kickbacks to Abacha and his family. Shortages have resurfaced periodically since 1999.
Source: Jay Oguntuwase-Asope, *The Guardian* (Lagos), August 12, 1998.

modeled on European-style processes to promote greater political integration across the continent. The AU's first item of business, largely promoted by Mbeki and Obasanjo, was to endorse the New Partnership for Africa's Development (NEPAD), through which African governments committed to specific political and economic reforms in return for access to Western markets and financial assistance. Western leaders endorsed NEPAD in principle at a summit of the world's largest economies in 2002, but were short on what specific actions they would take if African governments met their target reforms.

Despite its considerable geopolitical resources,

Nigeria's economic development profile is bleak. Nigeria is listed very close to the bottom of the UNDP's Human Development Index (HDI), 142 out of 174, behind India and Haiti. Gross national product (GNP) per capita in 2001 was $300, less than 2 percent of which was recorded as public expenditures on education and health, respectively. These figures compare unfavorably with the $860 per capita GNP for China and $390 per capita for India. On the basis of its per capita GDP, the Nigerian economy is the nineteenth poorest in the world in a 1997 World Bank ranking. For comparative purposes, the same study ranks Ghana as thirty-first poorest and India twenty-seventh.

Section ❸ Governance and Policy-Making

The rough edges of what has been called the "unfinished Nigerian state" can be seen in its institutions of governance and policy-making. What seemed like an endless political transition under the Babangida and Abacha regimes was rushed through in less than a year by their successor, Abdulsalami Abubakar, by 1999. President Obasanjo thus inherited a government that was close to collapse, riddled with corruption, unable to coherently perform basic tasks of governance, yet facing high public expectations to deliver considerable progress.

Organization of the State

The National Question and Constitutional Governance

After four decades as an independent nation, Nigerians are still debating the basic political structures of the country, who will rule and how, and indeed, even if the country should remain united. They call this fundamental governance issue the "national question." How is the country to be governed given its great diversity? What should be the institutional form of the government? How can all sections of the country work in harmony and none feel excluded or dominated by the others? Nigerian leaders have attempted to answer these questions in various ways. Since the creation of Nigeria by the British, one path has been reliance on the Anglo-American tradition of rule by law rather

than by individuals. Another path has been military guidance. Nigeria has stumbled along under hybrids of these two tendencies. As a consequence, the country has produced many constitutions but has yet to entrench constitutionalism.

Since the amalgamation of northern and southern Nigeria in 1914, the country has introduced, or nearly inaugurated, nine constitutions—five under colonial rule (in 1922, 1946, 1951, 1954, and 1960) and four after colonial rule: the 1963 Republican Constitution, the 1979 Constitution of the Second Republic, the 1989 Constitution intended for the Third Republic, and the current 1999 Constitution, which essentially amended the 1979 version. Despite the expenditure of huge sums on constitution making by the Babangida and Abacha regimes, Nigeria experienced the anomaly of conducting national elections in 1998–1999 without a settled constitutional document. Civil society groups, meanwhile, continue to advocate rewriting the 1999 Constitution.

In the United States, the U.S. Constitution is perceived as a living document and subject to interpretation, yet the document itself has endured for over 200 years with just twenty-seven amendments. In contrast, Nigerian constitutions have earned no such respect from military or civilian leaders, who have been unwilling to observe legal and constitutional constraints. Governance and policy-making in this context are conducted within fragile institutions that are often swamped by personal and partisan considerations. Military rule bolstered these tendencies and personalized governance and policy-making. With this in mind, we will discuss key elements of recent periods of military rule, their continued influence in the present, and the young institutions of the Fourth Republic.

Federalism and State Structure

Nigeria's First Republic experimented with the parliamentary model, in which the executive is chosen directly from the legislative ranks in a manner inspired by the British system. The First Republic was relatively decentralized, with the locus of political power in the three federal units: the Northern, Eastern, and Western Regions. The Second Republic constitution, which went into effect in 1979, adopted a U.S.-style presidential model. The Fourth Republic continues with the presidential model: a system with a strong executive who is constrained by a system of checks and balances on authority, a bicameral legislature, and an independent judicial branch charged with matters of law and constitutional interpretation.[18]

Like the United States, Nigeria also features a federal structure comprising 36 states and 774 local government units empowered to enact their own laws within their individual jurisdictions, but limited in scope by the constitution and federal laws. Together, these units constitute a single national entity with three levels of government. The judicial system also resembles that of the United States with a network of local and district courts, as well as state-level courts.

Under a true federal system, the formal powers of the different levels of government would be clearly delineated and the relationships among and between them defined. In Nigeria, by contrast, these institutions have been radically altered by military rule, and the military-authored 1999 Constitution reflects the contradictions of that period. The military perceived their role as preservers of the federation, and they brooked little dissent. Consequently, they left a constitution that retains enormous powers in the federal government, and the executive in particular. In addition, so many years of military rule left a pattern of governance—a political culture—that retains many authoritarian strains despite the formal democratization of state structures.

The control of oil wealth by this centralized command structure has further cemented economic and political control in the center, resulting in a skewed federalism in which states enjoy nominal powers, but in reality are totally dependent on the central government. The powers of the state and local governments are delineated by the federal constitution, and most of them receive their entire budget from what the federal government decides is their share of the oil revenues.

Another aspect of federalism in Nigeria has been the effort to arrive at some form of elite accommodation to moderate some of the more divisive dimensions of cultural pluralism. For example, recruitment of local elements into the army shortly after independence followed a quota system. Through such a system, it was hoped the army would reflect the country's complex ethnic makeup more closely. A similar practice, reflecting what Nigerians now refer to as "federal character," was introduced into the public service and formally codified the 1979 Constitution. (See "Current Challenges: Nigeria's Federal Character.")

Because federal character is also perceived as a tool of ethnic management, disputes about its application have tended to focus on ethnic representation rather than on representation of state interests. Although this principle was originally regarded as a positive Nigerian contribution to governance in a plural society, its application has tended to intensify rather than reduce intergroup rivalries and conflicts. In recent years, there have been calls for the use of merit over federal character in awarding public sector jobs. (See "Current Challenges: Federalism in Nigeria.")

The Executive

Evolution of the Executive Function

In the Second Republic, the earlier parliamentary system was replaced by a presidential system based on the American model. The president was chosen directly by the electorate rather than indirectly by the legislature. The rationale for the change was based on the experience of the First Republic; the instability and ultimate failure of that government, which was less a result of the parliamentary model than of underlying societal cleavages, left a bitter legacy. In addition, there was a widespread belief that a popularly elected president, a truly national figure, could serve as a symbol of unity. Finally, the framers of the Second Republic's constitution believed that placing the election of

Current Challenges: **Nigeria's Federal Character**

What is Nigeria's "federal character"? Federal character, in principle, is an "affirmative action" program to ensure representation of all ethnic and regional groups, particularly in the civil service. Although *federal character* is regarded as a euphemism for *ethnic balancing*, in practice it has provoked ethnic instability, rivalry, and conflict. Federal character goes beyond federalism in the traditional Western and territorial sense, although it definitely contains a territorial element. Federalism as a principle of government has a positive connotation (especially with regard to mitigating ethnic conflict); however, federal character elicits the unevenness and inequality in Nigerian politics, especially when it comes to the controversial use of ethnic-based quotas in hiring, the awarding of government contracts, and the disbursement of political offices.

The pursuit of ethnic balancing has had numerous ill effects, several of which are identified by Nigerian scholar Peter Ekeh.* First, federal charac-

ter has created benefit-seeking and autonomy-seeking groups in areas where they did not previously exist. Second, federal character and federalism have overloaded the political system in terms of personnel and other costs. Federal character has also "invaded the integrity of the public bureaucracy" by ignoring merit. Finally, the thirty-six states that currently exist in Nigeria are vying for control of the center in order to extract the greatest benefits, using ethnic quotas as a lever. None of these conditions is likely to change in the near future. Federal character, and everything that goes with it, appears to be a permanent part of Nigeria's political and social landscape.

---

*See Peter Ekeh, "The Structure and Meaning of Federal Character in the Nigerian Political System," in Peter Ekeh and Eghosa E. Osaghae (eds.), *Federalism and the Federal Character in Nigeria* (Ibadan: Heinemann, 1989).

---

the president in the hands of the electorate, rather than parliament, would mitigate the effects of a lack of party discipline in the selection of the executive.

The Second Republic's experiment with presidentialism lasted for only four years before it was ended by the 1983 coup. Although some Nigerian intellectuals call for a return to parliamentarism, the presidential model has become entrenched in the nation's political arena. The return of military rule in 1983 further concentrated power in the hands of the chief executive, first with head of state Major-General Muhammadu Buhari, until his removal in a 1985 palace coup. His successor, General Babangida, although obviously unelected, assumed the title of president, the first Nigerian military ruler to do so. After ousting Chief Shonekan in November 1993, Sani Abacha also assumed the title of president. Thus, when President Obasanjo took office in 1999, the first elected Nigerian president since Shehu Shagari in 1983, he inherited an executive structure that towered above all other arms of the federal government, far beyond the careful balance envisioned when the model was adopted in 1979.

The Executive Under Military Rule

The styles and leadership approaches among Nigeria's seven military heads of state varied widely. The military regime of General Gowon (1966–1975) was initially consensual, but as he clung to power for five years after the war, his authority declined, and he increasingly relied on a small group of advisers. Although all military leaders talked of "transitions to democracy," only Generals Obasanjo (1976–1979) and Abubakar (1998–1999) fulfilled the pledge of yielding power to an elected government.

After a few years of relatively consensual governance, the Babangida regime (1985–1993) drifted into a more personalized and repressive mode of governance. Abacha (1993–1998) outdid them all, however, and his harsh autocratic rule included the 1994 suspension of habeas corpus and the hounding of outspoken Nigerians into exile. General Abubakar, in contrast, moved quickly to release political prisoners, institute a rapid democratization program, and curb the abuses of the security services.

Current Challenges: *Federalism in Nigeria*

Despite the high-handed methods of its institution and reform, ironically, the federal system has enjoyed wide support within Nigeria historically. With the "national question" unanswered, however, the federal structure endures increasing strain. At the conclusion of the civil war in 1970, many had assumed that the question of national unity had been finally settled. Thus, attempts to include clauses on the right to secede in the constitutions of 1979 and 1989 were roundly rejected by the drafting committees. Yet the Abubakar transition period featured a number of public debates about secession, particularly among the Yoruba, and other groups have complained since 1999 about their continuing marginalization. Other widely held beliefs are now questioned by some elements in society. For example, will Nigeria continue to be a secular state, as outlined in the 1999 Constitution, and persist as a federation to accommodate the country's ethnic, cultural, and religious heterogeneity?

Some northerners have advocated turning Nigeria into an Islamic state, prompting fear among many Christians.

To resolve these issues, some Nigerians have called for a national conference to review the basis of national unity and even to consider the restructuring of Nigeria into a loose confederation of autonomous states, perhaps along the lines of the First Republic. Such calls were ignored by the military, which refused to permit any debate on the viability of a united Nigeria, thus maintaining the geographic status quo. President Obasanjo has so far resisted calls for a national conference. Instead, he created an expert commission to make recommendations for constitutional amendments, and the National Assembly has also stated its intention to debate constitutional reforms. A number of critical civil society groups continue to push for a national conference, however, and the issue is likely to regain attention after the 2003 elections.

Under military administrations, the president, or head of state, made appointments to most senior government positions.[19] Since the legislature was disbanded, major executive decisions (such as decrees) were subject to the approval of a ruling council of high-level military officers. By the time of Abacha's Provisional Ruling Council (PRC), however, this council had become largely unwilling to disagree with the head of state. Given this highly personalistic character of military politics, patron-client relationships flourished during this period. Not surprisingly, ethnic, religious, and regional constituencies have paid close attention to the pattern of appointments to the executive branch.

The military emerged structurally weakened from their long years in power, having been politicized and divided by these patron-client relationships. Within days of his taking office in 1999, President Obasanjo promptly retired over ninety military officers who had held political offices (such as military governorships) under the previous military juntas, seeing them as the most likely plotters of future coups. This lightning act,

unthinkable just a year before, caught the nation, including the military, by surprise, and the officers left quietly. Since 1999, the print media have reported rumors of several possible coup plots that were thwarted, but for the most part, the military has remained loyal and outside of politics.

Under Babangida and Abacha, the military was transformed from an instrument that guarantees national defense and security into another predatory apparatus, one more powerful than political parties. Three decades after the first military coup of January 1966, most Nigerians now believe that the country's political and economic development has been profoundly hampered by military domination and misrule.

In addition, President Obasanjo has paid close attention to keeping the military professionally oriented—and in the barracks. Because he is an ex-military head of state himself, this should not be surprising. U.S. military advisers and technical assistance have been invited to redirect the Nigerian military toward regional peacekeeping expertise—and to keep them busy outside of politics. So far, this strategy seems effective, but the military remains a threat should the civilians fail to gain popular approval.

The Obasanjo Administration

After the abrupt retirement of the political military officers, President Obasanjo raised the minimum wage dramatically, to regain some of the value lost from years of inflation. He also pushed international donors, though without success, to forgive much of Nigeria's debt (see Section 2).

Obasanjo then turned to the conflict-ridden Niger Delta. The initial goodwill he won by visiting the region and meeting local leaders, including youths, soon turned to hostility when he refused to negotiate claims by delta communities for greater control of the revenues from oil drilled on their lands. Instead, he proposed a Niger Delta Development Commission (NDDC) to disburse the 13 percent of oil revenues constitutionally mandated to return to the delta states. Community groups rejected the plan, governors of the Niger Delta states took Obasanjo to court, and youth militias returned to harassing the police and kidnapping oil workers for ransom. One such attack killed several policemen in November 1999, prompting Obasanjo to send the military after the perpetrators. Military units then destroyed the village of Odi and massacred many of its innocent inhabitants.[20] Obasanjo's NDDC, meanwhile, took two years for approval by the National Assembly, and little of its funds have so far reached the impoverished communities of the Niger Delta.

Obasanjo also sought to root out public sector corruption. His initial appointments to manage the oil industry drew early praise for their clean management and contracting policies, and the persistent fuel scarcities of the Abacha years largely disappeared. By 2001, however, familiar patterns of clientelism and financial kickbacks for oil licenses began to resurface. Obasanjo also proposed an Anti-Corruption Commission with sweeping statutory powers to investigate and prosecute public officials, but this commission also took over two years to be enacted, and until 2003, indicted only one minor official. Several months before the 2003 elections, however, the commission shockingly announced that several governors and prominent members of the National Assembly were under investigation, almost all of whom were Obasanjo opponents. Legislators said that the announcements were politically motivated, and promptly revoked the commission's authority. Its future remains unresolved.

In response to calls by civil society groups for some accounting for the injustices committed during years of military rule, Obasanjo set up the Peace and Reconciliation Commission in 1999. Unlike the famous Truth and Reconciliation Commission set up by South Africa at the end of the apartheid years, the Nigerian Commission did not have the power to grant amnesty in exchange for admissions of guilt, which would have better ensured that testimony would be accurate. Consequently, the stories and mutual recriminations given by former Abacha henchmen that riveted the nation in nightly television broadcasts created high political drama. The commission conducted some of its most sensitive inquiries in secret, and when it submitted its report in 2002 to the president, he refused to make its findings public. The report purportedly contains evidence that former military leader General Babangida arranged for the death of a prominent journalist in 1986. The billionaire Babangida, a major financial backer of the president's People's Democratic Party (PDP) and other parties, managed to get a court order blocking its publication, and the Obasanjo administration has so far refrained from pursuing the matter.

To some extent, President Obasanjo's own PDP members hampered his reform efforts. The PDP was a collection of powerful politicians from Nigeria's First and Second Republics, many of whom had grown rich from their complicity with the Babangida and Abacha juntas. These "big men" approached Obasanjo in 1998, and their political machines delivered him the election victory in 1999, an election in which former U.S. President Jimmy Carter and his observation team recorded numerous procedural violations. As apparent reward for this support, Obasanjo filled his cabinet with many of these dubious political kingpins and did not scrutinize their handling of ministry budgets. With a difficult reelection bid in 2003, Obasanjo again turned to these "fixers" to deliver a victory for him and the PDP. Not surprisingly, allegations of corruption at the highest levels of the Obasanjo administration have increased—and gone largely uninvestigated. Personal differences between President Obasanjo and PDP leaders in the National Assembly, particularly the Speaker of the

House, meanwhile, led them to instigate impeachment proceedings against the president in mid-2002, as will be discussed in Section 4.

The Bureaucracy

The bureaucracy touches upon all aspects of Nigerian government. The colonial system relied on an expanding bureaucracy to govern Nigeria. As government was increasingly "Africanized," the bureaucracy became a way to reward individuals in the patrimonial, prebendal system (see "Current Challenges: Prebendalism"). Bureaucratic growth was no longer determined by function and need; increasingly, individuals were appointed on the basis of patronage, ethnic group, and regional origin rather than merit.

It is conservatively estimated that federal and state government personnel increased from a modest 72,000 at independence to well over 1 million by the mid-1980s and beyond. The salaries of these bureaucrats presently consume an estimated 80 to 90 percent of government expenditures, leaving a paltry 10 percent or so for the other responsibilities of government, from education and health care to building the roads.

Para-statals

The largest component of the national bureaucracy in Nigeria is the state-owned enterprises, or **para-statals.** Para-statals in Nigeria are corporate enterprises owned by the state and established to provide specific commercial and social welfare services. They are a hybrid, somewhere between institutions that engage in traditional government operations, such as customs or the

---

Current Challenges: *Prebendalism*

Prebendalism, the peculiarly Nigerian version of corruption, is the disbursing of public offices and state rents to one's ethnic-based clients.* It is an extreme form of clientelism that refers to the practice of mobilizing cultural and other sectional identities by political aspirants and officeholders for the purpose of corruptly appropriating state resources. Prebendalism is an institutionalized pattern of political behavior that justifies the pursuit of and the use of public office for the personal benefit of the officeholder and his clients. The official public purpose of the office becomes a secondary concern. As with clientelism, the officeholder's "clients" comprise a specific set of elites to which he is linked, typically by ethnic or religious ties, and this linkage is key to understanding the concept. There are thus two sides involved in prebendalism, the officeholder and the client, and expectations of benefits by the clients (or supporters) perpetuate the prebendalist system.

As practiced in the Babangida and Abacha eras, when official corruption occurred on an unprecedented scale, prebendalism deepened sectional cleavages and eroded the resources of the state. It also discouraged genuinely productive activity in civil society and expanded the class of individuals who live off state patronage.

As long as prebendalism remains the norm of Nigerian politics, a stable democracy will be elusive. These practices are now deeply embedded in Nigerian society and therefore are more difficult to uproot. The corruption resulting from prebendal practices is blamed in popular discourse for the enormous flight of internally generated capital into secret accounts in overseas banking institutions. The lion's share of the $12.2 billion Gulf War windfall is believed to have been pocketed by Babangida and senior members of his regime and the Central Bank, an example of the magnitude of the systematic pilfering of public resources. General Abacha continued this pattern and is accused of diverting $5 billion from the Nigerian central bank. There are so many current officeholders in Nigeria who indulge in these practices, albeit at less gargantuan levels, that Transparency International regularly lists Nigeria among the most corrupt countries.

*Richard Joseph, *Democracy and Prebendal Politics in Nigeria: The Rise and Fall of the Second Republic* (Cambridge: Cambridge University Press, 1987) 55–68.

postal service, and those in the private sector that operate primarily for profit. In organizational terms, such para-statals are similar to private enterprises in having their own boards of directors. In principle, they are autonomous of the government that established them. In reality, however, such autonomy is limited since their boards are appointed by, and ultimately answerable to, the government through the supervising government ministry.

In general, para-statals are established for several reasons. First, they furnish public facilities, including water, power, telecommunications, ports, and other transportation. A second rationale for the establishment of para-statals is the need to accelerate economic development by controlling the commanding heights of the economy, including steel production, petroleum and natural gas production, refining, petrochemicals, fertilizer, and certain areas of agriculture. Third, para-statals are intended to provide basic utilities and services to citizens at low costs, held below the levels that would be needed by private firms to generate profit. Finally, there is a nationalist dimension that relates to issues of sovereignty over sectors perceived sensitive for national security.

Para-statals such as agricultural commodity boards and the Nigerian National Petroleum Corporation (NNPC) have served as major instruments of the interventionist state. They have been used to co-opt and organize business and societal interests for the purpose of politically controlling the economy and dispensing state largesse. These enterprises are major instruments of patronage and rent-seeking. In Nigeria, as in the rest of Africa, most para-statal enterprises are a tremendous drain on the economy. It is not surprising, therefore, that one of the major requirements of the economic structural adjustment program discussed in Section 2 is the privatization of most of these enterprises. Privatizing the para-statals remains a central part of reform strategy under the Obasanjo administration. The telecommunications and power industries are already up for sale, and parts of the oil industry are slated for auction in 2003.

Other State Institutions

Other institutions of governance and policy-making, including the federal judiciary and subnational governments (incorporating state and local courts), operate within the context of a strong central government dominated by a powerful chief executive.

The Judiciary

At one time, the Nigerian judiciary enjoyed relative autonomy from the executive arm of government. Aggrieved individuals and organizations could take the government to court and expect a judgment based on the merits of their case. This situation changed as each successive military government demonstrated a profound disdain for judicial practices, and eventually it undermined not only the autonomy but also the very integrity of the judiciary as a third branch of government.

The principal instrument that the Babangida and Abacha regimes used to achieve this outcome was a spate of repressive decrees that contained clauses disallowing judicial review. Such clauses were regularly inserted in government decrees barring any consideration of their legality by the courts, as well as any actions taken by government officials under them. Other methods included intimidation by the security services, the creation of parallel special military tribunals that could dispense with various legal procedures and due process, and disrespect for courts of record.

Through the executive's power of appointment of judicial officers to the high bench, as well as the executive's control of funds required for the running of the judiciary, the government can dominate the courts at all levels. In addition, what was once regarded as a highly competent judiciary has been undermined severely by declining standards of legal training as well as bribery.

The decline of court independence reached a new low in 1993 when, in what some analysts labeled "judicial terrorism," the Supreme Court endorsed a government position that literally placed all actions of the military executive beyond the pale of judicial review. The detention and hanging of Ken Saro-Wiwa and eight other Ogoni activists in 1995 (see Section 2) underscored the politicization and compromised state of the judicial system. With the return of civilian rule in 1999, however, the courts have slowly begun to restore some independence and credibility. The Supreme Court in particular has suddenly returned as a critical player in national political development after years of docility and self-imposed irrelevance. In early 2002, it passed two landmark judgments. The first struck down a 2001 election law that Obasanjo and the PDP-dominated legislature passed that would have prevented new parties from contesting the national elections in 2003. Second, the Court decided against the governors of Nigeria's coastal states over control of the vast offshore gas reserves, declaring that these were under the jurisdiction of the federal government.

State and Local Judiciaries.   The judiciaries at the state level are subordinate to the Federal Court of Appeal and the Supreme Court. Some of the states in the northern part of the country with large Muslim populations maintain a parallel court system based on the Islamic *shari'a* (divine law). Similarly, some states in the Middle Belt and southern part of the country have subsidiary courts based on customary law. Each of these maintains an appellate division. Otherwise, all courts of record in the country are based on the English common law tradition, and all courts are ultimately bound by decisions handed down by the Supreme Court.

How to apply the *shari'a* has been a source of continuing debate in Nigerian politics. For several years, some northern groups have participated in a movement to apply *shari'a* to all of Nigeria, and some even have advocated that it be made the supreme law of the land. The military government of Obasanjo blocked the expansion of *shari'a* in 1979. Demands for a broader application of Islamic law were made during the drafting of the 1989 Constitution, but these were again thwarted.

Prior to 1999, *shari'a* courts had jurisdiction only among Muslims in civil proceedings and in questions of Islamic personal law. In November 1999, however, the northern state of Zamfara instituted a version of the *shari'a* criminal code, which included cutting off hands for stealing, and stoning to death for those (especially women) who committed adultery. Eleven other northern states adopted the criminal code by 2001, prompting fears among Christian minorities in these states that the code might be applied to them and creating a divisive national issue. Although the *shari'a* criminal code appears to contradict Nigeria's officially secular constitution, President Obasanjo has so far been unwilling to take these states to court and appears to be pushing for a political solution.

State and Local Government

Because the creation of new states and local governments opens new channels to the oil wealth accumulated at the federal level, localities and groups are constantly clamoring for more. Sensing opportunities to buy support for their regimes, Babangida and Abacha nearly doubled the number of states and tripled that of local governments (see Table 5). Although they touted these moves as answering the "national question" by increasing opportunities for local self-determination, the limited fiscal and political autonomy of these units has in fact bolstered central government control. Several states have added local governments since 2000, but it is uncertain whether they have the constitutional authority to do so.

In response to this proliferation of states, the political parties have turned to the notion of six zones in Nigeria, correlated roughly with the major ethnic regions in the country: Hausa-Fulani, Igbo, Yoruba, and three minority-dominated areas. Political appointments are roughly balanced among the six zones and rotate over time.[21] For instance, the presidency is currently held by the southwest (Yoruba) zone; the next president, by informal agreement, will likely be from one of the Middle Belt minorities, the Northeast, or from the South-South zone—the Niger Delta. Virtually the entire process of constituting and reconstituting this federal arrangement, including the addition of a third level of local government, has occurred under the nondemocratic auspices of colonial and military rule.

The Nigerian experience has promoted a distributive approach to federalism. The lofty claims for federalism as a way of promoting unity through diversity are lost amid the intense competition among "local communities and elites for access to national patronage in the form of oil revenues that are collected, and then appropriated or redistributed, by the federal administration" through the states. (See Table 6.)

State governments are generally weak and dependent on federally controlled revenues. Most of them would be insolvent and unable to sustain themselves without substantial support from the central government, because of the states' weak resource and tax base. About 90 percent of state incomes are received directly from the federal government, which includes a lump sum based on oil revenues, plus a percentage of

Table 5

Political Divisions, 1963–1996					
1963	1967	1976	1987	1991	1996
					(Northwest zone)
Northern Region	North Central	Kaduna	Kaduna	Kaduna	Kaduna
			Katsina	Katsina	Katsina
	Kano	Kano	Kano	Kano	Kano
				Jigawa	Jigawa
	North Western	Sokoto	Sokoto	Sokoto	Sokoto
					Zamfara
				Kebbi	Kebbi
					(North-Central zone)
		Niger	Niger	Niger	Niger
	Benue-Plateau	Benue-Plateau	Benue-Plateau	Benue	Benue
				Plateau	Plateau
					Nassarawa
		Abuja	Abuja	FCT (Abuja)[c]	FCT (Abuja)
	West Central	Kwara	Kwara	Kwara	Kwara
				Kogi[a]	Kogi
					(Northeast zone)
	North Eastern	Bauchi	Bauchi	Bauchi	Bauchi
					Gombe
		Borno	Borno	Borno	Borno
				Yobe	Yobe
		Gongola	Gongola	Adamawa	Adamawa
				Taraba	Taraba
					(Southeast zone)
Eastern Region	East Central	Anambra	Anambra	Anambra	Anambra
				Enugu	Enugu
					Ebonyi
		Imo	Imo	Imo	Imo
				Abia	Abia
					(South-south zone)
	South Eastern	Cross River	Cross River	Cross River	Cross River
			Akwa Ibom	Akwa Ibom	Akwa Ibom
	Rivers	Rivers	Rivers	Rivers	Rivers
					Bayelsa
Mid-West Region	Mid-Western	Bendel	Bendel	Edo	Edo
				Delta	Delta
					(Southwest zone)
Western Region	Western	Ogun	Ogun	Ogun	Ogun
		Ondo	Ondo	Ondo	Ondo
					Ekiti
		Oyo	Oyo	Oyo	Oyo
				Osun	Osun
Lagos[b]	Lagos	Lagos	Lagos	Lagos	Lagos

[a]Kogi state was created by combining parts of Benue and Kwara states.

[b]Lagos was excised from the Western Region in 1954 and became the federal capital. In 1967, it also became capital of the new Lagos State, which included Badagry, Ikeja, and Epe districts from the Western Region.

[c]Abuja replaced Lagos as the federal capital in December 1991, although its boundaries were first delineated in the 1970s.

Source: Tom Forrest, *Politics and Economic Development in Nigeria* (Boulder, Colo.: Westview Press, 1993), 214; Darren Kew.

oil income based on population. The states and local governments must, however, generate more resources of their own to increase the efficiency of both their administrations and private economic sectors. In all likelihood, only Lagos and Kano states could survive without federal subsidies.

In the same way that states depend on federal handouts, local governments have remained dependent on both state and federal governments. This practice has continued despite reforms of the local government system initiated by the Babangida regime in 1988, supposedly to strengthen that level of government. The state and local governments have the constitutional and legal powers to raise funds through taxes. However, Nige-

rians share a pronounced unwillingness, especially those in self-employment, trade, and other informal sector activities, to pay taxes and fees to a government with such a poor record of delivering basic services. The result is a vicious cycle: government is sapped of resources and legitimacy and cannot adequately serve the people. Communities, in turn, are compelled to resort to self-help measures to protect these operations and thus withdraw further from the reach of the state. Because very few individuals and organizations pay taxes, even the most basic government functions cannot be performed (see Table 7).

The return of democratic rule has meant the return of conflict between the state and national governments,

Table 6

Percentage Contribution of Different Sources of Government Revenue to Allocated Revenue, 1980–2002

	Oil Revenue Petroleum Profits Tax	Mining Rents and Royalties	Nonoil Revenue Customs and Excise Duties	Others	Total
1980	58.1	25.7	12.3	3.9	100.0
1981	55.5	19.6	20.4	4.5	100.0
1982	44.5	27.3	21.5	6.7	100.0
1983	35.7	33.4	18.9	12.0	100.0
1984	44.8	32.4	15.2	7.6	100.0
1985	47.8	30.0	14.7	7.5	100.0
1986	40.5	25.3	14.6	19.6	100.0
1987	50.6	25.4	14.3	9.7	100.0
1988	46.7	31.5	15.9	5.9	100.0
	Oil Revenues (Combined)		**Nonoil Revenue**	**Other**	**Total**
1992	86.2		8.4	5.4	100.0
1993	84.0		8.0	8.0	100.0
1994	79.3		9.1	11.6	100.0
1995	53.2		8.1	38.7*	100.0
1996	51.1		10.6	38.3*	100.0
2001	79.7		17.6	2.7	100.0
2002	78.6		19.4	2.0	100.0
2003	78.1		19.9	2.0	100.0

*Beginning in 1995, the Nigerian government began including surplus foreign exchange as federally collected revenue in its accounting.

Sources: Federal Ministry of Finance and Economic Development, Lagos. From Adedotun Phillips, "Managing Fiscal Federalism: Revenue Allocation Issues," *Publius: The Journal of Federalism*, 21, no. 4 (Fall 1991), p. 109. Nigerian Federal Office of Statistics, *Annual Abstract of Statistics: 1997 Edition*. Nigerian Economic Summit Group, *Economic Indicators* (Vol. 8, no. 2, April–June 2002).

much like during the Second Republic (1979–1983). The primary vehicle for conflict since 1999 has been a series of "governors' forums," one for the seventeen southern governors, one for the nineteen northern governors, and one for all thirty-six governors. Ad hoc committees on specific issues have also arisen. The governors' forums have not only taken the federal government to court on a number of occasions, they have also made policy pronouncements and have sought to mediate between the president and National Assembly. Much as at the national level, the state-level executives have far more power than their legislatures. These state assemblies, however, have not been docile, and on several occasions they have moved to impeach their state governors.

A number of governors, particularly in the Igbo-dominated southeast, have increasingly turned to armed militias and vigilante groups to provide security in their states and to intimidate political opponents. Many of these groups were initially local responses to the corrupt and ineffective police force, but several of the governors have sensed the larger political usefulness of these groups. Consequently, and disturbingly, political assassinations and violence increased as the 2003 elections approached.

The Policy-Making Process

Nigeria's prolonged experience with military rule has resulted in a policy process based more on top-down directives than on consultation, political debate, and legislation. Yet four years of democratic government have seen some important changes, as the legislatures, courts, and state governments have begun to force the presidency to negotiate its policies and work within a constitutional framework.

First, we must explore how military rule shaped policy-making in Nigeria. Because of their influence in recruitment and promotions, as well as through their own charisma or political connections, senior officers often develop a network of supporters of the same or lower rank, creating what is referred to as a "loyalty pyramid."[22] Once in power, the men at the top of these pyramids in Nigeria have access to tremendous oil wealth, which is passed on through the lower echelons of the pyramid to reward support. Often these pyramids feature ethnic or religious affiliations (see the discussions of corruption in Section 2 and **prebendalism** in Section 3) such as the "Kaduna Mafia" of northern elites, but pyramids like the "Babangida" or "Abacha Boys" included a patchwork of officers beyond their

Table 7

Share of Total Government Expenditure (%)

	1961	1965	1970	1975	1980	1987	1992	1996	2001	2002
Federal Government	49	53	73	72	66	75	72	74	57	52.3
State Government	51	47	27	28	34	25	28*	26*	24	26
Local Government**	–	–	–	–	–	–	–	–	20	21.7
Total Expenditure (millions Naira)	336	445	1,149	10,916	21,349	29,365	128,476	327,707	1,008,780	1,111,950

* Note that 67% of state spending in 1992 and 49% of it in 1996 came from federal government oil earnings, part of which are allocated annually to all the states roughly in proportion to their population size.

**Local government expenditures are included in state government figures in 1961 and 1965, and federal figures from 1970 through 1996.

Sources: Central Bank of Nigeria, Annual Report and Statement of Accounts; Federal Office of Statistics, Abstract of Annual Statistics (Lagos: Federal Government Printer, 1961, 1965, 1970, 1975, 1980, 1987, and 1997). From Izeubuwa Osayimwese and Sunday Iyare, "The Economics of Nigerian Federalism: Selected Issues in Economic Management," Publius: The Journal of Federalism, 21, no. 4 (Fall 1991), p. 91. Nigerian Economic Summit Group, Economic Indicators (Vol. 8, no. 2, April–June 2002). 1990s percentage calculations by Darren Kew.

ethnic circle. In addition, the well-developed pyramids have allies or personal connections in the bureaucracy, business, and the private sector.

The personal ambitions of leaders commonly eclipse the corporate mission of the military to "save" the nation. Personal goals and interests often become the defining characteristic of the regime and its policies, with the only check on personal power being another coup. In many African countries, a coup signifies the ascension of one particular loyalty pyramid into power, often at the expense of others. Nigeria's first coup in 1966 appeared to signal the rise of a group of Igbo officers under General Ironsi, although he tried to maintain a more nationalist image. General Gowon helped to establish a collegial (or consensus) model of military governance in which important decisions were made by an ethnically balanced body consisting of the leaders of the major loyalty pyramids. The Muhammed and Obasanjo regimes also employed this model, as did Buhari and, at first, Babangida.

General Babangida, however, signified the turning point within the military when national concerns became increasingly subsumed by personal ambitions.[23] He was a master at playing the different loyalty pyramids off against each other, lavishing the nation's oil wealth on friends and buying the support of opponents he could not crush. Once in power, General Abacha made little pretense of accommodating other factions, instead ruthlessly centralizing nearly all government decision making and spreading little of the largesse for which Babangida was famous.

Abacha's personal plunder of the nation's revenues dispelled the notion that the military was a cohesive, nationalist institution capable of governing Nigeria any more efficiently than the civilians. A parallel structure of junior officers loyal to Abacha acted as his gatekeepers, circumventing and humiliating the military's normal chain of command. General Abubakar thus took the reins of a military in June 1998 that was divided and demoralized. Abubakar was more of a professional than his predecessors, purging the government of "Abacha boys" and swiftly returning the country to civilian rule. Despite having returned to the barracks, others in the military clearly yearn for their turn at the top. The civilian politicians appear well aware of this danger. It remains to be seen whether the civilians can forge a new role for the military and develop for themselves a sustainable coalition of support among civil society groups and public constituencies.

Because the military dominated Nigeria for three-quarters of its existence, civilian politics bears strong a resemblance to the politics of loyalty pyramids among the military.[24] Many of the current civilian politicians belonged to the loyalty pyramids of different military men—as bureaucrats, members of military cabinets, business partners to exploit Nigeria's oil wealth, and so on. Now that these civilians are in power, some of whom are former military themselves, they are taking up the reins of the civilian portions of these pyramids, although they do retain some influence with military figures as well.

Nigerians often refer to the politicians who sit atop these civilian loyalty pyramids as "big men." Unlike the military leaders, however, the civilian big men do not typically have access to formal coercive instruments, so to maintain their pyramids they must rely on financial kickbacks and promises of rents from the state: government jobs, contracts, and so on. (Section 4 discusses these clientelistic and prebendal patterns of the loyalty pyramids in greater detail.)

Thus, in patterns reminiscent of the struggles among military loyalty pyramids, the policy-making process today in Nigeria under democratic rule is a function of the clash of interests among the big men and their clients. The vice president, party leaders of the PDP, many of the ministers, and leaders in the National Assembly are all big men vying for larger rents from the state and increased influence and status. Ironically, President Obasanjo was not a big man when he was elected; he rode to power on the backs of these big men and their supporters now in intense competition with each other.

Consequently, policy-making during the Obasanjo administration, after the early honeymoon period when the president was able to get much of what he wanted, has developed a pattern. Obasanjo and his closest advisers formulate a policy and announce it. If legislation is required, the big men in the National Assembly struggle to have their interests appeased in the process. Once the legislation is passed or if no legislation is required, the powerful ministers who must implement the policy alter it to reflect their interests, and then the policy moves on down through the bureaucracy. Not surprisingly, if the policy involves financial disbursements, little of the funds actually reach their intended targets.

In short, civilian policy-making in present day Nigeria is a story of the president introducing reform policies, which are then filtered through the interests of the big men. Invariably, their interests conflict with those of the president and each other, which leads the policy to be blocked or significantly altered to the point that at times, the reformist agenda is lost or ineffectual. The president has grown increasingly adept at navigating these interests, but soon enough his reformist agenda took a backseat to his own overarching interest: re-election in 2003. On this point, however, his ministers were agreed, and policy-making by the administration was undertaken with the goal of getting the president reelected by any possible means.

Section ❹ Representation and Participation

Representation and participation are two vital components in modern democracies; however, Nigeria is at best a nascent democracy. Nigerian legislatures, when they have been allowed to function, have been sidelined or reduced to subservience by the powerful executive, and fraud, elite manipulation, and regular military interference have marred the party system and elections. Consequently, Nigerian society has found modes of participation outside the official structures. An important focus of this section will therefore be unofficial (that is, nongovernmental) methods of representation and participation through the institutions of civil society. Whereas the institutions of political society include such entities as parties, constitutions, and legislatures, those of **civil society** include professional associations, trade unions, religious organizations, and various interest groups.

The Nigerian experience described in this section emphasizes the complex nature of the relationship between representation and participation. It shows that formal representation does not necessarily enhance participation. In fact, there are situations in which the most important modes of political participation are found outside of and in opposition to the institutional modes such as elections and legislatures.

The Legislature

Not surprisingly, Nigeria's legislature has been a victim of the country's political instability. Legislative structures and processes prior to 1999 suffered abuse, neglect, or peremptory suspension by the executive arm. As a consequence, the politicians who took office at the state and federal levels in 1999 had little understanding of and less practice with legislative functions and responsibilities. In addition, they stood in the shadow of the overly powerful executive that had dominated Nigerian politics under the military.

Until the first coup in 1966, Nigeria operated its legislature along the lines of the British Westminster model, with an elected lower house and a smaller upper house composed of individuals selected by the executive. For the next thirteen years of military rule, a Supreme Military Council performed legislative functions by initiating and passing decrees at will. During the second period of civilian rule, 1979–1983, the legislature was structured similar to the U.S. system. As in the United States, Nigeria employed a bicameral structure, with both houses (Senate and House of Representatives) consisting of elected members. The Fourth Republic maintains the U.S.-inspired legislative system, called the National Assembly.

As part of the Babangida regime's transition program, the civilian members of the National Assembly, elected in July 1992, held meetings until mid-1993. Once seated, however, they were barred by military decree from deliberating on issues other than those dealing with uncontroversial topics. When Abacha took over in late 1993, he dismissed both houses, as well as all other elected officials at the state and local levels.

Only one woman sat among the 91 senators and two among the 593 representatives in the Third Republic, and only eight women were elected in 1999 to sit in the Fourth Republic's National Assembly. This reflects the limited political participation of Nigerian women in formal institutions, as discussed in Section 2. Election to the Senate is on the basis of equal state representation, with three senators from each of the thirty-six states, plus one senator from the federal capital territory, Abuja. The practice of equal representation in the Senate is identical to that of the United States, except that each Nigerian state elects three senators instead of two. Election to the Nigerian House of Representatives was also based on state representation but weighted to reflect the relative size of each state's population, again after the U.S. example.

An innovation added during the failed transition to the Third Republic is that local government structures now enjoy greater autonomy from control by the state governments. The federal executive has, however, dominated other branches of government, partly as a consequence of the frequency of military coups. It is standard practice among coup leaders to replace all elected representatives with ruling councils, handpicked by the military executive. Indeed, General Abacha's first act as head of state in November 1993 was to abolish all political institutions, including the duly elected national and state legislatures.

Thus, Nigerian legislatures under military government were either powerless or nonexistent. Even under elected civil administrations prior to 1999, however, Nigerian legislatures were subjected to great pressure by the executive and never assumed their full constitutional role. Because the executive and majority interests in the National Assembly belonged to the same party, this influence has been easily exercised through the actions of party machines and by outright bribery. This situation has been exacerbated by legislative dependence on the executive for their allowances and the resources to meet the relentless demands from their constituents for jobs, contracts, and other favors. This is the critical difference between the Nigerian and U.S. systems: in Nigeria, the president gathers and disburses public revenues, which the Assembly only influences by its right to pass the budget, whereas the U.S. Congress controls the public purse.

The National Assembly that took office in 1999 therefore began its work with great uncertainty over its role in Nigerian politics. Both the House and the Senate were overwhelmingly controlled by the People's Democratic Party (PDP), as was the presidency. Thus, many observers expected the familiar pattern of executive dominance of the legislature through the party structures to continue as it had under the Second and Third Republics.

Initially, these expectations were largely fulfilled. Legislators spent most of their time clamoring for their personal spending funds to be disbursed by the executive. Some of their first acts were to vote themselves pay raises and exorbitant furniture expenditures (the latter move provoking a protest strike by trade unions). Other legislators tested the legislative waters for the first time with a variety of radical bills that never emerged from committee, including one that would have asked the United States to invade Nigeria if the military staged another coup. The first Speaker of the House was forced to resign when a newspaper discovered that he had lied about his age and was too young to run for office. Dramatically, two Senate presidents were also forced to resign within the first year when the media unearthed their corrupt practices. The president, meanwhile, referred to legislators as "small boys" and rarely accorded them the respect of an equal branch of government.

Gradually, however, the National Assembly began to fight back and gain some relevance. The one constitutional power of the Assembly that President Obasanjo could not circumvent was the authority to approve the national budget. In 2001, negotiations between the president and Assembly leaders over the budget became deadlocked, and it was eventually passed several months after it was due. The 2002 budget negotiations were even more bruising, and the president was ultimately forced to sign a budget that was much higher than the revenues expected for that year. When oil revenues dipped even lower than expected, Obasanjo unilaterally chose to disburse only a portion of the budgeted funds to programs of his choosing. Among the funds withheld were those for the National Assembly. Unpaid and feeling disrespected, legislators gradually escalated their demands that Obasanjo negotiate. In August 2002, both the House and the Senate began impeachment proceedings against the president, despite being controlled by Obasanjo's own party. Alarmed at the deadlock, PDP party leaders sought desperately to mediate between the two arms of government. A face-saving compromise, and an apology from the president, was reached through a combination of negotiation and reported side-payments to key legislators.

The impeachment move was not so much a serious attempt to remove the president as it was a statement to Obasanjo that he had to deal with the legislature with respect and as an equal partner in governance. The motives of legislators were hardly pure, since most were primarily concerned with getting their personal slices of the budget, but the president had clearly overstepped his constitutional role by arbitrarily choosing which portions of the budget he would or would not respect. Some of the big men in the Assembly, particularly the Speaker of the House, have personal grudges against Obasanjo that were also at play in the impeachment move. Overall, however, the legislature emerged strengthened from the encounter.

Legislatures at the state level face a similar imbalance of power with the governors, who control large local bureaucracies and disburse the funds received from the federally shared revenues. The politics of these state assemblies have been chaotic and often vicious, with behavior ranging from throwing chairs to storming the assembly hall with supporters, and increasingly, the use of political violence.

The Party System and Elections

The unfortunate legacy of the party and electoral systems after independence in 1960 was that political parties were associated with certain regions and ethnic groups.[25] This extreme factionalization was encouraged by the tendency of most Nigerians to perceive politics as a zero-sum struggle (or winner-take-all) for access to scarce state resources. Unlike Mexico and, to some extent, India, Nigeria did not develop an authoritarian dominant-party system after independence that might have transcended some of these social cleavages. Instead, the multiparty system reinforced and deepened existing social divisions.

Nigeria's use of a first-past-the-post plurality electoral system produced legislative majorities for parties with strong ethnic and regional identities. All of the parties of the First and Second Republics were more attentive to the welfare of the regions from which they drew the most support than to the development of Nigeria as a whole. Control of the center, or at least access to it, ensured access to substantial financial resources. In a polity as potentially volatile as Nigeria, however, these tendencies intensified political fragmentation and resentment among the losers. Nigerian parties during the First Republic were dominated by

the largest ethnic groups and interests in each of the three regions. During subsequent democratic experiments, many of the more recent parties could trace their roots to their predecessors in the First Republic.

In the Second Republic, the leading parties shared the same ethnic and sectional support, and often the same leadership, as the parties prominent in the first civilian regime. The Unity Party of Nigeria, UPN (mainly Yoruba), was headed by former Action Group leader Chief Obafemi Awolowo, the Nigerian Peoples Party, NPP (mainly Igbo), was led by Nnamdi Azikiwe (formerly of the NCNC), the Peoples Redemption Party, PRP (organized and located around Kano city in northern Nigeria), was led by Mallam Aminu Kano, while the Great Nigeria Peoples Party, GNPP (organized around the Kanuri northeast), was a somewhat new tendency under Waziri Ibrahim. The dominant party in the Second Republic, the National Party of Nigeria (NPN), brought together a diverse cross-ethnic coalition, under a predominantly northern leadership that had been associated with the Northern People's Congress (NPC) under the previous civilian regime.

In its wavering steps toward the civilian Third Republic, General Babangida's administration in October 1989 announced a landmark decision to establish, by decree, only two political parties.[26] The state provided initial start-up funds, wrote the constitutions and manifestos of these parties, and designed them to be "a little to the right and a little to the left," respectively, on the political-ideological spectrum.

Interestingly, the elections that took place between 1990 and 1992 at local, state, and federal levels indicate that despite their inauspicious beginnings, the two parties cut across the cleavages of ethnicity, regionalism, and religion in their membership and electoral performance and demonstrated the potential within Nigeria to move beyond ethnicity.[27] Presidential victor Moshood Abiola, a southern Muslim, won a number of key states in the north, including the hometown of his opponent. Once the election was annulled, however, the more familiar north-south divisions reemerged, fostered by both the regime and, ironically, Abiola's most determined advocates.

As shown in Table 8, northern-based parties dominated the first and second experiments with civilian rule. Given this historical trend, it is significant that a southerner was able to win the presidency in 1993, the first time in Nigeria's history that a southerner defeated a northerner in elections to lead the nation. Southerners therefore perceived the decision by the northern-dominated Babangida regime to annul the June 12 elections as a deliberate attempt by the military and northern interests to maintain their decades-long domination of the highest levels of government.

Yet Abiola's victorious Social Democratic Party (SDP) was an impressive coalition of Second Republic party structures, including elements of the former UPN, NPP, PRP, and GNPP. The opposing National Republican Convention (NRC) was seen as having its roots in northern groups that were the core of the National Party of Nigeria (NPN).

New Alignments: Abacha's Ambition and Abubakar's Promise

Nigerians in general greeted General Abacha's 1993 coup and subsequent banning of the SDP and NRC with expressions of anger, while the response of party members, with a few exceptions, was muted. Southern-based human rights and prodemocracy groups, in alliance with student unions and other organizations, launched street demonstrations, and trade union strikes brought the economy to a halt by mid-1994. With the unions crushed and Abiola in jail by the end of 1994, Abacha started his own transition program in October 1995. It featured a series of elections from the local to the federal levels over the following three years in a manner reminiscent of the Babangida program.

Once the ban on political associations was lifted, some of the Second Republic party structures resurfaced and applied for accreditation with the election commission. To general surprise, a party favored by northern oligarchs was not registered, and most of the other parties led by powerful figures were also barred. In late 1996, the Abacha government registered only five parties, most of whose members had no public constituency and little political experience. By the time local government elections were held in January 1997, the few people who did vote had little idea for whom they were voting; some of the candidates confessed publicly that they had never even seen their party's manifesto.

During 1997, the five parties, which Chief Bola Ige, a prominent Yoruba political figure and victim of political assassination in 2002, branded "five fingers of a leprous hand," began to clamor for General Abacha to run for president. Public participation in delayed state assembly elections in December 1997 was abysmal, as each of the parties proclaimed, one after another, that Abacha was their candidate. Despite strong resistance from some of its leaders, the fifth party finally succumbed to the pressure and nominated Abacha in April 1998, making the presidential elections scheduled for August 1998 a mere referendum, endorsed by the chief justice of the Supreme Court as being legally permissible. The "transition" process had become a travesty.[28] Throughout the Abacha transition, the military influenced or became actively involved in the parties. Key generals in the regime would orchestrate party policies and provide supplementary funding for the groups already funded by the government. The government actively disqualified party candidates just days before the casting of ballots and peremptorily reversed some election results.

In 1996–1997, condemnation of the Abacha government came primarily from Lagos-based human rights and pro-democracy groups, exiles abroad, international nongovernmental organizations, and foreign governments. By April 1998, once Abacha's plan to be certified as president became a certainty, domestic opposition increased. A group of former governors and political leaders from the north (many former NPN and PRP members) publicly petitioned Abacha not to run for president. They were later joined by colleagues from the south, forming what they called the Group of 34 (G-34). Human rights and pro-democracy organizations began again to form alliances to organize protests, and critical press coverage recovered some of its former boldness. Even General Babangida voiced his opposition to Abacha's continuing as president. Although public disenchantment and apathy were pervasive after years of economic struggle and broken political promises, the only real obstacle to Abacha's plan for "self-succession" was whether the military would allow it.

Rumors of Abacha's ill health had circulated for a year, but his sudden death on June 8, 1998, was still a great surprise. The following day, General Abubakar, chief of Defense Staff, was sworn in as head of state. Shortly after, he promised a speedy transition to democracy and began releasing political prisoners. There were

Table 8

Federal Election Results in Nigeria, 1959–2003

Presidential Election Results, 1979–2003

	Victor (% of the vote)	Leading Contender (% of vote)
1979	Shehu Shagari, NPN (33.8)	Obafemi Awolowo, UPN (29.2)
1983	Shehu Shagari, NPN (47.3)	Obafemi Awolowo, UPN (31.1)
1993	M.K.O. Abiola, SDP (58.0)	Bashir Tofa, NRC (42.0)
1999	Olusegun Obasanjo, PDP (62.8)	Olu Falae, AD/APP alliance (37.2)
2003	Olusegun Obasanjo, PDP (61.9)	Mohammadu Buhari, ANPP (32.1)

Parties Controlling the Parliament/National Assembly by Ethno-Regional Zone, First to Fourth Republics

		Northwest	North-Central	Northeast	Southwest	South-South	Southeast
First	1959	**NPC**	**NPC** (NEPU)	**NPC**	AG	AG	NCNC*
	1964–65	**NPC**	**NPC**	**NPC**	NNDP* (AG)**	NNDP* (AG)**	NCNC
Second	1979	**NPN**	PRP (NPN, UPN)	GNPP (NPN)	UPN (NPN)	**NPN**	NPP* (UPN)
	1983	**NPN**	**NPN** (PRP)	**NPN**	UPN (NPN)	**NPN**	NPP**
Third	1992	**NRC**	SDP (NRC)	SDP (NRC)	SDP	**NRC** (SDP)	**NRC**
Fourth	1999	**PDP** (APP)	**PDP**	**PDP** (APP)	AD (PDP)	**PDP** (APP)	**PDP**
	2003	ANPP	**PDP** (ANPP)	ANPP (PDP)	**PDP** (AD)	**PDP**	**PDP**

Boldfaced: Ruling party
Italicized: Leading opposition
*: Coalition with ruling party
**: Coalition with opposition

1998 Local Government Elections*

	Total Council Chairs	Total States with majority (out of 36, plus FCT)
PDP	459	28 (including FCT)
APP	188	2 (one tied with PDP)
AD	100	6
Others	8	—

*Preliminary results December 9, 1998, in *The Guardian* (Lagos, Nigeria).

1999 State Gubernatorial and House of Assembly Elections (out of 36)

	Total Seats	House of Assembly majorities
PDP	21	23
APP	9	8
AD	6	5

Table 8 *(continued)*

Federal Election Results in Nigeria, 1959–2003

1999 National Assembly Elections

	Senate (out of 109)	House (out of 360)
PDP	63	214
APP	26	77
AD	20	69

Table 9

List of Acronyms used in Table 8

AG	Action Group
AD	Alliance for Democracy
APP	All People's Party
GNPP	Great Nigerian Peoples' Party
NAP	Nigerian Advance Party
NCNC	National Convention of Nigerian Citizens (formerly, National Council of Nigeria and the Cameroons)
NEPU	Northern Elements Progressive Union
NNDP	Nigerian National Democratic Party
NPC	Northern People's Congress
NPF	Northern Progressive Front
NPN	National Party of Nigeria
NPP	Nigerian People's Party
NRC	National Republican Convention
PRP	People's Redemption Party
PDP	People's Democratic Party
SDP	Social Democratic Party
UPN	Unity Party of Nigeria

immediate calls for Abiola's release and his appointment to head an interim government of national unity. Abiola's fatal heart attack on July 7, 1998, removed the last obstacle to the holding of entirely new elections, the preferred option of the Abubakar administration. New parties quickly formed, and even Yoruba political leaders agreed by August to participate, although they insisted that the next president should be a Yoruba to compensate their people for having been robbed of their first elected presidency.

Once again, political associations centered on well-known personalities—the big men—emerged around the country, and intense bargaining and mergers among the smaller groups took place. The G-34, the prominent group of civilian leaders who had condemned Abacha's continuation plans, tried to transform itself into a political party. They created the People's Democratic Party (PDP) in late August, minus most of the key Yoruba members of G-34, who joined a primarily Yoruba-based Alliance for Democracy (AD). At least twenty more parties applied for certification to the electoral commission, INEC, many of which were truly grass-roots movements, including a transformed human rights organization and a trade union party. The Abubakar administration evidently played no role in party formation, nor did it provide government funds for their functioning (unlike its two predecessors, the Babangida and Abacha regimes).

To escape the ethnic-based parties of the First and Second Republics, INEC required that parties earn at least 5 percent of the votes in twenty-four of the thirty-six states in the December 1998 local government elections in order to proceed to the state and federal levels. This turned out to be an ingenious way of reducing the number of parties for the most important elections and also to oblige them to seek to broaden their appeal. The only parties to meet INEC's requirements were the PDP, AD, and the All Peoples Party (APP); the APP included a mixture of groups from the Middle Belt, the southeast, and the far north. With the big men of the PDP wielding tremendous resources across the country, the AD and APP formed an alliance in the elections for the presidency in February 1999.

In comparison to the failed experiments of Babangida and Abacha, the transition process under Abubakar moved ahead peacefully, if problematically. One important challenge was the continuing unrest in the southern Niger Delta region. A number of minority groups there, in some areas engaged in low-level conflict since 1997, complained of being excluded from the process. In September 1998, they seized several production sites from multinational oil corporations and demanded more local government access, development projects, and a greater share of the oil wealth. Bayelsa state elections were disrupted and had to be rescheduled, as were some local government contests in the region. Voter turnout in the Niger Delta region for the presidential and National Assembly elections was abysmal; the political parties fraudulently inflated the returns.

The three registered parties rely on elite-centered structures established during previous civilian governments and transition programs. The PDP includes core members of the northern establishment NPN and the northern progressive PRP of the Second Republic. From the Second Republic, the AD drew key individuals from the Yoruba-dominated UPN and the APP (now ANPP) from the GNPP, a party dominated by the Kanuri-Middle Belt. The ANPP also featured southern politicians who had prominent roles in the five Abacha parties. Demonstrating the cross-ethnic alliances that have forged and reworked despite the political disruptions of a quarter-century, only the AD reflected a specific ethnic configuration. General Obasanjo and other Yoruba leaders joined PDP. In a fiercely contested nomination battle, Obasanjo was chosen as the PDP's presidential nominee, defeating Second Republic Vice President Alex Ekwueme, who is Igbo. Interestingly, Obasanjo again defeated Ekwueme for the PDP nomination in 2003. Obasanjo then went on to defeat the AD/APP alliance candidate, Chief Olu Falae, also Yoruba, in the presidential contest in February 1999.

ANPP is truly a multiethnic collection, drawing northern politicians of royal lineage, northeastern and Middle Belt minorities, Igbo business moguls, and southern minority leaders. AD appears to be as Yoruba-centric as its Second Republic UPN and First Republic AG predecessors. Yet like these earlier parties, it has attracted dynamic politicians from other areas such as Arthur Nwankwo, an Igbo. It is important to note the political pragmatism of the Abubakar administration (and the INEC) in registering the AD, despite its ethno-regional base, and allowing it to compete for the presidency in alliance with the then-APP. It made sense to accommodate rather than alienate the Yoruba people on account of the deep sense of grievance toward the federal government provoked by the 1993 annulment of Abiola's victory and the subsequent five years of bitter conflict.

The rapidity of the Abubakar-supervised electoral process benefited civilian politicians and recently retired military officers with access to substantial financial resources. The civil society groups that led much of the struggle against the Abacha dictatorship found themselves at a disadvantage in trying to influence, and participate in, this process.

Thus, the leaders of the Fourth Republic political parties essentially represent alliances of convenience among powerful individuals, the big men, who retain their own resource and client bases and lack a common ideology or clear policy agenda. In contrast to the parties of the First and Second Republics, the current parties (with the exception of the AD, which showed signs of partial disintegration by the end of the first electoral cycle) are not associated with a single predominant ethnic group. Ethnicity is still a critical factor in party politics, but the locus of competition is within the parties themselves rather than among the parties using the levers of government against each other, as in the interethnic competition of the earlier failed republics.

Because the current parties are mere alliances of convenience among the big men, however, they suffer an instability that their predecessors did not. They stand for little beyond the interests of their masters, so the loyalties among their members are weak, as are their connections to the wider populace. Squabbles among the leaders of the AD caused the party to implode not long after the election, and the APP faced a crisis of relevance. Thus, the Fourth Republic has enjoyed no real opposition movement at the national level. Without a viable opposition to challenge it, the ruling PDP was also prey to internal division. Bonds among the PDP leaders had grown so frayed by 2002 that the PDP Speaker of the House could spearhead impeachment moves against the PDP president. The approach of the 2003 elections to some extent reinvigorated all three parties, but they may well continue to unravel thereafter.

The Independent National Electoral Commission (INEC) complicated matters in 2002 when it registered three new political parties, each of them pragmatic alliances among disgruntled politicians from the existing parties, primarily the PDP, as well as a few new faces. One of the new parties merged with the APP to form the ANPP, the All Nigerian Peoples Party.

Late in 2002, however, the Supreme Court overruled the INEC's restrictive policies on registering parties, and dozens of new parties were permitted to contest the 2003 elections. In all, some thirty associations participated at the polls. Revealing its pro-Abacha roots, the ANPP nominated as its 2003 presidential candidate former head of state, General (retired) Muhammadu Buhari, a well-known supporter of the *shari'a* movement. The AD declined to nominate a 2003 presidential candidate in exchange for the PDP not mounting serious challenges against other AD candidates in the Yoruba region. However, the PDP reneged on the backroom deal and stunningly defeated the AD at all levels in five of the six southwestern states in 2003.

Political Culture, Citizenship, and Identity

Traditionally, institutions that represent and mobilize society in the political sphere include legislatures, political parties, trade unions, and other major elements of civil society. In the process, they help to shape, organize, and express political culture and identities, thus nurturing qualities of citizenship. During military rule, which held sway for about thirty years of the post-independence period, these institutions were proscribed and disbanded (in the case of legislatures and political parties) or muzzled (in the case of labor unions). Their roles have been largely assumed by other groups and institutions, including ethnic and religious organizations, the mass media, and professional and trade groups. In many of these circles, the state (federal government) is regarded as a distant entity of questionable legitimacy. The state's unwillingness or inability to deliver appropriate services to the populace, its rampant corruption, and the frequency of military coups have fostered a political culture of apathy and alienation among many Nigerians and militant opposition among particular communities and groups.

Thus, military rule left Nigeria with strong authoritarian influences in its political culture. Most of the younger politicians of the Fourth Republic came of age during military rule, so naturally they learned the business of politics from Abacha, Babangida, and their military governors. Nigeria's deep democratic traditions discussed in Section 1 remain vibrant among the larger polity, but they are in constant tension with the values imbibed during years of governance when po-

litical problems were often solved by military dictate, power, and violence rather than by negotiation and respect for law. This tension was manifest in the irony that the leading presidential contenders in 2003 were all former military men, one of whom—Buhari—was the ringleader of the 1983 coup that overthrew the Second Republic.

Modernity Versus Traditionalism

The terrain of political culture, citizenship, and identity is a contested arena within Nigeria. The interaction of modern (colonial, Western) elements with traditional (precolonial, African) practices has created the tensions of a modern sociopolitical system that rests uneasily on traditional foundations. Nigerians straddle two worlds, each undergoing constant evolution. On one hand, the strong elements in communal societies that promoted accountability have been weakened by the intrusion of Western culture oriented toward individuality. On the other hand, the modern state has been unable to free itself fully from rival ethnic claims organized around narrow, exclusivist constituencies.

As a result, exclusivist identities continue to dominate Nigerian political culture and define the nature of citizenship.[29] Individuals tend to identify with their immediate ethnic, regional, and religious (or subethnic, subregional, and subreligious) groups rather than with state institutions, especially during moments of crisis. Nigerians usually seek to extract as many benefits as possible from the state but hesitate when it comes to performing basic civic duties such as paying taxes or taking care of public property. Entirely missing from the relationship between state and citizen in Nigeria is a fundamental reciprocity—a working social contract—based on the belief that there is a common interest that binds them.

Religion

Religion has been a persistent basis of conflict in Nigerian history. Islam began to filter into northeast Nigeria in the eleventh and twelfth centuries, spread to Hausaland by the fifteenth century, and greatly expanded in the early nineteenth century. In the north, Islam first coexisted with, then gradually supplanted, indigenous religions. Christianity arrived later, but it expanded rapidly through missionary activity in the south dating from the early nineteenth century. The amalgamation of northern and southern Nigeria in 1914 brought together the two regions and their belief systems.

These religious cultures have consistently clashed over political issues such as the application of the *shari'a* criminal code in the northern states. For most Muslims, the *shari'a* represents a way of life and supreme (personal) law that transcends secular and state law; for many Christians, the expansion of *shari'a* law threatens the secular nature of the Nigerian state and their position within it. The pull of religious versus national identity becomes even stronger in times of economic hardship. The Babangida period corresponded to a rise in both Islamic fundamentalist movements and evangelical Christian fundamentalism. Where significant numbers of southern Christians are living in predominantly Muslim states (for example, Kaduna state), many clashes have erupted, with great loss of life and the extensive destruction of churches, mosques, and small businesses.

The Press

The plural nature of Nigerian society, with the potential to engender a shared political culture, can be seen in virtually all aspects of public life. The Nigerian press, for instance, has long been one of the liveliest and most irreverent in Africa. The Abacha regime moved to stifle its independence, banning several publications and threatening the suspension of others. Significantly, most of the Nigerian press has been based in a Lagos-Ibadan axis in the western part of Nigeria and has frequently been labeled "southern." In 1994, Abacha closed several of the most influential and respected southern Nigerian newspapers and magazines, including the *Guardian, Concord* (owned by Abiola), and the *Punch,* leaving less critical and more biased publishers intact. In this regard, he was following the nefarious example of his predecessor, Babangida, especially during the final and increasingly conflicted years of his rule. A northern paper, the *New Nigerian,* published in Kaduna, succumbed at times to overt sectionalism. The fact that the media are sometimes regarded as a captive of ethnic and regional constituencies has weakened its capacity to resist attacks on its rights and privileges.

Recently, however, independent television and radio stations have proliferated, and forests of satellite towers now span across Nigerian cities to support the boom in Internet cafés and telecommunications. The freer environment of democracy has also allowed investigative journalism to flourish. One Speaker of the House and two Senate presidents have been brought down by timely media exposés of their misconduct, and other public figures are being scrutinized in the press.

Interests, Social Movements, and Protests

Issues relating to political attitudes, political culture, and identities are still dominated and defined largely by elite, male, urban-based interests. These interests include ethnic as well as professional and associational groups. The few nonelite groups, such as urban-based market women's associations, often serve as channels for disseminating the decisions and agendas of male-dominated groups. In essence, nonelite and rural elements continue to be marginalized and manipulated by elites and urban groups. Lacking competence in the language of public discourse, namely English, and access to financial networks, nonelites have difficulty confronting, on their own, the decision-making centers of the state and society.

Elite and nonelite Nigerians alike come together in civic organizations and interest groups such as labor unions and student and business associations. Because the political machinery was in the hands of the military, Nigerian citizens sought alternative means of representation and protest in an effort to have an impact on political life. Historically, labor has played a significant role in Nigerian politics, as have student groups, some women's organizations, and various radical and populist organizations. Business groups have frequently supported and colluded with corrupt civilian and military regimes. In the last year of the Abacha regime, however, even the business class, through mechanisms like Vision 2010, began to suggest an end to such arbitrary rule. The termination of military rule has seen civil society groups flourish across Nigeria.

Labor

Organized labor once played an important role in challenging governments during both the colonial and postcolonial eras in several African countries, including Nigeria. Continuous military pressure throughout the 1980s and 1990s forced a decline in the once independent and powerful role of organized labor in Nigerian politics. The Babangida regime implemented strategies of **state corporatism** designed to control and co-opt various social forces such as labor. When the leadership of the Nigerian Labour Congress (NLC), to which all unions compulsorily belong, however, took a vigorous stand against the government, the government sacked the leaders and appointed conservative replacements. When prodemocracy strikes during the summer of 1994 by the National Petroleum Employees Union (NUPENG) and other sympathetic labor groups significantly reduced oil production and nearly brought the country to a halt, the Abacha regime arrested and disbanded its leadership.

The Nigerian labor movement has been vulnerable to reprisals by the state and private employers. First, the state has always been the biggest single employer of labor in Nigeria, as well as the recognized regulator of industrial relations between employers and employees. Second, ethnic, regional, and religious divisions have often hampered labor solidarity while being deliberately manipulated by the state.

Military policy to centralize and co-opt the unions caused their militancy and impact to wane, until General Abubakar removed the government-appointed union administrators in 1998 and allowed the unions to elect their own leaders again. Within a year, labor had regained its footing. National strikes in 2000 forced the Obasanjo government to forgo plans to raise the price of fuel, and strikes in 2001 and 2002 had similar positive impacts on wage increases.

Labor still claims an estimated 2 million members across Nigeria and remains one of the most potent forces in civil society. It therefore has a great stake in the consolidation of constitutional rule in the Fourth Republic and the protections that allow it to organize and act freely on behalf of its members and, more broadly, the masses of disadvantaged people in Nigeria.

The Business Community

Nigeria has a long history of entrepreneurialism and business development. This spirit, however, is compromised by the tendencies toward rent-seeking and the appropriation of state resources. Members of the Nigerian business class are often characterized as "pirate capitalists" because of the high level of cor-

rupt practices and collusion with state officials.[30] Many wealthy individuals have served in the military or civilian governments, or indirectly protect their access to state resources by sponsoring elected officials. Nevertheless, as economic and political conditions in Nigeria deteriorated, the state offered fewer avenues for businesspeople and can no longer provide even the necessary infrastructure for business development.

Private interests have proved surprisingly resilient, as organized groups have emerged to represent the interests of the business class and promote economic development generally. These associations have proliferated throughout Nigeria and in many areas represent diverse groups, from butchers, to manufacturers, to car-hire firms. In a number of cases, they have demonstrated social responsibility by building roads, schools, market stalls, and similar infrastructure, rather than relying on uncertain government provisions.

Many local or regional groups are also members of national organizations. National business associations, such as the Nigerian Association of Chambers of Commerce, Industry, Mines, and Agriculture (NACCIMA), the largest in the country, have taken an increasingly political stance pressing the military leadership to resolve the June 12 crisis and advocating better governance. In their bid to reduce uncertainty, halt economic decline, and protect their economic interests, large business associations increasingly perform what are clearly political roles. The continuing influence of the Economic Summit and other business associations in shaping government economic policies underscores this trend.

Other Social Groups

Student activism continues to be an important feature of Nigerian political life. University and other higher-level student groups play an important political role. Along with their teachers, they have suffered government harassment, banning, and attempts to engineer divisions in their unions and associations, including countless closings of the universities during the Babangida and Abacha regimes. Many professional associations of doctors and lawyers have also become champions of human rights. They often support campaigns conducted by human rights organizations, which have proliferated since the founding of the Civil Liberties Organization (CLO) in 1987.

The activities of these organizations increased

significantly with the introduction of the structural adjustment program (SAP). Marginal groups, including women and the young, the urban poor, and people in rural areas, perceived an imbalance in the distribution of the benefits and burdens generated by the SAP program. Not surprisingly, the flagrant display of wealth by senior members of the military alienated these groups and encouraged a "culture of rage" among youths, artisans, the urban poor, and the unemployed.

This rage over economic hardship and military oppression led to a sharp increase in the number of human rights groups and other nongovernmental organizations (NGOs) in the 1990s.[31] Greater funding for NGOs from governments and private foundations in Europe and the United States assisted the growth of this sector, most notably in the south but gradually in the north as well. They generally focus on such issues as civil protection, gender law, health care, media access, and public housing. Most are urban based, although efforts to develop rural networks are underway.

Personality conflicts, ethnic divisions, and intense competition for funding hampered the challenge posed by these civil society organizations to military dictatorship.[32] Prodemocracy efforts by NGOs peaked in the 1993–1994 struggle over June 12, when they managed to stage numerous successful stay-home strikes in Lagos and several other southern cities. The Campaign for Democracy in 1993 and then the National Democratic Coalition (NADECO) in 1994 built an antimilitary front among the NGOs that also included students, academics, some labor unions, and other groups. As Abacha moved forward with his "self-succession" campaign in 1997–1998, this sector once again was able to mount numerous street demonstrations and other protests to counter the regime's orchestration, even under very restrictive political conditions.

The return of political freedoms under the Fourth Republic in 1999 has allowed these groups, battle hardened from the Abacha years, to proliferate and become influential. Yet the end of military government has also left many of the prodemocracy and human rights groups without the strong central focus they had in the 1990s. Specialized groups are gradually supplanting the older, broader organizations, while many of the leaders of the prodemocracy struggles in the 1990s ran for office in the 2003 elections, although most were unable to dislodge the ruling politicians.

Civil society groups are, in short, making a substantial contribution to consolidating democracy in Nigeria. Their relationships with the political parties, however, remain largely distant. Nigeria's prospects for building a sustainable democracy during the Fourth Republic will depend, in part, on the willingness of many of these advocacy groups to increase their collaboration with the political parties, while maintaining a high level of vigilance and activism.

Section ❺ Nigerian Politics in Transition

Despite the slow progress of the Fourth Republic, Nigerians remain overwhelmingly in favor of democratic government over military rule. About 80 percent of respondents in a recent survey said that they still prefer democracy to any other alternative, but their frustration is growing with the slow pace of reform and continued corruption in politics.[33] Will democracy in Nigeria consolidate sufficiently to meet even minimal levels of public satisfaction before Nigerians are again willing to accept authoritarian rule? So long as the civilian politicians treat government offices more as personal feeding frenzies rather than as positions of public service, the clock is ticking closer to the hour of the next military coup.

Several patterns in Nigerian politics must change if the entrepreneurs in the military are to be kept in the barracks and democracy is to become more stable in Nigeria. First and foremost, the nation must turn from a system of politics dominated by big men—what is, for all intents and purposes, a semicompetitive oligarchy—to a more popular mode of politics that engages and addresses the fundamental interests of the public. Second, but ultimately determined by the first, Nigerians must conclusively settle the national question and commit to a political arrangement that reflects and respects the nation's great diversity but allows its government to move beyond limited ethnic struggles so that it may address the larger national interests of economic development and good governance.

The popular vote on June 12, 1993, in which

Moshood Abiola won many of the states outside his own ethnic region, provided a radical departure from the sectionalism of the past and offered a refreshing opportunity to develop a more national political agenda. June 12 was a historic breakthrough, the day the ordinary people of Nigeria rose against the ethnic, religious, and regional prejudices and the divisive politics with which colonialism and the political class had oppressed them for a half a century. Babangida's annulment of the June 12 election followed by Abacha's predatory rule, however, placed ethnicity, religion, and regionalism back firmly on the agenda. Nonetheless, and despite the flaws of the May 1999 elections, President Obasanjo was elected *despite* having lost the popular vote in his own ethnic region. Northerners, Igbos, and minority groups across Nigeria, rather than Obasanjo's own Yoruba ethnicity, voted for him overwhelmingly and put him into office. Nigeria's Fourth Republic must find ways of moving beyond patrimonial politics and develop a truly national political process in which mobilization and conflicts along ethnic, regional, and religious lines gradually diminish.

Political Challenges and Changing Agendas

Nigeria's fitful transition to democratic rule from 1985 to 1999 was halting in part because it was planned and directed from above. This approach contrasts sharply with the popular-based movements that unseated autocracies in Central and Eastern Europe beginning in the spring of 1989. Promises of democratic transition were made periodically during Nigeria's political history as a ploy by the military to stabilize and legitimize their governments. General Abubakar dutifully handed power to the civilians in 1999, but only after ensuring that the military's interests would be protected under civilian rule, and creating an overly powerful executive that reinforces **patrimonialism,** a system of power in which authority is maintained through patronage. His rapid transition program produced a tenuous, conflicted democratic government facing daunting tasks of restoring key institutions, securing social stability, and reforming the economy. The continuing strength and influence of collective identities, defined on the basis of religion or ethnicity, are often more binding than "national" (that is, all-Nigerian) ones and remain problematic. The parasitic nature of the Nigerian economy is a further source of instability. Rent seeking and

other unproductive, often corrupt, business activities remain accepted norms of wealth accumulation.

Nonetheless, Nigerians are sowing seeds of change in all of these areas. Attitudes toward the military in government have shifted dramatically. The decline in the appeal of military rule can be attributed to the abysmal performances of the Babangida and Abacha regimes in economic policies and governance. Many now recognize that the military, apart from its contributions to national security, is incapable of promoting economic and social progress in Nigeria. With the military discredited for the moment, the nature and outcome of the struggles among the big men will decide the direction of political and economic change. Thus, the current struggles among Nigeria's patrimonial big men may actually support democratic development in the long run if stable coalitions appear among them over time and if these political kingpins are generally willing to respect the democratic rules.

So far, they have generally confined their struggles within the constraints of the democratic system: taking each other to court, attacking each other in the media, introducing competing bills in the Assembly, and even threatening to impeach the president. All of these efforts actually strengthen the system not just by using it, but by forcing the personal struggles of powerful individuals into the public realm. These opposing coalitions of powerful individuals, who gather under the umbrellas of political parties, have used the system to police each other and keep each other's ambitions in check.

The next critical step down the long road of democratic development for Nigeria is the development of a viable, multiethnic opposition party that is also "loyal," meaning that it plays by the rules of the system. Opposition parties help to reduce corruption in the system because they have an interest in exposing the corruption of the ruling party, which in turn forces them to reduce their own corrupt practices. Furthermore, in order to unseat the ruling party and win elections, opposition parties need to engage the public to win their votes. In this manner, issues of interest to the public become of interest to the powerful individuals leading the parties.

The introduction of so many new parties in 2002 may facilitate the development of a viable, loyal opposition, especially if the PDP continues to be riven with internal division. On the other hand, these new parties may further dilute the opposition and allow the PDP to govern largely unchecked, except by its own factions. Even worse, if these parties manage to win only narrow ethnic constituencies, and if the electoral commission does not rigorously apply the multiethnic rules of contest, Nigeria might return to the ruinous ethnic politics of the past.

In addition to loyal multiethnic opposition, democratic development also requires that parties compete within the confines of the law and, more so, that elections stay generally free of rigging or other corrupt practices. The parties of the First and Second Republics, particularly the NPC and NPN, were willing to rig the system with reckless abandon, and they were able to do so primarily because they held unchallenged control over their own states, and thus the electoral systems within their states.

Although the elections of 1999 saw serious violations of the rules, the public and the international observers present were largely willing to accept them in order to get the military out of power. Nonetheless, Obasanjo, a former military ruler, and the PDP received extensive financial support from other retired military officers, including the same individual who annulled the 1993 elections, Ibrahim Babangida. In the 2003 election, the PDP and its tarnished backers showed that it was willing to circumvent the system as it did four years prior. Local election commissions were packed with PDP loyalists, while the national commission, appointed by the president, showed a willingness to alter the process to accommodate PDP interests. Also disturbing was the reliance by a number of governors and other leaders on local ethnic militias to harass and intimidate their competitors.

Ironically, however, because the PDP has such national dominance, the critical event may not have been the elections but the PDP party convention held late in 2002. To the degree that the party's list of candidates were acceptable to its powerful patrimonial leaders this reduced the temptation to rig, except in areas where PDP candidates faced significant competition. Yet the elections were still contentious: the ANPP's nomination of the pro-*shari'a* Buhari and 2003 election victories across northwest and north-central Nigeria promise to aggravate the Muslim-Christian, North-South divide, and in part explains why the Yoruba-dominated AD shifted its support to Obasanjo. If the opposition

parties emerging from the 2003 elections are able to organize a viable coalition to challenge the PDP, they will have an interest in cleaning up the electoral system.

Democratic development also requires further decentralization of power structures in Nigeria. The struggle on the part of the National Assembly and the state governors to wrest power away from the presidency has already begun this process. The administration's efforts to privatize government para-statals will also reduce the power of the presidency over time, since it will no longer control all the productive sectors of the economy. A more decentralized system allows local problems to be solved locally rather than engaging national institutions and the consequent interethnic competition. Decentralization also lowers the stakes for holding national offices, so that they are less likely to be viewed as life-or-death contests. Moving businesses out of government control and into the private sector will also attract individuals interested in making their fortunes from government into the private sector, where market forces will then regulate them.

Decentralization and a viable opposition movement of themselves, however, will not necessarily change the elite, and hence unaccountable, character of Nigerian politics. Civil society groups are the final link in democratic consolidation in Nigeria. These groups are critical players in connecting the Nigerian state to the Nigerian people. They aggregate and articulate the interests of the sector they represent into the policy realm, and they advocate on behalf of their members. If the political parties are to reflect anything more than the elite interests of the big men and their clients, the parties must reach out and build alliances with civil society groups. So far, however, the parties continue to be an elite business, and civil society groups must strike or find other ways to gain more than the cursory attention of party leaders. For opposition parties to become a viable opposition movement capable of checking the power of the PDP, they will have to build alliances with civil society groups in order to mobilize large portions of the population.

Foreign pressure also plays an important role in maintaining the quest for democracy and sustainable development. In recent years, major external forces have been more forthright in supporting civil society and democratization in Nigeria. The United States, Britain, and some member states of the European Union were quite visible in exerting pressure on Babangida to leave and in applying modest sanctions in support of democracy. This has been made possible, in part, by a changing international environment, especially the willingness of the major industrial countries and the international financial institutions to support democracy in the Third World. Nigeria's increasingly weak economy and enormous debt, now estimated at $33 billion, have made it susceptible to this kind of pressure.

Western commitment to development and democracy in Africa is not guaranteed. Much of the initiative for Africa's growth therefore needs to emerge from within. In Nigeria, such initiatives will depend on substantial changes in the way Nigerians do business. It will be necessary to develop a more sophisticated and far less corrupt form of capitalist enterprise and the development of entrepreneurial interests within Nigeria who will see their interests tied to the standard principles of democratic politics and private economic initiative. The middle class is beginning to grow under democratic rule, but it remains small and vulnerable to economic and political instability.

In addition, the project of building a coherent nation-state out of competing nationalities remains largely unfinished and under constant siege by resurgent ethnonationalism and religious fundamentalism. The challenge here is to achieve a proper balance between ethnic-based symbols and institutions and those of a "transethnic" nature. Ironically, because the parties of the Fourth Republic generally do not represent any particular ethnic interest—indeed, they do not represent anyone's interests except those of the leaders and their clients—ethnic associations and militias have risen to articulate ethnic-based grievances. Ethnic consciousness cannot be eliminated from society, but ethnicity should not become the main basis for political competition. If the current ethnic mobilization can be contained within ethnic associations arguing over the agenda of the parties, then it can be managed. If any of the ethnic associations captures one of the political parties or joins with the militias to foment separatism, instability will result.

Nigerian politics has been characterized by turmoil and periodic crises since the British relinquished colonial power in 1960. Over forty years later, the country is still trying to piece together a fragile democracy, and per capita incomes are scarcely higher than they were at independence. Despite a number of positive trends, the nation continues to wrestle with stagnation and decline of major productive sectors, collapsed infrastructure and institutions, heightened sociopolitical tension, an irresponsible elite, and an expanding mass culture of despondency and rage. Only a responsible government combined with sustained civil society action can reverse this decline and restore the nation to what President Obasanjo has called "the path to greatness."

Nigerian Politics in Comparative Perspective

The study of Nigeria has important implications for the study of African politics and, more broadly, of comparative politics. The Nigerian case embodies a number of key themes and issues that can be generalized to increase social science knowledge, and these themes deserve careful consideration. We can learn much about how democratic regimes are established and achieve stability by understanding the pitfalls Nigeria has encountered. By analyzing the historical dynamics of Nigeria's ethnic conflict, for example, we can identify institutional mechanisms that may be effective in reducing ethnic conflict in other states. We can also learn much about how viable and sustainable economies are developed by contrasting their evolution with Nigeria's. Each of these issues offers comparative lessons for the major themes explored in this book: the world of states, governing the economy, the democratic idea, and the politics of collective identities.

A World of States

Nigeria exists in two "worlds" of states: one in the global political economy and the other within Africa. We have addressed at length Nigeria's position in the world. Economically, Nigeria was thrust into the world economy in a position of weakness, first as a British colony and later as an independent nation. Despite its resources and the potential of oil to provide the investment capital needed to build a modern economy, Nigeria has grown weaker. It has lost much of its international clout, and, in place of the respect it once enjoyed in diplomatic circles, it was regularly criticized for persistent human rights abuses throughout the 1990s. The return of democracy in 1999 has restored some of Nigeria's former stature, but its economic vulnerability and persistent corruption keep it a secondary player in the world of states.

This chapter has quoted the statement, "As Nigeria goes, so goes the rest of sub-Saharan Africa." The future of democracy, political stability, and economic renewal in other parts of Africa, and certainly in West Africa, will be greatly influenced, for good or ill, by unfolding events in Nigeria. Beyond the obvious demonstration effect, the economy of the West African subregion can be revitalized by resumed growth of the Nigerian economy. International political, scholarly, and business attention has shifted steadily to the south of the continent, focusing chiefly on South Africa and its stable neighboring states of Botswana and Namibia. That shift portends a greater danger of marginalization, as Africa becomes divided into a zone of growth that attracts investment and a zone of decay.

Governing the Economy

Nigeria provides important insights into the political economy of underdevelopment. At independence in 1960, Nigeria was stronger economically than its Southeast Asian counterparts, Indonesia and Malaysia. Independent Nigeria appeared poised for growth, with a wealth of natural resources, a large population, and the presence of highly entrepreneurial groups in all regions of the country. Today, Nigeria is among the poorest countries in the world in terms of per capita income, while many of its Asian counterparts have joined the ranks of the newly industrializing countries (NICs). One critical lesson Nigeria teaches is that a rich endowment of resources is not enough to ensure economic development. In fact, it may encourage rent-seeking behavior that undermines more productive activities.[34] Sound political development must come first.

Other variables are critically important, notably, political stability from democracy and a capable developmental state. A developmentalist ethic, and an institutional structure to enforce it, can set limits to corrupt behavior and constrain the pursuit of short-term personal gain at the expense of national economic growth. Institutions vital for the pursuit of these objectives include a professional civil service, an independent judiciary, and a free press. Nigeria has had each of these, yet they were gradually undermined and corrupted under military rule. The public "ethic" that has

come to dominate Nigerian political economy has been prebendalism. Where corruption is unchecked, as in Nigeria, the Philippines under Ferdinand Marcos, and Latin American countries such as Mexico and Venezuela, economic development suffers accordingly.

Nigeria also demonstrates that sustainable economic development requires sound economic policy. Without export diversification, commodity-exporting countries are buffeted by the price fluctuations of one or two main products. This situation can be traced back to overreliance on primary commodity export-oriented policies bequeathed by the British colonial regime. Yet other former colonies, such as Malaysia and Indonesia, have managed to diversify their initial export base. Nigeria, by contrast, has substituted one form of commodity dependence for another; and it has allowed its petroleum industry to overwhelm all other sectors of the economy. Nigeria even became a net importer of products (for example, of palm oil and palm nuts) for which it was once a leading world producer. In comparative perspective, we can see that natural resource endowments can be tremendously beneficial. The United States, for example, has parlayed its endowments of agricultural, mineral, and energy resources into one of the world's most diversified modern economies. Meanwhile Japan, which is by comparison poorly endowed with natural resources, has one of the strongest economies in the world, achieved in large part through its unique developmental strategies. Each of these examples illustrates the primacy of sound economic policies implemented through consolidated political systems.

The Democratic Idea

Many African countries have experienced transitions from authoritarian rule.[35] With the end of superpower competition in Africa and the withdrawal of support from the former Soviet Union and the United States for Africa's despots, many African societies experienced a resurgence of popular pressures for greater participation in political life and more open forms of governance. Decades of authoritarian, single-party, and military rule in Africa have left a dismal record: arbitrary imprisonment and silenced political opposition; harassment of civic, professional, and religious institutions; stifled public discourse and free speech; and bankrupted treasuries and mismanaged economies. At the same time, a handful of elites have acquired large fortunes through wanton corruption. The examples, sadly, are plentiful. Consider Nigeria's "missing" $2.3 billion windfall in oil revenues after the Gulf War in 1991 or the fact that former Zairian president Mobutu Sese Seko's personal wealth was estimated to be several billion dollars—perhaps as much as half the external debt of the entire country. Or that Kenya's former president Daniel Arap Moi is considered among the richest men in Africa, a group to which Ibrahim Babangida and the late Sani Abacha of Nigeria have belonged. The devious ways in which these fortunes were acquired and dispensed make it difficult to give concrete figures. They do, however, suggest that the exercise of postcolonial authoritarian rule in Africa has contributed to economic stagnation and decline. The difficulty that such countries as Cameroon, Togo, and Zimbabwe have experienced in moving to democratic systems is a reflection, among other factors, of the ruling elites' unwillingness to cede control of the political instruments that made possible their self-enrichment.

Nigeria exemplifies the harsh reality of authoritarian and unaccountable governance. Corruption, fraud, mismanagement, and the restriction of political liberties were tolerated in the past by populations numbed into complacency by political repression and the daily struggles for economic survival. Nigeria has endured six military regimes, countless attempted coups, and a bloody civil war that claimed over 1 million lives. They have also seen a once-prospering economy reduced to a near shambles. Today, democracy has become a greater imperative because only such a system provides the mechanisms to limit abuses of power and render governments accountable.

Collective Identities

Nigeria presents an important case in which to study the dangers of ethnically based competition in a society with deep cultural divisions. How can multiethnic countries manage their diversity? What institutional mechanisms can be employed to avert tragedies such as the 1967–1970 civil war or the continuing conflicts that have brought great suffering to the former Yugoslavia and Rwanda? This chapter has suggested institutional reforms such as constitutionally encouraged multiethnic political parties, decentralization, and a strengthened federal system that can contribute to reducing tensions and minimizing conflict.

Insights from the Nigerian experience may explain why some federations persist and identify the factors that can undermine them. Nigeria's complex social situation, and its varied attempts to create a nation out of its highly diverse population, enhances our understanding of the politics of cultural pluralism and the difficulty of accommodating sectional interests under conditions of political and economic insecurity. Federal character in Nigeria has been distorted into a form of ethnic and regional favoritism and a tool for dispensing patronage. Yet the country has benefited in some ways from the attention devoted to creating state and local governments and from giving people in different regions a sense of being stakeholders in the entity called "Nigeria."

The challenges that Nigeria faces concern not only its people's frustrated hopes for a better life, stable government, and a democratic political order, but also the potential contributions that this country and its peoples could make to the entire continent and to the world at large. The nation's leaders in partnership with civil society must deliver responsive and prosperous democratic governance before public frustration reaches the point where military entrepreneurs, or ethnic and religious extremists, seize the opportunity to return Nigeria to the cycles of coups, decline, and possibly collapse.

Key Terms

authoritarian
legitimacy
accountability
unfinished state
jihad
acephalous societies
emirs
indirect rule
warrant chiefs
interventionist
clientelism
autocracy
rents
rent-seeking
structural adjustment
  program (SAP)
international financial
  institutions
balance of payments
privatization
self-determination
Economic Community of
  West African States
  (ECOWAS)
para-statals
shari'a
prebendalism
civil society
state corporatism
patrimonialism

Suggested Readings

Aborisade, Oladimeji, and Robert J. Mundt. *Politics in Nigeria,* 2nd Edition. New York: Longman, 2002.

Achike, Okay. *Public Administration: A Nigerian and Comparative Perspective.* London: Longman, 1978.

Adamolekun, L. *Politics and Administration in Nigeria.* London: Hutchinson, 1986.

Agbaje, Adigun. *The Nigerian Press: Hegemony and the Social Construction of Legitimacy, 1960–1983.* Lewiston, N.Y.: Edwin Mellen Press, 1992.

———. "Twilight of Democracy in Nigeria." *Africa Demos* 3, no. 3:5. Atlanta: The Carter Center of Emory University, 1994.

Beckett, Paul A., and Crawford Young, eds. *Dilemmas of Democracy in Nigeria.* Rochester, NY: University of Rochester Press, 1997.

Bienen, Henry. *Political Conflict and Economic Change in Nigeria.* London: Frank Cass, 1988.

Diamond, Larry. *Class, Ethnicity and Democracy in Nigeria: The Failure of the First Republic.* London: Macmillan, 1988.

Diamond, Larry, "Nigeria: The Uncivic Society and the Descent into Praetorianism," in Larry Diamond, J. Linz, and S. M. Lipset, eds. *Politics in Developing Countries: Comparing Experiences With Democracy*, 2nd Edition. Boulder, Colo.: Lynne Rienner Publishers, 1995, 417–491.

Decalo, Samuel. *Coups and Army Rule in Africa,* 2nd edition. New Haven: Yale University Press, 1990.

Dudley, Billy. *An Introduction to Nigerian Government and Politics.* Bloomington: Indiana University Press, 1982.

Ekeh, Peter P., and Eghosa E. Osaghae, eds. *Federal Character and Federalism in Nigeria.* Ibadan: Heinemann, 1989.

Falola, Toyin. *Violence in Nigeria: The Crisis of Religious Politics and Secular Ideologies.* Rochester, NY: University of Rochester Press, 1999.

Forrest, Tom. *Politics and Economic Development in Nigeria.* Boulder, Colo.: Westview Press, 1993.

Horowitz, Donald L. *Ethnic Groups in Conflict.* Berkeley: University of California Press, 1985.

Joseph, Richard A. *Democracy and Prebendal Politics in Nigeria: The Rise and Fall of the Second Republic.* Cambridge: Cambridge University Press, 1987.

Kew, Darren. "Political Islam in Nigeria's Transition Crisis," *Muslim Politics Report* (Council on Foreign Relations: New York), May–June, 1996.

Kirk-Greene, Anthony, and Douglas Rimmer. *Nigeria Since 1970: A Political and Economic Outline.* London: Hodder and Stoughton, 1981.

Lewis, Peter M. "Endgame in Nigeria? The Politics of a Failed Democratic Transition." *African Affairs* 93 (1994): 323–340.

Lewis, Peter M., Barnett R. Rubin, and Pearl T. Robinson. *Stabilizing Nigeria: Pressures, Incentives, and Support for Civil Society.* New York: Century Foundation, for the Council on Foreign Relations, 1998.

Lubeck, Paul. *Islam and Urban Labor in Northern Nigeria.* Cambridge: Cambridge University Press, 1987.

Luckham, Robin. *The Nigerian Military: A Sociological Analysis of Authority and Revolt, 1960–67* Cambridge: Cambridge University Press, 1971.

Melson, Robert, and Howard Wolpe, eds. *Nigeria: Modernization and the Politics of Communalism*, East Lansing: Michigan State University Press, 1971.

Nyang'oro, Julius, and Tim Shaw, eds. *Corporatism in Africa: Comparative Analysis and Practice.* Boulder, Colo.: Westview Press, 1989.

Olukoshi, Adebayo, ed. *The Politics of Structural Adjustment in Nigeria.* London: James Currey Publishers, 1993.

Osaghae, Eghosa. *Crippled Giant: Nigeria Since Independence.* Bloomington: Indiana University Press, 1998.

Oyediran, Oyeleye, ed. *Nigerian Government and Politics Under Military Rule.* London: Macmillan, 1979.

Reno, William. *Warlord Politics and African States.* Boulder, Colo.: Lynne Rienner Publishers, 1998.

Sklar, Richard L. *Nigerian Political Parties: Power in an Emergent African Nation.* New York: NOK Publishers, 1983.

Soyinka, Wole. *Open Sore of a Continent.* Oxford: Oxford University Press, 1996.

Suberu, Rotimi. *Federalism and Ethnic Conflict in Nigeria.* Washington, D.C.: U.S. Institute of Peace, 2001.

Watts, Michael, ed. *State, Oil, and Agriculture in Nigeria.* Berkeley: University of California Press, 1987.

Wunsch, James S., and Dele Olowu, eds. *The Failure of the Centralized State: Institutions and Self-Governance in Africa.* Boulder, Colo.: Westview Press, 1990.

Young, Crawford. *The Rising Tide of Cultural Pluralism: The Nation-State at Bay?* Madison: University of Wisconsin Press, 1993.

Suggested Websites

British Broadcasting Corporation: A 2002 interview with President Obasanjo.
news.bbc.co.uk/2/hi/talking_point/1800826.stm

Gamji: A collection of news stories from Nigerian newspapers, as well as opinion pieces and other news links.
www.gamji.com/

The Guardian, Nigeria's leading daily newspaper
www.ngrguardiannews.com/

Human Rights Watch reports
www.hrw.org/africa/nigeria.php

International Institute for Democracy and Electoral Assistance
www.idea.int/frontpage_nigeria.htm

Stanford University's Center for African Studies
www.stanford.edu/dept/AFR/

Notes

[1]Much of this context is recounted in James S. Coleman, *Nigeria: Background to Nationalism* (Berkeley: University of California Press, 1958).

[2]Obafemi Awolowo, *Path to Nigerian Freedom* (London: Faber and Faber, 1947), 47–48.

[3]Billy Dudley, *An Introduction to Nigerian Government and Politics* (Bloomington: Indiana University Press, 1982), 71.

[4]Robin Luckham, *The Nigerian Military: A Sociological Analysis of Authority and Revolt 1960–67* (Cambridge: Cambridge University Press, 1971).

[5]Peter Ekeh, "Colonialism and the Two Publics in Africa: A Theoretical Statement," *Comparative Studies in Society and History* 17, no. 1 (January 1975).

[6]Richard A. Joseph, *Democracy and Prebendal Politics in Nigeria: The Rise and Fall of the Second Republic* (Cambridge: Cambridge University Press), 55–58.

[7]Gavin Williams and Terisa Turner, "Nigeria," in John Dunn, ed., *West African States: Failure and Promise* (Cambridge: Cambridge University Press,1978), 156–157 .

[8]Michael J. Watts, *State, Oil and Agriculture in Nigeria* (Berkeley: University of California Press, 1987), 71.

[9]Watts, *State Oil and Agriculture in Nigeria,* 67.

[10]See Peter M. Lewis, "From Prebendalism to Predation: The Political Economy of Decline in Nigeria," *Journal of Modern African Studies* 34, no. 1 (1996), 79–103.

[11]Tom Forrest, *Politics and Economic Development in Nigeria,* 2nd Edition (Boulder, Colo.: Westview Press, 1995), 207–212.

[12]Dele Olowu, "Centralization, Self-Governance, and Development in Nigeria," in *The Failure of the Centralized State: Institutions and Self-Governance in Africa,* ed. James S. Wunsch and Dele Olowu (Boulder, Colo.: Westview Press, 1991), 211.

[13]Robert Melson and Howard Wolpe, *Nigeria: Modernization and the Politics of Communalism* (East Lansing: Michigan State University Press, 1971).

[14]Toyin Falola, *Violence in Nigeria: The Crisis of Religious Politics and Secular Ideologies* (Rochester, NY: University of Rochester Press, 1998).

[15]Billy J. Dudley, *Instability and Political Order: Politics and Crisis in Nigeria* (Ibadan: Ibadan University Press, 1973), 35.

[16]Pat A. Williams, "Women and the Dilemma of Politics in Nigeria," in Crawford Young and Paul Beckett, eds., *Dilemmas of Democracy in Nigeria* (Rochester, NY: University of Rochester Press, 1997), 219–241.

[17]Anthony Kirk-Greene and Douglas Rimmer, *Nigeria Since 1970: A Political and Economic Outline* (London: Hodder and Stoughton 1981), 49.

[18]Rotimi Suberu, *Federalism and Ethnic Conflict in Nigeria* (Washington, D.C.: U.S. Institute of Peace, 2001).

[19]Henry Bienen, *Armies and Parties in Africa* (New York: Africana Publishing, 1978), 193–211.

[20]Human Rights Watch, *The Destruction of Odi and Rape in Choba* (New York: Human Rights Watch, December 22, 1999).

[21]Suberu, *Federalism and Ethnic Conflict in Nigeria,* 119–120.

[22]Samuel DeCalo, *Coups and Army Rule in Africa* (New Haven: Yale University Press, 1976), 18.

[23]Larry Diamond, "Nigeria: The Uncivic Society and the Descent into Praetorianism," in Larry Diamond, J. Linz, and S.M. Lipset, eds., *Politics in Developing Countries: Comparing Experiences With Democracy,* 2nd Edition (Boulder, Colo.: Lynne Rienner Publishers, 1995).

[24]Joseph, *Democracy and Prebendal Politics in Nigeria,* 52–53.

[25]Richard Sklar, *Nigerian Political Parties* (Princeton: Princeton University Press, 1963).

[26]Babafemi Badejo, "Party Formation and Party Competitition" in Larry Diamond, Anthony Kirk-Greene, and Oyeleye Oyediran, eds., *Transition Without End: Nigerian Politics and Civil Society Under Babangida* (Boulder, Colo.: Lynne Rienner Publishers, 1997), 179.

[27]Eghosa Osaghae, *Crippled Giant: Nigeria Since Independence* (Bloomington: Indiana University Press 1999), 233–239.

[28]Peter M. Lewis, Barnett Rubin, and Pearl Robinson, *Stabilizing Nigeria: Pressures, Incentives and Support for Civil Society* (New York: Council on Foreign Relations, 1998), 87.

[29]Rotimi Suberu, *Public Policies and National Unity in Nigeria,* Research Report No. 19 (Ibadan: Development Policy Centre, 199), 9–10.

[30]Sayre Schatz, " 'Pirate Capitalism' and the Inert Economy of Nigeria," *Journal of Modern African Studies* 22, no. 1 (March 1984), 45–57.

[31]Adebayo Olukoshi, "Associational Life" in Diamond, Kirk-Greene, and Oyediran, *Transition Without End,* 385–86.

[32]Osaghae, *Crippled Giant,* 301.

[33]Peter Lewis, Etannibi Alemika, and Michael Bratton, *Down to Earth: Changes in Attitudes to Democracy and Markets in Nigeria,* Afrobarometer Working Paper No. 20, Michigan State University, August 2002.

[34]See Terry Lynn Karl, *The Paradox of Plenty* (Berkeley: University of California Press, 1997). And Michael Ross, "The Political Economy of the Resource Curse," *World Politics* 51 (January 1999), 297–322.

[35]Michael Bratton and Nicolas van de Walle, *Democratic Experiments in Africa* (Cambridge: Cambridge University Press, 1997).

CHAPTER 7

Iran

Ervand Abrahamian

Islamic Republic of Iran

Land and People

Capital	Tehran
Total area (square miles)	634,562 (slightly larger than Alaska)
Population	64.6 million

Annual population growth rate (%)		
	1975–2000	3.0
	2000–2015 (projected)	1.2

Urban population (%)	64.0

Ethnic composition (% of total population)		
	Persian	51
	Azeri	24
	Gilaki and Mazandarani	8
	Kurd	7
	Arab	3
	Other	7

Major language(s) (%)		
	Persian (Farsi)	58
	Turkic	26
	Kurdish	9
	Other	7

Religious affiliation (%)		
	Shi'a Muslim	89
	Sunni Muslim	10
	Zoroastrian, Jewish, Christian, and Baha'i	1

Economy

Domestic currency	Rial (IRR) US$1: 1743.9 IRR (2002 av.)
Total GDP (US$)	104.9 billion
GDP per capita (US$)	4690
Total GDP at purchasing power parity (US$)	374.6 billion
GDP per capita at purchasing power parity (US$)	5,884

GDP annual growth rate (%)		
	1997	3.4
	2000	5.9
	2001	4.6

GDP per capita average annual growth rate (%)		
	1975–2000	–0.7
	1990–2000	1.9

Inequality in income or consumption (1996–1997) (%)	Data Not Available for Iran

Structure of production (% of GDP)		
	Agriculture	18.9
	Industry	22.3
	Services	58.8

Labor force distribution (% of total)		
	Agriculture	30
	Industry	25
	Services	45

Exports as % of GDP	35
Imports as % of GDP	21

Society

Life expectancy at birth	69
Infant mortality per 1,000 live births	41

Adult literacy (%)		
	Male	83.2
	Female	69.3

Access to information and communications (per 1,000 population)		
	Telephone lines	149
	Mobile phones	15
	Radios	281
	Televisions	163
	Personal computers	62.8

Women in Government and the Economy

Women in the national legislature

Lower house or single house (%)	4.1
Women at ministerial level (%)	9.4

Female economic activity rate (age 15 and above) (%)	29
Female labor force (% of total)	27

Estimated earned income (PPP US$)		
	Female	2,524
	Male	9,088

2002 Human Development Index Ranking (out of 173 countries)	98

Political Organization

Political System   Theocracy (rule of the clergy) headed by a cleric with the title of Supreme Leader. The clergy rule by divine right.

Regime History   Islamic Republic since the 1979 Islamic Revolution.

Administrative Structure   Centralized administration with 28 provinces. The Interior Minister appoints the provincial governor-generals.

Executive   President and his cabinet. The president is elected by the general electorate every four years. The president chooses his cabinet ministers, but they need to obtain the approval of the *Majles* (parliament).

Legislature   Unicameral. The *Majles*, formed of 270 seats, is elected every four years. It has multiple member districts with the top runners in the elections taking the seats. Bills passed by the *Majles* do not become law unless they have the approval of the clerically dominated Council of Guardians.

Judiciary   A Chief Judge and a Supreme Court independent of the exective and legislature but appointed by the Supreme Leader.

Party System   The ruling clergy restrict all party and organizational activities.

Section ① The Making of the Modern Iranian State

Politics in Action

Iran shook the world, not to mention its own establishment, first in 1997 by electing Muhammad Khatami, a relatively unknown liberal cleric, as president of the Islamic Republic in a landslide victory, and then again in 2001 by reelecting him with even a larger majority. Khatami, a former director of the National Library, was a mild-mannered middle-ranking cleric, a hojjat al-Islam ("Proof of Islam"), not a high-ranking **ayatollah** or grand ayatollah ("Sign of God"). In the elections, he vigorously campaigned on the theme of creating "civil society" and improving the "sick economy." He stressed the importance of an open society that would protect individual liberties, freedom of expression, women's rights, political pluralism, and, most essential, the rule of law. He even authored books applauding Western thinkers such as Locke, Voltaire, and Rousseau. It was as if he were transferring principles found in political science textbooks into practical politics. His electoral campaigns also stressed the need for a "dialogue between civilizations." This was a far cry from the early days of the 1979 Iranian Revolution, when its leader, Grand Ayatollah Ruhollah Khomeini, had denounced the United States as the "Great Satan" and incited students to seize the U.S. embassy. This takeover and "hostage crisis" lasted 444 days and prompted a break in U.S.-Iranian diplomatic relations that lasts to this day.

Khatami's initial electoral success was especially surprising since much of the religious establishment had openly endorsed his conservative rival. Most commentators, both inside and outside the country, had considered the election a shoo-in for the conservative candidate. After all, he had been endorsed by an impressive array of establishment newspapers, radio stations, television programs, state institutions, quasi-state foundations, clerical organizations, and local mosques (Muslim houses of worship). They had warned that any opening up of the system could endanger the whole regime and that Khatami could become another Mikhail Gorbachev, the reformist leader who had inadvertently presided over the demise of the Soviet Union. Even the Supreme Leader of the Islamic Republic, Ayatollah Ali Khamenei, had implicitly endorsed the conservative

candidate. In the upset election, Khatami took 70 percent of the vote in a campaign that attracted 80 percent of the electorate. Much of Khatami's vote came from women, university students, and young adults throughout the country—even from those serving in the armed forces. He followed up his victory by trying to liberalize the press, establishing political parties, and initiating a "dialogue" with the United States. He even bolstered the case for liberalization by citing *Democracy in America,* the famous book by nineteenth-century French writer Alexis de Tocqueville. Khatami also assured the West that Iran had no intention of implementing the *fatwa* (religious decree) that Ayatollah Khomeini had placed on Salman Rushdie, the Muslim-born British writer. Khomeini had condemned Rushdie to death on the grounds that his book, *Satanic Verses,* blasphemed Islam and thus proved that its author was an apostate from Islam, which is a capital offense according to a narrow interpretation of Islamic law. The 2001 presidential elections further strengthened Khatami's mandate: he took 77 percent of the vote and increased his overall support by over 1 million.

These two presidential elections vividly illustrated the main dilemmas confronting the Islamic Republic that had been established by Ayatollah Khomeini in the aftermath of the 1979 revolution. The Islamic Republic of Iran today is a mixture of **theocracy** and democracy: it is a political system based on clerical authority as well as popular sovereignty, on the divine right of the clergy as well as the rights of the people, on concepts derived from early Islam as well as from modern democratic principles such as the separation of powers. The country has regular elections for the presidency and the *Majles* (Parliament), but a clerically dominated **Guardian Council** determines who can and cannot run in these elections. The president is the formal head of the executive branch of government, but he can be overruled, even dismissed, by the chief cleric known as the **Supreme Leader.** The president appoints the minister of justice, but the whole judiciary is under the supervision of the chief judge, who is appointed directly by the Supreme Leader. The *Majles* is the legislative branch of government, but its bills do not become law unless the Guardian Council deems them compatible with Islam and the Islamic constitution. In short, contemporary Iranian politics resonates with both *vox dei* (the voice of God) and *vox populi* (the voice of the people).

Geographic Setting

Iran—three times the size of France, slightly larger than Alaska, and much larger than its immediate neighbors—is notable for two geographic features. The first is that much of its territory is inhospitable to agriculture. A vast arid zone known as the Great Salt Desert covers much of the central plateau from the capital city, Tehran, to the borders with Afghanistan and Pakistan. A mountain range known as the Zagros takes up the western third of the country. Another range, the Elborz, stretches across the north. Rain-fed agriculture is confined mostly to the northwest and the provinces along the Caspian Sea. In the rest of the country, population settlements are located mostly on oases, on the few rare rivers, and on constructed irrigation networks. Only pastoral nomads can survive in the semiarid zones and in the high mountain valleys. Thus, 67 percent of the total population of 65 million is concentrated on 27 percent of the land—mostly in the Caspian provinces, in the northwest, and in the cities of Tehran, Qom, Isfahan, Shiraz, and Ahwaz. In the past, the inhospitable environment was a major obstacle to economic development. In recent decades, this obstacle has been partly alleviated by oil revenues. Iran is the second largest oil

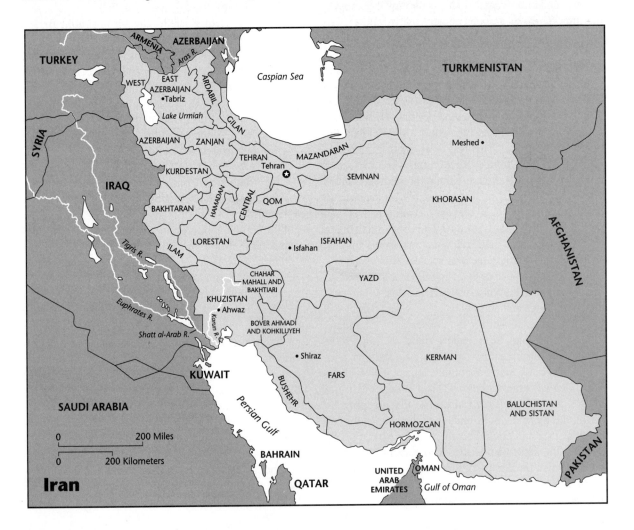

producer in the Middle East and the fourth largest in the world. Its oil wells help fuel many industrial economies. These oil revenues account for the fact that Iran is now urbanized and partly industrialized and can be described as a developing rather than a stagnant society. Nearly 63 percent of the population lives in urban centers; 68 percent of the labor force is employed in industry and services; 67 percent of adults are literate; life expectancy has reached sixty-nine years; and the majority of Iranians enjoy a standard of living well above that found in most of Asia and Africa.

Iran's second notable geographic feature is that it lies on the crossroads between Central Asia and Asia Minor, between the Indian subcontinent and the Middle East, between the Arabian Peninsula and the Caucasus Mountains. This has made the region vulnerable to invaders: Indo-Europeans in the distant past (they gave the country the name of Iran, Land of the Aryans), Islamic Arab tribes in the seventh century, and a series of Turkic incursions in the Middle Ages. The population today reflects these historic invasions. Some 51 percent of the country speaks Persian (**Farsi**), an Indo-European language, as their first language; 26 percent speak various dialects of Turkic, mainly Azeri and Turkmen; 8 percent speak Gilaki or Mazandarani, distant Persian dialects; 7 percent speak Kurdish, another Indo-European language; and 3 percent speak Arabic. Although since the Middle Ages, Europeans have referred to the country as Persia, Iranians have traditionally called their country Iran and their main language Farsi, after the central province (Fars) where the language originated. In 1935, Iran formally asked the international community to cease calling the country Persia.

Critical Junctures

Although modern Iran traces its roots to the ancient Iranian empire of sixth century B.C. and its Islamic religion to the Arab invasions of the seventh century, its current national identity, geographic boundaries, particular interpretation of Islam—**Shi'ism**—and political system were formed by four more recent critical junctures: the Safavid (1501–1722), Qajar (1794–1925), and Pahlavi (1925–1979) dynasties and the Islamic Revolution of 1979, which led to establishment of the current Islamic Republic.

Critical Junctions in Modern Iran's Political Development

1921	Colonel Reza Khan's military coup
1925	Establishment of the Pahlavi dynasty
1941–1945	Allied occupation of Iran
1951	Nationalization of the oil industry
1953	Coup against Mosaddeq
1963	White Revolution
1975	Establishment of the Resurgence Party
1979	Islamic Revolution
1979–1981	U.S. hostage crisis
December 1979	Referendum on the constitution
January 1980	Bani-Sadr elected president
March 1980	Elections for the First Islamic *Majles*
1980–1988	War with Iraq
June 1981	President Bani-Sadr ousted
October 1981	Khamenei elected president
1984	Elections for the Second Islamic *Majles*
1988	Elections for the Third Islamic *Majles*
1989	Khomeini dies; Khamenei appointed Supreme Leader; Rafsanjani elected president
1992	Elections for the Fourth Islamic *Majles*
1996	Elections for the Fifth Islamic *Majles*
1997	Khatami elected president on reform platform
2000	Reformers win elections for the Sixth Islamic *Majles*
2000	Khatami reelected president with a huge majority

The Safavids (1501–1722)

Modern Iran, with its Shi'i Islamic identity and its present-day boundaries, can be traced to the sixteenth century, when the Safavid family conquered the territory with the help of fellow Turkic-speaking tribes and established their dynasty. They revived the ancient Iranian titles of shah-in-shah (King of Kings) and Shadow of God on Earth, and proceeded to convert their subjects to Shi'ism forcibly. Although small Shi'i communities had existed in this area since the beginning of Islam, the vast majority had adhered to the majority Sunni branch (see "Background: Islam and Shi'ism"). The Safavid motivation for this drastic conversion was to give their state and population a distinct identity separate from the surrounding Sunni powers: the Ottomans in the west, the Uzbeks in the north, and the Afghans in the east.

By the mid-seventeenth century, the Safavids had succeeded in converting nearly 90 percent of their subjects to Shi'ism. Sunnism survived among the peripheral tribal groups: Kurds in the northwest, Turkmens in the northeast, Baluchis in the southeast, and Arabs in the southwest. It should be noted that the Safavids, despite their conquests, failed to capture from the Ottomans the two most holy Shi'i places located in modern Iraq: Karbala, the site of the martyrdom in 680 B.C.

of Imam Husayn, one of the most important figures in the history of Shi'ism, and Najaf, the main theological center.

In addition to the Sunni minority, Safavid Iran contained small communities of Jews, Zoroastrians, and Christians (Armenians and Assyrians). These small minorities lived mostly in Isfahan, Shiraz, Kerman, Yazd, and Azerbaijan. Jews had lived in Iran since ancient times, predating the great diaspora prompted by the Roman destruction of Jerusalem. Zoroastrians were descendants of those who retained their old religion after the Arab invasions. The Christians had lived in the northwest long before the advent of Islam. To strengthen their foothold in central Iran, the Safavids transported there some 100,000 Armenians, encouraging them to

Background: Islam and Shi'ism

Islam, with some 1 billion adherents, is the second largest religion in the world. Islam means literally "submission to God," and a Muslim is someone who has submitted to God—the same God that Jews and Christians worship. Islam has one central tenet: "There is only one God, and Muhammad is His Prophet." Muslims, in order to consider themselves faithful, need to perform the following four duties to the best of their ability: give to charity; pray every day facing Mecca, where Abraham is believed to have built the first place of worship; make a pilgrimage at least once in a lifetime to Mecca, which is located in modern Saudi Arabia; and fast during the daytime hours in the month of Ramadan to commemorate God's revelation of the Qur'an (Koran, or Holy Book) to the Prophet Muhammad. These four, together with the central tenet, are known in the West as the Five Pillars of Islam.

From its earliest days, Islam has been divided into two major branches: the Sunnis and the Shi'is. The Sunnis, meaning literally "followers of tradition," are by far in the majority worldwide. The Shi'is, literally "partisans of Ali," constitute less than 10 percent of Muslims worldwide and are concentrated in Iran, southern Iraq, Azerbaijan, and southern Lebanon. Although both

branches accept the Five Pillars, they differ mostly over who should have succeeded the Prophet Muhammad (d. 632). The Sunnis recognized the early dynasties that ruled the Islamic empire with the exalted title of caliph ("Prophet's Deputy"). The Shi'is, however, argued that as soon as the Prophet died, his authority should have been passed on to Imam Ali, the Prophet's close companion, disciple, and son-in-law. They further argue that Imam Ali passed his authority to his direct male heirs, the third of whom, Imam Husayn, had been martyred fighting the Sunnis in 680, and the twelfth of whom had supposedly gone into hiding in 941. The Shi'is are also know as Twelvers since they follow the Twelve Imams. They refer to the Twelfth Imam as the *Mahdi*, the Hidden Imam, and believe him to be the Messiah who will herald the end of the world. Furthermore, they argue that in his absence, the authority to interpret the *shari'a* (religious law) should be in the hands of the senior clerical scholars—the ayatollahs. Thus, from the beginning, the Shi'is harbored ambivalent attitudes toward the state, especially if the rulers were Sunnis or lacked genealogical links to the Twelve Imams. For Sunnis, the *shari'a* is based mostly on the Qur'an and the teachings of the Prophet. For Shi'is, it is also based on the teachings of the Twelve Imams.

become craftsmen and merchants, especially in the lucrative silk trade. The Safavids, like most other Muslim rulers but unlike medieval Christian kings, tolerated religious minorities as long as they paid special taxes and accepted royal authority. According to Islam, Christians, Jews, and Zoroastrians were to be tolerated as legitimate **People of the Book.** They were respected both because they were mentioned in the Holy **Qur'an** and because they had their own sacred texts: the Bible, the Torah, and the Avesta.

The Safavids established their capital in Isfahan, a Persian-speaking city, and recruited Persian scribes into their court administration. Such families had helped administer the ancient Iranian empires. They proceeded to govern not only through these Persian scribes and Shi'i clerics but also through local magnates: tribal chiefs, large landowners, religious notables, city merchants, guild elders, and urban ward leaders.

The Safavid army was formed mostly of tribal cavalry led by local chieftains. Financial constraints prevented the Safavids from creating a large bureaucracy or an extended standing army. Their revenues came mostly from land taxes levied on the peasantry. In theory, the Safavids claimed absolute power; Europeans labeled them Oriental despots. In reality, their power was limited, since they lacked a central state and had no choice but to seek the cooperation of many semi-independent local leaders. The central government was linked to the general population not so much through coercive institutions as through provincial and hereditary notables. It survived for the most part because the society below was sharply fragmented by geographic barriers (especially mountains) and by regional, tribal, communal, and ethnic differences. Moreover, some of the senior clerics resided in Najaf, safely out of royal reach. The monarch did not control society. Rather, he hovered over it, systematically orchestrating its many existing rivalries.

The Qajars (1794–1925)

The Safavid dynasty collapsed in 1722 when Afghan tribesmen invaded the capital. The invasion was followed by a half-century of civil war until the Qajars, another Turkic tribe, reconquered much of Iran. The Qajars moved the capital to Tehran and recreated the Safavid system of central manipulation and court administration, including the Persian scribes. They also declared Shi'ism to be the state religion even though they, unlike the Safavids, did not boast of genealogical links to the Twelve Imams. This was to have far-reaching repercussions. Since these new shahs did not pretend to wear the imam's mantle, the Shi'i clerical leaders could claim to be the main interpreters of Islam. In addition, many of them safeguarded their independence from the state by continuing to reside in Iraq and collecting religious contributions directly from the faithful in Iran. These contributions came mainly from wealthy merchants.

Qajar rule coincided with the peak of European imperialism. The Russians seized parts of Central Asia and the Caucasus from Iran and extracted a series of major economic concessions, including a monopoly to fish for sturgeon in the Caspian Sea and exemption from import duties, internal tariffs, and the jurisdiction of local courts. The British Imperial Bank won the monopoly to issue paper money. The Indo-European Telegraph Company got a contract to extend communication lines through the country. Exclusive rights to drill for oil in the southwest were sold to a British citizen. The later Qajars also borrowed heavily from European banks to meet lavish court expenses. By the end of the century, these loans had become so heavy that the Qajars were obliged to guarantee repayments by placing the country's entire customs service under European supervision. Iranians felt that their whole country had been auctioned off and that the shah had given away far too many concessions, or capitulations, as they called them.

These resentments culminated in the constitutional revolution of 1905–1909. The revolution began with shopkeepers and moneylenders demonstrating against the handing over of customs collections to Europeans. They suspected that the shah would renege on local debts in favor of repaying his foreign loans. They also protested that the government was not doing enough to protect native merchants and local industries. The protests intensified when the government, faced with soaring sugar prices due to political turmoil in Russia, publicly whipped two major sugar merchants.

The revolutionary movement peaked in 1906, when some 14,000 protesters took sanctuary inside the gardens of the British legation in Tehran and demanded a written constitution. After weeks of haggling, the shah conceded because the British diplomats advised compromise and because the unpaid Cossack Brigade, the regime's sole standing army, threatened to join the protesters. Led by Russians and named after the tsar's praetorian guards, the Cossack Brigade was the only force in Iran resembling a disciplined army. A British diplomat commented, "The shah with his unarmed, unpaid, ragged, starving soldiers, what can he do in face of the menace of a general strike and riots?"[1]

The 1906 constitution, modeled after the Belgian one, introduced essential features of modern government into Iran: elections, separation of powers, laws made by a legislative assembly, and the concepts of popular sovereignty and the nation (*mellat*). It also generated a heated debate, with some arguing that democracy was inherently incompatible with Islam and others countering that true Islam could not be practiced unless the government was based on popular support. Some even argued in favor of secularism—complete separation of religion from politics, church from state, clergy from government authority, the affairs of the next world from those of this world.

While retaining the monarchy, the new constitution centered political power in a national assembly called the *Majles*. It hailed this assembly as "the representative of the whole people" and guaranteed seats to the recognized religious minorities: Jews, Zoroastrians, and Christians. Significantly, no seats were given to the Baha'is, a nineteenth-century offshoot of Shi'ism. The clerical leaders deemed the Baha'is to be apostates from Islam and Baha'i to be a "sinister heresy linked to the imperial powers."

The constitution endowed the *Majles* with extensive authority over all laws, budgets, treaties, loans, concessions, and the composition of the cabinet. The ministers were accountable to the *Majles,* not to the shah. "Sovereignty," declared the constitution, "is a trust confided (as a divine gift) by the people to the person of the shah." The constitution also included a bill of rights guaranteeing citizens equality before the law, protection of life and property, safeguards from arbitrary arrest, and freedom of expression and association.

Although the constitution was modeled on the European liberal secular system of government, it made some concessions to Shi'ism. Shi'ism was declared Iran's official religion. Only Shi'is could hold cabinet posts. Clerical courts retained the right to implement the *shari'a* (religious law), especially in family matters. A Guardian Council formed of senior clerics elected by the *Majles* was given veto power over parliamentary bills deemed not to be Islamic. In short, popular sovereignty was to be restricted by a clerical veto power. In actual fact, this Guardian Council was not convened until the 1979 Islamic Revolution. Divisions within the clerical establishment as well as opposition from parliament forestalled implementation of the Guardian Council.

The initial euphoria that greeted the constitutional revolution gave way to deep disillusionment in the subsequent decade. Pressures from the European powers continued, and a devastating famine after World War I took some 1 million lives, almost 10 percent of the total population. Internal conflicts polarized the *Majles* into warring liberal and conservative factions. The former, mostly members of the intelligentsia, championed social reforms, especially the replacement of the *shari'a* with a modern law code. The latter, led by landlords, tribal chiefs, and senior clerics, vehemently opposed such reforms, particularly land reform, women's rights, and the granting of full equality to religious minorities.

Meanwhile, the central government, lacking any real army, bureaucracy, or tax-collecting machinery, was unable to administer the provinces, especially the regions inhabited by the Kurds, Turkmens, and Baluchis. Some tribes, equipped with modern breech-loading European rifles, had more firepower than the central government. Moreover, during World War I, Russia and Britain formally carved up Iran into three zones. Russia occupied the north and Britain the south. Iran was left with a small "neutral zone" in the middle.

By 1921, Iran was in complete disarray. The shah was gathering his crown jewels to flee south. The British, in their own words, were hoping to "salvage" some "healthy limbs" in their southern zone. Left-wing rebels, helped by the new communist regime in Russia, had taken over Gilan province and were threatening nearby Azerbaijan, Mazandaran, and Khorasan. According to a British diplomat, the propertied classes, fearful of communism, were anxiously seeking "a savior on horseback."[2]

The Pahlavis (1925–1979)

That savior appeared in February 1921 in the person of Colonel Reza Khan, the recently appointed commander of the 3,000-man Cossack Brigade. Carrying out a typical military coup d'état, he replaced the cabinet and, while paying lip service to the monarch, consolidated power in his own hands, especially the post of commander in chief of the armed forces. Four years later, he emerged from behind the throne, deposed the Qajars, crowned himself shah-in-shah in the style of his hero, the French emperor Napoleon, and established his own Pahlavi dynasty, adopting a name associated with the glories of ancient Iran. This was the first nontribal dynasty to rule the whole of Iran. To forestall opposition from Britain and the Soviet Union, he assured both countries that Iran would remain strictly nonaligned. A compliant *Majles* endorsed this transfer of power from the Qajars to the Pahlavis.

Reza Shah ruled with an iron fist until 1941, when the British and the Soviets invaded Iran to forestall Nazi Germany from establishing a foothold there. Reza Shah promptly abdicated in favor of his son, Muhammad Reza Shah, and went into exile, where he soon died. In the first twelve years of his reign, the young shah retained control over the armed forces but had to live with a free press, an independent judiciary, competitive elections, assertive cabinet ministers, and boisterous parliaments. He also had to confront two vigorous political movements: the communist Tudeh (Masses) Party and the National Front, led by the charismatic Dr. Muhammad Mosaddeq (1882–1967).

The Tudeh drew its support mostly from working-class trade unions. The National Front drew its support mainly from the salaried middle classes and campaigned to nationalize the British-owned company that had a monopoly over the drilling, refining, and sale of all petroleum in Iran. Mosaddeq also wanted to sever the shah's links with the armed forces. He argued that according to the constitution, the monarch should reign, not rule, and that the armed forces should be supervised by cabinet ministers responsible to parliament. In 1951, Mosaddeq was elected prime minister and promptly nationalized the oil industry. The period of relative freedom, however, ended abruptly in 1953, when royalist officers overthrew Mosaddeq and in-

stalled the shah with absolute power. Since this 1953 coup was financed by the U.S. Central Intelligence Agency (CIA) and the British, it intensified anti-British sentiment and created a deep distrust of the United States. It also made the shah appear to be a puppet of the foreign powers. Muhammad Reza Shah ruled much in the style of his autocratic father until he was overthrown by the 1979 Islamic Revolution.

During their fifty-four-year rule, the Pahlavis built a highly centralized state, the first in Iran's history. This state rested on three pillars: the armed forces, the bureaucracy, and the royal patronage system. The armed forces grew from fewer than 40,000 men in 1925 to 124,000 in 1941 and to over 410,000 in 1979. In 1925, the armed forces had been formed of a motley crew of cossacks, city policeman, and gendarmes (rural policemen). By the mid-1930s, they had the power to disarm the tribes and impose the will of the state on the provinces. By 1979, they constituted the fifth largest army in the world, the largest navy in the Persian Gulf, the largest air force in western Asia, and one of the best-equipped tank brigades in the Third World. They were supplemented with a pervasive secret police known as SAVAK—the Persian acronym for the Organization to Protect and Gather Information for the State.

The bureaucracy expanded from a haphazard collection of hereditary scribes, some without fixed offices, to twenty-one ministries employing over 300,000 civil servants in 1979. The powerful Interior Ministry appointed the provincial governors, town mayors, district superintendents, and village headmen. Since it also appointed electoral supervisors, it could rig *Majles* elections and provide the shah with rubber-stamp parliaments. Thus, the 1905–1909 constitutional laws survived only on paper. The Education Ministry grew twentyfold, administering 26,000 primary schools with some 4 million children and 1,850 secondary schools with 740,000 pupils. Meanwhile, the Ministry of Higher Education supervised 750 vocational schools with 227,000 students and thirteen universities with 154,000 students.

The Justice Ministry supplanted the *shari'a* with a European-style civil code and the clerical courts with a modern judicial system. This included district courts, provincial courts, and a Supreme Court. To practice in these courts, lawyers and judges had to pass government-administered exams based on European jurisprudence. The system was further secularized in the 1960s, when the shah decreed a controversial Family Protection Law. This contradicted the traditional interpretation of the *shar'ia* on a number of points. It raised the marriage age to twenty for men and eighteen for women. It allowed women to override spousal objections and work outside the home if they got court permission. It restricted polygamy by stipulating that husbands could marry more than one wife only if they first obtained permission from previous wives and the courts. For some, the state had extended its arm to reach into the most intimate area of existence: family life.

Other ministries experienced similar expansion. For example, the Transport Ministry built an impressive array of bridges, ports, highways, and railroads known as the Trans-Iranian Railway. The Ministry of Industries financed the construction of numerous factories specializing in consumer goods. The Agricultural Ministry attained prominence in 1962 when the shah made land reform the centerpiece of his much-heralded "White Revolution," which was designed partly to forestall the possibility of a communist-led "red revolution." The government bought land from large absentee owners and sold it to small farmers through low-interest, long-term mortgages. It also undertook the task of transforming small farmers into modern commercial entrepreneurs by providing them with fertilizers, cooperatives, distribution centers, irrigation canals, dams, and tractor repair shops. The White Revolution included the extension of the vote to women, the Family Protection Law, and a Literacy Corps to eradicate illiteracy in the countryside. Thus, by 1979, the state had set up a modern system of communications, initiated a minor industrial revolution, and extended its reach into even the most outlying villages.

The state also controlled a number of major institutions: the National and the Central Banks; the Industrial and Mining Development Bank, which channeled money to private entrepreneurs; the Plan Organization in charge of economic policy; the national radio-television network, which monopolized the airwaves (by the 1960s, most villages had access to transistor radios); and most important, the National Iranian Oil Company, which grew from a leasing firm in the 1950s to become a large exploring, drilling, refining, and exporting corporation.

The Pahlavi state was further bolstered by court patronage. Reza Shah, the son of a small landowner, used coercion, confiscations, and diversion of irrigation water to make himself one of the largest landowners in the Middle East. In the words of a British diplomat, Reza Shah had an "unholy interest in property," especially other people's property.[3] This wealth transformed the shah's court into a large military-landed complex, providing work for thousands employed in its numerous palaces, hotels, casinos, charities, companies, and beach resorts. This patronage system grew under Muhammad Reza Shah, particularly after he established his tax-exempt Pahlavi Foundation. By the 1970s, the Pahlavi Foundation controlled 207 large companies active in tourism, insurance, banking, agribusiness, mining, construction, and manufacturing.

Although the Pahlavi state looked impressive, it lacked solid foundations. The drive for secularization, centralization, industrialization, and social development won some favor from the urban propertied classes. But arbitrary rule, the 1953 coup, the disregard for constitutional liberties, and the stifling of independent newspapers, political parties, and professional associations produced widespread resentment, particularly among the clergy, the intelligentsia, and the urban masses. In short, this state was strong in the sense that it controlled the modern instruments of coercion and administration. But its roots were very shallow because of its failure to link the new state institutions to the country's social structure. The Pahlavi state, like the Safavids and the Qajars, hovered over, rather than embedded itself into, the society. Furthermore, much of the civil society that had existed in traditional Iran had now been suffocated by the modern state.

As if the Pahlavi state did not have enough social control, the shah in 1975 announced the formation of the Resurgence Party. He declared Iran to be a one-party state and threatened imprisonment and exile to those refusing to join the party. In heralding the new order, the shah replaced the traditional Islamic calendar with a new royalist one, jumping from the Muslim year 1355 to the royalist year 2535; 2,500 years were allocated to the monarchy in general and 35 years for the shah's own reign. The King of Kings and the Shadow of God also accrued two new titles: Guide to the New Great Civilization and Light of the Aryans (Aryamehr).

The Resurgence Party was designed to create yet another organizational link with the population, especially with the **bazaars** (traditional marketplaces), which, unlike the rest of society, had managed to retain their guilds and thus escape direct government control. The Resurgence Party promptly established bazaar guilds as well as newspapers, women's organizations, professional associations, and labor unions. It also prepared to create a Religious Corps, modeled on the Literacy Corps, to go into the countryside to teach the peasants "true Islam." The state was venturing into areas where previous rulers had feared to tread.

The Resurgence Party promised to establish an "organic relationship between rulers and ruled," "synthesize the best of capitalism and socialism," and chart the way toward the New Great Civilization. It also praised the shah for curbing the "medieval clergy," eradicating "class warfare," and becoming a "spiritual guide" as well as a world-renowned statesman. For his part, the shah told an English-language newspaper that the party's philosophy was "based on the dialectical principles of the White Revolution" and that nowhere else in the world was there such a close relationship between a ruler and his people. "No other nation has given its commander such a carte-blanche [blank check]."[4] The terminology, as well as the boast, revealed much about the shah at the height of his power—or, as some suspected, his megalomania.

The Islamic Revolution (1979)

On the eve of the 1979 Islamic Revolution that overthrew the shah, an exiled Iranian newspaper denounced the Pahlavis in an issue entitled "Fifty Indictments of Treason During Fifty Years of Treason."[5] It charged the shah and his family with establishing a military dictatorship; collaborating with the CIA; trampling on the constitution; creating SAVAK; rigging parliamentary elections; organizing a fascistic one-party state; taking over the religious establishment; and undermining national identity by disseminating Western culture. It also accused the regime of inducing millions of landless peasants to migrate into urban shantytowns; widening the gap between rich and poor; funneling money away from the small bourgeoisie into the pockets

of the wealthy comprador bourgeoisie (the entrepreneurs linked to foreign companies and multinational corporations); wasting resources on bloated military budgets; and granting new capitulations to the West—the most controversial being the extension of diplomatic immunity to U.S. military advisers in Iran.

These grievances were given greater articulation when a leading anti-shah cleric, Ayatollah Ruhollah Khomeini—from his exile in Iraq—began to formulate a new version of Shi'ism (see "Leaders: Ayatollah Ruhollah Khomeini"). His version has often been labeled Islamic **fundamentalism;** it would better be described as Shi'i populism or political Islam. The term *fundamentalism,* derived from American Protestantism, implies religious dogmatism, intellectual inflexibility and purity, political traditionalism, social conservatism, rejection of the modern world, and the literal interpretation of scriptural texts. Khomeini, however, was less concerned about literal interpretations of the Qur'an than about articulating resentments against the elite and the United States. He was more of a political revolutionary than a social conservative.

Khomeini denounced monarchies in general and the Pahlavis in particular as part and parcel of the corrupt elite exploiting the oppressed masses. For him, the oppressors consisted of courtiers, large landowners, high-ranking military officers, wealthy foreign-connected capitalists, and millionaire palace dwellers. The oppressed consisted of the masses, especially landless peasants, wage earners, bazaar shopkeepers, and shantytown dwellers. His proclamations often cited the Qur'anic term *mostazafin* (dispossessed) and the biblical promise that "the poor (meek) shall inherit the earth."

In calling for the overthrow of the Pahlavi monarchy, Khomeini injected a radically new meaning into the old Shi'i term *velayat-e faqih* (**jurist's guardianship**). He argued that jurist's guardianship gave the senior clergy—namely, the grand ayatollahs such as himself—all-encompassing authority over the whole community, not just over widows, minors, and the mentally disabled, as had been the interpretation previously. He insisted that only the senior clerics had the sole competence to understand the *shari'a;* that the divine authority given to the Prophet and the imams had been passed on to their spiritual heirs, the clergy; and that throughout history, the clergy had championed the rights of the people against bad government and

Leaders: *Ayatollah Ruhollah Khomeini*

Ruhollah Khomeini was born in 1902 into a landed clerical family well known in central Iran. During the 1920s, he studied in the famous Fayzieh Seminary in Qom with the leading theologians of the day, most of whom were scrupulously apolitical. He taught at the seminary from the 1930s through the 1950s, avoiding politics even during the mass campaign to nationalize the British-owned oil company. His entry into politics did not come until 1962, when he, along with most other clerical leaders, denounced Muhammad Reza Shah's White Revolution. Forced into exile, Khomeini taught at the Shi'i center of Najaf in Iraq from 1964 until 1978. During these years, he developed his own version of Shi'i populism by incorporating socioeconomic grievances into his sermons and denouncing not just the shah but the whole ruling class. Returning home triumphant in the midst of the Iranian Revolution, he was declared the Supreme Leader, the Founder of the Islamic Republic, the Guide for the Oppressed Masses, and imam of the Muslim community. In the past, Iranian Shi'is, unlike the Arab Sunnis, had reserved the special term *imam* only for Imam Ali and his twelve direct heirs, whom they deemed to be semidivine and thereby infallible. For many Iranians in 1979, Khomeini was charismatic in the true sense of the word: a man with a special gift from God. Khomeini ruled as Imam and Supreme Leader of the Islamic Republic until his death in 1989.

foreign powers. He further insisted that the clergy were the people's true representatives, since they lived among them, listened to their problems, and shared their everyday joys and pains. He claimed that the shah secretly planned to confiscate all religious endowments and replace Islamic values with "cultural imperialism." These pronouncements added fuel to an already explosive situation.

By 1977, Iran needed a few sparks to ignite the revolution. These sparks came in the form of minor economic difficulties and international pressures to curb human rights violations. In 1977–1978, the shah tried to deal with a 20 percent rise in consumer prices and a 10 percent decline in oil revenues by cutting construction projects and declaring war against "profiteers," "hoarders," and "price gougers." Not surprisingly, shopkeepers felt that the shah was diverting attention from court corruption and planning to replace them with government-run department stores and that he was intending to destroy the bazaar, which some felt was the "the real pillar of Iranian society."

The pressure for human rights came from Amnesty International, the United Nations, and the Western press, as well as from the recently elected Carter administration in the United States. In 1977, after meeting with the International Commission of Jurists, the shah permitted Red Cross officials to visit prisons and allowed defense attorneys to attend political trials. In the words of Khomeini's first postrevolution prime minister, Mehdi Bazargan, this international pressure had allowed the opposition to breathe again after decades of suffocation.[6]

This slight loosening of the reins, coming in the midst of the economic recession, sealed the fate of the shah. Political parties, labor organizations, and professional associations—especially lawyers, writers, and university professors—regrouped after years of being banned. Bazaar guilds regained their independence from the government party. College, high school, and seminary students, especially in the religious center of Qom, took to the streets to protest the quarter-century of repression. On September 8, 1978, known as Bloody Friday, troops in Tehran fired into a crowded square, killing hundreds of unarmed demonstrators. By late 1978, a general strike brought the whole economy to a halt, paralyzing not only the oil industry, the factories, the banks, and the transport system but also the civil service, the media, the bazaars, and the whole educational establishment. The oil workers vowed that they would not export any petroleum until they had exported the "shah and his forty thieves."[7]

Meanwhile, in the urban centers, local committees attached to the **mosques** and financed by the bazaars were distributing food to the needy, supplanting the police with militias known as ***pasdaran*** (Revolutionary Guards), and replacing the judicial system with ad hoc courts applying the *shari'a*. Equally significant, antiregime rallies were now attracting as many as 2 million protesters. The largest rally was held in Tehran in December 1978 on the day commemorating the martyrdom of Imam Husayn in the seventh century. Protesters demanded the abolition of the monarchy, the return of Khomeini, and the establishment of a republic to preserve national independence and provide the masses with social justice in the form of decent wages, land, and a proper standard of living.

Although these rallies were led by pro-Khomeini clerics, they drew support from a broad variety of organizations: the National Front; the Lawyer's, Doctor's, and Women's associations; the communist Tudeh Party; the Fedayin, a Marxist guerrilla group; and the Mojahedin, a Muslim guerrilla group formed of nonclerical intellectuals. The rallies also attracted students, from both high schools and colleges, as well as shopkeepers and craftsmen from the bazaars. A secret Revolutionary Committee in Tehran coordinated protests throughout the country, kept in telephone contact with Khomeini in exile in Paris, and circulated his tapes within Iran. This was a revolution made in the streets and propelled forward by audiotapes. It was also one of the first revolutions to be televised worldwide.

After a series of such mass rallies in late 1978, the *Washington Post* concluded that "disciplined and well-organized marches lent considerable weight to the opposition's claim of being an alternative government."[8] Similarly, the *Christian Science Monitor* stated that the "giant wave of humanity sweeping through the capital declared louder than any bullet or bomb could the clear message, 'The shah must go.'"[9] Confronted by this opposition and aware that increasing numbers of soldiers were deserting to the opposition, the shah decided to leave Iran. A year later, when he was in exile and dying of cancer, there was much speculation, especially in the United States, that he might have mastered the upheavals if he had been healthier, possessed a stronger personality, and received full support from the United States. But even a healthy man with an iron will and full foreign backing would not have been able to deal with 2 million demonstrators, massive general strikes, and debilitating defections from his own army rank and file.

On February 11, 1979—three weeks after the shah's departure from Iran and ten days after Khomeini's return—armed groups, especially Fedayin and Mojahedin guerrillas, supported by air force cadets, broke into the main army barracks in Tehran, distributed arms, and then assaulted the main police stations, the jails, and eventually the national radio-television station. That same evening, the radio station made the historic announcement: "This is the voice of Iran, the voice of true Iran, the voice of the Islamic Revolution." A few hours of street fighting had completed the destruction of the fifty-four-year-old dynasty that claimed a 2,500-year-old heritage.

The Islamic Republic (1979 to the Present)

Seven weeks after the February revolution, a nationwide referendum replaced the monarchy with an Islamic Republic. Of the 21 million eligible voters, over 20 million—97 percent—endorsed the change. Liberal and lay supporters of Khomeini, including Mehdi Bazargan, his first prime minister, had hoped to offer the electorate a third choice: that of a democratic Islamic Republic. But Khomeini overruled them on the grounds that the term *democratic* was redundant because Islam itself was democratic. The structure of this new republic was to be determined later. Khomeini was now hailed as the Leader of the Revolution, Founder of the Islamic Republic, Guide of the Oppressed Masses, Commander of the Armed Forces, and most potent of all, Imam of the Muslim World, since in Shi'ism, the term **imam** implies "infallible authority."

The constitution itself was drawn up in late 1979 by a constituent body named the Assembly of Religious Experts (*Majles-e Khebregan*). Although this seventy-three-man assembly was elected by the general public, almost all secular organizations as well as clerics opposed to Khomeini boycotted the elections on the grounds that the state media were controlled, independent papers had been banned, and voters were being intimidated by club-wielding vigilantes known as the **Hezbollahis** ("Partisans of God"). The vast majority of those elected, including forty **hojjat al-Islams** and fifteen ayatollahs, were pro-Khomeini clerics. They proceeded to draft a highly theocratic constitution vesting much authority in the hands of Khomeini in particular and the clergy in general—all this over the

The Shah's statue on the ground, February 1979.
Source: © Abbas/ Magnum Photos.

strong objections of Prime Minister Bazargan, who wanted a French-style presidential republic that would be Islamic in name but democratic in structure.

Khomeini submitted this clerical constitution to a national referendum in December 1979, at the height of the American hostage crisis. In fact, some suspect that the hostage crisis was engineered to undercut Bazargan. As soon as Bazargan threatened to submit his own secular constitution to the public, the state television network, controlled by the clerics, showed him shaking hands with U.S. policy-makers. Meanwhile, Khomeini declared that the U.S embassy had been a "den of spies" plotting a repeat performance of the 1953 coup. A month after the embassy break-in and Bazargan's resignation, Khomeini submitted the theocratic constitution to the public and declared that all citizens had a divine duty to vote. Although 99 percent of the electorate endorsed it, voter participation was down to 75 percent—this, despite full mobilizations by the mass media, the mosques, and the Revolutionary Guards. Some 5 million voters abstained. The clerics had won their constitution but at the cost of eroding their broad support.

In the first decade after the revolution, a number of factors helped the clerics consolidate power. First, few could afford to challenge Khomeini's overwhelming charisma. Second, the Iraqi invasion of Iran in 1980—prompted by Saddam Hussein's ambition to gain control over vital borders—rallied the Iranian population; after all, their homeland was in danger. Third, world petroleum prices shot up, sustaining oil revenues. The price of a barrel of oil, which had hovered around $30 in 1979, jumped to over $50 by 1981. Thus, despite war and revolution, the new regime was able to continue to finance social programs launched by the previous one. In fact, in the 1980s, modern amenities, especially electricity, indoor plumbing, televisions, telephones, refrigerators, motorcycles, and medical clinics, made their first significant appearance in the countryside.

The second decade after the revolution brought the clerics serious problems. Khomeini's death in June 1989 removed his decisive presence. His successor, Ali Khamenei, lacked not only his charisma but also his scholastic credentials and seminary disciples. Khamenei had been considered a mere hojjat al-Islam until the government-controlled press elevated him to the rank of ayatollah and Supreme Leader. Few grand ayatollahs deemed him their equal. The 1988 UN-brokered cease-fire in the Iran-Iraq War ended the foreign danger. The drastic fall in world oil prices after 1984 placed a sharp brake on economic development. By 1998, the price of a barrel of oil dipped down to less than $10. Even more serious, by the late 1990s, the regime was facing a major ideological crisis, with many of Khomeini's followers, including some of his closest disciples, now stressing the importance of public participation over clerical hegemony, of political pluralism over theological conformity, of populism over fundamentalism, and of civil society over state authority—in other words, of democracy over theocracy.

Themes and Implications

Historical Junctures and Political Themes

These historical junctures have shaped contemporary Iran, especially the way it deals with the democratic idea, its role in the world of states, its attempts to govern the economy and meet the rising expectations of its citizens, and its need to overcome internal ethnic divisions.

In internal affairs, by far the most important challenge facing the republic is the task of reconciling Islam with democracy. Iran has been Muslim since the seventh century and Shi'i Muslim since the sixteenth century. It has also aspired to attain democracy, mass participation, and popular sovereignty since the 1905 constitutional revolution. The dual aspirations for Islam and for democracy culminated in the 1979 Islamic Revolution and appeared to be reconcilable as long as the vast majority supported Khomeini and accepted his notion of the jurist's guardianship. Human rights did not seem to contradict the divine right of the clergy. As Khomeini liked to argue, Islam and democracy were compatible since the vast majority supported the clerics, had faith in them, respected them as the true interpreters of the shari'a, and wanted them to oversee the activities of state officials. Islam and democracy, however, appear less reconcilable now that the public has lost its enthusiasm for the clergy. Consequently, some Khomeini followers have continued to give priority to his concept of theocracy, but others have begun to emphasize the need for democracy. In other words, Khomeinism has divided into two divergent branches: political liberalism and clerical conservatism.

The fate of democracy in Iran is bounded by the very nature of the shari'a. Democracy is based partly on the two principles that all individuals are equal, especially before the law, and that all people have inalienable natural rights, including the right to choose their own religion. The shari'a, at least in its traditional and conventional interpretations, rejects both of these democratic principles. Formulated in the seventh century, the shari'a is based on the principle of inequality, especially between men and women, between Muslims and non-Muslims, between legitimate minorities, known as the People of the Book, and illegitimate ones, known as unbelievers. In addition, the shari'a, like all other religious law, not only considers rights to emanate from God rather than nature, but also deems the individual to be subordinate to the larger religious community. This is of special concern for Muslims who lose their faith or join another religion, since the shari'a can condemn them to death as apostates. This is no mere technicality; over 250 Baha'is and over 400 leftist prisoners have been executed on just such grounds. The latter were hanged after admitting that they did not believe in God, the Resurrection, and the divinity of the Qur'an. But there are many moderate clerics in Iran who want to reform the shari'a to make it compatible with the modern concepts of individual freedom and human rights. They also favor treating those who do not believe in religion in the traditional manner of "don't ask, don't tell."

In international affairs, the Islamic Republic is determined to remain the dominant power in the Persian Gulf, even though it attained this position under the shah thanks mainly to the United States. In his last years, the shah had become known as the American policeman in the Gulf region. By denouncing the United States as an "arrogant imperialist," canceling military agreements with the West, and condoning the taking of U.S. diplomats as hostages, Khomeini certainly asserted Iranian autonomy and authority in the region, but he also inadvertently prompted Saddam Hussein to launch the Iraq-Iran War. When his government ministers suggested renaming the Persian Gulf the Muslim Gulf to improve relations with Arab countries, all of which call it the Arab Gulf, Khomeini responded that it should remain what it had always been: the Persian

Gulf. Khomeini was as much an Iranian nationalist as a Muslim revolutionary.

Before he died, Khomeini initiated policies that have made it difficult for his successors to improve relations with the West, especially the United States. He called for revolutions throughout the Muslim world, denouncing Arab rulers in the region, particularly in Saudi Arabia, as the "corrupt puppets of American imperialism." He strengthened Iran's navy, and bought nuclear submarines from Russia. He launched a research program to build medium-range missiles and nuclear weapons. He denounced the proposals for Arab-Israeli negotiations over Palestine. He sent money as well as arms to Muslim dissidents abroad, particularly Shi'i groups in Lebanon, Iraq, and Afghanistan. He permitted the intelligence services to assassinate some one hundred exiled opposition leaders living in Western Europe, and he issued the *fatwa* death decree against the British writer Salman Rushdie. These policies helped isolate Iran not only from the United States but also from the European Community, human rights organizations, and the United Nations. Khomeini's successors have had to grapple with this heritage, especially since these acts have direct bearing on economic development and the prospects for obtaining foreign investment.

The Islamic Republic began with the conviction that it could rapidly develop the economy if it relied less on oil exports and more on agriculture and manufacturing. It blamed the shah for the one-export economy, the migration of peasants into the towns, the increasing gap in incomes, the continued high illiteracy rate, the lack of medical and educational facilities, and, in general, the low standard of living. It also blamed the former regime for failing to make Iran self-sufficient and instead making it vulnerable to the vagaries of the world economy by building assembly plants rather than factories that would produce industrial goods.

The new regime soon discovered that the country's underlying economic problems were formidable. Peasants continue to migrate to the cities because of the lack of both agricultural land and irrigated water. Industry remains limited because of the lack of capital. Real per capita income has fallen due to forces outside the control of the state, particularly the price fluctua-

tions of the international petroleum market. The real price of oil has plummeted; by 1999, it was less than it had been before the dramatic quadrupling of prices in 1974. Meanwhile, the population has grown to almost 64 million. In other words, the population has steadily increased, whereas the oil revenues have fluctuated widely. Not surprisingly, Iran continues to struggle with financial problems such as inflation, high unemployment, and capital shortages. To deal with this economic crisis, some have favored conventional state-interventionist strategies: price controls, five-year plans, and further redistribution of wealth through high taxation and social investment. Others have advocated equally conventional laissez-faire strategies: open markets, removal of state controls, more business incentives, and the wooing of foreign capital. Some clerics now openly admit that religion does not have answers to such problems as inflation, unemployment, and the volatility of world oil prices. This is a sharp contrast to the early days of the revolution, when Khomeini had confidently declared that Islam had all the solutions and that economics was a subject best left to "donkeys."

Finally, the Islamic Republic began with a broad collective identity, since 99 percent of Iran's population is Muslim. But this major asset has been squandered in the two decades after the revolution. The stress on Shi'ism naturally alienated the Sunnis, who constitute some 10 percent of the population. The triumph in neighboring Afghanistan of the Taliban, an ultraconservative Sunni organization supported initially by Pakistan and indirectly by the United States, complicated the situation. The Taliban armed Sunni dissidents in Iran; Iran, in turn, armed Shi'i dissidents inside Afghanistan. In addition, the regime's insistence on building the constitution on Khomeini's controversial concept of theocracy antagonized other top clerics as well as lay secular Muslims, who lead most of the political parties. Similarly, the inadvertent association of Shi'ism with the central Persian-speaking regions of Iran carries with it the potential danger of eventually alienating the important Turkic minority in Azerbaijan province. Thus, the Iranian regime, like most other developing states, has to solve the problem of how to allocate scarce resources without exacerbating ethnic, regional, and sectarian differences.

Implications for Comparative Politics

The Iranian Revolution, the emergence of religion in Middle Eastern politics, and the collapse of the Soviet Union convinced many Americans that a new specter was haunting the West: that of Islamic fundamentalism. Some experts on international relations predicted that "clash of civilizations" would replace the cold war; that the fault lines in world politics would no longer be over economics and ideology but over religion and culture; and that the main confrontation would be between the West and the Islamic world, headed by the Islamic Republic of Iran.[10] Islam was seen as a major threat not only because of its size but also because it was deemed "inherently bellicose," "militant," and antagonistic to the West.

These dire predictions have turned out to be gross exaggerations. It is true that the Islamic Republic began denouncing the United States, arming militants in other parts of the Middle East, and calling for a struggle, sometimes termed a *jihad* (crusade), against the West. But these rhetorical denunciations became muted as time passed, as reflected in the election of the reformist Muhammad Khatami as president. The call for Muslim unity has fallen on deaf ears, especially in Sunni countries, such as Saudi Arabia. External assistance to Shi'i Muslims was limited to Iraq, Lebanon, and Afghanistan, where, as part of the Northern Alliance, they helped the United States overthrow the Taliban in 2002. Islam has proved not to be a monolith. What is more, Iranians themselves, including the clerics, have divided sharply into ultraconservatives, conservatives, liberals, and radicals. They even use the Western terms *left, right,* and *center* to describe themselves. Iran shows that the notion of Muslim politics has as little meaning as that of Christian politics. In the same way that one does not study the Bible to understand modern Europe, one does not need the Qur'an to analyze Middle Eastern politics.

It is true that Iran is a major power in the Middle East. It has one of the region's biggest armies, a large land mass, considerable human resources, a respectable gross national product (GNP), and vast oil production. It has the largest navy in the Persian Gulf. In the days of the shah, this navy safeguarded the flow of oil to the West, but it now poses a threat to that same flow of oil. Iran also has plans, predating the Islamic Revolution, to build nuclear weapons.

But it is also true that Iran is in many ways a much weakened power. Its GNP is only about that of New Jersey, and its armed forces are a mere shadow of their former selves. The brutal eight-year conflict with Iraq made the military war-weary. The officer ranks have been decimated by constant purges. The country's military hardware has been depleted by war, obsolescence, and lack of spare parts. In the last years of the shah, military purchases accounted for 17 percent of the GNP. They now take less than 2 percent. Plans to build nuclear weapons are bogged down in financial, technical, and logistical problems. Iran is unlikely to obtain nuclear weapons, not to mention nuclear delivery capabilities, in the foreseeable future. Moreover, a U.S. fleet cruises the Persian Gulf, counterbalancing the Iranian navy, to say nothing of the increased American military presence in the region since the terrorist attacks of September 11, 2001.

It is true that Iran has viewed itself as the vanguard of the Islamic world. But that world turns out to be as illusory for its champions as for its detractors. The Muslim world is formed not of one unitary bloc but of many rival states, each with its own national self-interest. In theory, their rulers stress the importance of Islamic solidarity. In reality, they pursue conventional national interests, even if it necessitates allying with non-Muslims against Muslims. For example, at the height of the American hostage crisis, Iran obtained military equipment from Israel and the United States to pursue the war against Iraq. Similarly, in recent years, Iran has sided with Hindu India against Muslim Pakistan, with Christian Armenia against Muslim Azerbaijan, and with Russia against Muslim Chechnya. Those who see the future as a clash of civilizations and a replay of the medieval Christian-Muslim wars forget that the crusaders themselves, both Muslim and Christian, were often divided, with some siding against their own coreligionists. The Muslim world is no more united now than it was in the days of the medieval crusaders. Iran, like its neighbors, formulates state policies based on national interests, not on cultural and so-called civilizational sentiments.

Section ❷ Political Economy and Development

State and Economy

In 2002, Iran drafted a dramatically new investment law permitting foreigners to own as much as 100 percent of any firm in the country, to repatriate profits, to be free of state meddling, and to have assurances against both arbitrary confiscations and high taxation. Its intention was to attract foreign investments, especially from the European Union, and pave the way for joining the World Trade Organization (WTO). Iran's application to join the WTO in 1996 had failed in part because of its legal impediments against foreign investments and in part because of U.S. opposition. The new investment law was a far cry from the early days of the revolution when Khomeinists had vociferously denounced foreign investors as imperialist exploiters, waxed eloquent about economic self-sufficiency, and criticized the 1965 investment law, which limited foreign capital to less than 49 percent of any firm, as another example of the shah's selling out to the country to Western corporations. Although some leaders continued to warn against Western consumerism and cultural imperialism, the regime as a whole was now eager to attract foreign investment and to rejoin the world economy.

The Economy in the Nineteenth Century

The integration of Iran into the world system began in a modest way in the latter half of the nineteenth century. Before then, commercial contact with the outside world had been limited to a few luxury goods and the famous medieval silk route to China. A number of factors account for this nineteenth-century integration: the economic concessions granted to the European powers; the opening up of the Suez Canal and the building of the Trans-Caspian and the Batum-Baku railways; the laying of telegraph lines across Iran to link India with Britain; the outflow of capital from Europe after 1870; and, most important, the Industrial Revolution in Europe and the subsequent export of manufactured goods to the rest of the world.

In the course of the nineteenth century, Iran's foreign trade increased tenfold. Over 83 percent of this trade was with Russia and Britain; 10 percent with Germany, France, Italy, and Belgium; and less than 7 percent with countries in the Middle East. Exports were confined to carpets and agricultural products, including silk, raw cotton, opium, dried fruits, rice, and tobacco. Imports were mostly tea, sugar, kerosene, and such industrial products as textiles, glassware, guns, and other metal goods. Also in this period, modest foreign investment flowed into banking, fishing, carpet weaving, transport, and telegraph communications.

Contact with the West had far-reaching repercussions. It produced economic dependency, a situation common to much of the Third World, in which less developed countries become too reliant on developed countries; poorer nations are vulnerable to sudden fluctuations in richer economies and dependent on the export of raw materials, the prices of which often stagnate or decline, while the prices of the manufactured products they import invariably increase. Some scholars argue that this type of dependency lies at the root of the present-day economic problems in much of Africa, Latin America, and Asia, including the Middle East.

The nineteenth-century influx of mass-manufactured goods devastated some traditional handicrafts, especially cotton textiles. According to a tax collector in Isfahan, the import of cheap, colorful cotton goods undercut not only the local weavers, dyers, and carders but also the thousands of women who in the past had supplemented their family incomes with cottage industries and home spindles.[11] They naturally blamed foreign imports for their plight. Carpet manufacturers, however, benefited, since they found a ready market in Europe and North America.

The introduction of cash crops to be sold on the market, especially cotton, tobacco, and opium, reduced the acreage available for wheat and other edible grains. Many landowners ceased growing food and turned to commercial export crops. This paved the way for a series of disastrous famines in 1860, 1869–1872, 1880, and 1918–1920. Opium cultivation in Iran was particularly encouraged by British merchants eager to meet the rising demands of the Chinese market brought about by the notorious Opium Wars of the mid-nineteenth century.

Furthermore, the competition from foreign

merchants, together with the introduction of the telegraph and the postal systems, brought the many local merchants, shopkeepers, and workshop owners together into a national middle class aware for the first time of their common statewide interests against both the central government and the foreign powers. In short, the bazaars were transformed into a propertied middle class conscious of its shared grievances against the state. This awareness played an important role in Iran's constitutional revolution of 1905.

The Oil Economy

The real integration of Iran into the world system came in the twentieth century. Its main engine was oil. British prospectors struck oil in Khuzistan in 1908, and the British government in 1912 decided to fuel its navy with petroleum rather than coal. It also decided to buy most of its fuel from the Anglo-Iranian Oil Company, in which it was a major shareholder. Iran's oil revenues increased modestly in the next four decades, reaching $16 million in 1951. After the nationalization of the oil industry in 1951 and the agreement with a consortium of U.S. and British companies in 1955, oil revenues rose steadily, from $34 million in 1955 to $5 billion in 1973 and, after the quadrupling of oil prices in 1974, to over $20 billion in 1975 and $23 billion in 1976. Between 1953 and 1978, the cumulative oil income came to over $100 billion.

Oil became known as Iran's black gold. It financed over 90 percent of imports and 80 percent of the annual budget and far surpassed total tax revenues. Oil also enabled Iran not to worry about feeding its population, a problem that confronts many developing countries. Instead, it could undertake ambitious development programs that other states implemented only if they could squeeze scarce resources from their populations. In fact, oil revenues created what is known as a **rentier state,** a country that obtains a lucrative income by exporting raw materials or leasing out natural resources to foreign companies. Iran as well as Iraq, Algeria, and the Gulf states received enough money from their wells to be able to disregard their internal tax bases. The Iranian state became relatively independent of society. Society, in turn, had few inputs into the state. Little taxation meant little representation. It also meant that the state was totally reliant on one commodity, oil, whose worth was dependent on the vagaries of the world market.

Muhammad Reza Shah tried to reduce Iran's dependency on oil by encouraging other exports and attracting foreign investment into nonoil ventures. Neither policy succeeded. Despite some increase in carpet and pistachio exports, oil continued to dominate: on the eve of the 1979 revolution, it still provided 97 percent of the country's foreign exchange. The new nonoil industries faced difficulties finding export markets. Furthermore, Iran failed to draw external capital despite concerted efforts. Even after the oil boom, foreign firms, mostly U.S., European, and Japanese, invested no more than $1 billion. Much of this was not in industry but in banking, trade, and insurance. In Iran, as in the rest of the Middle East, foreign investors were put off by government corruption, labor costs, small internal markets, potential instability, and fear of confiscations. Apparently foreign companies did not share their government's confidence that Iran was an island of stability in the Middle East.

Society and Economy

Oil revenues financed Muhammad Reza Shah's development projects. It is true, as the opposition liked to publicize, that some revenue was squandered on palaces, bureaucratic waste, outright corruption, ambitious nuclear projects, and ultrasophisticated weapons too expensive even for many NATO countries. But it is also true that significant sums were channeled into socioeconomic development. GNP grew at the average rate of 9.6 percent every year from 1960 to 1977, making Iran one of the fastest-developing countries in the Third World at that time. The land reform project, the linchpin of the White Revolution, created over 644,000 moderately prosperous farms (see Table 1). The number of modern factories tripled from fewer than 320 to over 980 (see Table 2). Enrollment in primary schools grew from fewer than 750,000 to over 4 million; in secondary schools from 121,000 to nearly 740,000; in vocational schools from 2,500 to nearly 230,000; and in universities from under 14,000 to more than 154,000. The Trans-Iranian Railway was completed, linking Tehran with Tabriz, Meshed, Isfahan, and the Gulf. Roads were built connecting most villages with the provincial cities.

The expansion in health services was equally impressive. Between 1963 and 1977, the number of hospital beds increased from 24,126 to 48,000; medical clinics from 700 to 2,800; nurses from 1,969 to 4,105; and doctors from 4,500 to 12,750. These improvements, together with the elimination of epidemics and famines, mainly due to food imports, lowered infant mortality and led to a population explosion. In the two decades prior to the 1979 revolution, the overall population doubled from 18 million to nearly 36 million. This explosion gave the country a predominantly youthful age structure. By the mid-1970s, half the population was under sixteen years of age. This was to have far reaching repercussions in the street politics of 1977–1979 when young people were one of the driving forces leading up to the Islamic Revolution.

Socioeconomic development did not necessarily make the shah popular. On the contrary, his approach to development tended to increase his unpopularity with many sectors of Iranian society. The Industrial and Mining Development Bank channeled over $50 billion of low-interest loans to court-connected entrepreneurs, industrialists, and agribusinessmen. The shah believed that if economic growth benefited those who were already better off, some of the wealth that was produced would gradually trickle down to the lower levels of society. But in Iran, as elsewhere, the benefits of this development strategy got stuck at the top of society and never trickled down. By the mid-1970s, Iran had one of most unequal countries in the world in terms of income distribution.[12] Similarly, land reform, despite high expectations, created a small stratum of prosperous farmers but left the vast majority of peasants landless or nearly landless; over 1.2 million received less than 10 hectares (approximately 24.7 acres), not enough to survive as independent farmers (see Table 1). Not surprisingly, many of the rural poor flocked to the urban shantytowns in search of work.

The factories spawned by the shah's modernization program drew criticism on the grounds that they were mere assembly plants and poor substitutes for real industrial development (see Table 3). His medical programs left Iran with one of the worst doctor-patient ratios and child mortality rates in the Middle East. Educational expansion created only one place for every five university applicants, failed to provide primary

Table 1

Land Ownership in 1977	
Size (hectares)	Number of Owners
200+	1,300
51–200	44,000
11–50	600,000
3–10	1,200,000
Landless	700,000

Note: One hectare is equal to approximately 2.47 acres.
Source: E. Abrahamian, "Structural Causes of the Iranian Revolution," *Middle East Research and Information Project*, no. 87 (May 1980).

Table 2

Number of Factories		
Size	1953	1977
Small (10–49 workers)	Fewer than 1,000	More than 7,000
Medium (50–500 workers)	300	830
Large (over 500 workers)	19	159

Source: E. Abrahamian, "Structural Causes of the Iranian Revolution," *Middle East Research and Information Project*, no. 87 (May 1980).

Table 3

Industrial Production		
Product	1953	1977
Coal (tons)	200,000	900,000
Iron ore (tons)	5,000	930,000
Steel (tons)	—	275,000
Cement (tons)	53,000	4,300,000
Sugar (tons)	70,000	527,000
Tractors (no.)	—	7,700
Motor vehicles (no.)	—	109,000

Source: E. Abrahamian, "Structural Causes of the Iranian Revolution," *Middle East Research and Information Project*, no. 87 (May 1980), 22.

schools for 60 percent of children, and had no impact on 68 percent of the country's illiterates. In fact, the population explosion increased the absolute number of illiterates in Iran. The priority given to the development of Tehran increased disparities between the capital and the provinces. By the mid-1970s, Tehran contained half the country's doctors and manufacturing plants. According to one study, the per capita income in the richest provinces was ten times more than in the poorest ones. By the end of the shah's rule, Iran had the second highest (after Brazil) regional income disparity in the developing world.[13] According to another study, the ratio of urban to rural incomes was 5 to 1, making it one of the worst in the world.[14]

These inequalities created a **dual society** in Iran.

On one side was the modern sector, headed by the elites with close ties to the oil state. On the other side was the traditional sector comprising the clergy, the bazaar middle class, and the rural masses. Each sector, in turn, was sharply stratified into unequal classes. Thus, Iranian society was divided vertically into the modern and the traditional and horizontally into a number of urban as well as rural classes (see Figure 1).

The upper class—the Pahlavi family, the court-connected entrepreneurs, the military officers, and the senior civil servants—constituted less than 0.01 percent of the population. In the modern sector, the middle class—professionals, civil servants, salaried personnel, and college students—formed about 10 percent of the population. The bottom of the modern sector—the

Iranian society was divided sharply not only into horizontal classes, but also into vertical sectors—the modern and the transitional, the urban and the rural. This is known as a dual society.

Figure 1

Iran's Class Structure in the Mid-1970s

Upper Class

Pahlavi Family; Court-Connected Entrepreneurs; Senior Civil Servants and Military Officers	0.1%

Middle Class

Traditional (Propertied)	13%	Modern (Salaried)	10%
Clerics Bazaaris Small Factory Owners Commercial Farmers		Professionals Civil Servants Office Employees College Students	

Lower Classes

Rural	45%	Urban	32%
Landed Peasants Near Landless Peasants Landless Peasants Unemployed		Industrial Workers Wage-Earners in Small Factories Domestic Servants Construction Workers Peddlers Unemployed	

urban working class, which included factory workers, construction laborers, peddlers, and unemployed—constituted over 32 percent. In the traditional sector, the middle class—bazaar merchants, small retailers, shopkeepers, workshop owners, and well-to-do family farmers—made up 13 percent. The rural masses—landless and near-landless peasants, nomads, and village construction workers—made up about 45 percent of the population.

The government's own statistics reveal the widening inequality. In 1972, the richest 20 percent of urban households accounted for 47.1 percent of total urban family expenditures; by 1977, it accounted for 55.5 percent. In 1972, the poorest 40 percent accounted for 16.7 percent of urban family expenditures; by 1977, it accounted for 11.7 percent (see Table 4).

These inequalities fueled resentments against the ruling elite, which were expressed more in cultural and religious terms than in economic and class terms. Articulating these resentments was a gadfly writer named Jalal Al-e-Ahmad (1923–1969). A former communist who had rediscovered his Shi'i roots in the 1960s, Al-e-Ahmad shook his contemporaries by publishing a polemical pamphlet entitled *Gharbzadegi* (*The Plague from the West*). He argued that the ruling class was destroying Iran by blindly imitating the West; neglecting the peasantry; showing contempt for popular religion; worshipping mechanization, regimentation, and industrialization; and flooding the country with foreign ideas, tastes, luxury items, and mass-consumption goods. He stressed that developing countries such as Iran could survive this "plague" of Western imperialism only by returning to their cultural roots and developing a self-reliant society, especially a fully independent economy. Al-e-Ahmad inspired the long search for cultural authenticity and economic self-sufficiency.

These themes were developed further by another young intellectual, Ali Shariati (1933–1977). Studying in Paris during the turbulent 1960s, Shariati was influenced by Marxist sociology, Catholic liberation theology, the Algerian revolution, and, most important, Frantz Fanon's theory of violent Third World revolutions against colonial oppression as laid out in his famous book, *Wretched of the Earth*. Shariati returned home with what can be called a fresh and revolutionary interpretation of Shi'ism, echoes of which would later appear in Khomeini's writings.

Shariati argued that history was a continuous struggle between oppressors and oppressed. Each class had its own interests, its own interpretations of religion, and its own sense of right and wrong, justice and injustice, morality and immorality. To help the oppressed, Shariati believed, God periodically sent down prophets, such as Abraham, Moses, Jesus, and Muhammad. In fact, Muhammad had come to launch a dynamic community in "permanent revolution" toward the ultimate utopia: a perfectly classless society in this world.

Although Muhammad's goal had been betrayed by his illegitimate successors, the caliphs, his radical message had been preserved for posterity by the Shi'i imams, especially by Imam Husayn, who had been martyred in the seventh century to show future generations that human beings had the moral duty to fight oppression in all places at all times. Shariati equated Imam Husayn with Che Guevara, the famous Latin American guerrilla leader killed in Bolivia in 1967. According to Shariati, the contemporary oppressors were the imperialists, the feudalists, the corrupt capitalists, and their hangers-on, especially the "tie-wearers" and "the palace dwellers," the carriers of the "Western plague." He criticized the conservative clerics who had tried to transform revolutionary religion into an apolitical public opiate. Shariati died on the eve of the 1979 revolution, but his prolific works were so widely read and so influential that many felt that he, rather than Khomeini, was the true theorist of the 1979 Islamic Revolution.

Table 4

Measures of Inequality of Urban Household Consumption Expenditures

| Year | Percentage Share in Total Expenditures | | |
	Poorest 40%	Middle 40%	Richest 20%
1972	16.7	36.2	47.1
1977	11.7	32.8	55.5

Source: V. Nowshirvani and P. Clawson, "The State and Social Equity in Postrevolutionary Iran," in M. Weiner and A. Banuazizi (eds.), *The Politics of Social Transformation in Afghanistan, Iran, and Pakistan* (Syracuse, N.Y.: Syracuse University Press, 1994), 248.

Iran and the International Political Economy

Under the Shah

The oil boom in the 1970s gave the shah the opportunity to play a significant role in international politics. As the second most important member of the **Organization of Petroleum Exporting Countries (OPEC),** Iran could cast decisive votes for raising or moderating oil prices. At times, the shah curried Western favor by moderating prices. At other times, he pushed for higher prices to finance his ambitious projects and military purchases. These purchases rapidly escalated once President Richard Nixon began to encourage U.S. allies, such as the shah, to take a greater role in policing their regions. Moreover, Nixon's secretary of state, Henry Kissinger, openly argued that the United States should finance its ever-increasing oil imports, most of them from the Persian Gulf, by exporting more military hardware to the region. The shah was now able to buy from the United States almost any ultrasophisticated weapon he desired. Arms dealers began to jest that the shah read their technical manuals in the same way that some men read *Playboy.* The shah's arms buying from the United States jumped from $135 million in 1970 to a peak of $5.7 billion in 1977. Between 1955 and 1978, Iran spent more than $20.7 billion on U.S. arms alone.

This military might gave the shah a reach well beyond his immediate boundaries. He occupied three small but strategically located Arab islands in the Strait of Hormuz, thus controlling the oil lifeline through the Persian Gulf but also creating distrust among his Arab neighbors. He talked of establishing a presence well beyond the Gulf on the grounds that Iran's national interests reached into the Indian Ocean. "Iran's military expenditures," according to a 1979 U.S. congressional report, "surpassed those of the most powerful Indian Ocean states, including Australia, Indonesia, Pakistan, South Africa, and India."[15]

In the mid-1970s, the shah dispatched troops to Oman to help the local sultan fight rebels. He offered Afghanistan $2 billion to break its ties with the Soviet Union, a move that probably prompted the Soviets to intervene militarily in that country. The shah, after supporting Kurdish rebels in Iraq, forced Baghdad to concede to Iran vital territory on the Shatt al Arab estuary. This had been a bone of contention between the two countries ever since Iraq had come into existence after World War I. A U.S. congressional report summed up Iran's overall strategic position: "Iran in the 1970s was widely regarded as a significant regional, if not global, power. The United States relied on it, implicitly if not explicitly, to ensure the security and stability of the Persian Gulf sector and the flow of oil from the region to the industrialized Western world of Japan, Europe, and the United States, as well as to lesser powers elsewhere."[16]

These vast military expenditures, as well as the oil exports, tied Iran closely to the industrial countries of the West and to Japan. Iran was now importing millions of dollars' worth of rice, industrial tools, construction equipment, pharmaceuticals, tractors, pumps, and spare parts. The bulk of the rice and wheat, and a substantial portion of the tractors, medicines, and construction equipment, came from the United States. Trade with neighboring and other developing countries was insignificant. In the words of the Department of Commerce in Washington, "Iran's rapid economic growth [provided America with] excellent business opportunities."[17]

The oil revenues thus had major consequences for Iran's political economy, all of which paved the way for the Islamic Revolution. They allowed the shah to pursue ambitious programs that inadvertently widened class and regional divisions within the dual society. They drastically raised public expectations without necessarily meeting them. They made the rentier state independent of society. They also made the state highly dependent on oil prices and imported products. Iran was no longer a simple rentier state but an oil-addicted one, vulnerable to the world market. Economic slowdowns in the industrial countries could lead to a decline in their oil demands, which could diminish Iran's ability to buy such essential goods as food, medicine, and industrial spare parts. One of the major promises made by the Islamic Revolution was to end this economic dependency on oil and the West.

The Islamic Republic

The Islamic Republic began with high hopes of rapidly developing the economy and becoming fully independent of oil and the West. The results have been mixed, illustrating the constraints that political economy can place on society. The Pahlavi monarchy and the Islamic Republic may have differed in many respects, but they governed the same economy and therefore faced similar financial problems.

The main problem plaguing the Islamic Republic has been instability in the world oil market. This instability has occurred despite the efforts of OPEC to preserve prices by limiting production and setting quotas for its members. The price of a barrel of oil, which had quadrupled from $5 to $20 in 1974, peaked at $52 in late 1980 but plunged sharply thereafter, reaching $18 in 1985, hovering around $12 to $14 in the late 1980s and 1990s, and descending to a new low of $10 in 1999. This meant that Iran's oil revenues, which continued to provide the state with 80 percent of its hard currency and 75 percent of its total revenues, fell from $20 billion in 1978 to less than $10 billion in 1998. They did not improve until 2000, when they rose to $27 per barrel. Iran, still a rentier state, remains vulnerable to the vagaries of the international petroleum market.

The decline in the world price of oil was due to a number of factors outside Iran's control: the slackening of the demand in the industrialized countries (especially with the recession in the late 1990s); the glutting of the international market by the entry of non-OPEC producers, such as Britain and Mexico; and the tendency of some OPEC members to preserve their revenues by cheating on their production quotas. Iran's oil revenues were also affected by the war with Iraq and its own failure to raise production. In some years, Iran was not able to meet even its OPEC quotas. To raise production, Iran needs an influx of capital and new deep-drilling technology, both of which can be found only in the West. This explains the recent about-turn on foreign investments by the Islamic Republic.

This oil crisis has been compounded by the population explosion, the Iran-Iraqi war, and the emigration of some 3 million Iranians. The annual population growth rate, which had hit 2.5 percent in the late 1970s, jumped to nearly 4 percent by the late 1980s, mainly because the new regime encouraged large families. This was the highest rate in the world, causing a major strain on government resources, especially social services and food imports. The Iraqi war not only hurt the oil industry but also wrought as much as $600 billion in property damage—whole border cities were flattened. It also led to half a million Iranian casualties. The Islamic Revolution itself frightened many professionals and highly skilled technicians, as well as wealthy entrepreneurs, and industrialists into fleeing to the West. Of course, they carried their portable assets with them.

The overall result was a twenty-year economic crisis that lasted into the late 1990s. GNP fell 50 percent, per capita income declined 45 percent, and inflation hovered around 20 to 30 percent every year. The value of real incomes, including salaries and pensions, dropped by as much as 60 percent. Unemployment hit 20 percent; over two-thirds of entrants into the labor force could not find jobs. The absolute number of illiterates increased. Peasants continued to flock to urban shantytowns. Tehran grew from 4.5 million to 12 million people. The total number of families living below the poverty level increased. By the late 1990s, over 9 million urban dwellers lived below the official poverty line.[18] Shortages in foreign exchange curtailed vital imports, even of essential manufactured goods. The value of the currency plummeted. Before the revolution, the U.S. dollar had been worth 70 Iranian rials; by 1998, it was worth as much as 1,750 rials on the official exchange rate, and more than 9,000 rials on the black market. What is more, the regime that came to power advocating self-sufficiency now owed foreign banks and governments over $30 billion, forcing it to renegotiate foreign loans constantly.

Despite this ongoing economic crisis, the Islamic Republic scored some notable successes, especially after the war with Iraq ended. The Reconstruction Ministry, established mainly for the rural population, built 30,000 miles of paved roads, 40,000 schools, and 7,000 libraries. It brought electricity and running water to more than half of the country's 50,000 villages. The number of registered vehicles on the roads increased from 27,000 in 1990 to over 2.9 million in 1996. More dams and irrigation canals were built, and the Agricultural Ministry distributed some 630,000 hectares of confiscated arable land to peasants and gave farmers more favorable prices, especially for wheat. By the late 1990s, most independent farmers had such consumer goods as radios, televisions, refrigerators, and pickup trucks. The extension of social services narrowed the gap between town and country and between the urban poor and the middle classes. The overall literacy rate grew from 50 percent to nearly 76 percent, and by 2000 the literacy rate among those in the age range from six to twenty-nine years was 97 percent. The infant mortality rate fell from 104 per 1,000 in the mid-1970s to 25 per 1,000 in the late 1990s. Life expectancy climbed from fifty-five years in 1979 to sixty-eight in 1993 and further to sixty-nine in 2002, which is one of the highest in the Middle East. The UN estimates that by 2000, 94 percent of the population had access to health services and 95 percent to safe water. On the whole, the poor in Iran are better off now than their parents had been before the Islamic Revolution. Moreover, the country, despite initial setbacks, was able to become more self-sufficient in food production. By the mid-1990s, it was importing no more than 5 percent of its wheat, rice, sugar, and meat requirements. Furthermore, the regime was able to diversify foreign trade and become less dependent on the West. By 2000, Iran's main trade partners were Japan, South Korea, and Russia.

The Islamic Republic regime also made major strides toward population control. At first, it closed down birth control clinics, claiming that Islam approved of large families and that Iran needed workers. But it reversed direction once the ministries responsible for social services felt the full impact of this growth. The regime also realized that only food imports could meet the rising demands. In 1989, the government declared that Islam favored healthy rather than large families and that one literate citizen was better than ten illiterate ones. It reopened birth control clinics, cut subsidies to large families, and announced that the ideal family should consist of no more than two children. It even took away social benefits from those having more than two children. By 2003, the regime boasted that it had reduced the annual rate of population growth to 1.2 percent. It is an impressive accomplishment. It is also a sign that the regime is highly pragmatic when it comes to economic issues.

The 2000–2002 rise in petroleum prices further helped the situation. Oil revenues jumped from less than $10 billion in 1998 to over $28 billion in 2001. Foreign reserves increased to $4.8 billion, wiping out the external debt, stabilizing the currency, and improving the country's creditworthiness. Iran became one of the few developing countries to be free of foreign debt and was even able set aside some oil revenues as a hedge against leaner times. The GDP grew 6 percent in 2000 and 5 percent in 2001. The official unemployment rate fell from 16 to 12.5 percent, and inflation was reduced to 13 percent. The rial stabilized at 1,750 per U.S. dollar on the official rate and 8,000 in the unofficial rate. The government floated its first international bond and succeeded in attracting European investors despite American opposition. The World Bank lent Iran $232 million for medical services and sewage lines, again despite American opposition. Meanwhile, foreign investments—to the tune of $12 billion—have been contracted to flow into oil and gas ventures, petrochemicals, minerals, and car factories. What is more, the government could now afford to channel additional revenues into the infrastructure, especially into power stations, hydroelectric dams, and education. In the 1980 and 1990s, Iran had been considered one of the world's most inhospitable places for foreign investors. In the early 2000s, it was rated by European and Japanese investors as safe. The earlier oil bust had brought Iran economic stagnation; the new boom brought it some hope.

Section ③ Governance and Policy-Making

The political system of Iran is unique in the contemporary world. It is neither presidential, parliamentary, military, monarchical, nor totalitarian. Instead, it is a theocracy with some concessions to democracy. It is a theocracy for the simple reason that the clergy—in other words, the theocrats or the theologians—control most of the important positions. The system nevertheless contains an element of democracy, with some high officials, including the president, elected directly by the general public. Although this combination is unprecedented, similar ones could emerge in other parts of the Middle East if more Islamic countries have similar revolutions.

Organization of the State

The Iranian state rests on the Islamic constitution designed by the Assembly of Religious Experts immediately after the 1979 revolution. It was amended between April and June 1989 during the last months of Khomeini's life by the Council for the Revision of the Constitution, handpicked by Khomeini himself. These amendments were ratified by a nationwide referendum in July 1989, immediately after Khomeini's death. The final document, with 175 clauses and some 40 amendments, is a highly complex mixture of theocracy and democracy.

The constitution's preamble affirms faith in God, Divine Justice, the Qur'an, the Resurrection, the Prophet Muhammad, the Twelve Imams, the eventual return of the Hidden Imam (the Mahdi), and, of course, Khomeini's doctrine of jurist's guardianship. All laws, institutions, and state organizations have to conform to these "divine principles."

The Supreme Leader

The constitution named Khomeini to be the Supreme Leader for life on the grounds that the public overwhelmingly recognized him as the "most just, pious, informed, brave, and enterprising" of the senior clerics—the grand ayatollahs. It further described him as the Leader of the Revolution, the Founder of the Islamic Republic, and, most important, the imam of the whole community. It stipulated that if no single Supreme Leader emerged after his death, then all his authority would be passed on to a leadership council of two or three senior clerics. After Khomeini's death, however, his followers so distrusted the other senior clerics that they did not set up such a council. Instead, they elected one of their own, Ali Khamenei, a middle-ranking cleric, to be the new Supreme Leader. Most of Khomeini's titles, with the exception of imam, were bestowed on Khamenei. The Islamic Republic has often been described as a regime of the ayatollahs (high-ranking clerics). It could be more aptly called a regime of the hojjat al-Islams (middle-ranking clerics), since

few senior clerics want to be associated with it. None of the grand ayatollahs and few of the ordinary ayatollahs subscribed to Khomeini's novel notion of jurist's guardianship. On the contrary, most disliked his radical populism and political activism.

The constitution gives wide-ranging powers to the Supreme Leader. Enshrined as the vital link between

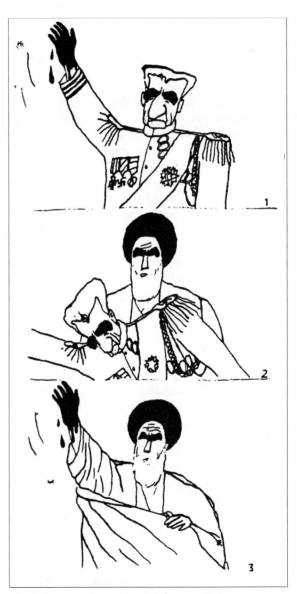

The shah turning into Khomeini, from an émigré newspaper. *Source:* Courtesy Nashriyeh.

the three branches of government, he can mediate between the legislature, the executive, and the judiciary. He can "determine the interests of Islam," "supervise the implementation of general policy," and "set political guidelines for the Islamic Republic." He can eliminate presidential candidates as well as dismiss the duly elected president. He can grant amnesty. As commander in chief, he can mobilize the armed forces, declare war and peace, and convene the Supreme Military Council. He can appoint and dismiss the commanders of Revolutionary Guards as well as those of the regular army, navy, and air force.

The Supreme Leader can nominate and remove the chief judge, the chief prosecutor, and the revolutionary tribunals. He can remove lower court judges. Even more important, he nominates six clerics to the powerful twelve-man Guardian Council. This council can veto parliamentary bills. It has also obtained (through separate legislation) the right to review all candidates for elected office, including the presidency and the *Majles.* The other six on the Guardian Council are jurists nominated by the chief judge and approved by the *Majles.*

The Supreme Leader is also authorized to fill a number of important nongovernment posts: the preachers (**Imam Jum'ehs**) at the main city mosques, the director of the national radio-television network, and the heads of the main religious endowments, especially the **Foundation of the Oppressed,** the successor to the privileged Pahlavi Foundation (see below). By 2001, the Office of the Supreme Leader employed over six hundred in Tehran and had representatives placed in most sensitive institutions throughout the country. The Supreme Leader has obtained more constitutional powers than dreamed of by the shah.

The later constitutional amendments expanded and transformed the Assembly of Religious Experts into an eighty-six-man house elected every four years. Packed with clerics, the assembly not only elected Khamenei as Khomeini's successor but also reserved the right to dismiss him if it found him "mentally incapable of fulfilling his arduous duties." In effect, the Assembly of Religious Experts has become an upper chamber to the regular *Majles.* Its members are required to have a seminary degree equivalent to a master's degree. Figure 2 illustrates the hierarchy established by the constitution.

The general public elects the *Majles,* the president, and the Assembly of Religious Experts. But the Supreme Leader and the Guardian Council decide who can compete in these elections.

Because the constitution is based on Khomeini's theory of jurist's guardianship, it gives wide-ranging judicial powers to the Supreme Leader in particular and to the clerical strata in general. Laws are supposed to conform to the religious law, and the clergy are regarded as the ultimate interpreters of the *shari'a.* In fact, the constitution makes the judicial system the central pillar of the state, overshadowing the executive and the legislature. Bills passed by the Islamic *Majles* are reviewed by the Guardian Council to ensure that they conform to the *shari'a.* All twelve members of this Guardian Council are either clerics or lay jurists knowledgeable in the *shari'a.* The minister of justice is chosen by the president but needs the approval of both the *Majles* and the chief judge. The judicial system itself has been Islamized all the way down to the district courts, with seminary-trained jurists replacing university-educated judges. The Pahlavis purged the clergy from the judicial system; the Islamic Republic purged the university-educated from the same judiciary.

The Executive

The President and the Cabinet

The constitution, particularly after the amendments, reserves some power for the president. He is described as the chief executive and the highest state official after the Supreme Leader. He is chosen every four years through a national election. He must be a pious Shi'i faithful to the principles of the Islamic Republic. He cannot be elected to more than two terms. He draws up the annual budget, supervises economic matters, and chairs the plan and budget organization. He can propose legislation to the *Majles.* He conducts the country's internal and external policies. He signs all international treaties, laws, and agreements. He chairs the National Security Council responsible for defense matters. He can select his own vice presidents and cabinet ministers. The minister of intelligence, however, has to be a cleric according to a separate parliamentary law.

The president appoints most senior officials, including provincial governors, town mayors, and

The general public elects the *Majles*, the president, and the Assembly of Religious Experts. But the Supreme Leader and the cleric-dominated Guardian Council decide who can compete in these elections.

Figure 2

The Islamic Constitution

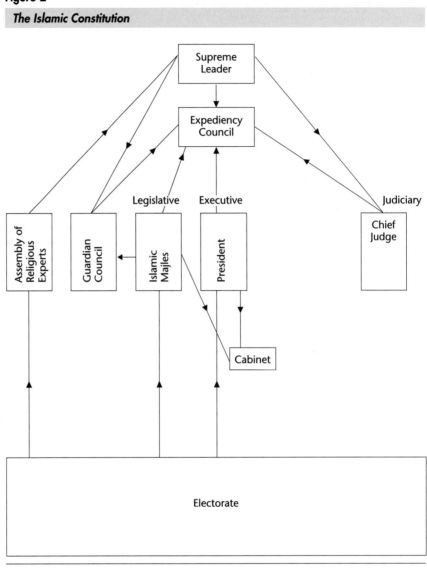

ambassadors. Furthermore, as head of the executive, he names the directors of some of the large public organizations, such as the National Iranian Oil Company, the National Electricity Board, and the National Bank.

Although during the revolution Khomeini often promised that trained officials would run the executive, clerics in fact have dominated the presidency. Of the four presidents since the revolution, three have been clerics: Khamenei, Rafsanjani, and Khatami (see "Leaders: Ayatollah Ali Khamenei," "Leaders: Hojjat al-Islam Ali-Akbar Hashemi Rafsanjani," and "Leaders: Sayyid Muhammad Khatami"). The exception, Abol-Hasan Bani-Sadr, was ousted in 1981 precisely because he denounced the regime as "a dictatorship of the mullahtariat," comparing it to a communist-led "dictatorship of the proletariat."

Leaders: *Ayatollah Ali Khamenei*

Ali Khamenei succeeded Khomeini as Supreme Leader in 1989. He was born in 1939 in Meshed into a minor clerical family originally from Azerbaijan. He studied theology with Khomeini in Qom and was briefly imprisoned in 1962. Active in the opposition movement in 1978, he was given a series of influential positions immediately after the revolution, even though he held only the middle-level clerical rank of hojjat al-Islam. He became Friday prayer leader of Tehran, head of the Revolutionary Guards, and, in the last years of Khomeini's life, president of the republic. After Khomeini's death, he was elevated to the rank of Supreme Leader even though he was neither a grand ayatollah nor a recognized senior expert on Islamic law. He had not even published a theological treatise. The government-controlled media, however, began to refer to him as an ayatollah. Some ardent followers even referred to him as a grand ayatollah qualified to guide the world's whole Shi'i community. After his elevation, he built a constituency among the regime's more diehard elements: traditionalist judges, conservative war veterans, and antiliberal ideologues. Before 1989, he often smoked a pipe in public, a mark of an intellectual, but put away the habit when he became Supreme Leader.

The Bureaucracy

The president, as the chief of the executive branch, heads a huge bureaucracy. In fact, this bureaucracy continued to proliferate after the revolution even though Khomeini had often taken the shah to task for having a bloated government. It expanded, for the most part, to provide jobs for the many college and high school graduates. On the eve of the revolution, the ministries had 300,000 civil servants and 1 million employees. By the early 1990s, they had over 600,000 civil servants and 1.5 million employees. The Iranian Revolution, like many others, ended up creating a bigger bureaucracy.

Of the new ministries, Culture and Islamic Guidance censored the media and enforced "proper conduct" in public life; Intelligence has replaced SAVAK as the main security organization; Heavy Industries manages the recently nationalized factories; and Reconstruction has the dual task of expanding social services and taking "true Islam" into the countryside. Its mission is to build bridges, roads, schools, libraries, and mosques in the villages so that the peasantry will learn the basic principles of Islam. "The peasants," declared one cleric, "are so ignorant of true Islam that they even sleep next to their unclean sheep."[19]

The clergy dominate the bureaucracy as they do the presidency. They have monopolized the most sensitive ministries—Intelligence, Interior, Justice, and Culture and Islamic Guidance—and have given posts in other ministries to their relatives and protégés. These ministers appear to be highly trained technocrats, sometimes with higher degrees from the West, but in fact are powerless individuals chosen by, trusted by, and related to the ruling clergy.

Semipublic Institutions

The Islamic Republic has set up a number of semipublic institutions. They include the Foundation of the Oppressed, the Alavi Foundation (named after Imam Ali), the Martyrs Foundation, the Pilgrimage Foundation, the Housing Foundation, the Foundation for the Publication of Imam Khomeini's Works, and the Fifteenth of Khordad Foundation, which commemorates the date (according to the Islamic calendar) of Khomeini's 1963 denunciation of the shah's White Revolution. Although supposedly autonomous, these foundations are directed by clerics appointed personally by the Supreme Leader. According to some estimates, their annual income may be as much as half that of the government.[20] They are exempt from paying state taxes and are allocated foreign currencies, especially U.S. dollars, at highly favorable exchange rates subsidized by the oil revenues. Most of their assets are property confiscated from the old elite.

The largest of these institutions, the Foundation for the Oppressed, administers over 140 factories,

---

Leaders: *Sayyid Muhammad Khatami*

Muhammad Khatami was elected president of the Islamic Republic in 1997 and reelected in 2000. He was born in 1944 into a prominent clerical family in central Iran. His father, an ayatollah, was a close friend of Khomeini. His mother came from a prosperous landed family. He studied theology in Qom and philosophy at Isfahan University. At the outbreak of the revolution, he was in charge of a Shi'i mosque in Germany. After the revolution, he first headed a state publishing house, then sat in the *Majles*, and then served as minister of culture and Islamic guidance. Arousing the wrath of the conservatives, he resigned from the last post in 1992 and took up the teaching of philosophy at Tehran University. He uses the title *sayyid* and wears a black turban to indicate that he is a male descendant of the Prophet. Although a cleric by appearance and training, he seems to many more like a university professor interested in political philosophy.

---

120 mines, 470 agribusinesses, and 100 construction companies. It also owns the country's two leading newspapers, *Ettela'at* and *Kayhan.* The Martyrs Foundation, in charge of helping war veterans, controls property of the old elite that was confiscated in 1979 but not handed over to the Foundation for the Oppressed. It also receives an annual subsidy from the government. These foundations together control $12 billion in assets and employ over 400,000 people. They can be described as states within a state—or rather, as clerical fiefdoms favored by the Supreme Leader.

Other State Institutions

The Military

The clergy have taken special measures to control the armed forces—both the regular military of 388,000, including 220,000 conscripts, and the irregular forces formed of 100,000 Revolutionary Guards established immediately after 1979 and 200,000 volunteers of the Mobilization of the Oppressed (*Basej-e Mostazafin*) created during the war against Iraq. The Supreme Leader, as commander in chief, appoints the chiefs of staff as well as the top commanders. He also fills the post of defense minister with his own confidants, who report directly to him, bypassing the president and the cabinet. Moreover, he places chaplains, who function like political commissars in communist party-states, in regular military units to watch over officers.

To further safeguard the republic against the regular army built by the Pahlavis, the new regime purged the top ranks, placed officers promoted from the ranks of the Revolutionary Guards in command positions over the regular divisions, and built up the Revolutionary Guards as a parallel force with its own uniforms, budgets, munitions factories, recruitment centers, and even small air force and navy. According to the constitution, the regular army defends the borders, while the Revolutionary Guards protect the republic. Despite these measures, political sentiments about the Islamic Republic remain unknown, if not ambivalent, in the regular military, especially among the 18,000 professionals in the navy, 45,000 in the air force, and 125,000 in the conventional army.

The Judiciary

The Islamic Republic regime Islamized the judiciary by enacting a penal code, the Retribution Law, based on a reading of the *shari'a* that was so narrow that it prompted many modern-educated lawyers to resign in disgust, charging that it contradicted the United Nations Charter on Human Rights. It permitted injured families to demand blood money on the biblical and Qur'anic principle of "an eye for an eye, a tooth for a tooth, a life for a life." It mandated the death penalty for a long list of "moral transgressions," including adultery, homosexuality, apostasy, drug trafficking, and habitual drinking. It sanctioned stoning, live burials, and finger amputations. It divided the population into male and female and Muslims and non-Muslims, and treated

Leaders: *Hojjat al-Islam Ali-Akbar Hashemi Rafsanjani Ali-Akbar*

Rafsanjani was born in 1934 into a fairly prosperous business and farming family in the heartland of the Shi'i and Persian-speaking provinces. He studied in Qom with Khomeini, found himself in prison four times during the 1960s, set up a number of commercial companies, including one that exported pistachios, and wrote a book praising a nineteenth-century prime minister who had made an abortive attempt to industrialize the country. Nevertheless, Rafsanjani remained active enough in clerical circles to be considered a hojjat al-Islam. After the revolution, he became a close confidant of Khomeini and attained a number of cabinet posts, culminating with the presidency in 1989. After serving two four-year terms, the maximum allowed by the constitution, he was given the chairmanship of the powerful Expediency Council. In some ways, his institutional power rivals that of President Khatami, but not, of course, that of Supreme Leader Khamenei.

them unequally. For example, in court, the evidence of one male Muslim is equal to that of two female Muslims. The regime also passed a "law on banking without usury" to implement the *shari'a* ban on all forms of interest taking and interest giving.

Although the law was Islamized, the modern centralized judicial system was not dismantled. For years, Khomeini argued that in a truly Islamic society, the local *shari'a* judges would pronounce final verdicts without the intervention of the central authorities. Their verdicts would be swift and decisive. This, he insisted, was the true spirit of the *shari'a*. After the revolution, however, he discovered that the central state needed to retain ultimate control over the justice system, especially over life and death. Thus, the new regime retained the appeals system, the hierarchy of state courts, and the power to appoint and dismiss all judges. State interests took priority over the spirit of the *shari'a*.

Practical experience led the regime to broaden the narrow interpretation of the *shari'a* gradually. To permit the giving and taking of interest, without which modern economies would not function, the regime allowed banks to offer attractive rates as long as they avoided the taboo term *usury*. To meet public sensitivities as well as international objections, the courts rarely implemented the harsh corporal punishments stipulated by the *shari'a*. They adopted the modern method of punishment, imprisonment, rather than the traditional one of corporal public punishment. By the early 1990s, those found guilty of breaking the law were treated much as they would be in the West: fined or imprisoned rather than flogged in the public square.

Subnational Government

Although Iran is a highly centralized state, it is divided administratively into provinces, districts, subdistricts, townships, and villages. Provinces are headed by governors-general, districts by governors, subdistricts by lieutenant governors, towns by mayors, and villages by headmen.

The Islamic constitution promises elected councils on each level of administration. The constitution declares that the management of local affairs in every village, town, subdistrict, district, and province will be under the supervision of councils whose members would be elected directly by the local population. It also declares that governors-general, governors, mayors, and other regional officials appointed by the central government's Interior Ministry have to consult local councils. These clauses creating local councils had been incorporated into the constitution mainly because of mass demonstrations organized in 1980 by the left—notably the Mojahedin and the Fedayin. The **Assembly of Experts** would have preferred to remained silent on the issue.

Despite these clauses, no steps were taken to hold council elections until 1999 when Khatami, the new president, insisted on holding the country's very first nationwide local elections. Over 300,000 candidates, including 5,000 women, competed for 11,000 council seats—3,900 in towns and 34,000 in villages. Khatami's supporters won a landslide victory taking 75 percent of the seats, including twelve of the fifteen in Tehran. The top vote getter in Tehran was Khatami's former interior minister, who had been impeached by the conservative *Majles* for issuing too many publishing licenses to reform-minded journals and newspapers. These local elections showed that the conservative clergy, despite their mosque pulpits, could not stem the reformist tide. They also showed that participatory democracy had come to the grass-roots level in Iran.

The Policy-Making Process

Iran's policy-making system is highly complex in part because of the cumbersome constitution and in part because factional conflicts within the ruling clergy have resulted in more amendments, which have made the original constitution even more complicated. Laws can originate in diverse places, and they can be modified by pressures coming from diverse directions. They can also be blocked by a wide variety of state institutions. In short, the decision-making process is highly fluid and diffuse, often reflecting the regime's factional divisions.

The clerics who destroyed Iran's old order remained united while building the new one. They were convinced that they alone had the divine mandate to govern. They formed a distinct social stratum as well as a cohesive political group. They followed the same leader, admired the same texts, cited the same potent symbols, remembered the same real and imaginary indignations under the shah, and, most important, shared the same vested interest in preserving the Islamic Republic. Moreover, most had studied at the same seminaries and came from the same lower-middle-class backgrounds. Some were even related to each other through marriage and blood ties.

But once the constitution was in place, the same clerics drifted into two loose but identifiable blocs: the Society (*Majmu'eh*) of the Militant Clergy, and the Association (*Jam'eh*) of the Militant Clergy. The former can be described as statists, populists, or radical reformers and the latter as laissez-faire (free-market) conservatives. The populists hoped to consolidate lower-class support by redistributing wealth, eradicating unemployment, nationalizing enterprises, confiscating large

The clerical regime and its two stilts: the sword and the oil wells. *Source:* Courtesy *Mojahed* (in exile).

estates, financing social programs, rationing and subsidizing essential goods, and placing price ceilings on essential consumer goods. In short, they espoused the creation of a comprehensive welfare state. The conservatives hoped to retain middle-class support, especially in the bazaars, by removing price controls, lowering business taxes, cutting red tape, encouraging private entrepreneurs, and balancing the budget, even at the cost of sacrificing subsidies and social programs. In recent years, the statist reformers have begun to emphasize the democratic over the theocratic features of the constitution, stressing the importance of individual rights, the rule of law, and government accountability to the electorate. In many ways, they have become like social democrats the world over.

The conservatives were originally labeled middle-roaders and traditionalists. The statists were labeled progressives, seekers of new ideas, and followers of the imam's line. The former often denounced the latter as extremists, leftists, and pro-Soviet Muslims. The latter countered by denouncing the free-marketers as medievalists, rightists, capitalists, mafia bazaaris, and pro-American Muslims. Both could bolster their arguments with apt quotes from Khomeini.

This polarization created a major constitutional gridlock, since the early Islamic *Majles* was dominated by the radicals, whereas the Guardian Council was controlled by the conservatives. Khomeini had appointed conservatives to the Guardian Council to preserve his links with the bazaars and to build bridges to the grand ayatollahs, who distrusted his whole revolutionary movement. Between 1981 and 1987, over one hundred bills passed by the *Majles* were vetoed by the Guardian Council on the grounds that they violated the *shari'a,* especially the sanctity of private property. The vetoed legislation included a labor law, land reform, nationalization of foreign trade, a progressive income tax, control over urban real estate transactions, and confiscation of the property of émigrés whom the courts had not yet found guilty of counterrevolutionary activities. Introduced by individual deputies or cabinet ministers, these bills had received quick passage because the radical statists controlled the crucial *Majles* committees and held a comfortable majority on the *Majles* floor. Some ultraconservatives had countered by encouraging the faithful not to pay taxes and instead to contribute to the grand ayatollahs of their choice. After all, they argued, one could find no mention of income tax anywhere in the *shari'a.*

Both sides cited the Islamic constitution to support their positions. The free-marketers referred to the long list of clauses protecting private property, promising balanced budgets, and placing agriculture, small industry, and retail trade in the private sector. The statists referred to an even longer list promising education, medicine, jobs, low-income housing, unemployment benefits, disability pay, interest-free loans, and the predominance of the public sector in the economy.

To break the constitutional gridlock, Khomeini boldly introduced into Shi'ism the Sunni Islamic concept of **maslahat**—that is, "public interest" and "rea-

sons of state." Over the centuries, Shi'i clerics had denounced this as a Sunni notion designed to bolster the illegitimate caliphs. Khomeini now claimed that a truly Islamic state could safeguard the public interest by suspending important religious rulings, even over prayer, fasting, and the pilgrimage to Mecca. He declared public interest to be a primary ruling and the others mere secondary rulings. In other words, the state could overrule the views of the highest-ranking clerics. In the name of public interest, it could destroy mosques, confiscate private property, and cancel religious obligations. Khomeini added that the Islamic state had absolute authority, since the Prophet Muhammad had exercised absolute (*motalaq*) power, which he had passed on to the imams and thus eventually to the Islamic Republic. Never before had a Shi'i religious leader claimed such powers for the state, especially at the expense of fellow clerics.

As a follow-up, Khomeini set up a new institution named the Expediency Council for Determining the Public Interest of the Islamic Order, known now as the **Expediency Council.** He gave this Expediency Council the task of resolving the conflicts between the Islamic *Majles* and the Guardian Council. He packed the council with thirteen clerics, including the president, the chief judge, the Speaker of the *Majles,* and six jurists from the Guardian Council. The Expediency Council eventually passed some of the more moderate bills favored by the statists. These included a new income tax, banking legislation, and a much-disputed labor law providing workers in large factories with a minimum wage and some semblance of job security.

The constitutional amendments introduced after Khomeini's death institutionalized the Expediency Council. The new Supreme Leader could now not only name its members but also determine its tenure and jurisdiction. Not surprisingly, Khamenei packed it with his supporters—none of them prominent grand ayatollahs. Even more important, he made its meetings secret and allowed it to initiate entirely new laws rather than restrict itself to resolving legislative differences between the Guardian Council and the *Majles.* In effect, the Expediency Council is now a secretive supraconstitutional body accountable only to the Supreme Leader. In this sense, it has become a powerful body rivaling the Islamic *Majles* even though it did not exist in the original constitution. By 2002, the Expediency

Council contained thirty-two members. These included the president; chief judge; Speaker of the *Majles;* ministers of intelligence, oil, culture, and foreign affairs; chief of the General Staff; commander of the Revolutionary Guards; jurists from the Guardian Council; directors of radio and television as well as of the Central Bank, Atomic Energy Organization, and National Oil Company; heads of the main religious foundations; chairman of the Chamber of Commerce; and editors of the main conservative newspapers. Seventeen were clerics. These thirty-two can be considered the most powerful men in the Islamic Republic.

Section ❹ Representation and Participation

Although the Islamic Republic is a theocracy, some supporters of the regime claim that it is still compatible with democracy. According to the constitution, the government represents the general electorate. The president is directly elected by the people, and the Supreme Leader is chosen by the Assembly of Religious Experts, which in turn is elected by the general population. What is more, the elected legislature, the Islamic *Majles,* retains considerable power, and according to one of the founders of the regime, it is the centerpiece of the Islamic constitution.[21] Another architect of the constitution has argued that the Iranian people, by carrying out an Islamic Revolution in 1979, implicitly favored a type of democracy that would be confined within the boundaries of Islam and within the rubric of jurist's guardianship.[22] But another declared that if he had to choose between the democracy and jurist's guardianship, he would not hesitate to choose the latter, since it came directly from God.[23] On the eve of the initial referendum on the constitution, Khomeini himself had declared: "This constitution, which the people will ratify, in no way contradicts democracy. Since the people love the clergy, have faith in the clergy, want to be guided by the clergy, it is only right that the supreme religious authority oversee the work of the ministers to ensure that they don't make mistakes or go against the law of the Qur'an."[24]

The Legislature

According to Iran's constitution, the *Majles* "represents the nation" and is granted many powers, including enacting or changing ordinary laws (with the approval of the Guardian Council), investigating and supervising all affairs of state, and approving or ousting the cabinet ministers. In describing this branch of government, the constitution uses the term *qanun* (statutes) rather than *shari'a* (divine law) so as to gloss over the fundamental question of whether legislation passed by the *Majles* is derived from God or the people. The rationale is that the divine law (*shari'a*) comes from God, but statutes (*qanuns*) are made by the people's elected representatives.

The *Majles* originally contained 270 seats and was elected every four years through secret direct balloting by all citizens over the age of fifteen. It now contains 290 seats and is elected by citizens over the age of sixteen. The *Majles* has considerable authority. It can pass *qanun* as long as the Guardian Council deems it compatible with the *shari'a* and the Islamic constitution. It can interpret legislation as long as these interpretations do not contradict the judicial authorities. It can choose, from a list drawn up by the chief judge, six of the twelve-man Guardian Council. It can investigate at will cabinet ministers, affairs of state, and public complaints against the executive and the judiciary. It can remove cabinet members—with the exception of the president—through a parliamentary vote of no confidence. It can withhold approval for government budgets, foreign loans, international treaties, and cabinet appointments. It can hold closed debates, provide its members with immunity from arrest, and regulate its own internal workings, especially the committee system.

Although the 1989 constitutional amendments weakened the *Majles* in relation to the presidency and the Expediency Council, the *Majles* nevertheless remains a highly important political institution in Iran. On occasion, it has changed government budgets, criticized cabinet policies, modified development plans, and forced the president to replace his ministers as well as the director of national radio-television. In 1992, 217 deputies circulated an open letter that explicitly emphasized the prerogatives of the *Majles* and thereby implicitly downplayed those of the Supreme Leader. Likewise, the Speaker of the House in 2002 threatened to close down the whole *Majles* if the judiciary violated parliamentary immunity and arrest one of his liberal deputies.

Political Parties and the Party System

The constitution guarantees citizens the right to organize, and a law passed in 1980 permits the Interior Ministry to issue licenses to political parties. But political parties were not encouraged until Khatami's 1997 election as president. Since then, three parties have been active, especially in the heated parliamentary elections of 2000: the Islamic Iran Participation Front and the Islamic Labor Party, both formed by Khatami supporters, and the Servants of Reconstruction created by Hojjat al-Islam Ali-Akbar Hashemi Rafsanjani, the former president and now chairman of the Expediency Council. According to the Interior Ministry, licenses have been granted to some seven hundred political, social, and cultural organizations, but all are led by people deemed politically acceptable by the regime. This limited form of political participation might be called "guided democracy." The real political opposition has been forced into exile, mostly in Europe:

- **The Liberation Movement.** Established in 1961 by Mehdi Bazargan, who became Khomeini's first premier in 1979, the Liberation Movement is a moderate Islamic party similar in ideology to Germany's Christian Democrats. Beginning in the early 1980s, the government gradually tightened control over its activities, especially after it criticized the Islamic Republic for prolonging the war with Iraq, giving too much influence to the clergy, and mismanaging the economy. In 2002, the judiciary banned the Liberation Movement as a subversive organization. Despite its religious orientation, the party advocates secularism and the strict separation of mosque from state.
- **The National Front.** Originating in the campaign to nationalize the country's oil resources in the early 1950s, the National Front remains committed to Mossadeq's twin political ideals of nationalism and secularism. Because the conservative clergy feel threatened by the National Front's potential appeal, they have banned the organization and forced it into exile.
- **The Mojahedin.** Formed in 1971 as a guerrilla organization to fight the shah's regime, the Mojahedin tried to synthesize Marxism and Islam. It interpreted Shi'i Islam to be a radical religion favoring equality, social justice, martyrdom, and redistribution of wealth. Immediately after the revolution, the Mojahedin attracted a large following among college and high school students, especially when it began to denounce the clergy for establishing a new dictatorship. The regime retaliated with mass executions and forced the Mojahedin to move their base of operations into Iraq. Not unexpectedly, the Mojahedin became associated with the national enemy and thereby lost much of its appeal within Iran.
- **The Fedayin.** Also formed in 1971, the Fedayin modeled itself after the Marxist guerrilla movements of the 1960s in Latin America, especially those inspired by Che Guevara and the Cuban revolution. Losing more fighters than any other organization in the guerrilla war against the shah, the Fedayin came out of the revolution with much revolutionary mystique and popular urban support. But it soon lost much of its strength because of massive government repression and a series of internal splits.
- **The Tudeh (Party of the Masses).** Established in 1941, the Tudeh is a mainstream, formerly pro-Soviet communist party. Although the Tudeh initially supported the Islamic Republic as a "popular anti-imperialist state," it was banned, and most of its organizers were executed during the period 1983 through 1989. It survives mostly in Europe.

Elections

Iran's constitution promises free elections. In practice, however, *Majles* elections have varied from relatively free but disorderly in the early days of the republic, to controlled and highly unfair in the middle years, and back again to free—and now orderly—in recent years. The main obstacle to fair elections has been the Guardian Council with its power to vet candidates. For example, in 1996, the Guardian Council excluded over 44 percent of some 5,000 parliamentary candidates by questioning their loyalty to the concept of jurist's guardianship. Other factors help restrict electoral freedom. The government-controlled radio-television network, the main source of information for the vast majority, favors some candidates, ignores others, and denounces yet others. The Interior Ministry can ban dissident organizations, especially their newspapers and meetings, with the claim that they are anti-Islamic and antirevolutionary. Ballot boxes are placed in mosques, and at the time the Revolutionary Guards supervise voting. Neighborhood clerics are on hand to help illiterates complete their ballots. Club-wielding gangs, the Hezbollahis, have been known to assault their opponents. Some elections are timed to coincide with high religious holidays. The Supreme Leader inevitably denounces those tempted to abstain as "secret agents of the devil." The electoral law, based on a winner-take-all majority system rather than on proportional representation, was designed to minimize the voice of the opposition. The Islamic Republic has had six *Majles* elections so far: 1980, 1984, 1988, 1992, 1996, and 2000.

The First Majles (1980)

In the election for the First *Majles* in 1980, shortly after the founding of the Islamic Republic, there were over 4,400 candidates, over 40 parties, over 200 dailies and weeklies, and thousands of workplace organizations in the bazaars, campuses, high schools, factories, and offices. The parties represented the whole range of the political spectrum from the far right, through the center, to the extreme left. By shattering the old state structures, the revolution had released a wide variety of political, social, and ethnic groups. It was as if, after years of silence, every professional and occupational association, every political party and ideological viewpoint, and every interest and pressure group rushed into the open to air its views, print its newspapers and broadsheets, and field its parliamentary candidates.

On the right was the Islamic Republican Party (IRP), which was established immediately after the revolution by Khomeini's closest disciples. It had the support of two highly conservative religious groups that had survived the old regime: the Fedayan-e Islam and the Hojjatieh Society. It also had the support of the Islamic Association of Bazaar Guilds, Islamic Association of Teachers, Islamic Association of University Students, the Association of Seminary Teachers of Qom, and, most important, the Association of the Militant Clergy in Tehran. Not surprisingly, it championed Khomeini's notion of jurist's guardianship.

At the center of the political spectrum was Bazargan's Liberation Movement. Bazargan had been appointed premier in February 1979 by Khomeini himself, but had resigned in disgust ten months later when the Revolutionary Guards had permitted students to take over the U.S. embassy. The Liberation Movement favored free markets, limited government, cordial relations with the United States, and a pluralistic political system in which all parties, religious and nonreligious, would compete in fair elections. The Liberation Movement also favored a regime built on its own liberal interpretation of Islam, one in which the clergy would guide and advise rather than rule. Bazargan was a former member of Mosaddeq's National Front, the organization instrumental in nationalizing the oil industry in 1951. But Bazargan, unlike Mosaddeq, liked to sprinkle his speeches with religious quotations.

Closely allied with the Liberation Movement was the National Front, a mere shadow of its former self, and its offshoots, the National Party and the Democratic National Front. These parties, like the Liberation Movement, were led by Western-educated, middle-aged professionals and technocrats. But unlike the Liberation Movement, they avoided making political use of Islam. Like their deceased mentor, Mosaddeq, they preferred to separate politics from religion and to treat the latter as primarily a private matter. The Liberation Movement can be defined as a liberal Muslim party; the National Front and its offshoots as liberal secular parties.

The left was fragmented even more into religious and nonreligious groups. The religious groups included such Muslim yet anticlerical ones as the People's Mojahedin, the Movement of Militant Muslims, and the Movement for the Liberation of the Iranian People. The nonreligious groups included a number of Marxist and ethnic parties: the Tudeh, the Majority and Minority Fedayin, the Kurdish Democratic Party, and at least a dozen small Marxist-Leninist parties. To complicate matters further, Abul-Hassan Bani-Sadr, a French-educated intellectual supporter of Khomeini who had been elected president of Iran in January 1980, was distancing himself from the Islamic Republican Party by fielding a number of his own candidates. Many of these political parties had their own student, labor, professional, and women's organizations. For example, in the early years of the revolution, there were over a dozen women's organizations in Tehran alone.

Not surprisingly, the elections for this First *Majles* were extremely lively, even though the IRP manipulated the state machinery, especially the Interior Ministry and the national radio-television network, to favor its candidates. On the eve of the voting, the minister of the interior declared that all were free to run, but only "true Muslims" would be permitted to sit in the forthcoming parliament.[25] Some 80 percent of the electorate participated in the first round.

The competition in the 1980 election was so intense in some constituencies, particularly Kurdistan, Kermanshah, West Azerbaijan, and the Caspian provinces, that the Interior Ministry stepped in, impounded the ballot boxes, harassed candidates, and postponed the second round indefinitely. The second round was not held until late 1981. By then, the regime had cracked down on the opposition, forcing Bani-Sadr into exile, banning many leftist parties, and executing hundreds of Mojahedin organizers.

Of the 216 deputies elected in 1980, 120 were supporters of the IRP, 33 of Bani-Sadr, and 20 of the Liberation Movement; 33 described themselves as independent. The independents included two Kurdish Democrats and five National Front leaders. The latter had their parliamentary credentials promptly rejected on the grounds that documents found in the recently occupied U.S. embassy "proved" them to be U.S. spies. The IRP had won only 35 percent of the popular vote but had collected over 60 percent of the filled seats. The Mojahedin, on the other hand, had won 25 percent of the popular vote but had not obtained a single seat. The electoral law based on majority rather than proportional representation had paid off for Khomeini.

Once the IRP carried out the second round and replaced the purged members, including Bani-Sadr's supporters, it gained a solid majority. This included 105 clerics—more than 38 percent of the *Majles*—making it by far the highest clerical representation in Iran's parliamentary history. Most were medium-ranking clerics serving as court judges and town preachers (Imam Jum'ehs). The others were white-collar employees and high school teachers, some of

whom were seminary graduates. Over 90 percent came from the propertied middle class. Their fathers had been clerics, bazaar merchants, guild elders, or small farmers.

The Second Majles (1984)

The elections for the Second *Majles* in 1984 were carried out under very different circumstances. The "spring of the Iranian Revolution" was over. The opposition was now either banned outright or else highly restricted in its activities. The IRP monopolized the political scene, manipulating state institutions and controlling a vast array of organizations, including large foundations, local mosques, Revolutionary Guards, and thousands of town preachers. Not surprisingly, it won a landslide victory, leaving a few seats to independent-minded clerics with their own local followings. Also not surprisingly, voter participation fell sharply, to less than 60 percent, even though Khomeini declared that abstaining was tantamount to betraying Islam.

Over 54 percent of the 270 deputies were clerics, almost all middle ranking. Most of the nonclerics had doctoral, master's, bachelor's, or associate's degrees or high school diplomas. Only eleven had not completed high school. Twenty-seven of the lay members had at one time or another attended seminary. As before, most were in their late thirties or early forties.

In 1987, Khomeini dissolved the IRP in preparation for the Third *Majles*. No reason was given, but the decision was prompted by the conflict between the radical statists demanding economic reforms and the conservative free marketers favoring the bazaars. One radical deputy claimed that "the party had been infiltrated by opportunistic time-servers pretending to be devout followers of the Imam's Line."[26] In the *Majles,* the radicals could muster 120 votes and the conservatives some 90; the remainder moved back and forth between these poles.

In dissolving the IRP, Khomeini declared that the clergy were free to establish two competing organizations as long as both opposed imperialism, communism, and capitalism and supported Islam, the Islamic Republic, and the jurist's guardianship. "Political differences," he commented, "are natural. Throughout history our religious authorities have differed among themselves. . . . Besides Iranians should be free to express themselves."[27] He could have added, "within reason and within the context of Islam as defined by myself."

In preparation for the next elections, the radicals left the Association of the Militant Clergy and formed their Society of the Militant Clergy. From then on, there were two rival clerical organizations: on one side, the statist reformers with their society and at least five major newspapers; on the other side, the conservative free marketers with their association and a major newspaper called *Resalat* (*Message*). The conservatives became known as the Resalat group. Both had adherents in the seminaries and among the local preachers (Imam Jum'ehs). This was political pluralism, but one restricted to those subscribing to Khomeini's interpretation of Shi'ism.

The Third (1988), Fourth (1992), and Fifth (1996) Majleses

The radicals won the lackluster 1988 elections for the Third *Majles*. In the new parliament, there were eighty-six clerics, a 23 percent decline from the previous assembly. This, however, did not signify the demise of clerical power. Some clerics had gone on to higher positions, especially to the Assembly of Religious Experts. Moreover, many of the new lay deputies were young protégés of the clerics recruited into their fold from the students who had taken over the U.S. embassy.

Although the radical clerics began the Third *Majles* with a clear majority, their influence soon ebbed because of Khomeini's death in June 1989 and because the new Supreme Leader Khamenei and President Rafsanjani began to adopt free-market policies as soon as the war with Iraq ended. During the war, both men had been vocal advocates of price controls, rationing, high taxes, nationalization, and large government budgets. Now, with the cease-fire, they argued that the only way to jump-start the economy was to encourage private enterprise and cut government expenditures.

Rafsanjani launched this new economic course for Iran in giving his eulogy for Khomeini. He downplayed Khomeini as the revolutionary leader of the downtrodden and oppressed and instead praised him as a world-famous statesman who had restored Iran's national sovereignty. He also praised him as a highly reputable scholar-theologian who had intellectually "awakened the moribund seminaries" from their "medieval graves."

In the following months, Rafsanjani, and to a lesser extent Khamenei, acknowledged that the revolution had been "guilty of excesses." They asked their followers to put away "childish slogans." They talked increasingly of realism, stability, efficiency, managerial skills, work discipline, expertise, individual self-reliance, modern technology, entrepreneurship, and business incentives. They warned that the worst mistake a state could make was to spend more than its revenue. Rafsanjani declared, "Some people claim that God will provide. They forget that God provides only for those willing to work." Khamenei sermonized on how Imam Ali, the founder of Shi'i Islam, had taken great pride in his plantations. Khomeini had often depicted Imam Ali as a humble water carrier; Khamenei now depicted him as an entrepreneurial plantation owner.

To ensure that the change of economic course would go smoothly, Khamenei handed over the two main newspapers, *Kayhan* and *Ettela'at,* to the conservative free marketers and authorized the Guardian Council to monitor the 1992 *Majles* elections. The Guardian Council announced that all candidates had to prove their "practical commitment to the Supreme Leader and the Islamic Republic." The Guardian Council further restricted the campaign to one week, permitting candidates to speak in mosques and run newspaper advertisements but not to debate each other in open forums. The head of the Guardian Council announced that he would use pesticides to cleanse parliament of anyone with "difficult attitudes." Seventy-five radical candidates withdrew. Forty were disqualified by the Guardian Council. Only a handful of radicals were allowed to be elected. Voter participation dropped to a new low. In Tehran, less than 55 percent of the eligible voters bothered to cast ballots despite Khamenei's pronouncement that it was the "religious obligation of everyone to participate."

Ayatollah Khalkhali, a vocal radical, was barred from running on the grounds that he did not have appropriate theological training. Yet the same Khalkhali had been considered qualified enough from 1978 to 1987 to sit as a high court judge dispatching hundreds of political prisoners to their deaths as enemies of the Islamic Republic. Khalkhali retorted that his candidacy had been rejected by conservatives who had sat out the revolution but were now weaseling their way into the Guardian Council. He warned that "true servants of the revolution," like himself, had been subjected to a political purge as a prelude to a future physical purge. Another disqualified candidate, who had earlier dismissed any talk of human rights as a "foreign conspiracy," now complained that the Guardian Council had grossly violated the UN Charter on Human Rights. It had failed to inform him of the charges brought against him, given him insufficient time to respond, and denied him the right to defend himself in a proper court of law.

The Guardian Council said, in turn, that its decisions had been kept out of the mass media in order to protect state secrets and the public reputations of those it had decided were unqualified to serve in the *Majles*. Those who had been purged were expected to be grateful for this sensitivity. It also argued that it had followed precedent, reminding the radicals that they themselves had used similar procedures to keep out "undesirables" from the previous three parliaments— undesirables such as the Mojahedin, the Fedayin, the Tudeh, the National Front, the Liberation Movement, and the "pseudo-clerics," who did not believe in jurist's guardianship.

The purge of the *Majles* was relatively easy to carry out. For one thing, the extensive constitutional powers entrusted to the Supreme Leader left the radicals vulnerable. As Hojjat al-Islam Mohtashami, a leading radical, complained, the institution of jurist's guardianship was now being used to clobber revolutionary heads. When radicals complained that they were being slandered as traitors for merely questioning the turn to free-market economic policies, their opponents countered that disobedience to the Supreme Leader was tantamount to disobedience to God. They argued that only proponents of "American Islam" would dare question the decisions of the Supreme Leader. They also reminded them that the new oath of office required parliamentary deputies to obey the Supreme Leader as "the Vice Regent of the Hidden Twelfth Imam." Khamenei may not have inherited Khomeini's title of imam, but he had obtained the new exalted position of the Hidden Imam's Spokesman.

The conservatives also effectively used populist rhetoric against the radicals. They described them as the "newly moneyed class" and as "Mercedes-Benz clerics." They accused them of misusing official positions to line their own pockets, open slush funds and secret foreign accounts, give lucrative contracts to their friends, sell contraband, and deceive the masses with unrealistic promises. "They," exclaimed one conservative, "act like a giant octopus, giving with one tentacle but taking away with the others." They also placed the responsibility for the country's economic malaise squarely on the shoulders of the radicals. They argued that a decade of statist policies had further increased poverty, illiteracy, inflation, unemployment, and slum housing. Before the revolution, these problems were blamed on the shah and his family. Now they were blamed on the "extremist pseudo-clerical radicals."

The purge was so decisive that the radicals suspended the activities of their Society of the Militant Clergy soon after the 1992 elections for the Fourth *Majles*. Some radicals went to head foundations and libraries. Some took up seminary positions. Others began to write for newspapers, occasionally arguing that the public should choose the Supreme Leader and that the Guardian Council should stay out of the whole electoral process. Yet others remained politically active, mildly criticizing the regime and quietly awaiting a better day.

This expectation was not far-fetched. The conservative majority in the Fourth *Majles* began to divide as soon as President Rafsanjani implemented a series of probusiness reforms. He relaxed price controls, liberalized imports, trimmed the ration list, disbanded courts that penalized price gougers, returned some confiscated property, and ended all talk of further nationalization, land reform, and income distribution. He also set up a stock exchange in Tehran and free-trade zones in the Persian Gulf. One bloc of deputies, associated with Supreme Leader Khamenei and the newspaper *Resalat,* supported these measures but also favored highly conservative cultural policies. They advocated strict control over the media, the silencing of liberal intellectuals, and the rigid implementation of the dress code for women. They were also reluctant to challenge the financial privileges of the large foundations or open up the economy to international and émigré capital; foreign competition was seen as a threat to the bazaar economy. These conservatives could muster some 170 votes in the *Majles*. Meanwhile, another bloc, also advocating laissez-faire policies but associated more with President Rafsanjani, favored foreign capital and greater cultural liberalization. They also favored balancing the budget by downsizing the large clerical foundations and cutting state subsidies. This bloc could muster some forty votes. The remaining sixty deputies were independent, voting sometimes with the majority and other times with the minority.

To get a working majority in the *Majles,* Rafsanjani had to water down his programs. He had to remove his own brother from the directorship of the national radio-television network. He could take only limited measures to privatize large enterprises, trim the foreign exchange privileges of the huge clerical foundations, and cut subsidies that absorbed much of the oil revenue. Moreover, he was unable to increase business taxes: all the taxes raised by the bazaar guilds together still constituted less than 9 percent of the government's annual tax income. Moreover, he had to shelve his daring bill designed to attract foreign investment. This bill would have raised the share that foreign interests could own in Iranian enterprises from 49 percent to 100 percent. It would have been a total policy reversal, since the Islamic revolutionaries had relished accusing the shah of selling the country to foreign capitalists. Rafsanjani now argued that he could not revive the ailing economy without an injection of massive foreign capital. The bill, however, met stiff resistance and failed to pass into law during Rafsanjani's terms as president.

Frustrated by these setbacks, Rafsanjani created a new political organization, the Servants of Reconstruction, to win control of the Fifth *Majles* that was to be elected in 1996. Although supported by many cabinet ministers and the popular mayor of Tehran who had made the capital more livable by building highways, libraries, and parks, this party won only 80 seats. Over 140 seats went to the conservatives endorsed by the Chamber of Commerce, the Association of the Militant Clergy, and the Teachers of Qum Seminaries. Some radical reformers even voted for the Servants of Reconstruction; most stayed away from the polls. The Fifth *Majles* turned out to be a continuation of the gridlocked Fourth *Majles.* The conservatives prevented liberalization—in either the economy or the media. Meanwhile, the Judiciary imprisoned the mayor of Tehran on trumped-up "embezzlement" charges and closed down the newspaper, *Zanan (Women),* which

was edited by Rafsanjani's daughter, on the grounds that it had offended religious susceptibilities. Rafsanjani's position was further weakened by term limits since the constitution stipulated that presidents could serve no more than two terms. This, together with Khatami's upset victory in the 1997 presidential election, opened the way for the Sixth *Majles* elections in 2000, the first to be both orderly and competitive since the founding of the Islamic Republic in 1979.

The Sixth Majles (2000)

The reformers—labeling themselves the Khordad Front after the month (in the Islamic calendar) when Khatami had won his first presidential election in 1997—ran a highly successful campaign in 2000. The Khordad Front brought together the Islamic Iran Participation Front (headed by Khatami's brother; the Society of Militant Clergy; the Islamic Labor Party and the Workers House, a quasi-union; the Servants of Reconstruction, at least, initially; and the Mojahedin Organization of the Islamic Revolution); a twenty-year-old group of radical technocrats and intellectuals not to be confused with the antiregime guerrilla Mojahedin; a new university campus organization called the Office for Strengthening Solidarity; and a host of Islamic associations, including the Islamic Association of Women. These associations had previously supported the regime but had recently spoken out in favor of a free press, government accountability, and fewer privileges for the clergy. Their views were articulated by a number of prominent intellectuals and journalists who had started their careers as staunch regime supporters—even as student occupants of the U.S. embassy in 1979–1980—but who had come to the conclusion that the democratic features of the constitution should take priority over the theocratic ones.

The best known of these reformist intellectuals was Abdol-Karim Soroush. Soroush had begun his political career as a militant supporter of Ali Shariati, the radical intellectual who had developed a revolutionary interpretation of Shi'ism that had greatly influenced Khomeini. But he now argued that Islam had become an overbloated ideology and should be limited to private ethics and individual morality. He and his fellow reformers often denounced intolerant conservatives as "religious fascists." If the works of Shariati and

Khomeini had been replete with such terms as *revolution, imperialism, cultural roots, martyrdom, the dispossessed,* and the *Western plague,* those of Soroush and the new reformers were full of concepts such as civil society, pluralism, democracy, freedom, equality, modernity, citizenship, dialogue, human rights, rule of law, and political participation. These new reformers not only championed liberal concepts but also tried to make them compatible with Islam.

These reformers took the Sixth *Majles* elections in 2000 in a landslide, winning 80 percent of the vote in a campaign that drew over 70 percent of the electorate. In elections held for the Assembly of Experts a few months earlier, the reformers had abstained, and consequently voter participation had dropped to 46 percent. Over 6,800 candidates competed for the 290 seats in the Sixth *Majles.* Although the Guardian Council axed some prominent reformers from the list of those allowed to run in the election, it permitted most of them to participate, probably because of pressure from the Supreme Leader Khamenei. The reformers won over 195 seats. Former president Rafsanjani, who in the last days had openly courted the conservatives, was humiliated in his bid to be elected to the *Majles.* He came in thirtieth in the first round of the Tehran election and quietly withdrew instead of continuing in the runoffs. Many supporters of secular parties, all banned from the campaign, voted for the reformers as a better alternative to the die-hard conservatives. Conservative candidates endorsed by the Association of Militant Clergy, Teachers of Qum Seminaries, and the bazaar Coalition of Islamic Societies won fewer than forty seats. The total number of "turbaned deputies" (clerics) fell to a new low of thirty-seven. Khatami's brother, who had created the Islamic Iran Participation Party, topped the winners in Tehran. Many prominent conservatives with long experience in high positions failed to get elected even in provincial constituencies. Even Qom, the country's religious capital, voted overwhelmingly for the reformers. After the elections, the London *Economist* magazine commented: "Iran, although an Islamic state, imbued with religion and religious symbolism, is an increasingly anti-clerical country. In a sense, Iran resembles some Roman Catholic countries where religion is taken for granted, without public display, and with ambiguous feeling towards the clergy. Iranians tend to mock their mullahs, making mild little jokes about them; they certainly want them out of their bedrooms. In particular, they dislike their political clergy."[28]

Political Culture, Citizenship, and Identity

In theory, the Islamic Republic should be a highly viable state. After all, Shi'ism is the religion of both the state and the vast majority of the population. It can also be described as the central component of popular culture. Moreover, the constitution guarantees basic rights to religious minorities as well as to individual citizens. All citizens, regardless of race, color, language, or religion, are promised the rights of free expression, worship, and organization. They are guaranteed freedom from arbitrary arrest, torture, and police surveillance. In short, the constitution incorporates the modern concepts of individual rights and civil society.

The constitution gives further guarantees to the recognized religious minorities: the Christian, Jews, and Zoroastrians. Although Christians (Armenians and Assyrians), Jews, and Zoroastrians form just 1 percent of the total population, they are allocated five *Majles* seats. They are permitted their own places of worship, their own community organizations, including schools, and their own marriage, divorce, and inheritance laws. The constitution, however, is ominously silent concerning Baha'is and Sunnis. The former are deemed defectors from Islam; the latter are treated as equal in theory to the Shi'is, but their status is not spelled out.

The constitution also gives guarantees to non-Persian speakers. Although 83 percent of the population understands Persian, thanks to the educational system, over 50 percent continue to speak non-Persian languages at home—languages such as Azeri, Kurdish, Turkic, Gilaki, Mazandarani, Arabic, and Baluchi. The constitution promises them rights unprecedented in Iranian history. It states that "local and native languages can be used in the press, media, and schools." It also states that local populations have the right to elect provincial, town, and village councils. These councils can watch over the governors-general and the town mayors, as well as their educational, cultural, and social programs.

These generous promises have often been honored more in theory than in fact. The local councils—the chief institutional safeguard for the provincial minorities—were not convened until twenty years after the revolution. Subsidies to non-Persian publications and radio stations remain meager. Jews have been so harassed as "pro-Israeli Zionists" that more than half—40,000 out of 80,000—have left the country. Armenian Christians had to accept Muslim principals in their schools. They also had to end coeducational classes, adopt the government curriculum, abide by Muslim dress codes, including the veil, and close their community clubs to Muslims. The Christian population has declined from over 300,000 to fewer than 200,000.

The Baha'is, however, have borne the brunt of religious persecution. Their leaders have been executed as "apostates" and "imperialist spies." Adherents have been fired from their jobs, had their property confiscated, and been imprisoned and tortured to pressure them to convert to Islam. Their schools have been closed, their community property expropriated, and their shrines and cemeteries bulldozed. It is estimated that since the revolution, one-third of the 300,000 Baha'is have left Iran. The Baha'is, like the Jews and Armenians, have migrated mostly to Canada and the United States, especially New York and California. This persecution did not ease until the election of President Khatami.

The much larger Sunni Muslim population, which forms as much as 10 percent of the total, has its own reasons for being alienated from the regime. The state religion is Shi'ism. High officials have to be Shi'i. Citizens have to subscribe to Khomeini's concept of government, a notion derived from Shi'ism. Few institutions cater to Sunni needs. There is not a single Sunni mosque in the whole of Tehran. The regime also tends to overlook the existence of Sunnis among Iran's Kurds, Turkmens, Arabs, and Baluchis. It is no accident that in the period 1979 through 1981, the newborn regime faced its most serious challenges in precisely the areas of the country where these people live. It succeeded in crushing the revolts by rushing in tens of thousands of Revolutionary Guards from the Persian Shi'i heartland of Isfahan, Shiraz, and Qom to the Sunni regions.

Thus, the Islamic Republic has its strongest cultural roots in the Persian Shi'i heartland. Its weakest roots are among the non-Shi'is: the Sunnis, Baha'is, Jews, Christians, and Zoroastrians. Its base among the Azeris, who are Shi'i but not Persian speakers, remains to be tested. In the past, the Azeris, who form 24 percent of the population and dwarf the other minorities, have not posed an ethnic problem. They are part and parcel of the Shi'i community. They have prominent figures, such as President Khamenei, in the Shi'i hierarchy. Many Azeri merchants, professionals, and workers live throughout the regions of Iran.

In short, Azeris can be considered well integrated into Iran. But the 1991 creation of the Republic of Azerbaijan on Iran's northeastern border following the disintegration of the Soviet Union has raised new concerns, since some Azeris on both sides of the border have begun to talk of establishing a larger unified Azerbaijan. It is no accident that in the war between Azerbaijan and Armenia in the early 1990s, Iran favored the latter. So far, the concept of a unified Azerbaijan has little appeal among Iranian Azeris. The recent elections show that the Sunni and Azeri populations remain politically integrated into Iran and that they place much of their hopes in Khatami and his reform movement.

Interests, Social Movements, and Protests

In the first two decades after its founding, the Islamic Republic often violated its own constitution. It closed down newspapers, professional associations, labor unions, and political parties. It banned demonstrations and public meetings. It incarcered tens of thousands without due process. It systematically tortured prisoners to extract false confessions and public recantations. And it executed some 25,000 political prisoners, most of them without due process of law. The United Nations, Amnesty International, and Human Rights Watch all took Iran to task for violating the UN Human Rights Charter as well its own Islamic constitution. Most victims were Kurds, military officers from the old regime, and leftists, especially members of the Mojahedin and Fedayin. Iran's Islamic Revolution, like many other revolutions in history, devoured its own children.

Although the violation of individual liberties affected the whole population, it aroused special resentment among three social groups: the modern middle class, educated women, and organized labor. The modern middle class, especially the intelligentsia, has been secular and even anticlerical ever since the 1905 revolution. Little love is lost between it and the Islamic Republic. Not surprisingly, the vast majority of those executed in the 1980s were teachers, engineers, professionals, and college students. In 1999, eighteen different campuses throughout the country, including Tehran University, erupted into mass demonstrations against the chief judge, who had closed down a reformist newspaper. Revolutionary Guards promptly occupied the campuses, killing and seriously injuring an unknown number of students. And again in late 2002, thousands of students protested the death sentence handed down by the courts to a reformist academic who was accused of insulting Islam.

Every year university students show their strength by commemorating December 7, the day in 1953 when three student demonstrators were shot dead by the shah's army. Youth and college students are now political forces to be reckoned with in Iran: over half the population was born after the 1979 revolution; and in 1997 there were more than 1.15 million students in higher education.

Educated women in Iran also harbor numerous grievances against the conservative clerics in the regime, especially in the judiciary. Although the Western press often dwells on the veil, Iranian women consider the veil one of their less important problems. Given a choice, most would probably continue to wear it out of personal habit and national tradition. More important are work-related grievances: job security, pay scales, promotions, maternity leave, and access to prestigious professions. Furthermore, judges often interpret the *shari'a* in a narrow fashion, treating women as second-class citizens, especially in marriage disputes, child custody disputes, and even criminal cases. They consider women to be wards of male relatives. Adult women are not allowed to travel without written permission from their male relatives. The conservatives also favor social policies to encourage women to stay home raising children rather than enter the university and the professions. Despite these patriarchal attitudes, educated women have become a major factor in Iranian society. They now form 54 percent of college students, 45 percent of doctors, 25 percent of government employees, and 13 percent of the general labor force, up from 8 percent in the 1980s. They have established their own organizations and journals reinterpreting Islam to conform with modern notions of

equality. One grand ayatollah has even argued that women should be able to hold any job, including president, Supreme Leader, and court judge, a position from which they have been barred since 1979. He also said they should have the right to abort fetuses in the first trimester; that compensation to a family for the loss of life of a relative, known as blood money, should be the same for men and women; and that wives should have the same rights as husbands in divorce cases.

Factory workers in Iran are another significant social group with serious grievances. Their concerns deal mostly with high unemployment, low wages, declining incomes, lack of decent housing, and an unsatisfactory labor law, which, while giving them mandatory holidays and some semblance of job security, denies them the right to call strikes and organize independent unions. Since 1979, wage earners have had a Workers' House—a government-influenced organization—and its affiliated newspaper, *Kar va Kargar* (*Work and Worker*), and, since 1999, the Islamic Labor Party to represent their interests. In most years, the Workers' House flexes political muscle by holding a May Day rally. In 1999, the rally began peacefully with a greeting from a woman reform deputy who had received the second-most votes in the 1996 Tehran municipal elections. But the rally turned into a protest when workers began to march to parliament denouncing conservatives who had spoken in favor of further watering down of the Labor Law. Bus drivers spontaneously joined the protest, shutting down most of central Tehran.

President Khatami's reform movement draws much of its core support precisely from these three social groups: college youth, women, and workers. In the 1997 and 2001, presidential campaigns, as well as in the elections for municipal councils and the Sixth *Majles,* crucial roles were played by the Islamic Student Associations, the Office of Student Solidarity, the Islamic Women's Association, and the Workers' House. The reformers were also supported by a number of newspapers, which have quickly gained a mass circulation even though they initially catered mainly to the intelligentsia. For example, the reformist *Hayat-e No,* launched in late 2000, had a circulation of over 235,000 by April 2001, almost double that of the long-established conservative newspaper *Ettela'at.*

Section ⑤ Iranian Politics in Transition

Political Challenges and Changing Agendas

As of 2002, President Khatami and his reform movement dominate both the executive and the legislative branches of Iran's government and continue to enjoy overwhelming support among the general electorate. But the conservative opposition still controls the judiciary and receives substantial support from the powerful religious foundations, Revolutionary Guards, and intelligence services. In political terms, this amounts to ongoing clash between reformers and conservatives. In institutional terms, it is a clash between the executive and the legislature against the judiciary. In ideological terms, it is a clash between democracy and theocracy. At times, the conflict is open, vociferous, and even violent. At other times, it is hidden, managed, and kept behind the scene. But it is ever present and underscores nearly everything that happens in Iran's politics. Khatami hopes to keep the conflict out of the streets and convince Supreme Leader Khamenei that alienating the general public would be fatal for the Islamic Republic, and he has tried to persuade Khamenei to nudge the die-hard conservatives to accept needed reforms.

Khatami has managed to score some successes. He placed reformers in charge of most cabinet posts. The Interior Ministry first went to Hojjat al-Islam Abdullah Nouri, an innovative interpreter of Islam. The Labor Ministry portfolio was given to the head of the Workers' House. Khatami also removed the previous intelligence minister and chief judge, and although he was unable to replace them with his own supporters, he managed to give these vital positions to less conservative clerics. He eased out military officers who had initiated the campus bloodshed, a general who had talked of cutting out the tongues of liberals, and a prison warden notorious for his cruelty. The new Intelligence minister brought to account officials responsible for a series of high-profile political assassinations, claiming that they had been out-of-control rogues; their leader conveniently "committed suicide" in prison. The culture minister issued some 200 newspaper licenses, relaxed censorship, which boosted both publishing and the film industry, and, in an act of great symbolic significance, made Mossadeq's home into a national heritage monument. The Justice minister named women judges to family courts for the first time since 1979. The Revolutionary Guards lost their autonomy and were merged into the Ministry of Defense. Moreover, the Revolutionary Guards and the Hezbollahi vigilantes

President Khatemi of Iran. *Source:* Angel Franco, *The New York Times,* November 10, 2001.

were instructed not to harass the public over dress codes, hair styles, videos, music cassettes, Internet cafés, and satellite dishes.

Meanwhile, reform deputies in the *Majles* have drafted a number of controversial bills. They proposed raising the legal marriage age for girls from nine to fifteen; giving women equal rights in divorce, and even the right to separate from husbands; and allowing girls to study in foreign universities. They tried to combat AIDS with safer-sex education, condom distribution, and even legalized prostitution. They favored ratifying the UN Declaration on All Forms of Discrimination Against Women. They drafted an investment law to attract foreign capital, a judicial law stipulating courts to have juries, and another one reiterating the constitutional ban on torture. They tried to get the Guardian Council to render its decisions in writing and to pass on its authority to vet parliamentary candidates to the Interior Ministry. Khatami warned of the dangers of "religious fascism" in Iran and openly argued that the long-term survival of the Islamic Republic would remain in doubt unless needed reforms were accepted. He even hinted that he would appeal directly to the public to obtain new constitutional powers. "We cannot speak of democracy if we are not ready to play by its rules," he declared. "The main feature of democracy is the right of people to change a government if they do not like it."[29]

The conservatives have fought back. The Guardian Council initially vetoed the new bills, but the Expediency Council, probably pushed by the Supreme Leader, eventually accepted some of them in watered-down versions. For example, the investment law was accepted. The marriage age was raised to thirteen, and divorced women were guaranteed a portion of their ex-husband's income. The Revolutionary Courts and the Special Court for the Clergy also waged a concerted campaign to silence the reformers. Over sixty newspapers, including the most popular ones, were banned for publishing supposedly antiregime materials in what became known as the "newspaper massacre." And a long array of prominent reformers and Khatami advisers, headed by Nouri, were accused by the courts of questioning the concept of jurist's guardianship and thus undermining not only the Islamic Republic but also Islam. In other words, they were accused of apostasy, blasphemy, and heresy. These measures,

however, were less dramatic than they sound. New newspapers replaced those that were closed down. The show trials boomeranged against the conservatives since the accused reformers were able to turn them into arenas for propagating their popular views. The reformers even equated the courts that were trying them to the Spanish Inquisition in medieval Europe. What is more, most of the defendants, after being charged with capital offenses, were given prison sentences and then, after relatively short intervals, were released through amnesties and appeals to the Supreme Leader.

The conflict between the reformers and conservatives has complicated Iran's foreign policy. Difference in foreign policy, which had existed from the early days of Khatami's administration, became stark in the aftermath of the September 11, 2001, terrorist attacks on the United States. Khatami promptly extended condolences to the American people, and his supporters held well-publicized candlelight vigils in Tehran. His foreign minister received his British counterpart in Tehran, promised help in the "war on terrorism," offered military assistance to American soldiers in Afghanistan, stepped up supplies to the Northern Alliance fighting the Taliban, and, once that regime was overthrown, extended financial and diplomatic aid to the pro-American administration in Kabul.

Supreme Leader Khamenei, however, continued to denounce Washington, implied that America had brought September 11 upon itself, and forbade any public debate about improving relations with the United States. His intransigence was ironically helped when U.S. President George W. Bush, in his January 2002 State of the Union address, lumped Iran together with Iraq and North Korea in an alleged "axis of evil" that supported terrorism and threatened world peace. President Khatami, however, while keeping his distance from the United States, has continued to improve relations with the rest of the world, especially with European and Arab countries. He paid state visits to Moscow, Rome, Tokyo, and Paris, where he laid wreaths at the Pantheon for French cultural icons Jean-Jacques Rousseau, Emile Zola, and Victor Hugo. He also signed contracts with European oil companies, attracted considerable foreign investment to Iran, and required foreign companies to pay for oil in euros rather than U.S. dollars.

Iranian Politics in Comparative Perspective

Iran is both like and unlike other developing countries. It is unlike most Third World countries in that it is an old state with institutions that go back to ancient times. It is also not a country that only relatively recently achieved independence since it was never formally colonized by the European imperial powers. Unlike many other developing nations that have a weak connection between state and society, Iran has a religion that links the elite with the masses, the cities with the villages, the government with the citizenry. Shi'ism, as well as Iranian national identity, serves as a social cement, giving the population a strong collective identity. Iran possesses rich oil resources that give it the potential for rapid economic growth that would be the envy of most developing countries. Finally, Iran produced two popular upheavals in the twentieth century: the constitutional (1905) and the Islamic (1979) revolutions in which the citizenry actively intervened in politics, overthrew the old regime, and shaped the new. Both of these revolutions were the result of authentic home-grown political movements, not foreign imports.

Yet Iran shares some problems with other Third World countries. It has failed to establish a full-fledged democracy. Its economy remains underdeveloped, highly dependent on one commodity, and unable to meet the rising expectations of its population. Iran's collective identity is strained by internal fault lines, especially those of class, ethnicity, and interclerical conflicts. And its ambition to enter the world of states as an important player has been thwarted by international as well as domestic and regional realities that have combined to keep the country pretty much on the global sidelines. This thwarted ambition has helped to undermine democracy and economic development in Iran.

Democracy has been constricted by theocracy. Some argue that Islam made this inevitable. But Islam, like Christianity and the other major religions, can be interpreted in ways that either support or oppose democracy. Islam, as interpreted by some Muslims, stresses the importance of justice, equality, and consultation. It has a tradition of tolerating other religions. Its *shari'a* explicitly protects life, property,

and honor. In practice, it has often separated politics from religion, statutes from holy laws, spiritual affairs from worldly matters, and the state from the clerical establishment.

Moreover, the theocracy in Iran originates not in Islam but in jurist's guardianship, a concept developed by Khomeini. On the whole, Sunni Islam considers clerics to be theological scholars, not a special political stratum. This helps explain why the Iranian regime has found it difficult to export the revolution to the rest of the Muslim world. The failure of democracy in Iran should be attributed less to Islam than to the confluence of crises between 1979 and 1981 that allowed a group of clerics to seize power. Whether they remain in power into the twenty-first century depends not so much on Islam but on how they handle the opposition, their own differences, and, most important, the country's economic problems.

The Islamic Republic of Iran is sharply divided over how to manage an economy beset by rising demands, wildly fluctuating petroleum revenues, and the nightmarish prospect that in the next two generations, the oil wells will run dry. Most clerics favor a rather conventional capitalist road to development, hoping to liberalize the market, privatize industry, attract foreign capital, and encourage the propertied classes to invest. Others envisage an equally conventional statist road to development, favoring central planning, government industries, price controls, high taxes, state subsidies, national self-reliance, and ambitious programs to eliminate poverty, illiteracy, slums, and unemployment. Khatami has charted a third road, combining elements of state intervention with free enterprise. This is strikingly similar to the social democracy favored in other parts of the world.

As the clock of history ticks, Iran's population grows, oil revenues fluctuate, and the per capita national income threatens to fall. Economic problems like those that undermined the monarchy could well undermine the Islamic Republic. The country's collective identity has also come under great strain in recent years. The emphasis on Shi'ism has antagonized Iran's Sunnis as well as its non-Muslim citizens. The emphasis on clerical Shi'ism has further alienated all secularists, including lay liberals, radical leftists, and moderate nationalists. Furthermore, the emphasis on Khomeini's brand of Shi'ism has alienated Shi'is who reject the whole notion of jurist's guardianship. The elevation of Khamenei as the Supreme Leader has also antagonized many early proponents of jurist's guardianship.

In sum, the regime has gradually reduced its social base of support to a bare minimum. Only time will tell whether the growing discontent in Iran will be expressed through apolitical channels, such as drug addiction, emigration, and quietist religion, or whether those seeking change will look to reformist movements such as that led by President Khatami and the reformist clerics remaining within the regime, or turn to more radical insurrectionary organizations or ethnic-based movements.

Finally, the Islamic Republic's initial attempt to enter the international arena as a militant force proved to be counterproductive. It has diverted scarce resources to the military, especially the Revolutionary Guards. It frightened Saudi Arabia and the Gulf sheikdoms into the arms of the United States. It has prompted the United States to isolate Iran, discouraging investment and preventing international organizations from extending economic assistance. It also alarmed neighboring secular Islamic states such as Turkey, Tadzhikistan, and Azerbaijan. In recent years, President Khatami has managed to overcome many of these problems. He has won over Iran's Arab neighbors and has established cordial relations with Turkey and Afghanistan. Most important, he has managed to repair bridges between Iran and the European Community. Whether he can do the same with the United States is an open question that will be answered by decision makers in Tehran and Washington.

Key Terms

ayatollah	*shari'a*
fatwa	bazaars
theocracy	fundamentalism
Majles	jurist's guardianship
Guardian Council	mosques
Supreme Leader	*pasdaran*
Farsi	imam
Shi'ism	Hezbollahis
People of the Book	hojjat al-Islam
Qur'an	*jihad*

rentier state	Foundation of the Oppressed
dual society	
Organization of Petroleum Exporting Countries	Assembly of Experts
	maslahat
Imam Jum'ehs	Expediency Council

Suggested Readings

Abrahamian, E. *Iran Between Two Revolutions.* Princeton, N.J.: Princeton University Press, 1982.

———. *Khomeinism.* Berkeley: University of California Press, 1993.

Akhavi, S. *Religion and Politics in Contemporary Iran.* Albany: State University of New York Press, 1980.

Bakhash, S. *Reign of the Ayatollahs.* New York: Basic Books, 1984.

Baktiari, B. *Parliamentary Politics in Revolutionary Iran.* Gainesville: University Press of Florida, 1966.

Bill, J. *The Eagle and the Lion.* New Haven, Conn.: Yale University Press, 1988.

Buchta, W. *Who Rules Iran?* Washington, D.C.: Washington Institute for Near East Policy, 2000.

Chehabi, H. *Iranian Politics and Religious Modernism.* Ithaca, N.Y.: Cornell University Press, 1990.

Dabashi, H. *Theology of Discontent: The Ideological Foundation of the Islamic Revolution in Iran.* New York: New York University Press, 1993.

Fischer, M. *Iran: From Religious Dispute to Revolution.* Cambridge, Mass.: Harvard University Press, 1980.

Halliday, F. *Iran: Dictatorship and Development.* London: Penguin, 1979.

Hooglund, E. *Twenty Years of Islamic Revolution.* Syracuse: Syracuse University Press, 2002.

Huntington, Samuel P. *The Clash of Civilizations and the Remaking of the World Order.* New York: Simon & Schuster, 1996.

Kazemi, F. "Civil Society and Iranian Politics." In A. Norton (ed.), *Civil Society in the Middle East.* Leiden: Brill, 1996.

Keddie, N. *Roots of Revolution.* New Haven, Conn.: Yale University Press, 1981.

Mackey, S. *The Iranians: Persia, Islam, and the Soul of a Nation.* New York: Penguin, 1996.

Milani, M. *The Making of Iran's Islamic Revolution.* Boulder, Colo.: Westview Press, 1994.

Mir-Hosseini, Z. *Islam and Gender.* Princeton, N.J.: Princeton University Press, 1999.

Moin, B. *Khomeini: Life of the Ayatollah.* London: Tauris, 1999.

Mottahedeh, R. *The Mantle of the Prophet.* New York: Simon & Schuster, 1985.

Schirazi, A. *The Constitution of Iran.* London: Tauris, 1997.

Suggested Websites

British Broadcasting Corporation
www.bbc.co.uk/persian/revolution

Guide to Iranian media, including English-language sources
www.gooya.org
Iranian Mission to the United Nations
www.un.int/iran.org
Radio Free Europe
www.iranreport@list.rferl.org
Weekly Digest of News
www.times@iranian.com

Notes

[1]Quoted in E. Browne, *The Persian Revolution* (New York: Barnes and Noble, 1966), 137.

[2]British Financial Adviser to the Foreign Office in Tehran, *Documents on British Foreign Policy, 1919–39* (London: Her Majesty's Stationery Office, 1963), First Series, XIII, 720, 735.

[3]British Minister to the Foreign Office, *Report on the Seizure of Lands,* Foreign Office 371/Persia 1932/File 34-16007.

[4]*Kayhan International,* November 10, 1976.

[5]"Fifty Indictments of Treason During Fifty Years of Treason," *Khabarnameh,* no. 46 (April 1976).

[6]M. Bazargan, "Letter to the Editor," *Ettela'at,* February 7, 1980.

[7]*Iran Times,* January 12, 1979.

[8]*Washington Post,* December 12, 1978.

[9]*Christian Science Monitor,* December 12, 1978.

[10]Samuel P. Huntington, *The Clash of Civilizations and the Remaking of World Order* (New York: Simon & Schuster, 1996).

[11]Mirza Hosayn Khan Tahvildar-e Isfahan, *Jukhrafiha-ye Isfahan* (The Geography of Isfahan) (Tehran: Tehran University Press, 1963), 100–101.

[12]International Labor Organization, "Employment and Income Policies for Iran" (Unpublished report, Geneva, 1972), Appendix C, 6.

[13]A. Sharbatoghilie, *Urbanization and Regional Disparity in Post-Revolutionary Iran* (Boulder, Colo.: Westview Press, 1991), 4.

[14]*Wall Street Journal,* November 4, 1977.

[15]U.S. Congress, *Economic Consequences of the Revolution in Iran* (Washington, D.C.: U.S. Government Printing Office, 1979), 184.

[16]U.S. Congress, *Economic Consequences of the Revolution in Iran,* 5.

[17]U.S. Department of Commerce, *Iran: A Survey of U.S. Business Opportunities* (Washington, D.C.: U.S. Government Printing Office, 1977), 1–2.

[18]Cited in H. Amirahmadi, *Revolution and Economic Transition* (Albany: State University of New York Press, 1960), p. 201.

[19]Cited in *Iran Times,* July 9, 1993.

[20]J. Amuzegar, *Iran's Economy Under the Islamic Republic* (London: Taurus Press, 1994), 100.

[21]A. Rafsanjani, "The Islamic Consultative Assembly," *Kayhan,* May 23, 1987.

[22]S. Saffari, "The Legitimation of the Clergy's Right to Rule in the Iranian Constitution of 1979," *British Journal of Middle Eastern Studies* 20, no. 1 (1993): 64–81.

[23]Ayatollah Montazeri, *Ettela'at,* October 8, 1979.

[24]O. Fallaci, "Interview with Khomeini," *New York Times Magazine,* October 7, 1979.

[25]*Kayhan,* March 6, 1980.

[26]*Kayhan,* April 21, 1987.

[27]*Kayhan-e Hava'i,* November 16, 1988.

[28]*Economist,* February 9, 2000.

[29]*New York Times,* August 27, 2002.

Glossary

abertura (Portugese for "opening"; *apertura* in Spanish) in Brazil, refers to the period of authoritarian liberalization begun in 1974 when the military allowed civilian politicians to contest for political office in the context of a more open political society.

accommodation an informal agreement or settlement between the government and important interest groups that is responsive to the interest groups' concerns for policy or program benefits.

accountability a government's responsibility to its population, usually by periodic popular elections and by parliament's having the power to dismiss the government by passing a motion of no confidence. In a political system characterized by accountability, the major actions taken by government must be known and understood by the citizenry.

acephalous societies literally "headless" societies. A number of traditional Nigerian societies, such as the Igbo in the precolonial period, lacked executive rulership as we have come to conceive of it. Instead, the villages and clans were governed by committee or consensus.

Amerindian original peoples of North and South America; indigenous people.

anticlericalism opposition to the power of churches or clergy in politics. In some countries, for example, France and Mexico, this opposition has focused on the role of the Catholic Church in politics.

Assembly of Experts nominates the **Supreme Leader** and can replace him. The assembly is elected by the general electorate but almost all its members are clerics.

authoritarian See **authoritarianism.**

authoritarianism a system of rule in which power depends not on popular legitimacy but on the coercive force of the political authorities. Hence, there are few personal and group freedoms. It is also characterized by near absolute power in the executive branch and few, if any, legislative and judicial controls. See also **autocracy; patrimonialism.**

autocracy a government in which one or a few rulers has absolute power, thus, a **dictatorship**. Similar to authoritarianism.

autonomous region in the People's Republic of China, a territorial unit equivalent to a province that contains a large concentration of ethnic minorities. These regions have some autonomy in the cultural sphere but in most policy matters are strictly subordinate to the central government.

ayatollah literally, "sign of God." High-ranking clerics in Iran. The most senior ones—often no more than half a dozen—are known as grand ayatollahs.

balance of payments an indicator of international flow of funds that shows the excess or deficit in total payments of all kinds between or among countries. Included in the calculation are exports and imports, grants, and international debt payments.

bazaars an urban marketplace where shops, workshops, small businessmen, and even export-importers are located.

Brahmin highest caste in the Hindu caste system.

bureaucracy an organization structured hierarchically, in which lower-officials are charged with administering regulations codified in rules that specify impersonal, objective guidelines for making decisions. In the modern world, many large organizations, especially business firms and the executives of developed states, are organized along bureaucratic lines.

bureaucratic-authoritarianism a term developed by Argentine sociologist Guillermo O'Donnell to interpret the common characteristics of military-led authoritarian regimes in Brazil, Argentina, Chile, and Uruguay in the 1960s and 1970s. According to O'Donnell, bureaucratic authoritarian regimes led by the armed forces and key civilian allies emerged in these countries in response to severe economic crises.

bureaucratic rings a term developed by the Brazilian sociologist and president Fernando Henrique Cardoso that refers to the highly permeable and fragmented structure of the state bureaucracy that allows private interests to make alliances with midlevel bureaucratic officers. By shaping public policy to benefit these interests, bureaucrats gain the promise of future employment in the private sector. While in positions of responsibility, bureaucratic rings are ardent defenders of their own interests.

cabinet the ministers who direct executive departments. In parliamentary systems, the cabinet and high-ranking sub-cabinet ministers (also known as the government) are considered collectively responsible to parliament.

cadre a person who occupies a position of authority in a **communist party-state;** cadres may or may not be Communist Party members.

caste system India's Hindu society is divided into castes. According to the Hindu religion, membership in a caste is determined at birth. Castes form a rough social and economic hierarchy. See also **Brahmin; untouchables.**

charisma the ability of a leader to attract an intensely devoted following because of his personal characteristics that supporters believe endows the charismatic leader with extraordinary and heroic qualities.

child mortality rate probability that a child will die before the age of 5 in the year(s) indicated. This is expressed as a rate per 1000 live births.

civil society refers to the space occupied by voluntary associations outside the state, for example, professional associations (lawyers, doctors, teachers), trade unions, student and women's groups, religious bodies, and other voluntary association groups. The term is similar to *society,* although *civil society* implies a degree of organization absent from the more inclusive term *society.*

clientelism (or patron-client networks) an informal aspect of policy-making in which a powerful patron (for example, a traditional local boss, government agency, or dominant party) offers resources such as land, contracts, protection, or jobs in return for the support and services (such as labor or votes) of lower-status and less powerful clients; corruption, preferential treatment, and inequality are characteristic of clientelist politics. See also **patrimonialism; prebendalism.**

cold war the term designates the hostile relations that prevailed between the United States and the USSR from the late 1940s until the demise of the Soviet Union in 1991. Although an actual (hot) war never directly occurred between the two superpowers, they clashed indirectly by supporting rival forces in many wars occurring in the Third World.

collectivization a process undertaken in the Soviet Union under Stalin in the late 1920s and early 1930s and in China under Mao in the 1950s, by which agricultural land was removed from private ownership and organized into large state and collective farms.

command economy a form of **socialism** in which government decisions ("commands") rather than market mechanisms (such as supply and demand) are the major influences in determining the nation's economic direction; also called central planning.

communism a system of social organization based on the common ownership and coordination of production. According to Marxism (the theory of German philosopher Karl Marx, 1818–1883), communism is a culminating stage of history, following capitalism and **socialism.** In historical practice, leaders of China, the Soviet Union, and other states that have proclaimed themselves seeking to achieve communism have ruled through a single party, the Communist Party, which has controlled the state and society in an authoritarian manner, and have applied **Marxism-Leninism** to justify their rule.

communist party-state a type of nation-state in which the Communist Party attempts to exercise a complete monopoly on political power and controls all important state institutions. See also **communism.**

comparative politics the study of the domestic politics, political institutions, and conflicts of countries. Often involves comparisons among countries and through time within single countries, emphasizing key patterns of similarity and difference.

comparativists political scientists who study the similarities and differences in the domestic politics of various countries (see **comparative politics**).

co-optation incorporating activists into the system while accommodating some of their concerns.

corporatism a pattern of organizing interests and influencing public policy in which the state gives favored status to certain interest groups; typically involves tripartite (three-way) consultations among representatives of business, labor, and government over economic policy. Corporatism can occur in democratic and **authoritarian** settings. However, it is usually criticized because it limits open debate and representative processes. See also **corporatist state; and state corporatism.**

corporatist state a state in which interest groups become an institutionalized part of the structure. See also **corporatism;** democratic corporatism; **state corporatism.**

country a territorial unit controlled by a single state. Countries vary in the degree to which groups within them have a common culture and ethnic affiliation. See also **nation-state; state.**

coup d'état literally "stroke of state," a French phrase used to describe the sudden, and often violent, overthrow of a government by a small group of people. Coups d'état are frequently carried out by military officers.

danwei a Chinese term that means "unit" and is the basic level of social organization and a major means of political control in China's **communist party-state.** A person's *danwei* is most often his or her workplace, such as a factory or an office.

decentralization policies that aim to transfer some decision-making power from higher to lower levels of government, typically from the central government to subnational governments.

developmental state a **nation-state** in which the government carries out policies that effectively promote national economic growth.

developmentalism an ideology and practice in Latin America during the 1950s in which the state played a leading role in seeking to foster economic development through sponsoring vigorous industrial policy. See also **import substituting industrialization.**

dictatorship (See **autocracy, authoritarianism, totalitarianism.**)

distributional politics the use of power, particularly by the state, to allocate some kind of valued resource among competing groups.

dual rule a system of administration used in China (adapted from the Soviet Union) that places a government body under the authority of both a higher-level government organization and a Communist Party organization.

dual society a society and economy that are sharply divided into a traditional, usually poorer, and a modern, usually richer, sectors.

Economic Community of West African States (ECOWAS) the organization established in 1975 among the sixteen governments in West Africa. Its goals are to strengthen and broaden the economies in the region through the removal of trade barriers among its members (such as import quotas and domestic content laws), freedom of movement for citizens, and monetary cooperation.

economic development the process by which an economy of a country grows in size and standard of living of its people improves. Economic development is most often measured by increases in the both the total and per capita (divided by population) **gross domestic product (or gross national income).**

economic liberalization attempts to dismantle government controls on the economy.

ejidatario recipient of *ejido* land grant in Mexico.

ejido land granted by Mexican government to an organized group of peasants.

Emergency (1975–1977) the period when Indian Prime Minister Indira Gandhi suspended many formal democratic rights and ruled in an **authoritarian** manner.

emir(s) traditional Islamic ruler. The emir presides over an "emirate," or kingdom, in Northern Nigeria.

executive the agencies of government that implement or execute policy. The highest levels of the executive in most countries is a president or prime minister and cabinet. The top executive officeholders supervise the work of administrative departments and bureaus.

Expediency Council a committee set up in Iran to resolve differences between the *Majles* and the Guardian Council.

export-led growth economic growth generated by the export of a country's commodities. Export-led growth can occur at an early stage of economic development, in which case it involves primary products, such as the country's mineral resources, timber, and agricultural products; or at a later stage, when industrial goods and services are exported.

Farsi Persian word for the Persian language. Fars is a province in central Iran.

fatwa a pronouncement issued by a high-ranking Islamic cleric.

favelas in Brazil, huge shantytowns of homes made out of cardboard, wood from dumps, and blocks of mortar and brick. These shantytowns create rings of extreme poverty around cities like Rio de Janeiro and São Paulo. Similar shantytowns can be found in other Latin American cities, although terms to describe them vary by country. In Peru, for example, these shantytowns are called *barriadas.*

federal character Nigeria's version of "affirmative action," applied to the civil service and all government agencies to ensure representation of all ethnic and regional groups and to prevent the dominance of any one group. In practice, federal character has tended to promote the employment of northern Nigerians at the expense of southerners.

Foundation of the Oppressed a clerically controlled foundation in Iran set up after the revolution there.

Four Cardinal Principles ideas first enunciated by Chinese leader Deng Xiaoping in 1979 asserting that all policies should be judged by whether they uphold the socialist road, the dictatorship of the proletariat, the leadership of the Communist Party, and Marxism-Leninism-Mao Zedong Thought. The main purpose of the Four Cardinal Principles was to proscribe any challenge to the ultimate authority of the

Chinese Communist Party, even during a time of far-reaching economic reform. The Principles have been reaffirmed by Deng's successors and continue to define the boundaries of what is politically permissible in China.

fundamentalism a term recently popularized to describe radical religious movements throughout the world.

Gini index a measure of economic equality based on income distribution or consumption expenditures. The Gini index range is 0–100 with a higher number indicating greater inequality.

globalization the intensification of worldwide interconnectedness associated with the increased speed and magnitude of cross-border flows of trade, investment and finance, and processes of migration, cultural diffusion, and communication.

Great Leap Forward a movement launched by Mao Zedong in 1958 to industrialize China very rapidly and thereby propel it toward communism. The Leap ended in economic disaster in 1960, causing one of the worst famines in human history.

Great Proletarian Cultural Revolution the political campaign launched in 1966 by Chairman Mao Zedong to stop what he saw as China's drift away from socialism and toward capitalism. The campaign led to massive purges in the Chinese Communist Party, the widespread persecution of China's intellectuals, and the destruction of invaluable cultural objects. The Cultural Revolution officially ended in 1979 after Mao's death and the arrest of some of his most radical followers.

green revolution a strategy for increasing agricultural (especially food) production, involving improved seeds, irrigation, and abundant use of fertilizers.

gross domestic product (GDP) the total of all goods and services produced within a country that is used as a broad measure of the size of its economy.

gross national income (GNI) a broad measure of the size of an economy. Similar to **gross domestic product,** but also takes into account income received from foreign sources. The World Bank started using the term gross national income rather than gross national product in its reports and statistics in 2002.

guanxi a Chinese term that means "connections" or "relationships," and describes personal ties between individuals based on such things as common birthplace or mutual acquaintances. *Guanxi* are an important factor in China's political and economic life.

Guardian Council a committee created in the Iranian constitution to oversee the *Majles* (the parliament).

guerrilla warfare a military strategy based on small bands of soldiers (the guerrillas) who use hit-and-run tactics to attack a numerically superior and better-armed enemy.

Hezbollahis literally "partisans of God." In Iran, the term is used to describe religious vigilantes. In Lebanon, it is used to describe the Shi'i militia.

Hindus India's main religion is Hinduism, and its adherents are called Hindus.

hojjat al-Islam literally, "the proof of Islam." In Iran, it means a medium-ranking cleric.

household responsibility system the system put into practice in China beginning in the early 1980s in which the major decisions about agricultural production are made by individual farm families based on the profit motive rather than by a **people's commune** or the government.

Human Development Index (HDI) a composite number used by the United Nations to measure and compare levels of achievement in health, knowledge, and standard of living. HDI is based on the following indicators: life expectancy, adult literacy rate and school enrollment statistics, and **gross domestic product** per capita at purchasing power parity.

illiteracy the inability of someone over the age of 15 to read, write, and understand a short, simple statement about their everyday life. Because of major differences in how illiteracy is measured and compiled in countries around the world, caution should be exercised when evaluating national figures and making comparisons.

imam leader. Iranians traditionally reserved this title for the twelve early Infallible Leaders of **Shi'ism.** During the Islamic Revolution, this title was bestowed on Khomeini to elevate him above the other grand ayatollahs.

Imam Jum'ehs prayer leaders in Iran's main urban mosques. Appointed by the **Supreme Leader,** they have considerable authority in the provinces.

import substituting industrialization (ISI) strategy for industrialization based on domestic manufacture of previously imported goods to satisfy domestic market demands. See also **developmentalism.**

Indian Administrative Service (IAS) India's civil service, a highly professional and talented group of administrators who run the Indian government on a day-to-day basis.

indigenous groups population of **Amerindian** heritage in Mexico.

indirect rule a term used to describe the British style of colonialism in Nigeria and India in which local traditional rulers and political structures were used to help support the colonial governing structure.

informal sector (economy) an underground economy.

International Financial Institutions (IFIs) generally refers to the International Bank for Reconstruction and Development (the World Bank) and the International Monetary Fund (IMF), but can also include other international lending institutions. See also **structural adjustment program (SAP).**

interventionist an interventionist state acts vigorously to shape the performance of major sectors of the economy.

interventores in Brazil, allies of Getúlio Vargas (1930–1945, 1950–1952) picked by the dictator during his first period of rulership to replace opposition governors in all the Brazilian states except Minas Gerais. The *interventores* represented a shift of power from subnational government to the central state. See also **politics of the governors.**

iron rice bowl a feature of China's socialist economy that provided guarantees of lifetime employment, income, and basic cradle-to-grave benefits to most urban and rural workers. Economic reforms beginning in the 1980s that aimed at improving efficiency and work motivation sought to smash the iron rice bowl and link employment and income more directly to individual effort.

jihad literally "struggle." Although often used to mean armed struggle against unbelievers, it can also mean spiritual struggle for more self-improvement.

jurist's guardianship Khomeini's concept that the Iranian clergy should rule on the grounds that they are the divinely appointed guardians of both the law and the people. He developed this concept in the 1970s.

land reform the process of reducing gross inequalities in the ownership of farm land by either confiscating or buying it from large owners and redistributing it to those who have little or no land.

legitimacy a belief by powerful groups and the broad citizenry that a state exercises "rightful" authority. In the contemporary world, a state is said to possess legitimacy when it enjoys the consent of the governed, which usually involves democratic procedures and the attempt to achieve a satisfactory level of development and equitable distribution of resources.

life expectancy the number of years a newborn infant can normally be expected to live. Considered to be one of the most fundamental measures of the level of health care available in a country.

Lok Sabha the lower house of parliament in India where all major legislation must pass before becoming law.

Maharajas India's traditional rulers—monarchs—who retained their positions during the colonial period but were removed from power when the Indian republic was established.

Majles Arabic term for "assembly"; used in Iran to describe the parliament.

maquiladora factories that produce goods for export, often located along the U.S.-Mexican border.

Marxism-Leninism the theoretical foundation of communism based on the ideas of the German philosopher, Karl Marx (1818–1883), and the leader of the Russian Revolution, V. I. Lenin (1870–1924). Marxism is, in essence, a theory of historical development that emphasizes the struggle between exploiting and exploited classes, particularly the struggle between the bourgeoisie (capitalists) and the proletariat (the industrial working class). Leninism emphasizes the strategy and organization to be used by the communist party to overthrow capitalism and seize power as a first step on the road to communism.

maslahat Arabic term for "expediency," "prudence," or "advisability." It is now used in Iran to refer to reasons of state or what is best for the Islamic Republic.

mestizo a person of mixed white, indigenous (Amerindian), and sometimes African descent.

middle-level theory seeks to explain phenomena in a limited range of cases, in particular, a specific set of countries with particular characteristics, such as parliamentary regimes, or a particular type of political institution (such as political parties) or activity (such as protest).

moderating power (*poder moderador*) a term used in Brazilian politics to refer to the situation following the 1824 constitution in which the monarchy was supposed to act as a moderating power, among the executive, legislative, and judicial branches of government, arbitrating party conflicts, and fulfilling governmental responsibilities when nonroyal agents failed.

mosque Muslim place of worship, equivalent to a church, temple, or synagogue.

Muslims followers of Islam.

nationalism an ideology that seeks to create a **nation-state** for a particular community; a group identity associated with membership is such a political community. Nationalists often proclaim that their state and nation are superior to others.

nationalization the take-over by the government of privately owned business firms.

nation-state distinct, politically defined territory with its own state, relatively coherent culture, economy, and ethnic and other social identities. See also **country.**

neo-imperialism imperialism describes a situation in which one country takes direct control of another country or territory, usually for the purpose of extracting economic benefits. Traditionally, imperialism involved the establishment of colonies. Neo-imperialism refers to the exercise of power over and exploitation of other countries in ways that may not involve formal conquest or colonization, such as through political or economic pressure.

New State (*Estado Novo*) in Brazil, an authoritarian government led by Getúlio Vargas in 1937 that legitimized its rule through state corporatism, massive public sector investment through para-statals, and paternalistic social policies.

newly industrializing countries (NICs) a term used to describe a group of countries that achieved rapid **economic development** beginning in the 1960s largely stimulated by robust international trade (particularly exports) and guided by government policies. The core NICs are usually considered to be Taiwan, South Korea, Hong Kong, and Singapore, but other countries, including Argentina, Brazil, Malaysia, Mexico, and Thailand, are often included in this category.

nomenklatura a system of personnel selection under which the Communist Party maintain control over the appointment of important officials in all spheres of social, economic, and political life. The term is also used to describe individuals chosen through this system and thus refers more broadly to the privileged circles in the Soviet Union and China.

nonaligned bloc a group of countries that refused to ally with either the United States or the USSR during the **cold war** years.

nongovernmental organization (NGO) a private group that seeks to influence public policy and deal with certain problems that it believes are not being adequately addressed by governments; examples include Amnesty International (human rights), Oxfam (famine relief), and Greenpeace (the environment).

North American Free Trade Agreement (NAFTA) a treaty among the United States, Mexico, and Canada implemented on January 1, 1994, that largely eliminates trade barriers among the three nations and establishes procedures to resolve trade disputes. NAFTA serves as a model for an eventual Free Trade Area of the Americas zone that could include most Western Hemisphere nations.

official international currency exchange rates the rate at which the central (government) banks will exchange one country's money for another.

oligarchy narrowly based, undemocratic government, often by traditional elites. See also **autocracy; authoritarianism.**

OPEC Organization of Petroleum Exporting Countries. Founded in 1960 by Iran, Venezuela, and Saudi Arabia, it now includes most oil exporting states with the notable exceptions of Mexico and former members of the Soviet Union. It tries to regulate prices by regulating production.

Other Backward Classes the middle or intermediary castes in India that have been accorded reserved seats in public education and employment since the early 1990s.

panchayats In India, elected bodies at the village, district, and state levels that have development and administrative responsibilities.

para-statals state-owned, or at least state-controlled, corporations, created to undertake a broad range of activities, from control and marketing of agricultural production to provision of banking services, operating airlines, and other transportation facilities and public utilities. See also **interventionist.**

patrimonialism a system of governance in which a single ruler treats the state as personal property (patrimony). Appointments to public office are made on the basis of unswerving loyalty to the ruler. In turn, state officials exercise wide authority in other domains, such as the economy, often for their personal benefit and that of the ruler, to the detriment of the general population. See also **authoritarianism; autocracy; prebendalism.**

patron-client networks see **clientelism.**

patron-client politics (or **network**) see **clientelism.**

People of the Book the Muslim term for recognized religious minorities, such as Christians, Jews, and Zoroastrians.

people's communes large-scale rural communities that were in charge of nearly all aspects of political, social, and economic life in the Chinese countryside from the late 1950s until the early 1980s, when they were disbanded and replaced by a system of household and village-based agricultural production.

personalist politicians demagogic political leaders who use their personal charisma to mobilize their constituency.

physical quality of life (PQLI) a measure, based on illiteracy, child mortality, and life expectancy, of how well the basic needs of life are being met. Similar to, but less sophisticated, than the **Human Development Index.**

political culture the attitudes, beliefs, and symbols that influence political behavior; often defined in terms of specific national political-cultural orientations.

political development the stages of change producing more modern and effective political institutions.

political economy the study of the interaction between the state and the economy, that is, how the state and political processes affect the organization of production and exchange (the economy) and how the organization of the economy affects political processes.

political institutions the formal rules, structured relationships, and organizations within the state and, more broadly, within the political sphere. Some key examples are the executive, legislature, judiciary, military, and political parties.

politics of the governors in Brazil, refers to periods of history in which state governors acquire extraordinary powers over domains of policy that were previously claimed by the federal government. The term refers most commonly to the Old Republic and the current state of Brazilian federalism.

populism gaining the support of popular sectors. When used in Latin American politics, this support is often achieved by manipulation and demagogic appeals.

prebendalism patterns of political behavior that rest on the justification that official state offices should be competed for and then utilized for the personal benefit of officeholders as well as of their support group or clients. Thus, prebendal politics is sustained by the existence of **patron-client networks.** See also **patrimonialism; clientelism.**

privatization the sale of state-owned enterprises to private companies or investors. Those who support the policy claim that private ownership is superior to government ownership because for-profit entities promote greater efficiency. Privatization is a common central component of **structural adjustment programs** to curtail the losses associated with these enterprises and generate state revenue when they are sold.

proletariat the industrial working class, which, according to **Marxism-Leninism,** is destined to seize power and replace capitalism with socialism.

proportional representation (PR) a system of political representation in which seats are allocated to parties within multimember constituencies, roughly in proportion to the votes each party receives. PR usually encourages the election to parliament of more political parties than single-member-district winner-take-all systems.

purchasing power parity (PPP) a method of calculating the value of a country's money based on the actual cost of buying certain goods and services in that country rather than how many U.S. dollars they are worth. PPP is widely considered to be a more accurate indicator of comparing standards of living, particularly in countries at very different levels of economic development.

Qur'an the Muslim Bible.

Rayja Sabha India's upper house of parliament; considerably less significant politically than the *Lok Sabha.*

rentier state a country that obtains much of its revenue from the export of oil or other natural resources.

rents above-market returns to a factor of production. Pursuit of economic rents (or "rent-seeking") is profit seeking that takes the form of nonproductive economic activity.

reservations jobs or admissions to colleges reserved by the government of India for specific social groups, particularly underprivileged groups.

revisionism a label used by the Chinese Communist Party during the late Maoist era (1965–1976) to refer to the ideology of those political parties (including the Communist Party of the Soviet Union) or individuals judged to have betrayed what they believed to be the true meaning of the theory and practice of **Marxism-Leninism.**

scheduled castes the lowest caste groups in India; also known as the untouchables. See also **untouchables.**

self-determination the right of a sovereign state or an ethnic or other group that shares cultural and historical ties to live together in a given territory and in a manner they desire. It is often the basis of the claim by a state or group for political independence and cultural autonomy.

sexenio the six-year administration of Mexican presidents.

shari'a Islamic law derived mostly from the **Qur'an** and the examples set by the Prophet Muhammad.

Shi'ism a branch of Islam. It literally means the followers or partisans of Ali. The other branch is known as Sunni, or the followers of tradition.

Sikhs an important religious minority in India.

social class common membership in a group whose boundaries are based on a common economic location, notably, occupation and income. Members of the same social class often share similar political attitudes.

socialism in a socialist regime, the state plays a leading role in organizing the economy, and most business firms are publicly owned. A socialist regime, unlike a **communist**

party-state, may allow the private sector to play an important role in the economy and be committed to political pluralism. In **Marxism-Leninism,** socialism refers to an early stage in development of communism. Socialist regimes can be organized in a democratic manner, in that those who control the state may be chosen according to democratic procedures. They may also be governed in an undemocratic manner when a single party, not chosen in free competitive elections, controls the state and society.

socialist democracy the term used by the Chinese Communist Party to describe the political system of the People's Republic of China. Also called the *people's democratic dictatorship.* The official view is that this type of system, under the leadership of the Communist Party, provides democracy for the overwhelming majority of people and suppresses (or exercises dictatorship over) only the enemies of the people. Socialist democracy is contrasted to bourgeois (or capitalist) democracy, which puts power in the hands of the rich and oppresses the poor.

socialist market economy the term used by the government of China to refer to the country's current economic system. It is meant to convey the mix of state control (socialism) and market forces (capitalism) that China is now following in its quest for economic development. The implication is that socialism will promote equality, while the market (especially the profit motive) will encourage people to work hard and foreign companies to invest.

state a unified political entity. The state comprises a country's key political institutions that are responsible for making, implementing, enforcing, and adjudicating important policies in that country. States have also been defined as those institutions within a country that claim the right to control force within the territory comprising the country and to make binding rules (laws), which citizens of that country must obey.

state capitalism strategy in which government guides industrial and agricultural development and sets political conditions for its success.

state corporatism a political system in which the state requires all members of a particular economic sector to join an officially designated interest group. Such interest groups thus attain public status, and they participate in national policymaking. The result is that the state has great control over the groups, and groups have great control over their members. See also **corporatism; corporatist state.**

state formation the historical development of a state, often marked by major stages, key events, or turning points (critical junctures) that influence the contemporary character of the state.

state-led economic development the process of promoting economic development using governmental machinery.

structural adjustment program (SAP) medium-term (generally three to five years) programs (which include both action plans and disbursement of funds) established by the World Bank intended to alter and reform the economic structures of highly indebted Third World countries as a condition for receiving international loans. SAPs often involve the necessity for **privatization**, trade liberalization, and fiscal restraint. See also **international financial institutions (IFIs).**

Supreme Leader the head of the Islamic Republic of Iran.

technocrats career-minded bureaucrats who administer public policy according to a technical rather than a political rationale. In Mexico and Brazil, these are known as the *técnicos.* For contrasting concepts, see **clientelism; prebendalism.**

theocracy state dominated by the clergy, who rule on the grounds that they are the only interpreters of God's will and law.

Third World used to refer to countries with a low or relatively low level of **economic development,** particularly as measured by **gross national income** or **gross domestic product** per capita. Synonymous with developing world.

totalitarianism a political system in which the state attempts to exercise total control over all aspects of public and private life, including the economy, culture, education, and social organizations, through an integrated system of ideological, economic, and political control. The term has been applied to both **communist party-states** and fascist regimes such as Nazi Germany.

township and village enterprises (TVEs) nonagricultural businesses and factories owned and run by local governments and private entrepreneurs in China's rural areas. TVEs operate largely according to market forces and outside the state plan.

unfinished state a state characterized by instabilities and uncertainties that may render it susceptible to collapse as a coherent entity.

untouchables the lowest caste in India's **caste system,** whose members are among the poorest and most disadvantaged Indians.

warrant chiefs employed by the British colonial regime in Nigeria. A system in which "chiefs" were selected by the British to oversee certain legal matters and assist the colonial enterprise in governance and law enforcement in local areas.

zamindars landlords who served as tax collectors under the British colonial government. The *zamindari* system was abolished after independence.

About the Editors and Contributors

Ervand Abrahamian is Distinguished Professor of History at Baruch College and the Graduate Center of the City University of New York. His recent publications include *Khomeinism: Essays on the Islamic Republic* (University of California Press, 1993) and *Tortured Confessions: Prisons and Public Recantations in Modern Iran* (University of California Press, 1999).

Amrita Basu is Professor of Political Science and Women's and Gender Studies at Amherst College. Her main areas of interest are social movements, religious nationalism, and gender politics in South Asia. She is the author of *Two Faces of Protest: Contrasting Modes of Women's Activism in India* (University of California Press, 1992) and several edited books, including *Localizing Knowledge in a Globalizing World, Community Conflicts and the State in India* (with Atul Kohli) (Syracuse University Press, 2002), and *Appropriating Gender: Women's Activism and Politicized Religion in South Asia* (Routledge, 1998).

Merilee S. Grindle is Edward S. Mason Professor of International Development at the John F. Kennedy School of Government, Harvard University. She is a specialist on the comparative analysis of policy-making, implementation, and public management in developing countries and has written extensively on Mexico. Her most recent book is *Audacious Reforms: Institutional Innovation and Democracy in Latin America* (The Johns Hopkins University Press, 2000).

William A. Joseph is Professor of Political Science at Wellesley College and an Associate of the Fairbank Center for East Asian Research at Harvard University. His research focuses on contemporary Chinese politics and ideology. He is the editor of *China Briefing: The Contradictions of Change* (M.E. Sharpe, 1997), co-editor of *New Perspectives on the Cultural Revolution* (Harvard University Press, 1991), and contributing editor of *The Oxford Companion to Politics of the World* (Oxford University Press, 2nd ed., 2001).

Mark Kesselman is Professor of Political Science at Columbia University. A specialist on the French and European political economy, his recent publications include contributions to *The Mitterrand Era: Policy Alternatives and Political Mobilization in France* (Macmillan, 1995), *Mitterrand's Legacy, Chirac's Challenge* (St. Martin's Press, 1996), and *Diminishing Welfare: A Cross-National Study of Social Provision* (Greenwood, 2002). He is the coauthor of *A Century of Organized Labor in France* (St. Martin's Press, 1997).

Darren Kew is Assistant Professor in the Graduate Program in Dispute Resolution at the University of Massachusetts, Boston. He studies the role of civil society in democratic development and conflict prevention in Africa. Professor Kew has written on elections, civil society, and conflict prevention in Nigeria. He has worked with the Council on Foreign Relations' Center for Preventive Action to provide analysis and blueprints for preventing conflicts in numerous areas around the world, including Nigeria, Central Africa, and Kosovo, and he has also observed elections in Nigeria.

Atul Kohli is Professor of Politics and International Affairs at Princeton University. His principal research interest is the comparative political economy of developing countries, especially India. He is the author of *Democracy and Discontent: India's Growing Crisis of Governability* (Cambridge University Press, 1990). His current research involves a comparative analysis of industrialization in South Korea, Brazil, India, and Nigeria.

Joel Krieger is Norma Wilentz Hess Professor of Political Science at Wellesley College. His publications include *British Politics in the Global Age: Can Social Democracy Survive?* (Polity Press, 1999) and *Reagan, Thatcher, and the Politics of Decline* (Oxford University Press, 1986). He was also editor-in-chief of *The Oxford Companion to Politics of the World* (Oxford University Press, 1993; 2nd ed., 2001).

Peter Lewis is Associate Professor at the School of International Service, American University. He has written extensively on Nigerian political economy, as well as on broader regional issues of participation, democratic transition, and economic adjustment in Africa. He is currently working on a study of the comparative political economies of Indonesia and Nigeria.

Alfred P. Montero is Assistant Professor of Political Science at Carleton College. His research focuses on the political economy of decentralization and comparative federalism in Latin American and European countries. He is the author of *Shifting States in Global Markets: Subnational Industrial Policy in Contemporary Brazil and Spain* (Penn State University Press, 2002) and co-editor of *Decentralization and Democracy in Latin America* (University of Notre Dame Press, 2003). He has also published his work in several edited volumes and journals such as *Latin American Politics and Society, Comparative Politics, Studies in Comparative International Development, Publius: The Journal of Federalism,* and the *Journal of Interamerican Studies and World Affairs.*

Index

---

*Numbers in boldface indicate the page where a key term is defined.